THE RISE AND FALL OF THE REHABILITATIVE IDEAL, 1895–1970

Spanning almost a century of penal policy and practice in England and Wales, this book is a study of the long arc of *the rehabilitative ideal*, beginning in 1895, the year of the Gladstone Committee on Prisons, and ending in 1970, when the policy of treating and training criminals was very much on the defensive.

Drawing on a plethora of source material, such as the official papers of mandarins, ministers, and magistrates, measures of public opinion, prisoner memoirs, publications of penal reform groups and prison officers, the reports of Royal Commissions and Departmental Committees, political opinion in both Houses of Parliament and the research of the first cadre of criminologists, this book comprehensively examines a number of aspects of the British penal system, including judicial sentencing, law-making, and the administration of legal penalties. In doing so, Victor Bailey expertly weaves a complex and nuanced picture of punishment in twentieth-century England and Wales, one that incorporates the enduring influence of the death penalty, and will force historians to revise their interpretation of twentieth-century social and penal policy.

This detailed and ground-breaking account of *the rise and fall of the rehabilitative ideal* will be essential reading for scholars and students of the history of crime and justice and historical criminology, as well as those interested in social and legal history.

Victor Bailey was Director of the Hall Center for the Humanities from 2000 to 2017 and the Charles W. Battey Distinguished Professor of Modern British History at the University of Kansas, USA.

"Professor Bailey has written an outstanding and important book. By tracing the rise and fall of the rehabilitative ideal within the English Justice system he raises vital questions about the nature of society. What is the purpose of prison? Is it ever possible to punish and reform at the same time? And, most importantly of all, to what extent does the corrosive nature of capital punishment inevitably dominate the discourse? Professor Bailey's writing is always clear, his analysis always razor-sharp. The product of a lifetime's scholarship, this book is sure to become the standard work on the subject. It is impossible to recommend it too highly."
   —Laurence Rees, author of *Auschwitz* and *The Holocaust: A New History*.

"*The Rise and Fall of the Rehabilitative Ideal* will quickly become the substantive text for those students and researchers of penal policy and punishment during the twentieth century. It offers a thorough and detailed historical account of the development of penal policy and related areas across a crucial period of change. This is a highly readable text, written by one of the leading scholars in the field, it skilfully marshals the complex terrain and makes a significant contribution to the historiography."
   —Helen L. Johnston, Professor of Criminology, University of Hull, UK.

"This excellent account of penal experimentation in England illuminates the forces behind waves of retribution and the constraints on rehabilitative hopes. Public opinion, party policies, the symbolic importance of capital punishment and the crucial but largely neglected role of the judiciary are all explored from a wealth of original sources. Bailey contests accounts of revolutionary turning points (Garland, Wiener, Foucault), emphasizing continuities in socialist critiques, contractarian liberalism, and the prejudices and legal doctrines found in the high courts, where changing sentencing practices nonetheless had huge impact. An epilogue sets the recent enormous increase of the prison population within this longer history. An essential book."
   —Professor Douglas Hay FRSC, Osgoode Hall Law School and Department of History, York University, Canada.

"Victor Bailey has been for many years a major authority on penal policy and the treatment of offenders in Britain. His study of the Young Offender, *Delinquency and Citizenship* (1987) was a pioneering, profoundly researched work of great interest to criminologists and historians, amongst others. This new work follows it up with a wide-ranging analysis of policy towards the adult offender, within the context of the idea of the rehabilitation of offenders, from the 1895 Gladstone Committee on Prisons down to the ending of capital punishment in 1969. The subject is addressed from a variety of approaches to penal policy and debate, from the slow abatement of the Victorians' stern penitential attitude through the beginning of a more progressive and thoughtful policy of penal reform emerging between the wars. A key section of the book takes us from the Criminal Justice Bill of 1938 through the trauma of the wartime and post-years to the piecemeal and generally disappointing measure of

1948. Much of the attention in these years focused on trying to end capital punishment which, as Bailey shows, was in many ways a distraction from the more profound issues of rehabilitation of offenders. Reformers in parliament and parts of the civil services found themselves frustrated by the conservatism shown amongst the judiciary even in the heyday of post-war reform. In the end, pioneered by radical politicians like Silverman, civil servants like Maxwell and Scott, and influential ministers like Hoare and Callaghan, capital punishment was finally brought to an end. Even so, questions on the right balance between retribution and rehabilitation remained unanswered. The slow march towards a rational sentencing policy went on. One of the many merits of this work lies in never claiming too much for its conclusions. Anyone concerned with law and justice within a democratic society will learn much from this fine book."

—Professor Lord Morgan FBA, King's College, London, UK.

"Victor Bailey provides us with a long overdue account of the evolution of penal policy in Britain between 1895 and 1970. Grounded in a careful and wide-ranging reading of a wide variety of sources, judicial, administrative, and political, his book forces scholars to question long-held assumptions about the character of the twentieth-century penal regime and the major influences that shaped it. In particular, he offers a sobering re-evaluation of the supposed triumph of the "rehabilitative ideal" during this period. His volume is full of valuable insights that better help us understand the penal crisis of our own age."

—Professor Randall McGowen, University of Oregon, USA.

"With *The Rise and Fall of the Rehabilitative Ideal, 1895–1970* Victor Bailey has provided the most thorough and judicious account of how modern English penal policy was formulated and re-formulated. Based deeply on government archives, it tells a complex story of multiple, often contending, influences—ideological, political and financial—that shaped how the governing class of civil servants and politicians developed, implemented and altered policies for dealing with criminal offenders, from an era in which 'crime' seemed a problem well on the way to solution to our era of intense preoccupation with crime."

—Martin Wiener, Mary Gibbs Jones Professor of History,
Rice University, USA.

"Deeply researched—and deeply felt—this long-pondered history authoritatively bridges the gap between the Radzinowicz/Hood 1984 history of English criminal justice 1750–1914 and the forthcoming post-World War II official history. Why did a rehabilitative ideal succeed in fending off judicial and popular fondness for corporal and capital punishment but fail to resist persistent retributive instincts which led to more than a doubling of the prison population? All this and more—much more—about a period continuing to mark the criminal justice system. This indispensable and accessible study explains why, wearing its considerable learning lightly and convincingly."

—R. M. Morris, Home Office 1961–97.

"This provides a much-needed survey of the realities of penal policy and prison experiences 1895–1970. Though work by other scholars has already suggested that aspects of the traditional conceptualisations of prison realities then may not have been as supposed, this admirable work provides the first comprehensive survey of penal policy and implementation. It frames contemporary thinking in their widest context, seriously examining the judicial dimension (and it is unique in so doing) alongside public opinion. It should provide a model for future work, as well as filling in a current gap in the literature, for crime and legal historians as well as criminologists."

—Judith Rowbotham, Research Professor in Law, Plymouth University, UK.

"This important study by Victor Bailey advances our understanding of punishment and rehabilitation by providing a long-term perspective on the evolution of penal policy and penal practice in England and Wales. The book makes a significant contribution to our knowledge about the twentieth-century penal system, from the Gladstone Committee of 1895 until the 1970s, by which time the rehabilitative ideal was in retreat. This rigorous unpicking of rehabilitation through an examination of the many manifestations of the penal system complements his earlier study of penal policy for young offenders. Like that book, this book will quickly become a widely consulted history of twentieth-century punishment."

—Professor Heather Shore, Leeds Beckett University, UK.

"In tracking the rise and fall of the rehabilitative ideal, Professor Bailey has given us an indispensable history of penal policy and policymaking in the twentieth century. Significantly, he highlights the limits to the reach of rehabilitation, both as an ideal and as a reality, helping to contextualise the large prison population of our current era. This book is required reading for historians and criminologists, who will find they turn to it frequently."

—Dr Lizzie Seal, Reader in Criminology, University of Sussex, UK.

"Professor Bailey has produced a comprehensive and detailed account of penal policy in England and Wales from 1895 to 1970. Based on meticulous research in government archives, *The Rise and Fall of the Rehabilitative Ideal* demonstrates the complexities of penal policy and the limits of the 'ideal' even when its influence was supposedly at its zenith. It also points to the salience of the continued existence of the death penalty throughout this period and restores it to its place within the wider policy debate."

—Dr Anne Logan, University of Kent, UK.

THE RISE AND FALL OF THE REHABILITATIVE IDEAL, 1895–1970

Victor Bailey

Routledge
Taylor & Francis Group

LONDON AND NEW YORK

First published 2019
by Routledge
2 Park Square, Milton Park, Abingdon, Oxon OX14 4RN

and by Routledge
52 Vanderbilt Avenue, New York, NY 10017

Routledge is an imprint of the Taylor & Francis Group, an informa business

British Library Cataloguing in Publication Data
A catalogue record for this book is available from the British Library

Library of Congress Cataloging-in-Publication Data
Names: Bailey, Victor, 1948- author.
Title: The rise and fall of the rehabilitative ideal, 1895-1970 / Victor Bailey.
Description: Abingdon, Oxon ; New York, NY : Routledge, 2019. |
Includes bibliographical references and index.
Identifiers: LCCN 2018052272 (print) | LCCN 2018054124 (ebook) |
ISBN 9780429022203 (Ebook) | ISBN 9780429666605 (Adobe Reader) |
ISBN 9780429663888 (ePub) | ISBN 9780429661167
(Mobipocket Encrypted) | ISBN 9780367077099 (hardback) |
ISBN 9780367077112 (pbk.)
Subjects: LCSH: Corrections--Great Britain--History--20th century. |
Imprisonment--Great Britain--History--20th century. |
Criminals--Rehabilitation--Great Britain--History--20th century.
Classification: LCC HV9345.A5 (ebook) | LCC HV9345.A5 B35 2019 (print) |
DDC 365/.661094209041--dc23
LC record available at https://lccn.loc.gov/2018052272

ISBN: 978-0-367-07709-9 (hbk)
ISBN: 978-0-367-07711-2 (pbk)
ISBN: 978-0-429-02220-3 (ebk)

Typeset in Bembo
by Taylor & Francis Books

Note: Chapters one and seven are taken from 'Order and Disorder in Modern Britain: Essays on Riot, Crime, Policing and Punishment', which is published by Breviary Stuff and are used with permission.

Cover image: The cover shows prisoners lining up outside their cells at HMP Strangeways, Manchester, 20 November 1948 (credit: Picture Post/Bert Hardy/ Getty Images)

MIX
Paper from
responsible sources
FSC
www.fsc.org   FSC® C013056

Printed and bound in Great Britain by
TJ International Ltd, Padstow, Cornwall

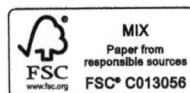

To Kathryn

To Kathryn

CONTENTS

ILLUSTRATIONS

Figures

Tables

Photographs

ACKNOWLEDGEMENTS

In writing this book I have incurred debts of many kinds. I am glad to be able formally to acknowledge some of them here. My thanks are due to the staff of The National Archives, who delivered a mountain of files to my desk over the years, and the staff of the Radzinowicz Library, Institute of Criminology, Cambridge University. I am grateful to the trustees and librarians for permission to quote from the collections of papers, which I list in the bibliography, and which are in their charge. In the hunt for illustrations, and for assistance with permissions, I want to thank Tom Gillmor, Tess Hines, and Lucinda Moore at the Mary Evans Picture Library, Paul Johnson at The National Archives, Nigel Wilkins at Historic England, Bev Baker at the National Justice Museum, and Michelle Gilbody, Crown Copyright section, HM Prison & Probation Service.

Chapter 1 of this book contains material which first appeared in my article "English Prisons, Penal Culture, and the Abatement of Imprisonment, 1895–1922," in the *Journal of British Studies*, vol. 36 (3), 1997, and Chapter 7 contains material which first appeared in "The Shadow of the Gallows: The Death Penalty and the British Labour Government, 1945–51," in *Law and History Review*, vol. 18 (2), 2000. I am grateful to Cambridge University Press, and to Paul Mangan of Breviary Stuff Publications, for permission to make use of the material here.

A Fellowship from the National Endowment for the Humanities, and research grants from the National Science Foundation and the American Philosophical Society, underwrote an extended trip to London, when the bulk of the research was completed. The Balfour Jeffrey Award, established by Takeru and Aya Higuchi, in recognition of research achievement in the humanities and social sciences, allowed me to take a final research trip to England. A grant from the Hall Family Foundation of Kansas City provided sabbatical leave for a year of writing. I am grateful to Don Hall, Bill Hall, and Angela Smart at the Hall Family Foundation for their generous support. Their grant-giving also helped make my tenure as director of the Hall Center for the Humanities the highlight of my academic career.

Three fellow historians scrutinized the entire book, and helped me avoid the solecisms we are all prey to, and clarify my arguments, although they are in no sense responsible for them. They are Randy McGowen, a superb historian of the death penalty; Alyson Brown, an equally superb historian of the prison system; and Laurence Rees, doyen of the historical documentary, and author of books which have changed our understanding of Nazi Germany. Laurence attended my Criminal Law and Penology class at Oxford University, where I first started thinking about the rise and fall of the rehabilitative ideal.

Many other people have helped me at various stages of my research. It would be impossible to enumerate them all here. I would, however, particularly like to express my gratitude to Lord Fenner Brockway, A. J. E. (Tony) Brennan, and R. M. (Bob) Morris for sharing their experiences of the penal system, and in the case of the two latter informants, of the Royal Commission on the Penal System. In the earliest research stage, I was supported fulsomely by John Croft, former head of the Home Office Research Unit.

The following scholars have given me research advice and encouragement over many years: E. P. Thompson, John Saville, Royden Harrison, Michael Ignatieff, Doug Hay, Allyson May, John Beattie, Elaine Reynolds, Joanna Innes, Vic Gatrell, Marty Wiener, Clive Emsley, Rosemary O'Day, Joanne Klein, David Cannadine, David Garland, Norval Morris, Sarah McCabe, Lord Asa Briggs, Sir Leon Radzinowicz, Roger Hood, Andrew Ashworth, Jane Morgan, Doug Reid, Sheila Blackburn, and Simon Stevenson.

I have been privileged to mentor a number of talented doctoral students, whose work has informed my own. They are Lisa Steffen, Jasonne Grabher, Karenbeth Zacharias, Karl Brooks, Christine Anderson, David Adams, Ryan Fagan, Emily Lowrance-Floyd, Alex Rosser, Mandi Barnard, and Andrew Avery.

Charlotte Endersby, editor of the Criminology and Criminal Justice list at Routledge, helped me inestimably by her intelligent and assiduous support. Reanna Young was an indulgent and adept production editor. Mary Brooks was my effective indexer once more. Mark Kaplan provided an office space beyond compare in Kritzer Hall.

In a special category are my family and those boon companions who make life convivial. They are my sister Pauline, my niece's family, Karen, Kevin, Freya and Jarl; Angela Elam and Cullen Holland, Ted and Judy Wilson, Purna and Sunita Bangere, Erin Nix, Eileen O'Hara, Nancy and John Hubbard, and Joan and Charles Battey, whose name dignifies my distinguished professorship. I wish also to memorialize two people who recently passed away: my mum, Lily, and my colleague, Henry Fortunato.

This book is dedicated to my wife Kathryn, who has been at my side throughout this elongated research venture. Her love, loyalty, strength, and sagacity are life-sustaining.

ABBREVIATIONS

ACPS	Advisory Council on the Penal System
ACTO	Advisory Council on the Treatment of Offenders
BL. Add. MSS	British Library, Additional Manuscripts
CAB	Cabinet Office Records
CC	Cabinet Conclusions
CM	Cabinet Minutes
CP	Cabinet Papers
CT	Corrective Training
Cr. App. R.	Criminal Appeal Reports
CrimLR	Criminal Law Review
DAP	Daily Average Population
DNB	Dictionary of National Biography
DPP	Director of Public Prosecutions
EC	Executive Committee
HA	Home Affairs
HAC	Home Affairs Committee
HO	Home Office
HORU	Home Office Research Unit
ILP	Independent Labour Party
ISTD	Institute for the Scientific Treatment of Delinquency (from 1951, Institute for the Study and Treatment of Delinquency)
JP	Justice of the Peace
KC	King's Counsel
LC	Legislation Committee
LCJ	Lord Chief Justice
LCO	Lord Chancellor's Office
LP	Lord President's Committee

M-O	Mass-Observation
MP	Member of Parliament
NACRO	National Association for the Care and Resettlement of Offenders
NCACP	National Campaign Against Capital Punishment
NCADP	National Council for the Abolition of the Death Penalty
Oxford DNB	Oxford Dictionary of National Biography
PCom	Prison Commission Papers
PD	preventive detention
PLP	Parliamentary Labour Party
PM	Prime Minister
POA	Prison Officers' Asssociation
POC	Persistent Offenders Committee
PP	Parliamentary Papers
PREM	Prime Minister's Office Papers
PS	penal servitude
QC	Queen's Counsel
RCCP	Royal Commission on Capital Punishment
RCPS	Royal Commission on the Penal System
TNA	The National Archives

In the footnotes and bibliography, the place of publication is London unless otherwise given.

ABOUT THE AUTHOR

Victor Bailey was Director of the Hall Center for the Humanities from 2000 to 2017, the first director to be invested with the Hall Center for the Humanities Directorship, and the Charles W. Battey Distinguished Professor of Modern British History at the University of Kansas. He was educated at the Centre for the Study of Social History at Warwick University, under E. P. Thompson and Royden Harrison, and the Institute of Criminology, University of Cambridge, under Sir Leon Radzinowicz and Roger Hood. He was a research officer at the Centre for Criminology, Oxford University; and a research fellow at the Institute of Historical Research, London University, and a senior research fellow at Worcester College, Oxford. He attended the University of Rochester, New York, as the R. T. French Visiting Professor of History. He has taught at the University of Oxford, Hull University, and Hamilton College.

He is the author of *Delinquency and Citizenship: Reclaiming the Young Offender, 1914–1948* (Oxford University Press, 1987); *This Rash Act: Suicide Across the Life Cycle in the Victorian City* (Stanford University Press, 1998); and *Charles Booth's Policemen: Crime, Police and Community in Jack-the-Ripper's London* (Breviary Stuff Publications, 2014). He was a contributor to the collection published as *Protest and Survival: Essays for E. P. Thompson* (Merlin Press, 1993).

LEGISLATIVE STAGES

A number of chapters presume knowledge of the various stages that legislation went through in the Houses of Parliament. This brief primer sets out the stages:

House of Commons

First reading: the short title of the bill is read out and is followed by an order for the bill to be printed. This first stage takes place without debate.

Second reading: a formal debate on the principles of the proposed legislation, followed by a vote to endorse or reject those principles.

Committee stage: a small committee is appointed to study the bill clause by clause. The composition of the Committee must reflect the size of the vote at second reading.

Report stage: the bill as amended (or not) by Committee returns to the Floor of the House. MPs decide to endorse or reject amendments passed in Committee. MPs not on the Committee can also propose amendments for discussion and decision.

Third reading: a formal short debate to conclude the report stage. Another vote on the bill's principles is usually called.

The bill then proceeds to the House of Lords where further amendments can be made. The bill returns again to the Commons for discussion on the Lords' amendments. This procedure is followed twice. It is rare for the Lords to re-insert any of their own amendments which have been turned down by the Commons.

The bill has only to receive the formal assent of the queen before becoming law.

INTRODUCTION

The rehabilitative ideal

I

This book is a study of the long arc of what we conventionally term the rehabilitative ideal. Above all, it is an evaluation of penal policy and penal practice in England and Wales between 1895, the year of the Gladstone Committee on Prisons, whose report is usually taken as the starting point of the rehabilitative ethic (the committee proposing that reform was to rank alongside deterrence as one of the objects of the English prison system), and 1970, by which date the policy of treating and training criminals was very much on the defensive.[1]

The theme that runs through this account of modern punishment is that historians and criminologists have exaggerated the dominance of the rehabilitative paradigm. This is due in part to the fact that scholars have focused heavily on only one strand of the penal system—the treatment of offenders after sentence—giving insufficient regard to what the criminal courts contributed to the penal equation. And it is due in part to the fact that scholars have too readily accepted the official rhetoric on penal policy and practice; have too rarely measured the rhetoric against the depressing and unchanging reality of prison conditions and prisoners' experience.

---

1   As a brief guide, "rehabilitation" considers the needs of the offender and, by the use of treatment strategies targeted at the individual offender, aims to reduce the likelihood of future re-offending. "Retribution" seeks the punishment to fit the crime. The calculation of punishment rests on the culpability, or blameworthiness, of the offender and the seriousness of the offence. It is concerned with issues of morality and criminal responsibility. "Denunciation" is a public expression of society's condemnation. It shares with retribution a focus on the morality of the act but, unlike retribution, looks beyond what should happen to the offender and examines the impact of a sentence on the community.

Punishment is examined in all its manifestations: judicial sentencing, law-making, and the administration of legal penalties. Particular emphasis is given to the interactions between the judicial and executive arms of the criminal justice system on the grounds that, as the Advisory Council on the Penal System stated: "The system of penalties imposed in court and the system of imprisonment have a close relationship, each influencing the other."[2] Since the precise nature of penal policy is influenced by the individuals in positions of authority, and by the political and administrative context within which they work, the book relies heavily on the papers of *mandarins* (in the Home Office, Prison Commission, and Lord Chancellor's Office), *ministers* (the Home Secretary, the Lord Chancellor, and the Cabinet), and *magistrates* (the Lord Chief Justice, High Court Judges, and justices of the peace). Yet not exclusively. The book also draws on measures of public opinion and on prisoner memoirs, on the publications of penal reform groups and prison officers, and on the research of the first cadre of criminologists. It incorporates the findings and recommendations of the reports of Royal Commissions and Departmental Committees and the frequent reports of the Advisory Council on the Treatment of Offenders, and it samples political opinion in both Houses of Parliament.

The emphasis of the book is on the adult offender, with only passing reference to the young delinquent. I am willing to concede from the outset that the rehabilitative ideal was honoured more in the observance than the breach, to invert the idiom's usual order, when it came to juvenile and young offenders.[3] My earlier book, *Delinquency and Citizenship*, was an attempt to argue exactly that. The present book places alongside that earlier account of penal policy for young offenders, the very different policy and practice that prevailed for adult offenders.[4]

The contours of penal policy and practice have attracted a good deal of historical and criminological attention in recent years. The outcome is a general consensus concerning the theory and content of what Francis Allen first termed "the rehabilitative ideal," and what David Garland has dubbed "penal-welfarism." Allen defined the rehabilitative ethic as the notion that

> the sanctions of the criminal law should or must be employed to achieve fundamental changes in the characters, personalities, and attitudes of convicted offenders, not only in the interest of the social defense, but also in the interests of the well-being of the offender himself.

2 Home Office, *Sentences of Imprisonment: A Review of Maximum Penalties* (HMSO, 1978), para 16, p. 7.

3 By the 1960s, almost 60 per cent of persons convicted of indictable offences were under 21, so this large body of offenders was in theory eligible for a "positivist" measure of corrective training or borstal detention. See also David Garland, "Beyond the Culture of Control," *Critical Review of International Social and Political Philosophy*, vol. 7 (2004), p. 175: "... 'rehabilitative' practices were more readily, more rapidly, and more extensively established for women and children than they ever were for adult males."

4 Victor Bailey, *Delinquency and Citizenship: Reclaiming the Young Offender 1914–1948* (Oxford, 1987).

He also maintained that this ethic was likely to flourish in a society whose cultural attitudes included two key assumptions: one, "a strong faith in the malleability of human behavior and human character," or a belief that treatment efforts can change the habits and values of individuals; and, two, "a sufficient consensus of values to permit practical agreement on what it means to be rehabilitated."[5] Both assumptions, Allen believed, were standard fare in post-war American society, and widely evident within English penal circles. Garland has offered a fuller outline of the intellectual framework and institutional structure of the years between 1890 and 1970, when, it is claimed, the tectonic plates of criminal justice shifted, from a classical liberal belief in proportionate punishment, to a "positivist" and "correctionalist" commitment to treatment and training. Punishment, particularly deterrent and retributive punishment, was increasingly viewed, we are told, as the remnant of a uniform and rigid "tariff" of sentencing, when what was thought to be required were penal measures tailored to the needs of the individual offender. Like Allen, Garland saw the rehabilitative ethic as "the hegemonic, organizing principle, the intellectual framework and value system that bound together the whole structure and made sense of it for practitioners."[6] Scrutinize any annual report by the Prison Commissioners, open the pages of any journal or newspaper, attend to any debate in Parliament, at any time between the 1920s and 1960s, and you will find the discussion of penal policy guided and shaped by the concept of the treatment and training of offenders.

The penal-welfare programme that emerged in the twentieth century was characterized first, it is claimed, by a number of rehabilitative signatures: pre-sentence, diagnostic reports; the classification and allocation of offenders to different institutions and regimes; indeterminate or semi-determinate sentences; the evaluation of eligibility for release from custody; and research into the efficacy of different treatments. Secondly, the programme was defined by specialist measures: probation, parole, custodial regimes of a re-educative nature, and the juvenile court. Indeed, for Allen, the juvenile court represented "the most important and ambitious effort yet undertaken by our law to give practical expression to the rehabilitative ideal."[7] A separate adjudication and sentencing system for juveniles rested on the cultural perception that they were less responsible for their delinquency, more amenable to reform. A key feature of the penal-welfare programme was the turn away from the merely punitive prison sentence, and *a fortiori* from the *short* prison sentence. Judges and magistrates were encouraged to use constructive non-custodial

---

5   Francis A. Allen, "The Decline of the Rehabilitative Ideal in American Criminal Justice," *Cleveland State Law Review*, vol. 27 (1978), p. 151. For Allen's earliest statement on this theme, see "Criminal Justice, Legal Values and the Rehabilitative Ideal," *Journal of Criminal Law and Criminology*, vol. 50 (1959), pp. 226ff. Allen was not alone *describing* the main traits of the rehabilitative ideal; he was presenting one of the earliest *critical appraisals* of it.

6   Garland, *The Culture of Control: Crime and Social Order in Contemporary Society* (Oxford, 2001), chap. 2, "Modern Criminal Justice and the Penal-Welfare State," *passim*; quote at p. 35. For the main tenets of "positivist" criminology, see chap. 1 *infra* at p. 19.

7   Allen, "The Juvenile Court and the Limits of Juvenile Justice," in idem., *The Borderland of Criminal Justice: Essays in Law and Criminology* (Chicago, 1964), pp. 48–9.

measures like probation, and avoid giving prison sentences that were too short for rehabilitative techniques to work.

Five other motifs have become accepted elements in the definition of penal-welfarism. First, the perception that crime was under control. As Garland declared, penal-welfarism was created "in a context defined by low crime rates and widespread confidence in the credentials of the state's crime control institutions."[8] Second, criminology played, as Lucia Zedner noted, "the role of handmaiden to the reformative project."[9] Criminology defined crime as a social problem that manifested itself in individual acts; individuals became delinquent because they were deprived of education, family socialization, or treatment for their abnormal psychology. In line with this definition, criminologists advised that character assessment was an important preface to sentencing, canvassed penal measures that focused attention upon maladjusted individuals, and sought to determine "what works" and why by studying the efficacy of specific custodial and non-custodial measures. Third, penal policy was a bipartisan affair. Labour, Liberal, and Conservative, with few exceptions, spoke the language of penal-welfarism, accepted the practical application of its principles, and were content to leave penal policy and practice to the administrators. Accordingly, the fourth motif, the development of the penal-welfare programme was, said Garland, "the colonization of a formerly legal terrain by 'social' authorities and professional groups."[10] The creation of new sanctions, new regimes, and early release mechanisms were the work of senior civil servants, expert advisers, and penal practitioners. These ideas and programmes, moreover, were linked to the welfare state and its social democratic politics, what David Marquand has called the era of "moral collectivism," or the moral-activist tradition, the foremost guardians of which were the mandarin class. And fifth, the limits or failures of penal-welfarism were ascribed to lack of resources, to the faulty- or under-implementation of "correctionalist" programmes, or to the shortage of research—rarely if ever to the theory of rehabilitation itself.

II

This description of the rehabilitative ideal has merit, yet it should be seen for what it is, an ideal type, a fabricated model that approximates the actual by selecting and accentuating particular elements. Lucia Zedner rightly challenged the entire construct. First, she wrote that "whilst welfarism might have dominated penal discourse, it is questionable whether it dominated *practice* in the way that Garland suggests."[11] She correctly notes that the fine, in which no reformative impulse inheres, was the most frequently used penal sanction between 1938 and 1980, its use tripling from 17 to 53 per cent, at the same time as the use of the probation

8   Garland, *The Culture of Control*, op cit., p. 33.
9   Zedner, "Dangers of Dystopias in Penal Theory," *Oxford Journal of Legal Studies*, vol. 22 (2002), p. 344. See also Francis Allen, "The Rehabilitative Ideal and the Decline of Social Purpose," in idem., *The Decline of the Rehabilitative Ideal* (New Haven, 1981), p. 6.
10 Garland, *The Culture of Control*, op cit., p. 36.
11 My emphasis. Zedner, "Dangers of Dystopias in Penal Theory," op cit., p. 344.

order, a manifestly reformative measure, fell from 15 to 7 per cent. To this, one can add that the practice of imprisonment was always deeply ambivalent: classification of prisons and prisoners, open prisons, psychological counselling, on one hand; corporal punishment, maximum security prisons, and preventive detention (a "positivist" measure of predictive restraint, yet far from rehabilitative) on the other.[12] Furthermore, what *was* the prison for most offenders in the era of rehabilitation? It is hard not to endorse the 1970 judgment of Norval Morris and Gordon Hawkins:

> a walled institution where adult criminals in large numbers are held for protracted periods, with economically meaningless and insufficient employment, with vocational training or education for a few, with rare contacts with the outside world, in cellular conditions varying from the decent to those which a zoo would not tolerate, the purposes being to lead the prisoners to eschew crime in the future and to deter others of like mind from running the risk of sharing their incarceration.[13]

"Training" in this context was largely the provision by educated, middle-class administrators of low-grade work to poorly educated, working-class men and women who had gone off the rails. Prisoners may have been deterred from returning, but few were ever truly rehabilitated. As Thomas Mathiesen argued, prison simply did not rehabilitate: the realities of prison life did not begin to equate to "treatment"; and inmates became "prisonized," internalizing the customs and culture of the penitentiary, which were anathema to moral and social improvement. Research increasingly proved that rehabilitative efforts inside prisons had little or no effect on recidivism.[14]

Secondly, Zedner is not convinced, either, that penal-welfarism dominated penal *discourse*. She questions whether welfarism ever enjoyed what Garland insists was "a broad professional consensus about the basic framework within which crime control should operate, and a widely shared sense of the goals and values that should shape criminal justice."[15] She is correct to insist that rehabilitation was not the sole objective of the penal

12 Andrew von Hirsch's review of Allen's *The Decline of the Rehabilitative Ideal* (New Haven, 1981) questioned whether the dominant penal ethic before the 1960s was exclusively rehabilitative, as Allen argued, and did so on the grounds that "the other vital element in the pre-1970's ideology" was predictive restraint, or "selectively incapacitating criminal offenders, based on predictions of their likelihood of returning to crime." This was a "positivist" measure, but not strictly rehabilitative. See *University of Pennsylvania Law Review*, vol. 131 (1983), p. 822, and note 17. See also Dennis Chapman, *Sociology and the Stereotype of the Criminal* (1968), p. 219.
13 Morris and Hawkins, "Rehabilitation: Rhetoric and Reality," *Federal Probation*, vol. 34 (1970).
14 Mathiesen, *Prison on Trial: A Critical Assessment* (1990), pp. 40–1.
15 Zedner, "Dangers of Dystopias in Penal Theory," op cit., p. 344. To extend the point, I argue in the first chapter that criminological "positivism," imported from Europe, was by no means the salient framework of thought in the debate on prisons. Penal thought was influenced more by a mix of humanitarian sensibility, ethical socialism, and the maxims of moral responsibility and just proportion (between crime and punishment). These were the key strands of "philosophical idealism," the credo of a number of well-placed penal practitioners, such as Evelyn Ruggles-Brise, the chairman of the Prison

framework. While the official vocabulary of modern penal policy, visible in legal statute or government publication, expunged the word "punishment," this was not true of popular culture. Public opinion remained more punitive than government policies, notably when it came to the retention of capital punishment. Rehabilitation co-existed with, and was inevitably affected by, the continued advocacy and use of the death penalty. Even Allen agreed that the reason for the survival of the "blameworthiness" principle was that "in many instances it expresses what might be called the popular understanding of criminality."[16] Zedner encapsulates this part of her critique by noting the disconnect between the rhetoric of rehabilitation and "a continuing commitment by the courts to classical legalism." The criminal law, she claimed, "has always been retributivist in its orientation, resting on the presumption of the responsible subject and geared toward the attribution of culpability."[17] In his exposition of the theology of punishment, Tim Gorringe underlined this view, concluding that while the focal point of faith moved from the atonement (or judgment) to the incarnation (or salvation), "[r]etributivism. . . always remained the backstop to penal policy."[18]

III

This final point alerts us to the role of the sentencing court. We start with an unlikely source. In Michel Foucault's *Discipline and Punish: The Birth of the Prison,* "confinement" or the "carceral" was the master obsession. The prison, argued Foucault, conducted on a strict timetable, with its regime of work, education and religion, brought a new economy of punitive power, coercing "the soul in the body" into the dominant morality. In the new penitentiaries, the objective of punishment was not to avenge the crime but to know and transform the criminal.[19] When it came to the criminal courts and sentencing, therefore, Foucault dealt with them only to the degree they were affected by the new correctional technologies and criminologies. He argued that the carceral system had the following effects:

> . . . an increasing difficulty in judging, as if one were ashamed to pass sentence; a furious desire on the part of the judge to judge, assess, diagnose, recognize the normal and abnormal and claim the honour of curing or rehabilitating . . .

Commission. This put restraints on how far the rehabilitative ethic would be taken. In the post-1945 period, "reform," or religious and moral impulses in reformation, morphed into "rehabilitation," as reform "became secularized, psychologised, scientized": see A. E. Bottoms, "An Introduction to 'The Coming Crisis,'" in Bottoms and R. H. Preston (eds.), *The Coming Penal Crisis* (Edinburgh, 1980), p. 2.

16 Allen, "The Law as a Path to the World," *Michigan Law Review,* vol. 77 (1978), p. 161.
17 Zedner, "Dangers of Dystopias in Penal Theory," op cit., pp. 344–5.
18 Timothy Gorringe, *God's Just Vengeance: Crime, Violence and the Rhetoric of Salvation* (Cambridge, 1996), p. 229. See also Wiener, *Reconstructing the Criminal: Culture, Law, and Policy in England, 1830–1914* (Cambridge, 1990), pp. 174–7, 322.
19 See D. Garland, *Punishment and Modern Society* (Chicago, 1990), chap. 6.

Their immense "appetite for medicine" which is constantly manifested—from their appeal to psychiatric experts, to their attention to the chatter of criminology—expresses the major fact that . . . it is the economy of power that they exercise, and not that of their scruples or their humanism, that makes them pass "therapeutic" sentences and recommend "rehabilitating" periods of imprisonment.[20]

He has a point, since the existence of a "carceral continuum," incorporating schools as well as prisons, meant that the process of punishing acquired affinities with educating or less coercive mechanisms. Yet, Foucault is misleading in this attempt to incorporate judging into his thesis. In the criminal courtroom, a different penal rhetoric was on display: the punitive idiom continued to be heard, punitive rituals continued to be performed, and moral sentiments continued to be expressed.

An understanding of the sentencing court requires the insights of other theorists. French sociologist, Emile Durkheim, theorized punishment as a moral process, its forms expressing moral judgments, corresponding with deeply held beliefs of the population at large. His central thesis was that punishment affirms vital social values against those who threaten those values, and is an essential means of doing so.[21] He would have endorsed the conviction of Victorian legal theorist, James Fitzjames Stephen, that the function of punishment was to express the community's hatred of the delinquent:

The sentence of law is to the moral sentiment of the public in relation to any offence what a seal is to hot wax. It converts into a permanent final judgment what might otherwise be a transient sentiment . . . In short, the infliction of punishment by law gives definite expression and a solemn ratification and justification to the hatred which is excited by the commission of the offence . . . The criminal law thus proceeds upon the principle that it is morally right to hate criminals, and it confirms and justifies the sentiment by inflicting upon criminals punishments which express it.[22]

In similar vein in 1918, American social psychologist, G. H. Mead, in his essay, "The Psychology of Punitive Justice," emphasized how the rituals of the criminal court provided the occasion for the release of society's hostility towards the law-breaker.[23] And David Garland argued compellingly that the higher courts

continue to speak in the traditional language of moral rhetoric [such that] the courts continued to appear "punitive" even at the high point of the treatment era . . . continued to give a place to the expression of sentiment and public condemnation.[24]

20 Foucault, *Discipline and Punish* (1977), p. 304.
21 See D. Garland, *Punishment and Modern Society*, op cit., chap. 2.
22 Stephen, *A History of the Criminal Law of England* (1883), vol. 2, p. 81.
23 Mead, "The Psychology of Punitive Justice," *American Journal of Sociology*, vol. 23 (1918), p. 591.
24 See D. Garland, *Punishment and Modern Society*, op cit., p. 72.

Accordingly, a comprehensive account of punishment must situate prisons and reformatories within the punitive context that the rituals and language of the criminal courts did so much to construct. Judges and magistrates enjoyed considerable discretion in the assessment of the gravity of the crime and in choice of penalty. As Glanville Williams affirmed as late as 1963,

> the attitude of the courts has always been that there is *in gremio judicis* [in the bosom of the law] a moral scale which enables the judge to pronounce what quantum of punishment is justly appropriate to what offence. This is the punishment that fits the crime.[25]

Judges have remained stubbornly faithful to the law's role as one of moral education, to the view of the offender as a rational actor with free will and moral responsibility, and to the censuring role of sentencing. The courtroom is a blaming institution. It is here that we find discussion of responsibility and punishment, where we find publicly conveyed the social condemnation of crime.[26] Nor did magistrates and judges alone *express* moral sensibilities; they also aroused and structured them. Until 1914, the lengthy reports of court cases in national and regional newspapers "helped to fix the moral tone of the country," according to Lord Justice Lawton.[27] Today, still, it is common practice for the press to include judicial remarks and declarations.

This means that there are contradictory conceptions of justice at work in penal practice. Many years ago, Francis Allen observed that criminal justice was two-faced: "It hedges its bets. It speaks, now of moral autonomy, now from deterministic assumptions."[28] He continued:

> The same public that is asked to support the criminal law and to condemn the criminal offense is also asked to embrace and provide financial resources for programs of correctional treatment that view offenders as the products of conditions over which they [have] little or no control.[29]

Garland has gone further by identifying "two contrasting visions" at work in criminal justice: "the passionate, morally toned desire to punish and the administrative, rationalistic, normalizing concern to manage."[30] Another way of describing these visions would be to contrast the durability of the liberal tradition and its attachment to a "classical" conception of the criminal law, with the "medicalization" of deviance and

---

25 Williams, "The Courts and Persistent Offenders," *Criminal Law Review* (1963), p. 733.
26 See L. Zedner, *Criminal Justice* (Oxford, 2004), chap. 5. See also Martin Wiener, "Murderers and 'Reasonable Men': The 'Criminology' of the Victorian Judiciary," in P. Becker and R. Wetzell, *Criminals and Their Scientists: The History of Criminology in International Perspective* (Cambridge, 2006), pp. 43–60.
27 Lord Justice Lawton, "The Law and Public Opinion," *The Riddell Lecture* (1975), p. 12.
28 Allen, "The Law as a Path to the World," op cit., p. 159.
29 Ibid., p. 166.
30 Garland, *Punishment and Modern Society*, op cit., p. 180.

individualized measures of rehabilitation. These tendencies were in a continuous process of dialogue in the twentieth century—though some would suggest that the different parts of the criminal justice system failed to talk to one another.[31] How the executive, legislative, and judicial branches of criminal justice interacted with one another, how the resulting tensions influenced policy and practice, are a vital consideration in this study of punishment.

IV

The subject of this book that requires special pleading is the attention given to the debate on the abolition of capital punishment. For too long, this emotional debate has been treated as something separate and different from what we conventionally define as penal policy. Yet there has always been an intimate dialogue between the "bloody code" and the other forms of punishment, especially imprisonment. As Malcolm Ramsay speculated many years ago, if imprisonment was seen, to use the official Victorian term, as a "secondary" punishment, "and then had to be made far tougher to supersede the death penalty, this goes far to explain why imprisonment has tended to be more repressive in character in Britain than elsewhere, as well as more extensively used."[32] Other countries contrived to make a cleaner break, simultaneously building prisons and restricting if not abolishing capital punishment. England abandoned the death penalty only slowly and with reluctance, even for offences against property. Imprisonment was not readily accepted as the supreme social sanction.

Moreover, while executions had not taken place in public since 1868, this did not mean executions had become "private." Hangings were still public occasions, and provoked intense public emotional response.[33] Over the years, steps had been taken to pare down the ritual trappings of the death penalty and to reduce the mounting tension of the days prior to an execution. The hoisting of a flag atop the prison and the tolling of a bell had been discontinued. The Royal Commission on Capital Punishment recommended the abandonment of the posting of notices on the prison gate before and after execution, in an attempt to remove the spectacle of crowds gathering outside the prison. In July 1955, the House of Commons was told this practice would end, though people continued to congregate in large numbers outside prison gates.[34]

31 See Derek Lewis, *Hidden Agendas: Politics, Law and Disorder* (1997), p. 227; Justice Stephen Tumin, Inspector of Prisons, in *Asking Around: Background to the David Hare Trilogy* (New York, 2001), p. 145.

32 Ramsay, "British Penal Policy: The Shackles of the Past," *Contemporary Review* (1980), p. 34.

33 See Claire Langhamer, "'The Live Dynamic Whole of Feeling and Behaviour': Capital Punishment and the Politics of Emotion, 1945–1957," *Journal of British Studies*, vol. 5 (2012).

34 See The National Archives (TNA), HO291/105; PCom9/429, Newsam, Permanent Undersecretary of State, Home Office, to Gowers, Chairman of the Royal Commission on Capital Punishment, 9 Dec. 1949. Newsam thought the Home Office should issue a notice to the press about the place and date of execution, and the fact that the sentence had been carried out. He added: ". . . it is necessary to take care not to give people any

Above all, the location of executions inside prisons inevitably had a profound impact on staff and prisoners, and on the efforts to create a more constructive prison environment. In every prison where the death penalty could be carried out, one or more cells were provided exclusively for the use of condemned prisoners.[35] A prisoner under sentence of death remained out of sight of, and contact with, other prisoners. He or she was visited by the governor and medical officer twice daily. Prison staff watched the prisoner night and day to ensure the gallows were not cheated by his suicide. The date of the execution was fixed by the sheriff, typically in the week following the third Sunday after the day on which the sentence had been passed, unless there was an appeal. The executioner and his assistant arrived at the prison on the day before the execution. They were given information as to the height and weight of the prisoner and were permitted to see the prisoner at exercise from some concealed vantage point, which allowed them to assess the length of the drop that would be required. The apparatus was tested before the day of execution with a bag of sand of roughly the same weight as the prisoner, and the bag was left hanging overnight to stretch the rope. The chaplain spent the last hour with the prisoner and stayed until the execution was over.

The hangman would enter the condemned cell on the stroke of the appointed hour, pull the prisoner's arms behind his back, and march him to the trapdoors in the execution chamber. The sheriff, governor, and medical officer entered the execution chamber; no public or press witnesses were allowed to attend.[36] The prisoner was placed on the drop so his feet were across the division of the trap doors. The executioner placed a white cap over the prisoner's head and a noose round his neck, while the assistant pinioned his legs. The executioner pulled the lever. At this point, wrote Syd Dernley, witnessing his first execution as a trainee observer in March 1949 in Winson Green Prison, Birmingham,

> [t]he whole floor seemed to collapse; Farrell [James Farrell, 19 years of age, an army deserter, hanged for strangling a young girl] plunged downwards and there was an enormous boom which must have been heard over half the prison as those massive doors crashed against the walls of the pit.[37]

The emphasis was on the speed of execution. Albert Pierrepoint, a veteran of over 400 hangings, prided himself on taking between nine and 12 seconds on average between entering the prisoner's cell and the drop. The medical officer went

reason for suggesting that prisoners are done to death in prison in a hole and corner manner; the fact of a judicial execution is a legitimate subject of public interest and there seems to be no reason for trying to shroud in official secrecy the date on which an execution will take place and the fact that it has taken place."

35 The next two paragraphs rely upon "Method of Execution," enclosed in TNA, HO317/4.
36 Press access to executions had been taken away by the 1890s: McConville, *English Local Prisons 1860–1900* (1995), p. 429; Gerald Robin, "The Executioner: His Place in English Society," *British Journal of Sociology*, vol. 15 (1964), p. 251.
37 Dernley with David Newman, *The Hangman's Tale: Memoirs of a Public Executioner* (1989), p. 12.

immediately to the pit and examined the prisoner to see that life was extinct. The shed was then locked and the body allowed to hang for one hour. Burial of the body took place in the prison graveyard during the dinner hour.

Margery Fry told fellow penal reformer Lord Templewood that she was "convinced that the possibility of having to deal with an execution discourages the type of men and women whom we want to see in the prison service from entering it."[38] Prisoners were locked in their cells during an execution. At the sound of trap doors, according to historian Bill Forsythe, "prisoners would roar a collective protest and revulsion and create a cacophony of noise by smashing their cell furniture."[39] Terence Morris, co-author of *Pentonville* (1963), likewise emphasized the malign effect of the gallows within prison walls. During his research "although there had been no executions at Pentonville for five years, two were to take place within weeks of each other," on April 24, 1959, of Joseph Chrimes (who killed in the course of a burglary) and on May 8 of Ronald Marwood (who murdered a policeman).[40] There was disorder before and after Marwood's execution.[41] Terence Morris concluded: ". . . in the last days of capital punishment the gallows cast a long shadow over almost every local prison in the country." In Holloway, the condemned cell was within the hearing of women serving sentences of corrective training, only one example of the glaring contradiction between vengeance and rehabilitation in the confines of the prison. As the Howard League's evidence to the 1930 Select Committee on Capital Punishment had asserted, "It is difficult to reconcile the existence in a prison, of the execution shed and reformative systems of training for citizenship." In Anne Logan's

---

38 See Anne Logan, *The Politics of Penal Reform: Margery Fry and the Howard League* (2018), p. 153. Fry made the same point to the Royal Commission on Capital Punishment, 1949–53. However, not all prison officers thought executions harmful. R. W. G. Rees, Chief Officer 1 at Liverpool had attended five executions: "On the morning of an execution, I have noticed an undefinable slight tension in the air, the Prison being unusually quiet—food complaints from prisoners at breakfast are rare & everyone seems eager to keep the bell scale running smoothly. In my opinion the inexorability of the law must inevitably impress itself on the minds of those in custody & in some measure have a deterrent effect on the recidivist class." See PCom9/1802, 11 Jun. 1949. So, too, a panel of governors from Wandsworth, Wakefield, Pentonville, Lincoln, and Swansea prisons submitted a memorandum to the Royal Commission on Capital Punishment stating that governors favoured execution by hanging, "which in their view was expeditious and humane." See *The Times*, 7 Oct. 1949, p. 2.

39 Bill Forsythe, "Loneliness and Cellular Confinement in English Prisons 1878–1921," *British Journal of Criminology*, vol. 44 (2004), p. 764. Forsythe cites Stuart Wood, *Shades of the Prison House* (1932), p. 377, who wrote that a forthcoming execution bred "an atmosphere of silent brooding in officers and men alike."

40 Morris, "A Lifetime with Pentonville," *Prison Service Journal*, issue 209 (2013), p. 36.

41 *Hansard*, vol. 605, 14 May 1959, col. 172; TNA, HO291/111, Cunningham to Home Secretary, 26 Jan. 1961; Terence and Pauline Morris, *Pentonville* (1963), p. 121; *The Times*, 20 Dec. 1991, David Waddilove, obituary, governor of Pentonville at the time of these two hangings, was "a passionate opponent of capital punishment." See also L. Seal, *Capital Punishment in Twentieth-Century Britain* (2014), p. 84.

words, for advocates of what the Howard League called "modern penal science. . . the death penalty was an unwelcome atavism."[42]

For the abolitionists, capital punishment was the antithesis of penal reform; the greatest contradiction to the principles of training for responsible citizenship. Roy Calvert, secretary to the National Council for the Abolition of the Death Penalty, wanted an enlightened treatment of all lawbreakers, and viewed the death penalty, according to his wife, "as the stranglehold which enabled the forces of reaction to keep their ground."[43] The fight over abolition became a test of the country's commitment to the reformative treatment of prisoners. Or as the *News Chronicle* declared at the height of the battle over capital punishment in 1948, abolition "has been regarded as the pinnacle of criminal reform which we must attain before we can hold up our heads in the modern world." For the retentionists, the demands for hanging (and flogging) testified to their concern over the problems of crime and punishment. Capital punishment was their sure and sovereign cure for all problems of crime. Even if we accept that "the death penalty began to appear. . . increasingly at odds with the 'politics of life' and the humanistic culture that were defining feature[s] of welfare state societies,"[44] the retentionists managed to keep the abolitionists at bay for a half century beyond 1914.

All through these years, the death penalty distracted Home Secretaries and the Home Department each time the royal prerogative of mercy for a convicted murderer was under consideration. On the strength of his time as Home Secretary in the 1960s, Roy Jenkins claimed that the death penalty pervaded the atmosphere of the Home Office, with the adventurous thought stifled by the "clinically strict regard for precedent and consistency."[45] The death penalty also gave an excuse for much of the press to beat their chests on the issue of crime and punishment. So, too, the most renowned set-piece, parliamentary battles in both Houses over penal policy invariably concerned this most retributive of icons. Why then is capital punishment treated by historians in isolation from other parts of the penal system? Yes, it was the only bodily punishment that still remained (with the exception of corporal punishment), it aroused visceral emotions that no other punishment did, it polarized political opinion, and it estranged parliamentary from public opinion in a way that no other penal policy did. To that degree, there is an argument for treating the death penalty as *sui generis*. Yet it is surely significant that the passage of the Criminal Justice Act of 1948, intended to steer penal policy towards rehabilitation, should have been so thoroughly distracted by the debate on capital punishment. It is likewise significant that this retributive penalty should still have attracted ardent defenders in the 1960s, at the supposed apex of the rehabilitative

---

42 TNA, PCom9/2236; Logan, *The Politics of Penal Reform*, op cit., p. 152.
43 Foreword to E. Roy Calvert, *Capital Punishment in the Twentieth Century* (1927; 5th ed. 1936), quoted in E. H. Jones, *Margery Fry* (1966), p. 124.
44 Garland, "Modes of Capital Punishment: The Death Penalty in Historical Perspective," in Garland et al. (eds.), *America's Death Penalty* (New York, 2011), p. 59.
45 Jenkins, "On Being a Minister," in V. Herman and J. E. Alt (eds.), *Cabinet Studies: A Reader* (1975), pp. 214–5. Reprinted from the *Sunday Times*, 17 Jan. 1971.

ideal. Indeed, the abolition of the death penalty was the most mesmerizing and influential theme in penal reform in the first two-thirds of the twentieth century. As Attorney-General Sir John Hobson said to Home Secretary Henry Brooke in February 1964, ". . . most discussions on crime and punishment usually come back to the death penalty and corporal punishment."[46] The death penalty was a dark cloud that hung over the entire penal system, periodically refreshing judicial, political, and public support for this iconic retributive measure. The progress of rehabilitation was constantly dogged by the retributive theatre of hanging. As such, the death penalty cannot easily be divorced from the wider structure of penalties; it is time we brought capital punishment into the wider discussion of penal policy and practice.[47]

The pre-eminent theme of this book is the degree to which the rehabilitative ideal established itself between 1895 and 1970. There were age groups for which rehabilitation became increasingly standard, namely, juveniles and young adults. For adults, however, there were severe limitations to the implementation of the rehabilitative ethic. Weaning judges off the "tariff" was a slow and unsuccessful business. The fine was used widely, but was hardly a rehabilitative sentence. Courts were willing to give probation a try or two, if the crime was not too serious, but after several failures, they would revert to the short, sharp shock of a prison sentence. The judiciary were encouraged by penal administrators and reformers to replace the short prison sentence with ones that allowed time for treatment and training; yet, three out of every four prisoners continued to be awarded short prison terms. Most offenders were still sent to prison for punishment, not rehabilitation. Judges also blocked any serious attempt to solve the problem of the persistent offender, whether professional or petty. Indeed, the influence of the judiciary runs through the entire book, whether for good (the massive abatement of imprisonment between 1880 and 1940), for ill (the stubborn defence of corporal punishment and the death penalty), or for the best (in the restraints they imposed on the more illiberal practices of the rehabilitative ideal). For all the treatment and training rhetoric, sentencing and penal practice was largely punitive for most adult offenders. It was not coincidental that the primary symbol of retribution, the death penalty, hung around until the tide of rehabilitation was beginning to go out.

---

46   TNA, HO291/518, Hobson to Brooke, 10 Feb. 1964.
47   Claire Valier, *Crime and Punishment in Contemporary Culture* (2004), begins her chapter on "The shadow of the death penalty" by quoting Michel Foucault's remark: "the practice of the public execution haunted our penal system for a long time and still haunts it today." No historian (or criminologist) would consider examining the *American* "carceral state" without parallel consideration of the death penalty. See Marie Gottschalk, *The Prison and the Gallows: The Politics of Mass Incarceration in America* (Cambridge, 2006).

1

ENGLISH PRISONS AND PENAL CULTURE, 1895–1922

The prison method is callous, regular and monotonous and produces great mental and physical strain. The deprivation of liberty is extremely cruel and if it is attended with treatment that deadens the spiritual nature and fails to offer any stimulus to the imagination, that coarsens and humiliates, then it stands condemned.

Arthur Creech Jones, conscientious objector, Wandsworth Prison, 1916–19[1]

I

The nineteenth century was the century of the penitentiary. Public and physical punishments (from whipping to the death penalty) were gradually replaced by the less visible, less corporal sanction of imprisonment. By the start of the Victorian era, imprisonment was the predominant penalty in the system of judicial punishments. For every 1,000 offenders sentenced at higher and summary courts in 1836 for serious (or indictable) offenses, 685 were punished by imprisonment in local prisons.[2] By mid-century, moreover, sentences of penal servitude in convict prisons were plugging the gap left by the end of

---

1   Papers of Arthur Creech Jones, Bodleian Library, Oxford, MS British Empire S 332, box 1, file 2, fols. 194–7, n.d.: manuscript account of his thoughts in Wandsworth prison; quoted with permission from Violet Creech Jones.
2   In addition, 33 were punished by death, 21 were fined, and 245 were transported; see Leon Radzinowicz and Roger Hood, *The Emergence of Penal Policy*, vol. 5 of *A History of English Criminal Law and Its Administration from 1750* (1986), p. 777. In a move to privatize punishment, public execution was abandoned in 1868; thereafter, hanging took place behind prison walls; see V. A. C. Gatrell, *The Hanging Tree: Execution and the English People, 1770–1868* (Oxford, 1994), pp. 589–611; R. McGowen, "Civilizing Punishment: The End of the Public Execution in England," *Journal of British Studies*, vol. 33 (1994), pp. 257–82.

transportation to Australia.[3] The 300 or so local prisons in the 1830s to which offenders were sent for anywhere between one day and two years (though typically for terms of less than three months), were locally controlled until 1877, and were less than uniform in regime. The separate system of prison discipline (or cellular isolation) increasingly prevailed over the silent system (or associated, silent labour), but it was subject to considerable local modification. Convict prisons were run by central government with less variability. Offenders sentenced to the longer terms of penal servitude spent the first nine months separately confined in a prison like Pentonville, the symbol since its foundation in 1842 of the penitential ideal, and the bulk of the sentence at a "public works" prison like Dartmoor, working silently in association, until release on licence. These differences aside, the regime behind the tall perimeter walls of most Victorian prisons inclined to one of hygienic and routinized order, cellular surveillance, and religious indoctrination.[4]

The first rays of reformist zeal were soon obscured by the clouds of deterrence that rolled in during the 1860s. One commission of inquiry after the next advised government to make the prisons more repressive, more deterrent, and feared. The task of making the prison regime exacting and uniform went to Edmund Du Cane, chairman of the Directors of Convict Prisons and an administrative martinet. From 1869 until his retirement in 1895, Du Cane turned the convict prison system into "a huge punishing machine," in the words of the Irish Fenian Michael Davitt,[5] and from 1877, when the Prison Act brought local prisons under central government control, he unified and streamlined the local prison structure. Two features distinguished Du Cane's penology: an inflexible adoption of deterrence as the primary aim of punishment, and a rigid adherence to the uniform enforcement by the prison authorities of the court-ordered punishment. Thus, Du Cane put into practice what the "classical school" of criminal law and penal policy had preached since the eighteenth century.

3 Transportation was the relocation of convicted criminals (including political prisoners) to established penal colonies. From the 1610s, convicts were sent to colonies in the Americas. For eighty years, between 1787 and 1868, some 160,000 convicts were transported to Australia.

4 See U. Henriques, "The Rise and Decline of the Separate System of Prison Discipline," *Past and Present*, no. 54 (1972), pp. 61–93; Victor Bailey (ed.), *Policing and Punishment in Nineteenth Century Britain* (1981), pp. 11–24; Michael Ignatieff, "State, Civil Society, and Total Institutions: A Critique of Recent Social Histories of Punishment," in M. Tonry and N. Morris (eds.), *Crime and Justice: An Annual Review of Research*, vol. 3 (Chicago, 1981), pp. 153–92; S. McConville, *A History of English Prison Administration, 1750–1877* (1981), chaps. 6–8, 11–13; M. DeLacy, *Prison Reform in Lancashire, 1700–1850* (Stanford, 1986); J. A. Sharpe, *Judicial Punishment in England* (1990), pp. 61–87; Clive Emsley, "The History of Crime and Crime Control Institutions, c. 1770–c. 1945," in M. Maguire, R. Morgan, and R. Reiner (eds.), *The Oxford Handbook of Criminology* (Oxford, 1994), chap. 4. Pentonville prison was initially used for convicts aged 18 to 35 who were sentenced to transportation for their first offense. They spent 18 (later reduced to nine) months in separate confinement before going to the penal colony. The period of separate confinement was applied to all penal servitude, or convict, sentences after 1857.

5 Quoted in Radzinowicz and Hood, p. 545.

Since individuals had freedom of choice in deciding whether or not to commit crime, they should be deemed to be responsible; hence, punishment, to be effective, should deter, and it should be strictly proportionate to the gravity of the crime. On the surface, the results of "classical" penal policy were impressive. Between 1879 and 1894, the daily average population in convict prisons fell by over half, from 10,880 prisoners to 4,770, and the population of local prisons fell by one-third, from 20,833 prisoners to 13,850. The drop in the prison population was probably less a function of prison discipline, however, than of the fall in recorded crime, a reduction in the minimum duration of penal servitude (from seven years to three years), and an increasing resort by courts to non-custodial penalties. For every 1,000 offenders sentenced at higher and summary courts in 1896 for indictable crimes, 516 were imprisoned, 19 sentenced to penal servitude, 194 fined, 120 bound over in their recognizances, and 34 sent to reformatory and industrial schools.[6] As the century of the prison drew to a close, the confidence in deterrent imprisonment was decidedly on the wane.

In 1895, two events brought the secret world of the Du Cane regime to public attention. The Departmental Committee on Prisons, under the chairmanship of Herbert Gladstone, issued its report, and Oscar Wilde, found guilty of homosexual acts, began a sentence of two years' imprisonment with hard labour.[7] In both cases, the medium that brought prison conditions to public attention was the press.[8] The Liberal newspaper, the *Daily Chronicle*, had taken the lead in January 1894 with a set of articles entitled "Our Dark Places."[9] It has long been presumed that the author of these articles was the assistant chaplain of Wandsworth prison, W. D. Morrison, but it now seems certain that the assistant editor, H. W. Massingham, wrote them, having toured a number of Her Majesty's prisons in the previous autumn.[10] Likewise,

6 See ibid., chap. 16, and p. 777; V. A. C. Gatrell, "The Decline of Theft and Violence in Victorian and Edwardian England," in V. A. C. Gatrell, B. Lenman, and G. Parker (eds.), *Crime and the Law* (1980), chap. 9. Du Cane's rigorous administration of the local prison system is exhaustively detailed in Sean McConville, *English Local Prisons, 1860–1900: Next Only to Death* (1995), chaps. 4–10. See also Bill Forsythe, "Du Cane, Sir Edmund Frederick (1830–1903)," *Oxford Dictionary of National Biography* (hereafter *Oxford DNB*), 2004.

7 Herbert Gladstone was first commissioner of works in the Liberal government and previously Parliamentary Undersecretary at the Home Office. See H. C. G. Matthew, "Gladstone, Herbert John, Viscount Gladstone (1854–1930)," *Oxford DNB* (2010).

8 *Report from the Departmental Committee on Prisons*, C. 7702, *Parliamentary Papers* (PP), 1895, vol. 56, p. 5. For a full account of the vigorous public campaign for a prison inquiry, see McConville, *English Local Prisons*, chap. 13. The Irish nationalists in Parliament, many of whom had been imprisoned for political offences, were also critical of prison administration. Their influence was strong enough to get one of their number, Arthur O'Connor, onto the Departmental Committee. See Michael Davitt, *The Prison Life of Michael Davitt, Related by Himself* (Dublin, 1882), pp. 10–18, and "Criminal and Prison Reform," *Nineteenth Century*, vol. 36 (Dec. 1894), pp. 875–89.

9 See John Stokes, *In the Nineties* (Chicago, 1989), pp. 96–9; A. F. Havighurst, *Radical Journalist: H. W. Massingham (1860–1924)* (Cambridge, 1974), p. 65.

10 See McConville, *English Local Prisons*, pp. 554–77; Stokes, p. 96; Radzinowicz and Hood, p. 574. See also W. D. Morrison, "Are Our Prisons a Failure?" *Fortnightly*

news of Oscar Wilde's prison treatment appeared in the columns of the *Daily Chronicle*, as did Wilde's two letters on prison reform written on release from Reading Gaol.[11] Massingham followed Wilde's case closely and urged W. T. Stead, editor of the *Pall Mall Gazette*, to do the same. "Don't forget the horror of the [prison] system," wrote Massingham, "which continually presses on my imagination since I went the round of the prisons. The whole thing is torture & nothing but torture. Oscar Wilde is being slowly starved to death, & is now little better than an hysterical imbecile."[12]

The main burden of the indictment against the Du Cane regime was that a highly centralized system of prison administration gave attention to "organization, finance, order, health of the prisons, and prison statistics," but treated prisoners "as a hopeless or worthless element of the community."[13] A prison regime characterized by inflexible discipline, rigid uniformity, and separate confinement was not even acting as an effective deterrent: prisons held, nay manufactured, increasing numbers of recidivists. The present principles of prison discipline, the Reverend Morrison charged, were so "debilitating," as evinced by the amount of insanity and suicide in local prisons, that they turned the casual offender into "a gaol-made criminal, the most dangerous class of all, and the most incorrigible."[14] In response to the growing dissatisfaction with the prison regime, the Gladstone Committee expressed the cautious hope that deterrence and reform could be pursued at one and the same time, as the "primary and concurrent objects" of prison treatment within a prison structure in which unproductive hard labour would be eliminated, the time spent in separate confinement reduced, and educational and trade-training services developed. More radical proposals followed for young offenders and recidivists, characterized by longer detention and special institutions.[15]

Meanwhile, between June 1895 and May 1897, Oscar Wilde served his sentence of two years' hard labour, a term that the Gladstone Committee judged to be more

Review, vol. 55 (Apr. 1894), pp. 459–69. For Morrison's evidence to the Gladstone Committee, see *Minutes of Evidence to the Departmental Committee on Prisons*, C. 7702-I, PP, 1895, vol. 56, pp. 158–84.

11 Letters, *Daily Chronicle* 27 May 1897; 24 Mar. 1898, reprinted in Oscar Wilde, *The Soul of Man and Prison Writings* (Oxford, 1990), pp. 159–67, 190–6. Wilde completed his sentence on 19 May 1897.

12 Quoted in Havighurst, p. 67. Massingham's description of Wilde was exaggerated, to judge from other evidence. See Richard Ellmann, *Oscar Wilde* (New York, 1988), pp. 479–532.

13 *Report from the Departmental Committee on Prisons*, C. 7702, PP, 1895, vol. 56, p. 11, par. 23.

14 Morrison, "Are Our Prisons a Failure?" p. 468. See Christopher Harding, "'The Inevitable End of a Discredited System'? The Origins of the Gladstone Committee Report on Prisons, 1895," *Historical Journal*, vol. 31 (1988), pp. 598–600; McConville, *English Local Prisons*, pp. 559–61, 581–3.

15 See W. R. Cornish and J. Hart, *Crime and Law in Nineteenth Century Britain* (Dublin, 1978), pp. 38–9; Radzinowicz and Hood, pp. 576–9; McConville, *English Local Prisons*, chap. 15.

than a man could endure. Each day during the first month, prisoners climbed the equivalent of 6,000 feet on the treadmill, a purely penal form of labour.[16] Wilde was declared unfit for first-class labour by the medical officer and so was excused from the treadmill. Each night, however, he slept on a bare plank bed. After the first month, Wilde worked in silence stitching mailbags or picking oakum (tearing old, tarry ropes into corkscrew strands for use in caulking the deck planking of ships).[17] In silence, too, he attended chapel each morning (twice on Sunday) and took daily exercise in single file for an hour in the open air. After the first three months, he could write four letters a year, all vetted and censored before they were dispatched, and see friends four times a year for no more than 20 minutes each time.[18] An attack of dysentery put Wilde into the prison infirmary for two months and led to some improvement in his dietary lot. Additional relief came in the shape of the Liberal lawyer R. B. Haldane, who, as a member of the Gladstone Committee, had the authority to enter any prison and make the governor produce any prisoner. He visited Wilde in Pentonville and agreed to get him books of his choice. He also visited the prisoner in Wandsworth and subsequently persuaded the Home Secretary to transfer Wilde to Reading, where he was assigned to light work in the garden and in book distribution. For his troubles, Haldane later received a copy of Wilde's celebrated work, *The Ballad of Reading Gaol* (1898), written on his release from prison.[19]

The rise of the prison as the main, not to say symbolic, form of punishment in the nineteenth century has concentrated the minds of a number of historians in the past 25 years. One question, above all, has guided their work: why, between 1780 and 1840, was the penitentiary conceived and constructed? And one explanation has taken centre stage: the origins of this revolution in punishment are to be found less in the humanitarian sensibility of prison reformers, whether evangelical or utilitarian (which an older historiography underlined), and more in the desire of elite groups to isolate the criminal class, to shape a disciplined workforce, and to cope with the social dislocations of a new industrial order. Humanitarian sensibility is traced back to its supposed source in economic interest or the will to power.[20] In 1985, however, David Garland's

---

16 See the illustration with caption of the treadmill or tread wheel at Preston Prison in 1902, *infra*.

17 Picking oakum was a common form of hard labour in Victorian prisons (as well as in poor law workhouses).

18 See Ellmann, p. 480; Wilde's letter to the *Daily Chronicle* 24 Mar. 1898, in Wilde, *The Soul of Man*, pp. 193–4.

19 R. B. Haldane, *An Autobiography* (1929), pp. 166–7; Ellmann, p. 495; Wilde, *The Ballad of Reading Gaol*, lines 559–70, in Wilde, *The Soul of Man*, pp. 186–7; McConville, *English Local Prisons*, pp. 598–9.

20 See Michel Foucault, *Discipline and Punish: The Birth of the Prison* (1975; reprint, 1977); M. Ignatieff, *A Just Measure of Pain: The Penitentiary in the Industrial Revolution, 1750–1850* (New York, 1978). See also Victor Bailey, "The Fabrication of Deviance: 'Dangerous Classes' and 'Criminal Classes' in Victorian England," in J. Rule and R. Malcolmson (eds.), *Protest and Survival: Essays for E. P. Thompson* (1993), pp. 221–56.

Punishment and Welfare offered a new approach to the origins of the modern English penal system.[21] In particular, Garland converted the blueprint offered by the Gladstone Report (1895) into the starting point of the "modern penal complex" and, in so doing, shifted the timing of the transition to "modern penality" from the birth of the penitentiary to the Edwardian period. Between 1895 and 1914, according to Garland, the conceptual domain defined by the "classical" jurisprudential principles of individual moral responsibility, deterrence, and just proportion between crime and punishment, and the Victorian penal structure that rested on these principles, were replaced by a new "positivist" criminology and by the "modern penal complex."[22]

The main tenets of "positivist" criminology, common to all the European "schools" of criminology, were, first, that criminal behaviour was determined by factors and processes that could be discovered by observation, measurement, and inductive reasoning, the methods used by the natural and social sciences. Second, since people were impelled to commit crime by constitutional and environmental forces beyond their control and, thus, were not responsible for their actions, treatment, and "medicalization," not punishment, was the most appropriate legal response. Third, the delinquent was fundamentally different from normal, law-abiding citizens. In the 20 years following Cesare Lombroso's *L'Uomo delinquente* (1876), the founding text of positivist criminology, numerous congresses, associations, and journals promoted a positivist diagnosis of criminal behaviour and linked it to a new model of criminal justice. Proportionate punishment was rejected in favour of a system of sanctions adapted to the reformability or "dangerousness" of the individual offender. An exclusively deterrent system of criminal justice was rejected in favour of one that would prevent, treat, and eliminate delinquency.[23] The proponents of this scientific criminology, along with advocates of the eugenic program (who claimed that criminality, like feeblemindedness and alcoholism, was a heritable "degenerate" characteristic), and prison administrators all took part, according to Garland, in the complex administrative and legislative process that lay the foundations of modern penality. The notable milestones on this 20-year legislative road were the Prison Act (1898), the Inebriates Act (1898), the Prevention of Crime Act (1908), and the Mental Deficiency Act (1913). Under these enactments, special institutions were established for the extended training or segregation of "habitual drunkards," "habitual criminals," and the "mentally defective." The new penal forms, finally, were part of a much wider social and political transformation,

21 David Garland, *Punishment and Welfare: A History of Penal Strategies* (Aldershot, 1985).
22 Ibid., chap. 1. See also David Garland, "The Criminal and His Science: A Critical Account of the Formation of Criminology at the End of the Nineteenth Century," *British Journal of Criminology*, vol. 25 (Apr. 1985), pp. 109–37.
23 Cesare Lombroso, *L'Uomo delinquente* (Milan, 1876). See L. Radzinowicz, *Ideology and Crime* (New York, 1966), pp. 50–6; David Matza, *Delinquency and Drift* (1964), chap. 1; Taylor et al., *The New Criminology* (1977), pp. 10–23; D. Garland, "Of Crimes and Criminals: The Development of Criminology in Britain," in M. Maguire, R. Morgan, and R. Reiner (eds.), *The Oxford Handbook of Criminology* (Oxford, 1994), pp. 37–42.

according to Garland. The new penality was tightly linked to the social principles and strategies that would become known as the Welfare State.[24]

Punishment and Welfare owes an obvious, if largely unacknowledged, intellectual debt to Michel Foucault's *Discipline and Punish* (1975). Garland and Foucault examined different fault lines, but they adopted the same method of sinking a shaft into the culture of a particular period and excavating its *episteme* or the deep structure of knowledge at work in that society. Moreover, Garland translated Foucault's conception of change by radical shifts from one discursive formation or *episteme* to another, into a recognizable historical and political reality. And last, Garland shared Foucault's view that the reforms we tend to describe as rational, progressive, and humanitarian in fact constituted a new strategy for the more effective exercise of social control: "Not to punish less, but to punish better . . . to insert the power to punish more deeply into the social body."[25]

More recently, Martin Wiener's *Reconstructing the Criminal* (1990), while critical of Garland's exclusively political interpretation of criminal policy, and while concerned to show the role of culture, values, and sensibilities in the shaping of penal history, presented an account of the transformation of criminal justice from the penal crisis of the 1890s to the outbreak of war in 1914 that differed little in essentials from that of Garland. In the last quarter of the nineteenth century, according to Wiener, society lost confidence in the inherent responsibility of individuals. Crime was increasingly ascribed, not to wilful utilitarian calculation, but to inherited mental or physical deficiency. Accordingly, reformers no longer sought to "remoralize" the criminal—to develop the moral character necessary for leading a law-abiding life—but to "demoralize" the criminal—to uncover the physiological and environmental (or "natural") roots of criminal behaviour. Wiener, like Garland, contended that the new image of criminal man owed a good deal to the force of the human sciences and, notably, positivist criminology. And the network of penal measures grounded on this new image of man represented, for Wiener, too, a major structural change in the penal complex.[26]

The shift in "mental frame" and the enactment of positive penology owed not a little, argued Wiener, to changes in Home Office personnel and to the reforming

---

24   Garland, *Punishment and Welfare*, chaps. 3–5, and *Punishment and Modern Society: A Study in Social Theory* (Chicago, 1990), pp. 206–9. And see Harding, p. 608. In recent years, Garland has enriched his approach to the history of "penality" by incorporating discussion of the links between penal institutions and cultural phenomena: see *Punishment and Modern Society*, chaps. 9–11. Nonetheless, he stands by his original conception of a new Edwardian "penal-welfare complex," characterized by "its distinctively positive approach to the reform of deviants, its extensive use of interventionist agencies, its deployment of social work and psychiatric expertise, its concern to regulate, manage, and normalize rather than immediately to punish, and of course its new 'welfarist' self-representation" (ibid., p. 128).

25   Foucault, p. 82.

26   Martin J. Wiener, *Reconstructing the Criminal: Culture, Law, and Policy in England, 1830–1914* (Cambridge, 1990), chap. 6.

Liberal governments of 1906–14. The first generation of career civil servants, "less moralistic or legalistic than their predecessors . . . more attracted to the idea of scientific administration," assumed positions of influence in the Home Office and Prison Commission in the 1890s.[27] A case in point was Evelyn Ruggles-Brise, who entered the Home Office in 1881 and replaced Du Cane as chairman of the Prison Commission in 1895. Likewise, a new generation of politicians took the tiller. Herbert Gladstone, who chaired the Gladstone Committee, became Home Secretary in the 1906 government and enacted the committee's two proposals concerning habitual criminals and young adult offenders. His successor, Winston Churchill, was more visionary still, instructing his officials to draft plans for a remedial penal system. By 1914, then, as Wiener concluded,

> the rationales of deterrence and disciplinary moralization were yielding to those of welfarist administration. After the First World War, the seeds planted in the late Victorian and Edwardian years came to fruition, and the criminal justice system was thoroughly reorganized according to the new vision of criminality and its solution.[28]

I wish to offer a different interpretation of the years 1895–1914, and, by extension, to 1922, one that seeks, first, to argue for a more limited alteration in the structure of criminal justice, second, to reconstruct the penal culture of this period in its full complexity, and third, to highlight what I take to be the truly significant change in penal practice in the quarter century following the Gladstone Report, the massive abatement of imprisonment.[29] These years are simply not intelligible in terms solely of an emerging positivism or medicalism. David Garland and Martin Wiener, in my view, placed far too much emphasis on positivist criminology and the associated alterations in the practice of criminal justice. The intellectual roots of what happened, and what failed to happen, in the realm of penality need to be sought elsewhere: in a radical humanitarianism, in the writings of the Philosophical Idealists, and in ethical socialism.[30] The most critical change in these years—the recognition of the worthlessness of short-term imprisonment, and the related "decentring" of the prison in the system of judicial punishments—needs greater

---

27 Ibid., p. 339. See Philip Priestley, "Brise, Sir Evelyn John Ruggles- (1857–1935)," *Oxford DNB* (2004). He was appointed in 1892 as Commissioner of Prisons; in 1895 as chairman of the Prison Commission.

28 Ibid., p. 379. McConville, *English Local Prisons*, chap. 12, also emphasizes the contribution of a new generation of Home Office clerks, including Ruggles-Brise, to penal change.

29 In this I have built on the suggestive remarks to be found in Radzinowicz and Hood, chaps. 1, 17; and W. J. Forsythe, *Penal Discipline, Reformatory Projects and the English Prison Commission, 1895–1939* (Exeter, 1990), chap. 1.

30 See Jose Harris's convincing assessment of the role of Idealist thought in the development of the welfare state: "Political Thought and the Welfare State, 1870–1940: An Intellectual Framework for British Social Policy," *Past and Present*, no. 135 (1992), pp. 117–39.

emphasis and evaluation than it has received. I begin this reassessment of the changes and continuities in the penal policy and practice of late Victorian and Edwardian England by arguing that alterations in the structure of the penal complex have been exaggerated in recent scholarship.

II

The first legislative response to the Gladstone Committee's report—a report that simply proposed ameliorating the cruelty and inhumanity of prison discipline, and the grafting of a limited number of treatment and training initiatives to the existing body of punishment and moral improvement—was the Prison Act 1898. The primary object of the measure, according to the Home Secretary, Matthew White Ridley, was "the creation of powers for applying differential treatment or classification . . . to our prison population."[31] The act established three separate divisions for those sentenced to imprisonment without hard labour. Prisoners placed in the first division, for example, were excused the first month of separate confinement. Yet significantly—and in fairness, the point is not lost on David Garland—a classification that was meant to determine the conditions under which an offender would serve his sentence was left, *pace* the positivist program, to the sentencing court, not the prison executive. The criteria to be followed by the courts, moreover, included both individualization—the offender's "character" and "antecedents"—and neoclassical concerns—the "nature of the offence" and "special provocation." Undaunted, Garland described the act's classification as a "discursive bridgehead to later and more fundamental changes."[32] In fact, the experiment was a failure since the courts seldom used any but the third and most severe classification. In 1912–13, 37 males and one female were placed in the first division, mainly for offences against the Elementary Education Acts; 869 males and 246 females got the second division, or roughly one per cent of persons admitted into local prisons.[33]

The 1898 act also conferred on the Home Secretary the power to make rules for prison administration without seeking fresh legislation, abolished all forms of penal labour (including the treadmill and hand-crank), and allowed local prisoners to earn remission of up to one-sixth of their sentence.[34] Of all the improvements

31 *Hansard*, vol. 55, 24 Mar. 1898, col. 837. See Garland, *Punishment and Welfare*, pp. 216–17. The most complete account of the 1898 Prisons Bill, and of the unsuccessful press and parliamentary campaign to deepen its reforming effect on the prison system, is in McConville, *English Local Prisons*, chap. 17. The Second Reading of the Bill prompted Oscar Wilde to write to the *Daily Chronicle* (24 Mar. 1898), to catalogue what he termed the "three permanent punishments authorized by law in English prisons": hunger, insomnia, and disease. See Wilde, *The Soul of Man*, pp. 190–6. See also McConville, *English Local Prisons*, pp. 708–10, 755–6.

32 Garland, *Punishment and Welfare*, p. 217. See W. D. Morrison, "Prison Reform I: Prisons and Prisoners," *Fortnightly Review*, vol. 63 (May 1898), pp. 781–9.

33 See *Report of the Indian Jails Committee, 1919–20*, Cmd. 1303, PP, 1921, vol. 10, pp. 447–50.

34 See the Advisory Council on the Penal System, *Sentences of Imprisonment: A Review of Maximum Penalties* (1978), p. 64.

made prior to the war, however, the most important concerned the term of solitary or separate confinement endured by every convict prisoner for the first few months of a penal servitude sentence and by every local prisoner sentenced to hard labour for the first month.[35] The playwright John Galsworthy first concentrated the official mind in an "Open Letter to the Home Secretary" in the *Nation* in May 1909, in which he charged that solitary confinement was detrimental to mental, moral, and physical health to no deterrent purpose.[36] Ruggles-Brise countered by arguing that solitary confinement was not retained on grounds of deterrence but "in order to give the necessary penal character to a sentence of penal servitude in the same way as a month's separate confinement is maintained in local prisons as the penal element of the sentence of hard labor."[37] He was willing, however, to limit the duration of strict cellular isolation to three months for all classes serving a sentence of penal servitude. Gladstone, now Home Secretary, agreed; hence, Galsworthy was told that a uniform term of three months' separate confinement for all convicts would come into force on April 1, 1910. For Galsworthy, it was "a big step in the right direction," but not the end of the campaign.[38] Winston Churchill's appointment as Home Secretary brought fresh hope.

As Churchill took up the reins of office, Galsworthy urged him "to strike the finishing blow at a custom which continues to darken our humanity and good sense." Churchill asked the prison commissioners for the main arguments against the total abolition of the system of separate confinement.[39] But Galsworthy left nothing to chance. He highlighted the detrimental effects of such confinement in his new play *Justice*, first produced in February 1910. The play's high point is a three-minute prison scene in which a young clerk, imprisoned for forgery, beats helplessly on his cell door, racked by the mental torture of solitary confinement. The scene, in which no word is spoken, profoundly affected the audience. Both Churchill and Ruggles-Brise went to see the play, the latter concluding that it was unfair because "it makes an abnormal case typical of the system."[40] Churchill, however, insisted on a reduction in the

---

35 More strictly, the period of separate confinement undergone by convicts was three months for the "Star" class, six months for "Intermediates," and nine months for recidivists and revokees. The practice of separate confinement harked back to the origins of the penitentiary in the 1840s, when it became official policy, from American example, to reform prisoners through "penitence" or silent reflection upon their crimes. See citations in note 4 *supra*.

36 *Nation* (1 and 8 May 1909). The *Nation* was the main mouthpiece of the New Liberalism.

37 The National Archives (TNA), London, Prison Commission (PCom.) 7/308; E. Ruggles-Brise memo, 10 Jun. 1909, PCom. 7/309.

38 TNA, PCom. 7/309; H. V. Marrot, *The Life and Letters of John Galsworthy* (1935), pp. 250, 677; E. Garnett (ed.), *Letters from John Galsworthy 1900–1932* (1934), p. 174.

39 Marrot, pp. 676–8.

40 J. Galsworthy, *Justice* (New York, 1910), pp. 81–4; E. Ruggles-Brise to W. Churchill, 21 Mar. 1910, TNA, PCom. 7/309. C. F. G. Masterman, Parliamentary Undersecretary at the Home Office, told Galsworthy at a *Nation* lunch in April that "he had turned the Home Office upside down with *Justice*"; quoted in Havighurst, *Radical Journalist*, p. 163.

term of separate confinement, and a compromise was reached with the Prison Commission whereby separate confinement would be limited to one month for all convicts, except for "old lags," who would continue to serve three months. If unsuccessful in his quest for abolition, Galsworthy took comfort from the reckoning that his writings had helped "to knock off 1000 months of Solitary Confinement per year."[41]

This change aside (which brought no improvement for the large body of *local* prisoners), the Victorian prison system remained essentially inviolate. Nothing better illustrates how the new rules introduced under the 1898 Prison Act were simply a development, on less repressive lines, of the older system of prison discipline, than the fact that 20 years on from the act, prison administration came under a barrage of criticism quite as heavy as that which had provoked the appointment of the Gladstone Committee. And it emerged that little had truly changed.

Ruggles-Brise's regime came under the critical scrutiny of the "absolutist" conscientious objectors, "unaccustomed travellers into this valley of shadow," as Margery Fry, Quaker secretary of the Howard League for Penal Reform, so appositely termed them.[42] Over 16,000 men were conscientious objectors during the First World War, but only the 1,350 who took up an "absolutist" position and refused alternative work were subject to the cycle of arrest, court-martial, prison, release, and arrest. The practice quickly developed of commuting the original sentence of two years' imprisonment with hard labour to 112 days, which, with "good conduct," meant just over three months in prison. Repeated sentences—and some conscientious objectors served three, four, and even five such sentences—meant that many conscientious objectors served more than two years' hard labour, the maximum sentence that could normally be imposed.[43] It also meant that

Galsworthy kept up the pressure with a Penal Reform League leaflet, *The Spirit of Punishment* (1910).

41 Marrot, p. 266; *The Times* 23 Jul. 1910, p. 4, letter from Galsworthy; TNA, PCom. 7/310. See Paul Addison, *Churchill on the Home Front 1900–1955* (1992), p. 113.

42 S. Margery Fry, "The State in Its Relation to Law-Breakers," *Friends Fellowship Papers* (May 1920), p. 67. Fry also mentioned the prison experiences of the militant suffragists. An earlier critique of the Edwardian prisons, which lent force to that of the conscientious objectors, grew out of the experiences of the suffragettes. One of the most sensitive accounts of the indignities of prison life was written by Lady Constance Lytton, who was imprisoned on four occasions for her suffrage activity; she went on hunger strike twice, the second time in Walton gaol, Liverpool, in January 1910, when she was forcibly fed. See C. Lytton and Jane Warton [the name she took in Walton gaol, when she was disguised as a working woman], *Prisons and Prisoners* (New York, 1914), pp. 96, 121, 178. See also S. McConville, "Hearing, Not Listening: Penal Policy and the Political Prisoners of 1906–1921," in L. Zedner and A. Ashworth (eds.), *The Criminological Foundations of Penal Policy* (Oxford, 2003), pp. 258–9; D. Scott and F. Spear, "Counterblast: 100 Years On: Constance Lytton/Jane Warton *Prisons and Prisoners, Howard Journal of Criminal Justice*, vol. 53 (2014), p. 428; Caitlin Davies, *Bad Girls: A History of Rebels and Renegades* (2018), p. 62, quoting the Fabian Society, which noted: "No female prisoner recorded her experiences until suffragists in large numbers were sent to Holloway."

43 Philip Viscount Snowden, *An Autobiography* (1934), vol. 1, p. 410; T. C. Kennedy, "Public Opinion and the Conscientious Objector, 1915–1919," *Journal of British Studies*, vol. 12 (1973), p. 113.

conscientious objectors underwent the first month's separate confinement at regular intervals; a first month of spare diet, bare wooden plank for a bed, work done in cellular isolation, and no contact with the world outside.[44] There was little advance here on Oscar Wilde's treatment. The "first month" regulation, in fact, was abandoned for second and subsequent terms as the war dragged on, and from January 1918, some conscientious objectors were permitted to talk during exercise.[45]

Not surprisingly, perhaps, conscientious objectors were horrified by the inhumanity of the prison regime, and especially by the dehumanizing effects of the silence rule. No conversation was allowed either with other prisoners or with prison warders, except to answer a warder's question or to make an official request. For rebelling against the silence rule, Fenner Brockway, the young socialist who, with Clifford Allen, had formed the No-Conscription Fellowship (which orchestrated the movement of resistance to conscription and acted as the guardian of the conscientious objectors), received eight months' solitary confinement and three months' bread and water.[46] If some conscientious objectors complained of the semi-starvation diet, some the intense cold, and some the monotony of sewing post-office mailbags, all conscientious objectors bore witness to the silence rule as the most arduous of all prison regulations.[47] Let Authur Creech Jones, a junior civil servant, socialist, and conscientious objector stand proxy for them all. At some date between 1916 and 1919, Creech Jones smuggled out his uncensored thoughts in prison. "The whole system," he declared, "is based on fear." You want to live a normal healthy life while in prison, he continued:

44 See David Boulton, *Objection Overruled* (1967), p. 220.
45 See J. W. Graham, *Conscription and Conscience: A History, 1916–1919* (1922), pp. 298–9. H. B. Simpson, Assistant Undersecretary of State in the Home Office, wrote this of Graham: "To me the lesson that this book & the whole story of the COs teaches, is plain—to attempt to force men to be soldiers if they are strongly opposed to military service on whatsoever grounds, is a mischievous & very costly waste of time & trouble": TNA, HO144/5802/311180.
46 See Boulton, p. 223; Hubert W. Peet, "Some Fruits of Silence," *Friends Quarterly Examiner* (Apr. 1920), pp. 127–30. Most of the leadership and the rank and file of the No-Conscription Fellowship were from the Independent Labour Party (ILP) and the Quaker Society of Friends; see Kennedy, "Public Opinion and the Conscientious Objector, 1915–1919," p. 107.
47 See R. C. Wallhead, "In Jail," *Socialist Review*, vol. 15 (Apr.–Jun. 1918), p. 175; Martin Gilbert, *Plough My Own Furrow: The Story of Lord Allen of Hurtwood as Told through His Writings and Correspondence* (1965), pp. 62, 66–8; E. Williamson Mason, *Made Free in Prison* (1918), pp. 134–5, 191–2; T. Corder Catchpool, *On Two Fronts* (1918), p. 171; S. Hobhouse, *An English Prison from Within* (1919), pp. 29, 33; A. Fenner Brockway, *Prisons as Crime Factories* (ILP pamphlet, 1919), pp. 4–8. If the silence rule were truly enforced, said Brockway, 90 per cent. of prisoners would lose their reason within a few months. See the comments made by the Poplar councillors imprisoned in September 1921 in N. Branson, *Poplarism 1919–1925: George Lansbury and the Councillors' Revolt* (1979), pp. 67–8.

But instead you meet your friends and you dare not speak. You dare not show any comradeship or even geniality. Often to speak pleasantly to an officer is to earn his rebuke. You must live in complete isolation, your self all hedged round as if you were a thing without a personality or soul. You must ever be stoical, never laugh, hum, whistle, sing or speak in case you are punished by bread & water diet and solitary confinement in a bare cell without work or reading material. The general result is that you are made cunning and crafty & adopt all manner of subterfuge to escape the vigilance of the warders. You go to church and have to sit under eyes that watch you as if you were hawks, you march 3 yards apart at exercise under the eyes of 3 or 4 officers, you work after your first month of solitary confinement under the stern face of an officer who stands on a raised platform, you sit in your cell and never sew but some eyes are not watching you through the spy hole in the door . . . It is this feeling of isolation at the worst and most miserable moments that ever come to men, this feeling of eternal surveillance, this deprival of initiative and stripping of men of their personality, this submission to ignorance and abuse which make men bitter and anti-social.[48]

By war's end, many of the conscientious objectors were broken in health.[49] But many also were eager to publicize further the state of English prisons and to effect some reform.

Margaret Hobhouse was the first to use letters written from prison. In *I Appeal unto Caesar* (1917), most of which was ghost-written by Bertrand Russell, acting on behalf of the No-Conscription Fellowship, Hobhouse pleaded the case of the absolutists, one of whom, Stephen, was her son.[50] Of greater importance was the Prison System Enquiry Committee established in January 1919, by the executive of the Labour (formerly Fabian) Research Department. Instrumental in the appointment of this Committee was Mrs. Hobhouse's younger sister, Beatrice Webb; the final report, published as *English Prisons To-Day*, was edited by two absolutists, Stephen Hobhouse and Fenner Brockway.[51] With Arthur Creech Jones's

48 Papers of Arthur Creech Jones, Bodleian Library, Oxford, MS British Empire S 332, box 1, file 2, fols. 194–7, n.d.: account of his thoughts in Wandsworth prison, quoted with permission from Violet Creech Jones. Creech Jones also noted: "We were always in touch with the ordinary prisoners. Many of them were incorrigible, infirm, maimed; some almost utterly depraved."

49 Nine conscientious objectors died in prison; approximately 60 others died later from the after-effects of prison treatment. See John Rae, *Conscience and Politics: The British Government and the Conscientious Objector to Military Service, 1916–1919* (1970), p. 226. Robin Page Arnot, who evaded conscription as a self-defined revolutionary socialist, so suffered in health that R. H. Tawney worked through Tom Jones, Assistant Secretary to the War Cabinet, to get him released from Wormwood Scrubs: Papers of Page Arnot, University of Hull Library, DAR 2/1–9.

50 Mrs. Henry Hobhouse, *I Appeal unto Caesar* (1917), pp. 44–70; Jo Vellacott, *Bertrand Russell and the Pacifists in the First World War* (Brighton, 1980), pp. 210–12. Mrs. Hobhouse visited Herbert Samuel, the Home Secretary, about her son's health in prison in early 1917: TNA, HO144/22259/328515/1.

51 See A. F. Brockway, *Inside the Left* (1942), pp. 126–8, and *Towards Tomorrow: The Autobiography of Fenner Brockway* (1977), p. 61. See also S. Hobhouse and A. F.

assistance, Hobhouse collected information from official documents (including a pirated copy of prison standing rules), from questionnaires completed by some fifty prison officials (until the Prison Commission nipped that in the bud), from agents of Discharged Prisoners' Aid Societies, and above all from 290 ex-prisoners, mainly ex-conscientious objectors.[52]

Witnesses who went to prison as a form of political demonstration, and who were more sensitive in mind and body than the average felon, were not, the Home Office complained, the best judges of the prison system.[53] Hobhouse defended the first-hand testimony, however, on the grounds that conscientious objectors could readily communicate their prison experiences and "that the mental effects observed in the course of imprisonment can be more easily isolated from the consequences of previous habits of crime, congenital abnormalities, and such concomitants of imprisonment as social ostracism." As the finishing touches were being applied to the report, an official appraisal appeared in the form of Ruggles-Brise's *English Prison System* (1921).[54] The contrast was telling: one displayed a defensive parental pride in the achievements of the past 25 years, while the other presented an unassailable case for the prosecution.

English Prisons To-Day was an exhaustive report of 728 pages (or over a quarter of a million words), describing and evaluating the various forms of imprisonment, the different kinds of prisoner, prison food and work, and medical and sanitary treatment. At times, indeed, the excess of detail detracts from the report's effectiveness. The report is certainly longer on exposure of prison conditions than on proposals for a thoroughgoing alternative. As McConville concluded: ". . . there was no attempt to set priorities or propose a programme; more importantly, there was no attempt to develop a penal philosophy." The latter were precluded, however, by divisions in the Prison System Enquiry Committee.[55] Once again, the silence rule, the first rule on the card that hung in every prisoner's cell, was named as the most pernicious feature of prison life.[56] But the silence rule was, the authors insisted, "only characteristic of the whole system. Self-respect is systematically destroyed and self-expression prevented in every phase of prison existence."[57] The effects of imprisonment, they claimed, "are of the nature of a progressive weakening of the mental powers and of a deterioration of the character in a way which renders the prisoner less fit for useful social life, more predisposed to crime, and in

Brockway, *English Prisons To-Day: Being the Report of the Prison System Enquiry Committee* (1922). For details of the membership of the Prison System Enquiry Committee, and for more on Hobhouse and Brockway, see pp. 35–6 *infra*.

52 See Stephen Hobhouse, *Forty Years and an Epilogue: An Autobiography* (1951), p. 176; Gordon Rose, *The Struggle for Penal Reform* (1961), pp. 108–9; TNA, HO45/11543/357055/33.

53 TNA, HO45/11543/357055/33.

54 Hobhouse and Brockway, p. 482; E. Ruggles-Brise, *English Prison System* (1921).

55 Brockway, *Inside the Left*, p. 129; personal interview with Fenner Brockway, Jun. 1980; S. McConville, p. 264.

56 Hobhouse and Brockway, pp. 561–2.

57 Ibid, p. 356.

consequence more liable to reconviction." The distinctive feature of prison life "is the sense of being in the grip of a huge machine which is felt to be repressive at every point, inhuman, aimless, tyrannical."[58] In all, *English Prisons To-Day* proclaimed that the guiding principles and effect of the Ruggles-Brise regime were barely distinguishable from those of its predecessor, the Du Cane regime. There could be no greater indictment of a quarter century during which the Gladstone Report had been implemented.[59]

At first, it looked as if *English Prisons To-Day*, along with Sidney and Beatrice Webb's *English Prisons Under Local Government*, and Mary Gordon's *Penal Discipline*, would provoke the Home Office to appoint a new prison enquiry committee. In May 1922, H. B. Simpson, Assistant Undersecretary, submitted in a private minute: "The only remedy is an inquiry by responsible & trustworthy persons who can take evidence & report . . . There is as much interest in the subject of prisons to-day as there was 30 years ago . . ." The prison commissioners agreed about the inquiry if not about the level of public interest. In August 1922, the Treasury made money available for the inquiry, but the next Home Secretary decided not to appoint a Commission. In November 1922, Arthur Locke, junior clerk in the department, judged that all three "reform" books had fallen flat, concluding: "Unless much clearer signs appear of a public desire for prison reform, there is no case for a laborious inquiry." Simpson still believed "the Prison 'reformers' are too much in earnest about it to allow their recent Report to become a *brutum fulmen* [an empty threat]," but Locke waspishly responded: "The case for any Royal Commission on which all & sundry reformers would air their very academic opinions grows smaller by degrees & beautifully less." In June 1927, Locke applied the closure in denigrating terms:

> For some years, the friends of various queer types of ex-prisoners have done their best to discredit prison administration, and have failed. We have had the Suffragettes, the Conscientious Objectors, the Poplarites, the Emergency Prisoners and the Communists . . . the very specious post-war agitation for an Inquiry into Prison Reform, which was engineered by the Conscientious Objectors and others . . . has died down, but it will not die out.[60]

Even so, *English Prisons To-Day*, according to Margery Fry of the Howard League, became "the Bible of penal reformers."[61] It inspired a number of parliamentary

---

58 Ibid., p. 561. Another continuing feature of prison administration was its dreary uniformity, encapsulated by Ruggles-Brise's 1911 comment, quoted in Hobhouse and Brockway, p. 97: "It is now 4:30 in the afternoon and I know that just now, at every Local and Convict Prison in England, the same things in general are being done, and that in general they are being done in the same way."

59 It should be added, however, that there had doubtless been a change in expectations since the Gladstone Report, sufficient to sharpen the post-war critique.

60 See HO45/11543/357055/72 and 79; HO45/18006/546730/12.

61 Enid Huws Jones, *Margery Fry: The Essential Amateur* (1966), p. 113.

questions concerning insanity among prisoners and the suicide rate in prisons.[62] More important, Sir Maurice Waller, the new chairman of the Prison Commission (as of August 1921), studied the volume and then, claimed Stephen Hobhouse, consulted both Sir William Clarke Hall (progressive London magistrate and Hobhouse's brother-in-law) and Margery Fry. Moreover, a member of the Prison System Enquiry Committee, Alec Paterson, who had helped draft the section on Borstal training, was appointed to the Prison Commission and was "the guiding and most beneficent spirit of that powerful body, revolutionising a large part of prison treatment by substituting educational methods for the rigid and stupid punitive regime."[63] This all perhaps exaggerates the direct influence of *English Prisons To-Day* since the new prison commissioners were already committed to a less repressive regime, and some of their immediate changes anticipated the recommendations of the Prison System Enquiry Committee.

Waller persuaded the Home Secretary in late 1921 to abolish the close cropping of convicts' hair and to allow prisoners to see visitors without intervening wire or bars.[64] But the volume doubtless strengthened Wallers's arm when it came to ending the rigours of the silence rule and separate confinement. A month after the book's publication, all prison governors were instructed to allow conversation between prisoners at labour and between warders and prisoners.[65] A few months later, convinced that solitude led to morbid introspection, revengeful feelings, and suicidal tendencies, the Prison Commission got Home Office approval to suspend, for an experimental period of six months, the stage of separate confinement at the start of every convict's sentence. These arrangements were ultimately made permanent.[66] And, finally, a statement of aims in the annual reports for 1924 and 1925 illustrated the new approach of the prison commissioners. Their object was to restore prisoners "to ordinary standards of citizenship" by promoting self-respect and a sense of personal responsibility. This in turn would require "vigorous industrial, mental, and moral training, pursued on considered lines by officers, teachers, and prison visitors of character and personality."[67]

Yet if improvements in prison administration were evident, helped forward by Hobhouse and Brockway, by some 18 MPs who shared the status of ex-prisoner, and by a reconstructed Prison Commission, the pace of penal change remained decidedly halting.[68] In many prisons, claimed Fenner Brockway in 1926, the new

62 For example, *Hansard*, vol. 156, 11 Jul. 1922, col. 1040. See also TNA, HO45/11543/357055/54 and 55.
63 Hobhouse, *Forty Years and an Epilogue*, pp. 178–9. For Paterson, see Victor Bailey, *Delinquency and Citizenship: Reclaiming the Young Offender, 1914–1948* (Oxford, 1987), pp. 195–6.
64 TNA, HO45/11033/428541.
65 See Rose, *The Struggle for Penal Reform*, p. 111; TNA, PCom 7/475.
66 TNA, HO45/13658/185668/21; Lionel W. Fox, *The English Prison and Borstal Systems* (1952), p. 68.
67 Quoted in Fox, pp. 70–1.
68 For details of ex-prisoner MPs, see Snowden, p. 410; Lord Pethick-Lawrence, *Fate Has Been Kind* (1942), p, 130; K. Robbins, "Morgan Jones in 1916," *Llafur*, vol. 1(1975), pp. 38–43. Another influence on penal change, particularly in staff conditions, was the unrest among prison officers, which found expression in the growth of the National Union of Police and Prison Officers, and in the 1919 strike.

interpretation of the silence rule had yet to find full expression.[69] In the case of men sentenced to imprisonment with hard labour, moreover, the preliminary period of separate confinement (reduced from 28 to 14 days in 1919) still obtained. In September 1924, Waller pressed for its abolition, but the Home Secretary demurred, and the issue was dropped.[70] Not until 1931 was the period of cellular confinement entirely abolished.[71] In short, this entire catalogue of evidence should give pause to those who insist that the Edwardian years witnessed the emergence of a new penal structure.

III

Garland is perhaps on firmer ground when it comes to the separate treatment of distinct categories of offender, recommended by the Gladstone Committee for young offenders aged 16 to 23 and for habitual criminals. Lengthy discussions, and some experimentation, preceded the Prevention of Crime Act, 1908, which brought into being the sentence of preventive detention, to rid society of the habitual criminal, and the Borstal training sentence, to stem the flow of new habitual offenders. Both measures are typically seen as basic components of the positivist restructuring of the penal system; both measures reflect the influence of the principles of individualization and indeterminacy. Even here, however, caution is required.

For habitual offenders, the 1908 act settled on a so-called "dual track" system.[72] In an awkward alliance of classicism and positivism, those deemed to be habitual criminals first paid for their crime in the coinage of just deserts (penal servitude), after which they were detained for their habitual criminality in the new currency of social defence (preventive detention). What looked to the judiciary like double sentencing made judges so uneasy that they became extremely averse to using the measure. By 1921, only 577 convicts had been sentenced to preventive detention.[73] The low number was a result not only of judicial scepticism but also of Churchill's determination, when Home Secretary, to restrict preventive detention to the dangerous professional criminal. The act, he believed, had pressed too largely on the persistent minor offender.[74] Churchill's intervention gave the kiss of death to this new form of detention. In 1911, only 53 men were sentenced to preventive detention, as compared with 177 in

69 A. F. Brockway in *Socialist Review* (Sept., Oct., and Dec. 1926).
70 TNA, HO45/13658/185668/21.
71 See TNA, HO45/11543/357055/71; "Editorial," *Howard Journal*, vol. 1 (1922), pp. 4–5. For a more in-depth appraisal of the prison reforms of the inter-war years, see Chapter 4 *infra*.
72 For discussion of the definition of habitual criminality adopted by the 1908 act—one that failed to distinguish clearly between the habitual professional and the habitual petty nuisance—see Wiener, p. 347; Radzinowicz and Hood, pp. 266–7.
73 S. Petrow, *Policing Morals: The Metropolitan Police and the Home Office 1870–1914* (Oxford, 1994), p. 111.
74 See pp. 47–8 *infra* for Churchill's critical approach to preventive detention.

the previous year.[75] If the sentence of Borstal training was less troubled by a conflict of penal philosophies, it fell well short of a full-blooded positivist transplant. Ruggles-Brise saw Borstal as an alternative to penal servitude for the dangerous criminal between 16 and 21 years of age and hence insisted on a regime that would build character via strict discipline, obedience, and uniform treatment. Up to and for some years beyond 1918 the conditions and regime of Borstal training were only one step removed from those of a convict prison.[76]

If the net is cast wider to include the Inebriates Act 1898 (establishing state reformatories for habitual drunkards), and the Mental Deficiency Act 1913 the overall conclusion persists. The first-mentioned statute reflects the shift of policy towards extended custody and medical treatment of habitual drunkards.[77] The other measure was one of which the eugenics movement could legitimately claim responsibility. Mental deficiency was thought to be hereditary, to be largely incurable, and to require the compulsory segregation of the "feeble-minded," not to mention limitation of their right to reproduce.[78] Two points establish the overall conclusion. First, evidence of the origins and workings of these acts suggest that Garland's notion of a shift in criminological understanding from the "moral" to the "medical" is overdrawn. Inebriate reformatories and mental deficiency institutions were used predominantly for females.[79] Most of the committals to inebriate reformatories were for either neglect or cruelty to children or drunk and disorderly behaviour.[80] The most convincing explanation of this policy is that, because women, in their role as mothers, were identified as the biological source of inebriety and feeblemindedness, female offenders became subject to a process of medicalization. But these new medical and psychiatric interpretations of female crime, and this is the point of importance, were, according to Lucia Zedner, "suffused with a highly moral view of what constituted deviance and what constituted normality in

75 Radzinowicz and Hood, p. 286. See also N. Morris, *The Habitual Criminal* (Cambridge, Mass., 1951), p. 80; Forsythe, *Penal Discipline, Reformatory Projects and the English Prison Commission, 1895–1939*, p. 243, and idem., "Reformatory Projects in British Prisons, 1780–1939: Recent Writings and Lessons from the Past," in *History and Sociology of Crime*, ed. P. Robert and C. Emsley (Pfaffenweiler, 1991), p. 54.

76 See Bailey, *Delinquency and Citizenship*, pp. 186–91, esp. p. 189.

77 See Wiener, p. 188; Radzinowicz and Hood, pp. 308–13.

78 Eugenics, based on the belief that the physical and mental condition of the population was determined more by heredity than environment, had an influential following up to 1914. Eugenists predicted race degeneration if the "unfit" were allowed to reproduce themselves more rapidly than the "fit." See G. R. Searle, *Eugenics and Politics in Britain, 1900–1914* (Leyden, 1976); M. Freeden, "Eugenics and Progressive Thought: A Study in Ideological Affinity," *Historical Journal*, vol. 22 (1979), p. 658; Jose Harris, *Private Lives, Public Spirit: A Social History of Britain 1870–1914* (Oxford, 1993), pp. 244–5.

79 See H. G. Simmons, "Explaining Social Policy: The English Mental Deficiency Act of 1913," *Journal of Social History*, vol. 11 (1977–8), p. 399; G. Hunt, J. Mellor, and J. Turner, "Wretched, Hatless and Miserably Clad: Women and the Inebriate Reformatories from 1900–1913," *British Journal of Sociology*, vol. 40 (1989), p. 246.

80 C. Harding and L. Wilkin, "'The Dream of a Benevolent Mind': The Late Victorian Response to the Problem of Inebriety," *Criminal Justice History*, vol. 9 (1988), p. 198.

women."[81] These theories, she argues, "fitted only too well with the long-standing belief that criminal women not merely broke the law but tended to exhibit fundamental flaws of character." And she concludes by saying that historians have neglected the extent to which medical responses were erected on "the foundation of older, culturally derived assumptions about women's character and behaviour."[82]

The second point relates to the abiding strength of the "tariff" principle of sentencing. The judiciary either committed offenders to inebriate reformatories only for terms similar to those they would have served in prison or refused to make use of them at all. The figures speak for themselves. There were approximately a quarter of a million committals to prison for drunkenness *annually* before 1914. Yet the total number of committals to inebriate reformatories between 1899 and 1913 was 4,590 (3,741, or 81 per cent, of whom were women). The daily average population never reached 1,000. By 1921, all the reformatories had closed.[83] The experiment of subjecting habitual drunkards to prolonged detention had proved a colossal failure. Only by a large stretch of the imagination, then, can penal measures that were full of philosophical ambiguity, that dealt with only a few hundred cases each year, and that were surrounded on all sides by more traditional forms of punishment be seen as composing a major alteration in the structure of criminal justice.

As a brief coda to this section, it is useful to refer to the failure, also, to establish penal labour colonies for those convicted of vagrancy. Garland struggles to explain this failure to establish the compulsory segregation of the "unemployable," which he sees as an essential deterrent underside to the "social security program" of labour exchanges and social insurance. He posits the undocumented interpretation that policy makers realized that they could instead employ the network of Borstals, preventive detention prisons, inebriate reformatories, and mental deficiency institutions.[84] I prefer the more prosaic explanation that the labour colony scheme expired because a sentence of three years' detention, even as a maximum, for the crime of vagrancy was deemed unduly drastic. Thus, the failure of the penal labour colony squares with the conclusion that judges (and public opinion) consistently adopted an extremely circumspect approach to the new scientific knowledges, and they remained stubbornly reluctant to impose long preventive sentences.

IV

The way we see criminal offenders, understand their motivations, and dispose of them as cases is heavily influenced by the intellectual frameworks of the time. What patterns of thought guided the ways in which criminals were seen,

81 L. Zedner, "Women, Crime, and Penal Responses: A Historical Account," in M. Tonry (ed.), *Crime and Justice: A Review of Research*, vol. 14 (Chicago, 1991), p. 308.
82 Ibid., pp. 343, 353. See Simmons, p. 393.
83 Hunt et al., p. 246; Radzinowicz and Hood, pp. 311–14.
84 Garland, *Punishment and Welfare*, pp. 227–8.

understood, and treated in the Edwardian era? Garland and Wiener reply that a traditional "moral" discourse retreated before the wave of scientific determinism. They argue that these years witnessed a major sea change in criminological discourse, from classical jurisprudence to positivist medicalism, which in turn led to a tectonic shift in penal structures.[85] This is not how I read the evidence. I am not convinced that a new positivist discourse, underwritten by the human sciences, dominated what could be seen, thought, and performed in the penal domain. I am not convinced that "demoralization," or a diminishing faith in the efficacy of individual willpower, was as pronounced or advanced as Garland and Wiener contend. Their interpretation underestimates the continued influence of humanitarianism as a causal factor in penal change, utterly ignores the Idealist framework of social and legal thought, and relegates the force of ethical and Christian socialism to a footnote. It is to these other discourses that I turn in order to document the complexity of Edwardian penal culture and to underline the continued and vital role of moral character in Edwardian penal thought.[86]

Historians now accept that cultural mentalities and sensibilities affect the ways in which we think about offenders. Yet too often these important moral, religious, and emotional forces are mere ghosts at the table of penal change. If we truly wish to include sensibilities in our explanatory framework, then humanitarianism should be seen not as surface rhetoric, masking more fundamental economic or political interests—the line taken by Foucault when he dismissed humanitarianism as "so much incidental music"—but as a causal factor in penal change. The humanitarian sensibility altered in character over the Victorian period. Early Victorian humanitarianism was a form of benevolence that regarded the "lower orders" with a charitable and superior eye. By the last quarter of the nineteenth century, humanitarians were no longer so seized by the personal moral inadequacies of those they would redeem. Newer humanitarian feelings were emerging. Humanitarians encouraged a compassion for the weak and infirm precisely because they were weak and infirm.[87]

In 1891, humanitarian ranks were bolstered by the arrival of the Humanitarian League. It was founded by the socialist pacifist Henry Salt, a former master of Eton public school who returned to a Thoreau-inspired, simple life in the Surrey

---

85 Wiener, p. 186.

86 I am not arguing that ideological forms were the only influence on the penal system; I am arguing that positivism was only one, and not the most important, framework of social and political thought in the Edwardian debate on prisons.

87 For the early nineteenth century, humanitarian concern for the protection from abuse of prisoners and lunatics, see T. W. Laqueur, "Bodies, Details, and the Humanitarian Narrative," in *The New Cultural History*, ed. Lynn Hunt (Berkeley, 1989), p. 179; Andrew Scull, *The Most Solitary of Afflictions: Madness and Society in Britain, 1700–1900* (New Haven, Conn., 1993), p. 380. See also Martin Wiener, ed., "Special Issue: Humanitarianism or Control? A Symposium on Aspects of Nineteenth Century Social Reform in Britain and America," *Rice University Studies*, vol. 67 (1981). And see T. L. Haskell, "Capitalism and the Origins of the Humanitarian Sensibility, Parts 1 and 2," *American Historical Review*, vol. 90 (Apr. and Jun. 1985), pp. 339–61, 547–66.

countryside. There he became the centre of a progressive literary circle, the most famous members of which were the Fabian socialist George Bernard Shaw and the ethical socialist Edward Carpenter. The League was particularly concerned with criminal law reform, the abolition of corporal punishment, and preventing cruelty to animals and children. In 1896, the League established a criminal law and prisons department to advocate improvements in prison conditions and penal policy. The department sought to humanize the conditions of prison life and to affirm that the true purpose of imprisonment was the reformation, not the mere punishment, of the offender.[88]

The most striking feature of the Humanitarian League is the way it acted as an unofficial hub of penal reform between the Gladstone Report of 1895 and the Prison System Enquiry Committee's volume, *English Prisons To-Day* (1922). One spoke of the reform wheel radiated out to the agitation that led to the Gladstone Report and the 1898 Prison Act. The League's activities were guided by W. D. Morrison, chaplain of Wandsworth prison, Christian socialist, and criminologist, and were supported by the Irish nationalist M. P. Michael Davitt, who was on the committee of the League's criminal law and prisons department.[89]

A second spoke led to the circle of progressives—Edward Carpenter, Havelock Ellis—who sought to live the new Ideal of Humanity, and who, with Morrison, condemned existing prisons—"whited sepulchres full of dead men's bones," in Carpenter's telling biblical allusion—and acted as conduits for a more "scientific" view of crime.[90] Carpenter and Ellis represented advanced opinion in the 1890s. Carpenter's lifestyle was a revolt against the oppressive conventionalities of Victorian life. He crusaded for a new ideal of social brotherhood and the honest human relation. Salt's friendship drew him into the Humanitarian League and into speaking and writing on behalf of penal reform. The prisons, Carpenter advised, should be transformed into "Industrial Asylums" in which prisoners would be educated for citizenship.[91] Havelock Ellis was a member of the Fellowship of the New Life, a group that viewed individual moral regeneration as the key to social reform (and from which the Fabian socialists had broken away in 1884). Ellis's Contemporary Science Series, in which his own contribution to "criminal anthropology," *The Criminal*, appeared in 1890, introduced Cesare Lombroso, the "criminal type," biological determinism, and the indeterminate sentence to an

---

88 See Rose, *The Struggle for Penal Reform*, pp. 56–7; Garland, *Punishment and Welfare*, p. 109; Wiener, p. 335. Salt and the Humanitarian League supported the *Daily Chronicle*'s 1894 campaign for a prison inquiry; see McConville, *English Local Prisons*, p. 580.

89 See Henry S. Salt, *Seventy Years among Savages* (1921), p. 140; George Hendrick, *Henry Salt: Humanitarian Reformer and Man of Letters* (Urbana, Ill., 1977), p. 77; Forsythe, *Penal Discipline, Reformatory Projects and the English Prison Commission, 1895–1939*, p. 23; Dan Weinbren, "Against *All* Cruelty: The Humanitarian League, 1891–1919," *History Workshop Journal*, vol. 38 (1994), pp. 92–5.

90 E. Carpenter, *Prisons Police and Punishment* (1905), p. 120.

91 See E. Carpenter, *England's Ideal and Other Papers on Social Subjects* (1895), pp. 1–22, and *Prisons Police and Punishment*, pp. 61–77; C. Tsuzuki, *Edward Carpenter, 1844–1929* (Cambridge, 1980), p. 113.

English audience. Not surprisingly, his remedy for crime was resolutely positivist: to replace the word "crime" with that of "disease," in the belief that criminals needed individualized treatment.[92]

Positivism also attracted W. D. Morrison. The Criminology Series he edited included the work of European positivists such as Lombroso and Enrico Ferri, and Morrison's own studies stressed the deterministic (particularly biological) sources of delinquency. But Morrison's criminology was, in fact, an eclectic, often contradictory, mix of positivism, practical prison experience, and Christian socialism. To judge from his introductions to the translations of continental theorists, moreover, Morrison's attraction to positivism grew out of deep dissatisfaction with the existing prison system, and hence his main approach was to mine the new theory for scientific sanction to the humanitarian-cum-evangelistic campaign for penal reform. Anyway, Morrison's enthusiasm for positivism gradually waned. He could not ultimately accept the Lombrosian theory of degenerate "criminal man." Nor could he support the indeterminate sentence, so foreign was it, he felt, to the English liberal tradition.[93]

A third spoke of the reform wheel ran from the "Tolstoyans" and humanitarians in the Penal Reform League to the socialists and pacifists of the Prison System Enquiry Committee. The Penal Reform League was founded in 1907, an outgrowth of the prison experience of the suffragettes and the new humanist spirit. It stood for the reclamation of criminals by a curative and educational prison system. The founder and first secretary was Arthur St. John, a Tolstoy disciple and a believer, with Salt and Carpenter, in the good in every individual. In truth, the league was a small body with no money to speak of and had little influence on the course of penal reform before 1914. This was not for want of trying. League leaflets, written by such humanitarians as the playwright, John Galsworthy, advocated penal reform. St John led deputations to the Home Office, where he complained that the prison system was having a disastrous effect on the minds and souls of prisoners and declared that the country needed a different spirit in prison administration.[94] Predictably, St John was asked to join the Prison System Enquiry Committee in 1919. Other committee members included the ubiquitous W. D. Morrison, Margery Fry, the secretary of the Howard League for Penal Reform (a 1921 amalgamation of the Howard Association and the Penal Reform League), Alexander Paterson, secretary of a voluntary society to assist discharged prisoners,

92 Havelock Ellis, *The Criminal* (1890). See Phyllis Grosskurth, *Havelock Ellis* (New York, 1980), pp. 69, 114–16; R. E. McGowen, "Rethinking Crime: Changing Attitudes towards Law-Breakers in Eighteenth and Nineteenth-Century England" (PhD diss., University of Illinois at Urbana-Champaign, 1979), pp. 311–14.

93 See McGowen, "Rethinking Crime," pp. 301–11; Radzinowicz and Hood, pp. 86–8; W. D. Morrison, "The Study of Crime," *Mind*, no. 4 (Oct. 1892), pp. 489–517; David Garland, "British Criminology before 1935," *British Journal of Criminology*, vol. 28 (1988), p. 7; C. Lombroso and W. Ferrero, *The Female Offender* (New York, 1916), introduction by W. D. Morrison, pp. v–xx.

94 See Galsworthy, *The Spirit of Punishment*; Arthur St. John, *Prison Regime* (1913), and *Reception Houses* (1918); TNA, HO 45/11543/357055/16.

Sidney and Beatrice Webb, and the guild socialist G. D. H. Cole. The chairman of the committee was Fabian socialist, Sydney Olivier, a friend of the Salts and fellow humanitarian.[95]

The secretary of the Prison System Enquiry Committee was Stephen Hobhouse. He emerged from prison determined to bear witness to the defects in prison conditions. "If some of our predecessors in the Society [of Friends] have a heavy responsibility fixed on them for assisting in the establishment of the false methods of to-day," wrote Hobhouse, in a reproachful reference to his Quaker forebears who had helped to construct the penitentiary model, "we may perhaps atone for this want of imagination by helping to inaugurate a new and more Christ like treatment of our erring fellow-creatures."[96] After two years' work on the report, Hobhouse was close to a nervous breakdown. Hence Beatrice Webb asked Fenner Brockway to join her nephew, Stephen, as joint editor. A year later a report appeared under the title, *English Prisons To-Day*. The two authors converted the searing personal testimony of the conscientious objectors into an impeachment of the prison administration of the Prison Commission Chairman, Sir Evelyn Ruggles-Brise. If one thread held together *English Prisons To-Day* it was that, whatever the prevailing theory of punishment, "the Prison System ought not to result in the brutalization, deterioration, or devitalisation of the criminal, but should, as far as possible, be humane in the best sense of the word."[97]

The humanitarian or "moral" approach of these various reform bodies was, for David Garland, little more than rhetoric that either served to mask power or provided legitimacy for the use of power. Thus, humanitarian values, he suggests, facilitated the acceptance by a conservative political and administrative elite of positivist penal measures.[98] This reductive approach underestimates the contribution of humanitarianism to penal debate and change. Humanitarianism exists at a

---

95 TNA, HO45/11543/357055/33; Stephen Hobhouse, *Forty Years and an Epilogue*, pp. 133–4. For the contribution of conscientious objectors to the Prison System Enquiry Committee, see pp. 26–7 *supra*. See also T. L. Hodgkin, "Fry (Sara) Margery (1874–1958)," *Oxford DNB* (2007). Fry was of Quaker background and conscience. She was secretary of the Penal Reform League, before amalgamation with the Howard Association, from 1918–1926; later chairman and vice-chairman of the Howard League. She was also a magistrate, especially supportive of probation, and the first education adviser to Holloway prison.

96 S. Hobhouse, "The Silence System in British Prisons," *Friends' Quarterly Examiner* (Jul. 1918), p. 263.

97 TNA, HO45/11543/357055/33; A. Fenner Brockway, *Inside the Left*, chap. 13.

98 Garland, *Punishment and Welfare*, pp. 108–9, 123. In fairness, Garland states that the approach of the penal reform groups to the "criminological programme" was "mediated by Christian evangelicalism, which allowed a large degree of policy support, but prohibited any total endorsement of the programme as a whole" (ibid., p. 109). In more recent work, moreover, Garland acknowledges the need to include sensibilities in the examination of penal policy and speculates on the contribution of humanitarian values to change in penal laws and institutions; see David Garland, *Punishment and Modern Society: A Study of Social Theory*, p. 198, and "Criminological Knowledge and Its Relation to Power: Foucault's Genealogy and Criminology Today," *British Journal of Criminology*, vol. 32 (1992), pp. 411–12.

different level than coherent and articulated theories like positivism, idealism, or socialism; it is at once more popular, vague, and elusive. Yet if humanitarianism's weight was felt less rationally, it was an essential feature of the emotional and intellectual environment of these years. It is misleading, moreover, *pace* Foucault, to see humanitarianism as the antithesis of social science. Rather, the Edwardian years point to a more complex relationship between the two. A reinvigorated humanitarianism accompanied the rise of positivist criminology. As a result, humanitarians began to use more deterministic language and to propose more "scientific" remedies. Yet humanitarians also modified and limited the effect of positivist theory by their emphasis on the suffering and dignity of individual prisoners. The gravamen of the reformers' critique was that the existing prison system manifestly failed to believe in, or to revive, the good in every prisoner. No one would wish to accept at face value all the claims of the humanitarian bodies, but humanitarian sensibility deserves full recognition in an explanation of Edwardian penal debate and change.

V

The penal culture of these years was also deeply touched by the ideas of the Philosophical Idealists, notably the work of the Oxford professor of moral philosophy, T. H. Green. This should occasion no surprise, given the considerable influence that Idealism is known to have exerted on social thought and public policy in the late Victorian and Edwardian years.[99] Yet Garland and Wiener make little or no mention of it. It is time to repair the neglect, starting with the bare essentials of this philosophical approach.[100]

Green believed that every man had the capacity for moral choice and the will to behave responsibly and that every man had to be encouraged to cultivate his "best self." For a man to realize his "best self," he had to will it; social institutions could not enforce self-realization. However, the state had an obligation to help the individual to further his "best self"; the state had a key role to play in creating the conditions for moral advancement. A framework of law guaranteeing certain rights (such as access to education) was the *sine qua non* of an individual's moral development. Rights, that is, were the powers given by the state to permit each

99 See Melvin Richter, *The Politics of Conscience: T. H. Green and His Age* (1964), p. 13, and "T. H. Green and His Audience: Liberalism as a Surrogate Faith," *Review of Politics*, vol. 18 (1956), p. 444. The most compelling assessments of the influence of Idealist thought on the structural transformation of welfare provision are Jose Harris, "The Webbs, the Charity Organisation Society and the Ratan Tata Foundation: Social Policy from the Perspective of 1912," in M. Bulmer et al. (ed.), *The Goals of Social Policy* (1989), pp. 51–5, and idem, "Political Thought and the Welfare State, 1870–1940."

100 The next paragraph is based on G. Himmelfarb, *Poverty and Compassion: The Moral Imagination of the Late Victorians* (New York, 1991), chap. 17; Adam B. Ulam, *Philosophical Foundations of English Socialism* (Cambridge, Mass., 1951), pp. 34–8; A. Vincent and R. Plant, *Philosophy, Politics and Citizenship: The Life and Thought of the British Idealists* (Oxford, 1984), pp. 2, 40, 52.

individual to develop his moral character and contribute his best to society. In pursuing his "best self," the individual also contributed to the "common good." Moral improvement, then, was the motor of social progress. Social transformation depended on the moral improvement of individual citizens. Two notions relevant for our purposes flowed from this philosophy.

One was a nondeterministic approach to human behaviour. "Idealist man" willed his own destiny "instead of being driven this way and that by external forces."[101] Though the state had the job of creating conditions that would enable men to realize their moral potential, state intervention was meant not to diminish individual responsibility but rather to offer a new way to promote it. The second notion was the cult of citizenship. Idealism dignified all men, even the poorest, as citizens capable of self-realization. The disadvantaged had to be helped to achieve self-development, either by state assistance or, more suitably, by voluntary social service. This belief in active citizenship underpinned the work, for example, of the university settlement movement.[102] These two notions contributed to the debate on Edwardian penal policy. The insistence on individual responsibility reinvigorated the classical philosophy and practice of punishment and provided an antidote to the excesses of positivism. The secular religion of citizenship converted a number of key prison reformers and practitioners to the belief that they had a civic duty to create penal environments in which prisoners could fit themselves for citizenship.

Idealism offered a philosophy of punishment and, indirectly, an image of "criminal man." Not for the Idealist, Lombroso's "born criminal," nor the notion of crime as degeneracy or disease requiring prolonged, if not indefinite, detention. Rather, the criminal was a moral and responsible being who had violated someone else's rights. Punishment was the state's way of securing "the future maintenance of rights." Among the rights to be maintained, however, "are included rights of the criminal himself." Green argued that

> this consideration limits the kind of punishment which the state may justly inflict. It ought not in punishing to sacrifice unnecessarily to the maintenance of rights in general what might be called the reversionary rights of the criminal, rights which, if properly treated, he might ultimately become capable of exercising for the general good.[103]

To be just, then, punishment ought to be proportionate to the importance of the right violated, and it ought to be "reformatory" in the sense that "it must tend to

101 T. H. Green, "Principles of Political Obligation," par. 7, in R. L. Nettleship (ed.), *Works of Thomas Hill Green*, vol. 2 (1886; 5th impression, 1906).

102 See J. Morrow, "Ancestors, Legacies and Traditions: British Idealism in the History of Political Thought," *History of Political Thought*, vol. 6 (1985), p. 510; S. Meacham, *Toynbee Hall and Social Reform, 1880–1914* (New Haven, Conn., 1987), pp. 12–14. See also Clement Attlee, *The Social Worker* (1920).

103 Green, para. 205.

qualify the criminal for the resumption of rights."[104] A similar theory of punishment was presented by neo-Hegelian philosopher and political theorist, Bernard Bosanquet, except that he warned against the tendency in "reformation theory" to treat the offender "as a 'patient', not as an agent."[105] In this manner, Bosanquet claimed, "it leads to the notion that the State may take hold of any man, whose life or ideas are thought capable of improvement, and set to work to ameliorate them by forcible treatment."[106] In a later work, Bosanquet argued that "the reformatory theory, in its purity, *is* arbitrary and cruel," for "Revenge may be exhausted by a term in prison; it is the work of reformation to the duration of which no sane man can profess to set a limit." In words that have contemporary resonance, he asked rhetorically:

> Could anything be conceived more brutalizing, arbitrary, and oppressive? . . . You want to annul the bad will, and in doing so, to help the offender against it so far as within reasonable limits you can. But to bind a man under the jurisdiction of some official expert in morals—say a gaol chaplain— till the latter should be satisfied of his reformation, would be a tyranny to which I find it hard to conceive a parallel.[107]

Punishment, in all, was "a negation of an evil will which has been realized in action; deterrence and reformation are subordinate aspects implied within it."[108] The correction of the *young* man was a different matter, however, since it involved "imperfect wills, which have not entered upon complete responsibility."[109]

The import of all this is that the Idealist movement, a dominant intellectual force by the 1890s, reinstated retribution as the key justification for punishment, with all that entailed: individual responsibility, just proportion, and the quest for uniformity in sentencing.[110] Moreover, the judiciary (which, strangely, Garland never includes within his "penal complex") was confirmed in its tendency to see the criminal law as an embodiment of the fundamental moral principles of the community and to guard against moves to limit their applicability. Attachment to classical notions of criminal justice was not a judicial peculiarity but was endemic among the prison service, even including prison doctors and psychiatrists. While top penal administrators were willing to accept that criminality might have a physical basis in "degeneracy," particularly in "feeblemindedness," at the level of the prison medical officer, continuity prevailed. Prison medical officers were preoccupied still with

104 Ibid., para. 206. See H. B. Acton, *The Philosophy of Punishment* (1969), p. 11; Paul Harris, "Moral Progress and Politics: The Theory of T. H. Green," *Polity*, vol. 21 (1989), p. 542. See also Henry Jones, *The Working Faith of the Social Reformer* (1910), p. 254.
105 B. Bosanquet, *The Philosophical Theory of the State* (1910), p. 223.
106 Ibid., p. 224.
107 B. Bosanquet, *Some Suggestions in Ethics* (1918), pp. 200–2, emphasis in original.
108 Ibid., p. 207.
109 Ibid., p. 183.
110 See Radzinowicz and Hood, pp. 18–19.

separating the malingerer from those who were unfit for prison discipline. Few of the "weak-minded," however, were transferred elsewhere, even after 1913 and the Mental Deficiency Act, and a more thoroughgoing mental diagnosis and treatment of prisoners was a rarity. For the most part, medical officers continued to serve the "moral" mission of the prisons.[111] But let us turn to the most powerful prison administrator, the chairman of the Prison Commission and devotee of T. H. Green, Evelyn Ruggles-Brise.

In explaining why this "humane and high-minded administrator, well versed in the literature of penology," a pillar of the International Penal and Penitentiary Commission, did so little to change the principles and practice of the prison regime in response to the Gladstone Report, Lionel Fox correctly highlighted Ruggles-Brise's own statements, "which suggest that he never really accepted the possibility of a system of treatment in which reform would hold a primary and concurrent place with deterrence."[112] In an address to the American Prison Association in Washington in 1910, Ruggles-Brise argued forcefully against a change in the "historic order of the factors of punishment"—to wit, retributory, deterrent, and reformatory. For support, he turned to the formula, "prescribed by one of the clearest and profoundest thinkers of the end of last century, Professor T. H. Green," whose definitions Ruggles-Brise then emulated. By "retributory," said Ruggles-Brise, he meant

> the determination of the human consciousness that the system of rights shall be maintained, and that he who offends against it shall be punished, and that the punishment shall be of such a nature as to deter him and others from anti-social acts.

By "reformatory," he meant

> the accepted axiom of modern penology that a prisoner has reversionary rights of humanity . . . and that no effort must be spared to restore that man to society as a better and a wiser man and a good citizen.[113]

On other occasions, too, Ruggles-Brise warned against a retreat from the classical traditions of punishment.[114]

Nothing, in Ruggles-Brise's opinion, had more retarded modern penology than the idea of a "criminal type" of persons predestined to crime. The idea challenged the entire system of punishment since the "criminal type" was hardly likely to be amenable to deterrent or reformatory influences. Fortunately, the tide of criminal anthropology ebbed

---

111 See S. Watson, "Malingerers, the 'Weakminded' Criminal and the 'Moral Imbecile': How the English Prison Medical Officer Became an Expert in Mental Deficiency, 1880–1930," in *Legal Medicine in History*, ed. M. Clark and C. Crawford (Cambridge, 1994), p. 229; Hobhouse and Brockway, pp. 257–85.

112 Fox, *The English Prison and Borstal Systems*, pp. 62–3.

113 E. Ruggles-Brise, *Prison Reform: At Home and Abroad* (1924), p. 193.

114 See *Report of the Commissioners of Prisons . . . for 1912–1913*, Cd. 7092, PP, 1914, vol. 45, pp. 22–3.

quickly, as Ruggles-Brise recorded in 1910: "The Lombrosian theories of the criminal-ne [*sic*] are exploded. Our own investigations now being conducted into the physiology of crime will, I think, fire the last shot at this deserted ship."[115] Ruggles-Brise had commissioned Dr. Charles Goring, medical officer at Parkhurst, to test Lombroso's theory by a large-scale examination of English convicts. Happily, Goring successfully demolished the "physical criminal type." But ironically his finding that the English prisoner was, on average, defective, either physically or mentally, gladdened the heart of all eugenists. It required Ruggles-Brise, in his preface to *The English Convict*, to warn that Goring's "theory of defectiveness . . . must not be pressed so far as to affect the liability to punishment of the offender for his act."[116] Ruggles-Brise also contested other planks of the positivist credo. He rejected both an entirely indeterminate sentence and anything that encroached upon judicial discretion in sentencing, "the most sacred principle of English Criminal Law."[117]

Other features of the positivist paradigm attracted Ruggles-Brise. He endorsed the principle of the "the individualization of punishment."[118] He recognized the merit of greater specialization in the treatment offered by each prison, adapted to different kinds of offender,[119] apropos of which he recommended a special institution for mentally defective prisoners requiring long, possibly permanent detention.[120] And he was generally supportive of preventive detention for habitual offenders.[121] But Ruggles-Brise's most valuable contribution was surely the urge to save young adult offenders from a career of crime. Moreover, the development of the Borstal training system owed something to positivist criminology, more to American example, but much more to the social conscience of a follower of T. H. Green. Only for young, feeble-minded, and gravely habitual offenders, those considered incapable of making moral choices, was Ruggles-Brise willing to waive the application of culpability, punishment, and moral reformation. He still saw the primary function of a humane administration to be "to secure obedience, discipline, order, and the habit of industry." "These things alone," he continued, "have a great moral value."[122]

---

115 E. Ruggles-Brise memo, 18 Apr. 1910, TNA, HO45/13658/185668/6.
116 Charles Goring, *The English Convict: A Statistical Study*, abridged ed. (1919), preface by E. Ruggles-Brise, p. vi. See Ruggles-Brise, *English Prison System*, pp. 198–212. See also Radzinowicz and Hood, pp. 21–6; Wiener, p. 357; Piers Beirne, *Inventing Criminology: Essays on the Rise of Homo Criminalis* (New York, 1993), p. 213. Hobhouse and Brockway's *English Prisons To-Day* confirmed the view that the criminal type was manufactured by the prison system.
117 Quoted in D. A. Thomas, *Constraints on Judgment: The Search for Structured Discretion in Sentencing, 1860–1910* (Cambridge, 1979), p. 27. See Radzinowicz and Hood, p. 268, n. 17; E. Ruggles-Brise memo, 13 Jul. 1910, TNA, HO144/18869/196919/3.
118 Ruggles-Brise, *Prison Reform*, p. 195.
119 Edward Marsh to W. Churchill, 23 Aug. 1910, in Randolph Churchill, *Winston S. Churchill: Companion Volume* (Boston, 1969), 2, pt. 2:1196.
120 E. Ruggles-Brise memo, 9 Apr. 1910, TNA, HO144/1085/193548/1.
121 Radzinowicz and Hood, pp. 269–71.
122 Ruggles-Brise, *English Prison System*, p. 3. Ruggles-Brise was liverishly unsympathetic, therefore, to the Penal Reform League's 1918 complaints about degrading prison garb,

The Idealist movement thus influenced British legal circles and prison administration. Legal and jurisprudential thinking, reinforced by philosophical idealism, clung fast to the classical principles of moral culpability, responsibility, and of measure for measure between crime and punishment. Penal officials held tight to traditional modes of uniformly administered discipline and remained sceptical of, if also open-minded about, the positivist view of crime as the determined outcome of biological or environmental conditions.[123] The upshot, I suggest, was a neoclassical philosophy and practice of punishment, by which I mean a continued legal appraisal of behaviour in terms of moral choice, at least for sane adults (modified only by minor mitigating factors), and a departure from voluntarism with regard only to the young, the insane, and the feeble-minded—in a word, those incapable of exercising free will—whose actions were largely determined. But determinist philosophies never came close to triumphing over older legal and penological imperatives. The Edwardian debate on prisons was guided less by the new positivist discourse and more by an Idealist framework of thought, with its stress on moral responsibility, just proportion, and the role of the state and citizens to secure the general protection of rights and to help the criminal resume the exercise of rights.

VI

The influence of "moral character," active citizenship, and the realization of the best possible self is evident, too, in ethical socialism. A fundamental strand of the ethical socialist tradition is a belief in the power of moral character both to improve individual conduct and to build a virtuous society.[124] The important point, for present purposes, is that the moral fervour of ethical socialism contributed to the critique of Edwardian prisons by way of conscientious objection to participation in the First World War and the Prison System Enquiry Committee of the Labour Research Department. At the cost of some repetition, it is worth traversing this ground again.

Socialist war resisters, many from the Independent Labour Party, made up three-quarters of the membership of the No-Conscription Fellowship. They made common cause with Quaker Christians and libertarians, grouping around the principle of resistance to compulsion where life and death were concerned.[125]

"spy hole" practice, and the exclusion of outside news; see TNA, HO 45/11543/357055/9.

123 See Forsythe, *Penal Discipline, Reformatory Projects and the English Prison Commission, 1895–1939*, p. 239; Garland, "British Criminology before 1935," p. 5. Idealism's influence might also explain, at least in part, the continued resort to voluntary agencies as an adjunct to the penal system, notably for discharged prisoners, probation, and Borstal aftercare. This feature of the penal system was of particular concern to Ruggles-Brise.

124 For Idealism's influence on ethical socialism, see W. H. Greenleaf, *The British Political Tradition* (New York, 1983), vol. 2, p. 139; and Himmelfarb, p. 261. See also N. Dennis and A. H. Halsey, *English Ethical Socialism* (Oxford, 1988), pp. 1–12.

125 See Clifford Allen in Julian Bell, ed., *We Did Not Fight* (1935), p. 28; T. C. Kennedy, *The Hound of Conscience: A History of the No-Conscription Fellowship, 1914–1919* (Fayetteville, 1981), p. 48; Vellacott, *Bertrand Russell*, p. 29. See also *Report of the Annual Conference of the I.L.P.* (1916), pp. 72–4. The treasurer of the No-Conscription

Stephen Hobhouse, a Quaker pacifist (converted by Tolstoy's *What I Believe*) and long-time social worker in London's East End, observed later that the Quakers' faith "did not divide us in spirit from the many deeply sincere Socialists and others who were holding out against the army on grounds partly ethical and partly political."[126] Hobhouse himself told the conscription tribunal in Shoreditch Town Hall that he chose conscientious objection "as a disciple of Jesus Christ and as an advocate of International Socialism."[127] The two main founders of the No-Conscription Fellowship, Fenner Brockway and Clifford Allen, were ILP socialists. Brockway edited the *Labour Leader*, the ILP's official journal. Allen, also a political journalist, opposed the "capitalist" war from the outset. In March 1916, requesting exemption from military service, he declared, "there is something of divinity in every human being, irrespective of the nation to which he belongs." As the war hastened the shift towards state power, Allen was attracted to guild socialism, a political movement advocating workers' control of industry and defiance of the state.[128] Robin Page Arnot, an ILP member, attempted to evade conscription in May 1917 as a self-proclaimed revolutionary socialist; he served 18 months in Wormwood Scrubs prison.[129] A significant number of these conscientious objectors made up the next generation of penal reformers. Their first contribution was to the Labour Research Department's enquiry launched in 1919.

The Prison System Enquiry Committee was a heavily socialist outfit, although a number of socialisms were represented: ethical, Fabian, and guild. The chairman was Sydney Olivier, a Fabian socialist who sought a social reconstruction in accord with the highest moral possibilities. Committee members included George Bernard Shaw, the Webbs, and G. D. H. Cole, the guild socialist.[130] Hobhouse and Brockway were, of course, the joint editors of the enquiry *English Prisons To-Day*, and they were assisted by Arthur Creech Jones, secretary of the Camberwell Trades and Labour Council, member of the Liberal Christian League, and also a conscientious objector. At times of greatest despair in prison, Arthur Creech Jones had been sustained by the faith

Fellowship was Edward Grubb, a Quaker and former secretary of the Howard Association for Penal Reform.

126 Leo Tolstoy, *What I Believe* (Geneva, 1888). S. Hobhouse's quote is in Bell, ed., p. 167. Hobhouse was from a wealthy Quaker family, but he renounced his inheritance of the family estate. For other details, see Hobhouse, *Forty Years and an Epilogue*, pp. 174–7; A. G. Rose, "Some Influences on English Penal Reform, 1895–1921," *Sociological Review*, vol. 3 (Jul. 1955), pp. 34–7; Martin Ceadel, *Pacifism in Britain 1914–1945* (Oxford, 1980), p. 43.

127 S. Hobhouse in Bell, ed., p. 166.

128 Quoted in Gilbert, p. 5. See J. M. Winter, *Socialism and the Challenge of War* (1974), p. 129. Bertrand Russell, chairman of the No-Conscription Fellowship during the final years of the war, also turned to guild socialism; see W. B. Gwyn, "The Labour Party and the Threat of Bureaucracy," *Political Studies*, vol. 19 (1971), p. 385.

129 See H. E. Roberts, "Years of Struggle: The Life and Work of Robin Page Arnot," *Labour History Review*, vol. 59 (Autumn 1994), pp. 58–63.

130 N. MacKenzie and J. MacKenzie, *The First Fabians* (1977), p. 62. See also Margaret Olivier, ed., *Sydney Olivier: Letters and Selected Writings* (1948), chap. 3. The other committee members were penal reformers; see p. 35 *supra*.

that humanity was one, that I was not a tool of the governing class to slay my fellow workmen in a senseless, suicidal slaughter, that I was trying in a poor way to bear testimony to the ideals of liberty, internationalism, & fraternity.[131]

In summary, I would submit that another strand to the penal culture of these years was an ethical-cum-Christian socialism, a socialism that appealed to the common good, to social service, and to the power of moral character to perfect the person and to reform society. The overarching conclusions to this discussion of Edwardian penal culture seem inescapable. First, the set of attitudes to crime and punishment associated with the European positivist movement—characterized by a search for the determining causes of crime in the physical, genetic, or psychological make up of those pre-disposed to such acts—succumbed to the fatal embrace of British humanitarian, Idealism, and ethical thought. If positivism extended a superficial "scientific" allure to calls for penal reform, the bedrock sensibilities remained heavily "moral." Second, the different groups examined here assisted the continuing adherence to a more traditional jurisprudence and penality by the combined force of their ideas and personnel. En bloc, these groups remained sceptical of the brave new world of positivist criminology and contributed to the widespread public disenchantment with the use of imprisonment.

VII

Let me turn to what I conceive to be the significant development, not to say achievement, of the years 1895–1922: the reduction in the number passing through the prison turnstile. In evidence to the Gladstone Committee, Sir Godfrey Lushington, late Permanent Undersecretary at the Home Office, uttered the immortal lines:

> I regard as unfavourable to reformation the status of a prisoner throughout his whole career; the crushing of self-respect; the starving of all moral instinct he may possess; the absence of all opportunity to do or receive a kindness; the continual association with none but criminals . . . the forced labour and the denial of all liberty. I believe the true mode of reforming a man or restoring him to society is exactly in the opposite direction of all these.[132]

Lushington's approach to criminal justice was shaped by a commitment to the classical Liberal ideal of the free and responsible individual. He was extremely sceptical of the

131 Bodleian Library, Arthur Creech Jones Papers, MS British Empire S 332, box 1, file 2, fol. 142: letter from Hounslow barracks, 9 Jan. 1917.

132 *Report from the Departmental Committee on Prisons, Minutes of Evidence*, PP, 1895, vol. LVI (C.-7702–1), q. 11,482, p. 401. See J. Pellew, "Law and Order: Expertise and the Victorian Home Office," in R. MacLeod (ed.), *Government and Expertise: Specialists, Administrators and Professionals, 1860–1919*, (Cambridge, 1988), pp. 68–9. See idem., "Lushington, Sir Godfrey (1832–1907)," *Oxford DNB* (2009).

reformatory claims of institutions and of the medicalization of criminal justice. The Gladstone Committee accepted the accuracy of Lushington's description but could not agree "that all of these unfavorable features are irremovable."[133] Nevertheless, the principal achievement of the years after Gladstone took place where Lushington pointed: outside prison. The main tendency of the period was not the expansion of preventive confinement, the emergence of new islands in the "carceral archipelago," but the extraordinary decrease in both the number of prisoners, especially those undergoing short sentences (and of the 200,000 committals to prison in 1909, no fewer than 125,000, or 61 per cent, were under sentences of two weeks or less, over half of which were imposed on first offenders),[134] and of the prison estate.

Detention in penal institutions was still the mainstay of the criminal justice system in the early twentieth century. The cardinal characteristic of the prison system was the enormous procession of persons sentenced for non-indictable (or less serious) offences or those receiving sentences in default of payment of a fine for such offenses as drunkenness, minor assaults, or contravention of borough by-laws. In 1899, prison receptions were running at 175,000 per annum, and the daily average population was about 14,500 in local prisons, 4,000 in the convict prisons. By 1903, receptions were close to 200,000, and the daily average population rose to 20,000. Thereafter, the numbers fell, but still in 1914 receptions numbered 150,000, and the daily average population stood at 18,000. Yet by 1918, receptions had plummeted to 30,000, and the daily average population was below 9,000. The pre-war peaks were never again ascended.[135] A number of factors explain this enormous decrease.

The Probation of Offenders Act, 1907, gave the courts another alternative to incarceration; the Children Act, 1908, excluded those aged under 16 from prison. Of vital importance, the Criminal Justice (Administration) Act 1914 did much to keep fine defaulters out of prison by allowing magistrates to give time for payment. Between 1910 and 1921, the numbers imprisoned annually for non-payment of fines dropped from 85,000 to 15,000. And the wartime combination of full employment and drinking restrictions resulted in a fall-off in the numbers imprisoned for minor offenses like drunkenness and vagrancy. The downward trend of the prison population, it should be stressed, was not the result of a decrease in crime but of the legislation mentioned previously, the effect of war, and perhaps most crucially, of judicial

---

133 *Report from the Departmental Committee on Prisons*, p. 12.

134 Victor Bailey, "Churchill as Home Secretary: Prison Reform," *History Today*, vol. 35 (1985), p. 11.

135 K. Neale, "Her Majesty's Commissioners 1878–1978" (Home Office, 1978, private circulation), pp. 19–20; E. H. Sutherland, "The Decreasing Prison Population of England," *Journal of Criminal Law and Criminology*, vol. 24 (1933), pp. 880–900. The figures specifically for women tell the same story. At the turn of the century, 50,000 women were annually committed to prison, largely for prostitution and drunkenness. In 1918, commitments were 14,922, a drop of 72 per cent. The daily average in local prisons fell from about 3,000 to 1,500 prisoners. See E. Ruggles-Brise memo, 22 Oct. 1918, TNA, HO45/11543/357055/9.

willingness to move away from custody in their sentencing practice.[136] A credible explanation of the judicial mindset requires separate investigation, but justices were influenced by the disenchantment with prison that pervaded the press and the Home Office from the 1880s and by their own experience of the revolving doors of short-term imprisonment. In addition, Home Secretaries, aware of the effect that sentencing practice had on penal administration, were increasingly prepared to supervise magistrates and judges, either directly by circular or indirectly via the lord chancellor.[137]

I am familiar, finally, with the fall-back position of the revisionist historians, which is to insist that non-custodial measures actually extended the field of intervention available to the courts. Modern criminologists speak of the "hidden discipline" of community corrections and suggest that it amounts to a qualitatively new and different pattern of penality. Perhaps so. For my part, I simply wish to insist that the revisionists' image of a prison system ingesting ever more prisoners into its insatiable maw is a gross exaggeration. We should be impressed rather with the pre-war mood of profound scepticism about imprisonment, local and convict, a mood that one Liberal politician in particular helped to shape.

Winston Churchill, Home Secretary for an animated 18 months in 1910–11, assisted the reductionist tendency. The first principle of prison reform, declared Churchill, "should be to prevent as many people as possible getting there at all. There is an injury to the individual, there is a loss to the State whenever a person is committed to prison for the first time."[138] His opening gambit was audacious by the standards of any former or subsequent Home Secretary: "to arrange matters so that next year there will be 50,000 fewer people sent to prison than this year."[139] He not only wanted to reduce by one-third the annual committals to prison but also to reduce by 10 to 15 per cent the daily average prison population and to abolish all imprisonment for periods of less than one month. To reduce this "gigantic number of useless and often pernicious committals"[140] and avoid the unnecessary familiarization of offenders with prison surroundings, four main lines of advance were explored by Churchill.

First, for the 5,000 lads aged 16 to 21 who were sent to prison each year for such offences as gaming and stone throwing, Churchill proposed a system of "defaulters' drill," or physical exercise, to be administered at the police station. Second, there was to be time to pay fines. Third, imprisonment for debt was to be abolished. Finally, Churchill proposed a "suspensory sentence" of imprisonment for petty offenders. As a result, first or

136 For the figures cited, see Sidney Webb and Beatrice Webb, *English Prisons under Local Government* (1922; reprint, 1963), p. 248; Ruggles-Brise, *English Prison System*, pp. 224–5; A. Rutherford, *Prisons and the Process of Justice: The Reductionist Challenge* (1984), pp. 123, 130; and Robert and Emsley, eds., *Lessons from a Reductionist Era*, pp. 59–60. The rate of indictable crime recorded by the police rose by less than 10 per cent between 1900 and 1921; see F. H. McClintock and N. H. Avison, *Crime in England and Wales* (1968), pp. 18–24.
137 For a full assessment of the abatement of imprisonment between 1880 and 1939, see chaps. 2 and 3 *infra*.
138 *Hansard*, vol. 19, 20 Jul. 1910, col. 1344.
139 W. S. Blunt, *My Diaries* (New York, 1922), pt. 2, p. 335.
140 W. Churchill minute, 13 Aug. 1910, TNA, HO144/18869/196919/1.

infrequent offenders would never go to prison for less than one month.[141] Once the prisons were emptied of their deadweight of petty criminals, Churchill envisaged a radical reorganization of the penal system. The prison population was to be classified into 20 main categories and distributed for specialized treatment to "a regular series of scientifically graded institutions."[142] Prisoners would be so distributed by a board of classification since no "scientific uniform system" could be administered through the courts. Churchill was in office too briefly to bring more than a few of his many planned reforms to fruition. Accordingly, his contribution to keeping people out of prison was characterized more by promise than accomplishment. Nonetheless, Churchill contributed to the mood of disenchantment with short-term confinement in "the general mixed prison," a mood that was rekindled in the post-war years by *English Prisons To-Day*.[143]

Churchill's tenure at the Home Office also serves to underscore a central ambivalence running through Edwardian Liberalism. The impulse towards scientific medicalization was continually balked by deep-rooted commitments to morality and liberty. This was noticeably evident in Churchill's approach to sentencing. Indeed, Churchill was more interested in the techniques of sentencing and commitment than in the administration of penal custody. His letters are far more concerned with who should or should not go to prison, and for how long, than what happened to them after they arrived. His thinking was dominated, moreover, by classical notions of justice, notably a just proportion between crime and penalty. He would have liked to set down a uniform scale of penalties for judges to follow. He had to make do with revising sentences piecemeal, searching the criminal calendars for cases of injustice, and exercising the prerogative of mercy to influence sentencing practice.[144]

Churchill was particularly disturbed by what he termed "the first fruits of the [Preventive Detention] Act": "It has greatly increased the severity of the criminal law, and the inequality of sentences," he wrote in June 1910.[145] Through new administrative rules, Churchill sought to mitigate the inequalities arising from the working of the act and to restrict the act's scope to the criminal who was a "danger to society," whose newest crime was a serious offence.[146] So, too, Churchill insisted that Borstal detention be reserved for those who had committed serious offences, by which he meant rape, robbery with violence, and burglary. Some check must be imposed, he minuted, on the increasing tendency of the courts to inflict sentences of three years' imprisonment at Borstal for offences that would ordinarily receive six months or less. And linking both provisions of the Prevention of Crime Act 1908 together, Churchill wrote:

141 Cabinet paper, R. Churchill, *Winston S. Churchill: Companion Volume*, op. cit., vol. 2, pt. 2, pp. 1198–203; TNA, HO45/10613/194534. For the full history of imprisonment for debt, see G. R. Rubin, "Law, Poverty and Imprisonment for Debt, 1869–1914," in G. R. Rubin and D. Sugarman (eds.), *Law, Economy and Society: Essays in the History of English Law 1750–1914* (Abingdon, 1984), pp. 241–99.
142 TNA, HO144/18869/196919/1.
143 See Webb and Webb, p. 248.
144 See Radzinowicz and Hood, pp. 770, 773; Addison, pp. 112–17; Thomas, pp. 40, 46–7.
145 TNA, HO45/10589/184160/23.
146 Ibid., 184160/25a. See also Thomas, pp. 41–5; Addison, pp. 118–19.

Within proper limits both the Borstal and Preventive Detention systems are desirable as being beneficial and humane refinements upon the ordinary prison system. Beyond those limits they cannot be defended and will quickly draw upon themselves a current of public displeasure. I should certainly not consent to be responsible for any system which can be shown to aggravate the severity of the Penal Codes.[147]

Churchill *was* ready to sanction prolonged detention (of up to two years) in curative labour colonies for habitual offenders convicted repeatedly of vagrancy and drunkenness, and he inclined to the eugenic in proposals to deal with the feeble-minded.[148] This could be expected of a young politician who had donned the coat of the New Liberalism in all its progressive and welfarist colours. The influence of positivist criminology was never such, however, as to shake Churchill's dependence on the classical principles of deterrence, just proportion, and uniformity of treatment. In the face of "scientific reform," he displayed a meticulous regard for what he termed "the rights of convicted criminals against the State."[149] He resisted the advance of indeterminate detention, the emblem of the new penology, except with regard to the segregation of mental defectives.[150] And he curbed the excesses, as he saw them, of the semi-indeterminate sentences of preventive detention and Borstal training.

VIII

The debate on English prisons between 1895 and 1922 was framed by the unchanging structure of a harsh prison system and the related determination to diminish the number of persons passing through prison gates. Despite the good intentions of the Gladstone Committee, the pace of progress in humanizing prisons was glacial. The prison discipline meted out to conscientious objectors during the war was almost identical to that suffered by Oscar Wilde, a quarter century before:

Deprived of books, of all human intercourse, isolated from every humane and humanising influence, condemned to eternal silence, robbed of all intercourse with the external world, treated like an unintelligent animal, brutalised below the level of any of the brute-creation, the wretched man who is confined in an English prison can hardly escape becoming insane.[151]

147 TNA, HO144/18869/196919/2.
148 See TNA, HO144/A60866/4; HO45/10520/138276/57; Radzinowicz and Hood, pp. 372–5; Addison, pp. 123–6; Searle, pp. 107–8. According to his friend, Wilfred Scawen Blunt, Churchill was "a strong eugenist"; see Blunt, p. 399 (entry for 20 Oct. 1912). When the Cabinet discussed the issue of "the unfit" in Dec. 1911, Churchill presented Dr. A. F. Tredgold's article, "The Feeble-Minded—a Social Danger," which warned of the peril of "national degeneracy." See Ted Morgan, *Churchill: Young Man in a Hurry, 1874–1915* (New York, 1982), p. 289.
149 *Hansard*, vol. 19, 20 Jul. 1910, col. 1354.
150 TNA, HO45/1085/193548/1. Churchill's contribution to the abatement of imprisonment is again addressed in chap. 2 *infra*.
151 Wilde, *The Soul of Man*, p. 193.

Is this Oscar Wilde or Hobhouse and Brockway? It hardly matters, since it could serve as an accurate description of the prison regime both in 1895 and 1921. The special measures proposed by the Gladstone Committee met with no greater success than the attempts to improve prison conditions. If Borstal training was lauded as a progressive step in the treatment of young adult offenders, the various forms of preventive detention for habituals, defectives, inebriates, and vagrants met with considerable judicial, administrative, and public scepticism, so much so that all withered on the vine. To see all this as a new penal structure, as an integral part of a "modern penal complex," seems wide of the mark.

Nor is it any more convincing to see positivism as the main ideological inspiration of the limited changes that did take place. Judges, prison administrators, and penal reformers were generally familiar with the ideas of individualization, classification, and indeterminacy, but true converts were thin on the ground, and their ranks became thinner as the first flush of enthusiasm dissipated. The new scientific knowledges, whether Lombrosian positivism or British eugenics, far from being incorporated into penal practice, were held at arm's length. Judges and prison officials remained loyal to the classical credo of moral culpability, a just measure of punishment, and uniformly administered discipline. In this, they were guided by a jurisprudence and a civic consciousness that drew inspiration from philosophic idealism. Lombrosian criminal man was born, his action the determined outcome of biological inheritance, his fate to be incarcerated in perpetuity to protect society against his dangerousness. By contrast, Idealist criminal man was a responsible agent, his action the willed violation of an explicit social right, his fate to have his bad will annulled by a punishment proportionate to the importance of the right violated. As such, the prisoner possessed an individual human worth, and the state had the duty to safeguard his "reversionary rights" by sending him out better fitted to assume the role of citizen. This philosophy shaped the idée fixe of a host of administrators, reformers, and social workers in the early twentieth century, and, as I have argued elsewhere, was the predominant influence on the patterns of criminal policy and practice in the 1920s and 1930s.[152]

If there was a sea change in prison policy and practice between 1895 and 1922, then it was surely the massive reduction in the number of short-sentence prisoners. The tightening of urban regulations in the nineteenth century had brought growing numbers of citizens into conflict with the law through drunkenness and street offences and growing numbers into the prisons, either directly or in default of fine payment. In their campaigns to make inroads into this mass of petty imprisonments, the reformers were aided by the pre-war Liberal home secretaries, Herbert Gladstone and Winston Churchill, by a war that for various reasons reduced the size of the social "residuum" from which much of the short-stay prison population was drawn, and by a change in judicial sentencing practice which the next chapter explores. From the vantage point of the present day, when the number of prisoners rarely ceases to rise, the steep drop in both prison receptions and daily average population in the first quarter of the twentieth century is remarkable. It was this statistical change on which Sidney and Beatrice Webb concluded their historical study of the administration of English prisons,

152 Bailey, *Delinquency and Citizenship*.

published simultaneously with Hobhouse and Brockway's *English Prisons To-Day*. Echoing Sir Godfrey Lushington's evidence to the Gladstone Committee, the Webbs wrote:

> The reflection emerges that, when all is said and done, it is probably quite impossible to make a good job of the deliberate incarceration of a human being in the most enlightened of dungeons. Even the mere sense of confinement, the mere deprivation of liberty, the mere interference with self-initiative—if in any actual prison the adverse regimen were, in practice, ever limited to these restrictions—could hardly ever, in themselves, have a beneficial result on intellect, emotions or character. We suspect that it passes the wit of man to contrive a prison which shall not be gravely injurious to the minds of the vast majority of the prisoners, if not also to their bodies. So far as can be seen at present, the most practical and the most hopeful of "prison reforms" is to keep people out of prison altogether![153]

153 Webb and Webb, pp. 247–8.

2

JUDGES, THE TARIFF, AND THE ABATEMENT OF IMPRISONMENT, 1880–1914

Probably no system in the world leaves so wide a discretion to the judges in the matter of punishment.

Sir James Fitzjames Stephen, "The Punishment of Convicts," Cornhill Magazine, vol. 7 (1863).

I

In 1982, Malcolm Ramsay plotted the daily average prison population, as well as the number of persons imprisoned per 100,000 of the total population in England and Wales, between 1775 and 1980 (see Figure 2.1).[1] What stands out vividly is the way the two trend lines plummet in tandem between 1880 and 1939, or for almost one-third of the two centuries under investigation. Only in the first decade of the twentieth century is there a reversal in the trend. In 1908 the prison population stood at 22,000, the level of 20 years before. Yet this turned out to be a momentary pause in the downward trend. The prison population continued to fall between 1908 and 1939, in what the Commission on English Prisons Today called the "longest period of decarceration in world history."[2] Such a dramatic abatement of imprisonment, a de-centring of the prison in penal policy, warrants interrogation if we are to understand the essential contours and content of inter-war sentencing and penal policy. Historians are familiar with this era of "decarceration," at least in statistical outline, yet it cannot be claimed that we have a firm grip on

1 Ramsay, "Two centuries of imprisonment," *Research Bulletin* (Home Office Research and Planning Unit), No. 14 (1982), pp. 45–7.
2 Commission on English Prisons Today, *The Principles and Limits of the Penal System* (2009), p. 2. The United States did not experience this level of abatement of imprisonment: M. Cahalan, "Trends in Incarceration in the United States since 1880," *Crime & Delinquency*, vol. 25 (1979), pp. 9–21.

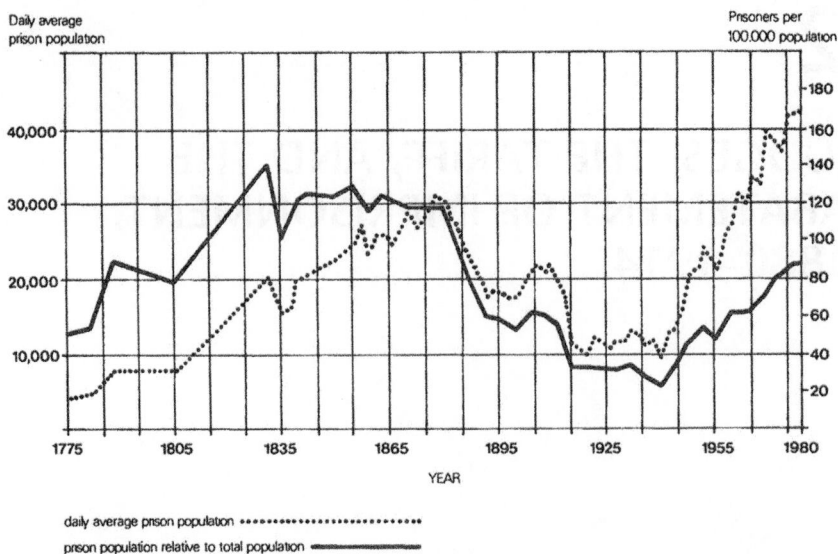

FIGURE 2.1 Daily average prison population and number of persons imprisoned per 100,000 of the total population, in England and Wales, 1775–1980

Source: Malcolm Ramsay, "Two centuries of imprisonment," *Research Bulletin* (Home Office Research and Planning Unit), No. 14 (1982), p. 47, reproduced with permission of Crown Copyright Section of HMPPS.

the reasons for the transformation. The purpose of the next two chapters is to offer an assessment of the judicial, administrative, legislative, and socio-economic factors that shaped this remarkable abatement of imprisonment between 1880 and 1940, this unprecedented recalibration of the tariff of punishment. While a multi-factorial analysis is inevitably required to explain such a dramatic drop in the prison population over five decades, the factor that has attracted too little attention, in our view, is judicial sentencing. Yet the entire subject begs the question: why did the judiciary, both high and low, alter their sentencing practices, without which decarceration would have been stillborn? Imprisonment appealed to a tariff-minded judiciary, since it can be measured out in periods of prison time, marking and denouncing the seriousness of the offence. For the judiciary, prison was "real" punishment, unlike probation or other non-custodial measures. Yet the magistracy and High Court judges, encouraged on occasion by the Court of Criminal Appeal, scaled back the sentencing tariff to an inordinate degree over the sixty years in question. One feature of this judicial activism was the unwillingness to accept those parts of the rehabilitative programme that required long preventive or indeterminate sentences. Living as we do in an age when penologists deride the judiciary for filling the prisons well beyond capacity by their sentencing decisions, it is salutary to discover that this is not always the case.[3]

3   As Andrew Ashworth wrote of a later period: "The fact that the courts choose to send offenders to prison in the exercise of their discretion does mean, in a sense, that they are

The abatement of imprisonment was not lost upon penal reformers and prison commissioners of the day. Sir Evelyn Ruggles-Brise, chairman of the Prison Commission, 1895–1921, provided the figures in Table 2.1 for committals (or receptions) on conviction, revealing a considerable drop over the course of the late Victorian and Edwardian years:

TABLE 2.1 Committals to prison on conviction, 1883 and 1914

Year ended 31 Mar.	Convicted of indictable, or "serious," offences tried at assizes and quarter sessions	Convicted of offences tried summarily		Total committals on conviction	Per 100,000 of population of country
		Indict	Non-indict		
1883	10,069	153,645*		163,714	622
1914	7,738	15,598	113,088	136,424	369

Source: Table adapted from E. Ruggles-Brise, *The English Prison System* (Macmillan, 1921), p. 219. *The figures for "Convicted of Offences tried Summarily" were not available for indictable and non-indictable offences *separately* in 1883.

Stephen Hobhouse and Fenner Brockway began their 1922 report, *English Prisons To-Day*, with an analysis of the diminishing prison population.[4] In 1876–77, when *local* prisons were brought under government control, the daily average population was 20,000; by 1913–14 (the year before the war) it was 14,300; by 1918–19, it was down to 7,000. The decrease in the number of female prisoners was proportionally greater than that of males. The daily average population for *convict* prisons for the same years was 10,000; 2,700; and 1,200, respectively. And Lionel Fox, Secretary to the Prison Commission, plotted the fluctuations in prison population between 1880 and 1932, the most striking aspect of which, he wrote, "is the totally different levels of population that are divided, roughly, by the decade 1908–1918."[5] In the early part of the twentieth century, the daily average prison population in both local and convict prisons exceeded 20,000; between 1920 and 1932, the figure rarely exceeded 12,000 (see Figure 2.2). The fall in prison population was precipitous during the First World War, notably of those committed for short prison sentences. Fox's finding of two different numerical plateaus, divided by the decade 1908–18, and the sharp fall in the prison population during the War years, indicate that an analysis of the abatement of imprisonment is best divided into three phases: 1880–1914, the 1914–18 war, and the inter-war years. This chapter deals with the first phase, the next chapter with the war and inter-war years.

responsible for the size of the prison population." See *Reducing the Prison Population in the 1980s: The Need for Sentencing Reform* (NACRO, 1983), p. 2.

4   Stephen Hobhouse and A. Fenner Brockway (eds.), *English Prisons To-Day: Being the Report of the Prison System Enquiry Committee* (1922), p. 3.

5   L. W. Fox, *The Modern English Prison* (1934), p. 221 (Graph A); p. 208. Fox was Secretary to the Prison Commission between 1925 and 1934.

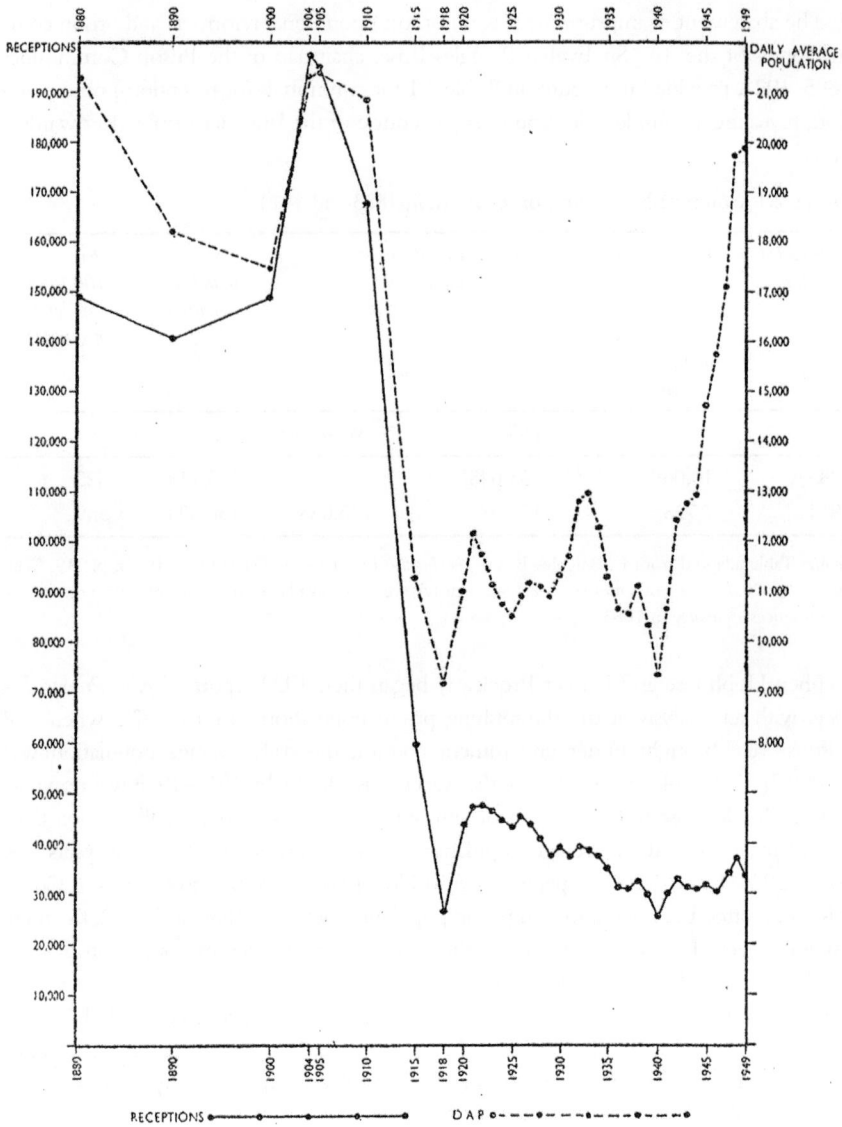

FIGURE 2.2 Graph showing the total annual receptions on conviction and daily average population in English prisons from 1880 to 1949

Source: Report of prison commissioners for 1951 (Cmd. 8356), p. 12, reproduced with permission of Crown Copyright Section of HMPPS.

II

We first need to pinpoint the numerical changes that were at the back of the fall in prison population. The main sources of a fall in prison population are changes in the *number of offences tried* (*and number of persons convicted*), changes in the *proportion of those convicted who are sentenced to prison*, and changes in the *length of time that people are sent to prison*.[6] The first change concerns trials for indictable or "serious" offences in England and Wales. The rate per 100,000 population declined by a third between the late 1850s and the pre-war years (or by 43 per cent, if the early 1860s and late 1890s are taken as benchmarks). This was due largely to a decline in the crimes of theft and violence. As importantly, for present purposes, the *absolute* number of trials also declined in the later Victorian years. The total number of trials for indictable offences in assizes, quarter sessions, and courts of summary jurisdiction fell from an annual average of 60,220 in 1881–85 to 55,405 in 1891–95 to 51,612 in 1896–1900 (before rising to 64,423 in 1906–10). These figures were a function of offences against property without violence, mainly larcenies, which made up 90 per cent of all indictable offences in these years. The total number of trials for larcenies fell from an annual average of 54,241 in 1881–85 to 49,489 in 1891–95 to 45,679 in 1896–1900 (before rising to 56,204 in 1906–10).[7] These figures say nothing about the *conviction rate*, however, and hence of the number available to be sentenced. The percentage of trials resulting in conviction for larceny increased over this period from 72 per cent in 1881–85 to 76 per cent in 1891–95, and to 80 per cent in 1896–1900. Even so, the *absolute* number of convicted offenders declined, if less markedly than the number of trials. Between 1881 and 1900, the number of trials fell by around 8,500, while the number of convictions fell by 2,400.

The second change concerns *the courts' custody rates*, or the proportion of offenders convicted of indictable offences who were sent to prison. The figures indicate a progressive mitigation of the sentences passed upon conviction, especially for property crimes. The percentage distribution of sentences for indictable offences against property without violence, delivered in higher courts and courts of summary jurisdiction combined, indicates the following. Penal servitude sentences declined to virtual insignificance between the 1860s (5 per cent) and the 1890s (1 per cent). In the 1860s, close to 90 per cent of those convicted of indictable

6   The next three paragraphs are based on figures dug out from the following sources: Edwin H. Sutherland, "The Decreasing Prison Population of England," *Journal of Criminal Law & Criminology*, vol. 24 (1933), pp. 880–96; L. Radzinowicz, "The Assessment of Punishments by English Courts," in Radzinowicz and J. W. C. Turner (eds.), *The Modern Approach to Criminal Law* (1945), pp. 110–22; R. M. Jackson, *The Machinery of Justice in England* (Cambridge, 1972), Table 13, p. 298; H. Mannheim, "Some Aspects of Judicial Sentencing Policy," *Yale Law Journal*, vol. 67 (1958), p. 976; R. Hood and A. Roddam, "Crime, Sentencing and Punishment," in A. H. Halsey and J. Webb (eds.), *Twentieth Century British Social Trends* (2000), pp. 690–9.

7   The rise in larceny trials and convictions in the first decade of the twentieth century was a consequence most likely of trade depression, price inflation, falling real wages, and high unemployment. It resulted in a temporary reaction against the mitigation of punishment, and in the advocacy of longer custodial sentences for recidivists, one legislative effect being the introduction in 1908 of preventive detention for habitual offenders.

larcenies were sentenced to imprisonment. By 1881–85, this figure had fallen to 65 per cent, by 1896–1900 to less than 50 per cent, and by 1911–14 the figure had come down to 35 per cent. Prison sentences increasingly made way for non-custodial penalties. Already by 1881–85, 28 per cent of those convicted of indictable larcenies were sentenced to fine, whipping, or released on a surety or recognizance. By the end of the century, over half of all larcenists (mainly juveniles and first offenders) were subjected to a fine or were released on a surety. Imprisonment fell off even more rapidly after the Probation of Offenders Act 1907. There was also greater leniency in the sentencing of serious property crime (burglary, breaking and entering, and robbery). Over one-third of those convicted in the early 1860s were sent to penal servitude, and 60 per cent received imprisonment. From the late 1880s onwards, penal servitude sentences declined, only 12 per cent receiving such a sentence by 1900. Imprisonment took up the slack, 79 per cent receiving such a sentence by 1900, though this figure fell to 66 per cent by 1914, as 14 per cent were released on a surety or recognizance (half of them with a probation order).[8]

The third change concerns *the length of sentences*. A remarkable drop took place in the number of "long" sentences passed in the 1880s and 1890s. The number of penal servitude sentences per 100,000 population fell from 5.86 in 1881 to 2.64 in 1895; and the number of sentences of imprisonment for one year and upward per 100,000 population fell from 4.73 in 1881 to 2.51 in 1895. Furthermore, by 1896, only 2 per cent of those convicted of indictable offences were being given penal servitude, and nine-tenths of these sentences were for five years or less. Imprisonment, with a maximum of two years, became the primary custodial sanction for all courts. Yet prison sentences got shorter in duration, and imprisonment started to give way to non-custodial penalties. The average length of a sentence of imprisonment declined from 48.3 days in 1880 to 34.4 days in 1894. By 1900, the average length of imprisonment had fallen to less than one month.[9]

8   Mitigation was slower for those convicted of felonious and malicious wounding. Penal servitude sentences declined from 10 per cent in the 1860s to 9 per cent in the 1890s. Eighty-seven per cent of those convicted of violent crime in the 1860s were imprisoned, falling slowly to 81 per cent in the late 1890s, then more rapidly to 71 per cent by 1914. Another way of presenting the statistical information drawn from the annual Judicial Returns is in this brief assessment of punishments. Taking all indictable offences sentenced at both higher and summary courts, *of every 100 offenders in 1880*, 77 were deprived of their liberty (73 imprisoned, four given penal servitude), 17 were released with or without conditions, and five were detained in reformatory schools. By *1913*, 57 were deprived of liberty (55 imprisoned, two penal servitude), 37 were released with or without conditions, three were detained in reformatories, and two were sent to Borstal detention.

9   The decreasing severity in the lengths of *penal servitude* sentences is evident from the following figures:

Length of term (in years)	1880	1913
Above 10 years	5.1	1.0
10 years and above 7 years	14.5	1.3
7 years	23.1	3.3
Below 7 years	57.3	94.5

As for specific types of indictable crime, a large proportion of larcenists were sent to prison for short periods. Of those convicted in 1881–85, 57 per cent were imprisoned for less than six months; 29 per cent for less than a month. These figures declined to 49 per cent and 27 per cent of all convicted by 1891–92, as non-custodial sentences were increasingly turned to.

It is evident, then, that from around 1880, courts tried and convicted fewer offenders, sent fewer convicted offenders to prison, and shortened the length of sentences of penal servitude and imprisonment (and increasingly resorted to non-custodial measures). The combination of these three changes led to a marked drop in the prison population. By the exercise of their discretion to send offenders to prison or not, and for how long, the courts changed the size and shape of the late Victorian prison population. It only remains to underline the contribution of the drop in the length of prison sentences. Troup, a senior clerk in the Home Office, in his evidence to the Gladstone Committee on Prisons, revealed that between 1883 and 1893, the number of committals to prison showed a decrease of only 3.3 per cent. As he extrapolated, if the number of offenders receiving prison sentences was only slightly down, the significant fall in daily average prison population must have been a function of shorter terms of imprisonment.[10]

III

How do we explain this remarkable abatement of imprisonment, and particularly the drop in the length of sentences of penal servitude and imprisonment? Above all, how do we explain the recalibration of the tariff of punishment that the judiciary installed in these years? One explanation, voiced at the time, is that the sharp fall in the incidence of property and violent offences in the last half of the nineteenth century reduced the anxiety about crime and encouraged mitigation of punishment by the courts. Recorded crime, especially offences against property, fell steadily from the 1860s to 1914, and especially thefts of food and clothing stolen by the poor from the poor. Violent robbery declined. Riot and arson practically disappeared. Violence fell sharply from the 1870s, as drinking diminished. Homicide halved from 1.6 per 100,000 in 1860 to 0.8 by 1914. A high proportion (up to one-third) of killings took place within families. Female crime diminished. The proportion of the population involved in crime narrowed, while the number of hardened professional criminals was reassuringly small.[11] The decline in serious

10 See C. Harding, "'The Inevitable End of a Discredited System'? The Origins of the Gladstone Committee Report on Prisons, 1895," *Historical Journal*, vol. 31 (1988), p. 594. Edmund Du Cane, former chairman of the Prison Commission, thought it possible that the shorter prison sentences for ordinary crimes were much the same as before, but the longer sentences had been diminished, "whether because the crimes are less serious or the courts more merciful there is no evidence to show." See "The Prison Committee Report," *Nineteenth Century*, vol. 38 (1895), p. 286.

11 V. A. C. Gatrell, "The Decline of Theft and Violence in Victorian and Edwardian England," in Gatrell et al (eds.), *Crime and the Law* (1980), pp. 301–16, 330–1. Gatrell's explanation for the decline in crime is wide-ranging, including a lower incidence of economic dislocation in the second half of the nineteenth century, modest increases in

crime was more than sufficient to convince Victorians that the war against crime was being won. As early as 1879, barrister Luke Owen Pike, could assert: "There never was in any nation of which we have a history, a time in which life and property were so secure as they are at present in England."[12] Judges were manifestly aware of the decrease of crime since the end of transportation. In evidence to the Commissioners appointed to inquire into the working of the penal servitude acts, Mr. Justice Lush stated: "There certainly has been a great decrease of crime of late years; to what cause or combination of causes attributable I do not know"; Lord Justice Bramwell concurred: "Generally speaking, I should say that all over England there is no doubt that crime has diminished" (though both justices made exceptions of the Irish population in Manchester and Liverpool).[13] This was thought to be influential. "The knowledge that crime is diminishing," declared the criminal registrar in 1894, "encourages judges and magistrates to deal with crimes more leniently."[14] Sir Francis Powell, MP, said the same in 1897: "There could be no doubt that judges and justices of the peace had diminished sentences, because they believed that there was now greater order in society than formerly, and that property was in greater security."[15] It all sounds plausible: less crime, less fear of crime, and less resistance on the part of the judiciary to penal moderation. Where today sentencing *severity* is largely a function of public and press anxiety about violent and sexual crimes, in the Victorian era sentencing *leniency* was a response to diminished public and press anxiety.

A second explanation concerns the expansion in the criminal jurisdiction of the magistrates' courts, and the devaluation of the gravity of many offences by transferring them to summary jurisdiction.[16] Legislation progressively transferred

prosperity for the lower social echelons, and the moral and environmental impact of the "moralizing missions," but he places a good deal of emphasis upon the balance of power between those who enforced the law and those who broke it, arguing that in this period the balance tilted decidedly in favour of the legal authorities. See Gatrell, p. 336. Note, however, that police numbers rose steeply after 1860, and their adoption of what we now call "zero tolerance," led to large numbers of arrests and convictions for such non-indictable offences as loitering, drunkenness, minor assault, and offences against various social and moral regulations, and led to magistrates' courts handing out a large number of short prison sentences.

12 Quoted in Gatrell, "The Decline," op cit., p. 241.
13 *Report of the Commissioners Appointed to Inquire into The Working of the Penal Servitude Acts (Kimberley Commission), Minutes of Evidence*, PP, 1878–9, vol. 37 (C.-2368.-1), q. 11691, p. 929 (Lush); q. 12086, p. 965 (Bramwell).
14 Quoted in Martin Wiener, *Reconstructing the Criminal: Culture, Law, and Policy in England, 1830–1914* (Cambridge, 1990), p. 258. On the other hand, judges were less tolerant of male violence, and dealt increasingly severely with the major crimes of violence: murder, manslaughter, and rape. See idem., *Men of Blood: Violence, Manliness and Criminal Justice in Victorian England* (Cambridge, 2004), *passim*.
15 Quoted in W. McWilliams, "The Mission to the English Police Courts 1876–1936," *Howard Journal*, vol. 22 (1983), p. 131. The decline in crime also influenced the approach to punishment of the executive and the legislature.
16 See Wiener, op cit., pp. 259–60; 264; McWilliams, op cit., p. 130; L. Radzinowicz and R. Hood, *A History of English Criminal Law and its Administration from 1750*, vol. 5 (1986), pp. 622–3; Gatrell, "The Decline," op cit., pp. 273–4; Douglas Hay, "Time, Inequality, and Law's Violence," in A. Sarat and T. R. Kearns (eds.), *Law's Violence* (Ann Arbor, 1992), p. 167. William McWilliams speculated that "perceptions of the

indictable offences from jury trials in the higher courts, to the jurisdiction of magistrates in petty sessions. The Summary Jurisdiction Act of 1879 extended summary trial to all offences committed by juveniles under 12 (except homicide), all larcenies by adults pleading guilty, and larcenies under 40 shillings in value when the accused consented. The Summary Jurisdiction Act of 1899 covered all offences by juveniles under 16 (except homicide). In consequence, by 1881–85, 82 per cent of all larcenists were dealt with summarily, rising to 89 per cent by 1901–05. Magistrates' courts were limited in their sentencing powers, including the term of imprisonment they could award, which was restricted to six months for any one offence. Shifting more and more of the criminal caseload from jury trials to summary courts automatically lowered the scale of punishment. By century's end, the 471 sentences of imprisonment per every 1,000 sentences for indictable offences rarely exceeded six months in length, and in 62 per cent of these sentences the length did not exceed one month.[17] The change in jurisdiction also led to greater use of non-custodial penalties: fines, release on recognizances, and probation.

A third possible explanation for the abatement of imprisonment by the courts is the influence of the transition in the ways of seeing criminals between the mid- and late-Victorian years. Martin Wiener documented how a mid-Victorian image of the criminal as a wilful, undisciplined savage in need of control was displaced by a late-Victorian image of a debilitated, unfit offender in need of help and revitalization. Criminals were seen less as rational, responsible human beings and more as victims of social deprivation or mental impairment. Weakness not wickedness was thought to induce criminality.[18] This led, we are told, to changes in sentencing. The courts, at

gravity of some offences themselves could have altered. . . . [A]s punishments became less severe, the offences to which such punishments applied could be viewed as less serious than had previously been the case." See "The Mission to the English Police Courts," op cit., p. 131. The courts were themselves a locus for communication of these penal norms: see Barry Godfrey, "Sentencing, Theatre, Audience and Communication: the Victorian and Edwardian Magistrates' Courts and Their Message," in *Les Témoins Devant La Justice: Une Histoire des Status et des Comportements* (Rennes, 2003), pp. 162–3.

17 J. Holt Schooling, "Crime, part II," *Pall Mall Magazine*, vol. 15 (1898), p. 356. Note, however, that the expansion in criminal jurisdiction of the lower courts, plus the enforcement of the many new social and moral regulations of the late Victorian years (such as parental failure to send a child to school, from 1876; or living off immoral earnings, from 1884), had the effect of turning the local prisons into a turnstile for short-term prisoners, whether by direct committal to prison or in default of payment of a fine. By the early twentieth century, the prisons were glutted with a stage army of vagrants, drunks, prostitutes, and offenders against social and moral regulations.

18 Wiener, *Reconstructing*, passim; idem., "Some Images of Man and their Relation to the Administration of the Criminal Law in Britain, 1830–1914," in T. G. Watkin (ed.), *Legal Record and Historical Reality* (1989), pp. 199–213. See also D. Melossi, "Changing Representations of the Criminal," *British Journal of Criminology*, vol. 40 (2000), p. 298; Nicola Lacey, "In Search of the Responsible Subject: History, Philosophy and Social Sciences in Criminal Law Theory," *Modern Law Review*, vol. 64 (2001), p. 365. I am persuaded that this image of criminal man might well have influenced the judiciary to abate the use of imprisonment, but I remain unconvinced that there was a *single* image

times with executive encouragement, began to divert a proportion of the delinquent group away from the prison system, offenders for whom regular prison discipline was deemed unsuitable. In the 1880s, Sir William Harcourt, when Home Secretary, delivered a series of speeches critical of juvenile imprisonment; ordered the review of all committals of children under 15; and put pressure on justices to send fewer young offenders to prison.[19] The number of offenders under 12 who were jailed fell from 866 in 1879–80 to 250 in 1885–86 to 18 in 1900. The number of offenders between the ages of 12 and 16 also fell, though less sharply.[20] Even faith in the reformatory and industrial schools began to ebb. Probation, release on recognizances without probation, and simple discharge were increasingly used by the courts for juveniles under 16 and young adults aged 16 to 21. The courts also steered women away from local and convict prisons, which became proportionately more male. The female proportion of the average population in local prisons fell from 22 per cent in 1870 to slightly over 15 per cent in 1912; and in convict prisons from 14 per cent in 1878 to slightly over 3 per cent in 1912.[21] Finally, resistance developed to imprisoning first offenders, vagrants, inebriates, and mentally or physically disabled offenders.[22] In the early twentieth century, official reports on vagrants, "the feeble-minded," and habitual offenders laid stress upon the failed Victorian strategy of treating individuals as responsible moral agents, and the associated resort to severe and uniform custodial penalties.[23]

of self and society lurking behind official characterizations of crime and punishment. When in the late-Victorian years a new "positivist" criminology sought to influence penal policy and practice, several competing images of criminal man were in circulation. If there was a new image of "psychological man," the image of "moral man" lived on in mandarin circles and among High Court Judges. See chap. 1 *supra*. See also Neil Davie, "Criminal Man Revisited? Continuity and Change in British Criminology, c. 1865–1918," *Journal of Victorian Culture*, vol. 8 (2003), p. 17.

19　Wiener, *Reconstructing the Criminal*, pp. 309–10, 313–15.

20　Ibid., p. 288; G. Behlmer, *Child Abuse and Moral Reform in England, 1870–1908* (1982), Table 7, p. 198. The 1908 Children Act put the seal on this approach, mandating that children under 14 could no longer be sentenced to imprisonment for any offence; and those aged between 14 and 16 could be committed to prison only if considered to be of "so unruly" or "so depraved" a character that they were unfit to be sentenced to reformatory detention. See Radzinowicz and Hood, *English Criminal Law*, op cit., pp. 628–9.

21　Wiener, *Reconstructing the Criminal*, note 5, p. 309. In explanation of this trend, it could be that the increase in summary jurisdiction disproportionately affected women, or that the "medicalization" of crime went further for females. See Lucia Zedner, *Women, Crime and Custody in Victorian England* (Oxford, 1991), *passim*; M. Feeley, "The Decline of Women in the Criminal Process: A Comparative History," in L. Knafla (ed.), *Criminal Justice History*, vol. 15 (1994), p. 269.

22　Wiener, *Reconstructing the Criminal*, pp. 319, 321, 335. The Probation of First Offenders Act, 1887, increased the pressure on magistrates to use recognizances in appropriate cases. In 1904, Sir Howard Vincent, who had inspired the Act, claimed that it "had saved from imprisonment some 70,000 persons in England and Wales:" *Hansard*, vol. 135, 3 Jun. 1904, col. 740.

23　See D. Garland, *Punishment and Welfare* (Aldershot, 1985), p. 61. The judiciary proved reluctant, however, to use the new state inebriate reformatories. See Radzinowicz and Hood, *English Criminal Law*, op cit., pp. 307–15.

Historians have offered a related explanation for the abatement of imprisonment in the growing disenchantment with the prison paradigm.[24] Victorian prison policy—uniformity, long prison sentences, and severe discipline—came under critical scrutiny from a number of quarters from the 1880s. In 1892, when Ruggles-Brise was appointed Commissioner of Prisons, Sir William Harcourt pressed him to "continue the good work of diminishing their (the convict prisons') population." By 1894, *The Times* asserted: "We are not all so sure as we once were of the good effects of a residence in prison . . ."[25] As we saw in chapter one, in the mid-1890s, the press single-handedly created a sense of crisis within the prison system. This press indictment culminated in the appointment of the Gladstone Committee on Prisons and a new Prisons Act. The most sceptical evidence before the Gladstone Committee, presented in February 1895, came from Sir Godfrey Lushington, Permanent Under-Secretary of State at the Home Office, who described the harsh reality of prison and its inherent unsuitability for reform:

> I regard as unfavourable to reformation the status of a prisoner throughout his whole career; the crushing of self-respect; the starving of all moral instinct he may possess; the absence of all opportunity to do or receive a kindness; the continual association with none but criminals . . . the forced labour and the denial of all liberty. I believe the true mode of reforming a man or restoring him to society is exactly in the opposite direction of all these. But, of course, this is a mere idea. It is quite impracticable in a prison. In fact, the unfavourable features I have mentioned are inseparable from a prison life.[26]

The Committee could not accept Lushington's view that "all these unfavourable features are irremovable . . ." "We think," declared the final report,

> that prison discipline and treatment should be more effectually designed to maintain, stimulate or awaken the higher susceptibilities of prisoners, to develop their moral instincts, to train them in orderly and industrial habits, and

---

24 See Wiener, *Reconstructing*, chap. 8 and pp. 341–2. See also G. Mair and L. Burke, *Redemption, Rehabilitation and Risk Management: A History of Probation* (2012), p. 15. Wiener emphasizes the influence of the complaints of overly harsh sentences and penal discipline voiced by Irish MPs in the Commons, "the first antiprison lobby." See ibid., pp. 327–8.

25 Shane Leslie (compiler), *Sir Evelyn Ruggles-Brise: A Memoir of the Founder of Borstal* (1938), p. 78; *The Times*, 17 Dec. 1894, p. 9.

26 I also used this quotation in chap. 1, though for a slightly different purpose. *Report from the Departmental Committee on Prisons, Minutes of Evidence*, PP, 1895, vol. 56 (C.-7702–1), q. 11,482, p. 401; also q. 11,485, p. 401. See Jill Pellew, "Lushington, Sir Godfrey (1832–1907)", *Oxford DNB* (2009). See also McConville, *English Local Prisons 1860–1900* (Abingdon, 1995), pp. 626–32. Lushington retired as Permanent Undersecretary in early 1895.

whenever possible to turn them out of prison better men and women physically and mentally than when they came in.[27]

Gladstone, in short, endorsed the idea of treatment *within* prison. And it declared that prison treatment should have "as its primary and concurrent objects deterrence and reformation." But it was Lushington's sceptical view that had the more lasting influence, especially since he went on to chair a departmental committee to examine reformatory and industrial schools, whose report warned against inserting the treatment ideology into custodial institutions. As for the Prisons Act, 1898, it led to a new set of prison rules for a less punitive prison regime, for greater classification of the prison population, and for reform to be the primary purpose of imprisonment, yet still the response was critical. As *The Times* stated in an editorial on the Act: "Administrators, no less than irresponsible critics, own that every prison is more or less a failure."[28] Moreover, the prison commissioners in their Report for 1898–99, conceded that for every type of criminal, "imprisonment should be the last and not the first resource."[29] It is feasible that this scepticism about the role of the prison persuaded the judiciary further to de-centre the prison, and even institutions for young offenders, in their sentencing practice.[30]

27 *Report of the Departmental Committee on Prisons*, PP, 1895, vol. 56 (C.-7702), para. 25, p. 8.
28 *The Times*, 26 Mar. 1898, p. 11.
29 Quoted in Wiener, *Reconstructing*, p. 371. Others in the prison service agreed. James Devon, medical officer at Glasgow prison, wrote in his 1912 book, *The Criminal and the Community*, ". . . . there are a great many people sent to prison who ought never to have been there at all. . . . in the majority of cases imprisonment not only does no good, but does positive and serious harm."
30 In 1900, 24,000 young people were held in reformatory and industrial schools; by 1913 the numbers had fallen to 19,000 (and by 1922, to 8,000). It has also been suggested that a new penal administrative generation was in place by the 1890s (in the shape of Evelyn Ruggles-Brise and C. E. Troup), one more attracted to the idea of scientific administration, working alongside politicians (such as H. H. Asquith, Herbert Gladstone, and Churchill) who were "more ready to extend administrative discretion to modify the judgment of the bench": Wiener, *Reconstructing the Criminal*, op cit., p. 339; Jill Pellew, *The Home Office 1848–1914* (1982), part II. This can be exaggerated as far as the administrative elite is concerned. Ruggles-Brise remained committed to voluntarist assumptions of personal responsibility, and viewed a prison system instituted only for the moral reformation of prisoners as "the dream of the philanthropist." "The reform of a man is incidental to the prison system, but is not its primary or essential condition. I believe that the prison system, by inculcating habits of obedience, and order, and discipline, and labour, fortifies a man and does not crush him." See TNA, HO45/13658/185668/6, Ruggles-Brise to Troup, 19 Apr. 1910. See also Peter Bartrip, "Troup, Sir Charles Edward (1857–1941)," *Oxford DNB* (2004). Troup, "a rather silent, heavy Scot," in Sir Harold Scott's description, was Permanent Undersecretary of State, 1908–1922: see Scott, *Your Obedient Servant* (1959), p. 28.

IV

Is it possible to get closer to the judicial mind, to discover how the judiciary was thinking about the tariff of punishment? The evidence has to be teased out from the interactions between the judiciary and the executive branch, which is the aim of the next three sections. The argument is that between 1880 and 1914 the judiciary decisively scaled back the tariff of punishment. The focus in these sections is on the Judges of the Queen's and King's Bench Division conducting assize courts in the country, and to a lesser extent on the approximately 5,000 magistrates who were entitled to sit at quarter sessions.

The criminal law was constructed on the principle of high maximum penalties for crimes, and few restraints on the judge's choice of sentence up to the maximum. Judges had extensive discretion in deciding the length of a prison sentence in felony cases, allowing them to mark the offender's culpability by their choice of days, months, or years in custody.[31] Such discretion run wild rendered anything in the nature of standardization or equality of sentences utterly impossible, but it also meant that judicial discretion was, as Ruggles-Brise, chairman of the Prison Commission, wrote in 1901, "practically unlimited in the direction of *lenity*."[32] One of the few restrictions on choice of sentence was the existence of the gap between the maximum term of imprisonment and the minimum term of penal servitude. The Penal Servitude Act 1864 put an end to the sentence of three years' penal servitude, and fixed the minimum term of penal servitude at five years for a first felony conviction, and seven years in the case of an offender with a previous conviction for felony. The result of this gap between imprisonment (two years) and penal servitude (five years, and frequently seven years) was that "once an offender was considered to have graduated beyond imprisonment, he would necessarily receive sentences of very great length if the practice was followed."[33] In practice, however, judges often stopped short of penal servitude and inflicted instead the more lenient sentence of imprisonment. Mr. Justice Lush told the Kimberley Commission: "I have always felt a great difficulty in leaping from two years [imprisonment], or rather 18 months (for it is rarely that the whole two years are given), to five years' penal servitude." He and his colleagues in the Criminal Code Commission were likewise critical of the seven years minimum, after a previous conviction for felony, a view also held by recorders and chairmen of quarter sessions, according to Lush:

Everybody that I have heard of is of opinion that the seven years minimum is too high, that it is very injurious [to the discretion of the judge], and that

---

31 Mr. Pickersgill, MP for Bethnal Green, stated: "there is probably no system in the world. . . a criminal system which has left so wide a discretion as our own to Judges in the apportionment of punishment." *Hansard*, vol. 336, 24 May 1889, col. 1002.

32 My emphasis. See D. A. Thomas, *Constraints on Judgment: The Search for Structured Discretion in Sentencing, 1860–1910* (Cambridge, 1979), p. 26. Ruggle-Brise was reporting on the Proceedings of the 5th and 6th International Penitentiary Congress.

33 Thomas, *Constraints on Judgment*, op cit., pp. 1, 12–13.

many sentences of imprisonment which are felt to be inadequate are passed in order to avoid that which would be an excess.[34]

Hence, the Penal Servitude Act 1879 installed a new general minimum of five years.[35] If a gap still existed between imprisonment (two years) and penal servitude (five years), the judges had at least freed themselves from the seven-year minimum for subsequent convictions.

Moreover, the cumulative principle, which asserted that offences should attract ever-increasing severity in order to deter repeat offenders, was losing its charms for the judiciary.[36] In the later Victorian decades, there were outright attacks on the practice of awarding cumulative sentences, in particular to petty property offenders. In the early 1880s, C. H. Hopwood, Liberal MP for Stockport, campaigned in Parliament to mitigate the severity of sentencing practices, a cause he further advanced as Recorder of Liverpool after his appointment in 1886. He claimed to have dealt with nearly 2,000 prisoners by 1889 without once imposing penal servitude. In 1896, *The Times* declared: "[w]hat Mr. Hopwood . . . does in a striking manner, all Judges do more or less. Penal servitude is awarded for much shorter terms than were once customary, and sentences of imprisonment are for shorter periods."[37] This sentencing approach drew endorsement from no less a quarter than that of Lord Chief Justice Coleridge.

On a motion for an inquiry into the principles followed by judges in sentencing offenders, the House of Lords focused on the cumulative principle. Coleridge confessed to "disregarding repeated convictions if the offences have been what I should call peccadilloes rather than serious crimes." Elaborating on the point, he said,

> that if a Judge punishes with great severity even the twentieth peccadillo, what is he to do in the case of a really grave offence? I have known a woman to be sent to penal servitude for 15 years for stealing a shovel. It may be quite true that she had previously stolen 16 or 17 other shovels, and it may appear to some that that would justify the 15 years' penal servitude; but I do not think so, and nothing will ever persuade me that I ought to punish an offender such as that woman as I ought to punish a person who has inflicted gross and detestable cruelty on man, woman, or child. In cases like this the punishment and the offence are not correlative . . . If you inflict severe sentences for such offences the weapon breaks in your hand.[38]

34 *Report of the Commissioners appointed to inquire into The Working of the Penal Servitude Acts (Kimberley Commission), Minutes of Evidence*, PP, 1878–9, vol. 37 (C.-2368.-1), q. 11573, p. 917; q. 11609, p. 921.
35 Thomas, *Constraints*, p. 25; *Hansard* (Lords), 21 Apr. 1890, col. 950 (The Earl of Kimberley).
36 See Wiener, *Reconstructing the Criminal*, op cit., p. 284.
37 *Hansard*, vol. 336, 24 May 1889, col. 1023; *The Times*, 21 Dec. 1896, p. 9. See also Wiener, *Reconstructing the Criminal*, op cit., pp. 283–4.
38 *Hansard* (Lords), vol. 343, 21 Apr. 1890, cols. 943–4. According to Mr. Pickersgill, at the autumn assizes at York in 1887, Lord Coleridge had before him a woman who had served ten years' penal servitude for stealing a door mat, and was then charged with the theft of a piece of linen. Coleridge sentenced her to three weeks' hard labour,

The opening contribution to this Lords' debate, from former Lord Chancellor, Lord Herschell, also suggested that the method of cumulative sentencing was on the defensive, and that lighter sentencing was in vogue:

> I hold strongly to the view that early sentences to the extent of the third or fourth, or even more—I am not at all fixing a limit at the moment—should be as light as possible, consistently with the gravity of the offence committed . . . I think, too, that the present tendency in some quarters to inflict lighter sentences, and to consider it unwise to inflict sentences of penal servitude for trivial offences, is a reaction in some degree, and I think a wholesome reaction, from the over-severity which has been shown in other quarters in the extent to which long terms of penal servitude have often followed upon even trifling and minor offences.[39]

By "other quarters," Herschell was referring to courts of quarter sessions:

> . . . it is rather at Quarter Sessions than at Assizes that the habit of passing very considerable terms of penal servitude after previous conviction is followed. I believe that this has, to some extent, arisen from the fact . . . that no sentence of less than five years' penal servitude can be passed, and that consequently between a sentence of 18 months' imprisonment and one of five years' penal servitude there is no middle course.[40]

Herschell was relieved to hear, therefore, that the Government proposed to reduce the minimum term of five years penal servitude to three years, which was authorized by the Penal Servitude Act 1891.[41] The remaining statutory gap between the maximum sentence of imprisonment (two years) and the minimum sentence of penal servitude (three years) could be bridged by the availability of early release on licence from a penal servitude sentence. These statements clearly took effect. To judge from the criminal statistics for the 1890s, while offenders convicted of minor larcenies still attracted sentences of penal servitude, the number of long sentences continued to recede.[42]

---

observing: "I do not know what is to become of punishment. If people are to be sent to ten years' penal servitude for stealing a door mat, what is to be done with men for half killing their wives?" See *Hansard*, vol. 336, 24 May 1889, cols. 1009–10.

39   Ibid., cols. 927–8.
40   Ibid., col. 928. However, Forrest Fulton, MP for West Ham North, who had served as counsel to the Treasury at the Central Criminal Court, told the Commons that in appeals to quarter sessions against excessive sentences passed by the metropolitan police magistrates, 10 per cent of cases were reduced from terms of imprisonment to a fine and terms of imprisonment reduced from, say, three months to one month. See *Hansard*, vol. 336, 24 May 1889, col. 1017.
41   Thomas, *Constraints on Judgment*, op cit., p. 24.
42   Ibid., p. 23; Wiener, *Reconstructing the Criminal*, op cit., p. 284.

In brief, judges, though not yet all chairmen of quarter sessions, were lowering the tariff of sentences for property crime. They began to see the long prison sentences given in the immediate aftermath of the end of transportation to Australia as excessive and unjust. Cumulative sentencing, in particular, increasingly appeared cruel and unjust.[43] While views differed among the 15 high court judges, most seem to have believed that to punish a small offence with lengthy imprisonment or penal servitude, by reason of the offender's previous career, was unjustifiable, and that length of sentence ought to be regulated, largely if not solely, by regard to the circumstances of the immediate crime. By 1896, H. B. Simpson, head of the Criminal Department in the Home Office, was resigned to "the growing disinclination to give long sentences of Penal Servitude for 'trifling' offences."[44] In response, the department was already examining a new kind of extended preventive sentence for habitual criminals, of which more in the following section.

V

Was the executive at all influential in guiding the tariff of punishment? The most direct way of executive review of sentences was the royal prerogative of mercy, which was exercised on the advice of the Home Secretary. Pardons under the prerogative were of three kinds: a free pardon, which wiped out the sentence and the conviction; a conditional pardon or commutation, which substituted one form of punishment (say penal servitude) with a milder punishment (say imprisonment); and remission, which reduced the amount of a sentence without changing its character (say six months' imprisonment reduced to four months).[45] For a start, applications to the Home Office on grounds of undue severity or sentence inequality depended on the prisoner and his supporters taking the initiative. The department took a restrictive view of the scope of the prerogative of mercy, rarely intervening, for example, with long sentences imposed under the cumulative principle.[46] And since applications were investigated according to the merits of each individual case, review did little to change wider sentencing practice. The more usual method of mitigating a penal servitude sentence was by releasing the prisoner on licence after serving the term to which the department thought he should have been sentenced.[47] In an 1899 memorandum to the Lord Chief Justice,

43 In an undated, unsigned note on the Prevention of Crime Bill, 1908, though probably written by Home Secretary Gladstone, it was claimed: "Judges abjure the cumulative sentence. [Ruggles-] Brise shows clearly. . . that not only do [Judges] shorten their sentences, but they constantly give short terms to most dangerous recidivists." Viscount Gladstone Papers, Add MSS 46094, fol. 124.

44 Quoted in Wiener, *Reconstructing the Criminal*, op cit., note 16, p. 343.

45 Edward Troup, *The Home Office* (2nd ed. rev., 1926), pp. 55–6. In addition to the review of non-capital sentences, the royal prerogative was used to commute the death penalty passed for murder.

46 Thomas, *Constraints on Judgment*, op cit., p. 29.

47 Ibid., p. 31.

the department revealed that since sentences passed by the courts had shown "an undeniable tendency to leniency," the department "has followed the awards of criminal courts of justice; and has endeavoured . . . to apply to past cases the punishments at present most generally prevailing."[48] Thus in non-capital cases, the power to grant penal servitude licences earlier than usual was used to reduce the effective length of sentences passed in the 1870s and 1880s, to lengths comparable with those being passed in the 1890s. To this end, as D. A. Thomas stated, "systematic review of all long sentences of penal servitude, after the prisoner had served ten, fifteen or twenty years, had been instituted . . . whether or not a petition was submitted by the prisoner or on his behalf."[49]

When all is said and done, however, the number affected by executive review was small. Winston Churchill told the Commons that the prerogative had been used 436 times between 1907 and 1909 by Gladstone, his predecessor as Home Secretary: 160 on medical grounds, 203 in simple mitigation of sentence. Between February 1910 and July 1911, when Churchill was Home Secretary, 395 cases were given remission of imprisonment.[50] Sir Edward Troup provided the figures for 1922, in which year there were 108 remissions of imprisonment, 32 on medical grounds and 35 "in what is described as 'simple mitigation of sentence,' that is, cases where increased weight is given, sometimes at the judge's own suggestion, to such circumstances as youth, provocation or mental disturbance . . ." In the same year, 28 penal servitude sentences were reduced by early grant of licence, nearly all "in simple mitigation of sentence."[51] If, as seems likely, no more than 300 to 400 sentences were mitigated during each Home Secretary's period of office, few of which received any widespread publicity, it is unlikely that executive review did much to influence general sentencing practice. Moreover, in more than a few of these cases, it was the judges themselves who provided the impetus to mitigation.

There were occasions when the executive was more direct in its guidance. In February 1884, Sir Edmund Du Cane, chairman of the Prison Commission, called the Home Office's attention to the judicial tendency to pass sentences of what he called "stock" lengths—five, seven, ten, 15 years of penal servitude (which duplicated the lengths of transportation sentences), to the almost entire exclusion of the years in between.[52] As a result, Home Secretary Harcourt (believing that the

---

48 TNA, HO144/943/A60866/1: "Notes on the Exercise of the Prerogative of Mercy," prepared by K. Digby, 10 Feb. 1899, p. 2.
49 Thomas, *Constraints on Judgment*, op cit., p. 34. In addition, the department acted to equalize sentences in four classes of crime: abortion, bestiality, infanticide, and carnal knowledge of young girls, on account of the similarity of circumstances under which the crime had been committed. See TNA, HO144/943/A60866/1.
50 *Hansard*, 26 Jun. 1911, col. 252; 17 Jul. 1911, col. 669.
51 Troup, *The Home Office*, op. cit., pp. 71–2.
52 TNA, HO45/18479/565861/1, Du Cane to Undersecretary of State, 4 Feb. 1884. See also Du Cane, "The Duration of Penal Sentences," *Fortnightly Review*, vol. 33 (1883), pp. 856–63. Godfrey Lushington, Assistant Undersecretary, minuted: ". . . Judges and Magistrates cannot be too often reminded that a year's penal servitude means a year's

authorities had "successfully tapped the fountains of crime," and that it was time to consider "whether severity may not be relaxed"), wrote to Lord Chancellor Selborne, asking him to share with the judges Du Cane's opinion "that the deterring and reformatory effect of imprisonment . . . would be as well and even more effectually accomplished if the average length of sentences were materially shortened." Harcourt's letter also asked the judges to examine the notion of laying down general rules for the greater uniformity of sentences.[53] A year later Du Cane followed up with another memorandum, this time for Lord Chief Justice Coleridge, hoping that it would prompt "a common agreement in certain principles" in the exercise of sentencing.[54]

In March 1885, the Lord Chief Justice sent the Lord Chancellor a resolution from the Council of Judges of the Supreme Court. The judges recognized the importance of preventing inequality or extreme severity in sentences, and so were willing to meet occasionally to exchange their views about sentencing. Yet they declined to pass any formal resolution "to determine the amount of the sentences . . . which ought to be imposed for any specified offences." Several of them wanted it to be known that "the severity of sentences usually passed some years ago might be diminished without detriment to the administration of the criminal law," but no formal resolution to that effect was moved, and the Lord Chief Justice was not convinced that such a resolution would have carried.[55] It seems that senior judges were averse to laying down any definite rules for guiding sentencing, and were not persuaded by Du Cane to confront systematically the pattern of "stock" lengths of penal servitude. The conclusion must be that Du Cane's letters had little obvious impact on the judges, though the latter were willing to introduce some mitigation of punishment.[56]

Yet ten years later, Lord Chief Justice Alverstone sent the Home Secretary a unique document, drafted by Alverstone and a committee of judges, which

penal servitude, and that a month's imprisonment means a month's imprisonment, and I should certainly recommend that a copy of Sir E. Du Cane's minute should be sent to the Lord Chancellor for him . . . to communicate it to the Judges, and that copies should be circulated to the Chairmen of Quarter Sessions and Recorders." TNA, HO45/9699/A50087/2, 8 Feb. 1884. See also Radzinowicz and Hood, *English Criminal Law*, op cit., p. 748.

53 Ibid., 565861/5, Harcourt to Lord Chancellor, 10 Dec. 1884.
54 Ibid., 565861/7, 16 Mar. 1885 memo.
55 TNA, LCO1/54, Lord Chief Justice to Lord Chancellor, 26 Mar. 1885.
56 The issue of "stock" lengths of penal servitude and imprisonment was raised ten years later by Francis Galton in "Terms of Imprisonment," *Nature*, 20 Jun. 1895, pp. 174–6, in which he argued that the length of prison sentences flowed from "such irrelevant influences as the associations connected with decimal or duodecimal habits and the unconscious favour or disfavour felt for particular numbers." Of course, not all Judges agreed about the mitigation of punishment. Justice Stephen challenged Du Cane's and Harcourt's proposals, as he did all mitigation of punishment. See Thomas, *Constraints on Judgment*, op cit., pp. 61–3; L. Radzinowicz, *Sir James Fitzjames Stephen* (1957), p. 32. In the following years, the Home Office was reluctant to press the issue. Home Secretary Matthews rebuffed parliamentary efforts to obtain a royal commission on sentencing: TNA, HO45/9699/A50087/4, 30 Jul. 1889.

established "a 'normal' standard of punishment" for six general categories of offence, applicable except where the case presented special features of aggravation or extenuation. The *obiter dicta* of the document, and the Home Office response to it, are revealing of executive and judicial thought. Under "Offences Against Property, Without Violence" the preamble stated:

> The inclination of the Court towards leniency of punishment which has marked the last 20 years has, on the whole, been justified by results. But, as the Reports published annually by the Home Office and the Statistics of Crime which they contain seem clearly to indicate, the leniency has gone too far in regard to those who are habitual criminals.[57]

For those who had been previously convicted of such property offences and "who appear to be seeking regularly to make a livelihood out of crime," the judges considered that a sentence of penal servitude should be the rule. They drew a distinction, however, between professional criminals and "occasional criminals." For persons "who from one cause or another have been temporarily disabled from earning wages and yield to the pressure of want; and again, persons who, although leading a generally honest life of work, do at times commit acts of dishonesty . . . as often happens, under the influence of drink," imprisonment was "sufficient punishment."[58]

The department welcomed this attempt to agree on normal standards of punishment. Yet significantly these officials also thought the resulting scale of punishment was insufficiently robust, indeed erred on the side of leniency, and failed to tackle the problem of the habitual offender. Frederik Dryhurst, senior clerk in the Criminal Department, believed that the proposed normal sentences for many of the crimes specified were lighter than customary. Moreover, the reason that had led judges to the view that the standard sentence could be reduced—"the marked and continuous decrease in crime against property without violence"—could not be used in support of lowering the standard of sentences for habitual criminals and for men guilty of violent forms of sexual crime. Dryhurst was particularly critical of the normal sentences for the offences of the habitual or professional criminal:

> It is easy to understand the reaction against the old-fashioned sentence of 12 and 15 years' p[enal] s[ervitude] for the pick-pocket or till-robber, shop-lifter or passers of bad half-crowns. But . . . why should such a man be able to secure his release at the end of his 3 years and 9 months only to prey upon the public until he is again caught? . . . I am afraid that this general lowering of the

---

57 TNA, HO144/943/A60866/3, Alverstone to Home Secretary, 2 Jul. 1901. For the "Memorandum of Normal Punishments in Certain Kinds of Crime," see R. M. Jackson, *Enforcing the Law* (1967), Appendix V, pp. 250–8.

58 Ibid. See F. D. Mackinnon, "Webster, Richard Everard, Viscount Alverstone (1842–1915)," *Oxford DNB* (2004).

standard of sentences will see such men free for a considerably larger portion of their lives to prey upon the community . . .[59]

Charles Murdoch, Assistant Undersecretary, agreed with his colleagues "that the margin of punishment may not be sufficiently wide" and queried whether the judges' scheme provided for sufficiently severe punishment for professional criminals:

> It will be a great gain that such persons should invariably be awarded a sentence of penal servitude from 3 to 5 years . . . but is the proposed punishment . . . especially in cases of burglary, housebreaking, and shop-breaking sufficient?[60]

Nothing of consequence came of the judges' scheme. Senior clerk C. E. Troup minuted: "The Judges have I believe guided themselves to some extent in their sentences by the lines laid down in their printed memo, but it has never reached Recorders or Q[uarter] S[essions]"—the courts, it has to be said, responsible for sentencing the vast majority of offenders whose crimes were the subject of the judges' memorandum.[61] The judges' memorandum and the departmental response suggest that the judiciary were more inclined to sentencing leniency than the executive, and if they were willing to pass sentences of penal servitude on the professional criminal, they were not looking to the kind of prolonged detention that department officials favoured.

What was by now evident was that the judiciary and the executive were at cross purposes when it came to dealing with the habitual offender. For judges like Sir Alfred Wills, the

---

59 Ibid., 31 Jul. 1901.
60 Ibid., 22 Oct. 1901. H. B. Simpson, Assistant Undersecretary and head of the Criminal Department, added that the cases in which sentencing diversity was most striking were those in which "old offenders are convicted of larcenies of a trifling character. It is scarcely an exaggeration to say that it is a mere chance whether an offender gets a few weeks' imprisonment or a term of 5, 7 or even 10 years' P[enal] S[ervitude]." He went on: "A special form of detention suitable for habitual offenders is a reform the desirability of which is shown by the daily experience of H[ome] O[ffice]—the records of men whose career of crime is impeded but scarcely checked by successive convictions." Simpson had in mind a form of detention "in which habitual criminals would be kept for 10 years or more without undue harshness. . . ." The result, said Simpson, would be that "the difficulty that HM Judges feel in securing uniformity in the sentences they pass on habitual offenders, would at all events be lessened," concluding: "The class of criminals in question no doubt appear (sic) much more frequently in Police Courts and at Quarter Sessions than at Assizes, but if the Judges were able to apply a rational treatment . . . the example set by them would speedily affect the practice of other Courts." See Ibid., 8 Aug. 1901.
61 Ibid., undated minute. In the 1906 debate on the Criminal Appeal Bill, Lord Alverstone also indicated that the agreement formed the basis of sentencing practice: "The judges of the High Court now work upon a memorandum to which we are all agreed, and during the last eight or ten years no one can say that High Court sentences have erred on the side of severity." See *Hansard* (Lords), vol. 157, 22 May 1906, col. 1085.

[i]ron severity and rigidity of our convict prisons is one of the things that makes most of us—myself certainly—shrink from the long sentences [of penal servitude] that are really the only things of any use, not to the prisoner, who in these cases is really irreclaimable, but to society . . .[62]

From Ruggles-Brise's vantage point at the Prison Commission, the hostility to long sentences meant that the system of penal servitude was futile for dealing with the habitual criminal. As he remarked,

In the seventies nearly ten thousand men would have been found in our Convict Prisons with sentences of ten years and over five years. In 1891 the minimum of Penal Servitude was reduced to three years and the number of convicts under these long sentences fell to some four or five hundred. This amazing change, though commendable in many ways as a protest against the undue severity of the Penal Law, yet undoubtedly had the effect of lessening the deterrence of Penal Servitude for the more dangerous class of confirmed recidivists.[63]

The only way out of this difficulty, Ruggles-Brise believed, was a separate measure of extended protection against the habitual criminal.

Yet still the judiciary acted to restrain departmental moves to expand the imprisoning process for habitual offenders. In May, 1901, Lord Chief Justice Alverstone forwarded to the Home Secretary a resolution passed by the Judges of the King's Bench Division stating that it was time to assess the desirability of modifying, in the direction of leniency, the discipline imposed in the later stages of the longer sentences of penal servitude, and the desirability of providing better means of dealing with habitual or professional criminals, in order to protect society against them.[64] In reply, Home Secretary Ritchie wrote that the only solution for the habitual thief, "whether pick-pocket, shoplifter, swindler of lodging-house keepers or burglar," was "to shut him up and keep him out of mischief." The problem was, where to incarcerate him?

. . . while the only place in which he can be shut up is the ordinary convict prison, there is, as is well-known, a growing indisposition to send him there, the judge and the public alike feeling that for such a purpose the discipline of the convict prison is too severe . . . [Figures from the judicial statistics] show the falling off in the number and length of sentences of penal servitude passed upon habitual thieves—a falling off doubtless due to the cause I have indicated.[65]

62 Wills to Ruggles-Brise, 26 Nov. 1896, in Leslie, *A Memoir*, p. 100.
63 Leslie, *A Memoir*, pp. 124–5.
64 See also Judge Alfred Wills' letter "Habitual Crime and Its Treatment," in *The Times*, 21 Feb. 1901.
65 TNA, PCom 7/286, Ritchie to Lord Chief Justice, 22 Mar. 1902.

Ruggles-Brise, chairman of the Prison Commission, had already advised that when the habitual criminal had served the sentence of imprisonment or penal servitude which the court considered appropriate to the offence, "there should be power to detain him in prison for a lengthened period, but under the milder conditions which would govern the stage of penal servitude," to which he gave the name "penal colony."[66]

While the Judges were averse to the term "penal colony," reminding them too much of the transportation system, they agreed that the habitual criminal might be placed for a significant proportion of the penal servitude sentence under the restraint of the fifth progressive stage. Accordingly, a Penal Servitude Bill was introduced in Parliament in 1904. The Courts were to be given power, where certain conditions of previous convictions and mode of life were met, to pass a sentence of penal servitude for any term not less than seven years, and to direct that after serving a portion of it under the general rules, the rest should be served in the "habitual offender division." However, the judges were less than enthused by the Bill, which was eventually withdrawn.[67] The entire episode indicated that judges would consign habitual offenders to longer terms of penal servitude only if a large proportion of the sentence was served in a less severe prison regime, and even then reluctantly.

Herbert Gladstone, Home Secretary from December 1905 to February 1910, was finally successful in gaining parliamentary approval for legislation to deal with habitual offenders. It was far from smooth sailing, however. After a year in office, Gladstone wrote to Lord Chancellor Loreburn pressing the case for "a King's pleasure sentence for old and incorrigible criminals," activated for "certain grave offences . . . on the fourth or fifth conviction," and bemoaning the fact that "[s]uccessive Home Secretaries have endeavoured to get the Judges to consent to a Commission to consider the proposal but in vain." For the "hardened criminal," said Gladstone, "[s]egregation for an indeterminate period under treatment less severe than in convict prisons but with compulsory work, is the only remedy." He added that such a punishment would act as a real deterrent, and (in an attempt perhaps to convince the Lord Chancellor and his judicial colleagues of the proposal) "it might be expected to lead to less harsh sentences in the earlier criminal stages of the offender's life. . . . [W]ith the ultimate power of the indeterminate sentence, Judges might be expected to shorten their sentences to give him a chance."[68] Under Gladstone's direction, the "single track" sentence of 1904

---

66 Ibid., Ruggles-Brise to Digby, 21 Nov. 1901.
67 Ibid., "Report of a Committee of Judges of the King's Bench Division Appointed to Inquire and Report upon Certain Matters in Connexion with the Treatment of Criminals, and Especially of Habitual Criminals," 6 Apr. 1903. See also *Hansard*, vol. 135, 3 Jun. 1904, cols. 722–71, Penal Servitude Bill.
68 Viscount Gladstone Papers, Add MSS 46018, ff. 153–4, Gladstone to Loreburn, 9 Oct. 1906. In December 1909, Gladstone informed Lord Chief Justice Alverstone that it had proved impossible to make the detention *indeterminate* "chiefly owing to the opposition of the Irish Members at a late period in the Session . . ." See Ibid., Add MSS 46068, ff. 1–5, 4 Dec. 1909. Ruggles-Brise wrote in his unpublished autobiography: "Personally, I

became the "double track" sentence of the Prevention of Crime Act 1908. The offender received both a sentence for the offence itself, and a sentence of preventive detention for the protection of society. The second part of the sentence was also fixed by the judge, within the range of not less than five years, nor more than ten years, with the executive having the right to release the offender when considered appropriate. We shall see shortly how the judges responded to this new measure.

VI

While the executive wanted greater standardization of sentencing, to remove what they considered to be the large disparity in the way offenders were dealt with—an important component of which was the longer preventive sentence for habitual offenders—they had been less active in pressing for mitigation of punishment or the abatement of imprisonment. Enter Winston Churchill who as Home Secretary in 1910–11 focused executive attention on these matters. Churchill embarked upon an ambitious reform of the English penal system along three main lines: improving prison conditions, keeping people out of prison, and reforming sentencing policy.[69] He concentrated on the last two lines. The first principle of prison reform, Churchill told the House of Commons in July 1910, "should be to prevent as many people as possible getting there at all."[70] Yet of the 200,000 committals to prison in 1909, no fewer than 125,000 or 61 per cent, were under sentences of two weeks or less, more than half of which were imposed upon first offenders. The quest for Churchill was how to avoid this unnecessary familiarization of offenders with prison surroundings. He challenged the department to tell him how "this gigantic number of useless and often pernicious committals can be abolished, or, at least, vastly abated."[71] Churchill hoped for a 33 per cent reduction in annual committals to prison, and a reduction in the annual average prison population of up to 15 per cent. No such radical prison plan had ever been contemplated, and it is not surprising that it was never implemented (though a circular went to every magistrate urging them to take greater advantage of the Probation of Offenders Act.)[72]

was in favour of the Indeterminate Sentence for the comparatively small number of dangerous criminals . . . But it became evident that in this country public sentiment would not accept anything so drastic as an indeterminate sentence." See Leslie, *A Memoir*, p. 126.

69 See "Abatement of Imprisonment," 25 Oct. 1910, British Library State Papers, BP 2/4 (15). See also Victor Bailey, "Churchill as Home Secretary: Prison Reform," *History Today*, vol. 35 (1985), pp. 10–3; Alan Baxendale, *Before the Wars: Churchill as Reformer (1910–1911)* (Oxford, 2011), chaps. 6–8.

70 *Hansard*, vol. 19, 20 Jul. 1910, col. 1344.

71 TNA, HO144/18869/196919, 13 Aug. 1910. See also A. Rutherford, *Prisons and the Process of Justice* (1984), p. 124.

72 With regard to the proposals for imprisonment for debt, grace for payment of fines, young adult offenders, and "suspensory sentences," Churchill minuted: "We must not

Churchill also sought to guide judicial sentencing practice. On taking office, Churchill had received the uncompromising advice of Sir Francis Hopwood, Permanent Undersecretary of State at the Colonial Office: "Keep an eye on the sentences passed by fat headed people and reduce them fearlessly whether they emanate from the Ermine or only the 'great unpaid'."[73] Churchill obliged by reducing sentences when he considered the punishment to be disproportionate to the crime. He did not wait for petitions of mercy; he searched the criminal calendars and visited the prisons for cases of injustice.[74] In October 1910, following his visit to Pentonville prison, he ordered the release of a number of youths serving short sentences for minor offences. He would later explain to the Commons that his visit was intended "to draw public attention in a sharp and effective manner" to the evil of imprisoning boys for trifling offences, and he defended his action on the grounds that the figures of such commitments since his visit showed "a marked decrease."[75]

Finally, Churchill also used his executive authority to reduce the severity, as he saw it, of the two new penalties introduced by the 1908 Prevention of Crime Act: borstal training (a new form of penal institution to which young offenders could be sent for a semi-determinate term of not less than one year nor more than three years' detention), and preventive detention for habitual criminals.[76] In both cases, he was determined to assert the importance of a fair proportionality between crime and punishment. He was particularly concerned that preventive detention would lead to "the ferocious sentences of the last generation." "I do not like the look of the first fruits of the [Prevention of Crime] Act," Churchill minuted on June 6, 1910, "It has greatly increased the severity of the criminal law, and the inequality of sentences." He also warned, "There is a great danger of using smooth words for ugly things. Preventive detention is penal servitude in all its aspects."[77] Churchill's attitude to preventive detention was guided by the distinction between the dangerous professional criminal, for which the Act was supposedly meant, and the

---

count too much upon the Courts. They are so numerous and diverse that only Parliament can secure uniformity. We must, therefore, be prepared to legislate on all these four subjects." See Ibid., 196919, 13 Aug. 1910.

73 Randolph Churchill, *Winston S. Churchill: Companion Volume 2*, part 2 (1969), pp. 1138, Hopwood to Churchill, 17 Feb. 1910. By the Ermine, Hopwood meant the high court judges; by the "great unpaid," the magistracy.

74 Paul Addison, "Churchill and Social Reform," in R. Blake and W. R. Louis (eds.), *Churchill* (New York, 1993), p. 63.

75 *The Times*, 3 Oct. 1910, p. 3; *Hansard,* vol. 21, 21 Feb. 1911, col. 1854. Churchill said he wanted to draw attention to the evil by which 7–8,000 lads of the poorer classes were sent to prison each year for minor offences, often in default of payment of fine.

76 TNA, HO144/18869/196919/2, Churchill memo, 30 Jun. 1910.

77 TNA, HO45/10589/184160/23, Churchill minute, 6 Jun. 1910; *Hansard,* vol. 19, 20 Jul. 1910, col. 1352. In response to Churchill's claim that preventive detention was only penal servitude under another name, Sir Robert Wallace, chairman of the County of London Sessions, stated from the Bench that if this were so, "he will beware of it—he thought it would be something quite different." See Waller to Gladstone, 11 Aug. 1910, Gladstone Papers, British Library, Add MSS 45994, ff. 255–61.

petty persistent offender. In a few of the cases where preventive detention had been imposed more for repetition than for gravity of offences, Churchill acted to remit the penalty. In due course, Churchill instructed police forces not to submit applications to the Director of Public Prosecution for authority to prosecute accused persons as "habituals" unless, in addition to the statutory qualifications, the offender was at least 30 years of age, had already undergone a term of penal servitude, and was charged anew with a substantial and serious offence.[78] Had these conditions been in force from the start, 86 of the 113 "habituals" convicted, or 76 per cent, would have escaped indictment. Churchill's intervention led to a marked drop in the number sentenced to preventive detention. In 1910, 177 men were sentenced to preventive detention; in 1911, the figure fell to 53.[79]

It is impossible to know what impact Churchill's determination to avoid increasing "the general aggregate severity of our penal code" had upon the judiciary. His was certainly the most concerted attempt by the executive to guide sentencing. We can perhaps conclude that his activity in the revision of sentences set an example of sorts to the judiciary, and confirmed them in their pattern of leniency in sentencing. As for Churchill's contribution to penal reform, it is impossible not to be impressed by the innovative force of his vision, but he was in office for too short a period to bring about the drastic reduction in the number of people sentenced to prison to which he aspired. Had he succeeded, he would have given massive executive and legislative backing to the judicial contribution to the abatement of imprisonment since 1880. In default, all that can be said is that his plans for a radical abatement of imprisonment forced the department to confront the problem of the large stage army of vagrants, inebriates, prostitutes, and petty larcenists who clogged the local prisons.[80]

VII

Another way of uncovering judicial thinking is to assess the role played by the appellate court for criminal cases established by the Criminal Appeal Act 1907.

---

78 See "Copy of Circular, dated 21 Jun. 1911, issued by the Secretary of State to Police Authorities," PP, 1911 (Cmd. 5629), vol. 65.

79 However, Churchill's more stringent rules proved no more successful at keeping the petty persistent criminal out of the net of preventive detention.

80 This problem was familiar to those working in the prison service. Dr. Smalley, in his report as Medical Inspector of Prisons in 1909, claimed, "Prisons are largely peopled by the very poor, the very ignorant, the physical and mental weaklings, the unemployable, and the unskilled, to say nothing of the drunkards." Quoted in Hobhouse and Brockway, *English Prisons To-Day*, op cit., p. 7. And Ruggles-Brise told Churchill, "If our prisons can be cleared of this useless, cumbrous, trouble-giving set of persons, whom it is hopeless either to deter or to reclaim under the existing methods of short sentences of imprisonment, I believe that all the objects which the Secretary of State has so much at heart will gradually be developed and advanced." See TNA, HO144/18869/196919/4, 9 Sept. 1910.

How useful were the Court's early deliberations in the formulation of sentencing policy? And is this a further example of judicial activity in the mitigation of punishment? The Act creating the Court gave those convicted of serious crimes by assizes or quarter sessions the right to appeal against either conviction or sentence.[81] The number of cases that came before the Court was not large. Between 1909 and 1914, applications for leave to appeal increased to over 400 a year, though the number heard by the Court averaged only 66, in half of which the sentence was reduced.[82] From the start, the appeal court issued a self-denying ordinance, saying in *Sidlow* it would not interfere with a sentence "unless it was apparent that the judge at the trial had proceeded upon wrong principles, or given undue weight to some of the facts proved in evidence."[83] A sentence was passed upon wrong principles when it was "extremely severe" or when it was "rather excessive." The case of *Sidlow* also ruled: "It was not possible to allow appeals because individual members of the Court might have inflicted a different sentence, more or less severe,"—though the Act empowered the Court to intervene "if they think that a different sentence should have been passed." This ruling provoked Herman Cohen, the first editor of the *Criminal Appeal Reports*, to criticize the Court for its "abdication of jurisdiction." "Surely," he wrote, "if no one of the three appeal Judges would have inflicted the given sentence, it is not only reasonable but imperative that they should reduce it."[84] The Court was also allowed to increase the sentence passed on an accused who appealed, in part to enhance sentencing uniformity, and in part to deter frivolous appeals, but this power was invoked in only 14 cases in the first 19 years.[85]

This approach meant that the Court made little attempt to lay down standard punishments for specific offences (despite Justice Darling's statement in *Woodman*, a case of larceny, that the Court "will tend to some kind of standardization of sentences").[86] The Court did establish a few general rules in the direction of mitigation of punishment. One was that the maximum penalty prescribed by statute should be reserved for the "worst cases" in any class of crime (*Harrison*).[87] If very

---

81 The Court of Criminal Appeal consisted of the Lord Chief Justice and all the puisne judges of the King's Bench Division. Typically, only three judges were present at the hearings. The LCJ always sat if possible.

82 Radzinowicz and Hood, *English Criminal Law*, pp. 767–8. The next three paragraphs have been assisted by idem., "Judicial Discretion and Sentencing Standards: Victorian Attempts to Solve a Perennial Problem," *University of Pennsylvania Law Review*, vol. 127 (1979), pp. 1336–40; Rosemary Pattenden, *English Criminal Appeals 1844–1994* (Oxford, 1996), p. 34–6, 255, 268–9, 295.

83 (1908) 1 Cr. App. R. 29.

84 Cohen, "The Court of Criminal Appeal," *Quarterly Review*, vol. 230 (1918), p. 351. Cohen did also write: "Acting in harmony with the spirit of the hour, they have sensibly lowered the standard of severity; the savage sentence is a thing of the past." Ibid., p. 352. See also Pattenden, *English Criminal Appeals*, op cit., p. 255.

85 P. Howard, "The English Court of Criminal Appeal," *American Bar Association Journal*, vol. 17 (1931), p. 150.

86 Rex v. Woodman, *Justice of the Peace*, 22 May 1909, p. 287.

87 (1909) 2 Cr. App. R. 94.

severe sentences were imposed for small crimes, it left no heavier sentence for graver crimes. A second rule was that penal servitude should not be imposed for a first offence; and a third rule was that the first term of penal servitude should be the minimum of three years. In subsequent years, there were signs the Court was willing to expand its remit. In *Goldstein* and *Borham*, the Court ruled against consecutive sentences of imprisonment with hard labour for a total term of above two years.[88] So, too, the Court looked to prescribe a lower tariff for some serious offences, and set down the principle that penal servitude ought not to be passed on a convicted person who had never been incarcerated (*Haddon*)[89] And the gravity of the offence became a limiting factor, ensuring that recidivists would not always incur prolonged punishment, unless they were sentenced to preventive detention as habitual criminals.

The Court of Appeal's response to preventive detention was not always easy to fathom, but the double-track nature of the sentence led to some confusion. In an early judgment (*Smith*), the Court reduced the preliminary period of penal servitude from five to three years, "for there was a good deal to be said for the contention that the sooner the period of preventive detention commenced the better." Ruggles-Brise was horrified by this decision, since it defeated the very principle for which they had striven, "that the persistent criminal shall be kept in 'Preventive Detention' *in addition* to the sentence of Penal Servitude which his crime merits."[90] Yet in *Taylor & Coney*, the Court again reduced the preliminary period of penal servitude from five to three years. In the case of young men, "where there may be some hope of reform," said Mr. Justice Darling, "the period of preventive detention, which might possibly do them some good should begin soon, and not be postponed for two years beyond the period from which it legally may commence."[91] There was some confusion, too, over the length of a preventive detention sentence. In December 1909, Home Secretary Gladstone complained to the Lord Chief Justice that "since the Act came into operation all the sentences imposed by the Courts have, with few exceptions, been for the minimum term of five years." Preventive detention, Gladstone advised,

> should be long enough to give the public a considerable respite from the attentions of the professional criminal, and also long enough to allow probationary release while a sufficient portion of the sentence remains to give effective sanction to the requirements of the licence.[92]

---

88 (1914) 11 Cr. App. R. 27; (1918) 13 Cr. App. R. 191. Borham was looking at serving a term of 33 months' imprisonment for receiving stolen goods; "this severe result does not receive our approval," said McCardie J.

89 Rex v. Haddon, *Justice of the Peace*, Feb. 1918.

90 TNA, HO45/10589/184160/15, Ruggles-Brise to Waller, 26 Nov. 1909.

91 (1910) 5 Cr. App. R. 168. The more relaxed regime for preventive detainees is described in chap. 5 *infra*.

92 Ibid., 184160/16, Gladstone to Lord Chief Justice, 4 Dec. 1909.

The appeal court never consistently obliged. In *Moran*, where the appellant was convicted of receiving stolen property, the Lord Chief Justice stated that a sentence of ten years' preventive detention, the maximum allowed by the Act, was "not desirable except for very grave offences." Finally, in *Jones*, the Court ruled that sentencers did not have the power to increase the sentence for the offence in order to allow them to pass a sentence of preventive detention: "the sentence for the offence charged should be the same as if no sentence of preventive detention was to follow."[93]

The Court of Criminal Appeal could only ever exercise a modicum of supervision. It tended to see the unusual or excessive cases; it was principally concerned to curb any serious departure by the sentencing judges. It never sought to provide systematic guidance to the sentencer faced with a *typical* case. Once the Court got into its stride, it varied sentence in roughly 40 cases a year, too few to provide guidance to the assize judges, let alone the courts of quarter sessions. The most that can be claimed, then, is that the appellate court set new lower benchmarks for certain punishments, promoted the view that the maximum penalty should be reserved for the worst examples of a crime, and set some retributive limits to the sentence of preventive detention. As such, the Court at least restrained any attempt to increase the severity of the tariff of punishment.

As a preliminary conclusion, we can say that between 1880 and 1914, the marked reduction in the prison population was largely the consequence of the judiciary having much less resort to the long sentences of penal servitude and imprisonment that had characterized the first two decades after the end of transportation. High court judges, in particular, gradually improvised a more lenient tariff of punishment for indictable crimes, persuaded perhaps by the fall in the crime rate and by a growing disillusionment with the prison. While judges remained averse to establishing sentencing benchmarks for each category of crime (and the Court of Criminal Appeal did little before 1914 to guide sentencing standards), they held fast to proportionality in punishment, and were rarely distracted by the "positivist" sirens, who sought to lure them on to the reefs of greater indeterminacy. While ministers and mandarins enacted ways of elongating sentences for the habitual offender, judges showed a marked reluctance to employ cumulative sentencing, let alone sentences of long terms of preventive detention.

By 1914, if the tariff of punishment was considerably more lenient with regard to the most serious crimes, the lower courts were still sending too many offenders to prison on short sentences for petty crimes. Yet radical change was imminent. The War years would do what Churchill had wanted, which was to "break in upon this volume of petty sentences for trifling offences from several different directions with a view to effecting a substantial and permanent reduction in them."[94]

---

93 Rex v. Jones, *Justice of the Peace*, 3 Dec. 1910, p. 580.
94 R. Churchill, *Winston Churchill: Companion Volume*, vol. 2, part 2, op cit., p. 1199, Churchill to Asquith, 26 Sept. 1910.

3

WAR, INTER-WAR, AND THE DECREASING PRISON POPULATION, 1914–1939

In the Criminal Courts the change in the course of a single generation is remarkable. In the last twenty years crime, in the sense of serious crime, has not decreased, but punishments have decreased in a remarkable degree. Many offences, for which twenty years ago severe sentences of penal servitude or imprisonment would have been imposed, lead nowadays to sentences of only a few weeks or months, and often no sentence at all is imposed, the case being dealt with under the Probation Act.

Alexander Maxwell, "The Punishment of Crime and the Crime of Punishment," a talk, mid-1930s.

I

Prior to the war, despite the fall in prison population, penal institutions were still clogged with large numbers of short-sentence prisoners. Three-quarters of these prisoners were either sentenced for a petty, non-indictable offence, or imprisoned as fine defaulters. This was well known at the time. Edmund Du Cane, former chairman of the Prison Commissioners, in an article on the Report of the Gladstone Committee on Prisons, recorded that of 118,976 sentences of imprisonment passed on males in the year 1893–94, 44,354 were for a week or under, and 55,527 from that to a month. In all, 100,000, or five-sixths of the whole, were sentenced to a month or under, leaving only 3,131 between six months and three, and 2,169 over six months.[1] Sir Edward Troup, Permanent Under-secretary of State, informed Home Secretary Churchill in September 1910 that sentences of 14 days and less formed 61 per cent of the total number received into prison (though

---

[1] E. F. Du Cane, "The Prison Committee Report," *Nineteenth Century*, vol. 38 (1895), p. 288. It was the large number of short prison sentences that made Du Cane so sceptical of the Gladstone Committee's recommendation that the prison system should emulate the treatment practiced by the existing reformatories, which to be effective required *long* prison sentences. See also idem., "The Prisons Bill and Progress in Criminal Treatment," *Nineteenth Century*, vol. 43 (1898), p. 814.

only 15 per cent of the daily average prison population). A high proportion were in prison for minor offences. In 1912–13, one-quarter of the males aged 16 to 21 who were imprisoned in London were serving seven-day sentences for such offences as obscene language, sleeping rough, drunkenness, and riding a bicycle without lights. However, between 1914 and 1919, the number of prison receptions and the daily average prison population went into freefall. The First World War proved to be a crucial watershed in England's penal profile. The forces in play this time were not judicial thought and practice, but the social and economic changes produced by the rigours of total war.

The decrease in prisoners received under sentence was dramatic, as Sir Evelyn Ruggles-Brise revealed (see Table 3.1). Likewise, the daily average local prison population fell 52 per cent in the case of males and 40 per cent in the case of females during the war years. Convict prisons also experienced this level of reduction in daily average population, at least with regard to male convicts (see Table 3.2).

How do we explain these remarkable figures? One factor was the continued fall in the incidence of adult crime.[2] The number of indictable offences reported to the police fell considerably in the first two years of the war, and while the figure increased in the final war years, it remained below that of 1913. The figures of the less serious, *non-indictable* offences were much more striking. The war years saw an enormous reduction in the volume of minor offences. Taking the figures of persons dealt with by the courts for minor offences typically resulting in imprisonment, the annual averages for 1910–14 and 1925–29 are strikingly different (see Table 3.3).[3]

2   This was not true of juvenile crime. The war years witnessed a significant increase in juvenile offending, at least among boys in large towns, where rates of larceny, malicious damage, and gambling rose by 40 per cent, reaching a peak in 1916. See "Juvenile Crime and the War," *Justice of the Peace*, 17 Jun. 1916, p. 261; Cecil Chapman, "War and Criminality," *Sociological Review*, vol. 9 (1916–17), p. 79. See also David Smith, "Juvenile Delinquency in Britain in the First World War," *Criminal Justice History*, vol. 11 (1990), pp. 119–37; R. L. Gard, *The End of the Rod: A History of the Abolition of Corporal Punishment in the Courts of England and Wales* (Boca Raton, 2009), pp. 59–61, 80–4.

3   See also H. Mannheim, *War and Crime* (1941), pp. 92–6. The fact that 10 per cent of the police force joined the colours on the outbreak of war, and were not replaced, presumably reduced the number of criminals who were apprehended. See Mannheim, p. 97. Another possible cause of the decline in crime is the changed intensity of policing of many non-indictable, or less serious, offences. Howard Taylor has argued that well before the War, under pressure from the Home Office, a major change in policy led to many fewer prosecutions of drunks and vagrants. Taylor takes his argument deep into the post-Great War era, claiming that the police deliberately switched their resources to prosecuting motoring offences rather than minor public order offences such as drunkenness. It is impossible to know for sure if more than 100 separate police forces were capable of such conscious manipulation of the crime figures, especially since the figures for drunkenness convictions rose again in the 1930s, so the police hardly stopped dealing with this public order offence. But it is at least possible that police strategy had some influence upon the declining prosecution of drunks and vagrants in the war years, over and above the fact that police strength was down. See Taylor, "Forging the Job: A Crisis of 'Modernization' or Redundancy for the Police in England and Wales, 1900–39," *British Journal of Criminology*, vol. 39 (1999), pp. 113–33. For a rebuttal, see R. M. Morris,

TABLE 3.1 Committals to prison on conviction, 1913–14 and 1918-19

Year	On indictment	Indictable offences tried summarily	Non-indictable offences	Proportion per 100,000 of the population
1913–14	7,738	15,598	113,088	360
1918–19	3,486	8,568	13,996	70
Decrease since 1913–14	55%	45%	88%	

Source: Table adapted from E. Ruggles-Brise, *The English Prison System* (Macmillan, 1921), p. 224.

TABLE 3.2 Daily average population of local prisons, convict prisons, and borstal institutions, 1913–14 and 1918–19

	Local prisons		Convict prisons		Borstal institutions	
	Male	Female	Male	Female	Male	Female
1913–14	12,116	2,236	2,609	95	841	87
1918–19	5,751	1,322	1,146	83	566	194

Source: Table adapted from E. Ruggles-Brise, *The English Prison System* (Macmillan, 1921), p. 223.

TABLE 3.3 Persons dealt with by the courts for minor offences, annual averages for 1910–14 and 1925–29

Offence	Annual Averages	
	1910–14	1925–29
Drunkenness	193,354	68,491
Assaults	43,032	29,000
Prostitution	10,682	3,278
Begging	25,419	4,803
Sleeping-out	8,594	2,163

Source: L. Fox, *The Modern English Prison* (Routledge, 1934), p. 209.

TABLE 3.4 Convictions for drunkenness in 1913 and 1918

Year	Males	Females	Total
1913	153,112	35,765	188,877
1918	21,853	7,222	29,075
Decrease since 1913	86%	79%	85%

Source: Table adapted from E. Ruggles-Brise, *The English Prison System* (Macmillan, 1921), p. 226.

Particularly impressive was the decline in offences of drunkenness (see Table 3.4).[4] The most decisive fall in drunkenness followed the establishment in June 1915 of the Central Control Board (Liquor Traffic), which was given powers of control over the sale and consumption of alcohol in any area scheduled by order in council. During 1916, the number of commitments for drunkenness fell from 41,329 to 21,399, or by 48 per cent. By 1918, almost the entire country lived in areas under Board control. The main restrictions were the limitation of hours for the sale of liquor (later opening in the morning, earlier closing in the evening, and a compulsory break in the afternoon); increased tax on alcoholic drinks, raising the price of beer and spirits (though higher wartime wages could have offset the impact of price rises); and decreased potency or weaker beer. To these influences was added a reduction in the quantity of drink available. The *per capita* consumption of alcohol fell, along with convictions for drunkenness and convictions for assault (assault and drunkenness tending to move together). Wartime regulations did nothing less than recast the drinking habits of the English people. Traditionally, higher wages and drunkenness convictions had gone arm in arm; during the war they parted company.[5]

The second cause of the fall in prison population was the enlistment of habitual petty offenders. For the year ending 31 March 1914, the percentage of male prisoners aged over 40 received on conviction formed 40 per cent of the total population; for the year ending 31 March 1916, this percentage had risen to 49. By contrast, during these years, the actual number of prisoners received of military age fell from 61,739 to 19,169. According to the commissioners, one of the most notable effects of the war on the prison population was that receptions were for the most part confined to the physically and mentally weak. The "country's call for men appealed as strongly to the criminal classes as to other classes . . ."[6] In addition, many young offenders were released from the borstal institutions to join the army.

The decline in convictions and prison receptions was also linked to the reduction of primary poverty as a result of the war economy.[7] Between 1914 and 1920, there was a significant increase in money and real wages, particularly for unskilled workers. The upshot was a reduction in the size of the underclass or "residuum,"

"'Lies, Damned Lies and Criminal Statistics': Reinterpreting the Criminal Statistics in England and Wales," *Crime, History & Societies*, vol. 5 (2001), pp. 111–27.

4   See also Henry Carter, *The Control of the Drink Trade: A Contribution to National Efficiency 1915–1917* (1918), pp. 233–9; H. Mannheim, *Social Aspects of Crime in England Between the Wars* (1940), pp. 164–7.

5   See Arthur Shadwell, *Drink in 1914–1922: A Lesson in Control* (1923), passim; *The Times*, 13 Aug. 1915, p. 7 (letter from Adeline Bedford, President of the Association of Lady Visitors to Prisons). See also A. E. Dingle, "Drink and Working-Class Living Standards in Britain, 1870–1914," *Economic History Review*, vol. 25 (1972), Figure 1, p. 609; M. E. Rose, "The Success of Social Reform? The Central Control Board (Liquor Traffic) 1915–21," in M. R. D. Foot (ed.), *War and Society* (1973), pp. 71–84.

6   Ann. Rep. of PC for year ended 31 Mar. 1916 (Cd. 8342), p. 6. See also Mannheim, *War and Crime*, op cit., pp. 99–100; Y. Jewkes and H. Johnston, "The English Prison During the First and Second World Wars," *Prison Service Journal*, issue 198 (2011), p. 48.

7   There was practically no unemployment during the war: F. W. Hirst, *The Consequences of the War to Great Britain* (1934), p. 281.

the 10 per cent of the population which before the war suffered from chronic malnutrition, chronic disease, and early death. For evidence, we can turn to Robert Roberts' memoir of slum life in Salford, particularly the chapter entitled "The Great Release" (from primary poverty). By late 1916, claimed Roberts, "abject poverty began to disappear from the neighbourhood," and before the end of the war "[n]early all the 'unemployables' had got jobs of some sort, taking over mostly part-time and casual tasks, whilst the former 'casuals' found regular work." There were fewer prosecutions for child neglect; petty crime fell, "including a great decline in the number of women imprisoned for prostitution," and greatly diminished numbers went to prison for begging and sleeping out.[8] By 1920, *The Times* was announcing that the tramp had been changed for the better by the war.[9] Jay Winter documented this change more thoroughly still, reaching the same conclusion: "By 1918, much of the residuum which had so exercised pre-war politicians, social administrators, and writers [including criminologists who clung to the notion of an hereditary, degenerate residuum of unemployables] had simply ceased to exist."[10] Control of the liquor trade and rent control (liberating more family income for food), the payment of separation allowances and the extension of health insurance to wives of men on active service; and wages that rose to keep pace with wartime inflation (with the greatest gains registered by the most poorly paid before the war) all contributed to the decline in these years of convictions and prison committals.

There were also changes in the way the courts dealt with the smaller number of cases that came before them. A very high percentage of convicted offenders had been sent to prison in default of paying a fine before the war. In 1910, close to 20 per cent of all persons sentenced to a fine were eventually imprisoned for non-payment; in 1913 the figure was 15 per cent. According to Ruggles-Brise, "about half of the population of Local Prisons, guilty perhaps of trivial offences and ordered to pay a small fine of a few shillings, were taken off directly to jail (without the opportunity of gradually redeeming their debt) . . ."[11] During the war years the position greatly improved. The annual average of such imprisonments for the five years 1910–14 was 75,434; the average for the next five years fell to 15,316.[12] In cases of all descriptions dealt with by fine at summary courts, the percentage of cases which came to prison by the end of 1916 had fallen to less than 5 per cent. The main reason for this remarkable decline in imprisonment was the provision of the Criminal Justice Administration Act 1914, which required courts

8   Roberts, *The Classic Slum* (Manchester, 1971), chap. 9 and pp. 176–7.
9   *The Times*, 12 Jan. 1920, p. 9.
10 Winter, *The Great War and the British People* (1986), pp. 21, 213–5, 232–45. Some parts of Winter's optimism have been challenged by L. Bryder, "The First World War: Healthy or Hungry?", *History Workshop*, no. 24 (1987), pp. 142, 150–5. But see R. McKibbin, *Classes and Cultures: England 1918–1951* (Oxford, 1998), p. 114.
11 Shane Leslie (compiler), *Sir Evelyn Ruggles-Brise: A Memoir of the Founder of Borstal* (1938), p. 118, quoting from Ruggles-Brise's unpublished autobiography.
12 Ann. Rep. of PC for 1959, PP, 1959–60, vol. 20 (Cd. 1117), p. 354, Receptions in default of payment of fines.

of summary jurisdiction to allow time for the payment of fines. Hobhouse and Brockway put some hard figures on this claim. The total number of committals to prison fell from 139,000 in 1913 to 20,000 in 1918. According to the two authors, "at least 50,000 of this must be put down to the Criminal Justice (Administration) Act . . . about 25,000 or so are to be attributed probably to the effect of employment and high wages, which enabled more fines to be paid."[13] In all, the drop in the number of fine defaulters entering prison was extremely sharp: no less than an 80 per cent decrease between 1908 and 1923.[14] To these figures, one can add the smaller figures of imprisonment for non-payment of amounts due in respect of affiliation orders, wife maintenance orders, and rates. Full employment at high wages again doubtless helped.

The Criminal Justice (Administration) Act 1914 was only one example, though the most important, of legislative influence on the abatement of imprisonment. Other changes in the criminal law also helped to keep people out of prisons during the war and immediate post-war years. The Children Act 1908 raised the minimum age for committal to prison to 16 (extended to 17 by the Children and Young Persons Act 1933). In 1907–08, three children under 12 and 566 between the ages of 12 and 16 were received into prison on conviction. By the mid-thirties the number of children imprisoned was miniscule. Under the Probation of Offenders Act 1907, an increasing number of persons were placed on probation. In 1910, the number under probation supervision was 10,217; in 1933 the number was 18,937, many of whom were juveniles. The Prevention of Crime Act 1908 reduced the number of young adults (aged 16 to 21) committed to prison, by creating the borstal system. By the end of the inter-war period, something like one-sixth of the prison population was being dealt with in borstal institutions. Finally, the Mental Deficiency Act 1913 (with the amending act of 1927) went some way to clearing the prisons of those mentally unfit for penal discipline. Dr. H. Freize Stephens, of the National Council of Mental Hygiene, told the Persistent Offenders Committee in 1932 that, since 1914, a large proportion of "weak-minded offenders" had been dealt with under the Mental Deficiency Acts. "It is computed that since they came into operation in 1914 the daily average prison population has been reduced by at least 200."[15]

The War was a major watershed in the use of the prison. Between 1914 and 1918, as a result of the social and economic changes that War enforced, assisted by legislation to encourage courts to give time to pay fines, the prisons were relieved of the large stage army of drunks, vagrants and prostitutes. It all confirms what the prison commissioners and others believed, that the solution of the penal problem was to be found, at least in part, in social and welfare reform. In 1911, Maurice Waller, named by Gladstone as a prison commissioner, wrote as follows:

13 Hobhouse and Brockway, *English Prisons To-Day*, op cit., p. 23. Ruggles-Brise claimed that the Act led to "a practical reduction of the prison population by some 50 per cent." See Leslie, *A Memoir*, op cit., p. 119.
14 Rutherford, *Prisons and the Process of Justice*, op cit., p. 126.
15 Persistent Offenders Committee, Summaries of Evidence, vol. 3, POC 59.

This prison business . . . is an integral part of the whole problem of the ineffective and anti-social and submerged . . . The whole business of dealing with social inefficiency has to be reformed—and prison reforms, limited in operation to the inside of prisons, cannot in so many cases be more than tinkering.[16]

The question now became: would all these wartime developments survive the end of total war?

II

The statistics indicate that the changes in the tariff of punishment and the associated abatement of penal servitude and imprisonment continued between 1918 and 1939.[17] The annual numbers of sentences of penal servitude, which before the War ranged between 850 and 1,000 for men, and between 40 and 50 for women, were halved in the 1920s.[18] Of all indictable offences dealt with by the courts, 49 per cent received imprisonment in 1908, 25 per cent in 1923, and only 19 per cent in 1938. The comparable figures for non-indictable, or less serious, offences were 13 per cent in 1908, 3 per cent in 1923, and 1 per cent in 1938. As Fox told a group of Recorders, in 1938, taking adult convicted offenders of all kinds (indictable and non-indictable), only 3 per cent were sent to prison.[19] In addition, the number of very long sentences fell. By 1934, of every 100 men received into prison only 16 were sentenced for periods exceeding three months; of every 100 females, only

16 Ann. Rep. of PC for year ended 31 Mar. 1919 (Cmd. 374), p. 6; Viscount Gladstone Papers, Add. MSS 45994, ff. 272–3, Waller to Gladstone, 10 Mar. 1911. Ruggles-Brise told Troup, 18 April 1910: "I am afraid that we must make up our minds that there is this irreducible minimum as a sort of hopeless residuum in all civilized communities. It is also my belief that this residuum will become smaller with each advancing generation, and to this most desirable end I submit that the Prison System of to-day is contributing its share . . ." TNA, HO45/13658/185668/6. And Churchill told Blackwell in January 1911 that "the treatment of vagrants and inebriates and, to a certain extent, the general treatment of petty offenders, may . . . prove incapable of a final or satisfactory solution except in conjunction with the final reform of the poor law." Quoted in Baxendale, *Before the Wars*, op cit., p. 146.

17 Again, I have pulled upon the statistical sources itemized in footnote 6 of chap. 2 *supra*. Howard Taylor has argued that despite the increasing rhetoric in these decades concerning the individualization of punishment, "the rationale of selecting and punishing a small sample of offenders to make an example to others clearly remained the dominant policy. Courts obviously allotted sentences by quota." He suggests, for example, that the tariff for 1936 "allowed assize courts to send two in three (66.5 per cent) of those convicted to prison, quarter sessions to send one in two (49.8 per cent), summary courts one in four (23.8 per cent) . . ." See Taylor, "Rationing Crime: The Political Economy of Criminal Statistics since the 1850s," *Economic History Review*, vol. 51 (1998), p. 588. It is an intriguing argument, but it fails to account for the considerable differences in the percentage of offenders sent to prison from each court, and implies that the tariff was something more than the loosely-defined, judicial norm we know it to be. There were marked variations by region and city in the practice of the courts.

18 Ann. Rep. of PC for 1927, PP, 1928–29, vol. 9 (Cd. 3292), p. 333.

19 TNA, LCO2/3352, Fox to Recorders, Dec. 1943.

nine were so sentenced.[20] By 1933, the American criminologist, Edwin Suther-land, was highlighting the fact that prisons were being closed in England, because there were too few prisoners to fill them. In 1913 there were 56 local prisons; in 1929, only 31, and two more prisons closed shortly afterwards.[21]

Clearly, the courts were using custody less and less in the first 40 years of the century. Instead, they relied upon non-custodial dispositions, notably fines, probation, and nominal penalties (absolute and conditional discharges, recogni-zances, and bind-overs). Even in the higher courts, which dealt with the most serious crimes, non-custodial measures rose from 12.9 per cent in 1907 to 21.6 per cent in 1920 to 33.1 per cent in 1937; the figures for magistrates' courts moved in the same direction, from 50 per cent in 1907 to 67 per cent in 1920 to 76 per cent in 1937. The fine deserves particular emphasis. A growing aversion to the imposition of short prison sentences, and the initial lack of an efficient probation system, led to greater use of the fine after the Great War.[22] Even for indictable offences, the proportion of persons fined amounted in 1932 to more than 1 in 5 of all persons found guilty of such offences. And the Criminal Justice (Administration) Act 1914 ensured that the majority of offen-ders paid up. Whereas in 1913, 75,000 were imprisoned in default of the pay-ment of fines, for both indictable and non-indictable offences; in 1932 the figure had fallen to 11,244. In short, the tariff of punishment changed markedly from the end of war to the end of the 1930s. The prison became even more decentred in the sentencing practice of the courts.

Once again, we seek to assess how and why the recalibration of the tariff of punishment continued apace. The argument is that while judicial activism remained important, the executive assumed a larger role than previously. First, beyond judicial and executive influence, there were important social improve-ments that led to fewer offenders coming before the courts at all. The inter-war years saw the arrival of forms of social assistance beyond the poor law, such as health insurance, war pensions, widows' and orphans' pensions, and mater-nity and child welfare services, which resulted in improved social conditions,

20 Another measure makes the same point. In 1937, the 800 male prisoners serving over three years' penal servitude or preventive detention accounted for only 9 per cent of the daily average population of 9,000 male prisoners.

21 Ann. Rep. of PC for 1929, PP. 1930–1 (3868), vol. 16, p. 921; Sutherland, "The Decreasing Prison Population of England," *Journal of Criminal Law and Criminology*, vol. 24 (1933), p. 880. For a one-off reduction to the prison population, the Report of the Geddes Committee noted that the Irish amnesty had led to 600 Sinn Fein prisoners being released from English prisons (leading to a reduction of 50 prison officers): *The Times*, 11 Feb. 1922, p. 4. The prison commissioners responded to the Geddes Com-mittee recommendations with the idea of a circular to all courts, stating that a number of commitments to prison still took place that might be met by inflicting a fine or using probation: TNA, Treasury papers, T161/170/515765.

22 H. B. Simpson showed just how more common fining was than imprisonment by citing the following figures: of 532,454 persons convicted in 1920, 495,585 were fined, only 29,565 were sentenced to imprisonment. "Crime and Punishment," *Edinburgh Review*, No. 482 (1922), p. 284.

helping some offenders to avoid imprisonment.[23] Mary Size, lady super-intendent of Liverpool prison in the mid-1920s, considered the old age pension a factor in the drop in the number of women habitual offenders:

> Fewer women were committed to prison for begging, wandering abroad without visible means of subsistence, hawking without a licence etc. . . . The pittance of 10/– [ten shillings] a week gave them a feeling of independence which they had not known before, and encouraged a self-respect that they would not forfeit by going to prison.[24]

The 1932 Report of the Royal Commission on Licensing also found "excessive drinking . . . greatly, even spectacularly, diminished," due to educational, recreational, and dietary improvements.[25]

For this and other reasons, the crime rate held reasonably steady in the inter-war period. The yearly figure for indictable crimes recorded as known to the police was 100,000 between 1900 and 1925. The figure moved upwards to 150,000 in 1930 and to 300,000 in 1939. Stated as notifiable offences recorded by the police per 100,000 population (aged 10 years and over), recorded crime in 1920 was only 5 per cent above the 1900 level, and barely increased up to 1927.[26] Not even the high unemployment rate of the inter-war years had any sizeable impact on the crime rate. The most consistent finding was that the increase in crime was largely limited to boys under 16, many of whom were not directly affected by unemployment.[27] As a result, no pressure ever built up on the courts to adopt a more punitive approach to crime. The courts certainly never allowed the condition of being out of work to affect their sentencing practice. The figures of drunkenness and vagrancy, cases in which imprisonment often resulted from failure to pay a fine, did not show any rise corresponding with the rise in unemployment. Between 1927 and 1931,

---

23 Sir Allan Powell and E. C. Blight, "Poor Law Relief" in *The New Survey of London Life and Labour*, director: Sir Hubert Llewellyn Smith, vol. 1 (London, 1934), 1st pub. 1930, p. 378.

24 Size, *Prisons I Have Known* (1957), p. 65.

25 Quoted in *Habitual Drunken Offenders*, Report of the Working Party (1971), Appendix D, p. 202.

26 The period between 1920 and 1939 was one of falling birth rates, the era of the one-child or no-child family; thus, the proportion of young people in the most crime-prone age groups was lower than at any period in the twentieth century. The crime increase of the 1930s prompted the Home Office to explore if it bore any relationship to the decrease in the number and duration of prison sentences. Publicly, the department insisted that no statistical connection existed between a more lenient sentencing and penal policy and the increase in the general volume of crime, and no group challenged this conclusion. See Fox, *The Modern English Prison* (1934), p. 213; G. Rusche and O. Kirchheimer, *Punishment and Social Structure* (1st pub. 1939; New York, 1968), p. 197.

27 Fox, ibid., p. 212. See also H. Mannheim, *Social Aspects of Crime in England Between the Wars* (1940), p. 134; TNA, HO45/17928/429843, 1922–39: "Unemployment and Criminality"; PCom 9/95.

the number of persons dealt with for drunkenness, assault, and begging and sleeping out went down, as did the number of persons sentenced to imprisonment for these offences. Accordingly, variations in the daily average population of the prisons did not correspond to the variations in unemployment. Between 1921 and 1930, unemployment rose from just over one million to two and three-quarter millions, yet the daily average prison population was 11,000 in 1921 and 11,676 in 1931.

Again, a factor in the mitigation of punishment was the extension of summary jurisdiction, which was further extended by the Criminal Justice Act 1925. By 1928, taking indictable offences as a whole, 54,231 persons had their cases finally disposed of by courts of summary jurisdiction, and only 7,155 were tried on indictment at quarter sessions (4,262) and assizes (2,893). Some of the judges, notably Mr. Justice Roche in his charge to the Grand Jury at the opening of the Worcestershire assizes, protested that too many serious offences were being dealt with by justices summarily, resulting in sentences which were too light for the offences concerned.[28]

Another factor persisted from the late Victorian era. Scepticism about the prison system was sustained by a number of authors, some of whom had personal experience of being imprisoned either for suffragette activities before 1914 or for wartime conscientious objection. The concluding paragraph of Hobhouse and Brockway's study of English prisons looked forward to giving offenders the opportunity to become good and useful citizens, eliminating "the long procession of men and women passing continuously in and out of prison gates, hardened and deteriorated by the rigours and deprivations of the regime . . ."[29] The epilogue to the Webbs' *English Prisons Under Local Government* (1922) declared that "the most practical and the most hopeful of 'prison reforms' is to keep people out of prison altogether!" And "we can keep people out of prison by the simple expedient of not sending them there."[30] To these influential voices was added the advocacy of the Howard League for Penal Reform (created in 1921 by merging the Howard Association and the Penal Reform League) and the Magistrates Association (formed in 1921), alongside the independent commentary on sentencing and penal matters by the weekly journal, *Justice of the Peace*. These bodies were particularly vocal concerning the futility of short prison sentences and the need for alternatives to imprisonment.

---

28 TNA, HO45/21673/433166/35; *The Times*, 28 Jan. 1927, p. 11.
29 Hobhouse and Brockway, *English Prisons To-Day*, op cit., p. 595.
30 S. and B. Webb, *English Prisons under Local Government* (1st pub. 1922; 1963 reprint), p. 248.

III

When the Webbs ascribed the fall in the number of persons committed to prison to the advances in law and practice of the past 20 years, including giving time for payment of fines and greater use of probation, they described these advances as "changes in the temper of the judicial authorities." They proceeded to encourage all courts to adopt "the new attitude of mind:" "It is suggested that if none of the judges and magistrates sent any higher percentage of recruits to join the sad army of the prison population than the present average for all the Courts, the aggregate total of commitments might possibly be reduced by as much as a quarter."[31] This passage prompts further consideration of the judiciary in the abatement of imprisonment in the inter-war years.

When justices spoke about their sentencing practice, their approach inclined to the lenient. Judge Atherley-Jones wrote a letter to *The Times* in 1920 in response to a charge of leniency by those presiding at the London Sessions, declaring, "I would rather be open to the reproach of undue leniency than its converse."[32] In the same year, Sir Robert Wallace, chairman of the London quarter sessions, stated that they had found that out of every 100 prisoners on probation, 96 never returned to a life of crime. Wallace also declared that the practice of sending young girls to prison for their first offence was "manufacturing criminals," and that at the other end of the age spectrum, it was a standing disgrace to criminal jurisprudence that a female offender who came before him had spent 44 years of her 81 years in prison.[33] Mr. Justice McCardie at the Glamorganshire assizes, having solicited the testimony of a police inspector about the future of persons bound over under the First Offenders Act, remarked that "in many cases first offenders have been saved from a future criminal life by the exercise of a wise mercy on the part of the Judge," adding that the inspector's words were important to every judge and magistrate.[34] In a letter to *The Times* in April 1924 on "Just Sentences," the Recorder of Tewkesbury encouraged the Home Office to issue a circular informing magistrates of the grounds (such as youth or period of time since last conviction) on which leniency may be entertained.[35] And, finally, Lord Hewart, Lord Chief Justice, addressing the International Prison Congress in London, October 1925, on alternatives to imprisonment, stated that

> there are few more effectual ways of manufacturing criminals than to send young offenders unnecessarily to prison . . . where, after serving some short sentence of complete futility, they may abandon for ever their repugnance to prison and all that it involves. Grave indeed is the responsibility of those who . . . send any youth or girl, or indeed any man or woman, to prison for the first time.[36]

31 Ibid., pp. 248–50.
32 *The Times*, 27 Jan. 1920, p. 8.
33 Hobhouse and Brockway, *English Prisons To-Day*, op cit., note 13, p. 51; *Justice of the Peace*, 26 Mar. 1921, p. 133.
34 "Punishment and Reclamation," *Magistrate*, vol. 1 (1928), p. 213.
35 *The Times*, 5 Apr. 1924, p. 13.
36 Hewart, "Alternatives to Imprisonment," in *Essays and Observations* (1930), pp. 270–1.

Academic lawyers seconded these judicial sentiments. Sir Paul Vinogradoff, Corpus Professor of Jurisprudence in Oxford, wrote in *Outlines of Historical Jurisprudence*, "of all methods of penalizing culprits, the one most usual in our days, imprisonment, appears to be the most unsatisfactory. There is nothing to recommend it but the ease of its application to large numbers of delinquents."[37]

As before, a more systematic way of taking the measure of the judicial mind is by way of the decisions of the Court of Criminal Appeal. The Court did not always err on the side of leniency. In *Hayley Morris*,[38] a case of unlawful carnal knowledge of girls under the age of 16, the Lord Chief Justice's remarks ultimately resulted in the Penal Servitude Act 1926, a private members' bill (with Conservative government support), the original title of which was Criminal Justice (Increase of Penalties) Bill. The Act increased the powers of the court to substitute penal servitude for consecutive terms of imprisonment. There were two groups of offences—fraud and sexual—for which the maximum sentence was one of imprisonment for one or two years. In view of the general practice of the courts against sentencing persons to more than two years' imprisonment in the aggregate, it followed that for these offences the prisoner was not liable in practice to greater punishment whether he committed one offence or a whole series of offences. The object of the new Act was to allow courts in cases where they could in theory sentence the prisoner to consecutive terms of imprisonment amounting in the aggregate to a period of not less than three years, to pass a sentence of penal servitude equal to the aggregate term of the consecutive imprisonment sentences, subject to a limit of seven years' penal servitude. In principle, the Act extended the sentencing discretion of judges, and increased sentencing severity.[39] It is hard to tell what impact the new Act had, though the one case we have found that came before the Court was reversed on appeal. In *Ascoli*, the prisoner was found guilty on six counts of obtaining credit by fraud other than false pretences, and was sentenced to three years' penal servitude. The Lord Chief Justice, who had inspired the Act, decided that the statute

> is clearly intended only to apply to cases where the maximum sentence by ordinary law, though sufficient for the particular offence or group of offences, is not sufficient for a considerable group taken together. The question is—is this such a case? . . . We think not. The ordinary law is adequate, and no recourse to the statute was needed.

He reduced the sentence to 12 months' imprisonment with hard labour.[40]

On the other hand, in case after case the Court reduced sentences, frequently substituting short terms of imprisonment for long years of penal servitude. In

37 "The Ends of Punishment," *Justice of the Peace*, 25 Dec. 1920, p. 537.
38 (1926) 19 Cr. App. R. 75.
39 TNA, HO45/12383/490292/6 and 10; *Hansard*, vol. 191, 19 Feb. 1926, col. 2303; *Hansard* (Lords), vol. 65, 21 Jul. 1926, col. 113.
40 (1927) 20 Cr. App. R. 156.

Maxwell, the Lord Chief Justice gave early guidance. The appellant was sentenced to five years' penal servitude for stealing two checks and larceny of a bicycle. Though only 40 years of age, he had 19 previous convictions, and had served short prison terms and one of four years' penal servitude:

> It is a difficult question whether a man of bad character should be sentenced solely with reference to the substantive offence with which he is charged, or whether his previous convictions should always be considered. But . . . it is clear that a heavy sentence should not be passed for a minor offence merely because the prisoner has previously committed serious offences.[41]

The sentence was reduced to 12 months' imprisonment. For the same reason, in *Clifton* the Court reduced a sentence of five years' penal servitude for larceny and false pretences to three months' hard labour.[42] A sentence of five years' penal servitude passed at Staffordshire quarter sessions in 1929 on Alfred Woodward for obtaining by false pretences several small sums of money, and previously convicted six times, was reduced by the Lord Chief Justice to nine months' imprisonment with hard labour, out of regard for the intrinsic nature of the offence. Lord Hewart observed, "It is all wrong to send a man to a long term of penal servitude because at some other time for some other offence he has received heavy punishment." And the list could go on.

The Court clearly disapproved of long sentences for small crimes merely because the appellant had committed serious crimes in early life and suffered long terms of detention. In *Knell*, the Lord Chief Justice noted that the appellant had been sentenced to three years' penal servitude for his first offence in 1901, when he was 22 years of age, remarking, "The sentences which were passed in these days were very different from those passed now."[43] In *Griffiths*, the Court reduced a sentence of four years' penal servitude and 12 month's imprisonment, concurrent, for office-breaking and bigamy, to 18 months' imprisonment, rejecting the principle that a sentence must necessarily be heavier than that passed on the prisoner on a previous conviction, even though the trial judge was reported as saying that the appellant's record "'illustrates the unfortunate effect of lenient sentences in the past, not only by magistrates but also by judges, and I think it illustrates, too, the unfortunate effect of unnecessary reductions of sentences by the Court of Criminal Appeal.'"[44] At least one trial judge was keeping track of the appeal court's decisions.

---

41 (1924) 18 Cr. App. R. 13.
42 (1924) 18 Cr. App. R. 101. A sentence of three years' penal servitude for office-breaking was reduced to 12 months' imprisonment: *Price* (1924) 18 Cr. App. R. 138. A sentence of five years' penal servitude for obtaining money by false pretences was reduced to 18 months' imprisonment: *Gumbs* (1926) 19 Cr. App. R. 74. A sentence of five years' penal servitude for the theft of £2 worth of milk and two £1 Treasury notes was reduced to 18 months' imprisonment: *Armstrong* (1926) 19 Crim. App. R. 154.
43 (1926) 19 Cr. App. R. 169.
44 (1932) 23 Cr. App. R. 153.

Age was an important consideration at both ends of the spectrum in reducing severe sentences. The Court came to the rescue of old offenders. In *Watson*, a sentence of five years' penal servitude for sacrilege (stealing eight pence from a church) on a 72-year-old was reduced to nine months' imprisonment. The appellant had 20 previous convictions, and some of his prior sentences had been for long terms "in circumstances in which they would not be inflicted today," said the Lord Chief Justice. The trial judge had claimed that had the appeal court not reduced a five years' penal servitude inflicted by him on Watson in 1923 for stealing a clock, the appellant would have been in prison and unable to commit the most recent offence. The LCJ struck back, "It is not easy to follow this reasoning, but it seems to imply that anyone imprisoned for crime should be sentenced for life."[45] Youth and prior good behaviour were also taken into account. In *Taggart*, the LCJ reduced a sentence of nine months' imprisonment for obtaining money by false pretences to probation, stating:

> It is not practicable, and if practicable it would not be desirable, to lay down a general rule, but there are many cases in which it is worth while to take some risk in order to save a young man or a young woman from prison and the consequences of imprisonment.[46]

Thereafter, the Court acted as if it were a general rule, substituting probation for imprisonment and borstal detention on grounds of youth and prior good record in other cases. Serious crimes were not excluded from this approach. In *Bowler*, the Court reduced a ten years' penal servitude sentence for rape to one of 18 months' imprisonment, since the appellant was 22 years old and of good previous character.[47]

On the "gap" principle, the Court was influenced by a long period of honest work, especially if there was a guarantee of employment, or by a long interval free from conviction, again reducing sentences of penal servitude to ones of imprisonment in consequence. In *Pomfret*, a sentence of five years' penal servitude for receiving was reduced to 15 months' imprisonment. The appellant had previous convictions and in 1927 was sentenced to three years' penal servitude. After release in 1929, he worked in various places, but for the last nine months had been unemployed. The Sheffield Discharged Prisoners' Aid Society had testified that "if he only had regular employment no more would be heard of his criminal exploits."[48] The Court also guided to a small degree the relationship of imprisonment to penal servitude. In 1932, the Court felt the need to inform judges that a

45 (1927) 20 Cr. App. R. 119. In *Tussler*, the Court reduced a sentence of seven years' penal servitude on a 73-year-old man for stealing clothing from a caravan, to 18 months' imprisonment, regard being had to the intrinsic nature of the crime and his age: (1920) 15 Cr. Ap. R. 59.
46 (1923) 17 Cr. App. R. 132.
47 (1924) 18 Cr. App. R. 6.
48 (1931) 23 Cr. App. R. 31.

sentence of three years' penal servitude was to be regarded as more severe than one of two years' imprisonment with hard labour. "It may be that there was once a period when a sentence of two years' imprisonment with hard labour was more severe than a sentence of three years' penal servitude," said the LCJ. "That time has gone by."[49]

And, finally, the Court's commitment to proportionality meant it was less than eager to lengthen sentences for the purpose of securing treatment and training. The principle was established as early as 1919 in *Oxlade*, the effect of which was that unless the law expressly recognized a special form of sentence, such as borstal training or preventive detention, the length of a sentence of imprisonment must depend upon the offender's crime and not upon the prospect of his benefiting by some system of training. Oxlade, aged 19, was convicted of housebreaking and attempted burglary, and was sentenced to two years' imprisonment in order that he could receive the benefit of "modified borstal" in prison. The latter was the Prison Commission's arrangement to segregate lads between 16 and 21 sentenced to three months' or longer into collecting stations and taught a trade. Lord Reading's judgment was unambiguous. Courts should not sentence lads between 16 and 21 to a longer term of imprisonment than is appropriate to the case "in order that he may get indirectly the benefit of the borstal system as administered in our prisons."[50] The proper sentence was six months. However, both trial and appellate judges were willing to assist the borstal experiment. The Lord Chancellor, Lord Cave, told the 1925 International Prison Congress held in London,

> It was, he believed, the general opinion among Judges and magistrates that, in order that the Borstal institution might have a fair chance of success, a sentence for the full term of three years, reducible by the offenders own exertions, afforded the best prospect of the conversion of a budding criminal into a useful member of society.[51]

Not all special forms of sentence were so indulged by the courts, however. The appellate judges could never quite get their heads around preventive detention.[52]

49 *Jones* (1932) 23 Cr. App. R. 208.
50 Rex v. Oxlade, 2 King's Bench Division (1919) 628.
51 *Magistrate*, vol. 1 (1925), p. 95. At the request of the Lord Chief Justice, Prison Commissioner Alec Paterson gave evidence to the Court suggesting that no young offender was either too bad or too good for Borstal. Hence, the court substituted borstal sentences in a number of cases. See Bailey, *Delinquency and Citizenship*, pp. 252–3. The borstal training system had the effect of increasing the length of custody for those aged 16 to 21. By 1937, one-sixth of the prison population (or 1,860 inmates) was being dealt with in borstal institutions, sent there for anywhere between two and three years. The prison commissioners could release on licence after six months (or after three months in the case of girls), but the average period of borstal detention in the 1920s was rather more than two years.
52 The Court's decisions can be grouped into three broad areas. The first concerned the requirement of at least a three-year term of penal servitude before preventive detention could begin. The second broad area concerned whether the jury were bound to convict

The Court would have preferred to send habitual criminals straight into preventive detention. In *Searle*, when reducing a sentence of three years' penal servitude and five years' preventive detention to one year's imprisonment, the LCJ said that in the opinion of the Court "it is an unfortunate circumstance that under the law as it now stands it is not possible to pass a sentence of preventive detention without first satisfying the condition of passing one of penal servitude. . ."[53] But the law was the law, so it was frequently decided that a court ought not to impose a penal servitude sentence merely in order to give itself power to impose preventive detention. Penal servitude had to be warranted by the substantive crime of which he was convicted. In *Thompson*, the Court quashed the convictions for obtaining goods by false pretences and of being a habitual criminal (and hence the sentence of three years' penal servitude and five years' preventive detention), the LCJ stating, "we do not think that a man of 63 years, bad as his record may be, should be sentenced to three years' penal servitude for obtaining a night's lodging with supper and breakfast . . ."[54] In other cases, the sentence was reduced to a term of imprisonment. Gradually, the Court was strangling the life out of this "positivist" or social defence measure.[55]

The Home Office got nowhere in its attempts in the 1920s to save the preventive detention sentence from extinction. It was evident from correspondence with Lord Chief Justice Reading in 1920 that the judiciary was deterred from using preventive detention by the provision requiring a preliminary sentence of penal servitude. As Reading wrote: "Three years' Penal Servitude followed by five or ten years Preventive Detention is a very serious sentence."[56] The department went to some length to allow courts to pass a sentence of preventive detention upon a prisoner who had been sentenced to at least nine months' imprisonment, even drafting a bill that would have allowed preventive detention after sentence for the substantive offence of at least six months' imprisonment, which would have increased the numbers eligible for preventive detention quite considerably. But

a prisoner as a habitual criminal who had previously been convicted as a habitual criminal and sentenced to preventive detention, or whether it had always to be established that the prisoner was a habitual criminal at the time he committed his last offence. The third area of appeal decisions concerned the interpretation of the phrase in the Act "is leading persistently a dishonest or criminal life." Only the first area is highlighted here, but the other two also contributed to the gradual demise of the preventive detention sentence. See Norval Morris, *The Habitual Criminal* (1st pub. 1951; 1973 repr.), pp. 41ff.

53 (1922) 17 Cr. App. R. 35. In *Wilcock* (1921) 16 Cr. App. R. 91, the Lord Chief Justice said, "I do not know why penal servitude has been required to precede preventive detention."

54 (1921) 16 Cr. App. R. 6.

55 Troup noted that the 1908 Act laid down a rigid definition of "habitual criminal"— "and the Court of Criminal Appeal has interpreted it so strictly as almost to defeat the object of the Act." *The Home Office* (2nd. rev. ed. 1926), p. 122.

56 TNA, PCom7/291: Reading to Shortt, 20 Oct. 1920; HO45/20331/197277/43: Reading to Shortt, 29 Oct. 1920. See A. Lentin, "Isaacs, Rufus Daniel, first marquess of Reading (1860–1935)," *Oxford DNB* (2011).

Lord Hewart, Lord Chief Justice from 1922, was unwilling even to reply to departmental persuasions, and nothing came of these Home Office initiatives.[57] It comes as no surprise, then, to read the internal note of prison commissioner, Alexander Maxwell, in June 1930:

> As regards major offenders who are habitually guilty of crime, it was hoped that the Preventive Detention system would provide an improved method of dealing with these people. The Report of the Prison Commissioners for 1928 shows that the Preventive Detention system is a failure, and that there is no value in maintaining this system if the Courts only sentence to Preventive Detention such small numbers as have been sentenced in recent years.[58]

The figures say it all. Between 1909 and 1939, 1,049 men began sentences of preventive detention, an annual average of 33.8. Very few women were so sentenced, one or two per year at most. The annual average for males between 1918 and 1939 was 25. The bulk of preventive detention sentences, 82 per cent, were for the minimum period of five years. Most of the prisoners were sentenced for crimes against property, rarely for crime involving violence or the threat of it, and most were familiar with the courts (having previous convictions) and with prison (having experienced penal servitude at least once before conviction as a habitual offender).[59] Finally, most telling of all, few of the prisoners awarded a penal servitude sentence received preventive detention. In 1912–13, out of 871 persons sentenced to penal servitude, 85 received preventive detention as well. The same figures for 1920–21 were 482 and 44. Nine-tenths of those offenders who received a severer punishment than a term of imprisonment were sentenced to penal servitude *without* preventive detention.[60] The Court of Criminal Appeal wielded its powers to defeat the object of the Act, and their decisions influenced the trial courts, not to mention the DPP and the police.

The Court of Criminal Appeal never succeeded in fashioning a coherent jurisprudence of sentencing, but then it never sought to do so. There is no evidence that the court set out to do more than avoid anomalies and rationalize current

57 TNA, HO45/20331/197277/47; Ibid., 197277/49: Lawrence to Home Secretary, 27 May 1921. See also chap. 5 of this study, *infra*. See R. Stevens, "Hewart, Gordon, first Viscount Hewart (1870–1943)," *Oxford DNB* (2008).
58 TNA, HO45/18006/546730/12, Maxwell to Undersecretary of State, 25 Jun. 1930. Maxwell also wrote that the Gladstone Committee (1895) had stressed that the offence was persistence in the habit of crime, and that punishing for the particular crime was insufficient. Yet, "in the last 35 years practically no progress has been made in the adoption of this principle," and no progress can be made without the concurrence of the judges: HO45/21673/433166/21, Maxwell, 9 Dec. 1930.
59 Norval Morris, *The Habitual Criminal*, op cit.
60 Hobhouse and Brockway, *English Prisons To-Day*, op cit., p. 464; L. Radzinowicz, "The Persistent Offender," in Radzinowicz and J. W. C. Turner (eds.), *The Modern Approach to Criminal Law* (1945), note 1, p. 172.

practice. The appeal judges never asked themselves, why is the tariff for offence "x" 18 months rather than nine months; five years rather than three years? Rarely was an attempt made to relate a sentence to the range of sentences for similar classes of crime. Hence, appellate judgments yielded less guidance to trial judges than was anticipated, and even less guidance to magistrates, who dealt with the majority of criminal cases.[61] What is evident, however, is that the Court of Criminal Appeal consistently lowered the severity of sentences, in response to a number of extenuating circumstances: youth and old age, good character and prior good record, periods of honest work, intervals free from conviction—and, in keeping with the principle that the punishment must fit the crime, however bad the appellant's prior record. One legal commentator in 1933 felt the Court had carried this latter principle too far, in view of the recent increase in burglary and housebreaking, and even accused the Court of putting the interests of the criminal above the security of the community.[62] If the reductionist message was clear, the question remains what influence did it have? Appellate decisions were haphazardly reported; only some decisions found their way into either *The Times*, the *Criminal Appeal Reports*, or the *Justice of the Peace*. [63] Cases were rarely cited as precedents in argument before the court. Yet Sir Edward Troup, Permanent Undersecretary of State at the Home Office between 1908 and 1922, observed in 1925: "Compared with forty or even twenty years ago, the tendency of the courts to leniency in their sentences is very marked: and this tendency has been accentuated by the frequent reduction of sentences by the Court of Criminal Appeal."[64] It is also arguable that the sentencing norms set down by the Court entered the legal ether. As Lord Chief Justice Hewart argued in 1927, "The consequences of that diffused and abiding knowledge are quite incalculable."[65] What was calculable, according to the 1932 Report of the Departmental Committee on Persistent Offenders, was the reductionist tendency in sentencing. As the report claimed, "The very long sentences which were often passed twenty years ago [or in the pre-war years] are now usually regarded as harsh and excessive and are seldom imposed."[66] And the Court indubitably axed the only sentence that sought to punish persistence in crime with long preventive sentences.

61 See Home Office, *Sentences of Imprisonment: A Review of Maximum Penalties* (ACPS, 1978), pp. 34–8, 200–1.
62 W. T. S. Stallybrass, "A Comparison of the General Principles of Criminal Law in England with the Progetto Definitivo Di Un Nuovo Codice Penale of Alfredo Rocco," *Journal of Comparative Legislation and International Law*, vol. 15 (1933), p. 241.
63 D. Seaborne Davies, "The Court of Criminal Appeal: The First Forty Years," *Journal of Society of Public Teachers of Law*, vol. 1 (1951), p. 426; D. A. Thomas, "Appellate Review of Sentences and the Development of Sentencing Policy: The English Experience," *Alabama Law Review*, vol. 20 (1968), p. 221.
64 Troup, *The Home Office* (2nd ed. rev., 1926), p. 71.
65 "Address of the Right Honourable Baron Hewart of Bury at the Twelfth Annual Meeting of the Canadian Bar Association, *Canadian Bar Review*, vol. 5 (1927), p. 572. See also Travers Humphreys, *Criminal Days* (1946), p. 55.
66 *Report of the Departmental Committee on Persistent Offenders* (Cmd. 4090), 1932, p. 9.

IV

To the reductionist impact of the Court of Criminal Appeal, we must add the role of the executive in the inter-war years. The prison commissioners continued to stress the limitations of a prison sentence. Chairman Waller wrote in June 1922: "The [Prison] Commissioners would draw attention, as always, to the primary point that people should not be sent to prison at all if it can possibly be avoided," and many persons, especially young ones, were being committed who might have been saved from imprisonment.[67] Harold Scott, also chairman of the Prison Commission, told Lord Dufferin in February 1937 that despite the improvements made in the prisons, "no one is more conscious than the Prison Commissioners that our prison system is still open to many criticisms. Imprisonment necessarily involves an unnatural mode of life and it should only be used in the last resort."[68] More importantly, the Home Office extended mitigation of punishment where it could, and held the line against attempts to bring greater severity to bear upon sentencing and the criminal code.

The department informed the Royal Commission on Capital Punishment in 1949 that in regard to commuted capital punishment sentences, Home Office policy had been modified between the wars in accordance with the general tendency of the courts to impose less severe sentences for serious offences than in the past. Between 1930 and 1939 few prisoners were detained for as long as 15 years, and an increasing proportion were released after serving periods between ten and 13 years.[69] The Home Office also showed itself willing to respond to public pressure to make infanticide a non-capital offence. Women convicted of new-born murder were never executed, yet they were still automatically sentenced to death. In 1922, the Infanticide Act effectively abolished the death penalty for a woman who deliberately killed her new-born child, while the balance of her mind was disturbed as a result of giving birth. By providing a partial defence to murder, the woman was punished as if she had been convicted of manslaughter. The first trial to invoke the new Act took place at Lincoln assizes in October 1922. A domestic servant, Emma Temple, pleaded guilty to murdering her new-born child, "adding that at the time she did not know what she was doing." The Crown accepted the plea. Mr. Justice Lush sentenced her to four months' imprisonment in the second division, observing that "he was most thankful that under the new [Infanticide] Act, which was a most wise and humane piece of legislation, it was not necessary to put a girl on trial for murder."[70] The department also supported those who sought further abatement of imprisonment. In 1935, officials helped to prepare a Private Member's Bill to amend section 4 of the Vagrancy Act 1824 as it related to

---

67 HO45/11543/357055: Waller, 21 Jun. 1922.
68 HO45/18006/546730/48: Scott to Dufferin, 26 Feb. 1937.
69 *The Times*, 5 Aug. 1949, p. 2.
70 *Infanticide Act*, 1922, 12 and 13 Geo. 5, c. 18; *The Times*, 31 Oct. 1922, p. 9. See also Daniel Grey, "Women's Policy Networks and the Infanticide Act 1922," *Twentieth Century British History*, vol. 21 (2010), pp. 441–63.

persons wandering abroad and lodging in barns or other places. The bill's purpose was to ensure that no person would be sent to prison for sleeping out just because he had not the money to buy himself a night's lodging.[71] The figure for persons received into local prisons on a summary conviction for sleeping out was the lowest on record in 1936 at 82 (65 men; 17 women). In 1913, the figure had been 3,239 (2,922 men).[72]

The department resisted attempts to increase severity in sentencing, first in relation to sexual offences against young persons, and secondly in relation to flogging as a punishment. In the early 1920s, a number of bodies—Children's Rescue Fund, National Council for Combating Venereal Disease—and a number of MPs (Viscountess Astor and Major Paget) complained of an increase of sexual offences against young children, and protested the inadequate penalties imposed by the courts for these offences.[73] Initially, the Home Office argued that there was no evidence of any increase in the number of these offences over a period of 25 years, and, as Home Secretary Bridgeman told the Home Affairs Committee, "the Home Office has no evidence to show that a strengthening of the penalties is required."[74] Blackwell minuted that cases of indecent assault varied greatly in gravity, but the majority (358 out of 499 in 1921) were punished with some severity, by imprisonment not fine. Nevertheless, a conference was held at the Home Office of the various pressure groups, which were now asking for a committee of inquiry. Blackwell tried to stem the tide by referring to the fall in the number of offences of carnal knowledge of girls under 13, despite the drop in the severity of sentences. In earlier years, five years' penal servitude, even seven, ten, and 12 years, had been commonly passed. The reason for shorter sentences, he told the conference, was probably the decisions of the appeal court, the trial judges taking notice of cases in which sentences were reduced on appeal. The Home Secretary declined to criticize the sentences passed by the courts, "and drew attention to the present movement in favour of a general reduction of sentences in criminal cases which react on the sentences passed in this class of cases."[75] He nonetheless conceded the appointment of a committee.

The report of the Departmental Committee on Sexual Offences Against Young Persons appeared in late 1925. The Committee accepted that there had been an increase in indecent assaults on children under 16 years of age since the end of the Great War (though a decrease in the worst types of sexual offences against young persons, such as sexual crimes with violence), and it found evidence of very inadequate sentences in some cases. The committee considered that imprisonment

---

71 See *Hansard*, vol. 299, 26 Mar. 1935, col. 1742, Brigadier-General Spears; 25 and 26 Geo. V, c. 20, Vagrancy Act, 1935.

72 Ann. Rep. of PC for 1936, PP, 1937–8, vol. 14 (Cmd. 5675), p. 705.

73 See TNA, HO144/4483/316579/20; *Hansard*, vol. 133, 10 Aug. 1920, col. 248 (Astor); *Hansard*, vol. 165, 20 Jun. 1923, col. 1439 (Paget); *Justice of the Peace*, 21 Jul. 1923, p. 545; *Hansard*, vol. 166, 12 Jul. 1923, col. 1651 (Briant).

74 Ibid., 316579/26, Home Affairs Committee, CP 307 (23), 3 Jul. 1923.

75 Ibid., 316579/42 and 64, Blackwell, 31 Jan. 1924; Blackwell and Anderson, Home Office conference, Mar. 1924.

was the most suitable penalty in these cases; it did not advocate flogging. No fewer than 43 recommendations were made by the committee, but few were implemented.[76] In September 1926, the Home Office issued a circular in which the courts were asked to think about the committee's recommendations that could be implemented without legislation, mainly to do with trial procedure.[77] The final act in this saga came in January 1932, when the National Union of Societies for Equal Citizenship asked the Home Office to receive a deputation, in part to press for the recommendations of the Sexual Offences Committee, including raising the maximum penalties for sexual offences against young persons. Blackwell correctly noted that the committee made no such recommendation, adding: ". . . it is quite useless to increase maxima, when the general drift of the Courts is so much towards leniency." The Home Secretary told the deputation that the maximum sentences were adequate, "and when there is undue leniency it is because the Courts have not chosen to exercise to the full the powers of punishment which are. . . placed in their hands by the legislature."[78]

The second area in which the Home Office held the line was in regard to flogging as a punishment. Men were sentenced to be whipped under five statutes: Knackers Act 1786 (slaughtering horses without a licence); Vagrancy Act 1824 (being incorrigible rogues); Treason Act 1842; Larceny Acts 1861 and 1916 and Garrotters Act 1863 (aggravated robbery with violence and garroting); and Criminal Law Amendment Act 1912 (procuration and living on the earnings of prostitutes).[79] As a penalty for adults and young adults, flogging was rarely used. In 1928, 13 persons over 21 and three persons aged between 16 and 21 were ordered the "cat" for criminal offences. In 1931, the total number flogged was 31, the majority (19) inflicted for the crime of robbery. Additionally, 11 were flogged in prison (the figure for 1927) for breaches of prison discipline, including violence against prison officers, which was a tiny number considering that 50,000 persons passed through English prisons every year.[80] In the 1920s, the department dealt with the issue on a case by case basis, often in response to complaints from penal reform bodies about judicial claims (like the one by Mr. Justice Darling in April 1920) that flogging deterred robbery with violence.[81]

---

76 *Report of the Departmental Committee on Sexual Offences against Young Persons*, PP, 1924–25, Vol. XV (Cmd. 2561), pp. 913–4, 967–8, 988.
77 *The Times*, 18 Sept. 1926, p. 12.
78 TNA, HO144/20112/548577/47, Notes of Deputation, 26 Jan. 1932. See also J. E. Hall Williams, "Sex Offences: The British Experience," *Law and Contemporary Problems*, vol. 25 (1960), pp. 334–41.
79 "Corporal Punishment," *Nation & Athenaeum*, 22 Feb. 1930, p. 694. Flogging with the cat-o'-nine-tails was restricted to offenders over 16 years of age. It was carried out privately in prison (since a sentence of flogging was almost always combined with a term of imprisonment), and it was applied to the bare upper back, with the recipient standing against a frame. Boy offenders could be birched. This was administered to the bare buttocks of the boy, usually carried out by a policeman in the local police station or in the court building itself.
80 R. L. Gard, *The End of the Rod*, op cit., pp. 84–7.
81 *Daily News*, 21 Apr. 1920, enclosed in TNA, HO45/10912/A54970/88.

There was also a request to allow justices to inflict corporal punishment in cases of cruelty to animals. The Home Office felt that if magistrates did not use existing powers, they would not use more drastic ones, and it was not for the executive to lecture them into doing so. As Locke minuted in July 1929, "For some years the efficacy of sentences of corporal punishment has been doubted in HO & all suggestions for its extension have been opposed."[82] It was departmental policy to remit flogging sentences imposed under the Vagrancy Act unless for importuning, gross indecency or gross violence. Locke recommended repealing section 10 of the Vagrancy Act, in so far as it authorized whipping for sleeping out, begging, or deserting family, but no time could be found for a bill. Locke also wanted repeal for indecent exposure, since the offence was "so often connected with some form of mental peculiarity, & persons guilty of grosser sexual offences cannot be whipped."[83]

Justices (Lord Darling; Sir Montagu Sharp, chairman of the Middlesex quarter sessions; Sir Ernest Wild, recorder; Sir K. F. Dickens, the Common Sergeant) continued to defend the use of flogging, and judges (Avery, Horridge, Swift) continued to impose flogging on criminals guilty of personal violence.[84] In 1932, the number of convictions of robbery with violence doubled, as did cases in which the cat or birch rod was ordered by the court (61 cases, exclusive of whippings of juveniles).[85] Indeed, courts made more frequent use of corporal punishment when dealing with robbery with violence than in earlier years. The yearly average for 1911–13 was four sentences of corporal punishment; for 1921–23, 17, and for 1932–34, 43.[86] Yet, the department held the line. Prison Commissioner Alexander Maxwell addressing overseas prison administrators, stated that the Home Office opposed corporal punishment for young offenders, and had tried unsuccessfully to abolish the power in 1933 in the Children Act, but as regards older offenders, "it cannot be said that there is a Home Office official view on this subject." Yet the department remained sceptical of the deterrent effect of flogging, except possibly in relation to prison offences. As officials noted, sentences of corporal punishment were always combined with imprisonment or penal servitude, and hence it was impossible to measure the deterrent efficacy of corporal punishment as distinct from the efficacy of long terms of imprisonment or penal servitude. Also, the department preferred to have an enquiry into the question before introducing legislation. In March 1937, Home Secretary Simon announced the appointment of the Departmental Committee on Corporal Punishment.[87]

82 TNA, HO144/22331/454147/90.
83 TNA, HO45/14178/436329/32, Locke, 29 Jul. 1929.
84 TNA, HO144/22312/440258/1; HO45/14178/436329/49.
85 TNA, HO45/17489/589571/36.
86 Ibid., 589571/65, Maxwell minute, 21 Jan. 1936.
87 Ibid., 589571/70. See also M. Hamblin Smith, late Medical Officer, Birmingham Prison, "The Case Against Flogging," *Spectator*, 8 Sep. 1933, enclosed in ibid., 589571/35.

More so than in previous years, the Home Office were in favour of keeping people out of prison, and they recognized the immense strides that had been made since the early years of the century.[88] A main factor in the reduction of the daily average prison population, they knew, had been the decrease in the length of sentences. As Locke pointed out, "the Courts already do their utmost, after persons are found guilty, to avoid sending any but the worst to more than seven months' imprisonment."[89] In 1925, of the 13,121 persons sentenced to imprisonment (out of 47,525 persons guilty of indictable offences), only 2,479 (or 1 in 19 of those found guilty) were sentenced to more than seven months' imprisonment. In 1923–24, only 500 women had been sent to prison for more than three months.[90] At the same time, the prison commissioners recognized that, as they put it in their report for 1925–26, "the short sentence remains an outstanding defect in our penal system. . ."[91] Still 60 per cent of the sentences of imprisonment were for periods not exceeding one month in 1930. Though the commissioners believed that three months was the minimum period required for training, 77 per cent of male receptions and 89 per cent of female receptions in 1931 were for periods of three months and under. Margery Fry put her finger on the problem:

88 Alec Paterson, the reforming prison commissioner, recognized the malign features of a prison sentence (while still believing that rehabilitation within prison was possible). As he wrote, "The Court has attached to it, as a ready handmaid for its use, a state or provincial prison. Once guilt is ascertained, the easiest method for the disposal of the prisoner is a sentence of imprisonment. It may or may not be the best method of disposal on psychological grounds, or on those of economy and common sense." Quoted in Rutherford, *Prisons and the Process of Justice*, op cit., p. 128.

89 TNA, HO45/19453/507631/2, Locke, 10 Jun. 1927.

90 The female offender met with greater sentencing leniency than the male. Hermann Mannheim's survey of the inter-war years noted that "the percentage of women decreases in conformity with the severity of the particular method of penal treatment." In 1933, 542 men and 23 women were sent to penal servitude, a ratio of 23 men to one woman; and 32,646 men and 4,404 women were sentenced to imprisonment, a ratio of eight men to one woman. Sentences of more than one year's imprisonment were passed upon 1,099 men and only 48 women, a ratio of 23:1. As for the severe sentence of preventive detention, during the years 1909 and 1930, 944 men and 23 women were awarded it, a ratio of 41:1. Adult women stood a much greater chance than men of being awarded probation. See Hermann Mannheim, *Social Aspects of Crime in England Between the Wars* (1940), p. 343; B. S. Godfrey et al., "Explaining Gendered Sentencing Patterns for Violent Men and Women in the Late-Victorian and Edwardian Period," *British Journal of Criminology*, vol. 45 (2005), 696–720.

91 Cited in M. Davies et al., *Criminal Justice*, 2nd ed. (1998), p. 280. Maxwell, Prison Commission, told the Undersecretary of State in June 1930, in a discussion of habitual offenders guilty of minor offences: "Many magistrates recognize the futility of short sentences but do not know what is the proper alternative." TNA, HO45/18006/546730/12. However, an undated Home Office minute (circa 1933), indicated that the futility of short prison sentences had been the subject of much public comment in recent years, the result of which was possibly reflected in the decrease in the number of sentences of 14 days or less, from 11,406 or 33 per cent of male committals in 1927 to 8,609 or 26 per cent in 1932: HO144/18869/196919.

while we have largely lost belief in the efficacy of prison in dealing with minor *offences*, the figures would seem to show that it is still used for compelling the payment of debts on much the same scale as before the War.[92]

Oliver Stanley, parliamentary Undersecretary of State, told the annual meeting of the Magistrates Association in 1932 that over 24,000 people were sent to prison either for non-payment of fines or for failure to comply with wife maintenance and affiliation orders, accounting for over 40 per cent of the 60,000 receptions into prison.[93] Fines were still frequently imposed on habitual drunkards and vagrants guilty of minor offences.[94] A few years later, Alexander Maxwell, Assistant Undersecretary of State, wrote that for every one criminal sent to prison for burglary or shop-breaking, at least eight persons were sent to prison for failing to pay sums of money.[95] It was also evident that out of the 11,543 cases of imprisonment in default in 1931, almost 7,000 had not been allowed time to pay, some of whom were young people under 21 years old, despite the Criminal Justice (Administration) Act of 1914.[96]

In a 1925 circular, the Home Office reiterated that justices should allow more time for payment of a fine whenever a defendant was anxious to pay it, but temporarily prevented from doing so.[97] But the problem persisted. In 1934 a Home Office committee recommended that no defaulter should be committed to prison without a second appearance in court, when the mind of the court had to be expressly directed to the question of imprisonment by enquiring into the defaulter's means; and that no one under 21 should be sent to prison for non-payment of a fine unless he had been first under supervision of a probation officer. The Money Payments (Justices Procedure) Act 1935 carried these recommendations into effect. It had the desired effect: committals for non-payment of fines fell from 10,542 in 1935 to 7,400 in 1936. The number of committals fell also for wife maintenance and affiliation orders and for rates.[98]

92 S. Margery Fry, "Debtor Prisoners," *Magistrate*, vol. 2, Oct.–Nov. 1932, p. 626.

93 See TNA, HO45/16943/399376/36. There were 11,000 committals for failure to pay fines, 6,000 committals for failure to pay sums due under maintenance or affiliation orders, and 3,000 committals for failure to pay rates.

94 TNA, PCom 9/59, Maxwell at the Annual Conference of Visiting Justices, 27 Nov. 1934.

95 Maxwell, *Debtor Prisoners* (issued by Penal Reform Committee of the Society of Friends, Mar. 1935), p. 3.

96 L. W. Fox, *The Modern English Prison* (1934), p. 200.

97 For circular, see *Magistrate*, vol. 1 (1925).

98 TNA, HO45/16736/687245/3, Home Office circular, "Imprisonment in Default of Payment," 8 Nov. 1935; G. Rusche and O. Kirchheimer, *Punishment and Social Structure* (1st pub. 1939; New York, 1968), p. 170; R. M. Jackson, *The Machinery of Justice in England* (Cambridge, 1972), p. 312. Another reason for the decline of committals for non-payment of fines may be found in the increase in the infliction of fines on a wealthier class of *motoring* offender. See *Report of the Departmental Committee on Imprisonment by Courts of Summary Jurisdiction in Default of Payment of Fines and Other Sums of Money*, PP, 1933–34, vol. 11 (Cmd. 4649), p. 75. Note also that the Criminal Justice Act, 1925, gave effect to the recommendations of The Committee on the Detention in Custody of Prisoners Committed for Trial, presided over by Mr. Justice Horridge, enabling offenders to be brought to trial more quickly.

The Home Office was also instrumental in promoting alternatives to imprisonment, especially probation. Until 1925, there was a marked diversity of practice in the use of probation, some courts (especially in London) appreciating the value of the system, other courts (especially in the rural areas) failing even to obtain the services of a probation officer. Moreover, in both perception and practice, probation was a method only for the young, many courts hardly ever using probation for adult offenders. Through the inter-war period, 75 per cent of all probation orders were imposed on persons under 21 years of age; between 40 and 50 per cent of all probation orders were made on juveniles (aged under 16).[99] Troup was thinking of the 15,000 persons sent each year to prison for terms of two weeks or less, when he declared that many could have been placed on probation. However, "The system is. . . still in its infancy, and it may be doubted whether many Justices have fully grasped its meaning and value."[100] The 1922 departmental committee on probation, and the associated Criminal Justice Act 1925, transformed probation from an optional extra to an organized national service. Opening the way for greater central oversight, the Act ushered in greater use of probation by the courts, and established probation as a credible measure for offenders in need of diagnosis and treatment.[101] By 1927, almost all petty sessional divisions had appointed a probation officer, if only part-time. The number of probation orders increased from 13,838 in 1925 to 15,094 in 1927, to 17,989 in 1930, and to 29,301 in 1938. By 1938, 15 per cent of adult indictable offenders were being sentenced to probation. For those aged 21 and over, almost one-third of those given a probation order were female.[102] Where probation contributed most to the abatement of imprisonment was with regard to 16 to 21-year-olds. The Home Office believed there were too many of this age group with no previous convictions being sent to prison in the early 1920s. A considerable number, it was thought, could be dealt with better by the use of probation. In July 1928, the Home Secretary urged all courts to avoid committing young offenders to prison if an alternative method of treatment could properly be adopted. The subsequent decline in the number of young offenders imprisoned suggested that courts were responding to this executive exhortation.[103]

V

There was a massive abatement of imprisonment between 1880 and 1939. The judiciary, with little executive or legislative guidance, converted the

---

99 V. Bailey, *Delinquency and Citizenship* (Oxford, 1987), Table 7, p. 319.
100 Troup, *The Home Office*, op cit., p. 140.
101 W. McWilliams, "The Mission Transformed: Professionalisation of Probation Between the Wars," *Howard Journal*, vol. 24 (1985), p. 260. The slightly greater availability from the 1920s in some cities of psychiatric examination of remand prisoners, on behalf of the courts, saved a few offenders from imprisonment.
102 R. Gard, *Rehabilitation and Probation in England and Wales 1876–1962* (2014), p. 114.
103 See V. Bailey, *Delinquency and Citizenship* (Oxford, 1987), p. 185.

severe Victorian tariff of punishment, erected in the immediate post-transportation years—in which minor property offenders regularly received long sentences of penal servitude in convict prisons—into a sentencing structure that relied, at first, on sentences of imprisonment that were by common consent no more than two years in length and typically shorter, and increasingly on the non-custodial penalties of discharge, fine, and probation. Almost single-handedly, though with no high strategy behind it, opposing every new initiative put before them, and standing on the dignity of the supposed independence of the judiciary from executive interference, the judges reduced the severity of sentencing for indictable offences, encouraging magistrates at quarter sessions to follow suit. They did so, not because they were familiar with the inside of prisons and the harsh prison discipline to be found there[104]—though they were doubtless aware of the challenge to the prison paradigm in the 1890s—but because they believed that the sentences handed down in the 1860s and 1870s were out of all proportion to the incidence and gravity of crime. Retributive (and deterrent) considerations were decisive in the recalibration of the tariff. Judges were able to adopt a more sanguine view of the threat and gravity of crime, because all indications were that the rate of property and violent crime was falling. After the 1860s, no moral panic equivalent to the scare over ticket-of-leave robberies disturbed the surface. The fall in the number of prison receptions and the daily average prison population would have been greater still before 1914 had not the passage of new social laws and the stricter police enforcement of existing regulations led magistrates' courts to send too many petty offenders to prison on short sentences. It took the War years to rid the prisons of this stage army of vagrants, drunks, and petty thieves. The change was a function less of judicial action than social and economic intervention and improvement, but at least the lower courts never again sought refuge in the kind of sentencing that had characterized the pre-war years. In the inter-war years, prisons were closed as the judiciary continued to reduce the length of prison sentences, declined to take full advantage of preventive detention, and awarded non-custodial penalties in ever larger numbers. It is second nature today to lay the problem of prisons bursting at the seams at the feet of the judiciary. It should come as some sort of relief that the judiciary has the discretion to change direction, and did so in spades between 1880 and 1939.

---

104 The poet, Wilfred S. Blunt, advised Churchill that the judges and visiting justices "do not understand the severity of the suffering inflicted by leaving the minds of prisoners for long periods of months and years deprived of any spiritual sustenance whatever": *My Diaries*, part 2 (New York, 1922), pp. 446–7.

4

PRISONS, PRISONERS, AND PENAL REFORM, 1922–1938

We ["brought up in the days when the doctrine of retributive justice was still vigorous"] recognize, for example, that prisons can seldom do men any good and will often do them harm, but we do not actually feel that it is wrong to send people to prison, because there is still at the back of our minds the glow surviving from the old theological conflagration, and we have a half-conscious feeling that however bad prisons may be, at any rate the offenders have deserved to be treated badly. The younger generation, however, who have never been under the influence of the old doctrine of retributive justice, see quite clearly that our present penal system is in its main elements indefensible.

Alexander Maxwell, "The Punishment of Crime and the Crime of Punishment," a talk, mid-1930s.

I

On 10 September 1922, Maurice Waller, chairman of the Prison Commissioners, wrote to Herbert Gladstone, whose private secretary Waller had been before the Great War, and from whom Waller had inherited his interest in prison matters. The war, said Waller, had produced severe disorganization in a service "where half the people of all ranks had been away for four years." As a result,

It wasn't till the middle of 21 that one was able to look at the big problems again and ask oneself the big questions—especially "what are prisons for": the question to which each generation gives a different answer, and sometimes each person! I think we want a new answer now, but the question does not admit of a very simple answer; it applies to too many different sorts of people, and goes too deep into problems of mental processes, education, and indeed also the very structure of a society. But I am sure the answer should be scientific, neither brutal on the one hand, nor neurotic on the other. You start with the protection of society—there is pretty fair agreement so far. Then comes the point "How will you best protect society." Generally speaking, segregate the ascertained incorrigibles, and do your best to re-educate the rest. This is not pampering—not at all, because proper re-education will be a more strenuous and objectionable business to most offenders than a prison sentence is now—much! But it will have a purpose. I agree with the view that merely punishing—for the sake of punishing—is bad psychology, and likely to do harm rather than good.[1]

This is the closest we have to a manifesto for change in prison administration from Waller, the person whom Margery Fry, Secretary of the Howard League for Penal Reform, had pressed the Home Secretary to appoint as chairman of the Prison Commissioners, and whom Fry eulogized in 1928 on his retirement for having "transformed our prison system":

A new breath of criticism, of experiment, of endeavour, has moved over what was a stagnant pool of self-satisfied, unintelligent routine. The prison service has been *thinking* in the last seven years, and the person who has thought hardest of all has been Maurice Waller . . . his most outstanding quality by far is this, that in an official position he could keep the unofficial mind, the sense of what might be, unblunted by dealing with what is.

Before Waller, said Fry, prisons were "almost completely isolated from the ordinary life of the community." She continued,

The public was not encouraged to ask what was done in its name, and the prison was surrounded by a spiritual barrier as formidable as its heavy wall. The breaking down of this barrier, the letting air into the vacuum chamber of prison life, is a greater achievement even than the reforms which have been accomplished in regime . . .[2]

Waller's appointment as chairman coincided with the publication of the Prison System Enquiry Committee's volume on prisons, *English Prisons Today*. This volume, according to Miss Fry, became a "Bible for the reformers," and while Waller was disappointed with the Brockway and Hobhouse book for dealing

1   Waller to Gladstone, 10 Sep. 1922, Viscount Gladstone Papers, British Library (BL), Add. MSS, 45994, folio 318: emphasis in original. See also Waller's personnel file in The National Archives (TNA), PCom7/741. He was private secretary to Lord Gladstone from 1906 to 1910.
2   S. Margery Fry, "Retirement of Sir Maurice Waller," *Howard Journal*, vol. 2 (1928), pp. 192–3: emphasis in original; "Prison Reforms," *The Times*, 7 Jul. 1928. See also Martin Wright, "The Howard League and the Prison Authorities," *Prison Service Journal*, No. 31 (1978), p. 19.

"almost entirely with the war period, and with the CO's (conscientious objectors), and with neurotics. Time, people, and circumstances were all special," it was probably not without its influence upon him.[3]

In 1922, Waller took the unprecedented step of recommending the appointment of a commissioner from outside the prison service, Alexander Paterson, aged 38. Paterson had been preparing for the role for many years. Following graduation from Oxford in 1906, he spent the next 16 years living among the poor in a two-room, riverside tenement in Bermondsey, working with the Oxford and Bermondsey Club for boys, penning *Across the Bridges*, in which he described the poverty and hardship of his neighbours (though not the structural and political reasons for such conditions), and serving in a number of capacities: as assistant director of the Borstal Association for the aftercare of borstal boys, as a voluntary probation officer at Tower Bridge Police Court, and as assistant director of the Central Association for the Aid of Discharged Prisoners.[4] In the latter capacity, he visited every convict prison monthly. His description of Dartmoor convict prison in 1906, where he went to visit a young Bermondsey man who had been sentenced to ten years' penal servitude for murdering his wife, vividly represents the prison regime he would later seek to change:

> As I walked along the endless landings and corridors in the great cellular blocks, I saw something of the fifteen hundred men who were then immured in Dartmoor. Their drab uniforms were plastered with broad arrows, their heads were closely shaven . . . Not even a safety razor was allowed, so that in addition to the stubble on their heads, their faces were covered with a sort of dirty moss, representing the growth of hair that a pair of clippers could not remove. The prison regime, resting primarily on considerations of safe custody and security, . . . had succeeded in making a large number of human beings into objects of ugliness and contempt . . . As they saw us coming, each man ran to the nearest wall and put his face closely against it, remaining in this servile position till we had passed behind him. This was a strictly ordered procedure, to avoid assault or familiarity, the two great offences in prison conduct . . . The men looked hard in body and in spirit, healthy enough in physique and colour, but cowed and listless in demeanour and response. No active brutality was practiced by the warders, save when an escaped convict was recaptured. Then it was the age-long tradition of the place that he should be taken down to a separate cell and be beaten indiscriminately.[5]

3   Gordon Rose, *The Struggle for Penal Reform* (1961), p. 108; Waller to Gladstone, 10 Sep. 1922, Viscount Gladstone Papers, BL, Add. MSS, 45994, folio 319.
4   Victor Bailey, *Delinquency and Citizenship* (Oxford, 1987), pp. 194–5; Sir Harold Scott, *Your Obedient Servant* (1959), p. 69; Catrin Smith, "Paterson, Sir Alexander Henry (1884–1947)," *Oxford Dictionary of National Biography*, 2004.
5   Quoted in S. K. Ruck (ed.), *Paterson on Prisons* (1951), p. 11. As R. Duncan Fairn observed, Paterson "left behind him no systematic treatise on penology;" what he left in the form of reports, minutes, and occasional papers was woven into a coherent pattern

Paterson always believed that prison induced a mental and moral deterioration in inmates. He was unconvinced by the notion of a "criminal type," but he believed in a "prisoner type": "of face and voice and mien acquired by men who spend many years in the half-light of prison . . ."[6] No improvement was to be expected in prisoners after two years' detention, Paterson advised the government of Burma in 1926: "He will get used to it, relapse into the half-light of a monotonous regime, lose count of time and space, and become daily more fitted to be a prisoner than a free man." Indeed, Paterson would become renowned for the aphorism, "It is impossible to train men for freedom in a condition of captivity."[7]

The focus of this chapter is a critical estimate of the prison commissioners' efforts to improve the material conditions, regime, and effectiveness of the penitentiary in the 1920s and 1930s. It was, after all, the material conditions and disciplines of the penitentiary that continued to fix the meaning of prison for those sent there. It is a story of good intentions yet limited gains, despite the promising circumstances of a declining prison population, and a public and parliamentary opinion sympathetic to penal reform. When measured against the testimony of prisoners and prison staff, who experienced at first hand the inter-war penitentiaries, the material improvements were modest, and came on stream slowly and at times grudgingly. The pace of change was still retarded by the detrimental influence of "less eligibility," which had long insisted that living standards in prison should be inferior to those attained by the law-abiding poor. While the decline in the number of inmates made it possible also to think seriously about schemes of classification of prisons and prisoners, as preface to a prison system geared towards rehabilitation, the prison commissioners' ambition far outran the practical difficulties they faced, especially the age and condition of the penal estate, and the dead weight of prisoners committed for short terms to the local prisons. Yet, if meaningful change in prison policy and practice was still tentative in the inter-war years, the efforts of the prison commissioners at least testified to a shift in values. The prison commissioners, and none more so than Alexander Paterson, the architect of the improved Borstal reformatories for young offenders, were guided by an *idée fixe* that can be encapsulated in the phrase, "liberal progressive reform." An integral feature of this religious and moral outlook was a set of attitudes to crime and punishment, associated with the European "positivist" movement yet without its illiberal extremes. Crime was thought to be influenced, without being entirely determined, by an offender's innate constitution and environment, and hence punishment ought to be adapted, at least to some degree, to the offender's individual rehabilitation. Not even the

by S. K. Ruck in *Paterson on Prisons*: Fairn, review of Ruck, *British Journal of Delinquency*, vol. 2 (1951), p.175.

6   Alexander Paterson, "Should the Criminologist Be Encouraged?" *Transactions of the Medico-Legal Society*, vol. 26 (1933), p. 183.

7   Quoted in Ian Brown, "A Commissioner Calls: Alexander Paterson and Colonial Burma's Prisons," *Journal of Southeast Asian Studies*, vol. 38 (2007), p. 297. Paterson was partial to the aphorism; another was "a prison is a monastery of men unwilling to be monks."

mutiny of convicts serving penal servitude in Dartmoor prison in 1932, which is examined in the following, served to deflect this reformatory approach to the penitentiary and its inmates.[8]

II

The prison commissioners had the important advantage of working in a setting characterized by a relatively small and stable prison population. Between 1922 and 1939, annual receptions into prison hovered around the figure of 45,000, and the daily average population in prison never went much over 11,000. The prison estate shrank in consequence. Between 1914 and 1932, 29 out of 56 prisons were closed, female wings were closed in at least eight prisons, and capacity, or certified accommodation, declined from 22,872 in 1908 to 19,600 in 1930.[9] The process was accelerated by the request for savings emanating in 1922 from the Geddes Committee.[10] No prison construction took place in the inter-war years, though a handful of borstal institutions for young offenders were opened. Of course, such retrenchment did not alter one fact, as Herbert Gladstone recognized in 1922: the old prison structures overseen by Waller were mostly unsuitable to requirements. With their tiered corridors of cells, radiating out from a central hub, they were admirably constructed for discipline, order, cleanliness, and security, but little else. "Is it possible to conceive," Gladstone wrote, "a prison worse adapted to its purposes than for example Strangeways in Manchester?"[11] Even so, the prison commissioners had the space, resources, and public support to allow experimentation in penal practice. The chairman of the Prison Commission also enjoyed considerable autonomy. Subject to the statutory rules made under the Prison Act 1898 (which transferred rule-making powers from Parliament to the Home Office), and to the Home Secretary's general consent, the Commission was responsible for formulating and applying policy, and for superintending and inspecting penal institutions. As the reviewer of Lionel Fox's *The Modern English Prison* recognized, "this elastic procedure has made it possible for changes to be effected in accordance with

---

8   For a fuller account of the "liberal progressivism" of the prison commissioners, the penal reformers, and some of the Home Office mandarins (notably Maurice Waller and Alexander Maxwell), including what I termed "The Social Conception of Delinquency," see chapter one above, *passim*; and Bailey, *Delinquency and Citizenship*, op cit., chaps. 1 and 8. The emphasis in this previous work is on the religious and moral impulses in reformation, not yet become secularized and psychologized.

9   A. Rutherford, *Prisons and the Process of Justice* (1984), pp. 131, 147; TNA, HO45/12934/191335/27; *The Times*, 14 Feb. 1922, p. 10; *Hansard*, vol. 262, 25 Feb. 1932, col. 537.

10 TNA, HO45/19680/430010/1.

11 Gladstone's review of S. Hobhouse's pamphlet, *Prisons of Today* (1922), Viscount Gladstone Papers, BL, Add. MSS, 46117, folios 5–12. In an unpublished essay, "Prison Reform 1895," dated 20 May 1924, Gladstone wrote, "The cost of complete reconstruction is too great for any Govt. to propose in present times... Reconstruction of all Prisons is what is now most wanted." See Add. MSS, 46117, folio 13.

experience and with developments in public opinion, without the delay which recurrent fresh legislation would have involved."[12]

What was the overarching objective of the prison commissioners? It was to regard imprisonment as an opportunity for training rather than for punishment. To attain this objective, two components were needed: one negative, one positive. On the negative side, Harold Scott explained many years later,

> we must do away . . . with any features of prison life that will be harmful to the physical or mental well-being of the prisoner. He must be properly housed, clothed and fed, and must have proper medical attention and opportunities for exercise. We must do away also with those features which would tend to take away the prisoner's self-respect or to emphasize the degradation of a prison sentence.[13]

Or, as the commissioners' refrain became: do not send a prisoner out worse than when he came in. The positive component was training, or the imparting to the prisoner the qualities—self-control, industry, appreciation of the other person's point of view—the lack of which, it was believed, led to the commission of crime and imprisonment.[14] The essential accessory to these two components was deemed to be the proper classification of prisoners, of which more later.

What were the specific changes the Waller regime sought to implement? To appreciate the changes, it is necessary to describe first the progressive stage system, which regulated the earning of remission of a portion of an offender's imprisonment as well as the allocation of privileges. There were three rates of earned remission: one-sixth of the whole sentence for local prisoners serving more than one month, one-quarter for male convicts, and one-third for female convicts. The earning of remission was regulated by the award of marks, entered weekly on the stage register which hung outside the local prisoner's cell door, given for good

12 "What Imprisonment Means," *Times Literary Supplement*, 19 Apr. 1934, p. 276. See also TNA, HO45/10913/A60340/75, E. Ruggles Brise, 25 Feb. 1919.
13 PCom9/39: Scott memo, 28 Oct. 1937; Templewood Papers (Cambridge University Library), Box X. 7/6a.
14 In their annual report for 1922–3, the prison commissioners defined their objects as follows: "… to construct a system of training such as will fit the prisoner to re-enter the world as a citizen. To this end the first requisite is greater activity in mind and body, and the creation of habits of sustained industry… Next comes the removal of any features of unnecessary degradation in prison life, and the promotion of self-respect, and education on broad lines calculated to arouse some intelligent interests … Finally we endeavour to awaken some sense of personal responsibility by the gradual and cautious introduction of methods of limited trust." Quoted in John Watson, "The Prison System," in L. Radzinowicz and J. W. C. Turner (eds.), *Penal Reform in England* (1946, 2nd ed.), p. 164. L. W. Fox's most succinct description of the administration's policy was an attempt "to justify the optimism of the [Gladstone] Committee against Sir Godfrey [Lushington's] pessimism [in his evidence to the Gladstone Committee]: *The Modern English Prison* (1934), p. 31.

conduct and industry. The marks were also translated into progressive stages. The stage system was, said Fox,

> a method of preserving discipline, the theory being that the well-behaved prisoner should have increasing "privileges" to look forward to as he passed from one "stage" to the next, and that fear of losing his privileges once they were earned would preserve him in well doing.[15]

For *local prisoners*, each of the first three stages lasted for four weeks. The routine of the first stage was separate cellular confinement; in the second stage the prisoner moved to associated labour in workshop or corridor, and secured a half-hour of exercise on Sunday plus a book of fiction in addition to the "educational book" each week. Entrance into the third stage, after two months, was marked by a visit of a family member or friend of 20 minutes' duration, and the chance to write a letter and receive a reply to it. The fourth stage, after three months, brought the maximum amount of privileges. A second visit and second letter were allowed six weeks after the first, and visits and letters were obtainable at the end of each succeeding four-week period. In fact, it was not until the fourth stage that the privileges could be said to count for anything. For a majority of prisoners, unfortunately, the remission and stage system were purely academic, since close to 60 per cent of the sentences of imprisonment were for periods not exceeding one month. Not until 1934 was any change made to the stage system for prisoners, when greater eligibility for concerts and lectures, library books, letters and visits, and cell recreations was realized.[16]

As for male *convicts*, a new progressive stage system was introduced in 1921–2, modifying "much of the rigour incidental to a sentence of penal servitude." There were to be four stages: ordinary, probation, superior, and special. "Each stage confers a little relaxation on the convicts," wrote former convict Wilfred Macartney, "exiguous enough in all conscience, but nevertheless eagerly sought for."[17] There were no rewards on first stage. A convict who had earned marks representing two years of the sentence (later reduced to one and a half years) would pass into the probation stage, when he could be brought out of the cell in the evening on certain days in the week to sit silently on stools, occasionally to take part in readings and lectures. A year later he could be admitted to the privileges of the superior stage, namely shaving and hair-cutting, a looking-glass and wash-stand, one hour's talking exercise on alternate evenings and on Sundays. After four years

---

15 L. W. Fox, *The Modern English Prison* (1934), pp. 79–80. See also G. Rusche and O. Kirchheimer, *Punishment and Social Structure* (New York, 1968; first pub. 1939), pp. 153–6; Ruck (ed), *Paterson on Prisons*, op cit., pp. 86–9.
16 See Ibid., pp. 78–81; TNA, PCom9/102, Fox memo, 23 Jan. 1933; L. Athill, "The British Prison: IV. Discipline," *Spectator*, 22 Oct. 1937, p. 677.
17 TNA, PCom7/283; Wilfred Macartney, *Walls Have Mouths: A Record of Ten Years' Penal Servitude* (1936), p. 259. See also Rose, *Struggle*, op cit., p. 114. "Convicts" were those sentenced to long terms of penal servitude for serious crimes, as distinct from "prisoners" who were sentenced to ordinary imprisonment for no more than two years.

of his sentence, with exemplary conduct, he could pass into the special stage, when in addition he would be allowed to earn a tiny gratuity for the purchase of tobacco and a weekly newspaper. There were also progressive relaxations in the number of letters and visits. No letter or visit was allowed for the first four months of the sentence, and not until the special stage could the convict have a letter and visit once a month. Rules drawn up in 1924 allowed notebooks and pencils to be issued when a convict had completed six months of his sentence, later reduced to three months, in order to enable a prisoner to take full advantage of any course of study, and on condition that no attempt was made to write about prison conditions or to keep a diary of his prison life. The main defects of the scheme were that stage privileges did not come into force until convicts had served two years, and they were permissive not compulsory, and thus subject to the discretion of governors.[18]

Beyond the privileges accorded by the progressive stage system, the prison commissioners introduced changes that sought the mitigation or amelioration of the punitive and harmful features of detention. The close cropping of convicts' heads and the broad-arrow mark on prison uniform were abolished.[19] Shaving was allowed (ideally, along with bathing, outside of labour hours). Purely penal labour in the form of the treadwheel and crank was phased out from 1896 (though oakum picking lived on); prisoners were increasingly employed in a variety of occupations in workshops, with an eight-hour working day. The "honour party" system was extended to local prisons, and selected prisoners were allowed to work on their own in a workshop or in the grounds under the direction of a "leader" drawn from their own number. The silence rule was relaxed: conversation was allowed in workshops, though the commissioners hastened to add that this did not mean idle gossip or persistent conversation.[20] Some governors had gone ahead of the commissioners: at Parkhurst convict prison, those undergoing long sentences, and the "weak-minded" class were already allowed to speak to one another.[21] A prisoner was to receive sufficient diet to enable him to perform the work allotted to him. Selected prisoners were allowed to associate for meals and recreation; evening classes and weekly lectures were instituted; an educational adviser to the governor was appointed in almost all prisons; prison libraries were improved; and voluntary workers were invited (unless they had been a conscientious objector during the war, and on condition they did not publicize their prison work) to pay social calls on male prisoners in their cells in the evenings and at weekends, expanding a

18 PCom9/112; HO45/14810/595074/1; Stuart Wood, *Shades of the Prison House* (1932), pp. 310, 317–8.
19 The mark of the broad arrow represented the badge of the Sidney family, one of whom was Master of the Ordnance in the sixteenth century. It was adopted to mark ordnance and other government stores and subsequently convict clothing. See TNA, HO45/ 12566/209069/1–2; PCom7/314.
20 For the prison commissioners' first attempt in March 1922 to define how far inmates should be allowed to talk, both among themselves and between officers and prisoners, see TNA, PCom7/475.
21 TNA, HO45/20330/197277/42, Colonel Hughes-D'Aeth, Governor of Parkhurst, 15 Jul. 1920.

service that before was restricted to women prisoners. No longer was a prisoner required to stand with his face to the wall whenever a visitor passed. New forms of physical exercise were to replace the deadly trudge around a ring. Visiting boxes were replaced by tables and chairs, though in the larger prisons, owing to the number of visits, the boxes continued to be used (the wires and bars at least replaced by clear glass). Compulsory attendance at chapel services on weekdays and Sundays was suspended (attendance became voluntary), and the high seats facing the prisoners in chapels for prison officers to surveil their charges were removed. The weekly news reading was meant to keep prisoners in touch with the outside world, as was the printed news sheet that took its place. Transfer by rail of prisoners between prisons was to be carried out in civilian clothes, not in prison dress and chains.[22]

In the wake of these changes the number of punishments for violation of prison regulations fell. In convict prisons the percentage of male prisoners punished decreased from 37.4 per cent in 1902–7 to 13.4 per cent in 1930; in local prisons the percentage punished decreased from 12.8 per cent in 1913–14 to 4.3 per cent in 1930.[23] It is difficult to know how to interpret these figures, however. It could mean that prisoners were now better-behaved, or that prison discipline was more lenient. The commissioners were at pains to argue that discipline was as firm as ever, but that a more constructive approach in the prisons led to a better response and better behavior by prisoners.[24] With this set of changes, the prison commissioners thought of themselves as in the van of prison reform. Soon after the 1925 London Congress of the International Prison Commission, Waller and Paterson reached the conclusion that the IPC might usefully draft a statement of what civilized countries considered to be the minimum standard of prison conditions. The two of them drafted an outline

---

22 For all these administrative changes, see TNA, PCom7/314; PCom7/465; PCom9/67; PCom9/141; HO45/20330/197277/42; HO45/20385/441758/2–7; HO45/15189/570791/5; HO45/16515/375684/55A; HO45/17515/656577/5; HO144/8278/504928/3; HO144/10565/467827/38; *Annual Report of the Prison Commissioners for 1923–24*, Parl. Papers (PP) 1924–25, XV (2307), pp. 353–4; "Prison Reform," *Justice of the Peace*, 19 May 1923, p. 393; "The New Prison Discipline," *Justice of the Peace*, 1 Dec. 1923, p. 824; Howard League, Minute Books, 24 Mar. 1927, "Education in Prisons Bill," Modern Records Centre, MSS 16B/1/1; *Hansard*, vol. 182, 8 Apr. 1925, col. 2247; G. D. Turner, "Five Years of Progress in Penal Administration," *Contemporary Review*, vol. 138 (1930), pp. 207–8; Sir Edward Troup, *The Home Office* (2nd ed. 1926), p. 117; Ruck (ed), *Paterson on Prisons*, pp. 82–5; H. Llewellyn Smith, *The New Survey of London Life and Labour* (1935), vol. 9, pp. 370–1. See also H. Cronin, *The Screw Turns* (1967), p. 53; Rose, *Struggle*, p. 111; W. J. Forsythe, *Penal Discipline, Reformatory Projects and the English Prison Commission 1895–1939* (Exeter, 1990), p. 175; H. Johnston, "Prison histories, 1770–1950s," in Y. Jewkes et al. (eds.), *Handbook on Prisons*, (2016), p. 35. The use of leg irons and cross chains for prisoners re-captured after escaping was also discontinued in 1922: HO45/11077/407837.

23 Edwin H. Sutherland, "The Decreasing Prison Population of England," *Journal of Criminal Law and Criminology*, vol. 24 (1934), p. 899.

24 See Fox, *The Modern English Prison*, pp. 85–6.

for the standard treatment of prisoners and circulated it in 1927 to various other countries.[25]

One other change in penal administration requires more extended discussion, since it was deemed by the Prison Commission to be the greatest change in the method of treatment since 1914. It concerns what Harold Scott in 1937 described as "the abandonment of the old faith in the value of solitary confinement," with the related issue of the legal distinction between sentences of imprisonment with and without "hard labour."[26] Since 1919, males imprisoned with hard labour had worked for the first 14 days in separate cellular confinement, and had slept on a plank bed rather than a mattress. In the large majority of sentences of imprisonment, courts could not resist adding "with hard labour." After 14 days, the conditions of imprisonment with hard labour were the same as those of simple imprisonment in the third division (very few prisoners were ever assigned by the courts to the first or second division). For women, there was no distinction of any kind between sentences with or without hard labour.[27] Convicts also spent a period of time at the start of a penal servitude sentence in separate confinement. In July 1922, the prison commissioners were considering whether to advise the Home Secretary to do away with separate confinement altogether, except as a punishment, "on the general ground," wrote Waller, "that solitude and introspection do nobody any good and generally do harm."[28] They decided to try the following new arrangements for an experimental period of six months.

All convicts on arrival at a convict prison would be placed in association immediately, undergoing no separate confinement. In the local prison, where convicts spent two or three weeks prior to removal, governors would have the discretion to leave the prisoner's cell door open, or place him in associated work, as

25 TNA, PCom7/61, Paterson to Waller, 28 Jun. 1928. See also B. Forsythe, "National Socialists and the English Prison Commission: The Berlin Penitentiary Congress of 1935," *International Journal of the Sociology of Law*, vol. 17 (1989), pp. 135–6.

26 Scott, 26 Feb. 1937, TNA, HO45/18006/546730/48. "Hard labour," or punishment by forced physical labour, including in Victorian times the crank and the treadwheel, was introduced to teach prisoners the value of hard work, and to deter others from committing crime. For the crank and treadwheel, see the illustrations *infra*. As far back as 1910, the chairman of the Prison Commission, E. Ruggles Brise, had called for the abolition of the distinction between sentences with and without hard labour, minuting on 29 Oct. 1910: "This distinction has long since ceased to have any meaning; it greatly hampers the administration: it confuses the Courts...": TNA, HO144/18869/196919/4. Troup explained that under the regime introduced in 1898, the treadwheel and crank had gone (though see the Preston treadwheel in 1902 in the illustrations *infra*), so there was no "hard labour" in the old sense. The plank bed survived for adult males under 60 years of age sentenced to hard labour, and that for only the first 14 days of the sentence: *The Home Office* (1926, 2nd. ed.), p. 117.

27 Separate confinement of women prisoners during the first month of their sentence had never been imposed by the prison rules: *Hansard*, vol. 138, 22 Feb. 1921, col. 745.

28 Waller to Polwarth (Prison Commissioner for Scotland), 30 Jun. 1922, TNA, PCom7/312. According to *The Times*, 7 Jul. 1928, Waller "hated solitary confinement; he refused to believe that a cell, however it might be equipped, could provide a proper environment for the regeneration of human character."

soon as it was thought desirable to do so, while retaining the right to insist the prisoner work in his cell with the door locked for the first few days.[29] As for local prisoners, men sentenced to hard labour for any period over one month would work in association from the start of their sentence, unless the governor thought a few days' separation was necessary on account of the physical or mental condition of the man on reception. Men sentenced to a month or less would be left to the governor's discretion, subject to the maximum limit of 14 days' separate confinement, as to whether the prisoner should be associated at once, kept in separate confinement for 14 days, or brought into association at some intermediate date. In their letter to the Home Secretary asking for agreement to these arrangements, the commissioners argued:

> The view has been held that it [solitude] led to meditation over past misdeeds, and repentance for them. But the Commissioners think, on the contrary, that it usually leads to morbid introspection, tendencies to suicide, or to sullen, morose, and revengeful feelings.[30]

The stumbling block for the Home Office was that these directions would reduce the distinction between a sentence of hard labour and a sentence of simple imprisonment almost to vanishing point. If a man with a hard-labour sentence were to be placed in association from the start, the only thing that would distinguish him from the man sentenced to simple imprisonment would be a plank bed without a mattress for the first 14 days. Any distinction based on the "hardness" of labour had long since disappeared. Indeed, the hard labour exacted during the period of separate confinement was thought to be the softer kind of work—sewing bags or picking fibre—because it had to be done in the man's own cell. Harder labour was done in association, though no distinction was made between "hard labour men" and "simple imprisonment men" in the type of work done. For this reason, while the Home Office accepted the experimental change for convicts, and a circular went out to prison governors in August 1922, the department deferred the "local prison" part of the commissioners' arrangements, on the grounds that the abolition of separate confinement would nullify or at least further whittle down the order for "hard labour," which increased the deterrent effect of a sentence. Hard labour was, for Ernley Blackwell, "almost a fraud upon the courts which pass it."[31] Waller himself accepted that judges and magistrates were still apt to think that a sentence of hard labour was a much more severe sentence than one of simple imprisonment. H. B. Simpson tried to hold the punitive line, arguing,

---

29 The experiment with convicts proved "a distinct success," and the provisional arrangement was confirmed: Waller to Home Secretary, 26 Sept. 1924: TNA, HO45/13658/185668/26.

30 Prison commissioners to Home Secretary, 7 Jul. 1922, PCom7/312.

31 Blackwell minute, 29 Jul. 1922, TNA, HO45/13658/185668/21; Waller minute, 14 Aug. 1922, PCom7/312.

The Prison Commissioners in their anxiety to get rid of everything in prison discipline that can be called "degrading" seem to have forgotten that a considerable proportion of prisoners ought to feel ashamed of their misdeeds and don't. It is surely part of a proper prison discipline to produce this effect on offenders whose moral sense is defective.

Finally, Blackwell, and the Permanent Undersecretary of State, Sir John Anderson, insisted that if separate confinement were abolished for local prisoners, hard labour should be retained, and means found for differentiating between "hard labour men" and "simple imprisonment men.".[32]

At this point, in December 1924, the commissioners decided to let the matter drop, though still of the view that separate confinement for prisoners in local prisons was undesirable in itself. Reality could not be given to the distinction between a hard-labour sentence and simple imprisonment.[33] In the meantime, the prison commissioners allowed the governor of Wandsworth prison, at his request, to allocate male prisoners between 21 and 26, in the so-called "special class," to their works party as soon as they were received, dispensing with the 14 days of separate confinement. And by the end of 1924, governors at several local prisons had in practice abolished separate confinement for all hard-labour prisoners.[34] However, it was not until 1931 that the 14 days separate confinement was formally abolished, leaving only the prescription of no mattress for the first 14 days of a hard-labour sentence passed on a man.

This entire discussion brings us to the positive side of the prison commissioners' general objective. The next chairman of the Prison Commission, Alexander Maxwell, concisely spelled out the commissioners' objection to "hard labour":

The conception of a hard labour sentence as something more severe and deterrent than an ordinary sentence of imprisonment is irreconcilable with the modern doctrine that the loss of liberty is the punishment, and that the period of imprisonment should be utilized not to inflict punitive tasks on the offender but to train him as far as possible in habits of industry.[35]

The idea by the 1920s was to train offenders to habits of industry by inducing an interest in work. Labour in prison was not meant to be penal but an essential part of the reformative training. All offenders should do a full day's work: eight hours of

32 Simpson minute, 13 Jul. 1923, HO45/13658/185668/23. For Simpson, assistant secretary, a classical scholar and authority on the criminal law, capricious and eccentric in later career, see Harold Scott, *Your Obedient Servant* (1959), p. 61. For Anderson, see G. C. Peden, "Anderson, John, first Viscount Waverley (1882–1958)," *Oxford DNB* (2016). For Ernley Blackwell, Legal Assistant Undersecretary of State, 1913–33, see Gladstone to Churchill, 19 Feb. 1910 in R. Churchill, *Winston Churchill: Companion Volume*, vol. 2, part 2 (1969), p. 1139.
33 Waller to Home Office, 24 Dec. 1924, HO45/13658/185668/26.
34 PCom7/312.
35 Maxwell minute, 28 Nov. 1929, TNA, HO45/13658/185668/29.

associated labour (plus two hours of cellular labour or, in lieu, two hours mental employment). This, however, was only part of the prison commissioners' over-arching goal. In their annual report for 1923, they described at length how they sought to mitigate the elements in prison life that led to physical and mental deterioration, to change the offender's anti-social outlook, and to restore the pris-oner to ordinary standards of citizenship:

> Since the offender has to return to ordinary life, take his place as a citizen, and earn his living, at some time in the future which is usually not far distant, our object is to fit him for those duties. The means to this end are fairly long hours of hard and steady work at an occupation which shall, if possible, give such industrial training as will enable him to earn a living; the removal of needless degradations and the encouragement of self-respect; and, in the evenings, well-considered education suitable for backward or unbalanced adults. To these are added visiting by voluntary workers of a strong character and perso-nal influence; and . . . such measures of trust as will awaken a sense of personal responsibility. The prison day should be hard, but the object is not mere severity . . . The aim is to make a citizen by quickening and directing the activities of both mind and body.[36]

Likewise, Paterson, guided by the Toc H ideals of friendship, fairmindedness, ser-vice, and the Christian nostrum of the value of the individual soul, was convinced that the primary aim of a prison system was to educate the offender. In response to those who would complain of undue leniency in the treatment of prisoners, Paterson coined his other renowned aphorism, "Men come to prison *as* a punish-ment not *for* punishment," to which he added, "It is doubtful whether any of the amenities granted in some modern prisons can in any way compensate for the punishment involved in the deprivation of liberty." He therefore challenged the supposed contradiction between reform and punishment:

> The changing of habits and the growth of self-control is an arduous and thorny process for any man or woman . . . There is then no real dilemma between a reformatory and punitive basis for prison treatment, for any training that is truly reformatory is also truly punitive.[37]

III

There is more to say about the discrete ways in which the Prison Commission sought to transform the penal system, and notably about its scheme to classify

---

36 Quoted in Fox, *The Modern English Prison* (1934), p. 40.
37 Ruck, *Paterson on Prisons*, op cit., p. 13; Paterson, *German Prisons* (1922), p. 3. See also K. Downing and B. Forsythe, "The Reform of Offenders in England, 1830–1995: A Circular Debate," *Criminal Justice History*, vol. 18 (2003), p. 152.

prisoners and prisons, but first we should offer an initial appraisal of the changes made to diminish the physical and mental deterioration of prisoners. Historians have had a tendency to take these changes at face value, citing chapter and verse from the annual reports of the prison commissioners. This, despite the warning from the Webbs at the end of their *English Prisons Under Local Government* that the commissioners' policy was "to ensure that the only source of authoritative information about what is going on in our prisons should be the series of annual reports by the Commissioners themselves . . ."[38] And this, despite the strong claim by criminologist, John Pratt, that official discourse in the form of the annual reports "has mainly determined 'the reality' of what prison is like and how the public at large have come to 'know' about this institution and the life contained within it," to the exclusion of alternative accounts by penal reformers, the press, or prisoners themselves.[39] Prisons were only ever inspected by "insiders," each assistant commissioner being responsible for the administration and inspection of a group of prisons or borstal institutions, which he visited twice a year. Visiting justices were attached to each prison, and in 1927 they began to hold an annual conference, sending resolutions for improvements to the Home Office, following each conference, which the department, in fairness, greeted as a source of independent comment and advice on prison administration.[40] In addition, the incontestability of official truth was buttressed by the Official Secrets Act 1920, which made it an offence for prison officials to disclose information about the prison system without permission, which the commissioners rarely gave.

We need to turn a critical eye upon the supposed ameliorations of prison life. For a start, the success of the system of progressive stage privileges was undermined by a number of weaknesses. First, the daily award of marks was cumbrous and its administration became more and more perfunctory. Full marks were invariably given, officers finding it easier to report prisoners for idleness, sending them to the governor for adjudication, than to incur the hostility of prisoners by taking off marks themselves. Second, the system rewarded conformism, the "good prisoner" who toed the line. It operated as a negative check on misconduct and idleness, not as an incentive to good conduct and industry, which is why the commissioners

---

38 S. and B. Webb, *English Prisons Under Local Government* (1963, first pub.1922), pp. 237–8.

39 John Pratt, *Punishment and Civilization: Penal Tolerance and Intolerance in Modern Society* (2002), p. 12. See idem., "Towards the 'Decivilizing' of Punishment?" *Social and Legal Studies: An International Journal*, vol. 7 (1998), p. 488; idem., "The Acceptable Prison: Official Discourse, Truth and Legitimacy in the Nineteenth Century," in G. Gilligan and J. Pratt (eds.), *Crime, Truth and Justice* (2004), p. 72. See also, Forsythe, *Penal Discipline and the English Prison Commission* (1990), p. 243.

40 E. Stockdale, "A Short History of Prison Inspection in England," *British Journal of Criminology*, vol. 23 (1983), p. 222; TNA, HO45/20084/482137/2–25. Judicial scrutiny of prisons provided no substitute. In Feb. 1939, the Home Office informed the Commons that during the preceding five years, only 12 visits had been paid by HM Judges to prisons. In view of the number of King's Bench judges, the average during this period was one visit per judge every ten years, or once during the average judicial lifespan. See Leo Page, *The Sentence of the Court* (1948), p. 62.

ultimately introduced a system of pay for work done. Third, privileges that took a prisoner time to earn (such as receiving visits and letters) were often needed for training purposes at an earlier stage of the sentence, which is why the commissioners started experimenting with the model (from American example) of giving privileges from the start of the sentence, requiring the prisoner to hold on to them by good behaviour.[41]

As for the other ameliorations, it was up to the first Lady Inspector of Prisons, Dr. Mary Gordon, who resigned in 1921, in her unofficial study, *Penal Discipline*, to acknowledge the fact of mental and physical deterioration during the prison sentence, and to issue a pre-emptive strike against promised mitigations. She wrote,

> The piano, concert, educational lecture, or other amusements and recreations, the newspaper . . . we bestow on our captive to enable her to bear our discipline better—to "lighten" the imprisonment . . . [T]he bitter pill of penal discipline cannot be disguised in this minute quantity of jam.

Gordon could see no point in trying to improve the local prison system, so few were deterred or reformed. The system was "a gigantic irrelevance—a social curiosity." A prison was a place of "suspended animation . . . .In it you hibernate—you don't do penance, you do 'time.'" She had no good word to say for the prison system. "I think it creates a criminal class, and directly fosters recidivism . . . and in need of decent cremation."[42] Gordon's scepticism about piecemeal ameliorations is borne out by other evidence. The adherence to the "less eligibility" maxim set narrow limits to the improvement of prison conditions.[43] In many prisons, especially ones with a daily average population of over a thousand, work and education were severely hampered by the restless atmosphere created by prisoners streaming in and out of the place. Prisoners continued to live under an iron compulsion, every act and movement controlled, any individuality stripped from them, addressed by number not name, with few opportunities to exercise initiative or judgment.[44] The squalor and unhygienic

41 TNA, PCom9/102, Fox memo, 23 Jan. 1933.
42 M. Gordon, *Penal Discipline* (1922), pp. 204–6 and 145. See also H. E. Barnes, review of *Penal Discipline, Journal of Social Forces*, vol. 2 (1924), pp. 604–5; *British Medical Journal*, vol. 1 (1941), p. 800 (obituary); B. Forsythe, "Women Prisoners and Women Penal Officials 1840–1921," *British Journal of Criminology*, vol. 33 (1993), pp. 537–8; D. Cheney, "Dr Mary Louisa Gordon (1861–1941): A Feminist Approach to Prison," *Feminist Legal Studies*, vol. 18 (2010), pp. 115–36. Arthur Locke in the Home Office claimed that Gordon's book contained nothing constructive, and offered no solutions: TNA, HO45/11543/357055/67.
43 See H. Mannheim, *The Dilemma of Penal Reform* (1939), pp. 56–9, 67–8; Rusche and Kirchheimer, *Punishment and Social Structure* (1968), pp. 151, 159.
44 Security also still dominated prisons. L. W. Fox, in an address to Recorders in Dec. 1943 stated, "It would not be unfair to say that for a long time after the Gladstone report there was still more sorrow in Whitehall over the one prisoner who escaped safe-custody than over the ninety and nine who escaped reform." See TNA, Lord Chancellor's Office, LCO2/3352.

character of "slopping out" each morning, as prisoners took their sewage to communal drains, went on as before. The initial period of total separation may have ended, use of the cellular system restricted to meals and sleeping, but local prisoners and convicts could still spend from 16 to 18 hours alone in their cells, especially at weekends when fewer staff were on duty.[45] In 1929, the deputy-governor of Parkhurst, in an internal memorandum on the harmful effects of a sentence of penal servitude, claimed that convicts spent from two-thirds to three-quarters of their sentence in solitary confinement.[46] In at least a quarter of the prisons no educational classes had been introduced by 1927. This was particularly the case in the convict prisons of Parkhurst and Dartmoor. At Dartmoor, no educational adviser had been appointed by 1928, and the Home Secretary ruled out any educational scheme until further experience of educational work had been gained from Maidstone and Parkhurst. Parkhurst became a storm centre in 1926–7, with disturbances breaking out over the new governor's dragooning of prisoners, and his decision to limit the number of prisoners attending lectures and concerts. In response, the local education authority refused to supply books to the prison or help appoint an educational adviser. A parliamentary reply indicated that in 1927–8, 85 per cent of Parkhurst convicts had attended no class, the reason being that many classes of convicts were ruled out: "such as aged convicts, hospital cases, weak-minded convicts, sexual perverts, violent and ill-conducted convicts."[47] Attempts to teach illiterate prisoners had been tried and abandoned at Pentonville and Wormwood Scrubs.[48]

His Majesty's prisons were lighted with thousands of gas jets ("Every prison stinks of gas," said prison governor, Lieut.-Col. Rich); not until 1935 were all the old gas lamps in cells and corridors replaced by electric lights, but the bulbs installed in cells were only 15 watts, a light that made it impossible for prisoners to read after dark.[49] Letters and visits were still painfully limited, and all letters were subject to censorship. The diet was still a monotonous and depressing round of porridge (or skilly), bread, suet, and cocoa. Dining in association was only slowly extended even among the Star and second division prisoners. As late as 1937, meals in

45 Cecil Chapman, *The Poor Man's Court of Justice: Twenty-Five Years as a Metropolitan Magistrate* (1925), p. 318; H. J. Woods, "Religion in the City of Cells," *The Congregational Quarterly*, vol. IV (1926), pp. 290–1. See also B. Forsythe, "Loneliness and Cellular Confinement in English Prisons 1878–1921," *British Journal of Criminology*, vol. 44 (2004), p. 761.

46 TNA, PCom9/43.

47 TNA, HO45/13776/498822/1–4, 23–4, 34, and 41; *Hansard*, vol. 217, 21 May 1928, col. 1580; *Hansard*, vol. 217, 23 May 1928, col. 1888–9; A. Fenner Brockway, *A New Way With Crime* (1928), p. 123. Parkhurst was a difficult prison, since it contained all the more difficult type of convicts, either mentally unstable or physically unfit for Dartmoor. See Sydney Moseley, *The Convict of To-Day* (1927), p. 97. See also Rose, *Struggle*, op cit., p. 115–6.

48 Howard League Minute Books, meeting of EC, 28 Sept. 1934, Pentonville, MSS 16B/1/2, Modern Records Centre.

49 Lieut.-Col. C. E. F. Rich, *Recollections of a Prison Governor* (1932), p. 250. See also Ann Smith, *Women in Prison* (1962), p. 170. It took until 1937 for all cells in the London prisons to be provided with 25-watt lamps: TNA, PCom9/140.

association for even a part of the population at Wandsworth prison was impossible without major structural alterations.[50] The silence rule may have been relaxed, but it created an Orwellian distinction. The offence was no longer mere talking, but talking after being told to stop talking.[51] If local prisons began working an eight-hour day, any general improvement of prison industries, especially the provision of new industries or machinery, was in the future. The prison commissioners admitted that there were still many prisons "where owing to the lack of workroom accommodation associated labour has to be carried on in the cell corridors." Again, the deputy-governor of Parkhurst insisted that the hours of labour were only 26 per week; convict prison industries required only unskilled or semi-skilled labour of an uninteresting kind; and the mark system no longer worked to incentivize hard work. Knowledge of the outside world was still largely confined to the chaplain's weekly summary of news, which was not improved until 1935, when a weekly news sheet produced at Maidstone prison was circulated to all prisons. The use of wireless sets was limited to educational purposes and third-stage recreation. The use of voluntary workers varied greatly, according to the class of prisoner (with younger and first offender prisoners given priority), to geographical location (prisons outside of cities being harder to supply with volunteers), and to the discretion of individual governors, not all of whom welcomed the new developments. In late 1926, moreover, to secure uniformity of treatment of short-sentence prisoners, the commissioners informed governors of local prisons that prisoners with sentences of a month and under (representing 60 per cent of all imprisonment sentences) would attend neither lectures nor concerts (except sacred music in the chapel), and would not be eligible for consideration for educational classes (in lieu of which they would perform an evening task).[52] Finally, no clear legal norms existed for complaints, so few prisoners complained, lest they worsen their plight. The custom at Parkhurst, and at other prisons too, was not even to hear convict witnesses when convicts were charged or made charges.[53]

Finally, on some issues the pace of change remained snail-like. Take smoking. Convicts who had reached the "special stage" of a penal servitude sentence, after four years, and preventive detainee convicts from the start of the sentence could spend part of their earnings on smoking materials; local prisoners were not allowed to have tobacco and anyway had no earned income. Waller informed the Home Office in early 1926 that the Prison Officers' Representative Board had forwarded a resolution asking the commissioners not to introduce smoking "lest trafficking

50   TNA, HO45/18006/546730/57.
51   As late as 1931, Blackwell could still minute: "As to 'talking' it has no doubt advantages but it is productive of a good deal of mischief in the way of trafficking, scheming etc.": TNA, HO144/20087/341623; *Hansard*, vol. 318, 24 Nov. 1936, col. 249.
52   TNA, PCom7/299; PCom9/41; HO45/17515/656577/5; Annual Report of PCom for 1934, PP, 1935–6, XIV (Cmd. 5153), pp. 462–5. Exercise facilities left much to be desired (PCom9/53: gymnastic apparatus, 1930), and boxing was discontinued in all prisons in Jun. 1931 (PCom9/198). The prison commissioners were nothing if not comprehensive, even formulating rules for the keeping of pet mice in convict prisons.
53   See Rusche and Kirkhheimer, op. cit., p. 157.

should take place in tobacco, and suspicion fall on officers." Waller minuted supportively: "We are making considerable calls on our staff for duties which are not wholly welcome to them, to which on the whole they are responding well. It will be sound policy to concede this point to their wishes."[54] As late as 1931, Maxwell was still not willing to allow convicted prisoners to smoke, and signaled that if it ever came, prisoners "should earn the privilege by a special effort in industry." He was willing to allow trial and remand prisoners at Brixton to smoke at exercise, and in 1934 the concession was extended to such prisoners at other prisons. Additionally, at all borstal institutions (for males and females), and at Wakefield and Maidstone prisons, for men, where pilot earnings schemes were in operation, inmates could purchase tobacco as soon as they started to earn, after 12 weeks at Wakefield, after 12 months at Maidstone.[55]

IV

Nowhere does the official information on the pace and direction of change in the prisons find less corroboration than in the writings of prisoners themselves. Historians value prisoner memoirs as important counterweights, subjective counter-discourses, or alternative knowledges to official rhetoric on the effects of imprisonment.[56] Yet they have also been seen as a flawed form of testimony. It is true that as a genre there is an over-representation of articulate "political" prisoners, or those who might be thought to suffer most from the indignities of prison life, and of offenders doing long sentences of penal servitude in convict prisons. And they are almost all gendered male. But is their testimony inherently unreliable? M. Hamblin Smith, medical officer of Birmingham prison, claimed that accounts of prison life by ex-prisoners were written by suffragettes and conscientious objectors, or by highly educated fraudsters, and could supply "no satisfactory account of the effect of prison life upon the ordinary type of prisoner." Harold Nicholson's *Daily Telegraph* review of Wilfred Macartney's *Walls Have Mouths: A Record of Ten Years' Penal Servitude* (which reached a sale of 35,000 copies in the first three weeks), contained the damning statement, "I am suspicious of books written by discharged prisoners. They are tempted to release their accumulated rancor by exaggerating small grievances and by dramatizing their own suffering." A riposte to this accusation appeared in Stuart Wood's *Shades of the Prison House*: "Surely there is nothing strange or unnatural in a person writing strongly about experiences which have made a deep and lasting impression upon him, nor does it follow that his experiences are exaggerated." Even Maxwell in the Home Office observed that it would

54 TNA, HO45/20055/468129/2: Waller minute, 30 Jan. 1926; HO45/18006/546730/48.
55 Home Office minute, 7 Dec. 1936: TNA, HO45/20055/468129/6–8.
56 Pratt, *Punishment and Civilization*, op cit., pp. 97–8; Alyson Brown and Emma Clare, "A History of Experience: Exploring Prisoners' Accounts of Incarceration," in C. Emsley (ed.), *The Persistent Prison: Problems, Images and Alternatives* (2005), p. 68; Alyson Brown, *Inter-War Penal Policy and Crime in England* (2013), p. 132.

be difficult to respond to Macartney, partly because he produces his effect less by specific statements than by his suggestions of the evil atmosphere of prison life, and partly because "the resulting impression that prison life is a very unpleasant and unnatural life—a fertile soil for evil—is not untrue."[57] So while accepting that those who recounted their prison experience in memoirs were hardly typical of the prison population, the evidence in prisoner testimonies is worth sampling—especially since no one can seriously claim that *official* testimony is inherently reliable.

First, memoirs served to give an impression of the overall role of the prison. They depicted the crushing burden of prison discipline. Prisoners had no choice but to accept the lack of dignity in the reception process, the stripping of identity (numbers substituted for names), the rigid routine, the silence, isolation and powerlessness, the incarceration in antiquated buildings, the deadweight of a century of retributive penal philosophy and practice. Conformity, passive obedience, subservience to prison rules, the "good prisoner" is what the system was in place to create, and woe betide anyone who kicked against the traces.[58] Secondly, prisoners displayed a universal cynicism towards the new changes in prison discipline. Stuart Wood was particularly sardonic:

> Prisons are no longer penal institutions, but schools for the inculcation of the ethics of civic responsibility . . . Even if books and reports did not tell me all this I should still know it is true, because I have heard these wonderful doctrines expounded, as it were, *ex cathedra*. For have I not sat in the chapel of a large convict prison listening to the Governor announcing the Millenium? . . . Six hundred somewhat sceptical lags were one day assembled at Parkhurst to hear the glad tidings. We learnt . . . that we had been sent to penal servitude not to be "punished," but "reformed."[59]

For Wood, the reforms of the 1920s were whitewash "to hide the essential rottenness of the structure." They were palliatives not remedies. "Society treats its criminals a little more humanely in its prisons, but its humanity is merely the

---

57 M. Hamblin Smith, *Prisons and a Changing Civilization* (1934), pp. 102–3. See also Vera Brittain, "The Forgotten Prisoner," in *Prisoners' Circle: Essays by Ex-Prisoners* (Prison Medical Reform Council, 1943), p. 3. For the libel action, Macartney v. Daily Telegraph, Ltd., see TNA, HO144/21206/492391/53 and 45; S. Wood, *Shades of the Prison House* (1932), p. v; Maxwell minute, 30 Jan. 1937: HO144/21206/492391/53. Macartney was convicted of spying for the USSR, and spent the years 1928–35 in Parkhurst prison. His memoir, *Walls Have Mouths*, was published by the Left Book Club.

58 W. Harris, "The Convict's Life," *Spectator*, 18 Sep. 1936, p. 448. Cf. Pratt, *Punishment and Civilization*, op cit., pp. 113–8. The humiliating routines suggest a continued desire to express punitive passions and moral censure. Cf. Harold Garfinkel, "Conditions of Successful Degradation Ceremonies," *American Journal of Sociology*, vol. LXI (1956), pp. 420–4.

59 Wood, op cit., p. 241. Wood was sentenced to three years penal servitude in 1915. As such, his experience pre-dated the improvements of the 1920s, but he paid close attention following release to changes in prison conditions.

surface humanity shown towards the caged bird."[60] "I write coldly," said Jim Phelan, "that the tangle of ideological contradictions called the English Jail System is one large and foolish lie, surrounded by a myriad smaller lies called reforms which hide the greater one."[61] Thirdly, prisoners were extremely aware of the limited application of the ameliorations, knowing from grim experience how illusory they could be. In part this was because of the discretion that staff possessed in the application of privileges. In Winchester in 1924, according to Wood, where the governor, a former naval commander, governed the prison as if it were a battleship, no effort was made "to introduce the social and recreational reforms sanctioned by the Home Office." Privileges had often to be wrung from the governor by prisoners. In part, it was because a large proportion of the inmates were not in prison long enough. As Wood explained,

> There is a general impression that all prisoners alike enjoy these privileges without distinction. That is quite wrong. They are granted to probably one-sixth of the entire prison population. Only men in the second and subsequent stages are eligible for such privileges, but the majority of prisoners do not get beyond the first stage owing to shortness of sentence.[62]

Not all memoirs relied solely on complaint. Macartney offered the essentials of a saner penitentiary:

> Permit talking, allow smoking, abolish flogging and bread and water; maintain discipline by the deprivation of remission and of privileges—that is to say, permit a man to smoke, associate with his fellows from the beginning of the sentence, and, in the event of bad behavior, take the privileges away.[63]

When it came to specifics, prisoners (and some prison staff) voiced much the same litany of grievances. "There was the early morning procession to the fetid 'recess,'" wrote Michael Davidson, imprisoned in Wormwood Scrubs for a homosexual offence, "an open bog used by about 50 people, carrying grotesquely one's jerry containing the stinking excretions of the night."[64] There was the ill-fitting, grey flannel uniform. Nothing, said prison governor Captain Gerold Clayton, "could be more degrading than the present quite shapeless clothing." "One's clothes," said Davidson, "were the first vehicle of humiliation one noticed: these sad grey garments seemed designed to make the biggest fool possible of one's appearance." This was an improvement, wrote Cicely McCall in the late 1930s, on what female

---

60 Ibid., p. viii.
61 J. Phelan, *Jail Journey* (1940), p. 303. Phelan served 13 years in Maidstone, Dartmoor, and Parkhurst prisons, starting his sentence of penal servitude for life in 1925. He was said to be a member of the Irish Republican Army.
62 Wood, op cit., pp. 371 and 402.
63 Macartney, op cit., p. 167.
64 M. Davidson, *The World, The Flesh and Myself* (1962), p. 175.

offenders in Holloway had to wear. "Women until quite recently were dressed as char-women, and their present costume is little better. Their underclothes are grotesque."[65] The working hours rarely approached the official claim of an eight-hour day. The anonymous author of an article in the *New Statesman and Nation*, fresh off a sentence of five years' penal servitude in Dartmoor and other prisons, claimed that working hours were less than five per day. The rest of the time was spent confined in cells. Others concurred. Prisoners insisted they were in solitary confinement for two-thirds of the time. And on weekends, said Macartney, who spent ten years in Parkhurst, "forty-three hours out of the forty-eight were spent alone behind a locked door, and frequently without a book to read."[66] Some prisoners, like Paul Pennyfeather in Evelyn Waugh's novel, *Decline and Fall*, appreciated the solitary condition. This is William Holt, a "political" prisoner, imprisoned for unlawful assembly and transferred to Wakefield: "There were times when I would have preferred solitary confinement to these 'liberties and privileges.' . . . After my work each day in the power-loom shed I returned to my cell with a monk-like joy."[67]

The cells left much to be desired. Prisoner B.2.15, with experience of Leicester, Leeds, and Wormwood Scrubs, was cold in the winter (when he slept in his clothes, and used canvas mail bags, his cell task, for bedding) and hot in the summer. Stuart Wood's cell in Dartmoor "was always extremely cold and wet as indeed were ninety per cent of the cells in this block." One of many impressions of the Scrubs that remained with Davidson was "the unvarying physical *cold* of the place."[68] Nor was it possible to read or write in the cell, according to Phelan, "as the little patch of light was only about four feet from the ground," gas-light sufficient only to allow the officer at the Judas-hole see if the prisoner was still there. "Dartmoor was not built or equipped for convicts who read or wrote."[69] Prison food was universally excoriated. "The food at Winchester [in 1924]," said Wood, "was simply awful: of bad quality, badly cooked, and always short weight, the men were half starved on food often little better than offal." The distance from the kitchens to the cell landings ensured, said governor Clayton, that "all these

65 C. McCall, *'They Always Come Back'* (1938), pp. 36–7. McCall was a prison officer in Holloway, and a qualified psychiatric social worker. She regretted the limited official interest in women's prisons, adding that "women's prisons, so far, have not produced a Macartney to describe their life." (p. 41). Cf. Pratt, *Punishment and Civilization*, op cit., pp. 105–6.

66 "Prison," *New Statesman and Nation*, 19 Mar. 1932, p. 355; Macartney, op cit., p. 93; McCall, p. 25; B.2.15, *Among the Broad-Arrow Men: A Plain Account of English Prison Life* (1924), p. 64. B.2.15 served 18 months imprisonment with hard labour in Leicester prison in 1918–19, having recently finished six months' imprisonment in Wormwood Scrubs.

67 W. Holt, *I Was a Prisoner* (1935), p. 52; idem., *I Haven't Unpacked: An Autobiography* (1939), p. 237. Holt was imprisoned for nine months for leading a demonstration of the local unemployed against the Means Test in 1932. He served time in Leeds (Armley) prison before transfer to Wakefield.

68 Wood, op cit., p. 348; Davidson, op cit., p. 174.

69 Phelan, op cit., p. 108.

attractive-sounding dishes were a pretty soggy and cool mess by the time they reached the prisoner." Macartney claimed that he asked Prison Commissioner Dr. East if a monotonous diet was harmful to a man's metabolism. When East said yes, Macartney asked "if 2,550 consecutive meals of margarine, cocoa, and cheese constituted monotony. He [East] said, 'Get out before I put you on report for insolence.'" He also claimed that the food he received in Germany as a prisoner of war was "cleaner and more nutritious and more palatable" than what he was given in Parkhurst. "In the early days of my sentence, from 1928 on, the food on certain days was uneatable even by a hungry man." An ex-burglar, who had also spent time in Parkhurst, in the first radio broadcast by a released prisoner, told his listeners that the midday meal was improved, but "the other two meals, breakfast and supper, are still the same as they were years ago."[70]

The ambiguities of the talking rule came in for derision. As Wood wrote of Dartmoor, "in order to support the illusion that the silence rule has been abolished the men are reported, not for talking, but for disobeying the order to 'stop that talking.'" The screws were particularly keen as lags exercised. As Macartney described it,

> Continual admonition to keep three feet from the man in front, and to stop talking, even when one had not uttered a word since exercise began, was very tiresome. "Open out! Close up! Stop that talking! You'll be down below [i.e. chokey]."[71]

Prisoners were counted perpetually, and searched periodically: the local prisoners in their cells, convicts in the bathhouse where they had to strip naked.[72] Prisoners were largely unpersuaded by the new prison privileges. At Parkhurst in 1928 the governor would not allow any concerts. Nor were there any educational classes. In Dartmoor, only 60 of the 500 prisoners went to classes; in Holloway 91 women out of 100 never saw the inside of a classroom, because their sentence was less than three months. Prisoners in the second stage and above were allowed to receive books from outside, subject to the chaplain's approval. Wood's experience in Wandsworth was that "the chaplain bans all books which he considers unsuitable on religious grounds." The prisoner was in conflict "with a spirit as inveterately hostile to freedom of thought as the Congregation of the Index." So, too, until 1933 when a newssheet was made available, "the amount and range of general news that the convict obtained was governed by the caprice of the chaplain," who read out news items in the chapel on Saturday for 30 minutes. Letters and visits were another bone of contention. For eight weeks after the date of conviction,

---

70 Wood, op cit., p. 372; Captain Gerold F. Clayton, *The Wall is Strong* (1958), p. 43; Macartney, op cit., p. 124; An Ex-Burglar, "Life in a Convict Prison," *The Listener*, 19 Feb., 1930, p. 313. Cf. Pratt, *Punishment and Civilization*, op cit., , p. 101.

71 Wood, op cit., p. 357; Macartney, op cit., pp. 86–7 and 148. See also B.2.15, op cit., p. 166; Phelan, op cit., p. 16. Cf. Brown and Clare, op cit., pp. 56–7.

72 B.2.15, op cit., p. 118; Macartney, op cit., p. 92; McCall, op cit., p. 194.

local prisoners in the Third Division could not send a letter. "This alone is sufficient, as I have known from actual cases, to drive men to despair and mental
anguish, if not desperation," said B.2.15. Convicts were allowed a letter on
reception, and a letter and a visit of half-an-hour after four months. For a convict
in Parkhurst, Dartmoor, or Maidstone, the privilege of visits was academic. The
cost of the trip was too high for relatives to afford. "I knew men in Parkhurst," said
Macartney, "[who] had not had visits for periods extending from two to ten
years!"[73]

And privileges were not rights. Whenever an escape occurred, said Phelan,
officers turned the clock back, and privileges were withdrawn. To complain was to
invite punishment. Macartney resignedly wrote, "the basic principle is that all
complaints against jailers are almost automatically treated as lies, and punished with
great severity." A convict could lay a complaint before the visiting magistrates, but
the judicial procedure was not encouraging: "A convict is not allowed to call evidence, not allowed to examine or cross-examine directly, not allowed to be
represented and not allowed to appeal." Officer or fellow convict could freely give
evidence against him. And magistrates were not averse to handing out sentences of
flogging, solitary confinement, or restricted diet (including dietary punishment
no.1, bread and water).[74] Prisoners also complained of the scant regard shown by
the medical staff. With few exceptions, said Macartney, Parkhurst's prison doctors
were "a heartless and indolent and incompetent crew."[75] This leaves only smoking
and sex. For the majority of prisoners, said B.2.15, being deprived of tobacco was
the chief punishment, especially in the early days of a sentence. Prison writings
typically omitted any mention of sex, in order not to offend the puritanical reader,
but Phelan made no bones about it: "Sex claimed everything—thought, vocabulary, fantasy, memory, and action."[76] Sublimation was the final repression in a
repressive world, unless resort was had to homosexuality.

A number of prison memoirs included mention of the prison staff, for good
reason. As Alyson Brown and Emma Clare have suggested, the prisoners' preferred
term for a prison officer, "screw," testifies to the power and pressure wielded by
custodial staff, and why inmate autobiographies so often described them "as powerful determinants of the harshness or otherwise of life for prisoners as well as of
the cultures of different prisons." In *Shades of the Prison House*, Stuart Wood
decreed that "one's treatment in prison depends upon two things—the type of
'screws' in charge of landing, exercise, and labour, and the opinions they form of

73 *New Statesman and Nation*, 19 Mar. 1932, p. 356; McCall, op cit., p. 139; Wood, op cit.,
     p. 397; B.2.15, op cit., p. 95; Macartney, op cit., p. 183. See also Cicely Craven,
     "English Prisons: Two Points of View," *Howard Journal*, vol. 4 (1936), p. 265.
74 Phelan, op cit., pp. 103 and 299; B.2.15, op cit., p. 99; Macartney, op cit., p. 410;
     Wood, op cit., p. 196. Cf. Pratt, *Punishment and Civilization*, op cit., p. 119.
75 Macartney, op cit., p. 103.
76 B.2.15, op cit., p. 45; McCall, op cit., p. 40; Phelan, op cit., p. 269. See also Harry
     Pollitt, *Serving My Time* (1940), p. 253.

one's character as a good or bad prisoner." Wood effectively encapsulated the old regime under which prison officers before the War had been trained:

> They had been for many years in a state of smouldering revolt against the appalling conditions of their own lot—the rigid discipline under which they had to perform their duties; the hovels in which they and their families had to live; the long hours of duty; the miserable scale of pay; the iniquitous system of the confidential report and half-sheet, and the heavy exactions in fines for trivial breaches of discipline.[77]

Immediately after the war, in the face of open revolt by police and prison officers, the Home Office had conceded an eight-hour day, pay and pension increases, and paid overtime, though not the right to join a trade union. In addition, a change of name was made, from prison "warder," which suggested a mere turnkey and disciplinarian, to prison "officer." By 1923, prison officer remuneration had fallen behind that of police officers, yet the 1923 Stanhope Committee declined to accept the claim for parity with the police, on the grounds that the tasks and responsibilities of prison staff were less than those of the police.[78] The post-war closure of many local prisons meant staff were posted to other prisons, creating a shortage of housing in some places and a serious reduction in promotion prospects—60 per cent of the officer grade retiring in the 1920s at the same rank as they had joined. The Geddes axe aggravated the position, leading to considerable reductions in staff between 1924 and 1926, to instances of officers supervising single-handed large parties of prisoners, and of inadequate staffing levels at weekends. Between 1921 and 1926, the number of male prison staff (officers and principal officers) fell from 1,964 to 1,760, and the ratio of prisoners to staff inched up from 5.44 to 5.74. It was hardly surprising, therefore, that the response of prison officers to the ameliorations of prison discipline was hostile. The Prison Commission, they charged, was giving preferential treatment to the criminal classes, making the officers' job harder and more dangerous. Captain Gerold Clayton, deputy-governor of Pentonville, was exasperated at seeing money allocated to facilities in borstal institutions, when there were Pentonville officers "whose quarters very nearly approximated to slums . . ." As the *Prison Officers Magazine* reminded the commissioners in 1923, "If the prisoner is to be reformed it can only be done through a good, well paid and contented staff."[79]

77 Brown and Clare, op cit., p. 64; Wood, op cit., p. 321–2, 386.
78 *Report of the Committee Appointed to Inquire into the Pay and Conditions of Service at the Prisons and Borstal Institutions in England and Scotland and at Broadmoor Criminal Lunatic Asylum*, 1923 (Cmd. 1959). For the dissatisfaction of the Prison Officers Representative Board with the recommendations of the Stanhope Committee, see TNA, PCom7/614; PCom7/724; HO45/11966/449102/1.
79 See *Report of the Committee of Inquiry into the United Kingdom Prison Services*, PP, 1979 (Cmd. 7673), p. 14; TNA, PCom9/129; PCom9/149; T. B. Gibson Mackenzie, "The British Prison," *Fortnightly Review*, vol. 137 (1932), p. 333–4; L. W. Fox, *The English Prison and Borstal Systems* (1952), p. 91; *Prison Officers' Magazine*, vol. XII (1936), p. 141.

The Prison Commission paid lip service to the idea that prison officers were not mere custodians, but were expected, as Scott wrote, "to co-operate in a national work of training and reformation."[80] Yet, in truth, the process of reform was marked by an almost total lack of consultation with junior staff, except via the inadequate channels of the Prison Officers Representative Board. Even prisoners remarked upon the plight of the prison officer. F. E. Baker, recently released from Maidstone, thought the officer was "the neglected link" of prison reform:

> Instead of being given a sense of dignity and responsibility, he is deprived of nearly all initiative and is driven into the degrading task of spying upon the actions of the men under his charge. His main duty is to report infractions of prison discipline.[81]

Not all prisoners thought the worst of the staff. Jim Phelan described Maidstone officers as "quiet, stolid, decent people." William Holt, sentenced to nine months' imprisonment for unlawful assembly (during a march of the unemployed against the Means Test), found the Wakefield staff to be human. "I believe that they did their best, considering that they were working within severe restrictions and rules. . ." To many prisoners, the prison staff was likewise controlled by the length and monotony of the daily regimen, and by the hundreds of Standing Orders "of an almost incredible stupidity," in Macartney's phrase. "The officers have to stand behind the cast-iron rules," wrote prisoner B.2.15, who did time in Leicester prison in 1918–19. He described well the "atmosphere where vigilance and suspicion are enthroned":

> The constant locking and unlocking of doors, counting and checking of men, searching and spying, inspection of cells to make sure that everything is in its proper place, keeping men always a certain distance apart . . . all tend towards a demoralizing effect on officers and prisoners.[82]

See also J. E. Thomas, *The English Prison Officer since 1850* (1972), pp.162–71; idem., "The Influence of the Prison Service," in N. Walker (ed.), *Penal Policy-Making in England* (Cambridge, 1977), p. 68; K. Daniel, "History of the POA," *Prison Service Journal*, No. 32 (1978), pp. 7–9. Prison staff were an expensive resource. The staff wages bill represented three-fifths of the total cost of prisons by the 1930s: Fox, 6 Oct. 1933: TNA, HO45/15189/570791/5; PCom9/149. Prison officer pay was twice revised upwards between 1935 and 1938: HO45/19680/430010/91; Sir Harold Scott, *Your Obedient Servant* (1959), p. 79.

80 Scott's brief for Lord Dufferin for Lords' debate, 3 Mar. 1937: TNA, HO45/18006/546730/48. For the substitution of "prison officer" for "warder," see TNA, HO45/11082/427916; PCom7/678.

81 Baker, "Star Convicts," *Howard Journal*, vol. IV (1936). Baker had recently served five years' penal servitude in Maidstone prison.

82 Phelan, op cit., p. 28; Holt, *I Haven't Unpacked*, op cit., p. 235; Macartney, op cit., p. 141.

The service needed urgent de-militarization. The senior appointments in the prison service still went too frequently to former Army and Navy officers, or to those from colonial police forces. They were, said Harley Cronin, who became the first general secretary of the Prison Officers' Association, "almost always sticklers for discipline—but too often they meant discipline as applied to the officer on the landing, not to the inmates of the cells."[83] The "screws" themselves were typically time-expired soldiers (and/or relatives of a serving officer, "moormen" in Dartmoor, for instance), and "like all soldiers," said ex-prisoner Charles Prior, "I found they treated people as units and not as human beings at all."[84] As far back as 1911, Prison Commissioner Waller had written, "Women officers is another mighty problem!. . . her position, training and previous education are such that if she is to be respectable she is inevitably dull—very dull."[85] Little changed over the next 20 years. In Holloway, according to Cicely McCall, the female officers had "no experience of the background and upbringing of the large bulk of the prisoners who come from a poorer social class than themselves."[86] Macartney thought that too many officers regarded convicts as a different "biological species," as a "lumpen-proletariat and, as such, worthy of no consideration." The final word belongs to Jim Phelan, sounding a mite Dickensian. The prison codes, he said, told of "progress, humanitarian methods, reforms, modernization." "They are made so much waste-paper, before they are printed, by the killem-an-eatem tradition of the third-generation jailers."[87]

V

Mary Gordon was cited earlier as a stick to beat the prison commissioners concerning the mitigation of the hardships of prison life—but in one important respect she was in harmony with what the prison commissioners strove to achieve. Once the dangers of imprisonment had been mitigated, it was essential to make a term of imprisonment a time of training. She recommended a clearing house for the differentiation of offenders by means of a psychological and sociological diagnosis. The feeble-minded would go to special institutions. Petty offenders would be dealt with chiefly through probation and the suspended sentence. The remaining group would be reformed or permanently segregated. She was especially critical of the short prison sentence, and recommended what she called "the smart sentence of

---

83 Cronin, *The Screw Turns*, op cit., p. 45. See also W. J. Brown, *Prison Problems* (Prison Reform Council, 1946), p. 9; TNA, PCom7/698; HO45/20099/492525/1–2: Aug. 1929, the Admiralty asked the Home Office to appoint retired naval officers as prison governors.
84 "Outcasts or Human Beings? A Discussion on Prison Reform," *The Listener*, 27 Oct. 1937, pp. 895–6. See Phelan, op cit., p. 111.
85 Waller to Gladstone, 9 Oct. 1911, Viscount Gladstone Papers, BL, Add. MSS 45994, folios 274–87.
86 McCall, op cit., p. 47.
87 Phelan, op cit., p. 121; Macartney, op cit., p. 144. The central problem, then as it is now, is that the job prison staff are asked to do—jailer and reformer—is inherently contradictory.

several months." For sure, the prison commissioners believed that an examination centre should supply the courts with information about each defendant, information which would be of service, should the offender be sentenced to imprisonment, in classifying prisoners and allocating them to different establishments or to separate parts of the same place. There were two main reasons for classification. The negative reason was, as Troup put it, "to prevent new offenders from being contaminated by association with those who are old in sin."[88] At one time, this had been done by the system of separate confinement. It was also secured by the system of three Divisions, introduced by the Prison Act of 1898. It rested with the sentencing court to decide in which division a prisoner was to be placed. The first division was little used; it was not always given to political prisoners for whom it was intended since the days of the suffragettes. The distinction between the second and third divisions was meant to separate persons who were not depraved and not of criminal habits from those who were. Courts struggled to understand the triple division, committing very few to the second division unless they were aged or infirm, and "it has long been to all intents and purposes a dead letter," said Lionel Fox in 1934.[89] The positive reason for classification was to make it possible to distribute different types of criminal to different forms of training. Paterson expressed the challenge as follows: "How shall thousands of offenders be so located in the establishments available, that they may be most effectively trained in association for a subsequent life of social freedom?"[90]

There was a familiar ring to this question. Winston Churchill in 1910 had declared, "Classification is the essence of penology." Churchill was determined to empty the prisons of their dead weight of petty criminals, to allow a more refined classification of inmates and to free the prison staff for new specialized tasks. As he wrote in an internal Home Office memorandum,

> Instead of having a lot of prisons of substantially the same type and reproducing the same features, scattered about all over the country, we should have a regular series of scientifically graded institutions which would gradually and increasingly become adapted to the treatment of every variety of human weakness.[91]

In place of only exceptions, such as borstal training or preventive detention, to "the dead level of the system," Churchill wished "to make the whole system increasingly one complete series of specialisations so that the general mixed prison should go with the general mixed workhouse into extinction." The Webbs, too, had recommended "a highly differentiated series of institutions, according to the ten or a dozen main classes into which the prisoners should be divided . . ." And

88   Troup, *The Home Office*, op cit., pp. 119.
89   TNA, HO45/12905/116578; *Hansard*, vol. 207, 21 Jun. 1927, col. 1664.
90   Ruck, *Paterson on Prisons*, op cit., p. 49.
91   Quoted in V. Bailey, "Churchill As Home Secretary: Prison Reform," *History Today*, vol. 35 (1985), p. 10.

the Commissioners' annual report for 1923–4 had included a passage on the desirability of dividing prisons into "training centers" and "places of detention."[92]

The difficulty faced by the commissioners, as Waller told the Home Office, was that classification within the limits of the prison had reached the point that governors could not properly separate the various classes of prisoners: men and women, young and old, first offender and recidivist, not to mention the "special" class of young recidivists between 21 and 25. As Paterson said, "We have probably gone as far as we can in this direction. Some of the partition walls within the prison . . . are so thin that a myopic bat could see through them."[93] Hence, said Waller, "the only method of achieving the desired result is to put different classes into different establishments."[94] The classification of prisoners within a prison had to be followed by classification according to the function of prisons themselves. Wakefield was reopened in 1922 and used as a special prison for prisoners sentenced to six months or over, collected from the North and Midlands regions. Gathered at Wakefield were first offenders or the "star class" and second division prisoners; "younger hopefuls" between 21 and 25 who had been in prison before, known as the "special class"; and "older hopefuls" with previous convictions but who were not regarded as persistent offenders. These three classes were kept in separate communities, subject to industrial training and an evening educational program. The privileges of association and earnings were granted to men on arrival, and lost only by misconduct or laziness. Prisoners could also share in the privileges of the community, such as freedom from being searched each time they went from workshop to cell. The first offenders were divided into houses and into groups called "crews," with a "stroke" chosen from their number in charge of their conduct. Prisoners were kept out of their cells from 6:30 in the morning until 9:30 at night. As L. W. Fox described the experiment, "It is in fact an attempt to provide something like a Borstal system for adults . . ." In the 1930s, Wakefield prison was occupied mainly by first offenders, the special class was limited to 20 per cent, and ordinary class prisoners were excluded.[95]

The commissioners hoped that Wakefield would point the way to classifying the local prisons, with those with the best industrial resources serving as training prisons, while the remaining prisons would serve as places of detention for those with short sentences. Paterson would soon elaborate on this statement. And at the beginning of 1925, the commissioners decided to experiment further in the classification of first

---

92 Ibid.; S and B. Webb, op cit., p. 246.

93 TNA, HO45/19453/507631/1. Prison administration now built up a classification consisting of four groups: (1) "star class," comprising prisoners of good character, with no serious previous convictions; (2) "special class" of prisoners between 21 and 25 years of age with previous convictions; (3) "ordinary class"; and (4) all young prisoners under 21.

94 HO45/19453/507631/1.

95 TNA, PCom9/39: Fox lecture, 6 Jul. 1927; Fletcher Allen, "The Wakefield Scheme," *The Humanist*, vol. 2 (1925), pp. 35–7; Sydney Moore, "Re-Making Men," *Congregational Quarterly*, vol. 5 (1927), pp. 25–31; *Howard Journal*, vol. 2 (1927), pp. 129–34; Colonel G. D. Turner (Inspector of Prisons; former governor of Wakefield Prison), "The Reclaimable Prisoner," *The Magistrate*, vol. 2 (1929), pp. 343–4.

offenders by collecting them at Wormwood Scrubs Prison in London. At the end of the year, it was decided to include men who had been convicted but had not been in prison before. A special system of stages with privileges was started, by which these star prisoners could gradually earn meals in association, evening classes, associated recreation, and talking exercise. As a Prison Commission memo explained,

> The system is based on privileges which a man has to not only earn but also keep, being of course liable to lose them for misconduct, or slackness; on honour and a spirit of common good and communal feeling, helping to raise the man in his own estimation and restore him to his manhood, so that he can feel when he again returns to daily life that all may still be well and that he leaves the prison walls at any rate no worse than when he entered.[96]

Many years later, Sir Harold Scott, former chairman of the Prison Commission, claimed that Wakefield was "the starting-point of Paterson's new deal in the 1920s"; and Harley Cronin, former general secretary of the Prison Officers Association, claimed that the Scrubs "was more or less the laboratory for Paterson's reforms."[97]

Convict prisons were also slowly being divided according to function. Parkhurst held large numbers of weak-minded and aged convicts. Waller turned his attention in late 1923 to convicts under 30, undergoing their first term of penal servitude. In June 1924, Mr. Lamb recommended to Paterson that part of Maidstone prison, namely Howard House, be given over to convicts under 26 (some of them young murderers who had been reprieved), and suitable convicts between 26 and 30 years of age, who would be formed into the "special training class," for whom an active and strenuous day would be devised as well as technical trade training. Paterson agreed that all convicts under 25, "including the Irish lads," should be housed in a separate prison, and sorted into three groups, to introduce a competitive element in work and recreation. In 1931, Chelmsford prison was re-opened as a training centre for 150 men aged 21 to 30, serving a second or subsequent sentence, in order to separate them from the more hardened convicts in Dartmoor and Parkhurst.[98] These initiatives were instances of a policy that sought to break up the old prison system. Yet at one point the commissioners had in mind a much more ambitious and comprehensive plan of classification. The plan is worth examining in detail, since it reveals that Alec Paterson, the doyen of reform in prison circles, did not invariably impress his colleagues, or secure the changes he desired.

In the autumn of 1925, as he sailed to Burma, Alec Paterson had drafted a systematic re-design of the entire prison estate. His scheme for the classification of prisons was a remarkable, though deeply flawed, document.[99] It provided for a

---

96 TNA, HO45/20947/448767/17; PCom7/298.
97 Scott, *Your Obedient Servant*, op cit.; Cronin, op cit., p. 17, 44–6.
98 TNA, PCom7/285: Lamb to Paterson, 26 Jun. 1924.
99 The next four paragraphs, and the quotations within, are drawn from Paterson's document, "A Scheme for the Re-Distribution of Prisoners Among the Prisons of England And Wales" (Nov. 1925), a 28-page report "Submitted to his colleagues by a Commissioner at Sea" held in TNA, HO45/19453/507631/1.

broad separation of adult prisoners into two classes, those who from age, personal qualities, and length of sentence were capable of being "trained for citizenship"; and those for whom the prospect of successful training was absent or remote. Each area of the country would be served by a group of prisons; in each group provision would be made for each class of prisoner, "so that classification would be complete within each area." This long document warrants close attention, since it is Paterson's most comprehensive manifesto for reform of the prison system, whose broad outlines would guide the Prison Commission for the rest of the inter-war period. His scheme of classification rested on the distinction between "trainable men" who would be collected at a training centre (like Wakefield), and "not so trainable" men who would be kept at places of detention. The majority of men in a place of detention would be serving very short sentences, and cleanliness and security would be the main desiderata. These prisoners would work on unskilled and repetitive tasks. Each training centre would hold first offenders, young men of the special class, and older recidivists, who would as far as possible be separated from each other. A Prison Reception Board would decide whether the prisoner was a subject for training or detention. The qualifications for training would be aged between 21 and 60; physically and mentally fit for 15 hours' training a day; a chance of being benefited by training; and sentenced to more than six months' imprisonment. Why insist upon a minimum period of six months? "To change the habits, the scale of values, and the point of view of a grown man," wrote Paterson, "is not a quick and easy operation, if the change is to be genuine and permanent."

Paterson then ran the existing numbers of receptions, daily average prison population, and sentence lengths, a computation that allowed him to claim that a quarter of the convicted prisoners (or 1,828 male local prisoners), having been sentenced to more than six months' imprisonment, would be available for training—especially as the courts would see the scheme's advantages and increasingly send men away for more than six months. For this number of "trainables," nine training centres for men would be needed, with populations ranging from 100 to 300. Training centres would possess several workshops for different types of work, and separate blocks to allow separation of first offenders from recidivists. They would also be divided into sections of no more than 50 men, each section in direct charge of a "leading personality," without which a section "will never realise its existence as an entity, or have any corporate life and spirit." There followed Paterson's proposed categorization of local and convict prisons for each region of the country, what he called "a jig-saw puzzle with many more pieces than spaces." In region number two, for example, Liverpool was to be the training centre, since Manchester was unsuitable: "It is cribbed, cabined and confined, clearly a place for detention rather than training." The five London prisons were in region number nine. Brixton would continue to act as an examination centre, Holloway would be a training centre for men stars, Wormwood Scrubs would be a training centre for the special class and recidivists, Wandsworth would host the large number of not-so-trainable recidivists and convicts, and Pentonville would be closed. The convicted women of Holloway were to be sent to Aylesbury. In 1923–4, only 500 women were sent to prison for more than three months, so the qualification for a female training centre was a sentence exceeding three months, though Paterson was already looking toward detention homes for the female petty recidivist. Since the division between trainable and not-so-trainable was applied to convicts also, Paterson proposed, first, that Lewes be re-opened to house 200 young recidivists under 30 years of age on their first sentence of penal servitude, who were currently "sunk in a cesspool of professional crime at Dartmoor and Parkhurst." This was the only way to reduce "the stage army of chronic recidivists." Maidstone would continue to receive first offenders. The remaining 1,000 or so middle-aged, largely professional criminals for whom detention not training was required, would go to Parkhurst (though they would spend the final 12 months of their sentence in the place of detention closest to their home), and Dartmoor would be closed.

Paterson ignored the collecting centres for young prisoners. He hoped "that these are a vanishing feature of prison administration," and trusted that by the time the scheme was in operation, there would be no more young prisoners. He was doubtless banking on the expansion of the borstal system to fill the void. He said little about borstal training for young adult offenders in this document, but we know from other sources how he was shaping the borstal system, and the future he imagined for it.[100] Paterson designed a system of institutional training, drawing on the public school model and ethos, to remove young offenders from "the evil environment of their homes and the wicked influences of their associates," and to teach them self-control, self-knowledge, and the qualities of good citizenship. Instrumental to this process of re-education were the personal influence of the housemasters on the boys, and the public opinion or corporate spirit of the lads themselves. At a central clearing house located at Wandsworth, later at Wormwood Scrubs, boys sentenced to borstal were classified according to degree of criminality, and sent to the institution most suited to their needs, including in the 1930s the minimum security or open borstals of Lowdham Grange and North Sea Camp. The training period was a minimum of two years, a maximum of three; inmates could be released on licence after six months, though the average period in the mid-1920s was rather more than two years. As for the future, Paterson envisioned Borstal both as an alternative to lengthy imprisonment for the potential recidivist, and as a substitute for short terms of imprisonment—in all, as the exclusive mode of custodial training for young adult offenders. Once probation was exhausted, lads would be sent to a "reception institution," where they would spend from three to six months. Most would be released on licence; if they failed on licence, they would be recalled to serve the rest of their sentence in an ordinary borstal institution. This plan of a provisional and a full sentence of Borstal, Paterson believed, would persuade the courts to commit lads to borstal training even for those less advanced in crime. Through a combination of classification, a flexible training programme, and after-care, young offenders would be given a new start in life. Paterson's ultimate ambition was a system in which the judiciary would pass a

100 See Bailey, *Delinquency and Citizenship*, op cit., chap. 8.

generic sentence, the prison authorities thereafter deciding on the length and nature of training.

Paterson concluded his long memorandum by hoping that the courts would respond positively to the new scheme.

> In course of time it may well be that for all ordinary offences Courts will do what we are already asking them to do in the case of lads, i.e. they will send everyone, who cannot be put on probation, for a period of training, and subsequently should training prove to have been ineffective, will commit them to a long period of detention.

Presently, by contrast, a period of training typically came after "a fruitless series of spells of detention." He also suggested that if aftercare or aid-on-discharge could not be organized efficiently by the local agencies, it ought to be nationalized. He was sanguine enough to recognize that it would be five or ten years before the scheme was fully operational. The first step, he said, was to explain the scheme to the Home Office and the Judges.

> To translate some sentences of 12 months' imprisonment into 12 months' training, and others into 12 months' detention, is to assume powers approximate to those of the Judiciary, and it is necessary that the sympathy and advice of the Judges should be secured at the outset.

In a passionate finale, Paterson argued that, if nothing else, discussion of the scheme would "clear our minds and suggest some programme that is founded upon a policy," as distinct from the present "isolated and spasmodic changes that do not appear to be related to and governed by any general principle." In a final sentence of Churchillian rhetoric, Paterson wrote,

> The highly civilized State is one that believes in its citizens, and indicates this belief in its system of government, its measure of education, and last but not least, in its treatment of the criminal.

The scheme was circulated confidentially to prison governors who responded positively, while urging that places of detention for the "untrainable" not be places in which all hope was abandoned. At this point in March 1927, Waller sent the scheme to the Home Office with the comment that here was "a considered policy for the future," and a system framed on the lines within would counteract "the evils and inefficiency of the general mixed prison."[101] Alas, the Home Office, at least in its internal deliberations, developed a stinging critique of Paterson's scheme. The main critic was Arthur Locke, Assistant Undersecretary, and H. B. Simpson's successor.[102]

101 TNA, HO45/19453/507631/1.
102 For Locke, see Harold Scott, *Your Obedient Servant* (1959), p. 62.

VI

Locke saw Paterson's scheme as an extension of the Wakefield "training centre" experiment to all prisons and prisoners, at great expense, without legal sanction, without evidence of the success of the Wakefield experiment, and—the most fatal part of the charge—resulting in all classes of prisoners, save the few regarded as trainable, being herded together in places of detention. The Wakefield scheme and its enlargement, said Locke, "are applications of the theory of one school of 'prison reformers' that the adequate classification of prisoners requires the classification and delocalization of prisons." In terms of expense, Locke was concerned that expensive new Wakefield's would prompt the public to ask,

> why does it already cost twice as much (over a million pounds) in 1925 to look after a daily average population of 10,509 as it did in 1898–9 to look after a daily average population of 17,687 when the cost was only just over half a million?

Locke might have added that the average gross cost per head of prisoners in local prisons was £35.10.10d in 1913, and £110.8.5d in 1920. Improvements in the pay and hours of prison staff explained much of this increase. Locke also felt that the scheme would require legal sanction. First, the Home Secretary should be asked to consider whether some prisons ought to be turned into "training centres," and whether Parliament should be asked to empower courts to send offenders to "training centres" for longer periods than they would send them to prisons. If the Home Secretary were convinced, legislation would be proposed and passed. Only then would the change be put into practice. Until then, courts could not be induced, as Paterson proposed, to pass longer sentences, and "if they are not so induced, Mr. Paterson's figure of 1828 melts away, and the bottom falls out of his elaborate redistribution of prisons." Locke was not convinced by Paterson's arithmetic, but even accepting the figure of 1828, in order to train them in nine training centres, all other prisoners had to be relegated to places of detention, and "the cream of the staff . . . and the most intense industrial and reformatory efforts would be concentrated on this small fraction of the prison population." What meanwhile were places of detention to hold? Locke's answer put the final nail in the coffin of Paterson's scheme:

> . . . they are to contain prisoners from near and from far; remand prisoners, trial prisoners and convicted prisoners . . . those debtors who are not exiled to Training Centres to do domestic tasks; first offenders and hardened recidivists; young prisoners and old prisoners; physically unfit prisoners; mental cases and prisoners of emotional temperament; trainable prisoners sentenced to seven months or less; untrainable prisoners sentenced to more than seven months; prisoners with even the shortest sentences; and convicts serving the last twelve months of their terms! Over any such "Place of Detention" one might well

write "Abandon hope, all ye who enter here." To herd 4/5ths of the DAP [daily average population] in such places is an astonishing outcome of a Scheme for counteracting "the evils and inefficiency of the general mixed prison".[103]

Locke's own calculations, using Paterson's tests for admission to a training centre, produced 956 trainable prisoners, 240 of whom were already at Wakefield. Only 716 new trainables would have to be catered for; while 7,000 untrainable local prisoners would be in places of detention.

All Locke could reasonably offer was a project for starting one new Wakefield or Training Prison (and he purposely used "prison," since the abandonment of the word had not been approved by the Home Secretary), and he sketched out a case for setting up a Royal Commission, which "might consider, and even bless, the Wakefield experiment," and thus justify asking Parliament for an extension of the experiment. He thought the time was not quite ripe for a Royal Commission, but it could be by late 1929. If Paterson knew that in two years' time "he may have an opportunity of vindicating the Wakefield experiment, that may do something to console him for the immediate loss of his Scheme." Locke was understandably sceptical of Paterson's assumption that prisoners under 21 would "disappear," but he was firmly of the view that the offender aged 16–21, along with those aged 21–25, "offers at once the most difficult, the most urgent and the most promising field for experiment and effort."[104] Emley Blackwell, Assistant Undersecretary of State, agreed with Locke's comments on Paterson's scheme, adding two further points, which displayed doubt about rehabilitative training and renewed faith in deterrence, especially of first offenders. A very large proportion of those sent to prison for the first time never came back to prison, said Blackwell. In the mid-1920s, the number of male *first* receptions was around 12,000. If any large number of these men *were* to become "gaol-birds," the daily average population would be much larger than 10,000. Second, too much reliance could be placed upon six or 12 months' "training":

> Some first offenders who go to Prison do not stand in need of any such manual training as they are likely to get in "Training-Centres" and as regards hardened criminals I doubt if that training will turn them into "good citizens" or cure them of "anti-social tendencies."
>
> I believe that imp[risonment] as it exists today does deter from crime both those who have had experience of it for the first time & the far larger number of potential criminals who in fact never go there at all! The bulk of the pr [ison] population are a comparatively small stage army.[105]

103 TNA, HO45/19453/507631/2–3: Locke's memorandum, 10 Jun. 1927. It clearly took the department some time to respond to Paterson's scheme. Locke was right to be sceptical of Paterson's assumption that young prisoners would disappear; in 1934, over 1,000 youths under 21 were sent to prison.
104 Ibid.
105 Ibid.

Blackwell's belief was ultimately borne out by the evidence. The after-career of prisoners received into prison for the first time on conviction of "finger-printable" offences revealed that of 30,151 prisoners received into prison for the first time during the years 1930–3, 24,326 or 81 per cent had not returned to prison a second time up to the end of 1935. Of course, some of these prisoners were in prison during some of these years, and others could have been reconvicted without earning a second prison sentence.[106]

Why did Paterson's signature penal scheme prove so unconvincing to the Home Office? The answer lies, of course, with the continued resort to places of detention where the bulk of the prison population would be incarcerated. Paterson had failed to solve the problem of the vast number of prisoners with short sentences. Years earlier, Churchill had known that before a scheme of effective classification could be imposed, he had to relieve the local prisons of the heavy duties of reception and discharge of prisoners on petty sentences, by abolishing all imprisonment for periods of less than one month. This is why he proposed the suspensory sentence and defaulters' drill, and encouraged greater use of probation. Paterson was surely familiar with the prison statistics (though he was no advocate of induction from statistics, preferring deduction from fundamental principles). Year after year, the annual reports of the prison commissioners pointed to the magnitude of short sentences. In 1927, out of 34,950 receptions of men sentenced to imprisonment, 11,406 or 33 per cent were for periods not exceeding a fortnight; out of 7,577 receptions of women sentenced to imprisonment, 3,170 or 42 per cent were for periods not exceeding a fortnight. Many of these short sentences were imposed as alternatives to fines, and many of the people serving these sentences were those who were repeatedly convicted for drunkenness. In 1928, 13,351 or 40.2 per cent of the men sentenced to imprisonment were for periods under one month; 3,223 or 54.1 per cent of the women sentenced to imprisonment were for periods under one month. By contrast, only 16.3 per cent of the men sentenced to imprisonment were for periods of six months and above; only 5 per cent of 12 months and over. Appendices to the annual reports included evidence from the governors and medical officers of Birmingham, Liverpool, and Holloway prisons to the effect that most female prisoners had multiple previous convictions for drunkenness and prostitution, were of low mental standard, and required some form of indeterminate sentence and release on license.[107]

Other telling figures appeared in the commissioners' statistical tables. Of the 40,449 convicted prisoners (male and female) received in 1928, 19,035 or 47 per cent, were imprisoned for "other non-indictable offences," more akin to nuisances

106 TNA, HO45/18006/546730/48: Scott's brief for Lord Dufferin, 3 Mar. 1937; Ann. Rep. of P. Com. for 1938, PP, 1939–40, V (Cd. 6137), pp. 130–1 (Appendix No. 10). See also Leo Page, "Outcasts or Human Beings?", *The Listener*, 27 Oct. 1937, p. 895.

107 Ann. Rep. of P. Com. for 1923–24, PP, 1924–5, XV (Cd. 2307), p. 345, 381; Ann. Rep. of P. Com. for 1927, PP, 1928–9, IX (Cd. 3292), p. 326, 346–9; Ann. Rep. of P. Com. for 1928, PP, 1929–30, XVII (Cd. 3607), p. 287; Ann. Rep. of P. Com. for 1929, PP, 1930–31, XVI (Cd. 3868), p. 917.

than to crimes, including drunkenness, prostitution, begging, sleeping out, and offences against the poor law and police regulations.[108] In 1929, for women, "other non-indictable offences" accounted for a staggering 67 per cent of imprisonments. It was no coincidence that Home Secretary, William Joynson-Hicks, following a tour of the nation's prisons, never missed an opportunity to tell the press, justices, and prison reform groups of the folly of short sentences, and to urge that if a man must go to prison, he must be sent there for a "sharp term of imprisonment."[109] Moreover, there is little doubt that Paterson and the other commissioners knew that for "short-timers," a prison could not be a place of training. Short sentences were, wrote the commissioners in 1924, "a standing hindrance to carrying out a proper scheme of training."[110] This is doubtless what induced Paterson in the first place to come up with a new classification of prisoners. His scheme fell short because it took the existing prison population for granted. Paterson simply redistributed what he found in the prisons in 1925. This resulted in what Locke objected to: training 20 per cent at most of the daily average population, herding the other 80 per cent into places of detention. What was needed, if inappropriate for a prison commissioner to provide, was the kind of holistic scheme presented by Churchill, in which imprisonment for periods of less than one month was abolished, as was imprisonment for debt, and provision was made for forms of long-term detention for vagrants, inebriates, and petty recidivists. Even then, the sentencing policy of the courts could have stymied any training scheme, since so few sentences were of the length Paterson required for training purposes, and courts were reluctant, per *R. v. Oxlade*, unless the law expressly recognized a special form of sentence, to base sentence length on the prospect of an offender benefiting from a system of training.

VII

Paterson and the commissioners were in no way deterred from continuing to advocate for a scheme of prison classification and training. In large part, they had the support of the penal reformers of the day. Fenner Brockway, who had co-authored the highly critical report, *English Prisons Today*, was by 1928 acknowledging that the commissioners had since 1920 "thrown over the theory upon which the modern prison system was built, and are now seeking both a new system and a new theory," and he encouraged them to make the prisons "a training ground for citizenship."[111] Throughout the 1930s, the commissioners enlarged the methods of classification,

108 Ann. Rep. of P. Com. for 1928, PP, 1929–30, XVII (Cd. 3607), pp. 339–41 (Table I).
109 See *New Statesman*, 26 Nov. 1927, pp. 193–4; *Spectator*, 26 Nov. 1927, p. 911; *The Times*, 12 Jan. 1928, p. 9; *The Law Journal*, 3 Dec. 1927, p. 394. See also press cuttings in TNA, HO144/10565/467827/46–7.
110 Ann. Rep. of P. Com. for 1923–4, PP, 1924–5, XV (Cd. 2307), p. 345. In Jun. 1932, Paterson stated, "The prison authorities of this country have faced the fact that in the case of short sentences it is idle hypocrisy to pretend that a prison can in any way be a place of training": *Transactions of the Medico-Legal Society*, vol. 26 (1933), p. 190.
111 A. Fenner Brockway, *A New Way with Crime* (1928), pp. ix, 14. It is remarkable that Brockway, along with the Webbs, despite their knowledge of official inefficiency in the

focusing particularly upon the most hopeful classes of the prison population, those who were regarded as *prima facie* most likely to profit. The borstal system removed from the prison population of some 11,000 persons, nearly 2,000, who served their sentence in one of seven borstal institutions for lads (one for girls), classified according to type of lad and type of treatment.[112] In London, it was possible to make a classification by prisons: Brixton for unconvicted prisoners on remand or awaiting trial; Wormwood Scrubs for those serving a first term of imprisonment and lads under 21 (whether awaiting trial or convicted); and Pentonville and Wandsworth for recidivists (with those under 30 concentrated at Wandsworth). Outside of London, Wakefield was set apart for the reception of all first offenders or "stars" from the North and Midlands serving sentences of six months or over, plus a number of selected "specials," young men aged 21–25 who had been in trouble before. The remaining local prisons tried to classify on the same lines, but it was difficult to segregate the different classes of prisoner for work, education, and training. For this reason, the commissioners adopted the policy of collecting particular classes of prisoner in sections of some local prisons: young male prisoners aged 16–21 with sentences of one month and over in Bedford, Bristol, Durham, Lewes, Winchester, and Liverpool, and young women prisoners aged 16–21 in Holloway; and prisoners who were of abnormal or sub-normal mentality in Birmingham, Lincoln, and Liverpool. Any of the latter who were suitable for psychological treatment were transferred to Wormwood Scrubs, where an experiment in psychiatric treatment of offenders started in 1934. Convicts were distributed over four prisons, Maidstone for first offenders not of criminal habits, Chelmsford for young convicts up to the age of 30 undergoing their first term of penal servitude (who had often passed through Borstal and prisons without effect, and who were on the road to becoming habitual criminals), and Dartmoor and Parkhurst for older convicts with previous prison sentences. Parkhurst also took men requiring medical care. Women convicts of the "star" class (not previously convicted, or not previously convicted of serious offences) were confined in Aylesbury prison, the "ordinary" class in Holloway.[113]

The idea of the specialist training prison was significantly advanced in one regard only in the thirties, and that was the opening in 1936 of New Hall Camp at Wakefield. Paterson, following a visit to North America in 1931, put forward the idea of a prison camp, an open prison run chiefly on the "public opinion" of the community of prisoners.[114] After a couple of false starts, work began in March

past, believed that re-adjusting the administrative machinery could convert the prisons into "moral hospitals."

112 Cicely Craven, "The Progress of English Criminology," *Journal of Criminal Law, Criminology & Police Science*, vol. 24 (1933), pp. 239–41.

113 TNA, HO45/18006/546730/48: Scott's brief for Lord Dufferin, 26 Feb. 1937; PCom/9/39: Scott memo, 28 Oct. 1937; *Hansard*, Lords, vol. 104, 3 Mar. 1937, col. 445; *Hansard*, vol. 338, 11 Jul. 1938, cols. 935–6. See also A. Paterson, "The Present Policy of the Prison Commission," *The Magistrate*, vol. 5 (1938), pp. 140–2.

114 TNA, PCom9/156; A. Paterson (New Hall Camp, Wakefield) to S. Bates (Head of Boys Clubs in USA and President of the Association for the After-Care of Prisoners), 27 May 1936, papers held by author.

1933 on reclaiming woodland and cultivating the land. Fifty prisoners were conveyed each day to and from the estate. In 1935, the commissioners asked the Home Office for agreement to establish a camp in the wood in which the prisoners would live and sleep during the week. Alexander Maxwell, Deputy Undersecretary of State, and former chairman of the Prison Commission, was in favour of the experiment:

> If in the early stages of the experiment we should be so unfortunate as to have one or two escapes or attempts to escape, there may be some public criticism, but the risk is small & ought to be taken. Safe custody is, of course, the basic principle of imprisonment, but we shall make little progress in the development of the idea that imprisonment shall so far as possible be used for training purposes, if we cling to the idea that for all types of prisoner the traditional fortress-like building is the only method of providing safe custody.[115]

Yet initially the prison commissioners took no chances. They decided to select only those serving a first term of imprisonment, and only those sentenced to 12 months or longer who had served at least one-third of their sentence: "This will mean that they have an appreciable amount of remission to lose if they abuse their position by escape or otherwise. No man guilty of homo-sexual offences will be chosen." In 1937, however, selected men serving long sentences of penal servitude were transferred to the camp from Maidstone prison. In time, there was to be hut accommodation for 100 men, in groups of ten, two groups of ten per hut, all of whom would live there permanently. No officer would patrol the camp at night. The prisoners themselves were to be relied upon to discourage attempts at escape. As the governor of Wakefield prison, Captain R. C. Williams, told the visiting justices conference, with good Borstal rhetoric, "it has been put to them [the prisoners] that they can play the game and so can we . . ."[116]

Women prisoners deserve separate attention, since if there was one category of prisoner for whom classification and training were an unmitigated failure, it was the female prisoner. The number of women prisoners fell rapidly, from a daily average population (in local and convict prisons, borstal institutions, and preventive detention prisons) of 2,484 in 1913 to 1,388 in 1921 to 888 in 1926 and to 674 in 1936. By this last date, women were only one-twentieth of the entire prison

---

115 TNA, HO45/16456/160787/42: Maxwell, 30 Oct. 1935.
116 HO45/16456/160787/47; HO45/20084/482137/20: Visiting Justices Conference, 24 Nov. 1936; Ann. Rep. of P. Com. for 1936, PP, 1937–8, XIV (Cmd. 5675), p. 30. See also Captain R. C. Williams, "The Wakefield Prison Camp," *The Magistrate*, vol. 5 (1938), pp. 143–4; Scott, *Your Obedient Servant*, op cit., pp. 86–8; H. Jones and P. Cornes, *Open Prisons* (1977), p. 5. One is left with the impression that Wakefield was a face-saver, perpetuating rotten conditions in the rest of the prison estate. Moreover, classification benefited only a small proportion of offenders, those in Wakefield, Maidstone, and Wormwood Scrubs. The Young Prisoners' Centres were only parts of the old slum prisons, which by their structure made "training" little more than an official phrase.

population. The more telling statistics, however, were those for receptions into prison. Receptions on conviction fell from 11,340 in 1921 to 3,869 in 1936.[117] As B. L. Jacot wrote in 1938, "the number of women to be found in prison has fallen to one quarter of the total to be found in gaol only a generation ago," and the fall in the number of receptions meant that "for every seven women taken. . . into the country's gaols a generation ago only one woman is imprisoned today."[118] Of the 3,869 receptions in 1936, 1,772 or 45.8 per cent were convicted of offences against the liquor laws and imprisoned in default of payment of a fine.[119] Most were elderly women (three-quarters were 40 years and older) who were imprisoned with clockwork regularity on short sentences for offences of drunkenness, what the governor of Birmingham prison called "a pathetic and hopeless collection of human wreckage."[120] Cicely McCall, a prison officer at Holloway from 1934, wrote of this revolving door of receptions:

> A woman may be discharged every Saturday morning, arrested every Saturday night and re-admitted to prison every Monday afternoon, and this may go on from the late twenties until she dies of old age. There is nothing in the judicial system, nor apparently in long-suffering human physiology, to stop it.[121]

As Jacot again wrote, "This band of fifteen hundred inebriates is the thorn in the side of prison administration."[122] In the 1920s, the commissioners' policy was to concentrate the small numbers of women in a few large centres, instead of dispersing them in small groups, which made it difficult to apply new methods of classification and training. By 1933, no fewer than 12 small wings of local prisons had been closed, leaving female wings in only five men's prisons: Manchester, Durham, Birmingham, Cardiff, and Exeter. Of these, Manchester held the largest number (114 prisoners in 1937). Holloway was the largest prison for women (366 prisoners

---

117 In 1928, sentences of imprisonment (excluding penal servitude sentences) for periods not exceeding a fortnight accounted for 10,688 or 31 per cent of male receptions, and for 2,536 or 42 per cent of the receptions of women: Ann. Rep. of P. Com. for 1928, PP, 1929–30, XVII (Cd. 3607), p. 9.
118 Jacot, "Women in Prison," *Quarterly Review*, vol. 271 (1938), p. 97.
119 Offences against the Intoxicating Liquor Laws accounted in 1931 for 48 per cent of the imprisonments of women, and for only 16 per cent of the imprisonments of men: Ann. Rep. of P. Com. for 1931, PP 1932–3, XV (Cd. 4295), p. 427.
120 TNA, PCom9/149; Ann. Rep. of P. Com. for 1927, PP, 1928–9, IX (Cd. 3292), p. 346 (Appendix I); Ann. Rep. of P. Com. for 1929, PP, 1930–1, XVI (Cd. 3868), pp. 911–9; Ann. Rep. of P. Com. for 1936, PP, 1937–8, XV (Cd. 5675), pp. 710–1; Ann. Rep. of P. Com. for 1937, PP, 1937–8, XIV (Cd. 5868), p. 17. See also M. Grunhut, *Penal Reform* (1948), pp. 160, 412–4; H. Mannheim, *Social Aspects of Crime in England Between the Wars* (1940), chap. VI; B. Forsythe, "Women Prisoners and Women Penal Officials 1840–1921," *British Journal of Criminology*, vol. 33 (1993), p. 526.
121 McCall, '*They Always Come Back,*' op cit., p. 88. See also Arthur Gardner, "English Prisons in 1936," *Howard Journal*, vol. 5 (1938), p. 116; Scott, *Your Obedient Servant*, op cit., p. 91.
122 Jacot, op cit., p. 101. See also Dr. M. Hamblin Smith, "Habitual Women Drunkards," *The Magistrate*, vol. III (1934), pp. 835–7; John Watson, *Meet the Prisoner* (1939), p. 160.

in 1937). Convict women were confined in Liverpool prison, except for a very few "stars" or first offenders, most serving sentences of life imprisonment, who were transferred to Aylesbury, and kept separate from the Borstal girls. The "ordinary" class of female convicts was sent to Holloway.[123]

Cicely McCall was deeply critical of the lack of classification in women's prisons: "In an age of specialization and classification, women law-breakers are still herded together with no more than the most elementary divisions, and such divisions as these are mainly differences in location not, except superficially, in training." Such classification as was attempted for local prisoners was confined to Holloway, though even there it was unsatisfactory, especially for first offenders. In one sewing workroom, the star and second division women sat on one side of the aisle and recidivists on the other, two yards apart: "Such," said McCall, "is the much-vaunted segregation of the first offender from contamination with habitual offenders."[124] It was also impossible to provide training suitable to their capacity (or incapacity) for different types of woman, including the stage army of drunks, vagrants, and prostitutes. Apart from the domestic work of the prison, employment consisted principally of some form of sewing. Dr. Morton, one-time governor of Holloway, proposed long-term detention in a special colony for chronic alcoholics, as did the National Council of Women, but the idea was too reminiscent of the failed experiment of inebriate reformatories under the 1898 Inebriates Act, which the courts had been reluctant to use. For women serving six months and upward, the National Council recommended a colony on the cottage home principle with facilities for domestic training and outdoor work. By 1937 even the commissioners were convinced that Holloway should be abandoned.[125]

The commissioners were aware that classification *in* prisons was difficult—that varying the regime of a prison in terms of work, discipline, and recreation within the walls of a single building was severely limited. This led them to underscore the danger of sending young lads to prison. In 1935, 1,600 young persons under 21 were committed to prison, half of them for one month or less, almost 40 per cent of whom had not previously been proved guilty of offences. Surely, the commissioners argued, for many of these lads probation or borstal would have been better.[126] The commissioners also sought to modify the classification of prisoners by the unexpected decision in 1932 to confine in local prisons, convicts of the

123 TNA, HO45/18498/655767/3; HO45/11631/447058/1–2; PCom9/192.
124 McCall, op cit., p. 93. See also PCom9/59: Annual Conference of Visiting Justices, 28 Nov. 1933.
125 G. D. Turner, "The Holloway 'Zoo'," *Spectator*, 18 Oct. 1930, p. 521; Cicely Craven letter to *Spectator*, 1 Nov. 1930. p. 634; J. Hall Morton, "Alcoholics in Prison," *Howard Journal*, vol. 2 (1929), p. 307; TNA, HO45/11056/216238; *The Times*, 28 Jul. 1938, p. 9. See also Watson, *Meet the Prisoner*, op cit., 171; Ann Smith, *Women in Prison*, op cit., pp. 168, 172.
126 For Alexander Paterson's statement to the Court of Criminal Appeal as to the treatment of young offenders, which was preface to the Court substituting sentences of borstal training in a number of cases where youths had been sentenced to terms of imprisonment, see *The Times*, 14 Jun. 1932, p. 5.

"ordinary" class with sentences of three years' penal servitude. They did so on the grounds that "there was no longer any material difference between the treatment accorded to the two classes of prisoners, and there was no reason why persons serving penal servitude should be kept in separate establishments from those serving terms of imprisonment." To prepare the way for this change, a chapter in the commissioners' annual report spelled out how little difference there was between the treatment of convicts and of local prisoners. The numbers involved were not great. The commissioners reckoned that 360 convicts would be scattered over the local prisons. By 1938, there were 99 men sentenced to penal servitude in local prisons, the largest number in Liverpool, Birmingham, Manchester, and Leeds. No attempt was made to keep convict and local prisoners separated. A crop of complaints from three-year convicts broke out in the wake of this decision. Convicts complained that they had to witness a procession of short-term prisoners in and out of prison; they were not getting the food they would have done at a convict prison; and they were subject, unlike those sentenced to imprisonment, to release on licence, not to mention the fact that they lost their smoking privilege. Governors accepted the change, though they claimed that some judges still remarked that they were passing a sentence of three years' penal servitude because two years' hard labour in a local prison was too severe. Naturally, this annoyed those serving three years' penal servitude in a *local prison*. As Stuart Wood in his prison memoir, *Shades of the Prison House*, stated: ". . . there is not one lag in a thousand who would not have preferred three years' penal servitude to twenty-one months in a local prison." And in subsequent years, both the Prison Officers Representative Board and the Visiting Justices Conference asked the commissioners to remove convicts from local prisons, the former claiming that it was difficult to find prison work for long sentence men. The commissioners held firm, believing that convicts wrongly regarded themselves as "a cut above the ordinary prisoners" and entitled to a separate prison. The chairman of the Prison Commission also revealed in 1937 that one of the main reasons the change had been made "was that it was unwise to have too big an aggregation of the more dangerous kind of prisoner in one place."[127] Ironically, the change was under discussion in the Home Office in the very same month, January 1932, as the Dartmoor mutiny.

VIII

On 24 January 1932, a prison mutiny without parallel in the history of English prisons broke out in Dartmoor. The riot lasted only a few hours, but it required a combined force of prison and police officers to bring it under control, who shot several prisoners with carbines, none fatally, as they attempted to escape over the walls, and not before extensive fire damage to the office-block of the prison had occurred. No prisoners escaped. Would this mutiny, a sensational spectacle covered heavily by the press, undermine political and public confidence in the direction of penal reform? So sensational was the press coverage that it prompted the King, via

127 TNA, HO45/20499/595278/1–2, 6; PCom9/164; Wood, *Shades*, op cit., p. 385.

his private secretary, to complain to the Home Secretary about the assistance the prison authorities must have given to the press. Would the mutiny strengthen the arm of those, like Lieut.-Col. Rich, who complained of "soft and sentimental extremists, whose views appear to have a very complete influence on the direction of Prison management"?[128] Dartmoor was the iconic convict prison. Convicts knew the transfer to Dartmoor as "a trip over the Alps." The prison was renowned for its moorland remoteness, its dense mists, its outdoor working parties, supervised by armed guards with permission to shoot escaping *felon* (though not *misdemeanant*) convicts. How they were supposed to discriminate in the heat of the moment was not vouchsafed. Even before the mutiny, the Home Office had decided to make a large reduction in the population of the prison, so unsuitable and costly was it as a locality for a prison. No new admissions had been received at Dartmoor since November 1931. The former Home Secretary, Joynson-Hicks, who always erred on the side of hyperbole, described Dartmoor in 1927 as "the cesspool of English humanity."[129] It had a capacity for almost 1,000 convicts, but at the time of the mutiny there were but 442 inmates. The latter were mostly hardened and, in some cases, dangerous recidivists, with multiple previous convictions (though often for mundane crimes), and who had served previous terms of imprisonment and penal servitude, and were now serving three years or more.

This is not the place to provide a detailed account of the mutiny and its after-math. For that we have Alyson Brown's excellent historical work.[130] What is clear is that within the short space of two weeks, Mr. Herbert du Parcq, KC, Recorder of Bristol, with the assistance of Prison Commissioner Paterson, listened to evidence in secret from senior staff, prison officers, and convicts, and compiled the report which was available to the press by 6 February.[131] Mr. du Parcq later told the Home Secretary that witnesses were encouraged to speak freely. "I told officers that they were at liberty to criticize their superiors, and convicts that they would be safe in making any complaints about officers."[132] Hence, all witness statements had to be treated as confidential. Blame for the riot was placed squarely by du Parcq on

128 TNA, HO144/20647/595645/10: Clive Wigram, 28 Jan. 1932, "The King cannot help feeling that it is undignified and unwise thus to make public our troubles."; Rich, *Recollections of a Prison Governor*, op cit., p. 48; *Daily Telegraph*, 25 Jan. 1932, p. 11.

129 Wood, *Shades*, op cit., p. 341; *Hansard*, vol. 264, 15 Apr. 1932, col. 1151 (Sir H. Samuel, Home Secretary); TNA, HO45/17321/174068/11–18; PCom9/98: memo by Maxwell, Jan. 1933, "Use of Fire Arms in Convict Prisons"; H. A. Taylor, *Jix: Viscount Brentford* (1933), p. 187. See also A. Barton and A. Brown, "Dartmoor: Penal and Cultural Icon," *Howard Journal of Criminal Justice*, vol. 50 (2011) pp. 478–91.

130 A. Brown, *Inter-War Penal Policy and Crime in England: The Dartmoor Convict Prison Riot, 1932* (Basingstoke, 2013), chaps. 2–3; A. Brown, "Challenging Discipline and Control: A Comparative Analysis of Prison Riots at Chatham (1861) and Dartmoor (1932)," in H. Johnston (ed.), *Punishment and Control in Historical Perspective* (2008), chap 10.

131 Report by Mr. Herbert du Parcq, KC: *On the Circumstances Connected with the Recent Disorder at Dartmoor Convict Prison*, PP. 1931–2, vol. 7 (Cd. 4010), p. 807. See G. R. Rubin, "Du Parcq, Herbert (1880–1949)," *Oxford DNB* (2004); *The Times*, 28 Apr. 1949, p. 7.

132 TNA, HO144/20647/595645/39.

a new type of young convict, described as "of the 'motor bandit' or 'gangster' class," who was capable by dint of leadership and intimidation of exercising undue influence over "the weaker-minded prisoners," and who were in touch with associates outside the prison with a view to escape; on the presence of "a few bad officers" who were guilty of "irregularities and worse"; and on the inability of the governor by force of personality to quell the growing disorder. Entirely above suspicion for du Parcq were any changes in prison administration, whether inclining to leniency or severity. The governor's decision to increase the minimum period from three to 12 months before a convict could change his work party (which some of the prisoners objected to) had not contributed to the disorder, said du Parcq.

> Nor do I think that the more humane and reformative treatment of prisoners which has been the aim of prison administration in this country for many years conduces to disorder, or that there is any reason to suppose that harsher treatment of the convicts would have prevented what took place.

One could be forgiven for seeing Paterson's influence behind this reassuring conclusion, though du Parcq insisted that Paterson scrupulously abstained from any endeavour to influence his judgement.[133] Newspapers followed du Parcq's lead as to the causes of the mutiny, and the moral to be drawn. The direction of reformative penal policy was not to be diverted into harsher channels by the difficulties of this exceptional prison. As *The Times* concluded, the report "leaves the present day theory and practice of British prison administration intact."[134]

It was a closer run thing than this, however. Two months after the Dartmoor mutiny, four prisoners attacked an officer in Chelmsford "model" prison for young convicts. Chelmsford prisoners, all 200 of them, were serving their first term of penal servitude or a term of imprisonment for a year or more, and were subject to strict discipline, a longer active day, and a strenuous programme of work and physical exercise. Disorder broke out again in December. Mark Benney, who did 18 months' imprisonment in Chelmsford, found it "a seething volcano of resentments," ascribing the trouble to inadequate staffing. The prisoners were so restless that "there was seldom less than a fifth of their numbers in the punishment cells." This recalcitrant fifth had to be brought to heel. "Pens" were constructed to receive these prisoners for silent and separate hard labour, restraint jackets and ankle straps were made available, and even injecting prisoners with hyoscine was considered though rejected by Dr. East. The climax came on Christmas Day and Boxing Day, when "a riot of cat-calls, shouting, thundering on cell doors ensued," which went on all night. For six weeks prisoners were confined to cells, at the end of which the prison staff was augmented by 20 new officers.[135] Likewise in

133 Report by Mr. Herbert du Parcq, pp. 838–40.
134 *The Times*, 8 Feb. 1932, p. 13.
135 M. Benney, *Low Company: Describing the Evolution of a Burglar* (1936), pp. 323–6, 330, 336–7; TNA, HO144/17948/597264/1–4; HO144/20648/595645/187; *Daily Herald*, 27 Dec. 1932, p. 8.

Parkhurst in 1935, convicts demonstrated against the decision not to grant special remission on the occasion of George V's Jubilee. The Home Secretary, Sir John Simon, had decided not to grant remission. Instead, prisoners received a dinner of roast beef and plum pudding, and were allowed to hear the broadcast of the Coronation Service.[136] It was with considerable difficulty that Scott, the chairman of the Prison Commission since 1932, had kept the Home Secretary before Simon, Sir John Gilmour, onside. As Scott wrote, "it was quite on the cards that he [Gilmour] might decide to make a drastic change in the control of HM Prisons." Scott continued,

> I had frequent interviews with him in which I tried to explain the principles which we were following in our administration. It was not easy, for Sir John had evidently come to the Home Office well primed by critics of prison reform . . .

There were also escapes from Dartmoor, Leicester, and other jails, though the prisons (if not the borstals) still ensured safe custody, with only 34 escapes or attempts to escape among 10,249 prisoners in 1933. With a sense of relief, Scott told his wife, "We keep our governors, and I think I've won the Home Secretary to our point of view."[137]

A special assize tried the Dartmoor mutineers, neither the Home Office nor the prison commissioners agreeing to treat the riot as a breach of prison discipline (for which corporal punishment could have been awarded), instead preferring criminal proceedings against the ring-leaders, followed by deterrent exemplary sentences of additional imprisonment. Thirty-one prisoners, 12 of whom were ex-borstal boys, were indicted under the Malicious Damage Act for the felony of riotous demolition of buildings. After a trial lasting 13 days, nine of the men were acquitted, five were convicted of the full offence, and 17 were convicted of the misdemeanor of malicious damage. Exemplary sentences totalling close to 100 years, ranging from six months to ten years, were added to the prisoners' existing sentences. In retrospect, the Home Office regretted the decision to prosecute the mutineers, since as Maxwell said, "a prosecution involves the disadvantage that publicity has an infectious effect on the behavior of prisoners generally, and a deleterious effect on prison discipline."[138] Justice Finlay held the trial to a narrow remit, instructing the jury to judge the prisoners not the prison administration. Yet prisoners were not always so obliging. The one prisoner who mounted his own defence, John Jackson, was critical of the Dartmoor regime when he stated, with echoes of Paterson's maxim that people are sent to prison *as* punishment not *for* punishment:

---

136 TNA, PCom 9/139: Scott's memo, 10 Jun. 1937.

137 TNA, HO144/20648/595645/187; Scott, *Your Obedient Servant*, op cit., pp. 72–5. See also Thomas, *The English Prison Officer*, op cit., p. 161.

138 Rex v. Burgess et al, Court of Criminal Appeal, leave to appeal refused, *The Times*, 28 Jun. 1932, p. 4. In 1937, the Home Secretary, Samuel Hoare, announced that one-quarter of the sentences imposed on the Dartmoor prison mutineers would be remitted: *Hansard*, vol. 330, 9 Dec. 1937, col. 549.

When we are sentenced to penal servitude, the object—the rightful object—is to segregate us from our fellow men. We were not sentenced to be deliberately badgered into insanity and killed with bad food . . . I mean food unfit for human consumption, in many cases. Nineteen hours in the cells, and the prison system which makes it a crime for one convict to say "good morning" to another. Those are the things which drive men to revolt.[139]

Jackson received six years' penal servitude for his part in the mutiny. According to the *Evening Standard* in May, the 11 men whose sentences were remitted for remaining loyal during the mutiny "agreed that the main source of discontent in the prison was the silence system." And a few years later, the convict Macartney, who spoke to those Dartmoor mutineers who were transferred to Parkhurst, insisted albeit at one remove that:

The Dartmoor mutiny was not planned; it was a wild outbreak against unbearable conditions. The brutality, the ceaseless nagging, the injustices, the foul food, and the wretched living conditions acted continuously upon the frayed nerves of these unfortunates until, able no longer to contain themselves, in two hours they swept the whole of the secret English prison system into front page news.

As he also wrote in the *News Chronicle*, the mutiny was "a spontaneous expression of unendurable agony."[140]

Herbert du Parcq's judgment was correct: the mutiny was not provoked by penal reform, because Dartmoor was untouched by constructive reform. He was wrong, however, to suggest that the prisoners had no substantial grievances. Dartmoor gave the lie to the vaunted ameliorations of prison discipline. Even Major Grew, governor of Dartmoor in the 1920s, was unimpressed by the so-called mitigations:

The archaic buildings, the insanitary cell blocks, and the memories that haunt this grim old place cry aloud to be destroyed. Against such an atmosphere the small reforms that I saw introduced and the many that have been made in recent years are as a few drops of rain in a vast Sahara.[141]

The view that the mutiny showed not the failure of prison reform, but its absence was pressed strongly by the Howard League, which Maxwell praised for avoiding "anything in the nature of agitation or sensationalism." As an editorial in the *Howard Journal* stated, "constructive Prison Reform has not

139 A. Brown, "The Amazing Mutiny at the Dartmoor Convict Prison," *British Journal of Criminology*, vol. 47 (2007), p. 282.
140 *Evening Standard*, 27 May 1932, in HO144/20648/595645/127; Macartney, *Walls Have Mouths*, op cit., p. 241; PCom9/28: *News Chronicle*, 16 Apr. 1937.
141 Quoted in Brown, *Inter-War Penal Policy*, op cit., p. 7.

been tried at Dartmoor." No more than 150 or one-third of the convicts attended classes or received regular visits from a prison visitor. The new governor, S. N. Roberts, who had no prior experience of a convict prison, further curtailed classes and visits, tightened up the silence rule, and stiffened up the discipline. Since his appointment the number of men in punishment cells had greatly increased. The daily hours of work had been reduced to no more than five and a half, due to staff reductions consequent upon the National Government's economy cuts, so men spent 18 to 19 hours a day in cellular confinement. In all, the League believed that "the secret of the trouble was the stagnation which characterizes all prisons, but which at Dartmoor had been raised to the highest power." Nor did the League believe that only the convicts suffered under the Dartmoor regime. It knew that du Parcq's report had suggested that prison officers regarded it as a "punishment" to be assigned to Dartmoor, and that there were actual instances of staff being sent to the prison who were under suspicion of offences in other prisons. Prison officers were also in a state of discontent, expressed most forcibly in the pages of the independent mouthpiece, the *Prison Officers' Magazine*, which used the mutiny as an opportunity to condemn the declining level of discipline in prisons, the pampering of inmates, and "Borstalizing" in prisons.[142] Pay cuts and potential job losses, especially if Dartmoor were to close, lowered staff morale even further. There seems little doubt that whatever shared ethos existed between staff and inmates in the isolation of Dartmoor, whatever legitimacy the Dartmoor regime once held in prisoners' eyes, was badly frayed by the time of the mutiny. For the Howard League, Dartmoor was "a symbol of the old penal system and a symbol of its failure, its folly, its wastefulness and its brutality."[143] Like the du Parcq report, then, the Howard League reinforced the image of Dartmoor as *sui generis*, and insisted that constructive and fundamental changes to the prison system should continue.

IX

A final accounting of the prison commissioners' inter-war policy and practice must await the findings of the next chapter. As an interim assessment, however, we can say that the commissioners believed they had introduced a clearer system of classification of prisoners, and especially in London, of prisons, and that they had created a training regime in a number of the local and convict prisons. This had been accomplished, moreover, without the burden of passing

---

142 *Howard Journal*, vol. 3 (1932), p. 6; Howard League, Minute Books, EC Meeting, 5 Feb. 1932, MSS 16B/1/1, Modern Records Centre; TNA, HO45/18006/546730/29, 44; HO144/20647/595645/71A: letter from E. R. Ramsay (of the *Prison Officers' Magazine*), 1 Feb. 1932, which began by stating "The trouble at Dartmoor was primarily caused by communist activity, its gangs and leaders." See also Brown, "The Amazing Mutiny," op cit., p. 280.

143 *Howard Journal*, vol. 3 (1932), p. 8.

new legislation, and with a minimum of public discussion, but simply by administrative fiat. Paterson was especially adept at launching and manipulating the informal experiment. In view of how little effort the commissioners put into carrying the prison staff with them, it was surprising that most governors accepted the new practices, though the Senior Officers Representative Board in 1930 raised the interesting point that the training centres would be employed to better advantage in training recidivists instead of "star" prisoners. Those most in need of training, the board opined, were left in the local prisons. While only a modicum of effort went into considering the statistics of the after-careers of offenders, the commissioners took some comfort from the fact that of the 30,000 people convicted for the first time of a serious offence between 1930 and 1933, over 80 per cent had not been returned to prison by 1935.[144] They also touted the fact that 60 per cent of borstal trainees were not reconvicted, and that the percentage not reconvicted of prisoners discharged from Wakefield prison since 1923 was, after 12 years, 83.6 per cent for stars, 48.2 per cent for the special class, and 47.3 per cent for ordinaries, for a combined total of 72.7 per cent. The results of the training prisons were encouraging. The problem lay with the provincial local prison, where still all manner of prisoner was to be found, including the "ins and outs," the floating population of debtors and drunks, and in which it was nigh impossible either to classify or to train. The prison commissioners recognized that 80 per cent of convicted prisoners were serving sentences of less than three months, 90 per cent were serving sentences not exceeding six months, making anything in the nature of an advanced scheme of training impracticable. For this reason, they were prepared to accept, as Scott did in 1933, that imprisonment necessarily involved such an unnatural mode of life that prison should be the last resort, but if imprisonment were needed, "let it be a substantial imprisonment during which something may be done for the offender."[145] Around the same time, Alexander Maxwell sounded equally resigned:

> Under our present system offenders of all ages and all types—hardened offenders, first offenders, educated people, uneducated ruffians, persons convicted of serious crime, and persons convicted of trivial offences—are congregated together in one common gaol, and very little progress in the way of training is possible.

144 Ann. Rep. of P. Com. for 1935, PP, 1936–7, XV (Cd. 5430), p. 29 and Appendix X. Nearly half of the total number of all prisoners were in prison for the first time in their lives. Terence Morris was right to point out that the presence of so large a proportion of first offenders who did not subsequently re-offend, suggesting "success" rates of the order of 80–90 per cent, gave the prison authorities "a false sense of the effectiveness of their regimes." Morris, *Crime and Criminal Justice since 1945* (Oxford, 1989), p. 31.

145 H. R. Scott, "The State of Crime in England and Wales," *The Magistrate*, vol. 3 (1933), p. 721. See also W. J. Forsythe, *Penal Discipline, Reformatory Projects and the English Prison Commission 1895–1939* (Exeter, 1990), p. 185.

Much was claimed for reformative training, but one had to guard against too rosy a view of these changes:

> When we say that modern methods in prisons are reformative, all we really mean is that they are not quite so de-formative of mind and character as the older methods. If prisons are to be transformed into really effective schools of training, an entire revolution of method would be necessary; most of the existing gaols would have to be abolished and an enormous increase of expense would have to be incurred.

Therefore, in Maxwell's opinion, the only official defence of the existing prison system was as follows:

> Prisons, as at present conducted, serve to frighten the great majority of the population into obeying the law. So long as only a small proportion of the population is sent to prison, we must put up with the evil effect which prisons are liable to have on that small proportion because of the advantage which accrues from scaring the great bulk of the population into obedience to the law. The view of the practical man is that though every effort should be made to minimize the evils of imprisonment, yet if some evils remain they must be tolerated, so long as only a small proportion of the population is subjected thereto. In other words, the value of prisons is negative. Just as salt was defined by the Irishman as "what makes potatoes taste nasty if you do not put it on," so prisons may be defined as what makes laws ineffective if you do not have them. Admittedly prisons do harm to a great many people who suffer imprisonment, but in the popular view this harm is insufficient to counterbalance the practical advantages. To those who attach value to human souls this conclusion will give little satisfaction.[146]

146 Maxwell, "The Punishment of Crime and the Crime of Punishment," circa 1933–5, private papers held by author.

5

THE PERSISTENT OFFENDER, 1908–1939

They [the Judges] have never accepted the theory on which the Act of 1908 was based that in convicting a man as a habitual & sentencing him to be detained for a long period under certain conditions the Court was dealing with him in that way by reason of his *record* & was not allotting punishment for the last offence of which he had just been convicted.

Ernley Blackwell, Assistant Undersecretary of State,
8 Jan. 1924, italics in original: HO45/20332/197277/73.

I

In 1934, Lionel Fox, Secretary to the Prison Commission, in *The Modern English Prison*, cited the statistics of recidivism that appeared in the 1932 Report of the Persistent Offenders Committee. Of the 39,000 sentences of imprisonment in 1930, 28,000 were imposed on people who had previously been found guilty of offences. More significantly, in 20,384 cases, the offenders had been in prison before. Many of them had repeated sentences of imprisonment.[1] Thus the prison commissioners were exceedingly aware that recidivism was both the strongest argument against the efficacy of imprisonment, and the greatest obstacle to reformatory treatment in prison. After all, the Gladstone Committee in 1895 had published statistics showing how the probability of a further prison sentence increased with each term of imprisonment. And prison, as the last resort of the selective process of criminal justice, had the innate tendency to assemble a high proportion of people with considerable criminal careers. Indeed, the daily average prison population was largely made up of the contingent of recidivists, whether hardened, professional offenders, for whom long sentences of penal servitude would alternate

---

1 Fox, *The Modern English Prison* (1934), pp. 167–8.

with several short sentences of imprisonment, or petty offenders who came to prison under short sentences. For neither group was it possible to develop an effective training programme. It was for this reason that the 1895 committee had recommended for "a large class of habitual criminals . . . [whose] real offence is the wilful persistence in the deliberately acquired habit of crime," a new form of sentence

> by which these offenders might be segregated for long periods of detention during which they would not be treated with the severity of first-class hard labour or of penal servitude, but would be forced to work under less onerous conditions.[2]

Confirmed recidivists were to be detained for longer than could be retributively justified by the nature of the immediate offence. This all culminated in Part II of the Prevention of Crime Act 1908.

The Act's provisions for preventive detention created a "double-track" or two-stage system, whereby the habitual criminal would receive a sentence of penal servitude for the offence, and one for the protection of society. Only when the former ended would preventive detention begin. For such a sentence to be passed, the jury had to find that the offender was an "habitual criminal," the proof of which was that since the age of 16, in addition to the new conviction, he had been previously convicted at least three times of crime, and that he was "leading persistently a dishonest or criminal life." When introducing the Bill in 1908, Home Secretary Gladstone announced that the second part of the sentence would be indeterminate, but Parliament insisted that the length of preventive detention be fixed by the judiciary for not less than five nor more than ten years, within which the executive could release the offender on licence if satisfied that there was a reasonable probability that he would abstain from crime. Gladstone also took pains to instruct Parliament that the operation of the Act was confined to "professional criminals" or "persistent dangerous criminals," hence the provision that there should be an antecedent sentence of three years' penal servitude for the immediate crime. It was not to be applied to those who were "a nuisance rather than a danger to society" or to the "much larger class of those who were partly vagrants, partly criminals. And who were to a large extent mentally deficient."[3] If this was still unclear, Home Secretary Churchill in 1910, laying before Parliament the Rules for carrying out the 1908 Act, stated:

2   Ibid., p. 168. See also L. Radzinowicz and R. Hood, "Incapacitating the Habitual Criminal: The English Experience," *Michigan Law Review*, vol. 78 (1980), pp. 1353–4.
3   See Radzinowicz and Hood, "Incapacitating the Habitual Criminal," op cit., p. 1365. See also S. Hobhouse and F. Brockway, *English Prisons To-Day* (1922), p. 442; L. Radzinowicz, "The Persistent Offender," in Radzinowicz and J. W. C. Turner (eds.), *The Modern Approach to Criminal Law* (1945), pp. 163–4.

Only the great need of society to be secured from professional or dangerous criminals can justify the prolongation of the ordinary sentence of penal servitude by the addition of such Preventive Detention . . . [T]he idea should not grow up that Preventive Detention affords a pleasant and easy asylum for persons whose moral weakness or defective education has rendered them merely a nuisance to society.

To ensure the Act was applied to a more restricted category of offenders, Churchill asked that police forces not seek the consent of the Director of Public Prosecutions to charge an offender with being an "habitual criminal," unless he was at least 30 years of age and had already been sentenced to at least one term of penal servitude. And, finally, Ruggles-Brise, chairman of the Prison Commission, in *The English Prison System*, confirmed that preventive detention was no protection against petty recidivism: "It does not touch that large army of habitual vagrants, drunkards, or offenders against bye-laws and Police Regulations, who figure so largely in the ordinary prison population." It was "an invaluable instrument for social defence" where the community was endangered by "a professed doer of anti-social acts being at large, and reverting cynically on discharge from prison to a repetition of predatory action or violent conduct."[4]

This is preface to the long and troubled history of the sentence of preventive detention, with which this chapter begins. It is a story of unmitigated failure. There were many reasons for the failure of the new sentence, but the most fundamental reason was the approach taken by the judiciary. The Judges of the King's Bench in their capacity both as trial judges and as members of the Court of Appeal, at times responding to signals sent by the likes of Churchill, at other times bewildered by the different philosophies of punishment encapsulated in the dual-track system (a mix of retribution, deterrence, and public protection), proved themselves incapable of meting out in any consistent manner the sentence of preventive detention. Their lead was followed by police forces and the Director of Public Prosecutions, who struggled to know exactly which offenders to charge as habitual criminals. The more the Home Office came up with ways to modify or adapt preventive detention, the more the judiciary dug in its heels.

This chapter also explores the three related issues which the 1932 Report of the Persistent Offenders Committee examined: the employment and psychological treatment of prisoners, and their after-care. Not to put too fine a point on it, the attempt to improve industrial employment in prisons was a miserable failure. If there is one metric that says everything, it is the continued high proportion of offenders, especially those in local prisons, working on sewing mailbags for post office use. Developments in the psychological treatment of prisoners were similarly meagre in the 1930s. Even the medical prison commissioner, Norwood East, sought to keep psychological treatment in bounds, arguing that only a small percentage of prisoners was in need of such treatment. And after-care remained the

4   Sir Evelyn Ruggles-Brise, *The English Prison System* (1921), p. 58.

Cinderella of the penal system, unable to transition from aid-on-discharge provided by voluntary agencies to the professional social service that ex-prisoners urgently required, and which would have recognized that after-care was one of the most crucial requirements of a truly rehabilitative programme.

II

For 20 years, until 1931, preventive detention was undergone by men in a purpose-built prison at Camp Hill on the Isle of Wight, surrounded by a forest of oak and Scots pine, on high ground about a mile from the town of Newport. A man could not qualify for preventive detention until after serving a term of at least three years' penal servitude, so the first arrivals were not received at Camp Hill until March 1912. By early 1914 there were 170 inmates, by 1915, 286 inmates, confined in six cell blocks, each of 50 cells and a common room for meals and association. The cells were slightly larger than those in the older prisons, and had a window to the open air. Since the man, having served his prior sentence of penal servitude, had received the full punishment for the actual offence, and since being an habitual criminal was a status not an offence, the treatment he received in preventive detention, though of a penal character, was more relaxed than that of penal servitude. A system of progressive grades was introduced, each grade having special privileges and a slightly distinctive dress. Detainees worked at trades or on agricultural work and were able to earn small sums of money for their work in addition to receiving small gratuities for good conduct. They could purchase goods in the prison store, including smoking materials. Men were trusted to return to their cells after work without supervision. The dietary was more liberal, more varied, and of higher quality. Conversation and social intercourse were more freely permitted. Visits and letters were on a more liberal scale than in the later stages of a penal servitude sentence. Certain men were allowed garden allotments which they cultivated themselves. Reformation was sought principally by making the men lead a regular life and work hard. Those being considered for discharge on licence were placed in single living-quarters in parole-line cabins for six months prior to discharge. An Advisory Committee of magistrates resident in the district interviewed each inmate to inform the decision to grant a licence. The after-care of prisoners was undertaken by the Central Association for the Aid of Discharged Convicts, which directed where the prisoner should work and live.[5]

Initially, then, the Camp Hill regime was markedly different from the punitive regime of ordinary prisons. Gradually, however, most of the privileges were extended to ordinary prisons; indeed, educational services improved faster in ordinary prisons than in Camp Hill. Inmates themselves were far from content. As

5　"Camp Hill Prison," *The Times*, 16 Feb. 1914, p. 3; F. E. Wintle (Governor of Camp Hill), "Preventive Detention at Work," *Howard Journal*, vol. 1 (1921), pp. 7ff; Hobhouse and Brockway, op cit., pp. 444–9; Report on the Recidivist, written by L. S. Brass, Criminal Division, for the International Prison Commission Congress, 1930, in TNA, HO45/20334/197277/107. See also Fox, op cit., pp. 170–1.

Alexander Maxwell, chairman of the Prison Commission, said in 1931, "All persons who have had experience of Camp Hill are agreed that the present system tends to generate a sense of injustice among the men and that the uncertainty has a bad effect on them."[6] For a start, inmates thought the decision to charge them as habitual criminals was too much in the hands of the police, and the habitual criminal indictment typically flowed from victimization by a detective who was hostile to them. Inmates also maintained that they were serving two sentences for one crime. A long sentence in Parkhurst or Dartmoor was punishment enough for any offence; to have to endure five or more years of extra punishment in Camp Hill was an injustice. Earl Russell had said as much during the debates in the House of Lords on the original bill: society was justified in inflicting one such pain on a prisoner, but not both.[7] The younger detainees (aged 35–45) complained that their crimes were no worse than convicts serving much shorter sentences. The judiciary did not help matters by misleadingly promising early release to those they were sentencing to preventive detention, if they behaved themselves in prison. Indeed, there was a general complaint against the uncertainty of the date of release. The discretionary system of licensing was resented and distrusted by detainees. Prisoners, said Maxwell, viewed the licensing system as one of "mysterious favouritism, to which they are constantly trying to find the key." The Governor told Maxwell that one of the prisoners' theories was that early releases were shared among the religious persuasions. Some prisoners joined the sect which was expected to get the next turn. And in 1924, 51 men serving a second term of preventive detention petitioned the Home Office to claim the benefit of the Court of Criminal Appeal's judgment in the case of *Norman*, which decided that a person once convicted as a habitual criminal should not always be regarded as such in law. The governor of Camp Hill reported that these men were in a state of unrest, and close to mutiny. The prison commissioners increased the armed guards from Parkhurst and obtained the assistance of soldiers stationed on the Isle of Wight.[8]

The number of women sentenced under the Act was very small, no more than half a dozen, so a separate establishment was out of the question. At first, female detainees were held at Liverpool Prison. By 1925, the Advisory Board of Liverpool prison was telling the Home Office that preventive detention was entirely unsuited to the female sex:

6   TNA, HO45/20334/197277/109: Maxwell to Undersecretary of State, 26 Oct. 1931. See also Max Grunhut, *Penal Reform* (Oxford, 1948) p. 398.
7   Persistent Offenders Committee, Summaries of Evidence, vol. 1, Major Pannall, governor of Camp Hill, p. 94; Harold Begbie, "The Life of the Convict: VII—Preventive Detention," *Daily Mail*, 15 Nov. 1926, cutting in TNA, HO144/10565/467827/38; PCom9/157. For Earl Russell, see Norval Morris, *The Habitual Criminal* (Westport, CT, 1973, 1st. pub. 1951), p. 39.
8   TNA, HO45/20334/197277/109: Maxwell to Undersecretary of State, 26 Oct. 1931; HO144/8497/A63099/71; *Report of the Departmental Committee on Persistent Offenders*, PP, 1931–2, XII (Cmd. 4090), p. 585.

It is too indefinite and women especially of the convict type are temperamentally unfit to endure it, with any prospect of benefit. The uncertainty of release brings after a time a kind of suppressed excitement which from day to day increases. The women do not settle down to it in the same way as they do to Penal Servitude which has a definite ending.[9]

In response, the medical inspector of prisons, William Norwood East, described the small group undergoing preventive detention as "irritable, irritating, and vindictive women of the worst type," for whom any reformation was unlikely. He also stated that since the disadvantages, medical and otherwise, of preventive detention flowed from the small number of women in this class, and that any increase was not to be expected, "no radical remedy, short of abolition, offers itself as a solution."[10] The prison commissioners agreed, and decided to take no action, either to alter the method of setting the date of discharge, or the location of these women. Later, however, women detainees were located in a separate wing at Aylesbury. Yet Assistant Undersecretary of State, Locke could still write in 1930: "P[reventive] D [etention] for women is really P[enal] S[ervitude] indoors, with mitigations: & much more irksome than for men at Camp Hill."[11]

How successful was the new sentence? Early soundings were encouraging. According to the prison commissioners, of the first 100 licencees, 27 were reconvicted, resulting in a 73 per cent success rate. It was readily admitted, however, that these men were discharged during the Great War when work was readily available, and when those of military age often join the armed forces. Over 150 licensed Camp Hill men enlisted in the Army or Navy. After the war the rate of success fell. Of the 454 detainees received between 1912 and 1921, 343 had been licensed and 52 per cent of them were doing well. The chairman of the Camp Hill Advisory Board, Arthur Andrews, JP, reminded the Howard League, however, that in view of the kind of men detained, they had expected only a 30 to 40 per cent. success rate.[12] At this stage, even Hobhouse and Brockway, in their unflattering appraisal of English prisons, concluded that "the preventive detention system succeeds in reinstating twice or even three times as many of its 'difficult and almost hopeless cases' as does penal servitude, when working upon the same 'recidivist' material." Earlier they had said, "Remarkable results they appear to be, judged by all penal precedents." There was no doubt, they also wrote, "as to the superiority, from the educative and reformative standpoint, of preventive detention over the convict system— assuming . . . that the men who come under them are in a

---

9   TNA, HO45/11020/394438/1–4; HO45/20333/197277/94: 25 Sep. 1925.
10 Ibid., East's minute, 7 Oct. 1925.
11 TNA, HO144/22287/415147: Locke, 1 Jul. 1930. In 1930, women under preventive detention were sent to Holloway; they proved to be a "severe trial" to the officers: Mary Size, *Prisons I Have Known* (1957), p. 104.
12 Extract from *Prison Commissioners' Annual Report*, 1918–19, in TNA, HO45/20331/197277/40; Andrews, "Results of Preventive Detention," *Howard Journal*, vol. 1 (1921), pp. 19–22.

condition to be re-educated or reformed." The only note of caution was provided by the testimony of a former detainee, who claimed that men came to Camp Hill too late, after long spells of penal servitude, in "a very bitter, rebellious state, and nearly always in a dazed and stupified (sic) condition of mind."[13] The success rate plummeted in the 1920s. The prison commissioners' annual report for 1928 contained a detailed account of the operation of preventive detention during its first 20 years. Between 1912 and the end of 1926, 392 men had been released on licence. Up to the end of 1928, 30 were known to have died and one certified insane. Of the remaining 361, there were 65 of whom no unsatisfactory report had been received (many of them released during the war); the remaining 296 had been reconvicted or had their licences revoked. This was an 18 per cent. success rate.[14] Of course, it could be argued that high reconviction rates were evidence not of the failure of preventive detention but evidence of what it prevented, if only temporarily. The 1908 Act had a double object, as Home Secretary Gladstone stated, "the prolonged detention of the irreclaimable and the release on licence, after an interval, of those in whose cases there might be some hope of reform."[15] It was not long, however, before it became common knowledge that preventive detention was less a corrective treatment, than a way of protecting society for a substantial time from those with a high crime risk.

In the face of this declining success rate, the prison commissioners felt obliged to re-visit the licensing system. As early as 1922, Ernley Blackwell, Assistant Undersecretary of State in the Home Office, noted that the 73 per cent successes shown a year ago had fallen to 39 per cent. He also remarked that the Advisory Committee put too much faith in the reforming influences of Camp Hill and recommended early licence too frequently. Licensing after only two to three years' detention had been served had not proved successful. Nine years' experience showed, said Blackwell, "that men of the habitual criminal class cannot be reformed by a comparatively short period of progressive stage treatment at Camp Hill." The position was aggravated by the reluctance of judges to impose the full term of ten years' preventive detention. Blackwell wanted release on licence to be more sparingly granted. Arthur Andrews, chairman of the Advisory Committee, pushed back, shifting responsibility for failure on to the after-care system. He pretty much won the day since, in early 1924, three and a half years was approved as the normal minimum before licence, though the commissioners had wanted four years or four-fifths of a five-year sentence. However, it was also agreed that a convict serving a second term of preventive detention (and no fewer than 61 were serving a second term) was not likely to be allowed a licence at all.[16] In the course of this internal discussion about discharge, the commissioners began to wonder, in view of

---

13 Hobhouse and Brockway, op cit., pp. 456, 459; ibid., p. 634 (Evidence of a preventive detention prisoner).
14 Ann. Rep. of P. Com. for 1928, PP, 1929–30, XVII (Cd. 3607), p. 294.
15 TNA, HO45/10589/184160/16: Gladstone to Lord Chief Justice, 4 Dec. 1909.
16 TNA, HO45/20332/197277/55, 64, 66, 73: Blackwell minutes, 6 Feb. 1922, 19 Feb. 1923; Andrews letter, 12 May 1923.

the cost of Camp Hill, whether male detainees should be put in a wing of a convict prison. The department would not hear of this, arguing that placing these men in a convict prison, implying that preventive detention was in reality but a form of penal servitude, would necessitate the frank admission that the experimental reform of habituals had failed, would lead to even fewer being sentenced to PD, and would likely bring the system to an end.[17] However, in 1931 it was decided to transfer existing detainees from Camp Hill to Lewes prison (with future entrants serving their preventive detention sentence at the convict prison where they served their penal servitude sentence). The commissioners pressed the department to introduce a system of allowing men to render themselves eligible by good conduct and industry for licence on the expiration of three-quarters of the sentence. What was in effect a semi-automatic system of earning remission would, the commissioners believed, soften the blow of being removed to Lewes. It meant that all detainees who behaved would be discharged after three and three-quarter years.[18]

Did preventive detention actually protect society from the person for whom it was designed, the "dangerous" and "professional" offender? As early as 1913, H. B. Simpson, chief clerk, was of the view that the "more dangerous and enterprising criminals usually escape the net, and Preventive Detention convicts are mostly thieves of a minor kind who have been thieves from childhood and never go far in crime."[19] Later evidence only confirmed this view. Criminologist Norval Morris examined the most serious of the last offences of the 325 males who were sentenced to preventive detention, and the previous convictions of these detainees, over the 18-year period 1928–45. All 325 had more than the three statutorily required previous convictions; 186 had 11 to 20 previous convictions, 63 had more than 20. All but seven of them had been sentenced to penal servitude a least once before their conviction as habitual criminals. As Morris concluded, "Assuredly none of them was a stranger either to the criminal courts or to the prisons." Yet the vast majority were sentenced to preventive detention having been indicted for offences against property (namely housebreaking, shopbreaking, obtaining by false pretences, and simple and minor larcenies), many of which netted trivial amounts. Only seven of the 325 habituals were sentenced for a crime involving violence, the threat of violence, or danger to the person (namely wounding, robbery, arson and extortion by threat). In practice, as Morris concluded, the 1908 Act "not infrequently impinged on criminals who can only be regarded as the habitual petty delinquent type, more of a nuisance than a danger to society, helpless rather than determined criminals."[20] The age profile of detainees suggests the same. Over the entire inter-war period, the average age of detainees only once sank below 40 years of age. In the thirties, the average age ranged from 42.9 to 55.7. Major Pannall,

17 TNA, PCom7/295; HO45/20332/197277/73: minute, 1 Jan. 1924.
18 TNA, HO45/20334/197277/109: Maxwell to Undersecretary of State, 26 Oct. 1931.
19 TNA, HO45/20331/197277/32.
20 Morris, *The Habitual Criminal*, op cit., pp. 64–6.

governor of Camp Hill, reported in 1931 that the average age of the 127 male detainees was 50.6. He added that the physical capacity of the men was low on account of age, and that only about 50–60 men were "normal." An article in *John Bull* in early 1931, written by a recently-released detainee from a second preventive detention sentence, with a criminal record dating back to 1896 for larceny and false pretences, claimed that many of the inhabitants of Camp Hill were "no more than gutter-pests and sneak-thieves," many being "the surviving victims of the age when brutally harsh sentences were imposed for first and petty offences."[21] And the Report of the Departmental Committee on Persistent Offenders found in Camp Hill men, mostly in their fifties and sixties, "with little mental capacity or strength of character . . . generally they are of the type whose frequent convictions testify as much to their clumsiness as to their persistence in crime."[22] In short, preventive detention was used predominantly against a type of offender for whom it was not intended, for offenders with a tendency to nuisance offences rather than professional crime, men on their way to institutionalization. Why did the Act press upon the persistent minor offender, despite the requirement of penal servitude as a prior condition to preventive detention? Presumably because the police and the courts were more willing to penalize repetition than severity of crime, and because the hard core of criminals could be adequately punished by sentences of penal servitude.

It follows that the number and proportion of habitual criminals sentenced to detention was simply too small to hinder the criminality of recidivists. In 1908 it was estimated that some 5,000 habitual criminals of the professional type existed, and that a prison for 500 inmates would be required. Camp Hill was built to take 400 inmates. As the prison commissioners' 1928 report stated,

> At the time of the passing of the Act it was contemplated that the new provisions would have an appreciable effect on recidivism, and that a substantial proportion of the offenders who had three or more convictions of crime would be sentenced to Preventive Detention.[23]

This had not happened. In 1928, 434 men were discharged from the convict prisons, of whom 308 had previous convictions, 254 had three or more previous convictions, and 134 of them had served prior sentences of penal servitude. Yet in recent years, the average number sentenced to preventive detention had been just 31 men, the majority of whom were sentenced to the minimum period of five

21 Persistent Offenders Committee, Summaries of Evidence, vol. 1, Major Pannall, governor of Camp Hill, p. 90; "Secrets of a Famous Prison," *John Bull*, 17 Jan. 1931, in TNA/HO45/21673/433166/20.
22 *Report of the Departmental Committee on Persistent Offenders*, PP. 1931–2, XII (Cmd. 4090), p. 611.
23 Max Grunhut, "The Treatment of Persistent Offenders," *Journal of Criminal Science*, vol. 2 (1950), p. 75; Ann. Rep. of P. Com. for 1928, PP, 1929–30, XVII (Cd. 3607), p. 290.

years. By another measure, the recidivist made up almost 50 per cent of adult male receptions convicted of serious crime, yet he was relatively untouched by the measure passed to combat him. Since this data coincided with a general tendency of the courts to pass fewer and shorter sentences—the number of penal servitude sentences fell from 1,182 in 1908 to 483 in 1928; and sentences of five years and over fell from 369 in 1908 to 83 in 1928—the commissioners were forced to conclude that in view of this reduction in periods of detention of convicts, of whom nearly 70 per cent were recidivists, "the increased 'protection of the public' effected by sentencing some 31 recidivists a year to Preventive Detention is almost negligible." It remained only for Arthur Locke in March 1930 to administer the *coup de grace*:

> The more I see of P[reventive] D[etention] the less I believe in it from *any* point of view. On 31 Dec last there were in Camp Hill only 113 men, 20 aged above 60, 76 aged 40–60, & 17 aged 30–40... I think it would be far better, & more economical, to pass sentences of from 7 to 10 yrs P[enal] S [ervitude] & let men earn 1/4 remission in earlier licences, than to maintain the P.D. system when at least half its purpose (reform) has admittedly never been achieved.[24]

Why did the Act reach such an insignificant proportion of those who could have been charged as habitual criminals? There are four interlocking explanations. The first is the impact of the Great War. Ruggles-Brise was convinced that the War, "by throwing all our Penal System into an inextricable confusion, destroyed the only hope of a satisfactory result by destroying the normal circumstances under which such a plan could operate and furnish evidence of its value."[25] The second explanation is the dual-track system of punishment, notably the requirement of a term of penal servitude as a precursor to preventive detention. For a start, if the particular offence of which the offender was convicted did not justify a penal servitude sentence according to the unwritten tariff, the court was precluded from passing a sentence of preventive detention. Additionally, the courts proved reluctant to add a sentence of preventive detention to a substantial term of penal servitude. Judges and juries baulked at the idea of adding at least five years to a three-year stretch for mere property crime. The measure was too drastic to be acceptable to those who had the responsibility of deciding whether to apply it.[26] The third

---

24 Ibid., p. 293; TNA, HO144/22239/A61266/75: Locke, 3 Mar. 1930. See also Morris, *The Habitual Criminal*, op cit., p. 27.

25 Shane Leslie (compiler), *Sir Evelyn Ruggles-Brise: A Memoir of the Founder of Borstal* (1938), p. 127.

26 In principle, the 1908 Act gave courts a way of escaping the binds of the tariff or retributive thinking. The invention of two separate names—"imprisonment" and "preventive detention"—provided courts with two separate philosophical compartments to operate within: retributive justice for ordinary sentences of imprisonment, social defence, or protection of society for sentences of preventive detention.

explanation is that since far fewer sentences of penal servitude were passed in the inter-war years than in 1908, despite an increase in the volume of indictable crime, a much smaller proportion of "habituals" became eligible for preventive detention.[27] Fourthly, the Act's procedural complications, prompting the Court of Criminal Appeal frequently to reverse the lower courts regarding, say, the interpretation of the phrase "is leading persistently a dishonest or criminal life"—made the police and the Director of Public Prosecutions reluctant to proceed, and prompted the assizes and quarter sessions to shy away from using the sentence. By the end of the 1920s preventive detention was a dead letter.[28]

III

Its demise was not for want of remedial efforts on the part of the Prison Commission and Home Office. From the beginning and throughout the 1920s the department tried to rescue the preventive detention measure from oblivion. These attempts are worth exploring since they reveal the judicial mindset in relation to habitual criminality, and the willingness of the Home Office, in response to pressure from some of the senior judges, to throw the net of preventive detention over a larger body of offenders, including those who were sentenced for their immediate crime to imprisonment, as distinct from the heavier penalty of penal servitude. As early as December 1909, Home Secretary Gladstone was urging L.C.J. Alverstone to issue a Court of Criminal Appeal judgment to persuade judges and magistrates to pass longer preventive detention sentences, in order both to give the public "a considerable respite from the attentions of the professional criminal" and "to allow probationary release while a sufficient portion of the sentence remains to give effective sanction to the requirements of the licence." The appeal fell on deaf ears, Lord Alverstone declaring that a sentence of three years' penal servitude plus five years' preventive detention was already very severe. Sentences imposed by the courts continued to be largely for the minimum term of five years.[29] Fast forward to 1920, and Home Secretary Shortt's request to Lord Chief Justice Reading, to discuss the working of the preventive detention system: the atrophy of the sentence was clearly not due to a reduction in the number of recidivists, said Shortt, since a substantial number of prisoners sentenced to penal servitude were recidivists. Rather, the problem was the narrow interpretation by the courts of the definition of a "habitual criminal." True to form, Reading defended the judiciary:

27   See Leo Page, *Crime and the Community* (1937), p. 353. In 1912, 845 penal servitude sentences were passed; in 1930, 536; and in 1935, 464.

28   Cf. Barry S. Godfrey et al, *Serious Offenders: A Historical Study of Habitual Criminals* (Oxford, 2010), chap. 3.

29   TNA, HO45/10589/184160/16: Gladstone to LCJ, 4 Dec. 1909. See also Radzinowicz and Hood, "Incapacitating," op cit., p. 1370.

The tendency of the Courts is to guard the person accused of being an habitual criminal by taking care that he shall only be found guilty if the conditions required by section 10 of the Prevention of Crime Act, 1908, are fulfilled.

It must be remembered that the accused is very often undefended and he is tried by the same jury that has just convicted him of an offence for which he is to be sentenced to a term of *at least three years' penal servitude.*

The Lord Chief Justice threw the Home Secretary a bone, however, by suggesting the abandonment of the provision requiring a sentence of penal servitude in order to qualify the habitual criminal for preventive detention:

I think it is this provision in the Act which accounts for the reluctance of the Judges to make fuller use of the system. Three years' Penal Servitude followed by five or ten years Preventive Detention is a very serious sentence. My suggestion would be to give power to the Court to sentence to such term as may seem right in addition to a term of Preventive Detention, or to give no sentence other than preventive detention . . .[30]

In February 1921, the Director of Public Prosecutions recommended amending the 1908 Act to allow courts to pass a sentence of preventive detention upon a prisoner who had been sentenced to penal servitude *or to at least nine months' imprisonment.* The Lord Chief Justice, Mr. Justice Lawrence, later Lord Trevethin, endorsed the DPP's view. He was so convinced of the futility of the preliminary sentence that he was ready to empower the judge to make it less than nine months, if he thought fit. Indeed, Lawrence believed that preventive detention was the only satisfactory way of dealing with serious crime and "we should do well to scrap our system of imprisonment and penal servitude altogether and substitute preventive detention." The Home Office drafted a Prevention of Crime Bill to provide *inter alia* that a person could be sent to preventive detention after a sentence for the substantive offence of six months' imprisonment or more. Such an alteration would have increased quite considerably the number of persons eligible for preventive detention, and (contra the original Act) would have brought within the scope of the scheme the merely frequent offender as well as the professional criminal. In addition, the minimum term of preventive detention was to be seven years and the maximum 12 years, presumably to ensure that an habitual criminal received more preventive detention than an occasional criminal received of penal servitude. The draft was sent to Lord Chief Justice Hewart in 1922. He never replied, and the bill made no further progress.[31]

30 TNA, HO45/20331/197277/42: Shortt to Reading, 14 Oct. 1920; PCom7/291: Reading to Shortt, 20 Oct. 1920; HO45/20331/197277/43: Reading to Shortt, 29 Oct. 1920.
31 TNA, HO45/20331/197277/47; Ibid., 197277/49: Lawrence to Home Secretary, 27 May 1921.

In the meantime, the prison commissioners raised the notion of extending the preventive detention system

> so that it may embrace not only those who come technically within the definition of Habitual Crime, but the great mass of the Penal Servitude population whose record shows that they belong indubitably to that class and are in reality a danger to society.

Their opening gambit was to seek permission to bring up the number of inmates of Camp Hill to 150 (from the 79 in custody in August 1920) by extending the preventive detention system to certain convicts undergoing penal servitude for five years and over, whose records showed that they came within the definition of "habitual criminal." The residue of their sentence would be commuted under section 12 of the 1908 Act. If this worked in the case of penal servitude for sentences of five years and over, it might be extended to all terms of penal servitude by slight amendment of section 12. A small committee consisting of Arthur Andrews, Sir Wemyss Grant-Wilson, and Mr. Waller was dispatched to find convicts undergoing penal servitude for commutation to preventive detention. They found only 18 candidates, all serving terms of five years or more, from Dartmoor, Parkhurst, and Portland. The unexpired residue of the sentences of 16 convicts was commuted to preventive detention, and they were removed to Camp Hill.[32] This appealed to Hobhouse and Brockway, who described the commissioners' recommendation of extending the preventive detention system to all terms of penal servitude as "a momentous one, and may well inaugurate a new and better epoch in the slowly moving development of prison reform in this country." They were of course persuaded by the "comparatively mild and educational regime" of Camp Hill. The recommendation also implied, they felt, that there was a strong case for the abolition or curtailment of the preliminary period of three years' penal servitude imposed upon men sentenced to preventive detention.[33]

The Home Office had asked Lord Chief Justice Hewart in 1922 how he felt about legislation giving power to impose preventive detention even where the offence was not punished by penal servitude, and in 1925 and 1926 about the unfortunate tendency of the courts to pass short terms of preventive detention (the courts imposing the minimum term of five years in 75 per cent of the cases). To not one of these letters had any reply been received, spurring Blackwell to minute:

> . . . the L[ord] C[hief] J[ustice] is not sympathetic on the subject of P[reventive] D[etention]. He never loses an opportunity in Ct. of C[riminal] A[ppeal]

---

32 TNA, HO45/20331/197277/46: report, Feb 1921; Ann. Rep. of P. Com. for 1919–20, PP, 1920, XXIII (Cd. 972), pp. 16–17; Ann. Rep. of P. Com. for 1921, PP, 1921, XVI (Cd. 1523), p. 436.

33 Hobhouse and Brockway, op cit., p. 465.

of pointing out that an offence must not be regarded as serious in itself merely because it has been committed by a man of bad record.

That doctrine is at the root of the objection felt by some Judges to the preliminary sentence of 3 yrs. P[enal] S[ervitude][34]

The Director of Public Prosecutions still urged the repeal of the provision requiring a penal servitude sentence in order to qualify the habitual criminal for preventive detention.[35] In June and July 1929, a flurry of letters to *The Times* on "hardened offenders," launched by Sir Arthur Conan Doyle advocating "perpetual segregation for irreclaimable criminals"—"the prison doors should never open again"—prompted Mr. Justice Horridge in his charge to the grand jury at the Sussex assizes to object to the idea of imprisonment for life. The flaw in the present law, said Horridge, was the requirement that the substantive offence warranted penal servitude before preventive detention could be given:

He never could understand that limitation. If a man was an habitual criminal and came before the Court for an offence for which a judge sentenced him for a year or eighteen months, surely the judge should have power to give detention in that case.[36]

Though the Lord Chief Justice was, said Locke, "temperamentally adverse to replying to letters," the Home Office decided to try again to get him to pronounce upon the idea, since as Locke also said, the Home Secretary "would hardly consider introducing a Bill unless he were assured that its main principles would be acceptable to the majority of the Judges, including the Lord Chief Justice . . ."[37]

In September 1929, Home Secretary Clynes wrote to Lord Hewart, asking for his view on a bill to enable the passing of sentences of preventive detention on habitual criminals sentenced to *six months'* hard labour or more, providing thereby "a proper method . . . of dealing with habitual criminals whose offences are not of the gravest," and also to increase the maximum term of preventive detention to 12 years, since detainees had shown themselves "hopeless subjects for reformatory effort, and their detention at Camp Hill has to be regarded mainly as securing the protection of society." This time the Lord Chief Justice replied. A judges' meeting, he reported, indicated that there was "a clear difference of opinion among the

34 TNA, HO45/20331/197277/89: Blackwell minute, 22 May 1925.
35 Ibid., 197277/83.
36 *The Times*, 20 Jun. 1929, p. 17; 9 Jul. 1929, p. 15; 13 Jul. 1929, p. 15; C. M. Knowles, "The Problem of the Old Offender," *Police Journal*, vol. 4 (1931), p. 506; *The Magistrate*, vol. 2 (1929), p. 332; TNA, HO144/10565/467827/89. Conan Doyle was known for his efforts to exonerate wrongly-imprisoned inmates, so his support for "perpetual segregation" came out of the blue. Cf. Sir Ernest Wild's statement in the Central Criminal Court, reported in *The Magistrate*, vol. 2 (1929), p. 292; Fenner Brockway, *A New Way with Crime* (1928), p. 161, in favour of indeterminate or long sentences for the "residuum" of 1,000 professional and habitual offenders.
37 TNA, HO45/20331/197277/104: Locke, 2 Aug. 1929.

Judges" on the question of extending the power to pass sentence of preventive detention, and that the judges were opposed to increasing the maximum sentence of preventive detention, "especially as the present maximum of ten years is rarely if ever served." Blackwell wrote cryptically, "We now know where we are on subject of the preliminary 3 years p.s.!" And Locke minuted, "I think this must be taken as fatal to legislation for some years to come."[38]

IV

In the shadow of these discussions of the 1908 Act and preventive detention, created ostensibly for those "professional criminals" who deliberately chose the gamble of crime, there occurred an intermittent debate about the "habitual petty delinquent," drunkards, vagrants, and beggars. Records were kept in 1927 of persons admitted to prison more than once during the year. They numbered 2,899 men and 1,203 women, a sample of what the prison commissioners called "the stage army of offenders who are continually passing in and out of the prisons." They accounted for 7,153 male and 4,659 female *receptions* in 1927. The crimes of the men on second commitment were largely against property without violence (in the case of indictable offences), and for drunkenness, begging and sleeping out, being found on enclosed premises, offences against the poor laws, and assaults (in the case of non-indictable offences). The crimes of the women were largely for drunkenness and prostitution. In fact, one-third of the men and half the women in this sample group of recidivists were habitual drunkards, though among the recidivist men there were also a large number of petty thieves.[39] A few years later, the commissioners estimated that a stage army of 700–800 men and 400–500 women accounted for the prisoners convicted of offences against the Intoxicating Liquor Laws.[40] The problem of the petty habitual offender, and the related issue of the short prison sentence, was not new. Churchill, after all, had proposed suspending short sentences of under a month, allowing sentences to accumulate until they tallied over a month in length. For "habitual drunkards, rogues and vagabonds," Churchill proposed a year's training for those convicted three times within a year; two years' training for those convicted six times within a two-year period.[41] Nothing came of his ideas. Home Secretary Gladstone, who inaugurated the preventive detention system, wrote a dozen years later in notes for his autobiography:

---

38   Ibid., 197277/106: Locke minute, 18 Oct. 1929. See also TNA, HO45/21674/ 433166/45.
39   Ann. Rep. of P. Com. for 1927, PP, 1928–9, IX (Cd. 3292), pp. 323–5. See also J. W. Rackstraw, "Vagrancy and Petty Crime," *Howard Journal*, vol. 2 (1929), pp. 352–5; Grunhut, *Penal Reform*, op cit., p. 390.
40   Ann. Rep. of P. Com. for 1931, PP, 1932–33, XV (Cd. 4295), p. 428.
41   Radzinowicz and Hood, "Incapacitating the Habitual Criminal," op cit., p. 1373. See also *Report from the Departmental Committee on Habitual Offenders, Vagrants, Beggars, Inebriates, and Juvenile Delinquents* (Scotland, 1895). The committee recommended extended confinement for persistent petty offenders.

> I held and hold strongly that [preventive detention] should include the hope-
> less persons of whom the Dartmoor Shepherd [a petty habitual thief whose
> long preventive detention sentence Churchill was appalled by] was a good
> example, who persist in a life of minor thieving & pilfering . . . But I found
> opinion was too strong for the inclusion of the Dartmoor Shepherd class and I
> reluctantly excluded them.[42]

In the 1920s, pressure to deal with this class of offender came from a number of
sources, including Visiting Justices and Boards of Visitors of prisons, and penal
reform bodies. The report of the Visiting Committee for Holloway Prison in 1921
complained about the short sentences imposed upon habitual offenders for drunkenness, solicitation, and loitering. For 1921–2, there were 1,775 receptions on
conviction into Holloway with sentences of one month and over two weeks, and
1,465 for two weeks or less. Forty-seven per cent of the total received had five or
more previous convictions; 57 per cent were imprisoned in default of payment of a
fine. The Visiting Committee wanted their fellow magistrates to be encouraged to
inflict longer punishment on these habituals. Waller could not agree more. Most of
these trivial offences, he said, should be dealt with in other ways than prison, but
where a sentence had to be given on an habitual offender, it should be a substantial
one. Yet as he told the Home Office, "you know that this is an immense controversial subject . . . It includes questions of separate homes for inebriates, prostitutes, vagrants etc.!" He concluded, "Prison life is not really suited for any of the
feebler wreckage of society." Locke concurred, "These short sentences encumber
prisons with a mass of flotsam which washes in & out & remains mere wreckage."
He hoped that an official commission considering prison reform might develop a
plan for dealing with the problem.[43] Other bodies chimed in on the subject. The
Women's Freedom League claimed prison was not the place for women habitual
petty offenders (indeed the League argued it was the present prison system which
was the cause of excess recidivism among women); they needed detention homes
to which entry would be voluntary. The Magistrates Association wanted non-
punitive preventive detention for weak-minded persons who committed petty
offences persistently. The Borstal Association recommended an institution for
"petty recidivists" on indeterminate sentences. The Howard League suggested
using the Mental Deficiency Act to take care of elderly defectives with ten or more
convictions against them. The International Prison Commission, which was held in
London in 1925, refreshed the concept of the indeterminate sentence for habitual
petty offenders. At four consecutive annual conferences of visiting justices and
boards of visitors, between 1927 and 1931, resolutions were passed and transmitted
to the Home Office calling for prolonged detention on non-punitive lines in Farm
Colonies for the mixed bag of petty recidivists. The 1929 conference also called for

---

42 Viscount Gladstone Papers, BL, Add MSS., 46118, folio 169.
43 TNA, HO45/21673/433166/1: Waller minutes, 26 Jun. 1922, 4 Jul. 1922; Locke
    minute 5 Jul. 1922.

a Committee of Inquiry to investigate the treatment of habitual offenders, including persons convicted of drunkenness, sleeping out, vagrancy, and begging, who were constantly serving short sentences.[44]

As early as 1927, the department were contemplating the appointment of an enquiry into the modes of dealing with offenders. "Such an inquiry [sic]," said Locke, "would no doubt bring out the consideration that prisoners in general, & especially 'short-sentence habituals' are largely a sort of residuum left over as not proper for other modes of dealing with offenders." But Locke did not think it advisable "to begin by tackling the residuum first."[45] By 1929, it was evident that if it became possible for preventive detention to be imposed when a sentence of only six or nine months' imprisonment was passed for the substantive offence, the offenders eligible for preventive detention might include the petty recidivist. When the Lord Chief Justice scotched any such legislative amendment, it followed therefore, as Locke realized, "that extensions of any modified P[reventive] D [etention] system to women petty recidivists, sexual recidivists & so on are also relegated, for the time being, to limbo."[46]

In June 1930, Maxwell, chairman of the Prison Commission, suggested the appointment of a committee of inquiry to review the whole problem of habitual offenders, including the small class who were sentenced to preventive detention; those who were sentenced to repeated terms of penal servitude (often with sentences of imprisonment sandwiched between such terms); and the large class of minor offenders presently awarded short prison sentences. Locke correctly diagnosed that for Maxwell, one of the most unsatisfactory features, "unsatisfactory in itself, and also enormously swelling the prison population and increasing the difficulties of handling the rest of the prison population satisfactorily, is the continued coming and going of 'ins-and-outs' or petty recidivists."[47] Would the committee of inquiry find a solution to this unsatisfactory feature of the prison system?

The first step was to find a chairman of the proposed committee. Maxwell wanted someone whose opinion would carry weight with the judiciary. In the past 35 years, said Maxwell, no progress had been made in the adoption of the principle that in sentencing a man to preventive detention, the court was dealing with him by reason of his previous record, not allotting punishment for the last offence, "and no progress can be made without the concurrence of the Judges." Accordingly, the Home Secretary asked Lord Chancellor Sankey to release Lord Atkin for the role, pleading that in any proposed amendment of the law "it is clearly desirable to carry

---

44 TNA, HO45/21673/433166/3, 7, 11; Borstal Association, Minutes of EC meeting, vol. 4, 19 Jan. 1928; *Howard Journal*, vol. 1 (1925), pp. 199–200; HO45/14099/145740/4; HO45/20084/482137/6, 10, 13; PCom9/59.
45 TNA, HO45/21673/433166/14: Locke's minute, 30 Mar. 1927.
46 TNA, HO45/20331/197277/106: Locke minute, 18 Oct. 1929.
47 TNA, HO45/18006/546730/12: Maxwell, 25 Jun. 1930; HO144/10565/467827/89: Locke, 19 Jul. 1929. See Duncan Fairn, "Maxwell, Alexander (1880–1963)," *Oxford DNB* (2004). Maxwell was chairman of the Prison Commission between 1928 and 1932, becoming Deputy Undersecretary of State, and in 1938, Permanent Undersecretary of State.

the Judges with us, and for this reason the Report ought to be the report of men whose opinion the Judges would respect." But Sankey opposed the request, since it would create extra work for the other judges. A Scottish judge was then sought and found in a former member of the Scottish Bar, and former Judge President of the Natal Division of the Supreme Court of South Africa, Sir John C. Dove-Wilson. Maxwell himself was appointed to the Committee, as was Mr. du Parcq, who would later be asked to take charge of the inquiry into the Dartmoor Mutiny. And since medical and psychological questions were bound to arise in connection with the treatment of alcoholics and persistent offenders who were "weakminded," Dr. East, medical commissioner of prisons, was put on the Departmental Committee on Persistent Offenders. The Home Office, in the words of Blackwell, wanted above all "a practical Report which wd. form a basis for legislation in the near future."[48]

V

The Committee held 39 meetings and examined 66 witnesses.[49] No shorthand notes of the evidence were taken, so Johnston, assistant principal in the Home Office, prepared a precis of the evidence, compressing into a few pages a clear statement of the important points which emerged from the rather rambling questioning of each witness.[50] To judge from these summaries, and from memoranda submitted by various pressure groups, there was close to unanimity on the need to abandon the prior sentence of penal servitude. The Magistrates Association called for it, as did Sir Ernest Wild, Recorder of the City of London, the Chief Constable of Manchester, and the previous and present Director of Public Prosecutions. Sir Emley Blackwell, speaking for the Home Secretary, recommended altering the statutory conditions, including "reducing the length of the preceding sentence for the substantive offence to, say, one year's or six months' imprisonment," adding in supplementary evidence that if the requirement as to primary sentence was reduced, "the police could then have a number of petty recidivists indicted and brought under the operation of the Act." The supplementary point was also made by Edward Tindal Atkinson, the DPP: "If the requirement as to the prior sentence were modified, there would of course be nothing in law to prevent persistent petty offenders being indicted and sent to preventive detention."[51]

48 TNA, HO45/21673/433166/21: Maxwell, 18 Nov. 1930; 9 Dec. 1930; Sankey to Clynes, 23 Feb. 1931; Blackwell, 8 Jan. 1931.
49 Thirteen of the witnesses were working as medical superintendents in prison or in psychiatric hospitals, which says something about the expanding legitimacy of the medical world in penal reform.
50 TNA, HO45/21674/433166/38. Johnston also wrote the preliminary draft of the report.
51 Persistent Offenders Committee, Summaries of Evidence, vol. 3, POC 74, Council of Magistrates' Association; vol. 1, POC 17, Sir Archibald Bodkin, former DPP; vol. 2, POC 41, Sir Ernest Wild, KC, Recorder of the City of London; vol. 1, POC 15, John Maxwell, Chief Constable of Manchester; vol. 1, POC 1, Sir Emley Blackwell, Assistant

The second point upon which there was good deal of unanimity was the need to find new ways of handling the petty persistent offender. The Howard League divided persistent offenders into "professionals," "ins-and-outs," and a middle group of recidivists suffering from some mental or psychological abnormality which lead them commit sexual crimes. The "ins-and-outs" of local prisons had multiple convictions, a large percentage were alcoholics, and they were "a nuisance to society." For this residuum, more or less permanent segregation was recommended in colonies or industrial villages, in which family settlement would be allowed. Likewise, the Magistrates Association recommended detention for not more than two years for those who habitually committed offences involving drunkenness, vagrancy, or disorderly conduct. Dr. J. H. Morton, governor of Holloway, thought the female shoplifter presented the largest problem among persistent petty recidivists, for whom he recommended preventive detention, provided the minimum term came down to two or three years. For the drunks and prostitutes, he suggested hostels where they would sleep at night but work outside during the day. For persistent drunks, the governor of Manchester prison, Mr. W. Young, thought a state inebriate reformatory was required, an idea seconded by M. Hamblin Smith, medical officer of Birmingham prison. Hamblin Smith added that the largest class of recidivists were those unable to cope with the demands of society "by reason of mental conflict, or of what may be called (for want of a better term) 'inadequate personality,'" for whom the Mental Deficiency Act ought to be amended "so that the persistent commission of vicious and/or criminal acts is sufficient evidence *per se* of mental defectiveness."[52]

One witness deserves extended discussion, since he was also the only person who sought to place the subject of the persistent offender into the larger structure of penal policy and practice. Not surprisingly, the evidence that Alexander Paterson gave drew heavily upon the system of prison classification he had devised in the mid-1920s.[53] He first sought to show by statistics that some forms of recidivism were much diminished by comparison with the pre-war years. Imprisonment for alcoholic offences was a shadow of its former self. The number of professional and persistent criminals was much smaller: "The recidivist army of 1909 no longer figures either in the convict or local prisons of 1929." To explain this reduction in recidivism, Paterson hymned the alternatives to imprisonment: probation, reformatory schools, and borstal training. He also acknowledged "the potency of the

Undersecretary of State, pp. 17–19; supplementary evidence, p. 34; vol. 1, POC 2A, E. H. Tindall Atkinson, DPP.

52 Persistent Offenders Committee, Summaries of Evidence, vol. 2, POC 31A, Dr. Morton, governor and medical officer, Holloway prison; vol. 2, POC 23, Young, governor of Manchester Prison. Dr. G. B. Griffiths, medical commissioner of prisons from 1923 to 1930, wondered if legislation, like the Mental Deficiency legislation, could be introduced to deal with repeat petty offenders suffering from gross social inadaptability, by a sentence of indefinite detention, in an institution run entirely by a medical man. See Persistent Offenders Committee, Summaries of Evidence, vol. 3, POC 65.

53 See chapter 4 *supra.*

first sentence of imprisonment and the impotence of subsequent sentences." This brought him to the real recidivist problem: "The recidivists are a stage army, crossing and recrossing the prison gates . . . every fresh sentence multiplies the chance of further sentence." Paterson's conclusions flowed from this statistical preface. First, social conditions—housing, education, and work—were critical to the reduction of crime. Secondly, the recidivist army could be reduced further by expanded use of the main alternatives to imprisonment, and by insisting that courts should certify that every alternative had been considered, adding reasons why none would suffice, before being allowed to commit an adolescent offender to prison. Paterson also recommended a new alternative for delinquents, the deprivation of leisure in the evening or on weekends, what would eventually be implemented years later in the shape of the attendance centre. His third conclusion concerned adult offenders, notably the men who were unchanged for having passed through all forms of adolescent training, who made up "the greater part of the recidivist population." For these offenders, remand homes for examination, diagnosis, and classification were essential. The probation system should be strengthened; imprisonment avoided:

> It is often but a clumsy piece of social surgery, tearing a man away from the social fabric of home and work and club and union that he has woven round himself, causing distress to others, and rendering his replacement in social and industrial life a matter of grave difficulty.

He proposed to abolish all prisons, especially all locals.

> The English local prison to-day contains an *omnium gatherum* of innocent and guilty, young and old, weak and defiant, and is trying with one staff and under one roof to perform a great variety of functions towards them, examining the men awaiting trial, detaining the old recidivists, trying to train the younger and less expert in crime.[54]

Instead, Paterson wanted a Board of Welfare (not the Prison Commission) to administer the probation system and all institutions, including training centres for first offenders (who had committed serious crimes) and young recidivists under 30 years of age, and for first and second offenders of any age, and places of detention for those who persisted in crime, who required safe custody. There would be different kinds of training centre, according to the type of offender, including hutment camps. The short, sharp prison sentence would be outlawed. Whether for training or detention, no sentence would be for less than six months. Courts would fix a minimum (to reflect the gravity of the offence) and a maximum (no longer

---

54 Persistent Offenders Committee, Summaries of Evidence, vol. 3, POC 61 and 61A, Alexander Paterson. This evidence also appears in S. K. Ruck, *Paterson on Prisons* (1951), chap. 4. The quotation is in Ruck, p. 62.

than the maximum fixed by law for each offence) in each case. "Thus a man convicted of arson might receive a sentence of one to five years." A licensing board would determine the date of release within the court-imposed limits, and inmates would be discharged on a strict licence. For the "residuum of habitual criminals," which had demonstrated its unfitness for freedom, Paterson resigned himself to the indeterminate sentence, though he was under no illusion that it was possible to know which prisoner was likely to go straight on discharge.[55] Already Sir Ernest Wild, Recorder of the City of London, had treated the committee to his view of such a sentence: "I consider that the indeterminate sentence is unfair and unEnglish [sic]; that it is an excrescence of foreign origin; that it allows amateurs to meddle with sentences, and tends to undermine Judicial responsibility."[56]

The Report of the Persistent Offenders Committee roughly followed Paterson's distinction between training and detention. The Committee believed that the judicial authorities would embrace an extension of their powers to allow them to order detention of such character and length, either for the training of offenders or for the protection of society. Before presenting the specific recommendations of the committee, it is necessary to see how they categorized persistent offenders. The prison authorities, they said, recognized three main types: the offenders who chose a life of crime, many of whom were young and still amenable to "reformative treatment"; the offenders of "weaker mentality and weaker moral character" who drifted into crime due to their inability to cope with life; and "pathological cases" amenable to medical and psychiatric treatment.[57] The committee's first recommendation was of a sentence of *detention for two to four years*, to fill what they called "an illogical gap" between borstal training and preventive detention. "For the many persistent offenders who are between the ages of 21 and 30 and for the many persistent offenders over the age of 30 whom it would be undesirable or impracticable to indict as 'habitual criminals,'" there was only imprisonment or penal servitude for the substantive offence. Yet of the total number of persons convicted of indictable offences in 1930, close to 14,000 or 25 per cent were aged between 21 and 30. Out of 15,712 receptions in prisons for indictable offences in the same year, 5,724 or 30 per cent were of persons between 21 and 30. It was also recognized that the persistent offender was usually engaged in crime of an unspectacular character, notably housebreaking and larcenies. Larcenies consisted largely of thefts of small sums of money or of articles valued at under £5. Thefts of property valued at over £100 formed only 2 per cent of the thefts known to the police. The new

55   Ibid.
56   vol. 2, POC 41, Sir Ernest Wild, KC, Recorder of the City of London.
57   *Report of the Departmental Committee on Persistent Offenders*, PP, 1931–32, XII (Cmd. 4090), p. 560. Many years later, the Permanent Undersecretary of State, C. C. Cunningham, claimed that it would have been impossible at the time to attempt a scientific enquiry into the validity of these distinctions (between three types of persistent offender), but that the failure to realize their relevance to the treatment needs of the different types of offender was the main reason why the two new sentences proved so ineffective and so wasteful of the prison system's resources: 13 Aug. 1963, TNA, HO291/518, CRI 15/1/8.

sentence, then, was meant for persistent offenders, especially those in the early stages of a criminal career, who would benefit from training, and for others "whose criminality appears to be mainly determined by mental inertia and other innate negative qualities," and whose detention was required for public protection. An offender would have to be convicted of an offence punishable by imprisonment for two years or by penal servitude, and (referring to personal qualities) by reason of his "criminal habits or tendencies" his detention was necessary for the prevention of crime. No recidivism in the sense of previous convictions would be required.[58]

The committee's second recommendation was of a sentence of *prolonged detention for not less than five and not more than ten years*, for "the 'professional' criminals who deliberately make a living by preying on the public"; for those "who practice thefts or frauds on a comparatively small scale—the victims being usually poor people on whom the loss of a small sum may inflict a more serious injury than the loss of valuable property on persons of means"; and for "certain sexual offenders . . . particularly those who commit repeated offences against children or young people and those who corrupt boys," the first occasion on which "dangerousness" was explicitly extended to sexual crimes. The committee's report claimed that some of these offenders would be suitable, at least in the first instance, for the shorter detention sentence. For prolonged detention, an offender would have to be convicted of a "crime" and have been at least three times previously convicted of crime, and by reason of his "criminal habits and mode of life" his detention was expedient for public protection. "Crime" was defined to cover the more serious offences against property and against the person, including certain sexual offences. For both forms of detention, there would be release on licence at any time after one-third of the sentence had been completed, and power to licence after the offender had completed three-quarters of his sentence, conditional on good conduct and industry. The licence would run until the end of the sentence and for 12 months beyond. Significantly, it was later acknowledged by the Home Office that: "No hard and fast line can be drawn between the types of offenders for whom the shorter sentences are appropriate and the types for whom the longer sentences are necessary."[59]

In addition, the committee suggested that the treatment in training institutions should be akin to what was being tried at Wakefield and Chelmsford, and should adapt the principles underlying borstal training to offenders aged 21 to 30. The report even suggested that places of detention should have officers acting like borstal housemasters, "maintaining personal touch" with small groups of inmates, and for some offenders the hutment camp on the lines of Lowdham Grange borstal should be tried. In all, the committee moved close to what Paterson had long tried to implement:

---

58 Ibid., pp. 571–3. See also Max Grunhut, "The Treatment of Persistent Offenders," *Journal of Criminal Science*, vol. 2 (1950), p. 79.
59 Ibid., pp. 574–7, 585–7; TNA, HO45/21674/433166/58.

Our proposals for sentences of detention will facilitate the policy of setting aside special establishments for selected classes of offenders and will enable the Prison Authorities to develop the policy that so far as practicable the period for which the offender is committed to their custody should be utilized for his training.[60]

It should be emphasized that the new sentences were to be available to the courts in lieu of a sentence of imprisonment or penal servitude. There was to be no requirement of a prior prison sentence. Courts would send offenders directly to detention. Moreover, the committee recommended the repeal of the requirement in the 1908 Act that there must be a finding by the jury of habitual criminality before such a sentence could be imposed. There would be no special procedure for giving the Court information as to the prisoner's habits or mode of life, only such information regarding the offender's character and record as was obtained in the normal course before passing sentence. The decision as to whether a person was or was not a habitual criminal as well as the length of his sentence was to rest entirely in the discretion of the judge (which is what the judges had proposed as far back as 1903).[61] Finally, the committee recommended that it was time to get rid of the distinction between penal servitude and imprisonment. For many years, the report argued, "there has been no material difference between the conditions under which sentences of penal servitude and sentence of imprisonment are served." This would deliver a simpler penal landscape. Only two designations would exist, Imprisonment and Detention. *Imprisonment* would describe all ordinary sentences up to life sentences, the aim being to apportion a term for the offence, "and in that sense are retributive in character." *Detention* would describe all sentences based on the character of the offender with the aim either of reformative training or safe custody. There would thus be three types of detention: borstal training, detention for periods of two to four years, and prolonged detention for five to ten years.[62]

The report was welcomed as a statesmanlike document (*Law Journal*), "fertile and farseeing in its proposals for the future" (*Justice of the Peace*), and initiating "a mild revolution in our treatment of crime" (*Spectator*). Criminologists agreed: "one of the most important contributions ever made towards the solution of this highly controversial and complicated problem."[63] In retrospect, these warm approbations seem

60 Ibid., pp. 581–2, 621.
61 Ibid., pp. 616–8; TNA, HO45/20334/197277/115; HO45/21674/433166/37.
62 Ibid., pp. 605–7. The only evidence of a "scientific" or positivist approach to the problem of the persistent offender was relegated to the back of the report. One committee member, Dan Griffiths, a schoolmaster, submitted a reservation, a plea for the view that the criminal was "an ill-adjusted or ill-equipped product of a faulty heredity and environment—in a very imperfect world." Of the 120 preventive detainees seen at Camp Hill, "The brand they overwhelmingly bore was poverty, physical and mental." See *Report of the Departmental Committee on Persistent Offenders*, PP, 1931–32, XII (Cmd. 4090), pp.624–8; Cicely Craven, "The Report of the Departmental Committee on Persistent Offenders," *Howard Journal*, vol. 3 (1932), pp. 69–70.
63 *Law Journal*, vol. 73, 11 Jun. 1932. p. 404; *Justice of the Peace*, vol. 96, 25 Jun. 1932, p. 428; *Spectator*, 10 Jun. 1932, p. 4; L. Radzinowicz, "The Persistent Offender," in

wide of the mark. None of them recognized that the report remained far from transparent concerning the treatment of the petty persistent offender, despite the fact that a good bit of the evidence the committee received had focused upon this type of offender. The treatment of recidivist inebriates did not figure constructively in the report, the Committee simply declaring that there was little advantage in the revival of special provisions relating to habitual drunkards in the Inebriates Act 1898. Nor were prostitutes or vagrants specifically provided for. No hostels or industrial villages were recommended for these "in-and-outs."[64] We have it on Maxwell's good authority, in a discussion on the report at the Annual Conference of Visiting Justices, that: "We did spend a good deal of time over the habitual drunkard. That is a problem upon which we came to the conclusion that there is no remedy that we could devise." As for the remaining stage army of petty offenders, those convicted on indictment of small thefts or frauds and sent through the prisons on repeated sentences of six or nine months, the committee seems to have put its faith in the new sentence of two to four years' detention, though the report is opaque on the issue. Again, we must rely upon Maxwell's later statement:

> There is the other type of petty offender who habitually steals small things—we think these should be dealt with quite severely. We are impressed by the number of people who defraud poor people to whom the loss of a few shillings or pence is really a serious matter . . . I do not see why the man who perpetually takes small things should not be dealt with by the proposed sentence of detention for three or four years.[65]

The sentence of two to four years' detention, then, was the Committee's main proposal for dealing not only with the young offender aged 21–30, but also with the large number of persistent offenders for whom a sentence of five to ten years would be inappropriate in view of the nature of the offence. The Committee did not *unwittingly* widen the net, *pace* Professor Radzinowicz, but *knowingly* accepted the long-term incarceration of the habitual petty offender. Of course, this all begged the question of how the judges would respond to the new proposed power. As Maxwell admitted to the visiting justices,

> I recognize that a great many courts would at present feel much hesitation in imposing such a sentence but my own view is that there is no use at all in shutting up that type of man who is perpetually committing these small crimes for a few weeks or months. It would be much better to subject him to a long term.[66]

Radzinowicz and J. W. C. Turner (eds.), *The Modern Approach to Criminal Law* (1945), p. 169.

64 *Howard Journal*, vol. 3 (1932), pp. 18–9; Leo Page, *Crime and the Community* (1937), pp. 357–8; Ann Smith, *Women in Prison* (1961), p. 188.

65 TNA, PCom9/59: annual conference of Visiting Magistrates, 29 Nov. 1932.

66 Ibid. A few years later, Maxwell observed that the scheme devised by the Persistent Offenders Committee would have the advantage that "if the local prisons were relieved of the numerous persistent offenders who at present return again and again on sentences

Home Secretary Samuel hoped to introduce a bill based on the Committee's proposals, but first he wrote to Lord Chief Justice Hewart asking for the opinion of
the judges on the report. Four months later, in a terse response, Hewart transmitted
the views of the judges of the King's Bench Division. They accepted that the
existing legislation as to habitual criminals should be repealed, and that the court
should decide whether a sentence of detention should be passed in the same way as
other sentences—though they wanted the accused person to be given notice that
the court would pass a sentence of detention if he were convicted of the crime
charged. Then the judges departed from the committee in two ruinous regards.
One, "We are not satisfied that there is sufficient reason for introducing sentences
of detention for two to four years." And, two, if sentences of prolonged detention
were to be given in lieu of any other sentence, "we think it of great importance to
retain also the power to pass such a sentence in addition to a sentence for the
offence charged in the indictment." Otherwise, since detention was to be less penal
than imprisonment or penal servitude, "a persistent offender might be more lightly
treated than a criminal who could not be so described."[67]

Maxwell wrote a long internal note in response to the judges' views. On the
sentence of two to four years' detention, he observed that unlike for offenders of
criminal habit under 21, for whom there was borstal training, for the offender over
21 there was no power to commit for a period of training. Nor was there power to
commit persistent offenders to detention for the protection of the public except for
the limited class who qualified for the existing scheme of preventive detention.[68]
He went on to show that few of the cases for which the shorter sentence of
detention was proposed came before assize court judges. Of the 15,842 persons
sent to prison in 1931 on conviction for indictable offences, 13,880 were dealt
with by the Courts of Quarter Session and the Courts of Summary Jurisdiction.
Thus of every 100 persons sent to prison for indictable offences only 12 came
before the judges, and these 12 were typically guilty of a serious crime, so the
courts were able to pass a long term of imprisonment or penal servitude. In consequence, "the personal experience of the Judges gives them no indication of the
difficulties which are experienced by other Courts in dealing with persistent
offenders." Maxwell believed that recorders and chairmen of quarter sessions
would make "substantial use" of the new sentence. As for the idea that the court
should be given an option of passing a sentence of prolonged detention *simpliciter*
or of passing a dual sentence of imprisonment or penal servitude plus detention,

of eighteen months or a year or less, it would be possible to make further progress in
improving prison conditions . . . ": *Treatment of Crime* (1938), Sidney Ball Lecture, 16
Nov. 1937, Barnett House Papers No. 21, p. 23.
67 TNA, HO45/21674/433166/45: Samuel to Lord Chief Justice Hewart, 25 Jul. 1932;
Ibid., 433166/55: Hewart to Home Secretary, 22 Nov. 1932.
68 TNA, HO45/21674/433166/55. Maxwell's first response to the judges' rejection of
sentences of detention for two to four years was to write: "Whether they regard the
existing system of sending this 'stage army' of offenders through the prisons on repeated
sentences of six months or nine months as inevitable, is not clear. . ."

Maxwell countered that the objection to a dual sentence was one of the chief objections to the existing law (which the judges themselves had often voiced), and that detention was not to be "less penal" than imprisonment or penal servitude. Loss of liberty for an extended period of detention would inevitably be punitive and deterrent. Life in detention, especially for the younger men, would be active and strenuous.[69]

This is where the matter rested for the time being.[70] In 1933, in the House of Lords, Lord Polwarth, former chairman of the prison commissioners for Scotland, asked if the government intended to introduce legislation to give effect to the recommendations of the report of the Committee on Persistent Offenders. He was told only that the government was closely examining the committee's recommendations.[71] In fact, the recommendations did not seriously form the subject of legislative activity until the Criminal Justice Bill 1938, of which more in the next chapter. We turn instead to the recommendations of the Persistent Offenders Committee of which we have not yet made mention: first, the industrial employment and after care of prisoners, and second, the mental condition and psychological treatment of offenders. Both subjects warrant examination over the wider canvas of the inter-war years.

VI

The Persistent Offenders Committee was under no illusions about the existing arrangements for employing prisoners:

> Most of the people who come to prison repeatedly are indifferent workers, untrained and ill-fitted by temperament or habit for steady employment; and prison does little to remedy their industrial efficiency. The kind of work a man learns to do in prison is seldom of much use outside, and he does not acquire in a prison workshop the habit of working with speed and concentration.[72]

There were three main categories of prison labour: domestic work (cleaning, cooking, laundry); building and maintenance work (altering and erecting prison buildings, the upkeep of heating and lighting services); and manufacturing articles required for prison use or for other government departments. The manufacturing industry that occupied most prisoners was still the making and repairing of mail

---

69 Ibid.
70 On 29 Jul. 1932, Home Secretary Samuel met Miss Craven and Roy Calvert of the Howard League to discuss the report. He said that, subject to Cabinet consent, he hoped to introduce a bill based on the proposals of the Committee. See TNA, HO45/21674/433166/46.
71 *Hansard* (Lords), vol. 87, 29 Mar. 1933, cols. 147–66.
72 *Report of the Departmental Committee on Persistent Offenders*, PP, 1931–32, XII (Cmd. 4090), p. 590.

bags for the General Post Office. Brushes and mats were made for the Admiralty and War Office. Other industries included the weaving of cloth for prison use on handlooms, bootmaking, tailoring, tinsmithing, basketmaking, and printing. These industries, said the Committee, "are apt to be regarded by the prisoners rather as prison-invented tasks than as serious work."[73] If the types of prison work left much to be desired, so too did the condition and pace of prison workshops, and the length of the working day. All the Committee chose to do was to recommend a special inquiry into the employment of prisoners and their re-absorption into the workforce.

These findings came as no surprise either to the prison commissioners or the penal reform lobby. For years, the parlous state of prison labour had been acknowledged. Two early statements say it all. In March 1921, Margery Fry, secretary of the Howard League, wrote to *The Times* about the unpaid character of English prison labour: "Most of the work done in our prisons to-day has the characteristic wastefulness of slave labour."[74] A month later, in an internal minute, the Comptroller of Industries, who was charged with the superintendence of all prison industries, wrote, "More and more the prison population becomes a mass of unskilled labour . . . More and more we are reverting to long hours of cellular employment in which labour cannot be other than of an elementary nature."[75] Until associated labour for long hours became the rule, he said (and he aspired to eight hours associated labour per day), the earning capacity of prisoners would not improve. Part of the problem was that the smaller county gaols had no workshops in which associated labour could take place. Prisoner B.2.15 wrote that inmates in Leicester prison "are obliged to go through with their sentences on cell work, with doors open after the first month."[76] Another part of the problem was that government departments, who were the only customers, had a wartime backlog of stores and were submitting no new orders. Hobhouse and Brockway's *English Prisons To-Day* underlined the absence of industrial training, the "punitive element" that still characterized all prison work, and the unsatisfactory state of the workshops, even where there were any. Perhaps the most telling statistic was that of the number of prisoners employed on mail bags, the staple industry of most local prisons. In 1920–21, under the heading of manufactures, of the 5,908 prisoners employed, 2736 or 46 per cent were mail-bag makers. This figure stubbornly refused to decline over the next few years. By 1928, the figure had fallen to 44 per cent; by 1931–32, the figure was back up to 47 per cent. Why was this? Simply because the industry could be carried on in prisoners' cells or on the floor of the halls, and prisoners of every kind—short sentence prisoners, unskilled prisoners, even the mentally defective—could be taught quickly, and with little waste of material, this type of manufacture. Yet even the commissioners accepted that the

73   Ibid.
74   *The Times*, 29 Mar. 1921, p. 4.
75   PCom7/343: 25 Apr. 1921.
76   B.2.15, *Among the Broad-Arrow Men: A Plain Account of English Prison Life* (1924), p. 77.

work "provides no sort of industrial training" and the prisoner looked upon the work "as an artificial prison task."[77]

In October 1922, Waller, the new chairman of the Prison Commission, had insisted that at every prison, however small, there had to be industry better than mail bags on which the longer sentenced prisoners could work. Assistant commissioner Mr. Lamb, said Waller, had inspected several smaller prisons in which he found "nothing but mail bag making going on in the place." This was true of Leicester, Oxford, Portsmouth, and Bedford. The employment returns of other prisons were equally unpleasant reading:

> Manchester with about 740 male prisoners, had no less than 400 employed on mail bags, cotton teasing, and oakum picking. Pentonville had about a quarter of the prison on mail bags. Wormwood Scrubs, a specially good industrial prison, actually had 127 men so employed out of its small population.[78]

Waller realized, of course, that mail bags could not be altogether avoided, since they were useful for those in separate confinement, those on short sentences, and for evening labour. It should be added that mail bag making was not carried out in borstal institutions, nor by females.[79]

What else did Waller's appointment as chairman bring with it? In May 1922, Waller informed the Home Secretary that the prison commissioners had several projects in mind for making prison labour more remunerative. In the best of the industrial shops, they intended to implement a full eight hours work day. The first necessity, however, was a market for the products, for which it was essential to reach an accord with the trade unions, to allow some prison goods to be sold on the outside market. Waller took heart from the interest which Labour Party members were taking in prison matters. "If this Party has, in fact, made the progressive training and teaching of prisoners a part of its programme, the Commissioners welcome the fact," and were prepared to ask for the party's assistance. In addition, Waller wanted an extension of the government market, by having the liberty to tender for work to all government departments, whether or not tenders had been invited from the trade, and a greater assignment of government work without tender. A Treasury circular went out in January 1923 asking all departments to order direct from the prison commissioners articles the prisons were able to supply. Waller pressed forward with the idea of gaining access to the outside

---

77 Ann. Rep. of P. Com. for 1921, PP, 1922, II (Cd. 1761), p. 1031; Hobhouse and Brockway, *English Prisons To-Day*, op cit., p. 110, and ch. VII, "Prison Labour;" Ann. Rep. of P. Com. for 1928, PP, 1929–30, XVII (Cd. 3607), pp. 332–3 (Appendix 6); Col. G. D. Turner, "Unemployment in Prisons," *Spectator*, 15 Oct. 1932, p. 476; L. W. Fox, *The Modern English Prison* (1934), pp. 246–7 (Appendix E).

78 TNA, PCom7/78.

79 Women prisoners were not employed on mail bag making presumably because the task required a modicum of brute force, and because the prison authorities had sufficient tailoring work for them.

market, Paterson consulting with Sir David Shackleton, the Chief Labour Adviser of the Ministry of Labour, to find the best way of doing this. Spreading prison products over a larger variety of industries was Shackleton's advice. But Home Secretary Bridgeman thought the question a thorny one and preferred not to rush into it.[80]

Another step taken in 1923 was to appoint a prisoners' employment committee from within the department, including Paterson, and to hire Mr. A. Newlands, late deputy director general of factories at the War Office, to advise on the reorganization of prison industries. Newland's report pulled no punches. As Fox wrote in July 1925, after reading the report,

> It is not necessary to be an expert to appreciate that the present state of affairs is deplorable, and is not only thoroughly uneconomical—how uneconomical it is impossible to tell—but fails utterly even in the prime object of the Commissioners—"to enable the prisoners to acquire habits of industry."[81]

The system failed for three main reasons, according to Newlands. First, the dislocation of industrial work by continued interruptions for shaving, bathing, visits, or absence of instructors. Governors readily granted individual prisoner requests for change of party or employment. Newland even suggested that governors "have generally ceased to bother about prisoners' work and spend more time and interest on their recreation." Second, there was no direct incentive to industry, since industry was not in practice a factor in earning remission. The prisoners' movements were listless and leisurely; there was no "snappiness of action" at work. Third, officers had no incentive to improve prison labour. His general view was that "a prisoner is much more likely to learn habits of idleness than habits of industry, and rarely does any work that is either educative or of value in helping him to earn a living." Industries were carried on by out-of-date methods, with antiquated equipment, under instructors who had picked up their knowledge in the prison. Newland's analysis of industries illuminated a familiar problem. Of a total prison population of 10,831 in 1925, only 6,611 were engaged in manufactures, and of these 2,865 were making mail bags, the others being employed in 23 different industries scattered over all the prisons, "in only four of which was work of any educative value at all being done." As if this were not bad enough, the commissioners had no way of knowing whether a given contract had resulted in profit or loss, nor were they able to compare one prison with another in efficiency. Fox's conclusion was damning: "A prolonged and detailed expert inquiry has shown a state of affairs which would almost justify the criticism that half a million of public money is being annually 'poured down the sink.'" The Permanent

80 TNA, HO45/16547/433045/1: Waller minute, 30 May 1922. Ibid., 433045/3 for Treasury circular dated 12 Jan. 1923. Ibid., 433045/5 for Home Secretary Bridgeman, 24 Mar. 1923.
81 TNA, HO45/16562/457719/9: Fox, 28 Jul. 1925.

Undersecretary of State, Sir John Anderson, in September 1925, could only concur: "This Report makes it clear that radical changes are necessary in the organization of prison industries & in the attitude of the higher prison staff towards prison labour."[82]

Newland's report was not short on recommendations. They included stopping all interference with hours of labour and unnecessary changes of occupation; creating an incentive to work in addition to remission of sentence; centralizing and specializing the industries in prisons; and allowing the sale of manufactured articles on the open market. As an incentive to labour, Newland suggested payment for prisoners who did work in excess of a prescribed amount—"not on the present miserable scale paid to debtors and trial prisoners . . . but on broad liberal scales even to that approaching the Trades Union rates of remuneration outside." The report also suggested clearing the decks of mail-bag making by using machinery. This would ultimately set free 2,000 men for other types of manufacturing.[83]

What became of this raft of recommendations? Little or nothing is the answer. This was particularly the case with regard to the entry of prison-made goods into free markets. As Max Grunhut said, "Almost throughout its whole history prison labour has been denounced by trade and free labour as unfair competition." A case in point was the protest by the United Society of Brushmakers in July 1909: "We regard the competition between the labour of the free worker & the prison worker as derogatory to the best interests of the law-respecting and tax paying worker." But it was not only prison goods for market that attracted protest. At times, man-ufacturers and trade unions also objected to prisons manufacturing for government departments, and even to prisoners working on the structure, maintenance, and repair of prison buildings. In 1906, it was a ships fender manufacturer from Liver-pool objecting to goods made in Durham prison; in 1907 it was the Federation of Sailmakers arguing that mail bag work should be given to outside contractors instead of prisons. In 1919, the building of 250 quarters for officers at 30 different prisons was authorized by the Treasury, on condition that prison labour was used on the construction as much as possible. In 1924, an additional 150 quarters was authorized. In consequence, between 1920 and 1928, the National Amalgamated Society of Operative House and Ship Painters and Decorators, the National Fed-eration of Building Trades Operatives, and the Carpenters' and Joiners' Union objected to the use of prison labour on this construction work. In 1933, it was the British Brush Manufacturers Association objecting to the making of brushes and brooms in prisons, including manufacture for sale to government departments. The prison commissioners always held the line, arguing that the number of prisoners employed was too small to represent any negative impact on the trade in question, or that the amount of building work done in connection with prisons was a tiny fraction of the building work throughout the country. In addition, the commissioners reminded critics that they were responsible for employing

82 TNA, HO45/16562/457719/9: Fox, 28 Jul. 1925; Anderson, 8 Sep. 1925.
83 TNA, PCom7/79.

prisoners while in custody, for their training to fit them for employment on release, and for the overall cost of the prison estate to the public. Finally, it was pointed out that the Gladstone Committee on Prisons in 1895, following communication with the Parliamentary Committee of the Trades Union Congress, reported that anything for the use of a government department may be manufactured by prison labour, and that there was no objection even to the sale of prison goods in the outside market, provided they were not sold below the market price, and that every consideration was shown to the plight of particular industries to avoid damage to the wages and employment of free labour. The rider to the reply was invariably that, notwithstanding this agreement, the commissioners had felt it wise to restrict prison manufactures almost entirely to work for government departments, though the supply of work was at times inadequate. In an era of high unemployment, the prison commissioners took the line of least resistance, preferring to appease trade union opinion by relying exclusively on a state-use system of prison employment—though, as Hobhouse and Brockway justifiably remarked, even government work was necessarily competitive with free labour. It does all indicate that if there was one area of prison administration where the principle of "less eligibility" had its most enduring effect, it was prison industry.[84]

The labour movement seemed rather more attracted to the idea of paying prisoners the trade union rate of wages, with a sum deducted for cost of maintenance, perhaps in the knowledge that this would never come about. A limited advance was made, however, towards a system of payment to prisoners for work done. As early as 1922, Waller stated that the commissioners would probably accept a system of payment, but a grant of money would be required to start it.[85] In 1929, the Howard League raised £250 for an experimental scheme in the mat-making shop at Wakefield Prison for special class prisoners between 21 and 26 years of age, later transferred to and enlarged at Nottingham Prison, before returning to Wakefield in 1931 and extended to the entire Wakefield population. When Alexander Maxwell first informed the Home Office of this private grant, he added that a wage scheme posed practical difficulties, not least the fact that much of the work done in prisons was hard to measure, but payment

> would be the strongest incentive to work and would lead to an increase of output . . . [I]t would be a good thing to make the prisoner feel that in prison—as in the outside world—his own efforts determine what he gets.

84 Grunhut, *Penal Reform* (Oxford, 1948), chap. "Prison Labour;" TNA, HO45/15528/143172/1, 5, 14, 49; HO45/16547/433045/26; PCom7/341; PCom9/137; Hobhouse and Brockway, op cit., pp. 118–9; Cf. H. Mannheim, *The Dilemma of Penal Reform* (1939), pp. 75–7; Gordon Hawkins, "Prison Labor and Prison Industries," *Crime and Justice*, vol. 5 (1983), p. 101.
85 TNA, HO45/16547/433045/1: Waller, 17 Aug. 1922.

A standard minimum output was fixed for the mat shop and a small payment was made for each week's output in excess of this standard. The maximum amount payable was a sum equivalent to 2/6d a week for each member of the party. The payments were based on the output of the shop to encourage team spirit in the party. The results were encouraging: the output of matting rose considerably, and the scheme had a good effect on the behaviour of the prisoners. Any further extension of the payment scheme had to await the recommendations of the departmental committee on prison industries.[86]

Otherwise, conditions of prison labour only deteriorated. In 1930, to provide employment for an increased number of prisoners in custody, it was necessary to return to manufacturing mailbags by hand instead of using machinery. By 1931, something approaching an eight-hour day in associated labour for every prisoner had been achieved, but then as part of the economy measures demanded by the economic crisis of that year, staffing was reduced in the prisons, leading to a reduction in hours of associated labour. The length of the workday sank to six and a half hours, and the time of actual work was closer to five hours. (A longer working day was not restored until 1934 in nearly all prisons).[87] By June 1932, the chronic shortage of work in the prisons led Home Secretary Samuel to appoint a committee to review the question of prison industries, following the recommendation of the Report of the Committee on Persistent Offenders. Major Isidore Salmon, chairman of J. Lyons and Co., and Conservative MP, who was known for his interest in the prison estimates in the House of Commons, was appointed to chair the departmental committee. Appointed to the committee were Miss Margery Fry; J. J. Maxwell, the Controller of Prison Industries; W. C. Crook, a manufacturer of footballs, who had visited a number of European prisons to examine their methods of employing prisoners; and A. Hollins, general secretary of the National Society of Pottery Workers, who carried weight with the trade unions. The new chairman of the Prison Commission, Harold Scott, was also appointed for a telling reason: "The problem which has to be faced is one of the most difficult in prison administration and on its solution any advance in prison methods depends."[88]

The Departmental Committee on the Employment of Prisoners, which reported in November 1933, first documented the nature of the prison population and how prisoners were employed. To find work for 13,000 people housed in 38 institutions in different parts of the country was always going to be supremely difficult. Then there was the ebb and flow of the prison population, over which the prison authorities had little control, being at the mercy of the courts. Of the receptions of convicted prisoners, one-half were labourers, and fewer than one-third were skilled workers. Many of them, especially the younger prisoners, had never been in regular employment. As to "the quality of the human material which passes through

86 TNA, HO45/22974/542336/1, Maxwell, 19 Aug. 1929; HO45/18006/546730/16, 29; PCom7/90; Ann. Rep. of P. Com. for 1929, PP, 1930–31, XVI (Cd. 3868), pp. 931–2; *The Magistrate*, vol. 2 (1931), p. 510.
87 Ann. Rep. of P. Com. for 1930, PP, 1931–32, XII (Cd. 4151), p. 796; TNA, HO45/18006/546730/48: Scott, 26 Feb. 1937; PCom9/218.
88 TNA, PCom9/182.

the prisons," the report cited the evidence of medical commissioner Dr. W. Norwood East:

> Some are of poor physique, indifferent mental capacity or temperamentally unstable. In short the human material in prison differs considerably from that in the general labour market. It is seldom efficient, it is often indifferent, and is sometimes useless.[89]

Practically all the work done in the prisons was for the prison service or for other government departments, the report confirmed, and the bulk of it was carried on within the prison walls. In addition to the work done in workshops, prisoners were also required to work each day in their cells for a couple of hours, mainly making by hand mail bags, coal sacks, or hammocks, or picking oakum (would this Victorian task never die out?) or cotton.[90] The hours of associated labour were down to five a day at most; the incentives to labour were negligible since the award of marks by officers, which determined remission of sentence and the earning of privileges under the progressive stage system, had become too automatic to serve as "a positive stimulus to industry." Possibly the most embarrassing figure in the report was the one that deflated the value of the work of prisoners engaged on manufacturing and building work, from that given by the prison commissioners in successive reports as £322,848 to what the Committee considered the true value of £82,500.[91]

This was preface to the final chapter, a discursive and disordered one, in which the Committee expressed its strongest views on present conditions and future practice. The report reiterated the difficulties caused by the poor quality of labour, by the number of prisoners serving short sentences, by the greater classification of prisoners (which meant that prisoners of certain categories could not be put in the same working parties), and by "the shortage of simple work suitable for unskilled and short-term prisoners." It pondered the question of training, concluding that, with the exception of Borstal inmates and long-sentence prisoners under the age of 30, it was not practicable to teach prisoners a trade:

> The most that can be done is to provide work which will accustom a prisoner to habits of industry and to the speed which is required in outside employment, and in that way improve or at least maintain his fitness for employment on release.[92]

---

89   Ibid.; *Report of the Departmental Committee on the Employment of Prisoners*, PP, 1933–34, XV (Cmd. 4462), p. 122.
90   Prisoners picking oakum had to untwist tarry ropes into strands, which were used to caulk ships.
91   *Report of the Departmental Committee on the Employment of Prisoners*, PP, 1933–34, XV (Cmd. 4462), pp. 141, 147. See also S. Margery Fry, "Prison Labour," *Howard Journal*, vol. 4 (1934), p. 19.
92   Ibid., p. 164.

And while it accepted that prisoners should in the main be employed on government work, it encouraged more gardening and agricultural work, and saw no objection to outside work being undertaken subject to the conditions laid down almost 40 years earlier in the Report of the Gladstone Committee.

The report then moved to its main recommendations. The *primus inter pares* was more work: "suitable employment is the most important factor in the physical and moral regeneration of the prisoner. The crux of the whole problem is the provision of a sufficiency of simple work." Once the shortage of work was solved, an eight-hour day of associated labour should be restored (plus the extra staffing this required); workshops should be modernized (including sewing and laundry machines in women's prisons); the speed and efficiency of work should be improved; and a system of payment to prisoners should be introduced (along with scientific methods of work measurement), though it was impracticable to usher in a system of trade union wages. In addition, the report recommended that industries should be concentrated in selected prisons, for which the policy of prison classification should be extended, in order to obtain more homogeneous prison populations. If this resulted in prisoners being removed further away from relatives and friends, the sending and receiving of letters would alleviate the hardship—which only prompts Homeric laughter.[93] Finally, the report sent a shot across the bow of prison governors by criticizing their present attitude to the employment of prisoners: "We have found some Governors pessimistic, even obdurately pessimistic, in regard to improvements in the organization of prison industries."[94] Shortly after the report appeared, however, prison governors protested against the allegation that they did not take any interest in the industries of their prisons.[95]

The general principles laid down in the Salmon Report were accepted by the prison commissioners, though they recognized that they had been presented with a long-range programme, which would take time to put into force. They considered the proposal that an industrial commissioner be appointed, and in 1934 hired John Lamb with the title of Director of Prison Industries. According to Harold Scott, Lamb was "a tubby, rosy-faced, twinkling-eyed human dynamo, who had held a series of responsible jobs in the motor car industry." His methods were "direct and unorthodox."[96] What did he achieve? Lamb first appointed industrial managers at three of the largest prisons. Then he reorganized the mail-bag, hammock, and coal-sack industries, with new methods of work and greater supervision. Power sewing machines were installed in Holloway; a new carpentry shop started at Chelmsford; clog making reorganized at Liverpool; and the mat industry installed with new machinery at Lewes. Also, he secured more orders from government departments. Steps were taken to re-establish the longer working day for prisoners in association. An eight-hour day was secured at Bedford, Birmingham,

93   Ibid, p. 174.
94   Ibid., pp. 172, 185.
95   TNA, PCom9/183.
96   Harold Scott, *Your Obedient Servant* (1959), p. 83; Bailey, *Delinquency and Citizenship*, op cit., p. 245.

Chelmsford, Lewes, and Wandsworth in 1934; at Bristol, Gloucester, Leeds, Leicester, Liverpool, Norwich, Oxford, Portsmouth, and Winchester in 1935. By 1938, eight hours associated labour was restored to all prisons, only for it to break down under the impact of war. The experimental system of wages was extended to all borstal institutions, and to Maidstone convict prison and the preventive detention prison at Portsmouth by 1935. At the latter, a reduction in the number of men reporting sick resulted, since sick men did not earn. By 1937, a wages scheme was in place at Chelmsford, Dartmoor, and Parkhurst convict prisons, and a start was made on local prisons with an experimental scheme at Winchester.[97] Governors typically reported that output increased and the general prison atmosphere improved. Harold Scott, chairman of the Prison Commission, was able to crow that by 1938 English prisons were close to full employment, with nearly 75 per cent of prisoners being productively employed.[98] What he failed to point out was that the manufacture of mail bags still represented 38 per cent of all prison manufacturing, and it was only by this staple occupation that 75 per cent of prisoners were productively employed.[99] It could also be pointed out that this level of employment should have been the minimum standard achieved throughout the inter-war period. How else could the prison authorities in good conscience have continued to urge the judiciary to make their sentences of imprisonment more substantial for training purposes?

VII

The Report of the Persistent Offenders Committee was convinced that the employment of prisoners "should not be considered in isolation as a problem of internal prison administration without reference to the prisoner's subsequent career as a free man, or to the organizations concerned with helping him." If the first was an administrative matter of finding work for prisoners, the latter "represents the development of a time-honoured philanthropy which makes heavy calls upon wide human sympathy and personal services by voluntary workers."[100] The Committee received uncompromising evidence concerning the inadequacy of after-care for local prisoners, which was a matter for the local Discharged Prisoners' Aid Societies. The latter depended for their funds on charitable subscriptions, apart from a capitation grant from the state of two shillings per prisoner.[101]

---

97 However, men serving less than three months were not eligible for earnings, "on the score that such short sentences were intended to be more purely deterrent than longer sentences": Mark Benney, *Gaol Delivery* (1948), p. 4.

98 TNA, HO45/17543/679178/2–3; Ann. Rep. of P. Com. for 1934, PP, 1935–36, XIV (Cd. 5153), p. 490; Ann. Rep. of P. Com. for 1936, PP, 1937–38, XIV (Cd. 5675), pp. 727–30; TNA, HO45/20084/482137/24: Scott, 2 Nov. 1937; HO45/22974/542336/15–16: 12 Nov. 1937; B. L. Jacot, "Women in Prison," *Quarterly Review*, vol. 271 (1938), p. 107; Harold Scott, *Your Obedient Servant* (1959), p. 83.

99 Grunhut, *Penal Reform*, op cit., pp. 205–6.

100 *Report of the Departmental Committee on Persistent Offenders*, PP, 1931–32, XII (Cmd. 4090), p. 593.

101 This compares with the sum not exceeding £2 which justices were authorized to pay to each discharged prisoner under the Discharged Prisoners' Aid Act of, wait for it, 1862.

In too many cases, after-care was merely aid-on-discharge: each prisoner was handed a meagre dole of ten to 15 shillings to keep him afloat for a few days. No wider conception or scope and purpose of after-care had developed. Paterson, in particular, was outspoken:

> The help which the Aid Societies can give to ex-prisoners is hopelessly inadequate. There are 5,000 discharges from Manchester Prison each year and the average amount of money which the local Aid Society can spend on each case is about 10/-. Even in the case of first offenders in local prisons only a fraction can be properly assisted. There are 70 discharges from Wormwood Scrubs [a first offenders' prison] every week, but there is only one agent to find work for them and he probably finds work for one or two each week.[102]

The Persistent Offenders Committee recommended "that the allied problems of the employment of prisoners and of their re-absorption into the industrial system constitute a suitable subject for special inquiry."[103] The Salmon Committee, Part Two, picked up the mantle, but its efforts to bring greater co-ordination and continuity to after-care work collided with what had always been after-care's Achilles' heel, voluntary effort, or as it was called in 1920, "patronage."

This very word appeared in the title of the chapter by Evelyn Ruggles-Brise on aid to discharged prisoners in *The English Prison System*. At this date, 1921, there was a network of discharged prisoners' aid societies attached to local prisons, affiliated to a Central Discharged Prisoners' Aid Society. As local prisons began to be closed for lack of patrons, and as prisons like Wakefield began to provide for special groups of offenders, the simplicity of one society per prison disappeared. By 1933, the 26 local prisons were served by over 50 local aid societies. Harold Scott, chairman of the Prison Commission, described this confusing environment: "At some prisons two or three or more societies are responsible for the prisoners, while some societies are concerned with prisoners in two or three or more prisons."[104] Convict and preventive detention prisoners discharged on licence were the responsibility of the Central Association for the Aid of Discharged Convicts, formed in 1911, and subsidized by public funds not charitable contributions. Convicts were helped by associates drawn from the probation service, Toc H, and the Society of Friends. The Central Association was Winston Churchill's brainchild, and his words ought to have been the mantra of all after-care work:

---

102 Persistent Offenders Committee, Summaries of Evidence, vol. 3, POC 61A. Similar sentiments were expressed by Cicely Craven and Roy Calvert on behalf of the Howard League: "At present aftercare for local prisoners is hopelessly inadequate, and with some aid Societies the system of aftercare is so antiquated that it would be better to sweep it right away and start afresh. Possibly the best way of getting a new vision of aftercare would be by approaching the subject from the industrial side. If a man has been trained in prison, he needs employment on discharge, not a small sum of money nor grand-motherly supervision." See Ibid., POC 63A.

103 *Report of the Departmental Committee on Persistent Offenders*, PP, 1931–32, XII (Cmd. 4090), p. 593.

104 Scott, "Employment of Discharged Prisoners," *The Magistrate*, vol. 4 (1936), p. 995.

It seems to me of the highest importance to fortify a prisoner strongly against undue pressures as soon as he returns to the world. I cannot feel easy in my mind that the fact of his having been a convict is not in many cases crushing and fatal.[105]

No small number of prisoners and prison officers echoed this statement in the inter-war years. Stuart Wood in *Shades of the Prison House* was vehemently critical of the help given to ex-prisoners in the 1920s. Wood declared that what happened to the criminal on release, not prison treatment, was "the fundamental problem of reclamation." Three factors were at stake, social, economic, and industrial:

So long as your criminal is ostracized by the so-called respectable elements of society; so long as he is vomited forth from prison homeless, friendless and often penniless; so long as the ranks of industry are closed to him by social prejudice, so long will the problem of recidivism remain insoluble!

The combined resources of the discharged prisoners' aid societies, said Wood,

cannot, and do not, provide permanent work for more than five per cent. of the adult criminals who pass through their hands . . . [T]he established after-care organisations never found me work of any description, or offered to do so.[106]

Cicely McCall contended that if the government were to provide "efficiently trained after-care workers," many Holloway prisoners might be spared re-conviction.[107] These statements were reinforced by *The New Survey of London Life and Labour*, which reported that of the 9,643 male prisoners discharged from Pentonville, Wormwood Scrubs and Wandsworth in 1933, 667 or 7 per cent were found work or returned to former employers by the two prisoners' aid societies serving these prisons. The after-care on behalf of convicts was seemingly more effective. The report of the Central Association for the Aid of Discharged Convicts for 1932 claimed that out of 567 convicts discharged in 1931, of whom 462 required work to be found for them, work was found for 213 or close to half of them.[108]

---

105 TNA, HO45/13658/185668/5: Churchill memo, 7 Mar. 1910.
106 S. Wood, *Shades of the Prison House* (1932), pp. vi, 169.
107 McCall, *'They Always Come Back,'* (1938), p. 92.
108 *The New Survey of London Life and Labour*, vol. 9 (1935), p. 373; Fox, *Modern English Prison*, op cit., pp. 165–6. The Central Association for the Aid of Discharged Convicts reported that during 1928, 547 men were discharged from the convict prisons to its care. Finding work for these men was hard: 158 were fit for light employment only, which was seldom available for unskilled labourers; 13 were unfit to earn their living; and 35 were medically described as of low mentality. The report also claimed, "Owing to the disorganized state of our leading industries, especially in the north of England, this task is at present exceptionally difficult. There are queues of unemployed men of

The Salmon Committee on the After Care of Prisoners reported in May 1935. In the course of its deliberations, it had flown the kite of bringing under one direction the work of the Central Association for the Aid of Discharged Convicts and that of the Central Discharged Prisoners' Aid Society. So opposed were the prisoners' aid societies to such centralization, however, that the Committee limited itself to proposals for the reorganization of the work of the societies. The committee found that the Central Discharged Prisoners' Aid Society was not functioning well as an agency for coordinating and stimulating the work of the local societies, and hence recommended that central control be entrusted to a new National Association of Discharged Prisoners' Aid Societies, on which the local societies would be represented. Also, there would be one prisoners' aid society for each committal area, requiring aid societies with no local prison to serve to merge with the new committal area societies. This was further illustration of the fact that the classification of prisons and prisoners that was so dear to the prison commissioners, leading to dispersal of prisoners around the country, ran contrary to the local aid societies, whose mainspring was local interest in the care of local prisoners. As for the after-care work itself, the Salmon Committee wanted local societies to do much more than make small cash grants to prisoners at the prison gate. The primary object of after-care, the Committee declared, should be re-instating the ex-prisoner in employment. Unsurprisingly, the local aid societies, deep-rooted voluntary bodies, jealous of their independence of official control, fought a rearguard action against these proposals, but without success.[109] Changes were made. Yet any improvement in after-care came slowly, evident from a flurry of letters to *The Times* in September and October 1938, prompted by a letter from "An Unemployed Ex-Convict," a former black-coated professional, who complained that "the present D[ischarged] P[risoners'] A[id] organization represents but a mere scratching of the surface of the problem." And John A. F. Watson, former Secretary of the National Association of Prison Visitors, hardly the severest critic of the prison authorities, was forced to conclude in 1939:

> Aftercare—at any rate so far as the local prisoner is concerned—virtually does not exist . . . This neglect of aftercare is the weak spot in our whole system, and until we devise some means of friendly supervision for every ex-prisoner who needs it, much good work done inside prison will continue to go to waste.[110]

experience and good character in every town." See Ann. Rep. of P. Com. for 1928, PP, 1929–30, XVII (Cd. 3607), p. 305.

109 *Report of the Departmental Committee on the Employment of Prisoners, Pt. II: Employment on Discharge*, PP, 1934–35, XI (Cmd. 4897), p. 97; TNA, PCom9/182; PCom9/183; Central Discharged Prisoners Aid Society, annual meeting report, Jun. 1935, p. 18, MSS 67/4; Leo Page, "The Discharged Prisoner," *Howard Journal*, vol. 5 (1938), p. 47. The Discharged Prisoners' Aid Societies issued their own report, the Whitbread Report.

110 *The Times*, 15 Sep. 1938, p. 6; ibid., 1 Oct. 1938. See also Mannheim, *Dilemma of Penal Reform*, op cit., pp. 93–4; John A. F. Watson, *Meet the Prisoner* (1939), p. 201.

VIII

The Persistent Offenders Committee, which included William Norwood East, medical commissioner of prisons, also approached the question of the psychological treatment of prisoners, though with considerable caution. The report rejected the idea of extending the definition of mental deficiency to include "all incorrigible criminals," not wishing to give the ameliorations of an institution for mental defectives to those "dangerous habitual criminals" who committed serious crimes, and unconvinced that petty recidivists would derive any lasting benefit from segregation among defectives. Nor did the committee agree with the view that "crime is a disease, or that it is generally the result of mental disorder." Nor finally had any witness given the committee

> any precise information concerning the curative value of psychological treatment in any large number of law-breakers, and the results on the whole have been inconclusive in the few convicted offenders who have been so treated during the currency of their sentences.

However, they did believe that a certain amount of persistent crime was the result of an abnormal mental condition—committed by offenders who were mentally subnormal though not certifiably defective, who were emotionally or temperamentally unstable, or who were repeat sex offenders or thieves—and that certain delinquents "may be amenable to psychological treatment." Since "the application of this method of treatment in criminal cases is in its infancy and is likely to remain so for many years to come," the committee recommended that a medical psychologist be attached to one or more penal establishments, that selected cases be placed voluntarily under treatment, a systematic follow-up conducted over a prolonged period, and the results published. For those affected with mental abnormality, the report did not propose special establishments.[111]

From this opening paragraph, it should be evident that psychiatry was still struggling to find a secure berth within the inter-war prison system. The committee's report, while willing to recognize offenders who were mentally subnormal or abnormal (though not certifiably defective under the Mental Deficiency Acts 1913 and 1927), was reluctant to widen the boundaries of mental treatment. It certainly

---

111 *Report of the Departmental Committee on Persistent Offenders*, PP, 1931–32, XII (Cmd. 4090), pp. 596–602, 623; HO 144/20113/548577/73: memo, circa Feb. 1935. See also, "Persistent Offenders," *Law Times*, vol. 173 (1932), p. 427. Dr. E. O. Lewis, "Mental Deficiency and Criminal Behaviour," in L. Radzinowicz and J. W. C. Turner (eds.), *Mental Abnormality and Crime* (1944), p. 95, provided the following definition: "'Mental Defectiveness' is a condition of arrested or incomplete development of mind existing before the age of eighteen years whether arising from inherent causes or induced by disease or injury." The four degrees of mental defect were "idiots," "imbeciles," "feebleminded," and "moral defectives."

stopped short of the approach described in Dr. Maurice Hamblin Smith's evidence to the committee. The largest class of recidivists, said Smith, medical officer of Birmingham Prison, consisted of persons "unable to adjust themselves to the demands of Society by reason of mental conflict, or of what may be called (for want of a better term) 'inadequate personality.'" These people, he continued, were mentally defective or mentally abnormal, but not certifiable under the existing law because they did not exhibit intellectual defect. Amend the definition, said Smith, "so that the persistent commission of vicious and/or criminal acts is sufficient evidence *per se* of mental defectiveness." Such persons could then be detained and an attempt made to deal with the mental conflict behind the recidivism by means of psychotherapy.[112] Instead, the committee's report leaned towards the evidence of W. A. Potts, psychological expert to the Birmingham justices and medical officer to the Birmingham Mental Deficiency Act Committee, who thought the majority of persistent offenders were not mentally defective, or insane, or mentally inefficient, but ordinary individuals "who may have some physical handicap or latent disease or infection, temporarily affecting their mentality, or who are miserable or unhappy, and who frequently have wrong ideas, ideals, outlook on life, and mistaken sense of value."[113] And the committee clearly listened to the evidence of Professor Cyril Burt, psychologist in the Education Department of the London County Council, who was sceptical of applying psychoanalysis and psychological treatment on any systematic basis:

> The science has not advanced to the stage at which legislation could be passed requiring or empowering a court to consider this method as a means of dealing with an offender. What is needed most of all is further research into the possibilities and success of different methods of treatment.[114]

It is the purpose of this section of the chapter to examine the advances made by psychiatry within the penal system, and the reasons for its limited influence.

The aim of psychiatry in the inter-war prisons was threefold: first, the pre-sentence, psychiatric examination of remand prisoners on behalf of the criminal courts; second, the certification of convicted prisoners who were insane or mentally defective and their transfer to mental institutions; and third, the care of prisoners who were not certifiable under the Lunacy or Mental Deficiency Acts, but who on account of an abnormal mental condition, required special consideration in prison. First, the remands. In 1920, there were 1,611 remands to prison for psychiatric examination, or 4.5 per cent of receptions under sentence. By 1938, the figure was 2,770 or 8.7 per cent of receptions. In the course of these examinations in 1931, prison medical staff found 281 remand prisoners to be insane and 182 to be mentally defective. At sentencing stage, criminal courts issued 183 orders in 1920 under

112 Persistent Offenders Committee, Summaries of Evidence, vol. 2, POC 52, 52A.
113 Ibid., POC 46.
114 Ibid., POC 51.

the Mental Deficiency Acts, 283 orders in 1930, and 332 orders in 1938.[115] The rise in number was confirmed by the Visiting Committee of Liverpool Prison in their report for 1929 which stated that the courts were taking greater care to recognize mental infirmity. More cases, they claimed, were certified as lunatics or mental defectives and sent to institutions instead of being sentenced to imprisonment.[116] There was a system in force at Wormwood Scrubs prison in London for dealing with young remand prisoners. Each one was subject to a physical, mental, and psychological examination, and a staff of voluntary women workers provided additional information about home environment and the circumstances leading to the crime. According to *The New Survey of London Life and Labour*, "Some magistrates consult these reports before passing sentence, but these unfortunately are in a minority." At this prison, too, a psychological examination was made of adolescents before they were drafted to the various borstal institutions.[117]

One of the most innovative ways of supplying courts with diagnostic facilities appeared in Birmingham, at the behest of the justices themselves, and with the cooperation of the prison commissioners. In 1919, Dr. Maurice Hamblin Smith, the psychoanalytically-oriented medical officer of Portland prison, was transferred to Birmingham Prison; his duty was to report on the mental condition of defendants sent there on remand, with a view to helping justices decide how best, on conviction, to deal with these cases. The justices also appointed Dr. W. A. Potts to act as examiner in cases which were not sent to the remand part of the prison. In any case where a person was charged before the court and mental instability was exhibited, either by conduct or repeated commission of the same class of offence (especially sex offences), the court would direct a remand in custody without bail, or a remand on bail (or an adjournment) on condition that the person charged voluntarily consulted the court doctor.[118] Hamblin Smith believed that "there was a prima facie case for the mental examination of all sex offenders before

115 See Nigel Walker, "Crime and Penal Measures," in A. H. Halsey (ed.), *Trends in British Society since 1900* (1972), p. 531 (Table 15.5); N. Walker and S. McCabe, *Crime and Insanity in England*, vol. 2 (Edinburgh, 1973), pp. 53, 74; Nigel Walker, "Crime and Penal Measures," in A. H. Halsey (ed.), *Trends in British Society since 1900* (1988), p. 629 (Table 15.4); Barbara Wootton, *Social Science and Social Pathology* (1st pub. 1959; 1967), p. 205.
116 TNA, HO45/13635/147974/32.
117 *The New Survey of London Life and Labour*, vol. 9 (1935), p. 372; TNA, PCom9/11. See also B. Forsythe, "Mental and Social Diagnosis and the English Prison Commission 1914–1939," *Social Policy and Administration*, vol. 24 (1990), p. 248.
118 TNA, PCom7/740/15, 24; HO45/18736/438456/14; W. A. Potts, "The Birmingham Scheme," *British Medical Journal*, 3 Apr. 1920, p. 472; C. Craven, "The Progress of English Criminology," *Journal of Criminal Law, Criminology & Police Science*, vol. 24 (1933), pp. 237–9; W. Norwood East, "In Memoriam: Maurice Hamblin Smith," *Howard Journal*, vol. 4 (1936), p. 269. See also Pat Carlen, "Psychiatry in Prisons: Promises, Premises, Practices and Politics," in P. Miller and N. Rose (eds.), *The Power of Psychiatry* (Oxford, 1986), p. 247; P. Bowden, "Pioneers in Forensic Psychiatry. Maurice Hamblin Smith: The Psychoanalytic Panacea," *Journal of Forensic Psychiatry*, vol. 1 (1990), pp. 104–5; Pamela Cox, "Girls, Deficiency and Delinquency," in D. Wright and A. Digby (eds.), *From Idiocy to Mental Deficiency* (1996), p. 190.

conviction," a view endorsed in 1926 by the Committee on Sexual Offences against Young Persons.[119] After the remand period, if the court decided to convict, it called the prison medical officer or the court doctor to give evidence before passing sentence. Imprisonment was resorted to when the court considered that "a period of detention under medical supervision is the proper method of dealing with the case," though a significant number were saved from imprisonment by this mechanism. During the year ending August 1920, 151 offenders were treated by Hamblin Smith, of which 39 (or less than 26 per cent) were sentenced to imprisonment, 16 were placed on probation (sometimes on condition that the probationer submit himself to the medical practitioner for treatment), 59 were dismissed or adjourned, 15 were found insane, and 14 were dealt with under the Mental Deficiency Act. According to Hamblin Smith's 1922 report on the scheme, "it is now very rare to get a mental defective or a psychosis case from the city of Birmingham on conviction."[120] Hamblin Smith also supervised those sent from outlying prisons for observation, under a scheme introduced by the commissioners in 1924. The scheme worked well in the first few years, though by 1931 Potts was complaining that few cases were referred to him (only 30 per annum), most of which were mental defectives, and that justices "appeared to fail to realise how many cases were suitable for physical or psycho-therapeutic treatment."[121] The Bradford justices introduced a similar scheme under which a remand for examination was ordered where the offender had previous convictions, or was charged with cruelty, sexual offences, theft, or arson.[122]

Other parts of the country were not so well served. As a result, the use made by the courts of the Mental Deficiency Acts was less than the incidence of defect among offenders brought to trial demanded. And sex offenders were hardly ever remanded for a medical report before being sent to prison, even where repeated sentences of imprisonment had been imposed. As late as 1934, moreover, in an official circular, the Home Office felt the need to chastise those courts of summary jurisdiction which *after* sentencing an offender to imprisonment had sent to the prison a request that the prisoner be kept under mental observation. This ran the risk that a sentence of imprisonment would be passed in a case where the court might have considered some other method, had they known more about the offender's mental condition. Observation should *precede* sentence, the Home Office insisted.[123]

119 TNA, HO144/4483/316579/64; L. Radzinowicz and J. W. C. Turner (eds.), *Mental Abnormality and Crime* (1944), p. xviii; J. E. Hall Williams, "Sex Offences: The British Experience," *Law and Contemporary Problems*, vol. 25 (1960), p. 337.
120 Hobhouse and Brockway, op cit., pp. 52–3; E. Clephan Palmer, "New Way with Crime," *Daily News*, 29 Jul. 1925; Hamblin Smith, "Medical Examination of Delinquents," *Journal of Mental Science*, vol. 68 (1922), pp. 258–9.
121 Persistent Offenders Committee, Summaries of Evidence, vol. 2, W. A. Potts, POC 46A.
122 M. Bligh, *Doctor Eurich of Bradford* (1961), p. 255.
123 TNA, HO144/20113/548577/73: circular 20 Apr. 1934; Ann. Rep. of P. Com. for 1930, PP, 1931–32, XII (Cd. 4151), p. 44.

The second aim of psychiatry in the inter-war prisons was the certification of *convicted* prisoners. A number of convicted prisoners were found after reception to be insane or mentally defective, known in unforgiving prison parlance as "the barmies." In 1919–20, 89 convicted prisoners were removed under the Criminal Lunatics Act 1884, section 2, and 102 prisoners under the Mental Deficiency Act 1913, section 9. In 1931 in local prisons 98 convicted prisoners were certified as insane, and 45 as mentally defective; in convict prisons seven men were certified as insane and two as mentally defective. This was a tiny proportion of all prisoners. During the five-year period, 1932–36, 0.73 per cent of prisoners received into prison were certified to be insane, and 0.41 per cent to be mentally defective.[124] Despite the Mental Deficiency Acts, then, the prisons were unable to rid themselves of as many defectives as they would have liked. This was particularly the case in the first post-war years when local authorities, responsible for providing and paying for specialized institutions, refused to accept prisoners who had been certified as defective, and when the Ministry of Health refused to allow poor law institutions to be used for the same purpose. By the end of the 1920s, the prison commissioners were complaining less, suggesting that local medical officers of health were accepting the certifiable defective prisoner, though Dr. H. Freize Stephens, medical superintendent of Coleshill Hall, the first mental deficiency institution in Birmingham, claimed in 1931 that there was still a shortage of accommodation for mental defectives. Additionally, it proved so difficult to find institutional places for certifiable males aged 16 to 21 that in 1920 Feltham borstal was reserved for the mentally handicapped boys.[125]

The third aim of psychiatry concerned the residue of *uncertifiable* offenders. Even when the evidently insane and defective had been eliminated, there remained a number of cases, not certifiable under the Acts but found to be of "subnormal, retarded, or unstable mentality," who were unfit for ordinary prison discipline. In his annual report for 1926, the medical commissioner stated that these people "form a sub-normal group and include the simple feeble-minded and those of border-line intelligence whose offences are due to their low intelligence and high suggestibility, and who are relatively incapable of social rehabilitation on account of their low mentality." The group also included cases of senility and "weakmindedness due to alcoholic excess."[126] As early as 1924, the prison commissioners, while insisting that such weak-minded cases did not belong in prison, decided to

---

124 *Hansard*, vol. 207, 14 Jun. 1927, col. 837: prisoners in England and Wales removed to mental institutions in each of the ten years 1916–17 and 1925–26; W. Norwood East, "The Modern Psychiatric Approach to Crime," *Journal of Mental Science*, vol. 85 (1939), p. 661: address to Prison Medical Officers' Annual Conference, 5 Apr. 1939.

125 N. Walker and S. McCabe, op cit., pp. 24–5, 42; TNA, HO144/22258/316627/6; HO144/3117/129758/24; Persistent Offenders Committee, Summaries of Evidence, vol. 3, Dr. Freize Stephens, POC 59. See also H. G. Simmons, "Explaining Social Policy: The English Mental Deficiency Act of 1913," *Journal of Social History*, vol. 11 (1977–78), p. 400.

126 Cited in A. Fenner Brockway, *A New Way with Crime* (1928), p. 133; TNA, HO45/12939/208316/36.

concentrate those men serving three months' imprisonment or more (later lowered to one month) in special units in Birmingham, Liverpool, Lincoln, and Wormwood Scrubs. Female prisoners were collected in three prisons. By May 1925, 141 male prisoners and 22 female prisoners were at these centres. The numbers were small but their impact on prisons was larger.[127] Cases of uncertifiable mental disease and defect were, according to Norwood East in 1932, "a bad example generally to the other prisoners and a drag on the efficiency of the prison." Since these men would be eligible for sentences of preventive detention, as outlined in the Persistent Offenders Committee, East thought it would be worthwhile to open "a special establishment for their custodial care and so . . . free the prisons from their deadweight."[128] But if prisoners who presented abnormal mental characteristics, and were deemed unfit for ordinary prison discipline, were grouped together, the question remains: apart from a slightly more relaxed work regime, what was done for these inmates? What psychological treatment was ever given by prison medical officers? The answer must be that there was barely any psychological treatment for prisoners, and none were sent to clinics beyond the prison walls.

A good part of the reason for the meagre advances of psychiatry in prisons was that the Home Office and the prison commissioners always believed that too much was claimed for these sciences as they entered the prison field.[129] A case in point was the response to a 1923 address to the Magistrates' Association by M. Hamblin Smith, medical officer of Birmingham Prison, on the mentality and grading of offenders. Delinquency could be caused by mental conflicts arising from problems in the patient's environment, Smith said, but delinquency could be caused by mental conflicts arising in another way:

> Mental conflict may result from the repression of experiences and desires which are, for any reason, unacceptable to the conscious mind of the patient . . . [T]he essential point which we have to grasp is that the patient is unaware of the real cause of his anti-social action, inasmuch as this cause lies in the unconscious mind.

Having mounted his psychoanalytic hobbyhorse, Smith galloped forward:

> I do not assert, as some have done, that *all* cases of delinquency are due to these mental conflicts. But there is no doubt that the numerical incidence of this cause of delinquency is very large. That 25 per cent of offences arise from such conflict is, in my opinion, a conservative estimate.

---

127 N. Walker and S. McCabe, op cit., p. 42.
128 TNA, PCom9/182.
129 A. Paterson, "U.S. Way with Crime," *The Times*, 10 Jul. 1931, p. 16. See also Edward Glover, *The Roots of Crime* (1960), pp. 37–8.

He predicted that in the future, offenders would be carefully graded in keeping with the form of mental abnormality which they presented, but "the intensive psychological investigation of our patient's mentalities is the essential preliminary to such grading."[130] It so happened that Sir Edward Troup, Permanent Undersecretary of State at the Home Office, also addressed the Association, with a paper that urged the importance of uncovering the motive, circumstances, character and mentality of the offender, adding,

> The last thing any Court should do, however, is to accept evidence from any person styling himself or herself a psychologist or psycho-analyst. Psychology is a great and difficult science; and it is the last science that should be touched by the amateur. Only mischief can come of listening to foolish persons who have dabbled a little in the obscene publications of Freud and his school.[131]

Indeed, the entire senior staff of the department was aroused by Hamblin Smith's address. Assistant principal Fox was disappointed that while making clear the desirability of a psychological examination of offenders, "he gives no indication of what is to be done to or with offenders where their psychopathic states and/or the mental conflicts in their subconscious minds have been isolated—except that they will be 'treated, in an institution or otherwise' and that 'the institution will be adjusted to the patient not the patient to the institution': apparently the conditions of 'Erewhon' with 'one patient, one institution.'" Blackwell, assistant Undersecretary of State, appended a marginal note at the same point in Smith's paper: "What about the liberty of the subject? How long is he to be detained while Hamblin Smiths study him and search for abnormalities and mental conflicts?" And when Smith stated that "treatment without examination can only be described as scandalous," Blackwell scratched, "Why assume that it is a case for 'treatment' and not simply one for punishment?" Not to be outdone, Assistant Secretary H. B. Simpson weighed in with:

> I feel sure his view is only applicable to a very small number of the cases that come before Courts of S[ummary] J[urisdiction]. The offences these Courts have to deal with are mostly due to normal not to abnormal conditions.

To judge from earlier notes, Simpson also felt that punishment sought to provide persons in danger of becoming criminal with a motive for remaining honest, and "imprisonment may have such an effect on 'psycho-pathological' persons as well as others." Moreover, he thought psychoanalysis was still in its infancy, and hence psychotherapy was mere guess work.[132]

130 TNA, HO45/16943/399376/19.
131 HO45/17943/451656. Troup's view was unchanged from 1910, when in response to an outside suggestion that a course of lessons in psychology should form part of the prison routine, he minuted wryly, "I am against adding the study of psychology to the other severities of imprisonment." See HO45/10612/194214, 29 Jun. 1910.
132 TNA, HO45/12939/208316/24: Fox, 22 Nov. 1923; Simpson, 23 Nov. 1923; HO45/18736/438456/9.

Another case in point was the 1932 response of Alexander Maxwell, transitioning from his role as chairman of the Prison Commission to that of Deputy Undersecretary of State at the Home Office, to the Howard League's recommendation that an independent medical commission, consisting of psychiatrists and psychotherapists from outside the prison medical service, should examine the Dartmoor mutineers awarded additional terms of imprisonment or penal servitude. Maxwell was adamant:

> None of the men is mentally defective or in the view of our Medical Officers mentally abnormal. There is, unhappily, no ground for the optimistic view of the Howard League that psychology can provide any curative treatment for offenders of this type. The Persistent Offenders Committee were at pains to collect all the evidence they could on this subject, and it was clear that the psychologists themselves make no claim to be able to "cure" adult offenders, except perhaps in some rare cases of an exceptional character where the patient wants to be cured . . . The responsibility for the treatment of these and similar cases must be left to the officials of the Prison Department, and the only line of progress is to pursue the present policy of encouraging prison Medical Officers to keep themselves acquainted with modern psychological knowledge and to give as much attention as possible to the psychological study of prisoners.[133]

Maxwell also wrote, "Knowledge is not advanced by attempting to describe moral differences in psychological or medical terms."[134] It is hard to resist the conclusion that the approach of the prison administration was that most prisoners were "bad" not "mad," and that prisons were about punishment not treatment.

The only real advance of psychiatry in prisons was in the realm of research. The prison commissioners recognized that there was a field for research in the study of prisoners who while not certifiable, presented abnormal mental characteristics. Studies by M. Hamblin Smith and W. Norwood East, both members of the prison medical staff, and by Grace Pailthorpe, took their place in the only substantial corpus of scientific criminology in England before 1939, characterized by a medico-psychological approach, and geared to solving practical problems, notably how to treat the residuum of socially inefficient, emotionally unstable, and mentally abnormal prisoners, including the group of offenders labelled as psychopathic personalities.[135] For a start, prison medical officers stayed faithful to the pre-war rejection of the eugenic theory that a large proportion of prisoners were feeble-

133 TNA, HO144/20648/595645/167: Maxwell, 13 Sep. 1932.
134 Maxwell, "The Punishment of Crime and the Crime of Punishment," a talk, circa 1933–35, private paper in author's possession.
135 See D. Garland, "British Criminology before 1935," *British Journal of Criminology*, vol. 28 (1988), pp. 2–10; idem., "Of Crimes and Criminals: The Development of Criminology in Britain," in M. Maguire et al. (eds.), *The Oxford Handbook of Criminology* (Oxford, 1994), pp. 45–9.

minded through hereditary transmission, and that the underclass of mental deficients, paupers, and criminals, what would by the 1930s be called the "social problem group," had to be prevented from breeding. The eugenic camp's last throw of the dice came in 1934 with the Departmental Committee on Sterilization. The committee recognized a concentration in the lowest social stratum of physical and mental defectives, chronic unemployables, recipients of public relief, and criminals of below average physique and mentality, but recommended only the *voluntary* sterilization of persons suffering from mental defect or disorder. Norwood East had memorialized the Sterilization Committee, concluding firmly,

> eugenic sterilization as a means of combating delinquency appears previous, unwarranted and possibly harmful to the race. As a punitive measure it is outrageous. As a therapeutic measure it is otiose, may incite to sexual crime and lead to a false sense of security in the public mind.[136]

The final nail in the coffin of eugenics came when "eugenic prophylactics" were proposed by the Nazis at the 1935 International Penitentiary Congress in Berlin, which Alexander Paterson was hard pressed to defeat.[137]

Of the two leading prison medical officers, Hamblin Smith was the most radical. In his first major publication, *The Psychology of the Criminal*, he set out his credo

> that conduct is the direct result of mental life, that misconduct, like all other forms of conduct, results from mental causes. The particular act with which a man is charged in Court is only a symptom produced by these mental causes.[138]

Hamblin Smith was, in his own words, "a convinced and a quite unrepentant Freudian."[139] In 1922, under his direction, Grace Pailthorpe began her psychoanalytical investigations in Birmingham prison, before moving to Holloway prison, courtesy of a research grant from the Medical Research Council. Between 1923

---

136 B. Forsythe, "Mental and Social Diagnosis and the English Prison Commission 1914–1939," *Social Policy and Administration*, vol. 24 (1990), pp. 238–40; "Report of the Departmental Committee on Sterilisation," *The Lancet*, 27 Jan. 1934, p. 209; Sir Bernard Mallet, "The Social Problem Group," *Eugenic Review*, vol. 23 (1931), pp. 203–5; D. Caradog Jones (ed.), *The Social Survey of Merseyside*, vol. 3, (1934), p. 395; Ralph Crowley, "The Role of Sterilisation in the Prevention of Mental Defect and Disorder," *Howard Journal*, vol. 4 (1934), pp. 35–7; TNA, PCom9/123: memo, 27 Mar. 1933. For an earlier discussion of sterilization within the Home Office when Churchill was Home Secretary, see TNA, HO144/1098/197900; CAB 37/108/189 (1911).

137 B. Forsythe, "National Socialists and the English Prison Commission: The Berlin Penitentiary Congress of 1935," *International Journal of the Sociology of Law*, vol. 17 (1989), pp. 132–42; idem., "Mental and Social Diagnosis and the English Prison Commission 1914–1939," *Social Policy and Administration*, vol. 24 (1990), p. 249–50.

138 Cited in Arthur Gardiner, "In Memoriam: Dr. M. Hamblin Smith," *Penal Reformer*, vol. 3 (1936), p. 15.

139 Smith, *Prisons and a Changing Civilisation* (1934), p. 130.

and 1927, Pailthorpe investigated female prisoners between 16 and 30 years of age, and inmates of preventive and rescue homes for girls and young women; 100 cases in each investigation. Her manuscript was submitted in 1929, but the Council insisted upon a number of changes, so *Studies in the Psychology of Delinquency* did not see the light of day until 1932, in the same year as her own book, *What We Put in Prison*. What did Pailthorpe's work add to the subject? For a start, she objected to the prevailing tendency "to regard the criminal as a member of a separate class; a class apart, inherently and permanently evil," instead endorsing Hamblin Smith's view that crime was a sub-branch of normal behaviour.[140] In *Studies in the Psychology of Delinquency*, the more academic of the two texts, of the 100 women prisoners investigated, 36 per cent were of defective or subnormal intelligence, and 64 per cent of normal intelligence. "This confutes the generally held opinion," she observed, "that criminals become such because they are sub-normal intellectually." Closer to the truth, she felt, was that criminals became so "through defect in sentiment development," which she described as "strikingly lacking in any other than egoistic sentiment." Eighty-four per cent of the prisoners, she claimed, were deficient in sentiment development. She also identified two other categories of prisoner apart from the Defective Group: the Psychopathic Group and the Adapted Group. More importantly, for present purposes, she concluded that, excluding mental defectives, there were 56 prisoners "for whom psychological treatment in one form or other is necessary." Psychoanalysis could usefully be applied in 19 per cent of the cases; for the rest, she advocated segregation, permanent supervision in the community, or education. To carry out the suggestions for treatment, she put forward two methods: a central clearing station to which all offenders would go on first conviction, and small laboratories to test the value of the different schools of psychology.[141] In the more accessible text, *What We Put in Prison*, Pailthorpe identified the unconscious mental life as the dominant factor in delinquent behaviour. Trying to "drive out the devil" by reform of the prisoner while in prison would only drive the "'devil' *deeper in*." The only hope was to help delinquents "reach their unconscious mind, so that by the resolution of the hidden cause of guilt there is no longer any reason for defensive measures against it."[142] Pailthorpe's work had little immediate impact on the criminal justice system, but it was influential on the establishment in 1932 of the Institute for the Scientific Treatment of Delinquency, whose goal was to examine and treat out-patient cases of anti-social conduct while on remand or probation, especially children and young adults. The institute's own psychopathic clinic opened in 1933, becoming the Portman Clinic in 1937.[143] The Home Office kept aloof.

140 Grace W. Pailthorpe, *What We Put in Prison* (1932), p. 21.
141 Pailthorpe, *Studies in the Psychology of Delinquency*, Medical Research Council (1932), pp. 16, 97–9.
142 Pailthorpe, *What We Put in Prison* (1932), p. 132.
143 Edward Glover, "The Diagnosis and Treatment of Delinquency," in L. Radzinowicz and J. W. C. Turner (eds.), *Mental Abnormality and Crime* (1944), pp. 269–70; N. Rose,

Norwood East had serious reservations about Pailthorpe's full-blooded advocacy of psychological treatment, and he was particularly sceptical of how many prisoners would benefit from psychotherapy. Indeed, East was always at pains to damp down the excessive claims of psychiatry. At the Howard League's Summer School in Oxford in August 1937, while affirming that crime was the result often of mental disabilities other than insanity and mental defectiveness, and that a "modern scientific approach to the criminal problem is by means of psychological investigation and treatment," East also insisted that "there is at present no substantial and authoritative body of evidence which can be utilized to estimate its ultimate value." Psychological treatment, he continued,

> has been hailed by some as the essential and most successful method of preventing crime and of treating criminals regardless of the fact that of 30,157 prisoners received into prison for the first time during the years 1930–33, 24,326, or 80.7 per cent. had not, as far as is known, returned to prison a second time up to the end of 1935.

He concluded his talk by asserting that biological, psychiatric, ethical, and social factors contributed to the formation of the criminal habit, and hence moral and social as well as medical methods of treating crime were required: "The majority of law breakers are ordinary men, ordinarily motivated and amenable to ordinary legal processes."[144] Indeed, in a 1939 report that East co-authored, of which more in the following, it was claimed that only 10–20 per cent of criminals displayed abnormal features, defined widely to include "minor degrees of defect, mild psychotic or psycho-neurotic reactions and manifestations of abnormal personality types."

Even so, in keeping with his view that psychological treatment of criminals, whether conducted in prison or elsewhere, was still in the experimental stage, East pressed the Home Office to implement the proposal of the Persistent Offenders Committee to appoint a medical psychologist to undertake the examination and treatment of certain mentally abnormal prisoners. In January 1934, Dr. William Henry de Bargue Hubert, a psychoanalytically-oriented psychiatrist, was appointed as part-time medical officer at Wormwood Scrubs prison, though free from the routine work of a medical officer.[145] A circular went to all male prisons informing governors of the appointment, and asking medical officers to be on the lookout for suitable subjects for

The Psychological Complex: Psychology, Politics and Society in England, 1869–1939 (1985), p. 201; Claire Valier, "Psychoanalysis and Crime in Britain during the Inter-War Years," British Society of Criminology, *Selected Proceedings*, vol. 1 (1998); M. Shapira, *The War Inside: Psychoanalysis, Total War, and the Making of the Democratic Self in Postwar Britain* (Cambridge, 2015), pp. 143–8.

144 *Justice of the Peace*, vol. 101 (1937), p. 622; East, "The Modern Psychiatric Approach to Crime," *Journal of Mental Science*, vol. 85 (1939), pp. 654, 661.

145 Paul Bowden, "Pioneers in Forensic Psychiatry. William Henry de Bargue Hubert (1905–47): Reformer and Expert Witness," *Journal of Forensic Psychiatry*, vol. 7 (1996), pp. 323–8.

psychological treatment. They were advised that prisoners should be under 40, serving sentences of not less than six months for indecent exposure, homosexual or abnormal sex crimes, arson, and other crimes "considered to be due to obsession or hysterical reactions." Adolescents who showed evidence of "pronounced mental instability" were also to be considered for submission. Cases were to be selected from the early recidivist group, where the penal or borstal system had failed or was likely to fail. Prisoners certifiable under the Lunacy and Mental Deficiency Acts were not to be submitted. And, finally, prisoners had to be willing to cooperate in psychological treatment.[146] The research ended on the outbreak of war in 1939 and *Report on the Psychological Treatment of Crime* by East and Hubert was published in the same year.

In this four-year study, 406 cases were investigated, drawn from a borstal group (63 cases), an adolescent group (41 offenders under the age of 23 serving prison sentences), an adult group (97 offenders over the age of 23 serving prison sentences), and the sexual offenders (205 homosexuals, exhibitionists, and offenders against women and girls). Two hundred and fourteen of the 406 cases were approved for treatment. Those treated had been out of prison for four years at most, and many for shorter periods, or were still serving their sentence, so the report presented no figure or percentage of cures. Case histories were recorded, however, in which it appeared probable that psychotherapy had led to some social adjustment. Hence, the first conclusion of the report was

> Psychotherapy as an adjunct to an ordinary prison sentence appears to be effective in preventing, or in reducing the chance of, future anti-social behavior provided the cases to which the treatment is applied are carefully selected.

The report added, however, that psychotherapy "is, and is likely to remain, a specialized method of treatment usefully applied to but a comparatively small number of disorders." Moreover,

> it is more than probable that skilled direction, management, specialized training and other general psychiatric methods of treatment are applicable to a very much larger number of cases and to a wider range of conditions than is psychotherapy alone.[147]

This led the co-authors to their two main recommendations: probation, with the requirement that the offender was to submit himself to mental treatment (for which more psychiatric clinics were needed); and the creation of "a penal institution of a special kind." The new institution was to serve four functions: first, as a clinic and hospital where cases could be investigated and treated by

146 TNA, PCom9/186.
147 W. Norwood East and W. H. de B. Hubert, *Report on the Psychological Treatment of Crime* (1939), pp. 153–5.

psychotherapy and other means (as well as serving as a centre for criminological research); second, as a place in which "selected cases could live under special conditions of training and treatment," especially those unchanged by the prison system; third, as a colony for the offender "who had proved himself quite unable to adapt himself to ordinary social conditions"; and, fourth, as an observation and treatment centre for borstal boys.[148] This was quite the *pot pourri* of functions, not to mention patients: those requiring active psychiatric treatment, those included for research purposes, and a further group of cases for psychiatric management (those unsuitable for the observation wings of ordinary prisons or for whom reformative measures seemed useless).

An intriguing annotation to this report is that even before it appeared, Maxwell, the Permanent Undersecretary of State at the Home Office, was talking to the prison commissioners about the recommendations that East and Hubert proposed to make. In a letter to East himself in August 1938, Maxwell wrote that the Criminal Justice Bill, being readied for the autumn, included a clause which gave courts the power to make a probation order with a direction that the offender should submit to mental treatment, either as an out-patient or as a resident patient, for a period not exceeding 12 months. But an additional clause would now be needed, said Maxwell, empowering a court to pass, instead of a sentence of imprisonment, a sentence of detention for a period not exceeding three years in a special institution for offenders in need of mental treatment. Maxwell was uncertain whether the proposed institution should be under the control of the prison commissioners or the Board of Control. He preferred the prison commissioners, if persistent offenders convicted of serious crimes were the medical cases being detained, but the Board of Control, if offenders had no prior record of persistence in serious crime.[149] Was this a recommendation that East and Hubert intended to make, but which never got into the final report? In the report, under the heading "Offenders requiring detention," the authors simply stated, "We should like to see cases for prison treatment sentenced for six to 12 months' imprisonment." Moreover, the report added another paragraph which seems to echo the same preliminary discussion:

We . . . do not consider a sentence of detention in a special institution for psychological treatment is practicable until a great deal more experience is gained in the matter. Perhaps not even then, for on certain occasions such a sentence would detain a prisoner for a longer period than would be appropriate, and if he misconducted himself seriously in an institution it might be necessary to transfer him to an ordinary prison although sentenced to a special form of detention. We do not think this could be justified in the present state of medical knowledge or public opinion.

148 Ibid., p. 159.
149 TNA, HO45/18736/438456/38: Maxwell to East, 31 Aug. 1938.

The next paragraph then stated, "We consider a new institution for convicted offenders under the administration of the Prison Commissioners is required."[150] The question of the future use of psychiatric methods in prisons was to be considered following publication of the East and Hubert report in 1939. The war put paid to that. In the annual report of the prison commissioners for 1949, an appendix on psychological treatment at Wormwood Scrubs prison referred to East and Hubert's proposal of a new institution, adding the cryptic remark, "It has not been possible hitherto to implement this recommendation. After the publication of the report, psychological treatment fell into abeyance for over 3 years owing to war conditions."[151]

IX

If recidivism or the habitual criminal was the core problem of inter-war penal policy and practice, which most mandarins, ministers, and judges believed to be the case, no solution to the problem came close to success in these years. A good part of the problem was that legislation was chasing a phantom. The number of hardened professional criminals, whom the law ostensibly targeted, was small, and anyway these people typically committed crimes of such severity that a long tariff-based sentence sufficed. As a result, the habitual criminal laws caught in their nets the petty property offender and the inadequate recidivist, which only brought the law into disrepute. The other part of the problem was that judges displayed extreme aversion to sentencing for the habit of persistence in crime. They declined to take advantage of the opportunity provided by the 1908 law to escape the restraints of "just deserts." The sentence of preventive detention expired from inanition. The Report of the Persistent Offenders Committee offered a new beginning, though one that again placed full trust in the judicial body as the sole arbiter of punishment. Since the Criminal Justice Bill 1938 fell on the outbreak of war, it was still unknown if what was proposed for persistent offenders by the 1932 committee would give judges the confidence to sentence the criminal as opposed to the crime. In other respects, too, the inter-war years were thoroughly disappointing. If the corner were ever to be turned with recidivism, if ex-prisoners were ever to be assured of employment, it was essential to overhaul the equipment, personnel, and payment systems of prison labour, and to convert the after-care system from a ramshackle and inadequate voluntary outfit into an effective professional organization. Small steps were taken in these directions, but prisoners would have been hard pressed to discover any meaningful

150 East and Hubert, *Report on the Psychological Treatment of Crime* (1939), p. 160.
151 Ann. Rep. of P. Com. for 1949, PP, 1950–51, XIV (Cd. 8088), Appendix to Chapter 7. Norwood East went on to publish the results of his study of 4,000 consecutive cases received at Wormwood Scrubs boys' prison between 1930 and 1938 in *The Adolescent Criminal* (1942); and 18 of his essays were collected together in *Society and the Criminal* (1949).

improvement. Nor was the recidivist the subject of any systematic form of social or psychological treatment in prison. Psychological knowledge had not advanced to the stage at which it was possible to diagnose cases with precision, and the mandarins were acutely suspicious of anything that was new and still protean.

6

WAR AND CRIMINAL JUSTICE LEGISLATION, 1938–1948

I conceive myself in this field of social reform to have two duties imposed upon me. First of all, to do everything in my power to keep people out of prison; and, secondly, if they get into prison, to prevent them coming back there—precisely, I would suggest, the duties that are upon your [the magistrates'] shoulders, that you are carrying out in the country day by day . . . I take the view . . . that, however intelligently and scientifically and sympathetically prisons are administered, prison life must in the nature of things be an unnatural kind of life . . . and that being so, the more we use alternative methods of dealing with crime and delinquency, the more likely we are to enable men and women in every walk of life to be able to keep their position in the community and not to become outlaws.

Sir Samuel Hoare, Home Secretary, The Magistrate, Nov.–Dec. 1938

I

In the inter-war years, changes in penal policy and practice emerged from a loose coalition of senior administrators, penal reformers, politicians, and criminologists: what I have called elsewhere the "liberal progressives."[1] The ideological underpinning for these changes was an amalgam of Christian humanism, philosophical Idealism, and "positivist" thought. This meant, in practice, a commitment to the softening of the punitive edges of incarceration; to the provision of training for a modicum of prisoners, especially the youngest ones, humane detention for the rest; and to the continued abatement of imprisonment, in favour of non-custodial

---

1 See Victor Bailey, *Delinquency and Citizenship* (Oxford, 1987), chaps. 1 and 8. Ian Loader, "Fall of the 'Platonic Guardians': Liberalism, Criminology and Political Responses to Crime in England and Wales," *British Journal of Criminology*, vol. 46 (2006), pp. 562–5. See also Nick Ryan, *Penal Policy and Political Culture in England and Wales* (Winchester, 2003).

penalties. This was never more evident than in the final years of the 1930s, when the new Home Secretary, Sir Samuel Hoare, eager to burnish his family's penal reform credentials, asked his officials to piece together the threads of administrative and social work experience, plus the recommendations of a handful of official reports on various aspects of penal practice, into a ground plan for penal reform. Little did any of the main parties to this task imagine that they were about to embark upon a ten-year odyssey, involving three notable stages. First, the 1938 Criminal Justice Bill, the first comprehensive penal measure since the Prison Act 1898, a departmental bill, short on vision, long on piecemeal reform, which was perforce abandoned on the outbreak of war in 1939. Second, a war-time and post-war increase in the volume of crime and the number of prisoners, and a related revival of the punitive ethos, voiced most stridently by the senior judges. And third, the 1948 Criminal Justice Act, which bore strong traces of the earlier bill, particularly in its provisions to restrict imprisonment for young offenders and devise prolonged detention for recidivists, yet which came close to falling foul of, and was certainly overshadowed by, the controversy surrounding the abolition of the death penalty. The outcome was a penal measure which was accepted *faute de mieux*, which already looked long in the tooth if not outdated, and which left much to the imagination when it came to the structural provision and internal regime of the new modes of incarceration.

"When I became Home Secretary in [May] 1937," Sir Samuel Hoare recalled a decade later,

> I was struck by an anomaly. On the one hand penal reform had, compared with other social reforms, made little or no advance in 50 years. On the other, a mass of invaluable material had been accumulated by practical experience and expert inquiries for creating an up-to-date and efficient prison system.[2]

Hoare was referring to the proposals to be found in the Select Committee on Capital Punishment 1930; the Persistent Offenders Committee 1932; the Committee on Social Services in Courts of Summary Jurisdiction 1936; and the Committee on Corporal Punishment 1938. Within a few days of taking office, Hoare had the opportunity on the Prison Vote to inform the House of Commons of his "hereditary interest in prison administration." He claimed kinship with Elizabeth Fry, the early-nineteenth century prison reformer, who was his great, great aunt. In what Hoare claimed as "my most successful speech in the House of Commons," he listed the first impressions he had formed in talks with his departmental advisors. One, it was time to extend the experiment of giving prisoners privileges from the start of their sentence, appealing to their fear of losing them, rather than starting with no privileges and having to earn them. Convicts in Chelmsford, Parkhurst, and Dartmoor were to be given the chance to earn wages, and spend them, from

---

2 *Evening Standard*, 28 Nov. 1946 in Viscount Templewood Papers, Cambridge University Library, Pam. 2.

the start of their penal servitude. This would complete the extension of such schemes to all persons under long terms of detention, with the exception of those two or three hundred convicts serving sentences of three years in local prisons. Two, Hoare expected to carry further the classification of offenders, especially for adolescent and habitual criminals, for which legislation might be required. Three, something had to be done about "the problem of the central prisons, out-of-date buildings in the middle of our great cities."[3] The only sour note was struck by James Maxton, the Scottish socialist and fierce parliamentarian, who had served a year in prison in 1916 for sedition.

> I cannot associate myself with the sort of "Oxford Group" spirit of general good will and congratulation that seems to prevail, and the idea that every-thing is going swimmingly so far as prisons are concerned . . . The general standard of life in the prisons remains what it was, and the essential conception of imprisonment remains precisely the same as it was.[4]

Hoare was fortunate in his permanent officials, who were accustomed both to administering the penal system and to making policy for the benefit of their political masters. Alexander Maxwell, whose appointment as Permanent Under-secretary of State Hoare personally secured, had served as chairman of the Prison Commission between 1928 and 1932, and as Deputy Undersecretary of State at the Home Office since 1932. He was a seasoned and talented administrator, whose intellectual grasp and capacity for work made him chief strategist of the advance in penal law and administration which the new Home Secretary desired.[5] Alongside Maxwell was Harold Scott, who had been chairman of the Prison Commission since 1932. His prior service in the Home Office stretched back to Churchill's Home Secretaryship in 1910.[6] He was a decisive and energetic executive. His fellow commissioners were Alec Paterson and Dr. Norwood East.[7] But how best to proceed? In early June 1937, Hoare asked Scott what small changes, such as improving prison libraries and the prison diet, could be made quickly. He also wondered if in the next year or two a new prison for women could be built out-side London. "I am aware that I speak in almost complete ignorance of all these questions and that there may be little or nothing that we can do," said Hoare. "I feel, however, that the moment to make changes . . . is when a new Home

---

3   *Hansard*, vol. 324, 4 Jun. 1937, cols. 1315–19. See also "A New Way with Prisoners," *Spectator*, 11 Jun. 1937, p. 1081; "Crime and Reclamation," *The Times*, 15 Jul. 1937, p. 15; T. Edmund Harvey, "The Home Secretary's Opportunity," *Contemporary Review*, vol. 152 (1937), pp. 668–75.
4   Ibid., Maxton, col. 1338.
5   See Duncan Fairn, "Maxwell, Alexander (1880–1963)," *Oxford DNB* (2004); Maxwell, *Treatment of Crime* (1938), Sidney Ball Lecture, 16 Nov. 1937, Barnett House Papers No. 21.
6   See Anon., "Scott, Sir Harold Richard (1887–1969)," *Oxford DNB* (2011); *The Times*, 20 Oct. 1969.
7   Viscount Templewood, *Nine Troubled Years* (1954), p. 229.

Secretary comes into office and a new chapter is rightly or wrongly considered to have begun."[8] In late June, Hoare asked for a programme of work for the next two or three years. Scott submitted a detailed agenda of prison reforms, including accommodation, clothing, employment, libraries, medical, and aid-on-discharge, and advised the Home Secretary that the most urgent need was legislation providing for the more effective treatment of young and persistent offenders. On 20 July, Hoare wrote that he was particularly in favour of the proposed legislation. He wanted to show the legislative proposals to Lord Chancellor Hailsham and Attorney-General Somervell, the latter having promised to help him with the judges.[9]

In the meantime, Hoare decided to go on a tour of prisons, to talk with the people in the know about the institutions, and to absorb the proposals put forward by the recent official inquiries into probation, preventive detention, and corporal punishment. He went to Dartmoor, Wandsworth, Winchester, Parkhurst, Wormwood Scrubs, Holloway, and Pentonville, writing a note after each visit. He interviewed the likes of Willie Gallacher, Communist MP; Sir Vivian Henderson, chairman of the Conference of Borstal Visiting Committees; and Florence Earengey, barrister and Holloway prison visitor. Hoare later told George Lansbury, former leader of the Labour Party, that since he came to the Home Office, "I have realised the almost religious fervour which some of our prison administrators are bringing to bear upon the treatment of crime."[10] The Home Secretary was laudably seeking to inform himself about his new brief. It was quite in character. Hoare was a conscientious politician, exceedingly efficient (as he had shown with the India Bill) at handling large bodies of papers and piloting legislation through the Commons. He was also realistic about his function:

> As at the India Office, so now in the Home Office, I was a gatherer rather than a sower. The harvest was ready, drilled and cultivated by skilled men and women, and needing only to be cut and winnowed in a combine machine.[11]

Rarely was Hoare's work leavened by any grander vision. Unlike Churchill, he never developed a feel for the penal system in its entirety, and never himself imagined innovative ways of abating imprisonment. The new Criminal Justice Bill was very much a departmental bill, aiming to supplement the administrative changes

8   TNA, PCom9/139: Hoare, 7 Jun. 1937.
9   PCom9/138: R. R. Scott (Permanent Undersecretary of State), 14 Jun. 1937; PCom9/139, Scott, 10 Jun. 1937; Scott, 8 Jul. 1937; Hoare, 20 Jul. 1937. For a Dec. 1937 review of the changes in prison administration since Hoare took office in May, see PCom9/140.
10 *Daily Herald*, 3 Aug. 1937 in TNA, HO45/18006/546730/65; *The Times*, 10 Sep. 1937, p. 14; Viscount Templewood Papers, Cambridge University Library, Box X:7, 10: Henderson interview, 1 Nov. 1937; Gallacher interview, 15 Dec. 1937. Ibid., Box X:8: Hoare to Lansbury, 20 Jan. 1938.
11 Templewood, *Nine Troubled Years*, op cit., p. 231. See also *Oxford Dictionary of National Biography* (Oxford, 2004), "Hoare, Samuel" by R. J. Q. Adams.

made by the prison commissioners in the past decade, and implement the proposals of the various official committees.[12]

In November 1937, Hoare submitted to Cabinet a memorandum on reform of penal law, which indicated that a new bill would cover amendments of the law concerning probation, new measures for persistent offenders, giving power to the courts of summary jurisdiction to pass sentences of borstal training (as a crucial step to avoiding, ultimately prohibiting, the imprisonment of young offenders), and the wiping away of many of the retributive terms still in use—what Hoare when introducing the bill in the House of Commons would describe as "the remnants of former dispensations, now little more than the stage properties of Victorian melodrama: penal servitude, hard labour, ticket-of-leave, the name 'criminal lunatic.'"[13] He might have added the term "convict" and "Director of Convict Prisons." Prior to the Cabinet meeting, a number of ministers sent their views on the memorandum to Hoare. Viscount Hailsham said, "you can count on my hearty support for your proposals," though he disliked the change of name of criminal lunatic, preferring "to call a spade a spade." Sir John Simon, Chancellor of the Exchequer, agreed with the general lines, though expressed surprise that 80 per cent of those who went to prison for the first time never returned. "I know that it is true of Wakefield . . . but I had not appreciated that this is true of prisoners of all sorts. It seems an argument for sending people to prison!" said the former Liberal Home Secretary. Cabinet gave Hoare the authority to draft a bill for submission to the Home Affairs Committee.[14] In December 1937, Hoare told the HAC that the main objects of the bill were to improve the probation system, give courts new powers of dealing with young offenders in place of imprisonment, provide new methods of dealing with persistent offenders, and make better arrangements for offenders who required mental investigation and treatment. New alternatives to imprisonment were proposed, namely Task Centres and Howard Houses, and Observation Centres were proposed for young persons aged 17–21 under remand or committed for trial or sentence. Once the new arrangements were in place, and

12 According to R. A. Butler (junior minister, Ministry of Labour), Hoare "has caused a good deal of antipathy by managing to crowd out some other Cabinet Ministers at the gate and get in with his Prison Reform Bill. . . There is naturally a good deal of jealousy but he is increasing daily in administrative ability, not concealing that he does not suffer fools gladly." Quoted in J. A. Cross, *Sir Samuel Hoare, a Political Biography* (1977), p. 281.

13 TNA, CAB 24/273, CP 282 (37): Reform of Penal Law; HO45/17666/805270/3. One hundred years earlier, Jeremy Bentham had denounced hard labour for "giving a bad name to industry, the parent of wealth, and setting it up as a scarecrow to frighten criminals with."

14 TNA, CAB 23/90 (Penal Reform), Cabinet meeting, 24 Nov. 1937; LCO 2/3338: Hailsham to Hoare, 10 Nov. 1937; HO45/17666/805270/3 (Sir John Simon). Simon was anxious about the preventive detention proposals: "I do not say that I am against the idea, though I always have a certain feeling of doubt. . . at an extension of the powers of the executive to determine at its discretion the length of time that a grown man, not certified to be insane, may be kept in detention. The totalitarian States, I imagine, exercise the power freely. . ."

probation and borstal treatment had been brought up to date, it was proposed that courts of summary jurisdiction would be prohibited from sentencing to imprisonment persons under the age of 21. The HAC approved the general framework of the bill, adjourning detailed consideration until their next meeting.[15]

In February 1938, the Home Secretary turned to the prison building programme, informing the Chancellor of the Exchequer:

> our buildings compare most unfavourably with those of many other countries. They are for the most part even more out-of-date than our law. Only one prison (Camp Hill) and two Borstal Institutions . . . have been built in this century—the remainder are at least 50 and in many cases 70, 80 or even a 100 years old . . . the time has come, and is indeed overdue, when we must face a comprehensive programme of new building spread over a period of many years if the provisions of the Bill and the progressive policy of the Prison Commissioners are not to be stultified by lack of suitable accommodation.[16]

Hoare enclosed a long memorandum from the prison commissioners, which set out a six-year plan of improvements. The first step was to erect a new prison for 350 women on a country site near London. Once the women and girls were removed from Holloway and Aylesbury, Pentonville would be sold to the London County Council, and the recidivist men detained there would be housed at Holloway and Aylesbury. Feltham borstal would become an Observation Centre, taking all lads under the age of 23 who were under remand or committed for trial, and all lads sentenced to borstal training and awaiting allocation—in short, the greater part of the lads then detained in the Boys' Prison at Wormwood Scrubs. Finally, a new borstal and a new prison for men were required. The new prison could possibly be used for the first crop of preventive detainees. It seems the Chancellor approved at once the new women's prison and the sale of Pentonville; the observation centre and a new boys' borstal were left open until the penal reform bill was further along; and the proposal to build a new prison for men was dropped. Hoare announced the closing of Pentonville prison and the building of a new women's prison in July 1938; and in March 1939 on the Home Office vote in the Commons, he announced that he was looking for a suitable site for the women prisoners who were to be moved from Holloway. (Land was bought at Stanwell in Middlesex, but the envisaged camp for women was never built). He also made

15 TNA, CAB 26/22, HA 57 (37), 17 Dec. 1937; LCO2/3338, for HAC 16th conclusion (37), Dec. 20. 1937; CAB 26/23, HAC 1st conclusions (38), 7 Feb. 1938. In January 1938, the Penal Reform Group of the House of Commons submitted a memorandum to the Home Office asking for the Penal Reform Bill to include much greater classification of prisoners, different types of institution, psychological treatment, and a measure of self-government. See TNA, HO45/18006/546730/90; Howard League Minute Book, EC meeting, 3 Jan. 1938, MSS 16B/1/3, Modern Records Centre, Warwick University.

16 TNA, HO45/19680/430010/91: Hoare to Chancellor (Simon), 4 Feb. 1938.

clear that the penal reform bill and prison buildings were joined at the hip. The housing "will be an integral part of the whole scheme of penal reform that we are discussing upstairs in connection with the Criminal Justice Bill. These are two essential sides of the same programme."[17]

Thus far, nothing had been said about judicial corporal punishment. On the assumption that the Departmental Committee on Corporal Punishment would fail to submit a unanimous report, Maxwell had initially advised the Home Secretary to omit the subject from the penal reform bill. However, when in December 1937 the Home Office got wind of the Cadogan committee's unanimous recommendation to abolish corporal punishment, Maxwell suggested incorporating the proposals into the Bill.[18] The Committee duly reported in March 1938, and questions were soon being asked in Parliament about the government's attitude towards the committee's recommendations. In June 1938, Hoare and the Secretary of State for Scotland, John Colville, circulated to the Cabinet a joint memorandum on this controversial subject. Under existing law, magistrates' courts had the power to punish by whipping boys under 14 years of age convicted of any indictable offence. The committee recommended that this power should be abolished, especially since most juvenile courts had in practice abandoned what they considered an ineffective method of dealing with young offenders. Corporal punishment for adults was in practice restricted to three classes of offence: procuring, living on the earnings of prostitution, and robbery with violence.[19] The committee recommended the repeal of corporal punishment as a penalty for offences against the criminal law. In the report, figures collected from the subsequent records of 440 men convicted of robbery with violence during the period 1921–30 showed that a sentence of imprisonment or penal servitude *without* corporal punishment was no less effective than a similar sentence combined with it. Finally, prisoners and borstal boys could be awarded corporal punishment for mutiny or incitement to mutiny, and for gross personal violence to a prison officer. The committee concluded that these powers should continue to be available, but for prisoners only, not borstal inmates. It did so because "for potential offenders against prison discipline the fear of imprisonment is no longer available as a deterrent."[20]

According to the Cabinet memorandum, the press had largely accepted the Cadogan report's conclusions, and none of the *national* newspapers had opposed the recommendations. The only body of opinion that objected to abolishing corporal punishment for adult offenders was that of the Judges of the King's Bench

---

17 Ibid.; TNA, PCom9/139: press cuttings arising from Hoare's 27 Jul. speech in the Commons; *Hansard*, vol. 338, 27 Jul. 1938, cols. 3150–64; *Daily Telegraph and Morning Post*, 28 Jul. 1938, p. 14; *Hansard*, vol. 344, 6 Mar. 1939, col. 1808.

18 TNA, HO45/17666/805270/8A: 11 Dec. 1937. See also Bailey, *Delinquency and Citizenship*, p. 140.

19 The reason these offences were subject to corporal punishment was a function of emergency legislation in the wake of a "moral panic" over the ostensible frequency of the crimes.

20 CP 142 (38), Corporal Punishment, Joint Memo, 16 Jun. 1938; Cabinet 29 (38), meeting 22 Jun. 1938.

Division. The latter even proposed extending existing powers by empowering courts to order corporal punishment for the offence of unlawful carnal knowledge of a girl under 13 and possibly for the offence of rape. The judges gave no grounds for their opinion.[21] At the Cabinet meeting on 22 June, Hoare and Colville advised Cabinet to accept the committee's recommendations, and to include the necessary provisions in the Criminal Justice Bill, "where they would fall into proper perspective in a wider measure of penal reform." The Earl Stanhope, President of the Board of Education, thought it probable that the House of Lords would take the same line as it had done in 1932 in connection with the Children and Young Persons Bill, which was to retain the existing powers of whipping. Hoare held his ground. As he stated in his autobiography, "I could not regard corporal punishment as morally wrong, but neither could I find evidence to show that it was an effective deterrent as a judicial punishment."[22] During the preparation of the Criminal Justice Bill, Hoare also had to confront the issue of capital punishment. According to his autobiography, *Nine Troubled Years*, he took the line "that as capital punishment had always been given a unique place in the administration of justice, its abolition should be the subject of specific and not general legislation."[23] The death penalty found no mention in the King's Speech in October 1938 which promised the Criminal Justice Bill.

II

The bill was published in November 1938.[24] As expected, it provided improvements in the organization and staffing of the probation service in order to extend the use of probation. Also, when making a probation order (or discharging an offender conditionally or unconditionally), the courts were first to proceed to a *conviction*. For "mental cases," magistrates were allowed to remand an offender on bail for up to three weeks for medical examination and report, to be paid for out of public funds, to assist the court in deciding how to deal with him. Also, offenders suffering from mental illness or abnormality could be put on probation with a condition that they submit for 12 months to treatment, either residential or non-residential. The consent of the person was required before such an order could be made. For the persistent offender, there were to be two forms of sentence, corrective training and preventive detention, with a dividing line drawn at the age of 30. For young offenders, the bill prohibited imprisonment for those under 16,

---

21 See E. Royalton Kisch, *Consistent Principles in Criminal Punishment* (1939), p. 11 enclosed in TNA, HO45/18479/565861/11. See also Hermann Mannheim, "The Report of the Departmental Committee on Corporal Punishment," *Modern Law Review*, vol. 2 (1938), p. 55.

22 Templewood, *Nine Troubled Years* (1954), pp. 233–4. See also Templewood Papers, Box X, 8 (16). Notes on interview with Lord Roche.

23 Ibid., p. 247.

24 Sir Harold Scott, *Your Obedient Servant* (1959), p. 93: "It was published in 1938, provoking a good deal of controversy. . ."

placed restrictions on the imprisonment of the 16–21 age group, and provided for its abolition in the lower courts for all under 21. To ensure the abatement of imprisonment for adolescents, the bill included remand centres for those aged 17–23 awaiting trial or on remand; compulsory attendance centres for persons aged 12–20, depriving offenders of their leisure time on Saturday afternoons and evenings for a maximum of 60 hours; and Howard Houses or residential hostels, from which offenders would go out to work, for persons aged 16–20. There was also the provision allowing direct committal to borstal training by the lower courts. Finally, detention within the precincts of the court or at the police station was reaffirmed; the anachronisms were abolished (penal servitude, hard labour, prison divisions, and tickets-of-leave); and corporal punishment was to be abolished except in prisons. Power was also taken to do away with the Prison Commission by merging prison administration with the general administration of the Home Office.[25] One thing is clear: the emphasis of the bill was on the young and trainable; hardly any notice was paid to the age groups above 30. The provisions of the bill regarding persons over 21 were limited mainly to implementing the proposals of the Persistent Offenders Committee, of which more later.

The Criminal Justice Bill was greeted positively by the main penal reform groups and by the press, who thought it portended a great advance in penal policy and practice.[26] The bill got rid of the obsolete Victorian terminology. It put faith in prevention, not cure, and sought to prevent the young offender from becoming the recidivist. It put faith in long-term training, not short-term imprisonment. And it turned against the repeated, incremental sentences of a gradually more severe character for habitual criminals.

Sir Samuel Hoare moved the Second Reading of the Criminal Justice Bill on 29 November 1938. True to form, he declared two main justifications for the bill: "to effect an immediate reduction in the number of young people received into prison"; and "protecting society against the pests who continually inflict damage and suffering upon their fellow men and women," what Hoare described as "this hard core of the criminal problem." He concluded by asserting that it was "the most comprehensive penal Bill that has ever been introduced into this House." In

25   TNA, HO45/17668/805270/85; Gordon Rose, *The Struggle for Penal Reform* (1961), pp. 224–8.
26   *The Times*, 17 Nov. 1938, p. 15; *Daily Telegraph and Morning Post*, 12 Nov. 1938; *Law Journal*, 26 Nov. 1938, p. 360; T. Edmund Harvey, MP, "The Criminal Justice Bill," *Contemporary Review*, vol. 155 (1939), p. 37; Margery Fry, "The 'Penal Reform' Bill," *Fortnightly*, vol. 151 (1939), pp. 10–11. Hermann Mannheim observed that the bill "has taken up the fight against the short-term prison sentence," especially for young offenders, and that the keynote of the bill was "on the lines of individualization, reformation, de-stigmatization. . . to *de-stigmatize* institutional treatment and to provide a *greater variety* of its methods. . . also to *restrict* its application to the indispensable minimum. . ." in *The Dilemma of Penal Reform* (1939), pp. 134, 219 (italics in original). Leon Radzinowicz declared, ". . . the bill . . . will act as a dynamic factor in accelerating and intensifying the process of further transformation of the system of English penal repression along the course hitherto pursued": "The Present Trend of English Penal Policy," *Law Quarterly Review*, vol. 55 (1939), p. 288.

the ensuing debate, there were few outright opponents of the Bill, though some members were critical of particular clauses. Replying for the Labour Party, Frederick Pethick-Lawrence reassured the government that the bill "will not be treated in this House from any party point of view," an approach reinforced by J. R. Clynes: "There are no party interests in this Bill; there are no votes in it; it is mainly designed to aid a voteless and a helpless group of outcasts . . . This Measure is a social and a national necessity . . ." Harold Nicholson emphasized the provenance of the bill:

> It is the formulation of a 30 year process of experience on the part of prison governors, of prison visitors, of the Prison Commissioners . . . of experience on the part of several committees and commissions, and also . . . on the part of those who have experienced in their own persons the dangers and disadvantages of incarceration.[27]

Only corporal punishment aroused any heat. The Home Secretary was accused of inconsistency by Conservative member, Sir Thomas Moore:

> My right hon. Friend said that statistics prove that the "cat" is not a deterrent, but at the same time he has retained it as a deterrent against attacks on prison warders. Surely, by doing so, he has proved to us that, in his view, it is a deterrent against attacks on prison warders, and therefore, surely, it must be a deterrent against the outside crimes of robbery with violence or criminal assault.[28]

Moore wanted to give judges discretion to inflict the "cat," not alone for crimes of robbery with violence but also for attacks on women, children and old people, and gross cruelty to animals. The Opposition benches came to the defence of the clause. George Benson urged the Home Secretary to stand firm, in view of the departmental committee's unanimous report in favour of abolition. "In view of that careful examination and that mass of statistics I am not prepared to accept unsupported the testimony of judges, ladies, or archangels." Sir Stafford Cripps tweaked the Colonel Blimps of the House who

> will continue to tell us that they became what they are owing to the good doses of corporal punishment which they received when they were at Eton or some other suitable seminary; and as they are what they are we shall be more than ever impressed with the evil results of corporal punishment.[29]

27 *Hansard*, vol. 342, 29 Nov. 1938, cols. 267–86 (Hoare); cols. 286–97 (Pethick-Lawrence). *Hansard*, vol. 342, 1 Dec. 1938, col. 631 (Clynes); col. 702 (Nicholson).
28 *Hansard*, vol. 342, 29 Nov. 1938, col. 346.
29 *Hansard*, vol. 342, 29 Nov. 1938, col. 354 (Benson); *Hansard*, vol. 342, 1 Dec. 1938, col. 710 (Cripps). See also *The Times*, 1 Dec. 1938, p. 15: "The Bill has many critics of detail, but very few outright opponents."

This was knockabout stuff as preface to turning Moore's argument on its head: "If corporal punishment will not deter, and has not in experience deterred, in cases of robbery with violence, what conceivable evidence or argument can there be that it will have a deterrent effect in the case of prison offences?" This issue returned to haunt the Committee Stage of the Criminal Justice Bill.

This was how Hoare himself described the position:

> By the time that the Bill had reached the Committee Stage, a raging agitation against abolition had been started by my old diehard opponents of Indian days, and by large sections of the Press. The front-line troops of the Party passed many resolutions in favour of flogging in the meetings of the National Union of Conservative Associations.[30]

In the country opinion was more evenly balanced. In 1938, asked whether they approved or disapproved of the proposal to abolish flogging and birching except for prison offences, 47 per cent of respondents approved, 45 per cent disapproved. A year later the figures were 44 per cent approve; 54 per cent disapprove.[31] In Standing Committee, in March 1939, two attempts were made to retain corporal punishment as a judicial penalty, but each amendment was defeated, and the abolition clause was carried by 32 votes to 17.[32] This was only the first skirmish. The Chief Whip told the Home Secretary that 203 Conservative members intended to support an amendment to delete the clause during the report stage. In the face of this backbench revolt, the Cabinet decided in June to allow a free vote on the clause dealing with flogging at report stage. Hoare was opposed to a free vote, feeling that the House of Lords would, in consequence, be more likely to reject the clause, particularly if the vote was close and relied upon Opposition members.[33] In the event, the report stage was never taken. It is impossible to know whether the clause would have survived the remaining legislative stages. More than likely, a compromise proposal would have been cobbled together, based on the distinction between the young delinquent and his adult counterpart, since the controversy centred less on the juvenile than on the adult offender.

The clause of the bill providing for new sentences of Corrective Training and Preventive Detention also requires discussion. The Persistent Offenders Committee had made two recommendations for this type of offender. First, a sentence of detention for two to four years for those in the early stages of a criminal career, who would benefit from training, and for others (notably petty persistent offenders) whose detention was required for public protection. Second, a sentence of prolonged detention for not less than five and not more than ten years for professional

---

30 Templewood, *Nine Troubled Years*, op cit., p. 234.
31 George H. Gallup (ed.), *The Gallup International Public Opinion Polls: Great Britain 1937–75*, vol. 1 (New York, 1976), 1938, pp. 9, 12; 1939, p. 20.
32 See CAB 129/56/36, C (52) 386, 4 Nov. 1952: Appendix 3, 1938–9.
33 Templewood, *Nine Troubled Years*, op cit., p. 234. See also Bailey, *Delinquency*, op cit., pp. 144–5.

criminals, for those who persistently committed thefts or frauds on a small scale, and for certain sexual offenders. When the Criminal Justice Bill was under construction in early 1938, Harold Scott insisted upon a clear distinction between detention for those likely to profit by a period of training, and those whose detention was necessary for the protection of the public.[34] Hence, the bill provided for two types of sentence (though technically three types): corrective training for a period of not less than two and not more than four years on persons between the ages of 21 and 30 whose records, characters, and habits were such as to make a sentence expedient for the training of the offender; and preventive detention for a term of not less than two and not more than four years on persons over the age of 30, if by reason of the offender's criminal record and mode of life such a sentence was expedient for the protection of the public. In both cases, the person had to be convicted on indictment of an offence for which the court had power to pass a sentence of imprisonment for a term of two years or more, and the person had to have one previous conviction. Thirdly, for offenders with records of repeated crime (previously convicted at least three times of an offence specified in the First Schedule, or previously convicted of an offence for which he was sentenced to corrective training or preventive detention), it was proposed that preventive detention sentences could exceed four but should not exceed ten years.[35] In short, only for a restricted group of offenders was *prolonged* preventive detention prescribed. The two to four years' sentence was clearly regarded as the norm, which was not the intention of the Departmental Committee, but none the worse for that.

Shortly before the Second Reading of the Bill, the Law Officers and the Director of Public Prosecutions (DPP), Sir Edward Atkinson, offered advice on the clause. The Attorney-General, Sir Donald Somervell, thought the distinction between training and public protection was still unclear, since the court was enjoined to consider the protection of the public as well as the expediency of corrective training for the offender. He might well have added that it was also stated that "persons sentenced to corrective training *or preventive detention . . . shall be given such employment and subjected to such methods of *training* and discipline as may be best fitted to lead to their *reformation* [my italics]." In response, the Home Office explained that it had been decided to make a sentence of corrective training rest on the same grounds as the sentence of borstal training. As for the DPP, he would have preferred the maximum term of preventive detention to be set at 14 or 15 years:

> In my experience of habitual criminals these persons in 99 cases out of 100 are wholly irreclaimable . . . I am glad to see that you have included a number of sexual offences in the First Schedule because I have occasion to

---

34 TNA, HO45/17666/805270/37.
35 See *Criminal Justice Bill*, PP. 1938–9, vol. 2 (4), 2 Geo. 6, pp. 325–6, 367–8.

deal with habitual sexual offenders who do not come within the Prevention of Crime Act, 1908, and are a serious menace to society.[36]

During the Second Reading debate, Pethick-Lawrence indicated that he felt some
misgivings about these proposals. For a start, he was disturbed by long confine-
ments, particularly for young people. Those subject to corrective training were by
definition under 30 years of age, and those subjected to preventive detention need
not be much more than 30. Second, he wanted corrective training to be reformative and to differ from a prison sentence, and hence was troubled by the statement
that it was proposed to set aside "prisons or parts of prisons" for these purposes.
Third, the First Schedule, which was said to refer only to very serious offences,
went wider than that.

> I understand that if a man who stole twopence from an offertory box he
> would, theoretically, come under this Schedule of offences . . . [I]t shows that
> the classification under Schedule I is not so watertight as the right hon. Gen-
> tleman would lead us to think.[37]

The Howard League endorsed all three reservations. Margery Fry added that the
felonies for which a sentence of two years' imprisonment could be given were of
varying gravity, and "one would like to see a more careful definition of the actions
which are to mark the species of habitual criminal."[38]

At Committee Stage, Sir Samuel Hoare's amendments tightened up the conditions under which these sentences could be given. Corrective training could only
be ordered if the offender had *twice* been convicted of an offence for which on
indictment a sentence of two years' imprisonment could be passed. In the original
clause, only *one* such previous conviction had been required. Preventive detention
of two to four years could be ordered if the offender had been previously convicted on indictment at least *twice* of an offence of the type specified previously.
This increased the number of previous convictions, and stipulated that the offences
must have been actually tried on indictment and not merely be indictable offences.
The last point applied also to cases of prolonged preventive detention.[39] Benson
tried unsuccessfully to secure an amendment to the statement that corrective
training may be served in "part of a prison;" and Robert Turton suggested the
adoption of a new type of corrective training (between one and two years) for
petty persistent offenders (those previously convicted at least five times of an
offence for which the court had power to pass a prison sentence for a term of three

36 TNA, HO45/17666/805270/72: Attorney-General to Home Secretary, 8 Nov. 1938;
    Ibid., 805270/75: DPP to Maxwell, 9 Nov. 1938.
37 *Hansard*, vol. 342, 29 Nov. 1938, col. 294.
38 Howard League Minute Book, EC meeting, 28 Nov. 1938, MSS 16B/1/3; Margery
    Fry, "The 'Penal Reform' Bill," *Fortnightly*, vol. 151 (1939), pp. 17–18.
39 W. A. Elkin, "Progress of Criminal Justice Bill," *The Penal Reformer*, vol. 6 (1939), p.
    13.

months or more), the type of offender that once again had got lost in the shuffle.[40] It should be pointed out, also, that the bill contained no provisions directly relating to the treatment of those persistent offenders who were mentally abnormal.

The bill emerged from committee in April 1939 and that was the end of the road. At the outbreak of war, Hoare was asked to join the War Cabinet on condition that he free himself from Home Office business, and at the end of September, Maxwell informed the Home Secretary:

> On the assumption that the Bill cannot come into operation for a couple of years or more there would be advantages from the point of view of those who are charged with the responsibility of getting the Bill right in all its complex details, if we started afresh after the war. As you know, the present Bill was originally prepared very hurriedly and still has many imperfections.[41]

Despite parliamentary pressure to keep the bill alive, the House was informed on 9 November that the government was not able to proceed with the bill. As the Howard League concluded, "The Criminal Justice Bill was the first and most important legislative casualty of the war."[42] The second casualty was the loss of the long-awaited prison-building programme.

The Criminal Justice Bill would have been the apex of the prison commissioners' inter-war attempts to improve the methods of classifying and training criminal offenders. It would have consolidated and enhanced the essential approach to adolescent offenders, which was to limit and ultimately prohibit the use of imprisonment and offer training elsewhere. For young offenders, the bill sought to improve the scope of the existing alternatives to imprisonment—probation and borstal—and add new alternatives to prison in the shape of remand centres, attendance centres, and Howard Houses. For offenders who suffered from mental illness or abnormality, the bill looked to increase the scale of pre-sentence examination, and make treatment available as a condition of probation. For recidivist offenders, the bill sought to encroach further upon the tariff mentality of the judiciary by allowing courts to punish persistence by longer detention sentences. As such, the legislation was janus-faced: it would have reduced the resort to incarceration at the same time as incarcerating more people for longer periods. And the measure was silent on a number of important matters. What would young offenders actually do in attendance centres? What would the regime be in corrective training and

40 L. Radzinowicz, "The Persistent Offender," in Radzinowicz and Turner (eds.), *The Modern Approach to Criminal Law* (1945), note 1, p. 170 (Turton); note 2, p. 171 (Benson).

41 Maxwell, 26 Sept. 1939 in Templewood Papers, Box X: 9.

42 *Hansard*, vol. 353, 14 Nov. 1939, col. 532; *Howard Journal*, vol. 5 (1940), p. 225; *Justice of the Peace*, vol. 103 (1939), pp. 705, 745. The Archbishop of Canterbury commiserated with Hoare at the loss of the Bill, Hoare replying: "I could not be more sorry about the Criminal Justice Bill. It was the result of years of work and common effort not only of the Department, but of a great body of social workers outside Whitehall." See Hoare to Archbishop, 17 Nov. 1939 in Templewood Papers, Box X: 9.

preventive detention, and where would recidivists be housed? Corrective training was to consist of "such methods of training and discipline as may lead to reformation," but this was the object which the prison commissioners had pursued in all prisons for the past 20 years. Would corrective training mean anything more than the kind of regime for young convicts to be found in Chelmsford prison? Would preventive detention, to be available for shorter periods, be any different from the purely custodial regime it had hitherto been?[43] Nor was there any mention of the East-Hubert recommendation to develop a separate establishment for mentally abnormal offenders.

Finally, as was true of all penal reform at the time, it was a leap in the dark. S. W. Harris, Assistant Undersecretary of State, observed in 1938,

> Attempts also have been made from time to time to estimate the success of different methods whether probation, Home Office Schools, Borstal Institutions or Prisons but none of these efforts has been correlated with the result that we are largely in the dark as to the relative advantages of different systems.[44]

S. K. Ruck, former Assistant Director of the Borstal Association, and secretary of The New Survey of London Life and Labour, likewise claimed in 1940,

> The revolution in the methods of treating crime which took place during the last generation . . . was not effected as the result of any proved insufficiency of the old methods or demonstrable efficiency of the new. It is only within the last dozen years that any attempt has been made to analyse the comparative results of the various methods of treatment . . . The change was thus wholly empirical . . .[45]

The same can be said for the measures in the Criminal Justice Bill. All the prison commissioners could offer by way of support was a general impression about the effect of different types of sentence (for example, that imprisonment with corporal punishment was no more effective than without it), and the claim that certain sentences were *prima facie* misguided (for example, that imprisonment was

---

43 See S. K. Ruck, "Developments in Crime and Punishment," in Radzinowicz and Turner (eds.), *Penal Reform in England* (1st. ed. 1940; 2nd ed., 1946), pp. 30–1.

44 TNA, HO45/21948/884452/1A. The Criminal Statistics for 1938 published the results of an investigation by the Metropolitan Police of the reconviction rates during a five-year period of all persons recorded as having been convicted for the first time of finger-printable offences. Using only the crude criteria of age and sex to distinguish one offender from another, "it made little difference how the court had dealt with the offender": R. A. Butler, *Penal Reform and Research* (Liverpool, 1960).

45 Quoted in E. R. Guest, "'Criminal Science' and Punishment," *Journal of Comparative Legislation and International Law*, vol. 30 (1948), pp. 46–7. See also S. K. Ruck, "Developments in Crime and Punishment," op cit., p. 12.

inappropriate for young offenders).[46] For the most part the bill had to be taken on faith.

III

The war years brought a significant number of crime-creating forces to bear on the country. Criminologist Hermann Mannheim documented some of the most important ones: the unprecedented population movements as a result of the conscription of military personnel and civilian workers, and of the evacuation scheme, movements that resulted in a severe dislocation of home life and parental control; the closing of schools in the evacuation areas, leaving city children to run wild; the closing of social clubs, hostels, and evening institutes for adolescents over school age; rationing, the scarcity value of commodities, and the black market; the blackout and the protection it afforded lawbreaking; and the opportunities for theft provided by air-raid damage.[47] Not surprisingly, indictable offences known to the police rose from 283,220 in 1938 to 478,394 in 1945, or by just under 70 per cent (though the increase in London was, for whatever reasons, only half the national figure). The increase was especially marked in the receiving of stolen property, though increases were registered also in sexual and violent crime. Only frauds and false pretences and offences of drunkenness posted a decline. Offences committed by women more than doubled in number during the war years, evidence probably of a newfound, wartime independence. Juvenile delinquency was especially affected by the war. Between 1938 and 1944, the proportion of offenders in the 8–17 age group increased by 70 per cent in the case of boys, and 120 per cent in the case of girls.[48]

Inevitably, these figures had an impact on punishment. After the initial reduction in the daily average prison population by special discharges (all prisoners with less than three months to serve, and all Borstal inmates who had served not less than six months of their term, were immediately released), bringing the number down from 11,400 to 5,750, and notwithstanding the increase to one-third of the amount of remission earned—the pre-war level of prison population was passed in 1942, and by late 1944 the figure was over 14,000, rising to 14,800 in June 1945.

46 Alexander Maxwell, *Treatment of Crime* (1938), op cit., p. 24; Memo on misguided or excessive sentences, 14 Nov. 1938, Templewood Papers, Box X:8 (19).

47 Mannheim, "Crime in Wartime England," *The Annals of the American Academy of Political and Social Science*, vol. 217 (1941), pp. 128–32; idem., *War and Crime* (1941), pp. 138–42. See also Bailey, *Delinquency*, op cit., pp. 270–1; Mark Roodhouse, *Black Market Britain, 1939–1955* (New York, 2013), Pt. II.

48 Mannheim, *War and Crime* (1941), pp. 129–37; idem., *Group Problems in Crime and Punishment* (1955), pp. 102–3; Viscount Templewood, *Crime and Punishment*, op cit., pp. 6–7; Home Office, *Habitual Drunken Offenders*, Report of the Working Party (1971), pp. 202, 204 (Appendix F). See also T. Morris, *Crime and Criminal Justice since 1945* (1989), pp. 34–5; Harold L. Smith (ed.), *Britain in the Second World War* (Manchester, 1996), p. 17, and chap. 6; Bailey, *Delinquency*, pp. 269–70; Barry S. Godfrey et al., *Crime, Regulation and Control During the Blitz* (2016), chap. 6.

This was an increase of almost 50 per cent in the space of five years.[49] Sorting by gender reveals that the daily population of women in prison doubled during the war. These population changes were not due to an increase of *men* sentenced to imprisonment, but to a decrease in the use of the short sentence, especially of a month or less, due to the decrease in the committals for drunkenness, and an increase in sentences of one to 12 months' imprisonment.[50] By contrast, there was a substantial increase in the number of *women* sent to prison on conviction. It is not possible to discover whether courts were imposing heavier sentences than they would have imposed before the war for offences of similar gravity, or whether more of the offences dealt with by the courts were such (like looting) as to call for substantial sentences of imprisonment. Another interesting fact is the increase in the proportion of first offenders (without previous proved offences) when compared with the pre-war years, arguably a sign of the temptations and changed value system of wartime.[51]

The short prison sentence was not, however, dispensed with for offenders under 21. In 1938, the number of persons under 21 sentenced to imprisonment was 1,226 males and 88 females; in 1944, the corresponding figures were 3,021 males and 904 females, and most of these sentences were for three months or less. At the same time, the proportion of male offenders aged 17–21 placed under the supervision of probation officers declined.[52] For the juvenile offender, greater use was made of corporal punishment and punitive detention in remand homes. Sentences of corporal punishment on boys under 16 reached a peak of 531 in 1941, compared with 48 in 1938, but fell sharply from this peak. By 1945, only 25 sentences of corporal punishment were awarded by magistrates' courts.[53]

The post-war years brought little relief. Between 1945 and 1950, the number of indictable offences known to the police declined from 478,394 to 461,435 (though to begin with the number rose to 498,576 in 1947). However, this overall decline

49 TNA, PCom 9/1386. Two-thirds of Holloway prisoners were discharged in September 1939, the remainder evacuated to Aylesbury: Mary Size, *Prisons I Have Known* (1957), p. 129.

50 See H. Mannheim, "Comparative Sentencing Practice," *Law and Contemporary Problems*, vol. 23 (1958), p. 561: "Prison sentences for males not exceeding one month numbered 51 per cent of all cases in 1938 and 26.1 per cent in 1945, whereas sentences of one month to twelve months rose from 43.8 per cent to 63.8 per cent and sentences of over twelve months rose from 5.2 per cent to 10.1 per cent."

51 TNA, LCO 2/3342: notes to deal with Templewood's motion on penal reform, 23 Nov. 1946; W. A. Elkin, "English Prisons in Six Years of War," *Howard Journal*, vol. 7 (1946–7), pp. 104–12; Joseph Trenaman, "English Prisons in 1947," *Howard Journal*, vol. 7 (1948–49). See also Ann Smith, *Women in Prison* (1962), pp. 246–7; A. Rutherford, *Prisons and the Process of Justice* (1984), note 43, p. 61.

52 Margery Fry, "The Criminal Justice Bill," *Political Quarterly*, vol. 19 (1948), p. 114; Alexander Maxwell, "Penal Reform, 1898–1948," *Magistrate*, vol. 8 (1948), pp. 165–6. See also Raymond L. Gard, *Rehabilitation and Probation in England and Wales, 1876–1962* (2014), p. 172.

53 R. L. Gard, *The End of the Rod* (Boca Raton, 2009), p. 115; Bailey, *Delinquency*, pp. 277–8; Smith, *Britain in the Second World War*, op cit., pp. 91–5; Phoebe Hall et al., *Change, Choice and Conflict in Social Policy* (1975), note 19, p. 318.

was due to a fall in offences against property, and masks sizeable increases in the number of sexual offences and crimes of violence against the person. It is the latter crimes, including armed robberies, plus the continued high level of young men found guilty of indictable offences between 1945 and 1948, that sustained the belief that the country was in the throes of a post-war "crime wave." Again, the impact on punishment was soon evident. The daily average prison population was 17,000 by 1947, exceeding 20,000 in July 1948. And again, the increase was a function of the larger proportion of prisoners convicted for indictable offences carrying longer sentences.[54] These figures of crime and punishment, as we shall see, sharpened the debate about penal reform in the post-war years. There was a good deal of unanimity around the view that the war had debased the country's moral standards, as a result of which crime and delinquency had increased. The divide came over the methods needed to turn back this tide. For the judiciary it was time to get tough with offenders. For Viscount Templewood, sponsor of the 1938 bill as Home Secretary, it was incumbent upon the government of the day "so to adapt its penal machinery as to make it as easy as possible for a moral renaissance to be carried into effect." In the Lords in November 1946, Templewood moved to resolve that in view of the serious increase of crime, "this House is of opinion that a comprehensive measure of penal reform should be passed into law without delay."[55]

The story of post-war penal reform began much earlier than Templewood's intervention. In May 1942, Herbert Morrison, Home Secretary in the wartime Coalition government, suggested to Maxwell, Permanent Undersecretary, that a committee might be appointed to examine the reformative treatment of prisoners. Maxwell informed Morrison that a general enquiry into prison treatment had been considered several times in the past 20 years, but the Home Office view had been "that we are likely to make more progress by having special enquiries made into special aspects of this complex problem." Hence, Maxwell advised resuscitating Lord Roche's 1938 committee on the Courts of Summary Jurisdiction, informing his chief that the view of Sir Claud Schuster, Permanent Secretary to the Lord Chancellor's Office, had been that,

> we were mistaken in introducing the Criminal Justice Bill before reforming the Courts of Summary Jurisdiction. The main responsibility for the treatment of offenders rests on the lay Justices of the Peace, and unless their work can be improved, for example by the appointment of full-time clerks properly qualified and properly paid, there is little chance of proper use being made of any new penal provisions.

54 Home Office, *Delinquent Generations* (1st. pub., 1960; 2nd impression, 1961), p. 11 (Appendix I, Table 1); Lord Windlesham, *Responses to Crime*, vol. 2 (Oxford, 1993), p. 66; Morris, *Crime and Criminal Justice*, op cit., pp. 90–1, 96; A. Bottoms and S. Stevenson, "'What Went Wrong?': Criminal Justice Policy in England and Wales, 1945–70," in D. Downes (ed.), *Unravelling Criminal Justice* (1992), pp. 4–5.
55 *Hansard* (Lords), vol. 144, 27 Nov. 1946, col. 415.

Maxwell, however, saw some value in having committee backing for the principles on which the Criminal Justice Bill was based:

> One of the main difficulties is that many of the Judges, and the legal profession generally, are naturally wedded to the principle that the business of the Courts is to weigh out doses of punishment proportionate to the particular offence, and it is difficult to reconcile this principle with the doctrine that offenders who need corrective training should be sentenced on their records to comparatively long terms of detention with discretion to the prison authorities to release them when the training is thought to have become effective. The Courts naturally do not like a system which leaves to the administrative authorities this kind of discretion to "interfere," as they regard it, with their sentence.[56]

Morrison decided to wait for a memorandum from Harold Laski, political scientist and member of the National Executive Committee of the Labour Party, whose Committee on Reconstruction Problems, with Laski as secretary, had recently published *The Old World and the New Society*, a plan for the post-war organization of virtually every feature of British life.[57]

Laski advised the appointment of a royal commission to ready public opinion for a criminal justice bill: "to get an enquiry going which will create the expectation of post-war innovation now while the public mind is attuned to the idea of innovation." He wanted attention drawn to the "painfully small part played by the judges in the reform of the Criminal Law" (as evinced by their hostility to "the revision of penal concepts in the light of advancing medical knowledge," and to the indefinite sentence); to the "painfully small contribution to the study of criminology made by the legal profession, not least on its academic side" (with the exception of Cambridge, the field "is the hunting ground, in this country, of the amateur"); and to the need to discuss the recruitment of prison staff and the employment (in prison and on release) and education of prisoners. He warned against weighing the commission down with a judge as chairman "and a flock of barristers and solicitors among its members." He wanted young, energetic members who would "realise that their task is to create the opinion which will lead to the establishment of the scientific study of crime in Britain":

> The law has produced no one of the first rank in criminology since Bentham; Charles Goring stands in lonely eminence among the officers of the prison service—compared to the United States, the Soviet Union, and pre-Hitler Germany, the British contribution to progress is disappointing.[58]

---

56 TNA, HO45/21948/884452/1: Maxwell memo, 22 May 1942.
57 Isaac Kramnick and Barry Sheerman, *Harold Laski: A Life on the Left* (1993), p. 447.
58 TNA, HO45/21948/884452/1, Laski letter and memo, 13 Jun. 1942.

There things remained until January 1944, when, prompted by an article by Margery Fry entitled *The Future Treatment of the Adult Offender*, Morrison met with Maxwell. Fry had asked, "What then are the desiderata we can formulate for an immediate penal programme for after the War?" What she thought was needed included a treatment authority, "to whom should be handed over the duty of prescribing and supervising treatment, whether institutional or other, of defined classes of persons, and in particular of young persons"; the destruction of prisons "whose every brick is stamped with century-old ideas of confinement, contempt and gloom"; the recruitment and training of staff, including trained psychiatrists; the abolition of capital and corporal punishment; and the provision of Attendance Centres and Howard Houses as provided for in the 1938 bill.[59] The decision arrived at in January was to provide Morrison with a statement of the department's policy on the treatment of offenders in the form of a White Paper. In preparing this statement, it was recognized that an informed public opinion was essential, particularly if there was to be a change in the powers of the court to prescribe the form and length of punishment, which led in turn to consideration of an advisory council:

> In view of the substantial measure of agreement on policy it was considered unnecessary . . . to appoint another Royal Commission or Departmental Committee to consider these problems . . . but that it might be desirable to have an Advisory Council on the lines suggested by Mr. Harris for juvenile delinquency . . . but of wider scope.[60]

As for the prisons, the department recognized that the ordinary local prison had had its day: "The future requires a system of regional prisons which will be adapted to serve as Training Centres on modern lines, with a limited number of special prisons for men serving very long sentences," and "a place where psychopathic and mentally subnormal prisoners can be segregated for observation and treatment."[61]

S. W. Harris, Assistant Undersecretary of State, affirmed that in planning for reconstruction, the problem of crime and the treatment of offenders "must find an appropriate place," and that the Home Office would greatly benefit from a "Standing Committee of advisers to whom special questions could be referred for consideration."[62] At this point, in early March 1944, Harris and Fox, chairman of the Prison Commission, were not convinced that reviving the Criminal Justice Bill, with or without amendment, would suffice. They advised several separate bills, one to implement the recommendations of the Roche Committee on summary jurisdiction, one amending and consolidating the law relating to probation, one amending and consolidating the Prison Acts. This approach was confirmed on 17

---

59 Fry, "The Future Treatment of the Adult Offender," enclosed in TNA, PCom 9/1428. The article appeared in *Agenda*, Nov. 1943.
60 TNA, HO45/21948/884452/2; PCom 9/1428.
61 PCom 9/1428.
62 Ibid.

March by a meeting on post-war penal reform between *inter alia* Maxwell, Harris, and Fox. The Home Secretary was to be advised to set up an advisory council, whose primary function would be "to consider and to advise on such proposals as might be referred to it by the Secretary of State." The major proposals of the Criminal Justice Bill, starting with juvenile offenders and ending with persistent offenders, would be referred to it, as would a White Paper on penal reform if such were to be issued. It was thought "it would be better that the proceedings of the Council should not be published."[63] Legislation was then prioritized as follows: a bill to give effect to the Roche Committee proposals; a bill dealing with remand homes and approved schools; a probation bill on the lines of the 1938 bill; a children and young-persons bill (dealing with offenders up to the age of 21); a prisons bill; and a bill to deal with persistent offenders. On 23 March, Morrison announced the appointment of an advisory council "to assist in the preparation of a programme of reforms," and at the end of March, opening a probation hostel in Birmingham, he took the opportunity to sketch out the line of post-war developments in penal reform, including pulling down or blowing up the old prison buildings.[64] The *New Statesman*, in an anonymous and hard-hitting article, which has the sound of Laski about it, applauded the appointment of a permanent advisory council: "It should be the biggest step forward in this field since . . . Mr. Churchill became a prison reformer after seeing Galsworthy's *Justice*." Above all, prison administrators would now be subject "to a constant stream of criticism, enquiry, and suggestion from laymen in this field." Lawyers had done little or nothing for criminal law; reformers within the Home Office had "rarely shown any profound imagination." The council presaged the possibility that "we shall begin at last to develop that clinical and statistical study of crime in its social context in which this country has been backward for something like two generations."[65]

In early April 1944, Morrison informed Prime Minister Churchill that he intended providing a written answer to a parliamentary question on reintroducing the pre-war Criminal Justice Bill, along the lines that many of the proposals in the 1938 Bill, improved by further consideration, might find a place in the programme of reforms that was presently under development. In a typically muscular response, Churchill advised against raising this topic: "So many people are having very hard things demanded of them, and our prisons have been vastly reformed in the last 30 years or so." Sir Samuel Hoare, with whom Churchill had clashed incessantly on the India Bill, had made "a great feature of prison reform," said the PM, but "[h]e was pretty well adrift from realities at that time." "I should recommend waiting," said Churchill, "for a gentler age than that in which we are condemned for a while to dwell." "I hope you will not think that I, too, am 'adrift from realities,'" said

---

63   TNA, HO45/21948/884452/3.

64   *Daily Herald*, 29 Mar. 1944; *The Times*, 29 Mar. 1944: cuttings enclosed in TNA, HO45/21948/884452/7.

65   "A Courageous Initiative," *New Statesman*, 1 Apr. 1944, p. 222.

Morrison, "if I return to the charge and stake out a claim for a Penal Reform Bill in our legislative programme of social reconstruction after the war." He promised no "sentimental journey in quest of ways and means of making life easier for the offender," but "a realistic attempt to tackle the economic problem of saving the community from the losses and suffering caused by the anti-social activities of criminals." Churchill relented: "By all means mature your proposals."[66]

First the Advisory Council on the Treatment of Offenders (ACTO) had to be appointed. Professor Laski accepted membership: "It is a chance to put British penal treatment at the head of modern efforts . . ." Dame Lilian Barker, former governor of the girls' borstal at Aylesbury, and first woman assistant commissioner of prisons, agreed to serve: "The war was a bitter blow to me, for it meant all the plans already drawn up for a new Holloway & girls Borstal had to be put away." They were joined by Hartley Shawcross, Recorder of Salford, and a supporter of the Howard League, who served until he was appointed Attorney-General in August 1945; George Benson, Labour MP, and chairman of the Howard League for Penal Reform; Miss Margery Fry, magistrate, and vice-president of the Howard League; Violet Creech Jones, magistrate, and an advocate of voluntary social service on behalf of children (whose husband, Arthur Creech Jones, had been imprisoned as a conscientious objector in the First World War); Lady Allen of Hurtwood, an advocate for children's rights and welfare (whose husband, Clifford Allen, had also been imprisoned as a conscientious objector); Leo Page, a leading authority on the work of magistrates; John Lees-Jones, Conservative MP and former chairman of the National Association of Discharged Prisoners Aid Societies; and the Bishop of Bristol. The council initially contained no medical psychologist, though in April 1946, Dr. Emmanuel Miller, a medical practitioner with expertise in psychological and psychiatric aspects of delinquency, was appointed. The vice-chairmanship went to Sir Alexander Maxwell, the chair to Mr. Justice Birkett, King's Bench judge.[67] The council was composed of 20 members exclusive of the chair. In general, male members were drawn from the legal and other professions, female members from the voluntary social service sector. The *Prison Officers' Magazine* complained that no one, except Lilian Barker, had practical prison service experience.[68] Politically the council represented all shades, though it tilted leftwards. Behind the council, preparing the agenda of topics for consideration, was the Administration of Justice Standing Committee, composed of Maxwell, Harris, Fox, and Frank Newsam.

66 TNA, HO45/21948/884452/6: Churchill to Morrison, 13 Apr. 1944; Churchill minute, 10 May 1944.
67 *Hansard*, vol. 402, 3 Aug. 1944, cols. 1598–9; TNA, HO45/25841/887177/2; "Birkett, (William) Norman," by Claude Rogers, *Oxford Dictionary of National Biography*, 2004. Discussing possible new ACTO members in September 1949, Birkett suggested to Newsam, Deputy Undersecretary of State, "some Psychiatrist who was not wholly mad (if such an one there be!)": HO 45/25841/887177.
68 *Prison Officers' Magazine*, May 1944, enclosed in TNA, HO45/21948/884452/14. See also Anne Logan, "Women and the Provision of Criminal Justice Advice," *British Journal of Criminology*, vol. 50 (2010), p. 1080.

Home Secretary Morrison gave the council its marching orders at its first meeting on September 5, 1944. He told council members that he wanted them to advise and assist the Home Office "in developing a comprehensive policy of reforms, and to maintain constant touch with the implementation of that policy." The burden of the effort would fall on the department but his officers should not work in isolation:

> I am anxious that our departmental ideas shall be broadened, humanized and improved by discussions with and suggestions from men and women who will look at the subject from various angles and contribute ideas based on experience in various spheres of work.

Specifically, Morrison mentioned—what was a daunting list—the information required by magistrates' courts and clerks to the justices, in order to decide upon the appropriate treatment of the various types of offenders; the development of the probation service as a skilled profession requiring training and expertise; the provision of alternatives to sentences of imprisonment; the problems connected with juvenile delinquency; and the subject of prison reform.[69]

It was the last-mentioned subject on which ACTO gave its advice between June and October 1945, as the new Labour government, elected in July, settled into office. The council accepted the Home Secretary's suggestion that they consider a prison commission memorandum on the development of the prison system in the aftermath of the war. The document is worth examining at length since it represents what Lionel Fox would later term a "Five Year Plan," which the Advisory Council approved, and since it impacted the shape of the post-war Criminal Justice Bill, especially the corrective training clause. The memorandum first laid out three factors of uncertainty which bedevilled any future planning. One was the suspended animation of the 1938 bill. When would legislative effect be given to the bill's provisions? The commissioners were particularly concerned with the treatment of persistent offenders. There are "some 2,000 prisoners serving sentences of Penal Servitude or imprisonment who would qualify for this form of sentence under the formula of the 1938 Bill." If courts used new statutory powers of long-term detention to the full, the consequences for prison population and its accommodation would be severe. Second, the size of the prison population had risen inexorably during the war years. The commissioners

> have no statistical guidance to explain why the recent increase has taken place [though why no thought was given to the trend of longer prison sentences is hard to understand], and they feel themselves quite unable to assess the effect on the post-war level . . . of the unknown and unpredictable social and economic conditions.

---

69 TNA, HO45/20729/893948/2; HO45/21948/884452/3A.

Third, how long would it be before priority would be given to starting an extensive prison-rebuilding programme? All that could be done for the time being was to supplement existing accommodation by the use of surplus camps and hostels as these became available.[70]

The Prison Commission memorandum then turned to the point of departure for post-war development, which was the "conception of 'training' as the governing principle of the prison regime . . ." Prisoners would be separated into short-sentence prisoners (less than four years), separated further into "trainable" and "untrainable," and long-sentence prisoners (four years or more). Persistent offenders were considered separately. Future development would be based on the assumption "that training in the fullest sense can only be given in a homogeneous establishment set apart for the purpose, to which prisoners selected as 'trainable' are transferred from their local prisons." Only one training centre existed before October 1944, Wakefield prison for prisoners of the "star" class, at which date Maidstone prison was set aside as a training centre for selected prisoners of the ordinary class. The commissioners fixed 12 months as the normal minimum sentence for a training centre, which would give eight months of training, allowing for remission. As for the type of man to be sent, the necessities of war had impelled the commissioners "to take a more generous view of the extent to which most ordinary prisoners can be trusted," which is what led to the setting up of the training centre at Maidstone. This was an important change because the hard core of the prison problem was not the "star" prisoners in Wakefield (70–80 per cent of whom would not return to prison), but "the 20–30% of 'first-timers' who do come back to prison, since it is from among these that the 'habitual criminals' of the future will be recruited." These were the men "on whom any scheme of training ought to concentrate." Finally, it was pointed out that to each training centre a camp like New Hall at Wakefield would be attached. And in London, trainable adult stars were already grouped in Wormwood Scrubs and Feltham (the latter experimenting with communal dormitories and dining rooms).[71]

The regime of training centres was spelled out in the memorandum: a prison day spent out of the cell as much as possible: eight hours in the shops, one hour of outdoor exercise; prison work that bore some resemblance to the kind of skilled and semi-skilled work for private firms that war demand made possible; earnings schemes that incentivized industry and good conduct; education that was an integral part of a "training for citizenship"; and improved health and hygiene. As part of the latter point, the commissioners pointed towards a special psychiatric establishment for prisoners who were mentally subnormal or affected by psychopathic

---

70 TNA, HO45/21949/884452/29: Maxwell to Fox, 20 Jun. 1945; PCom 9/1386; L. W. Fox, "A Survey of the Prison Administration for England and Wales since 1945," *Howard Journal*, vol. 8 (1951), p. 81. When asked to explain the *post-war* increase in the prison population, Maxwell ascribed it to the increase in crime: PCom 9/451, 22 Nov. 1947; 6 Feb. 1948.

71 Ibid. The general principles on which the prison system had been developed since 1895 was set out in the official pamphlet, *Prisons and Borstals* (1945).

conditions; provision "to enable the use of chamber-pots in cells to be dispensed with, though this problem does not appear capable of either cheap or easy solution"; and improvements in the methods of cooking and serving of food.

The commissioners made no claim to train the men in local prisons serving short sentences. As for the remaining 1,700 to 1,800 men with bad records serving sentences of 12 months or more in the local prisons (most of whom would qualify for preventive detention under the formula in the 1938 bill), it was proposed to concentrate them in the larger local prisons of their region, where there were better facilities for such training as could be given in a local prison.

Turning to long sentence prisoners (serving four years or more), provision would be needed for over 900 prisoners: 300 of the "star" class, 100 "trainable" ordinaries, and 500 "non-trainable" ordinaries, most of whom would be qualified for preventive detention under the formula of the 1938 bill. The number of very long sentences was limited; in 1941 only 119 men were serving sentences of five years and upwards. Star convicts would continue to go to Camp Hill; the bulk of the ordinary class would remain at Parkhurst. Dartmoor was being used for military convicts. Then there were the persistent offenders. In 1944 there were over 2,300 men serving sentences of 12 months or more who might have been eligible for preventive detention sentences of up to four or in some cases ten years under the 1938 formula. For these it might be necessary to find accommodation in special "detention" prisons. As for psychiatric and mentally abnormal cases, it was accepted in principle that a special prison would be set up as a combined hospital and colony. Prison psychiatric work had stopped almost entirely on the outbreak of war. It was reinstituted in 1943 when Dr. John Mackwood was appointed as part-time psychotherapist at Wormwood Scrubs. In the next three years, fewer than 30 prisoners with long enough sentences received treatment, including electric convulsive therapy. Not until 1948 did ACTO examine the means of treatment for offenders showing "psychopathic characteristics." However, the council ultimately advised against the East-Hubert proposal of an institution entirely within the penal system, preferring a special type of sentence, for a maximum period of two years' detention and treatment, in a special institution removed from the prison atmosphere. At this point nothing came of either approach.[72]

Finally, the memorandum dealt with the female prisoner. The increase in the female prison population since 1941 had been proportionately greater than in the male. Over 1,700 women were either unconvicted, sentenced to borstal detention, or serving sentences of penal servitude or imprisonment by April 1945. Increases had been seen in four main classes of offences, all linked to war conditions: shoplifting (clothes rationing), child neglect (the broken home), brothel-keeping (the 'armed camp' syndrome), and industrial absenteeism. Women prisoners were in

---

72 Annual Report of PCom for 1949, PP, 1950–1 XVIII (Cmd. 8088), Appendix to chap 7; TNA, HO45/21949/884452/16; HO45/20729/893948/2; PCom9/454. See also B. Richards, "Psychology, Prisons and Ideology: the Prison Psychological Service," *Ideology and Consciousness*, vol. 2 (1977), pp. 10–11.

Holloway or Aylesbury (star convicts), or in separate wings of a number of local prisons. There was no training centre for women. The commissioners wanted to create two training prisons on home-cottage, minimum security lines, with a third prison for recidivists. Women prisoners would do domestic work "directed towards training better housewives rather than better housemaids." In late 1946, Askham Grange open prison, near York, was opened, and the commissioners recalled Mary Size from retirement to head the new venture.[73]

ACTO devoted three days to consideration of the prison commissioners' memorandum, hearing evidence from the commissioners, the Superior Officers Representative Board, and the Prison Officers Association. In early October 1945, Birkett submitted the Council's views, which consisted of no more than urging the creation of one more girls' borstal, and hostels to accommodate the staff at women's prisons.[74] If the plans for the post-war quinquennium were approved by ACTO, they sat uneasily alongside the existing state of the prisons in 1945 and the next few years. This was particularly the case in the local prisons, where the population rose rapidly during the war years. In its report for 1942–3 the Howard League declared, "The war has put the prison clock back almost to 1922." A year later, Margery Fry claimed something similar: "in many of our prisons, the undoubted ameliorations of the last 20 years have been almost entirely lost under the pressure of the War, and recovery will need great efforts." At the 27th meeting of ACTO in March 1947, Fry raised the large number of suicides in prison between 1942 and 1944.[75] W. H. Hammond, imprisoned for a year in 1942 as a conscientious objector, covertly interviewed 62 prisoners serving their first, typically short, prison sentence, concluding (albeit 36 years later) that "the concept of any imprisonment as treatment, in however remotely a therapeutic sense, was simply derisory to the local prison inmates whom I met . . ."[76] Many other conscientious objectors replied to a questionnaire prepared by the Howard League about their wartime prison experience, which Mark Benney in *Gaol Delivery* fashioned into an exposure of the degradations that still featured in prisons: the revolting sanitary conditions—"the disgusting business of 'slopping-out'"; the severity of cell tasks; the shortage of evening classes; and 18 hours solitary confinement out of 24 banged up in the cell, due to a return of the one-shift system of staff working. Benney recorded some wartime improvements, such as prisoners being allowed to converse at exercise; the rescinding of the rule depriving a prisoner of a mattress for the first fortnight (the only remaining vestige of hard labour); and the greater provision of skilled and

73   Ibid. See also Howard League, *Annual Report, 1946–7*, p. 7; Size, *Prisons I Have Known* (1957), chaps. 12–15; "Britain's First Open Prison for Women," *Manchester Guardian*, 18 May 1949.
74   TNA, HO45/21949/884452/39: Birkett, 6 Oct. 1945.
75   *Howard Journal*, 1941, p. 7, cited in H. Mannheim, *Group Problems*, op cit.; Fry, "The Future Treatment of the Adult Offender," p. 2, in TNA, PCom9/1428; HO45/21988/903499/23.
76   Hammond, "A Study of the Deterrent Effect of Prison Conditions," *Howard Journal*, vol. 15 (1977), p. 20; "Doing Time," *New Society*, 2 Jun. 1977, p. 458.

semi–skilled employment as well as outside working parties (mainly farming). Yet he also accused the commissioners of allowing relaxations of the regime to prove illusory: "of a kind of official thinking which attempts to pervert all reforms back to the pattern of the *ur*-gaol . . ."[77] But it wasn't only the conscientious objector who was critical of the prison regime. A temporary prison officer working at Holloway in late 1944 told Mass Observation that the regular officers were "extremely dull, mentally and physically," having "the same look of hopeless apathy as the prisoners themselves." Officers treated the prisoners harshly: "[w]hatever the prisoner does is wrong, and after a few weeks inside the prisoners resign themselves to their fate."[78] A different spin was put on the issue of prison staff by the recently-conceded Prison Officers Association. The hours worked by prison officers had been reduced in 1939 from 48 to 44 per week. In response, the commissioners had contracted the prisoner's working day in local prisons to what it had been in 1931, and increased the time for which prisoners were locked in their cells. Even so, the POA in early 1941 demanded a large increase in prison staff to counteract an increase in violence against officers.[79] Even the chairman of the Prison Commission accepted as late as 1951 that the local prisons remained an *omnium gatherum* of prisoners, for whom little constructive training was provided, and they bore the brunt of overcrowding, with 2,000 prisoners sleeping three to a cell.[80]

IV

By August 1945, the war was over and a Labour government had been elected with a majority of 146 over all other parties. Britain became a laboratory of social engineering. Twenty per cent of the economy was taken into public ownership, and the framework of the welfare state was erected. The condition of criminal

---

77 Benney, *Gaol Delivery* (1948), p. 51 and *passim*. See Sydney Jacobson, "Inside Holloway Prison," *Picture Post*, 13 Sep. 1947, p. 8; William Douglas Home, *Now Barabbas* (1947); idem., "The Worst of Prison," *Picture Post*, 15 Mar. 1947, pp. 10–12; idem., *Half-Term Report* (1954), pp. 192–4, 199–201. Home was court-martialled for refusing to attack a town full of civilians; he served eight months in Wormwood Scrubs and Wakefield prison. See also M. Nellis, "British Prison Movies: The Case of 'Now Barabbas'," *Howard Journal*, vol. 27 (1988).

78 Mass Observation Archive, File Report 2198, Holloway Prison by a Prison Officer, 7 Jan. 1945.

79 TNA, HO45/25407/241357/51, 55, 57, 71.

80 TNA, CAB 134/635, PC (47) 16, Joint Memo by the Home Secretary and Secretary of State for Scotland: Employment of Prison Labour; L. W. Fox, "A Survey of the Prison Administration for England and Wales since 1945," *Howard Journal*, vol. 8 (1951), p. 84. Before the annual meeting of the Holloway Discharged Prisoners' Aid Society, Sir Harold Scott, Commissioner of the Metropolitan Police, and former chairman of the Prison Commission, remarked that prisons in Britain were a disgrace: "There is only one thing to be done with them, and that is to dynamite them": *The Times*, 14 May 1946, p. 4.

justice became an integral part of this post-war programme of social advance.[81] James Chuter Ede, the new Home Secretary, had the task of winning a place for penal reform. *The Times* declared in an editorial of 12 March 1946 that this was an overdue reform.[82] A month later, Ede decided to introduce a Criminal Justice Bill along the same lines as the 1938 measure. At the legislation committee in early July, however, Ede was asked by Herbert Morrison, leader of the House of Commons and manager of the legislative and parliamentary machine, to withdraw the bill until next session.

At the start of 1947, Morrison in his capacity as Lord President of the Council asked Chuter Ede to submit a policy paper in support of the proposals in the Criminal Justice Bill, following consultation with Lord Chancellor Jowitt.[83] The latter was clearly in no mood for leniency. In mid-January, he was lobbying the Lord Chief Justice, Rayner Goddard, saying he hoped

> the Judges will not be lenient to these bandits [who] carry arms [and] shoot at the Police . . . I may be written down as a Colonel Blimp, but you know I do take the view, which I think you share, that we have got rather soft and woolly in dealing with really serious crime.[84]

Goddard responded by declaring in at least three Court of Criminal Appeal cases (though none were armed bandits) that he would not hesitate to increase sentences for grave crimes: "In the state of crime in this country the time has now come when sentences must be severe . . ."[85] From the start of the legislative process, Jowitt began to bluster about the softness of the prison commissioners and the need for judicial severity. In a letter of 28 February to Chuter Ede, Jowitt stated that he was not opposed to imprisonment for young persons, so long as they were not able to associate with the older criminals. Hence he wanted a "Children's Prison." "No doubt the Prison Commissioners," Jowitt continued, "would want to call it a 'Rest Home' or something of the sort." No young person would want to return there, since he would be subjected to "the most stern and rigorous discipline," rather like the public school of old. Jowitt also recommended a prison for hardened offenders,

81   See R. Hood, "Hermann Mannheim (1889–1974) and Max Grunhut (1893–1964)," in J. Beatson and R. Zimmermann (eds.), *Jurists Uprooted: German-speaking Émigré Lawyers in Twentieth-Century Britain* (Oxford, 2004), p. 731.

82   *The Times*, 12 Mar. 1946, p. 5.

83   TNA, HO45/21951/884452/73 and 99.

84   TNA, LCO 2/3830: Jowitt to Lord Chief Justice Goddard, 15 Jan. 1947. Sir Hartley Shawcross was offered the position of Lord Chief Justice, but he declined it. Shawcross recommended Goddard for the position. See Fenton Bresler, *Lord Goddard* (1977), pp. 113–14.

85   Ibid: Goddard to Jowitt, 22 Jan. 1947; *McBain* (1946) 31 Cr. App. R. 113; *Gibbon* (1946) 31 Cr. App. R. 143; *Lawrence* (1946), 31 Cr. App. R. 179. Cf. P. Polden, *Guide to the Records of the Lord Chancellor's Department* (1988), p. 260 on the widening rift between "progressive" opinion in the Home Office and the "reactionary" views of the judges, including the Lord Chancellor.

for whom reform was impossible. He asked the Home Secretary to solicit the opinion of the Lord Chief Justice:

> He [Goddard] has done much already to correct the undue sloppiness of some of his brother Judges. So long as you have a public opinion and a press which abhors every judicial officer who resorts to severity and applauds every such officer who resorts to leniency, so long will you fail to decrease the extent of crime.[86]

Chuter Ede replied to say that Jowitt's request for a children's prison corresponded closely with the ideas that underlay detention centres (a new measure for young offenders that ACTO proposed as a substitute for corporal punishment), but then took the fight to Jowitt, reminding him that it was the judges not the prison commissioners who handed down inadequate sentences, and who had neglected to use the preventive detention provisions of the 1908 Act.[87] In mid-March, Jowitt wrote again, this time to endorse the detention centre proposal, but to insist it not be used for young men aged 18–21 who had committed serious crimes, for whom a prison was needed for full deterrent impact. He was unrepentant about his earlier insinuations concerning the prison leadership:

> I do not, of course, blame the Prison Commissioners for the excessive leniency shown by the Judges. Judges are too touchy about their position. It is, however, the fact, as you know, that the alteration of sentences, which has been made on the advice of the Prison Commissioners has made the Judges hesitant to impose more severe sentences. My real case against the Prison Commissioners is this. As I see it, you have to balance the reformation side and the deterrent side. The Prison Commissioners are men of great humanity and great experience in dealing with people in prison . . . My criticism is that prison life is now so tolerable that it has ceased to have sufficient deterrent effect . . . This I regard as primarily due to the Prison Commissioners, for on their advice successive Home Secretaries, knowing them to be very high-minded men with great experience in dealing with criminals, have naturally enough acted. This does not mean that I advocate the rack or the thumb-screw.

Jowitt concluded that the deterrent effect of punishment required underlining:

> I think it most unfortunate that at this moment of time with this large amount of juvenile crime you should proclaim the new experiment that under no conditions would any young person be whipped for anything he does out of prison.[88]

---

86 TNA, HO45/21951/884452/99: Jowitt to Chuter Ede, 28 Feb. 1947.
87 Ibid: Chuter Ede (Home Secretary) to Jowitt (Lord Chancellor), 11 Mar. 1947.
88 Ibid: Jowitt to Chuter Ede, 19 Mar. 1947.

This letter reflected the divide that existed between the Home Secretary and the Lord Chancellor by the 7 March meeting of the Lord President's Committee. Chuter Ede had indicated the main lines of the Criminal Justice Bill, which would broadly follow the 1938 bill, except that it would not include the provisions for compulsory attendance centres, Howard Houses, or detention at a police station overnight; these would be replaced by detention centres in which persons between 14 and 21 might be detained for up to three months (or exceptionally up to six months). He also set out the bill's amendment of the law relating to probation (notably the power to include in a probation order, with the offender's consent, a provision requiring him to submit to treatment for his mental condition for a period not exceeding 12 months), and the new restrictions on the imprisonment of young persons (by raising the minimum age for imprisonment to 15 in the case of courts of assize and quarter sessions, and to 17 in the case of summary courts). He also laid out the two new forms of sentence for persistent offenders, "extended training" and preventive detention, the latter for as much as 14 years. Ede recognized that controversy would gyrate around the abolition of corporal punishment.[89] The Lord Chancellor had expressed his "grave misgivings" about the abolition of corporal punishment, and certain other provisions of the bill, such as the proposal for detention centres, which was "open to criticism on the ground that they provided too lenient a form of punishment." The bill, he said, "might well lead to serious protest from the Bench and he would like to have an opportunity of consulting the Lord Chief Justice and one or two other senior judges before any final decision was taken." Sir Hartley Shawcross, the Attorney-General, had leapt to the defence of the provision to abolish corporal punishment, adding that he thought the bill should also provide for the abolition of capital punishment. The sting in the tail was then administered by Shawcross: "The attitude of the Bench to past proposals for the reform of the criminal law did not suggest that their judgment in this matter was reliable." Ede accepted that the punishment of offenders should be deterrent, but Government supporters felt strongly about the abolition of corporal punishment and "the Labour Party were deeply committed by their attitude in 1938."[90]

On the same day, Jowitt wrote to the Lord Chief Justice for help in drafting a counter-paper. It was evident just how resistant the Lord Chancellor was to the bill:

> I am personally opposed to the whole tenor of the Paper and shall have to consider my position very seriously if it goes forward in this way. I believe that the quantity and quality of the crime being committed today is such as to make it necessary for the Judges to have drastic powers at their disposal and I regard all these suggestions of calling prisons "Detention Centres" and the like . . . as sentimental sloppiness.[91]

89 Ibid., 884452/100: LP (47) 8th meeting, 7 Mar. 1947.
90 Ibid: 884452/102B: Law Officers' Department, Apr. 1947.
91 TNA, LCO 2/3340: Jowitt to Lord Chief Justice Goddard, 7 Mar. 1947.

He recognized that the judges, among whom he numbered himself, would be accused yet again of obstructing reform of the criminal law, "but I do not care what is said so long as I am not made a party individually or collectively to a measure which I believe to be fundamentally unsound."[92] In reply, Goddard restricted himself to the following point:

> I cannot think that it is seriously suggested that if boys of say 17 or 18 are charged with rape or other serious offences such as attempted murder or shooting with intent that one should be able to do nothing except send them to what is called a detention centre.[93]

For someone who had enjoyed a draft of the Criminal Justice Bill since autumn 1946, this was a shamefully ill-informed reading of the measure. Nothing in the bill restricted judges from sentencing young persons to imprisonment if the gravity of the crime warranted it. Goddard had already informed the Home Secretary that he and a number of other judges did not agree that corporal punishment should be abolished, but "we would support a proposal that flogging with the cat should be abolished and corporal punishment with a birch or cane retained."[94]

The battle between the Home Secretary and Lord Chancellor raged through the spring and early summer. In late March, Jowitt shared with the Home Secretary the memorandum which he was asked to prepare in the wake of the meeting of the Lord President's Committee. He underlined the change on the ground since 1938: " . . . we are confronted with a wave of juvenile crime which is more extensive and more serious than anything then prevailing." He believed corporal punishment was a deterrent in some cases, and that judges should have the increased power to flog "in all cases involving violence, particularly where women and children are concerned." He accepted that the detention centre may do good if the discipline was sharp and the work hard. Yet he also laboured under the same confusion as the Lord Chief Justice in thinking that no person under 21 could be sent to prison for a period of more than six months.[95] In fact, courts of assize and quarter sessions would have for offenders between 16 and 21 all the powers they already had to impose sentences of imprisonment, provided they were satisfied, after considering information as to the circumstances, that imprisonment was the only appropriate method of dealing with the offender. Nothing in the Bill prevented these courts from imposing long sentences on young offenders for serious crimes. The provisions restricting imprisonment for young persons applied only to courts of summary jurisdiction. For example, the latter courts could not impose imprisonment on a person under 18 years of age if it could order him to be detained in a detention centre. In the meantime, Jowitt continued his round of

---

92 Ibid.
93 Ibid: Goddard to Jowitt, 10 Mar. 1947.
94 TNA, HO45/21951/884452/86.
95 Ibid: 884452/99: Jowitt to Chuter Ede, 28 Mar. 1947.

prison visits "trying to study the problem at first hand." His visit to Aylesbury women's prison had confounded him:

> . . . when I think of the easy life these women are having compared with the hardships which the ordinary housewife is going through I well realise that the material advantage lies on the side of the criminal . . . I do not myself believe that the experience of a sojourn at Aylesbury will have any deterrent effect on the women who are being kept there or on those to whom they recount their experiences when they get out . . . Is there no halfway house between the horrors of the past and the fun and games—and let me add the lipstick and cigarettes for the older women—of the present?[96]

Of course, these comments had no direct bearing on the Criminal Justice Bill, since the latter did not alter, in one direction or another, the conditions of prison treatment. All the bill did was to create a single form of prison sentence, imprisonment, and allow the nature of the treatment of an offender sentenced to imprisonment to be determined according to the character, record, and requirements of the individual by the prison authorities. The powers so given were not new. It had always been the function of the commissioners to manage prisons in such a way as to secure that sentences were given effect from both deterrent and reformative points of view. But then this was part of Jowitt's problem, describing the prison commissioners to the Attorney-General as "a most well intentioned body of men whose judgment I profoundly distrust . . ."[97]

By mid-June 1947, the Home Secretary and Lord Chancellor had minimized their differences, the only remaining substantial divergence of opinion between them being the abolition of corporal punishment. As Ede minuted on 10 June, "The only point between us is the flogging issue on which I do not propose to give way." At the Cabinet meeting on 19 June, Ede simply stated that the abolition of corporal punishment would be included in the bill, which would "by enabling prisoners to be classified in a more rational way, lead to very desirable reforms in the treatment of offenders, though its full effect would not be felt until more could be done to replace out-of-date prison buildings." Although favouring retention of the birch, Jowitt accepted that "for political reasons it would be very difficult to do less than had been proposed in the Bill introduced in 1938." Accordingly, the Cabinet approved the abolition of corporal punishment (retaining it only for grave offences against prison discipline), and agreed to consider at a later meeting the government's approach to the abolition of *capital* punishment.[98]

The Criminal Justice Bill was published on 4 November 1947. Like its 1938 predecessor, the post-war bill concerned two main categories: young and persistent

---

96   Ibid: 884452/102A: Jowitt to Chuter Ede, 10 Apr. 1947.
97   TNA, LCO 2/3340: Jowitt to Shawcross (Attorney-General), 19 Apr. 1947.
98   TNA, HO45/21951/884452/99: Home Secretary's minute, 10 Jun. 1947; CAB 128/10, CM (47) 55th Conclusions, Cabinet meeting, 19 Jun. 1947. See also TNA, PREM 8/739, CP (47) 182, minute 18 Jun. 1947.

offenders. It sought to keep young offenders out of prison, notably by providing new alternatives to imprisonment, and to keep recidivists under "corrective train-ing" or in long-term "preventive detention." It also abolished corporal punishment (except in prisons), swept away the anachronistic nomenclature of "hard labour" and "penal servitude," and provided for improvements in the organization and staffing of the probation service, and the mental treatment of probationers.[99] The bill introduced no entirely new forms of punitive, *non-custodial* measures for *adults*, and except for young offenders, placed no curbs upon the use of imprisonment. On the following day, the national and metropolitan press accorded the bill a rea-sonably positive welcome. *The Times* remarked that the bill "derives from a common stock of liberal thought to which men of all parties and of none have contributed." The *Manchester Guardian* worried that the required accommodation for detention centres and probation homes and hostels would not be ready in time. The *Daily Telegraph* was unconvinced about the abolition of corporal punishment. All commented upon the absence of a provision to abolish the death penalty. In the *Evening Standard*, former Labour Home Secretary, J. R. Clynes, objected to weakening the arm of the law under the title, "Keep the 'Cat'!"; Viscount Tem-plewood's riposte to Clynes appeared in that week's *Observer*. [100]

V

Before moving to the Second Reading of the Criminal Justice Bill on 27–8 November 1947, it is worth noting that some of the proposals had been con-siderably modified as the legislation was being prepared in the department. In the 1938 bill, attendance centres were meant to deprive boys of their leisure, acting as an alternative to short terms of imprisonment for minor offences or to default in payment of fines. In October 1945, the Administration of Justice Standing Com-mittee examined the problems of giving effect to the proposal. One such was the aim of the measure: was it wholly punitive, or was reformative treatment to be attempted? The committee asked the principal probation officers for their views;

99 The bill introduced the possibility of probation with a condition of mental treatment. Norwood East argued that the new Act was "an important and progressive step towards the medical treatment of offenders:" "Medical Aspects of the Criminal Justice Act 1948," *Journal of Criminal Science*, vol. 2 (1950), p. 121. Edward Glover of the ISTD begged to differ: "There is no sign that those who framed the Bill have been converted to the psychological point of view, or that they are prepared to strike at the roots of the problem. On the contrary the new Criminal Justice Bill is largely a measure of prison reform . . . a timid, unimaginative and cheese-paring measure." Quoted in Gard, *Rehabilitation and Probation*, op cit., p. 196.

100 Press cuttings in TNA, HO45/21953/884452/128B. The bill also gave superior courts powers to impose a fine on conviction on indictment of felony, which the Lord Chief Justice supported: TNA, LCO 2/3340, Goddard to Napier, 12 Mar. 1946. It made formal provisions for absolute and conditional discharge. And the bill originally pro-posed to abolish the Prison Commission and transfer its duties to a department of the Home Office; however, the Home Secretary, bowing to the will of Standing Com-mittee, withdrew the clause.

they unanimously declared that attendance centres were wrong in principle. The opposition of the standing committee and later of ACTO ensured the provision was dropped. As Maxwell explained to Ede,

> There will be no possibility of establishing at such centres the tradition of discipline and good order which can be built up in an institution or a club: consequently anything in the nature of reformative training will be impossible . . . [101]

In early 1944, Harris reminded Maxwell that the Cadogan committee had recommended a form of sharp punishment to replace the birching of boys under 14 years of age. This might be met, said Harris, "by some effective way of enabling the Court to order up to a month's detention in a Remand Home."[102] In April 1946, the department examined the issue in the context of devising alternatives to imprisonment. The first idea was to replace attendance centres with detention for not more than three months in a remand home for persons under 17, or in a remand centre for persons between 17 and 21. In the same month, however, ACTO proposed a sentence of three months' disciplinary detention, spent "under conditions different from those which obtain in a remand home." The department eventually recommended for persons between 14 and 21, detention for up to three months or, exceptionally, up to six months, the prime purpose being "to bring [young offenders] up with a jerk and make them realise that they cannot flout the law with impunity."[103] The new bill provided for detention centres. The Howard League representatives on the Advisory Council, no less than those representing the judiciary and magistracy, supported the detention centre concept. Of course, there were mixed motives for accepting detention centres: for some, it was a sop to placate the opposition to the abolition of corporal punishment; to others it was a way of persuading courts to stop imprisoning young offenders. The wider context of this decision was the rise in juvenile crime, and the consequent need on the government's part to replace corporal punishment with a deterrent alternative, one which incorporated features of the military detention centre or "glasshouse" of the war years.[104]

There were changes also to the provisions for persistent offenders. The 1938 bill had proposed that persons sentenced to corrective training or preventive detention

101 See Bailey, *Delinquency*, op cit., pp. 294–5; Gard, *The End of the Rod*, op cit., p. 119.
102 Ibid., p. 295.
103 Ibid., p. 296. For the lineal descent of the detention centre concept, see Valerie Choppen, "The Origins of the Philosophy of Detention Centres," *British Journal of Criminology*, vol. 10 (1970), pp. 158–63. In her 1938 memoir, Cicely McCall suggested sending girls to a detention camp for six months, and if while there she was made to work really hard "the shock and the contrast might well pull her up short in her drifting, shiftless life"; "*They Always Come Back*," op cit., p. 254.
104 Ibid.; Phoebe Hall et al., *Change, Choice and Conflict*, op cit., p. 320; J. Muncie, "Failure Never Matters: Detention Centres and the Politics of Deterrence," *Critical Social Policy*, vol. 28 (1990), p. 55.

should be in separate establishments from persons sentenced to imprisonment. The proposal for segregating persons under 30 undergoing corrective training had been based largely on the expectation that the experiment in Chelmsford would prove successful. However, according to Fox,

> . . . the experiment of concentrating young men at Chelmsford for more strenuous training than was normally given in prison had proved a complete failure and the Commissioners were satisfied that these young men ought to be in establishments where they mixed with older men, preferably of better character, and so came under their sobering influence.[105]

The young men at Chelmsford, said Fox, were tough characters—"cynical, unresponsive, uncooperative, and difficult to handle"—and commonly belonged to gangs. So, too, segregation ignored the fact that under the five-year plan drawn up by the prison commissioners, all persons serving sentences of some length would be sent to training centres. As Maxwell informed the Home Secretary in late April 1946,

> To provide a separate establishment for persons sentenced to, say, four years' corrective training would be wasteful and illogical, since the treatment of a person sentenced to four years' imprisonment will under the new scheme be indistinguishable from the treatment of a person sentenced to, say, four years' corrective training.[106]

Similar considerations applied to preventive detention. For Fox, most of the population of Dartmoor and Parkhurst, "and the cream (or scum) of the larger local prisons," ought to be in preventive detention, for whom the highest standard of discipline and active work should be enacted. "There must be no more of the 'Home for the Aged Convict' spirit which has been inherited from Camp Hill in dealing with them . . ." Such considerations suggested that in practice "there would be no substantial difference between a prison set apart for Preventive Detention prisoners and a central prison for long-sentence recidivist prisoners." Hence, said Fox,

> If the Commissioners can place recidivists with long sentences of imprisonment in the same prisons as recidivists with sentences of Preventive Detention, they may be able to manage somehow, but to provide duplicate prisons for what are, so far as treatment goes, virtually identical categories will be beyond their powers for a period which cannot be foreseen.[107]

105 TNA, HO45/21950/884452/75: 18 Apr. 1946 meeting.
106 Ibid: Maxwell to Home Secretary, 29 Apr. 1946.
107 Ibid., 884452/76: Fox memo, "Provisions Dealing with Persistent Offenders."

Since the training given to those serving a corrective training or a preventive detention sentence would be identical with the training given in training centres or "central" (the present "convict") prisons, the provision for segregation in special places of persons sentenced to corrective training or preventive detention was omitted from the bill. Maxwell forecast a challenge to this move, but thought it was defensible:

> There will no doubt be opposition to this proposal on the ground that if an offender is "with a view to his reformation and the prevention of crime" given a longer sentence than he would otherwise get, he ought to be subjected to a different regime from the ordinary prison regime. The answer to this objection is that the regime is to be improved for all persons whose sentences are long enough to enable them to be given any course of training, that the Bill of 1939 was based on the assumption that comparatively little could be done to improve the treatment of persons sentenced to imprisonment, that the new policy is to effect a great improvement in the treatment of all prisoners with substantial sentences, and the dropping of the provision for the segregation of persons sentenced to corrective training or preventive detention marks an advance and not a retrogression.[108]

All very inventive—but if the department had now brought the provisions for persistent offenders into line with its five-year plan for the penal future, it had surely undermined the new special measures. Courts would not now be enabled to substitute a sentence of training or detention for a prison sentence—*but simply lengthen the prison sentence*. It all begged the question: would courts use novel protective and punitive methods if they were no more than longer terms of imprisonment with no clear variations of treatment and conditions, and especially if people so sentenced were mixed with the rest of the prison population? This was an ominous beginning to the supposedly new approach towards persistent offenders.

The department also wanted the removal of the complications about over and under 30 years of age. It decided that corrective training should be available for persons of all ages and not just for those under 30, and preventive detention should be available for persons over 30 who had the necessary qualifications. In other words, the shorter detention sentence would be based on record and character without regard to age, and the longer sentence would be for the worst cases, though limited to the over-30s. In the first months of 1947, ACTO considered the Lord Chancellor's suggestion that corrective training should be from two to seven years (as opposed to a maximum of four years), and preventive detention from seven to 14 years (as opposed to a maximum of ten years). The council was unanimously opposed to an extension of the maximum for corrective training on the following ground:

108 Ibid: Maxwell to Home Secretary, 29 Apr. 1946.

A 4-year sentence of corrective training would mean, with the remission of one-quarter proposed, actual detention for a term of 3 years, and this it was felt was as long as was necessary to train any person who was susceptible of training at all.[109]

The council saw no objection to extending the range of preventive detention sentences from ten to 14 years since the primary purpose of the sentence was custodial, though they attached importance to preserving the provision that the Secretary of State may direct the prison commissioners to authorize release on licence earlier in any particular case. One Council member, Leo Page, wanted the power to impose preventive detention sentences of indefinite duration for hardened and professional criminals, but he recognized that 14 years was as much as Parliament would be willing to accept.[110] Chuter Ede informed Jowitt accordingly, explaining the reluctance to go beyond four years for corrective training as follows. If a prisoner's crime and record were such that a severer sentence was necessary, the judges had the power to pass such a sentence under existing law:

> The use of the provisions relating to corrective detention will only be justifiable if a Court decides that for the purpose of the prisoner's training a longer sentence is requisite than the Court would otherwise pass . . . [I]f the sentence were made longer than four years, I think I should be exposed to the criticism that my object was to facilitate the imposition of severe sentences passed for the purposes of deterrence under the guise of sentences passed for purposes of corrective training.[111]

VI

At the Second Reading of the Criminal Justice Bill the passion for the measure was muted, perhaps because it was essentially a rehash of the 1938 bill, and perhaps because it was supported in principle by all shades of sociological and political opinion, both inside and outside of the House. Throughout both days of the

---

109 Ibid., 884452/99: minute for Maxwell, 20 Feb. 1947. As for release on licence, while the Persistent Offenders Committee, 1932, thought it should be permissible for *corrective trainees* at any time after the prisoner had served *one-third* of his sentence, the prison commissioners insisted that at least *two-thirds* of the sentence should be served, as it was in the case of an ordinary prison sentence; and while the 1932 Committee thought that *preventive detainees* should be eligible for release at any time after he had served *one-third* of his sentence, the prison commissioners prescribed that *five-sixths* of this should be served, with a possibility of release after two-thirds for selected cases.

110 TNA, LCO 2/3340: Maxwell to Snagge, 28 Mar. 1947; Page, "Soft Justice," *Quarterly Review*, No. 571 (1947), pp. 56–70.

111 TNA, HO45/21951/884452/99: Chuter Ede to Jowitt, 26 Feb. 1947. Clause 21 of the Criminal Justice Bill, concerning corrective training and preventive detention, received a minimum of discussion in the Commons. Out of a total of 16 days allocated to the committee stages of the Bill, only 1 hour 40 minutes was spent discussing clause 21.

debate a quorum was barely maintained.[112] Only the provision for the abolition of corporal punishment, and the absence of a provision for the abolition of capital punishment, stirred the blood.[113] Chuter Ede began by paying tribute to Sir Alexander Paterson, who had recently passed away, for his conviction "that it was our duty . . . to send prisoners out into the world better men than they were when they came into prison." He also made it clear that the bill did not limit the power of the courts, within the maximum penalties prescribed for various crimes, to deal severely with offenders where severity was warranted. At the end of his speech, Ede stated that the government believed the time was not opportune to include in the bill a provision for the suspension or abolition of capital punishment. Though the government could not see their way to making it part of the measure, they nonetheless agreed to leave the matter to a free vote of the House.[114] One of the more significant interventions in the debate came from George Benson, who was a member of ACTO. The bill, he said, can be summed up in one sentence: "It regulates the power of the courts to pass sentences; and it gives the Home Secretary power to establish institutions. It gives a very large blank cheque to the Home Office." For this reason, he expressed astonishment that no one had yet asked what the detention centre is to be, or what a four-year sentence of corrective training is to mean.[115] Finally, George Younger, Undersecretary of State at the Home Office, wrapped up the debate by noting that "the resistance to the proposals for abolition [of corporal punishment] which was manifested when the previous Bill was before this House, has very much diminished in the meantime."[116] Opinion did seem to have hardened against corporal punishment, with the Magistrates Association opposed to it, though the public was split evenly on whether the law should allow boys to be birched. In the Commons, the clause abolishing the punishment for adults and juveniles was passed without a division.[117] It was quite otherwise in the House of Lords.

112 See Norval Morris, "The Criminal Justice Bill 1947—A Cook's Tour," *Res Judicatae*, vol. 4 (1948), p. 23.
113 The preoccupation with the controversy over capital punishment meant that the bill went through Parliament virtually undiscussed. In November 1960, a *Times* leader pointed out, "In 1948 the issue of capital punishment and corporal punishment succeeded in depriving the Criminal Justice Bill of the close scrutiny it deserved." See TNA, HO291/792, Home Office Press Summary, 15 Nov. 1960.
114 *Hansard*, vol. 444, 27 Nov. 1947, cols. 2129–50.
115 *Hansard*, vol. 444, 28 Nov. 1947, col. 2269. See also Anne Dunlop and Sarah McCabe, *Young Men in Detention Centres* (1965), p. 1.
116 *Hansard*, vol. 444, 27 Nov. 1947, col. 2351.
117 *Youth Astray*, Report on the Treatment of Young Offenders published by the Conservative Party Committee on Policy and Political Education, Conservative Central Office, 1946. The report supported the findings of the Cadogan Committee on corporal punishment. George Gallup, *The Gallup International Public Opinion Polls: Great Britain 1937–75*, vol. 1, 1937–64 (New York, 1976), p. 160. To the question, "Do you think that the law should allow boys to be sentenced to birching?", 45 per cent said yes, 46 per cent said no. See also Gerald Gardiner and Nigel Curtis-Raleigh, "The Judicial Attitude to Penal Reform," *Law Quarterly Review*, vol. 65 (1949), p. 212.

On the Second Reading of the Criminal Justice Bill in the House of Lords on 28 April 1948, Lord Chief Justice Goddard sounded a full-throated critique of the Criminal Justice Bill. Though a member of the House of Lords since 1944, this was his maiden speech, which he felt impelled to deliver "because I suppose I am the head of the Criminal Judiciary." In his remarks he focused less on questions of policy than on the practical application of the bill. True to form, his debate style inclined to anecdotal evidence drawn from legal practice, not jurisprudential abstractions. He objected to the modern tendency to consider that punishment should never be punitive:

> If we are to punish only with a view to reformation, what is one to do, for instance, with the ordinary motor manslaughter case? . . . Then there are other cases, such as the bigamist . . . Then there is the professional abortionist; and the homosexual who corrupts small boys. These are cases with which every Judge has to deal at every Assize . . . I have never yet understood how you can make the criminal law a deterrent unless it is also punitive.[118]

Turning to corporal punishment, he claimed that he and the other judges would be willing to forego the "cat," if the birch remained, especially for young offenders up to 25 or 30 years of age. He concluded by saying that the judiciary had a right to know

> what corrective detention consists of and what will be the discipline or other training which will take place in the detention centres. I know at present more or less what happens to a man if I send him to prison for nine months. I think I ought to know what happens if I send him for a period, which may be two years, of corrective training.[119]

This was preface to the unusual step for a Lord Chief Justice of tabling several motions amending the bill. In particular, he moved an amendment to confine the clause for the abolition of power to pass a sentence of whipping to the abolition of flogging with the cat-o'-nine-tails. Whipping with a birch rod would continue. The class of case Goddard had in mind was that of robbery with violence and assaults with intent to rob, assaults with intent to choke, and living upon immoral earnings.[120] Viscount Samuel opposed the amendment, strongly stating, "I earnestly hope that this House will now join with the other House of Parliament in abolishing this last relic of the Middle Ages in the maintenance of some form of physical torture as a penalty for crime."[121] In a thinly-attended House the amendment was carried by 29 votes to 17. Unless the

118 *Hansard* (Lords), vol. 155, 28 Apr. 1948, cols. 490–1.
119 Ibid., col. 495.
120 *Hansard* (Lords), vol. 156, 2 Jun. 1948, col. 192; TNA, HO45/21960/884452/238; HO45/21962/884452/252B. See also P. A. Bromhead, *The House of Lords and Contemporary Politics, 1911–1957* (1958), pp. 71, 175; "Rayner Goddard" by K. J. M. Smith, *Oxford Dictionary of National Biography* (2004).
121 *Hansard* (Lords), vol. 156, 2 Jun. 1948, col. 210.

government were to throw over the Report of the Departmental Committee, the retention of whipping with the birch as a judicial punishment could not be accepted. The Commons rejected the Lords' amendment by reinserting the clause in its original form by 232 votes to 62, and the Lords gave way.[122] Lords Goddard and Schuster also felt there were too many clauses in the bill relating to the provision of institutions which there was no immediate prospect of bringing into existence. This was provoked by Lord Templewood's amendment, accepted by the government, to provide for attendance centres, but their concerns included detention centres and corrective-training establishments. Moreover, Goddard (on this occasion supported by Templewood) asked of what corrective training was to consist.[123] In preparing Lord Chorley's reply to Goddard, the Home Office made a revealing statement about the wide variety of persons they deemed eligible to receive corrective training:

> At one end of the scale are those who persist in committing serious offences, such as housebreaking, but are still young enough or not too hopelessly committed to a life of crime for reformation to be attempted. At the other end of the scale are the petty recidivists, of whom the persistent bicycle stealer mentioned by Lord du Parcq in the Second Reading debate is a good example. There is the persistent sexual offender, the man who specialises in obtaining money by false pretences, and so on. A large number of persons will be eligible to receive this new sentence and they will have little in common except the length of the sentence they will have to serve.[124]

VII

The Criminal Justice Act became law on 30 July 1948. It was hoped the measure would achieve two things: one, to keep young people out of prison by extending the eligibility for borstal, restricting the powers of courts to send them to prison, and providing for remand centres and detention centres; and two, to tackle on fresh lines the problem of persistent offenders, by providing for corrective training and a new type of preventive detention. These sentences were, once more, attempts at classification by court decision. Mandarins and criminologists believed they were urgently needed. W. F. Roper's 1948 survey of one prison's population concluded,

> The general prison population . . . is made up of a quarter first offenders, one-third recidivists and the remainder in an intermediate position, many of them in process of graduation into habitual offenders. Probably rather over a half of the general prison population are habitual offenders or near-habituals who pass

---

122 *Hansard*, vol. 453, 15 Jul. 1948, cols. 1546–71.
123 TNA, 21961/884452/245, 252B; *Hansard* (Lords), vol. 156, 3 Jun. 1948, cols. 321–2; 15 Jun. 1948, col. 804.
124 TNA, HO45/21960/884452/238A: Note on Corrective Training.

through the courts like a stage army, leaving prison only to offend again and reappear in court.[125]

If the 1948 Act was not the "penological dinosaur" of one criminologist's judgment, it certainly looked long in the tooth, implementing recommendations that harked back to official committees of 1930s vintage.[126] It was the 1938 bill in all important regards, with a slightly more punitive gloss in the shape of the detention centre. And, of course, it failed to bring an end to the penological giant of capital punishment which continued to stalk the land. It was a testimony to the philosophy of that earlier decade, in the sense that it inclined more to a social and environmental conception of delinquency than to an increasing advocacy of psychological observation and treatment.[127] And it was a testimony to the experience and humanitarianism of an inner circle of liberal progressives, many of whom were members of ACTO and who helped fine tune many of the Act's provisions. ACTO has been reproached for being under the thumb of the Home Office, and for failing to make its early reports available to the public.[128] Yet the council deliberated independently on the charges from the Home Secretary. Moreover, it was appointed to provide advice to the Home Secretary, not to rock the boat, and anyway there was no deep divide between the aims and policies of the prison commissioners and those of the penal reform lobby. All gathered under the same liberal progressive umbrella.

One of the more frequent impressions was that the Act gave a blank cheque to the prison commissioners, with the translation of new sentences and new facilities into effective penal reform depending on them. This was particularly true of the provisions for persistent offenders, which the commissioners found difficult to implement. The criminal courts used corrective training with an early enthusiasm, and used preventive detention more liberally than before. So much so that by January 1950 the Lord Chief Justice informed the Lord Chancellor:

> I may say that we are doing our best in the Court of Criminal Appeal to check the tendency of all Courts to pass sentences of corrective training or preventive detention far too freely: it is what always happens; because a new thing can be done everyone thinks they ought to do it in every case, with the result that far too many sentences of this sort are being given before the machinery is working to deal with them.[129]

---

125 Roper, "A Comparative Survey of the Wakefield Prison Population in 1948," *British Journal of Delinquency*, vol. 1 (1950), p. 20.

126 T. Morris, *Crime and Criminal Justice*, op cit., p. 77.

127 See Bailey, *Delinquency and Citizenship*, op cit., p. 303.

128 Mick Ryan, *Penal Policy and Political Culture in England and Wales* (Winchester, 2003), pp. 18–19. Cf. Bailey, *Delinquency*, op cit., p. 303.

129 TNA, LCO 2/3352: Goddard to Lord Chancellor, 4 Jan. 1950. See also *Howard Journal*, vol. 8 (1949–50), p. 33; Gordon Rose, *The Struggle for Penal Reform* (1961), p. 236.

The LCJ's observations came in response to a Commons debate in December 1949 on corrective training. Conservative MP John Maude, who tabled the motion, cited Home Office figures revealing that within six months of the Act coming into force in April 1949, 732 men and 36 women were serving corrective training sentences, and of these 768 trainees, 389 men and eight women were in local prisons. All prisoners sentenced to corrective training were received initially into local prisons to assess their suitability for training. The other half were in prisons set aside for corrective training, dotted around the country: Chelmsford, 233; Holloway, 28; Liverpool, 54; Sudbury Park (an open prison), 6; and in the two regional training prisons, Wakefield and Maidstone, only 26 and 24, respectively. Mr. Younger, Undersecretary of State for the Home Department, openly confronted how far it was possible to implement corrective training with a prison population around the 20,000 mark, with 2,000 prisoners sleeping three to a cell, and with a shortage of prison staff:

> The latest figure of the numbers who have received this sentence since the system began is 1,028 men and 48 women. Now, as there was virtually no spare space anywhere within the prisons at the time this new system was introduced, it was not to be expected that the Prison Commissioners could immediately make completely suitable provision for the large number of people who have been sentenced to this particular type of training.[130]

The initial experience with corrective training underlined how the Criminal Justice Act 1948 gave the prison commissioners considerable administrative latitude. It was evident that the success of the new legislation would depend on the vigour and insight with which the executive used the powers given by the Act to establish and run new types of institution or to restrict the use of imprisonment, and on how well the executive communicated its aims to the judiciary. The latter clearly felt ill-informed about the purpose and regime of most of the new forms of sentence, as they began to use them.[131] As in 1938, moreover, the Act was still a leap in the dark in terms of evidence of efficacy. On the Second Reading, Labour MP, Major Wilfrid Vernon sought to amend the bill to allow grants to be given to conduct research into the causation, prevention, and treatment of crime. The department's note on the new clause was telling, "It is doubtful if there is at the present time any case for devoting public money to investigations of this kind by any outside organization . . ."[132] Home Secretary Ede nonetheless agreed to the amendment. This

---

130 *Hansard*, vol. 470, 2 Dec. 1949, cols. 1467–1500. See also H. Scott, "Punishment or Reform?" *Magistrate*, vol. 9 (1951), p. 152.
131 TNA, LCO 2/3352: Goddard to Jowitt, 4 Jan. 1950.
132 TNA, PCom 9/1428. The clause was 77(1), enabling the Home Secretary to spend public money on "the conduct of research into the causes of crime and the treatment of offenders." See J. P. Martin, "The Development of Criminology in Britain 1948–60," *British Journal of Criminology*, vol. 28 (1988), p. 37.

was for the future. In December 1949 it was still necessary for George Benson, ACTO member, to call for

> years of intensive research into the whole problem of sentencing and . . . the treatment of delinquents which must be based on very accurate information as to what happens, not merely to delinquents in bulk . . . but to specific types of delinquents, because different types respond to different forms of sentence in different ways . . . Only by a very carefully controlled system of follow-up can we know how a particular type responds to a particular sentence. At the present moment we do not know that.[133]

---

133 *Hansard*, vol. 470, 2 Dec. 1949, col. 1479.

Prisoner at hard labour in his cell at HMP Wormwood Scrubs, London, 1895. The prisoner is on the crank, a pointless form of cell labour. Prison officers could make the labour harder by tightening the crank screw, hence their nickname, "screws."
Source: The National Archives.

UNE FEMME PENDUE EN ANGLETERRE
EXÉCUTION DE L'EMPOISONNEUSE MARY ANSELL

Execution of Mary Ann Ansell at St. Albans County Gaol, 19 July 1899. Ansell was an 18-year old, domestic servant. She sent a cake to her younger sister in Leavesden asylum, who died as a result of phosphorous poisoning. One hundred MPs petitioned for her reprieve on grounds of mental unsoundness. A special medical inquiry took place, but no mercy was granted.
Source: Mary Evans Picture Library.

Exterior, 'D' Wing, HMP Wormwood Scrubs. "The Scrubs" is a Victorian-built, local prison located in inner West London. It has five main wings, A to E.
Source: Crown copyright, 1999.

Prisoners on the tread wheel at Preston Prison, Lancashire, 1902. The tread wheel was a large hollow cylinder of wood on an iron frame with steps about seven inches apart. The prisoner trod on the steps, his weight causing the wheel to revolve. Originally introduced to grind flour, by 1902 it had no purpose other than to punish.
Source: The National Archives.

Feeding prisoners at HMP Wormwood Scrubs, 1895.
Source: The National Archives.

Female prisoners at work in the sewing shop at HMP Wormwood Scrubs.
Source: The National Archives.

Prisoners returning to their cells for their midday meal at HMP Wormwood Scrubs, 1900.
Source: Mary Evans/Peter Higginbotham Collection.

Suffragettes released from HMP Holloway, London, 31 July 1908. They were greeted by cheering crowds and given a medal, the Holloway brooch. Many had influential friends, and sought to make conditions better for women imprisoned in Holloway. Source: The March of the Women Collection/Mary Evans Picture Library.

Convicts in church at HMP Portland with warders on raised seats, 1910. Portland prison in Dorset was built in 1848 to hold convict prisoners. They worked in the Admiralty Quarries, providing stone for the construction of the breakwaters of Portland Harbour. In 1921 Portland became a Borstal institution for young offenders. Source: Illustrated London News Ltd/Mary Evans.

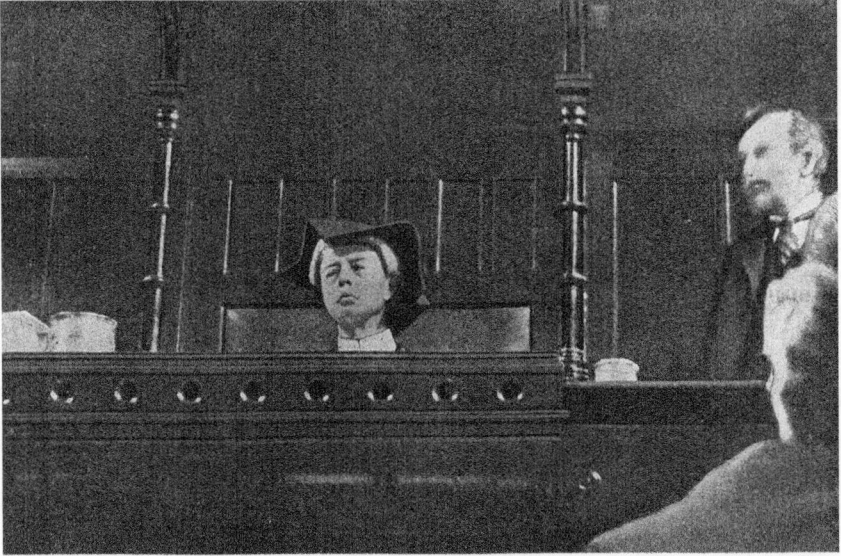

Mr. Justice Avory sentencing Thomas Henry Allaway to death at Winchester Assizes, July 1922 for murder. It is a rare image of a judge wearing the black cap as he pronounces the death penalty. Allaway was hanged at Winchester on 19 August 1922. Source: Mary Evans Picture Library.

Mutiny at HMP Dartmoor, Princetown, Devon, 24 January 1932. Convict mutineers set fire to the office block of buildings. The prison was renowned for making convicts quarry the barren moorland by hand under armed guards. It has been earmarked for closure on a number of occasions. It is still in use.
Source: Illustrated London News Ltd/Mary Evans.

Procession of Judges at Westminster Abbey in the 1930s, a custom before the opening of the Law Courts, showing the mace bearer and the Lord Chancellor.
Source: Mary Evans Picture Library.

Police hold back a crowd of sightseers outside HMP Strangeways, Manchester before the execution of Dr. Buck Ruxton, 21 May 1936. Ruxton was a Parsee doctor who killed his wife through jealousy at her supposed infidelity, and her maid after the latter inadvertently witnessed the crime. A petition for clemency was signed by 10,000 people.

Source: Hulton Archive/Getty Images.

Prison officers watching over prisoners sewing mailbags at HMP Strangeways, Manchester, 20 November 1948. Strangeways prison was designed in the 1860s by Alfred Waterhouse, with the help of Joshua Jebb, surveyor general of prisons. There were two imposing gateways, and a central dodecagonal (twelve-sided) hall, with wings A to F radiating from it.
Source: Picture Post/Bert Hardy/Getty Images.

Prison officers watching over prisoners as they take their daily outdoor exercise at HMP Strangeways, Manchester, 20 November 1948. The prison had a permanent gallows, and 100 hangings were carried out between 1869, when the prison opened, and 1964. The prison had to be considerably rebuilt after the major riot of 1990. Source: Picture Post/Bert Hardy/Getty Images.

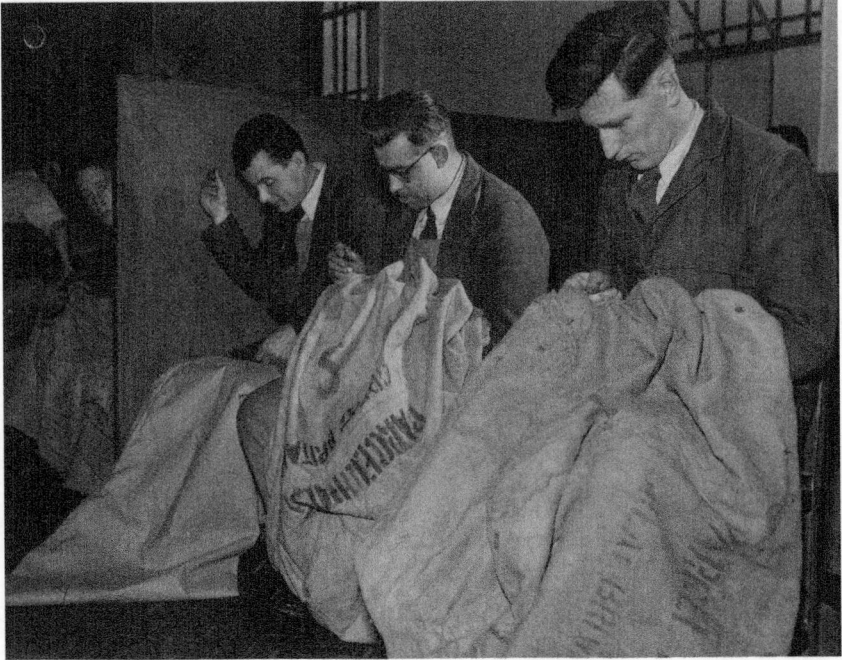

Prisoners sewing mailbags in HMP Oxford in the 1950s.
Source: Photograph reproduced with the kind permission of the National Justice Museum.

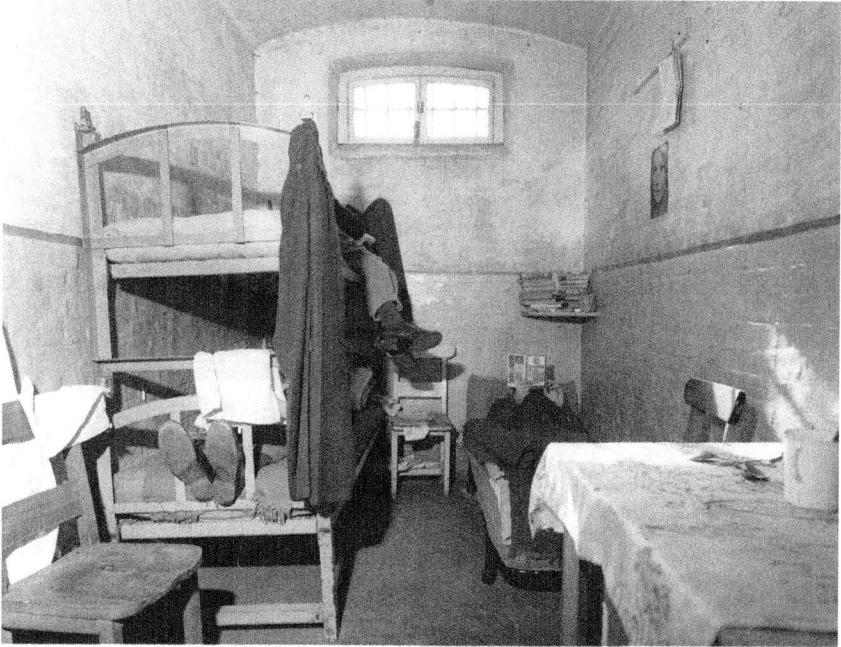

"Threeing up," or three prisoners sharing a cell designed for one at HMP Pentonville, 1969. "The Ville" in North London opened in 1842. It was built to implement the "separate system" of prison discipline, becoming the template for English prisons. 120 men were hanged at Pentonville prison between 1902 and 1961, or almost 15 per cent of all twentieth-century hangings for murder in England and Wales.
Source: Photograph reproduced with the kind permission of the National Justice Museum.

"Slopping out" or emptying chamber pots at HMP Brixton, London, 1973. "Slopping out" continued in many prisons until the mid-1990s.
Source: Photograph reproduced with the kind permission of the National Justice Museum.

7

LABOUR GOVERNMENT, ABOLITION, AND THE ROYAL COMMISSION ON CAPITAL PUNISHMENT, 1945–1953

> It is queer to look back and think that only a dozen years ago the abolition of the death penalty was one of those things that every enlightened person advocated as a matter of course, like divorce reform or the independence of India. Now, on the other hand, it is a mark of enlightenment not merely to approve of executions but to raise an outcry because there are not more of them.
>
> As I Please, *by George Orwell (Copyright George Orwell, 1946)*
> *Reprinted by permission of Bill Hamilton as the Literary Executor*
> *of the Estate of the Late Sonia Brownell Orwell*

I

The punishment prescribed by English law for murder in the first half of the twentieth century was death. A judge had to pronounce this sentence upon a person convicted of murder except in two special classes of cases: persons under eighteen years of age at the time of the offence and pregnant women.[1] He had no

---

[1] From 1887, executions for those under eighteen were virtually abolished by use of the royal prerogative of mercy. The Children Act 1908 formally abolished the death penalty for persons under sixteen; the Children and Young Persons Act 1933 confirmed the existing practice of reprieve by ending capital punishment for those under eighteen. The Sentence of Death (Expectant Mothers) Act 1931 prohibited the death sentence on a pregnant woman. In addition, by the 1922 Infanticide Act, a woman charged with the death of her "newly born"—a term undefined in the Act, and narrowly interpreted by the courts, but enlarged in 1938 to apply to the death of a child under twelve months of age—would be punished for the commission of manslaughter rather than murder. This change meant little in practice, because no woman had been executed for the murder of her baby since 1849. It simply brought law and practice into conformity. See Gordon Rose, *The Struggle for Penal Reform* (1961), pp. 202, 206; Christopher Hollis, *The Homicide Act* (1964), p. 13; P. G. Richards, *Parliament and Conscience* (1970), p. 37.

discretion to impose any less severe sentence. While retribution survived only in a symbolic form elsewhere in the criminal law, capital punishment, as Oxford criminologist Max Grunhut maintained, was a "powerful relic of retaliation in kind." The law still reflected the ancient concept that every murderer forfeits his life because he has taken another's life: "He that smiteth a man, so that he die, shall be surely put to death."[2]

The law reformers of the early nineteenth century had successfully whittled the number of capital offences down to the four that remained in the twentieth century: murder, treason, piracy with violence, and arson in government dockyards and arsenals. But they and their successors, while restricting the application of the death penalty to the gravest crimes, had failed to secure the complete abolition of capital punishment. The only proposal of the Royal Commission on Capital Punishment (1864–6) to be accepted was the prohibition of public execution; from 1868, executions were carried out within prison confines. The six subsequent attempts between 1866 and 1891 to divide murder into two degrees, capital and non-capital, which the Royal Commission had also proposed (on the model widely used in the United States), all failed. By 1918, the influence of the abolitionists was at its nadir. But from that point on, things improved rapidly. The emergence of the Labour Party in 1906, and its rise to become the main opposition to the Conservative Party by the 1920s, changed the parliamentary dynamics of the capital punishment debate. For the first time, abolitionists had the sympathetic ear of a principal political party.[3]

The achievements of the first two Labour governments of 1924 and 1929–31 were limited. Nonetheless, by the end of the 1930s, the number executed each year was at an all-time low; support for abolition in Parliament and among the public was arguably at an all-time peak. Little wonder that hopes ran high in abolitionist circles when the first Labour government with a parliamentary majority was elected in 1945, at the end of the Second World War, on a floodtide of popular support for a juster, more humane society. It was confidently expected that the 1938 Criminal Justice Bill, abandoned at the outbreak of war, would be resurrected, and that a clause eliminating the death penalty for murder would find a place in the new version. The 1947 bill, like its precursor, aimed to eclipse the idea of retribution by further extending the principle that punishment should fit the criminal, not the crime. What better moment to abolish capital punishment, the last relic of a barbarous penal code, the one punishment in which reformation has no place?[4]

2   Max Grunhut, "Murder and the Death Penalty in England," *Annals of the American Academy of Political and Social Science*, vol. 284 (1952), p. 158; *Exodus* 21:12.

3   For the crusade against capital punishment, from Sir Samuel Romilly's early nineteenth-century efforts to prune the Fatal Tree, to the inter-war activities of the Labour Party and the National Council for the Abolition of the Death Penalty (NCADP, established in 1925), see Victor Bailey, "The Shadow of the Gallows: The Death Penalty and the British Labour Government, 1945–51," *Law and History Review*, vol. 18 (2000), pp. 311–18.

4   For details of the 1938 and 1947 Criminal Justice Bills, see chap. 6 *supra*, and Victor Bailey, *Delinquency and Citizenship: Reclaiming the Young Offender, 1914–1948* (Oxford, 1987), pp. 255–65, 291–302.

Thus, there were great expectations; abolitionists felt victory to be within their grasp. In November 1945, the executive committee of the National Council for the Abolition of the Death Penalty advised members that the end of the war and the election of a Labour government "should bring success to our efforts for Abolition within the next few years," to ensure which "we must create from one end of the country to the other a public opinion insistently demanding Abolition." Yet three years later, following intense discussion of the subject both within and without Parliament, the abolitionists were disappointed, divided, and almost empty-handed. Anticipating the end of the death sentence for murder, abolitionists had to settle for a Royal Commission on Capital Punishment (1948–53), whose terms of reference restricted it to the possible means of limiting the operation of the death penalty, as distinct from its abolition. Few abolitionists expected an unimpeded procession towards abolition. They knew they still had worthy opponents in the senior judges, some of the principal Home Office mandarins, and the entire House of Lords. Yet few abolitionists expected the death penalty to become the paramount issue in the parliamentary debates on the Criminal Justice Bill and in the press and public discussion of the impending penal reform. Few would have forecast that the only revolt of Labour MPs (or the Parliamentary Labour Party) seriously to embarrass the Attlee government would arise over capital punishment. Few would have predicted that one of the two issues on which the House of Lords would exercise its delaying power would be capital punishment.[5] Clearly, something went terribly wrong for the abolitionists.

Exactly what went wrong, why, and with what outcome is the theme of this chapter. How and why did the Labour government, despite its massive majority in Parliament and a long-standing commitment to abolition, fail to get rid of the death penalty? Why was this "window of opportunity" to abolish capital punishment shut for another decade and a half? The answers to these questions will be sought primarily in the realm of government and Parliament. This is not as limiting as it may sound. An enduring condition of the conflict over capital punishment was that its crucial battles were fought in the main legislative fora. To *limit* the use of the death penalty, executive fiat in the form of more reprieves would suffice; but to *abolish* the penalty required changes in the law of murder that only Parliament could make. Moreover, the subject evoked such widespread lay interest, not to say passion, that the struggle over it had to be fought out in full view of the public. Accordingly, the answers to these questions have an essentially political character. Above all, the Labour government failed to take full responsibility for the death penalty. This, in turn, arose from the inclination of the government to see capital punishment as peripheral to its main business, as an issue best left to the private conscience of individual MPs, and hence to a free rather than a "whipped" vote of

5   NCADP, miscellaneous publications, MSS 16B/ADP/4/4/9/l, Modern Records Centre, University of Warwick Library. The other issue on which the Lords used their delaying power was the nationalization of iron and steel: see K. O. Morgan, *Labour in Power, 1945–51* (Oxford, 1985), pp. 62, 84; R. F. V. Heuston, *Lives of the Lord Chancellors, 1940–1970* (Oxford, 1987), p. 127.

the House of Commons.[6] The bulk of the government's troubles flowed from these peculiarities of the debate over the death penalty. There is, however, an additional explanation of the government's failure, one particular to the 1940s, yet one that lends wider significance to the entire evaluation.

The postwar world was much less hospitable to penal reform than the abolitionists had anticipated. For a start, the war crimes trial at Nuremberg, which began on 20 November 1945, affected the post-war mood. Judgment on the 22 war criminals was delivered in October 1946; twelve of the accused were sentenced to death, and ten were immediately hanged.[7] For some people, Nuremberg lent justification to a retributive approach to indigenous murder. More influential was the rise in officially recorded crime and the "moral panic" the figures generated.[8] The press was full of the senseless violence of juvenile gangs and of the sordid and meaningless nature of contemporary homicide, a theme taken up by George Orwell in his 1946 essay on the changed character of murder.[9] This crime-wave narrative had an effect upon penal thought, notably by reinvigorating the belief that punitive measures could not be surrendered. The reforming tide of the 1920s and 1930s can be exaggerated, as we have argued, but there is no doubt that this tide was turned back in the 1940s by the combined pressure of the senior judges, the Lord Chancellor, and the House of Lords, and with the effective deployment

6   The members of Parliament who have the job of delivering each party's vote in the House of Commons are known as "whips"; hence, a "whipped" vote is one in which MPs have no choice but to vote for their party; a free vote is when MPs are allowed to vote the way their conscience dictates. The free vote is generally permitted when the subject is deemed to be an issue that cuts across party lines. Almost all bills dealing with capital punishment have been put to free votes on some or all of their stages. However, capital punishment rarely cut across party lines, despite the pretence that it did. For most of the twentieth century, Labour and Liberal MPs typically voted against capital punishment, while Conservative MPs typically voted in favour. See Christie Davies, "The British State and the Power of Life and Death," in S. J. D. Green and R. C. Whiting (eds.), *The Boundaries of the State in Modern Britain* (Cambridge, 1996), p. 343.

7   One of those condemned to death, Martin Bormann, was sentenced in absentia; Hermann Goring cheated the hangman by committing suicide. See Peter Calvocoressi, *Nuremberg: The Facts, the Law and the Consequences* (New York, 1948); Werner Maser, *Nuremberg: A Nation on Trial* (New York, 1979).

8   See Harold L. Smith (ed.), *Britain in the Second World War* (Manchester, 1996), pp. 16–18; Terence Morris, *Crime and Criminal Justice since 1945* (Oxford, 1989), pp. 34–7, 96 (Table 7.2). For the concept of the moral panic, see Stanley Cohen, *Folk Devils and Moral Panics: The Creation of the Mods and Rockers* (1972). See also, Stanley Cohen and Jock Young (eds.), *The Manufacture of News: Social Problems, Deviance, and the Mass Media* (Beverly Hills, 1973).

9   Orwell contrasted the "domestic poisoning dramas" of the prewar era with the cause celebre of the war years, the Cleft Chin Murder, in which an American army deserter and an eighteen-year-old ex-waitress murdered a taxi driver with £8 in his pocket. "The background," explained Orwell, "was not domesticity, but the anonymous life of the dance-halls and the false values of the American film." See "Decline of the English Murder," in George Orwell, *Decline of the English Murder and Other Essays* (Harmondsworth, 1965), p. 12. See also Harry Hopkins, *The New Look: A Social History of the Forties and Fifties in Britain* (1963), pp. 207–8; Peter Hennessy, *Never Again: Britain, 1945–51* (New York, 1994), pp. 445–6.

of majority public opinion. Inevitably, the debate over the abolition of the death penalty became embroiled in this pronounced attack upon reformist sentiment. The fact that at one of the most propitious moments for abolition, an impassioned debate ended with the survival of this retributive symbol, should tell us something about the political, judicial, and popular resistance to the reforming ethos in punishment. In the post-war struggle to lay the ax once and for all to the gallows tree, a struggle that, as James Christoph affirmed, "cut more deeply into British life . . . than at any time since the first two decades of the nineteenth century," we have one of the more instructive moments in the history of modern British penology.[10]

II

In 1945 a Labour government was elected with a majority of 146 over all other parties (393 MPs out of 640). James Chuter Ede, the new Home Secretary, had the task of winning a place for penal reform in the post-war programme of social reconstruction. In April 1946, he decided to introduce the Criminal Justice Bill of 1938, subject to a few modifications.[11] At this point, it was still an open question whether a provision to abolish or suspend the death penalty would get into the new bill. It is to this issue we first turn. The aim is to explain the Labour government's conduct in the lead up to the Second Reading of the Criminal Justice Bill in November 1947, by which time the government had decided to omit an abolitionist clause from the bill, but to allow a free vote in the House of Commons if an abolitionist amendment were introduced.[12]

In March 1947, the pace picked up. Herbert Morrison, leader of the House of Commons, asked Chuter Ede to submit a policy paper on the Criminal Justice Bill. Of most significance, for present purposes, is the Home Secretary's view that any amendment to abolish or suspend capital punishment

> should be resisted on the ground that it is inappropriate that such a far-reaching change in the law should be included in a Criminal Justice Bill, and that, if any such change in the law were to be effected it should be after full consideration in a separate Bill dealing solely with this subject.

10 James B. Christoph, *Capital Punishment and British Politics* (1962), p. 190.
11 TNA, HO45/21950/884452/75 and 77. The press and penal reform lobby felt that a scheme of penal reform deserved a place in Labour's program. See *The Times*, 12 Mar. 1946, p. 5; TNA, HO45/21951/884452/99.
12 In this task I have been helped by Gordon Rose, *Struggle* (1961); Elizabeth Tuttle, *The Crusade against Capital Punishment in Great Britain* (1961); and James Christoph, *Capital Punishment* (1962). The authors did their work, however, before the Cabinet and other official papers were available to public scrutiny. More recently, Lord Windlesham used some of the relevant official papers in his study of penal policy-making: Windlesham, *Responses to Crime*, vol. 2, *Penal Policy in the Making* (Oxford, 1993), chap. 2. And Sir Leon Radzinowicz reviewed the lead-up to the Royal Commission on Capital Punishment, 1949–53: *Adventures in Criminology* (1999), pp. 245–52.

At the Lord President's Committee meeting held on 7 March, therefore, Chuter Ede remarked that most controversy was likely to centre on the abolition of *corporal* punishment.[13] Indeed, the main dispute that broke out between Home Secretary Ede and Lord Chancellor Jowitt was over corporal punishment. Ede stood his ground, reminding the meeting that on the matter of abolishing corporal punishment, "the Labour Party were deeply committed by their attitude in 1938."[14] He had an ally in the Attorney-General, Sir Hartley Shawcross, who said he strongly supported the abolition of corporal punishment. Additionally, Shawcross argued that the bill should provide also for the abolition or suspension of the death penalty and that "[t]he attitude of the Bench to past proposals for the reform of the criminal law did not suggest that their judgment in this matter was reliable," a brave line from a young government law officer.[15] Even so, Lord Chancellor Jowitt was invited to put his reservations on paper and allowed to consult the Lord Chief Justice and certain other senior judges about the proposals.[16]

The exchange of views at the meeting of the Lord President's Committee also spurred the law officers into action. In early April 1947, Shawcross and Sir Frank Soskice (the Solicitor-General) sent a strongly worded statement to both Jowitt and Chuter Ede. The proposed abolition of flogging, the law officers proclaimed, "carries out what has always been Labour Party policy." Corporal punishment had neither deterrent value nor reformative effect. They took the same view about capital punishment:

> If, as it is agreed, the present Bill provides a suitable opportunity for the abolition of flogging, we can see no reason why it should not be equally appropriate for the abolition of capital punishment if the abolition of such punishment is

13 TNA, HO45/21951/884452/99; "Criminal Justice Bill," memo by Home Secretary, 2 Mar. 1947, Lord President's Committee (hereafter LP) (47) 39, attached to Cabinet Papers (hereafter CP) (47) 182, 16 Jun. 1947, Cabinet Office (hereafter CAB) 129/19. The Lord President's Committee was a sub-cabinet body; it had referred to it questions of domestic policy not assigned to other committees.

14 LP (47) 8th meeting, 7 Mar. 1947, CAB 132/6. In the 1930s, the birching of young offenders (to whom corporal punishment was effectively restricted) had been almost abandoned by the courts. The wartime rise in delinquency, however, led to renewed birching. See Geoffrey Pearson, *Hooligan: A History of Respectable Fears* (1983), p. 261 n. 92.

15 Ibid. The Attorney-General and Solicitor-General were the chief legal advisers to the Executive. See J. Ll. J. Edwards, *The Law Officers of the Crown* (1964), pp. 174–5, and chap. 9, *passim*. The Labour Party was congenitally distrustful of the senior judiciary and legal profession. The fact that Lord Chancellor Jowitt boasted in late 1947 that he had never appointed "a member of my own Party" to be a judge corroborated the doubts about him, which had their origin in his thin socialist credentials. He generally took a detached attitude to Cabinet quarrels and party-political questions. See Robert Stevens, *Law and Politics: The House of Lords as a Judicial Body, 1800–1976* (Chapel Hill, 1978), pp. 336–7, and *The Independence of the Judiciary* (Oxford, 1993), pp. 78–9, 114; "Message from Britain: The Lord Chancellor's Address in Cleveland," *American Bar Association Journal*, vol. 33 (1947), p. 1180.

16 See Jowitt to Lord Chief Justice, 7 Mar. 1947, LCO 2/3340; Jowitt to Ede, 28 Mar. 1947, TNA, HO45/21951/884452/99.

otherwise desirable. We do not think that the Labour Party in the House would be likely to accept the position that this matter could not be dealt with in the present Bill unless an assurance were given that special legislation would be introduced. The case in favour of abolition of capital punishment seems to us overwhelming and the grounds for its abolition very similar to those above urged for the abolition of flogging.

Moving to a loftier moral plane, they wrote feelingly:

> The knowledge that society is deliberately hunting a man to his death, and when it has caught him taking away his life with the hideous trappings of legal execution, cannot fail to lessen the respect for the sanctity of human life . . . It is absolutely no answer to say that the convicted man has himself taken human life, since by carrying out the act of execution society is rendering itself culpable of precisely the same act as that for which the condemned man has been convicted.

They strongly urged, therefore, that the opportunity be taken in the bill to give effect to "what has been for many years a humanitarian conception associated with the Labour movement. There can, we think, be no excuse for what is virtually a running-away from an obvious opportunity to introduce this overdue reform." The law officers had firmly nailed their colours to the mast. In his cover letter, Shawcross added that strong views were held in the party on corporal and capital punishment and the government could be defeated if they opposed abolition, with the whips on.[17]

In May 1947, the Criminal Justice Bill was slotted for the 1947–8 session. The abolitionists were relieved, since it would allow time in the present Parliament to override a veto of the House of Lords, which a later date would not have done. The Lords still had the power to delay a bill's passage for two years (though the government had plans further to abbreviate their delaying power). The Cabinet now had to resolve how they wished to deal with corporal and capital punishment. At the Cabinet meeting of 19 June, Ede refused to give way on the flogging issue, and Jowitt finally conceded that "for political reasons it would be very difficult to do less than had been proposed in the Bill introduced in 1938."[18] On the

17 Shawcross had been associated with the Howard League for Penal Reform in the 1920s and had been a member of the Advisory Council on the Treatment of Offenders, the body established in August 1944 by Herbert Morrison, when Home Secretary, to plan post-war penal reform. See *New Statesman*, 21 Feb. 1975, pp. 234–6; Bailey, *Delinquency*, p. 288. Shawcross had always opposed capital punishment, but in 1945–6, he acted as the chief British prosecutor at the Nuremberg trial: *Life Sentence: The Memoirs of Lord Shawcross* (1995), p. 130. The citations in this and the previous paragraph are all drawn from TNA, HO45/21951/884452/102B. See also Shawcross to Jowitt, 16 Apr. 1947, HO45/21951/ 884452/102B; Jowitt to Shawcross, 19 Apr. 1947: LCO 2/ 3340.
18 CP (47) 182, 16 Jun. 1947, "Criminal Justice Bill," memo by Home Secretary, TNA, CAB 129/19; minute by F. Graham-Harrison, Assistant Private Secretary to the Prime

desirability of abolishing the death penalty, ministers were divided. Retentionists (Morrison undoubtedly, Ede and Jowitt presumably) argued that public opinion was not yet ready for abolition, that the abnormal amount of robbery with violence made abolition unwise, that the judges "were convinced that the fear of capital punishment was a real deterrent" and an effective alternative punishment was wanting, and that abolition at home would make it hard to justify its retention in the colonies and in the British Zone of Germany. Abolitionists (Shawcross indubitably, Aneurin Bevan most probably, and Shinwell possibly) argued that there was no firm evidence of its deterrent effect (particularly in the case of unpremeditated murders), that the opinion of His Majesty's judges was unreliable, and that the government supporters in Parliament who had studied the matter were unanimously in favour of abolition. In the face of such a divergence of opinion, the prime minister suggested that the Cabinet return to the issue at a later meeting.[19]

For the next month, the Home Office worked on the question. The guiding light in these internal discussions was the Permanent Secretary of State, Sir Alexander Maxwell. He was particularly concerned about the parliamentary strategy that seemed to be evolving. The plan was to introduce the bill without a clause abolishing capital punishment. Then, in the Second Reading debate, the suggestion would be made that, since the question aroused differences of opinion transcending party lines, the government would leave the matter to a free vote of the entire House. (This would, in fact, be the course ultimately followed by the Cabinet.) For Maxwell, pitfalls abounded on this path. "To leave the matter to a free vote of the House," he argued, "would be an indication that the Government had not made up its mind on the question." If an abolitionist clause was introduced on a free vote, this would only inspire the House of Lords to delete the clause from the bill and defend their action on the ground that the government had given no clear lead to Parliament. At that point, the government would feel unable to leave the matter any longer to a free vote and thus would have to decide "either to propose that [the] Lords amendment be rejected or to propose it be accepted and to put the Whips on." All this, it has to be said, bears an uncanny resemblance to the difficulties that soon overtook the government.

Maxwell's advice, therefore, was to take the bull by the horns. Unless the government was prepared to resist an amendment proposing abolition, however strong its supporters in the Commons,

---

Minister, 18 Jun. 1947, Prime Minister's Private Office (hereafter PREM) 8/739; Cabinet Minutes (hereafter CM) (47) 55th conclusions, Cabinet meeting, 19 Jun. 1947, CAB 128/10.

19 CM (47) 55th conclusions, Cabinet meeting, 19 Jun. 1947, CAB 128/10. The prime minister was no partisan on the question of capital punishment, even though he had been involved in the 1920s in securing the abolition of the death penalty for military offences (except for treachery, mutiny, and desertion to the enemy). See J. H. Brookshire, *Clement Attlee* (Manchester, 1995), p. 155. This campaign is described more fully in John McHugh, "The Labour Party and the Parliamentary Campaign to Abolish the Military Death Penalty, 1919–1930," *Historical Journal*, vol. 42 (1999), pp. 233–49.

their right line would be to take the initiative and to insert in the Bill as introduced a Clause for the abolition of the death penalty. If the Government are going ultimately to accept a Clause to this effect, and to resist any attempt on the part of the House of Lords to delete it, their better course would be themselves to propose the Clause.[20]

Maxwell's thinking imposed itself on the Home Secretary's July 8 memorandum for Cabinet discussion.[21]

At the meeting of July 15, 1947, it became crystal clear that the Cabinet was trapped in a logical circle of its own creation. The discussion went something like this. Since ministers could not agree on the merits of the question, the right course was to tell the Commons that because there were differences of opinion transcending party lines, the matter would be left to a free vote of the House. If this resulted in an abolitionist amendment, however, one that was accepted by the Commons but then rejected by the Lords, the government would be in an awkward position. There was much to be said, therefore, for uncoupling the death penalty question from the Criminal Justice Bill. But such was the sentiment in the House and Party that a *quid pro quo* of an uncoupling would be a government promise of abolitionist legislation in a later session. For this, ministers had to agree that the death penalty ought to be abolished. But this was exactly what ministers could not agree upon![22]

Not until early November 1947 did the Cabinet return to the issue. It was then learned from Herbert Morrison that his recent meeting with the Parliamentary Labour Party (PLP) indicated that while government supporters would accept the absence in the bill of a provision for the abolition of capital punishment, they had every intention of moving an abolitionist amendment. The Cabinet resolved that in these circumstances the decision on this issue should be left to a free vote.[23] The next day the bill was published.

The main principle of the Criminal Justice Bill was warmly received by the press. "Modem penal doctrine," said *The Times*, "has firmly established that simple retribution . . . is not a proper objective of secular justice." There was less unanimity concerning the government's decision to omit an abolitionist clause. *The Times* inclined towards an abolitionist position. "Capital punishment is so repulsive that no civilized people would continue it unless convinced that there is no other means of protecting life." On the day of the bill's Second Reading, the same paper

20 Minutes of 25 Jun. and 1 Jul. 1947, TNA, HO45/21959/884452/203. By July 1947, the Parliamentary Penal Reform Group, organized by the Howard League, had got 187 (mostly Labour) MPs to sign a memorial to the Home Secretary asking him to include in the Criminal Justice Bill a provision to suspend the death penalty for a five-year experimental period. See Christoph, *Capital Punishment*, pp. 36–7.
21 CP (47) 200, 8 Jul. 1947, "Abolition of the Death Penalty," memo by Home Secretary, CAB 129/19.
22 CM (47) 61st conclusions, Cabinet meeting, 15 Jul. 1947, CAB 128/10.
23 CM (47) 84th conclusions, Cabinet meeting, 3 Nov. 1947, CAB 128/10.

declared that the experiment of suspending capital punishment for five years "would provide both parties to the controversy . . . with the facts required for a final settlement of their difference." The secretary of the NCADP, Frank Dawtry, complained that the bill's intention to fit treatment to the criminal, not the crime, "will seem to be contradicted if the death penalty remains, for most murderers are first offenders." "Who could have imagined," said C. H. Rolph in the *New Statesman*, "that this immensely powerful Government, containing probably more idealists to the square vote than any of which there is biographical record, would reject the opportunity afforded by a great penal reform Bill to abolish the death penalty?"[24]

On 27 November 1947, the Second Reading of the Criminal Justice Bill took place. At the close of his speech, Home Secretary Ede stated the government's position on capital punishment. The reasons for retaining the death penalty were, first, that it acted as a deterrent; second, the war and post-war rise in crime made it dangerous to experiment with abolition; and, third, little public support existed for such an experiment. However, "recognising that this is a matter on which very strong individual conscientious feelings are held and that the division does not follow the usual party lines," the government, said Ede, would "leave the final decision to a free vote of the House," and "no attempt will be made to coerce the conscience of any individual hon. Member." (No one thought to ask whether this meant minister as well as backbencher.) For the Opposition, Osbert Peake promised that any vote on capital punishment would be free on his side of the House also. He himself felt that capital punishment should be retained in view of the increases in violent crime.[25]

Sydney Silverman, a left-wing Labourite and outspoken leader of the abolitionists in Parliament, greeted the bill as "a great act of courage and a great act of faith," before noting caustically that the increase in violent crime had led the previous (Templewood)[26] and present (Ede) Home Secretaries to change their minds about capital punishment in precisely opposite directions; and that the same increase led Ede to conclude that corporal punishment (inflicted in the main for violent crime) should be abolished, while capital punishment (for a crime known to be little affected by general crime waves) should be retained. These confusions aside, Silverman acknowledged that the government "have done wisely and generously, in agreeing to leave this matter to the free, unfettered, judgment of Members of the House."[27] Otherwise, the Second Reading debate passed off

24 *The Times*, 5 Nov. 1947; *Daily Telegraph*, 5 Nov. 1947; *The Times*, 27 Nov. 1947; *Observer*, 9 Nov. 1947, press cuttings in TNA, HO 45/21953/884452/1288. See also *Manchester Guardian*, 11 Nov. 1947, press cutting in HO45/21962/884452/263; "Cat and Hangman," *New Statesman*, 15 Nov. 1947, p. 387.

25 *Hansard*, Commons, vol. 444, 27 Nov. 1947, cols. 2150–1, 2161.

26 Templewood (formerly Sir Samuel Hoare) was now president of the Howard League and a publicly proclaimed abolitionist.

27 Ibid., cols. 2186–9. For Silverman, see Emrys Hughes, *Sydney Silverman: Rebel in Parliament* (1969), p. 90; Christoph, *Capital Punishment*, p. 42; Sarah McCabe, "Silverman, (Samuel) Sydney," *Dictionary of National Biography, 1961–70* (Oxford, 1980), pp. 941–4.

without incident, and the crucial vote on the death penalty was postponed for several months.

What conclusions can we draw from this recital of the government's conduct? There are, I would submit, four possible explanations for its behaviour. The first is that given by the Home Secretary during the Second Reading debate: a cocktail of deterrence, public opinion, and crime rates. It has considerable validity. The senior judges, Lord Chancellor Jowitt, and Chuter Ede all subscribed to the deterrent efficacy of the death penalty. They also took notice of, and were not above exploiting, opinion polls that indicated there were at least two retentionists for every abolitionist. When a deputation from the NCADP came to see him in July 1947, Ede specifically asked for the Council's view on the results of a recent Gallup Poll.[28] And Ede and Jowitt were not alone in underlining the war and post-war crime rise. The recorded incidence of murders and crimes of violence was markedly higher than before the war.[29]

There is evidence, secondly, for an explanation that emphasizes the desire not to lose the Criminal Justice Bill by including a clause that could arouse controversy. Just prior to the bill's publication, Morrison and Ede appealed to Labour backbenchers to save the possible (a penal reform bill) by foregoing the perfect (a bill that also abolished capital punishment).

Thirdly, the Home Secretary, it is claimed, became captive of the departmental view, more strictly of the supposedly retentionist views of Sir Alexander Maxwell, the Permanent Secretary, and Sir Frank Newsam, the Deputy Undersecretary. The evidence is far from clear cut. In 1961, Gordon Rose implied that Maxwell and Newsam both shared the retentionist views of the former Permanent Secretary, Sir John Anderson (1922–32). James Christoph pointed out that, in an interview, Ede had claimed that both officials were "at heart" abolitionists. Fenton Bresler maintained that Newsam was a decided retentionist and hence unpopular with the abolitionists. Herbert Morrison's biographers declared that Maxwell "was a strong believer in the abolition of capital punishment." For my part, I have found nothing to suggest that Maxwell was anything other than abolitionist in sentiment; Newsam may well have been retentionist.[30] To

---

28   7 Jul. 1947, TNA, HO45/21959/884452. The Gallup poll had asked, "In this country most people convicted of murder are sentenced to death. Do you agree with this or do you think that the death penalty should be abolished?" The result was: agree, 69 per cent; abolish, 24 per cent; no opinion, 7 per cent. See George H. Gallup (ed.), *The Gallup International Public Opinion Polls: Great Britain, 1937–75* (New York, 1976), vol. 1, p. 156.

29   The number of indictable (or serious) offences known to the police rose by 76 per cent between 1938 and 1947. More specifically, the annual average of cases of murder (of persons aged over one year) increased from 95 between 1936 and 1939 to 121 between 1945 and 1948. Crimes of violence against the person (committed by persons aged 17 and above) rose from 1,467 in 1938 to 2,952 in 1948, or from 4.7 to 8.9 per 100,000 population. Indictable sexual offences known to the police rose by 54 per cent between 1945 and 1950. See Rose, *Struggle*, p. 215; Morris, *Criminal Justice*, p. 96. And see the start of section III of chap. 6 *supra*.

30   Rose, *Struggle*, p. 215; Christoph, *Capital Punishment*, p. 70, n. 10; Fenton Bresler, *Reprieve: A Study of a System* (1965), p. 75; Donoughue and Jones, *Morrison*, p. 310.

what extent was Chuter Ede a captive of the departmental view? The character of the man points in that direction. Ede was a moderate, cautious, and practical politician, certainly no innovator, and, as such, likely to listen to his permanent officials. It is a telling point against him, moreover, that he was abolitionist both before and after his stint as Home Secretary, but retentionist when in office. Above all, Ede believed that so disputatious a subject as capital punishment required separate legislative treatment, as did officials in the Home Office and the Cabinet Office.[31] Perhaps, then, Ede was a mite captive, though the departmental view was not uniformly retentionist.

The preceding account of Cabinet thinking leads me to suggest a fourth explanation for the government's behaviour, one that underscores the incompatibility between a Parliamentary Labour Party chock-full of radical idealists and abolitionists, on the one hand, and a Cabinet with only a few committed abolitionists, on the other.[32] Only Shawcross and Soskice had fire in their bellies on this issue. They were up against the leader of the House, the Home Secretary, and a Lord Chancellor wielding the club of His Majesty's judges. Yet if the abolitionists were outgunned, the combination of strong backbench support for abolition and ministerial division together scuppered the idea of a separate bill to suspend or abolish the death penalty, and impelled the strategy of the free vote in the House of Commons. The Cabinet sought to find a way out of its difficulties by throwing the burden on the House by a free vote.

III

In early December 1947, abolitionists from the major parties (though pre-dominantly Labour Members of Parliament) decided to press for a five-year sus-pension of the death penalty rather than its complete abolition, presumably because this would attract a wider body of parliamentary support. The scene was set for a debate and free vote on the Report Stage of the Criminal Justice Bill, on the most controversial, and for some the most crucial, reform in the penal system. It would

Maxwell served on the Royal Commission on Capital Punishment, 1949–53, for which see *infra*, p. 276.

31 For more on Ede, see Francis Williams, "Chuter Ede," *Spectator*, 1 Oct. 1948, pp. 423–4, and *Nothing So Strange* (1970), p. 233; Morgan, *Labour in Power*, pp. 54–5; Kevin Jefferys (ed.), *Labour and the Wartime Coalition: From the Diary of James Chuter Ede, 1941–1945* (1987), pp. 8–9. Ede revised his views on capital punishment in the 1950s when serious doubts were raised about the conviction of Timothy Evans, who was executed on Ede's watch. Ede began to campaign for abolition of the death penalty and for a posthumous free pardon for Evans. See Jefferys, *Labour and the Wartime Coalition*, pp. 15–16. And *infra*, pp. 288–9.

32 Norman Brook's minute of 18 Nov. 1947, TNA, PREM 8/739, indicated that not more than five Cabinet ministers would vote for abolition, while ten or eleven sup-ported the view that the time was not opportune to abolish the death penalty. Norman Brook was secretary to the Cabinet from 1947 to 1962, and an enormously influential adviser to four prime ministers: Attlee, Churchill, Eden, and Macmillan. See Peter Hennessy, *Cabinet* (Oxford, 1986), p. 18; K. Theakston, "Brook, Norman Craven, Baron Normanbrook (1902–1967)," *Oxford DNB* (2011).

soon become clear that, by gambling on a free vote, the government had opened a bag of political troubles.[33]

In mid-March 1948, Prime Minister Attlee agreed, at Herbert Morrison's prompting, that the Cabinet ought again to discuss the question of whether ministers should be free to vote according to conscience on the amendment for the abolition of the death penalty. The previous Cabinet decision—that ministers should be free to vote for abolition—had the disadvantage that the division list would show afterwards that government members were not united in support of the advice given the Commons by the Home Secretary. The Cabinet agreed that members of the government who could not vote for retention of the death penalty should abstain from voting. All ministers and junior ministers outside the Cabinet were so informed, as was the PLP[34] This was a heavy blow to the Silverman group, who were banking on the votes of sympathizers in the ministry. Ministers began to search their consciences.[35]

At the Report Stage of the bill on 14 April 1948, the first order of business was the Silverman amendment, by now bearing the signatures of 147 Members of Parliament, proposing that for a period of five years the death penalty should be suspended and sentence of life imprisonment substituted.[36] For a number of speakers in the debate, wartime events had manifestly reinforced their moralist convictions. Supporters of capital punishment argued that if it was morally right to hang war criminals, then it was right to use the death penalty for murderers at home. "We have just been hanging our defeated enemies after the trials at Nuremberg," said Quintin Hogg, Conservative MP for Oxford, and the Attorney-General had prosecuted them "not as an act of war but as an act of what was claimed to be justice." If we were going to say that it was wrong in all circumstances to take life, Hogg continued, "then the time to say so was before Nuremberg and not immediately after." By contrast, opponents of capital punishment underlined the penchant for Britain's wartime enemies to use the death penalty. "It is not insignificant," said Elwyn Jones, who had been a member of the prosecution team at Nuremberg, "that one of the first acts of the Nazi Government was to restore the death penalty . . . Our democracy is a democracy that does not need

33 Christoph, *Capital Punishment*, p. 42. Some abolitionists were by now less optimistic about the outcome. In January 1948, Margery Fry told Professor Kinberg: "I'm very much afraid we are going to be defeated. A tremendous rise in crime . . . has made people jumpy and vindictive." Quoted in E. H. Jones, *Margery Fry* (1966), p. 220.

34 CM (48) 27th conclusions, Cabinet meeting, 8 Apr. 1948, TNA, CAB 128/12; Norman Brook minute, 19 Mar. 1948, TNA, PREM 8/739. At a stormy meeting of ministers outside the Cabinet, many objected strongly to the abandonment of the free vote. See Windlesham, *Responses to Crime*, p. 60.

35 Griffiths to Attlee, 14 Apr. 1948, PREM 8/739; Donoughue and Jones, *Morrison*, p. 430. The abolitionist cause was probably weakened by a series of shocking murders in the months prior to the vote, including the murder of a policeman, all of which were given banner headlines in the press. See Christoph, *Capital Punishment*, p. 45.

36 *Hansard*, Commons, vol. 449, 14 Apr. 1948, col. 986. The amendment had been tabled by an all-party list of sponsors.

the terror of the death penalty." In fine, the capital punishment debate in 1948 had a strong moral tone, whether retributive or humanitarian in sentiment.[37]

When the House divided on the Silverman clause, 245 voted yes, 222 voted no. By a slim majority, the Commons had approved a major change in the law of murder for the first time in almost a century. Immediately a roar of cheers went up. R. H. S. Crossman later explained the emotional outburst:

> For once the machine had been defeated by conscience; and a longstanding Party pledge had been fulfilled despite the dictates of expediency . . . It was a glorious victory. The violence of the jubilation revealed the frustration of a Party which longs to be able to choose between right and wrong and is constrained time after time to make do with the lesser evil.[38]

To its embarrassment, the government drew the bulk of its support from the Conservatives (no less than 134 of them). Of the 289 Labour Members who took part in the division, 215 voted for the clause (or three to one in favour). Party lines were thus clearly drawn on the issue, despite the government's argument that opinion transcended such lines. The most remarkable fact, however, is that of the 72 government members in the Commons, only 28 voted against the amendment, while 44 availed themselves of the right to abstain, several pointedly remaining on the front bench during the division. Out of fourteen cabinet ministers eligible to vote in the Commons, nine voted against the amendment (including Attlee, Morrison, Bevin, and Ede), while Cripps, Bevan, and Harold Wilson (president of the Board of Trade) were present but abstained.[39] Another nine senior ministers not of Cabinet rank and 32 junior ministers abstained, including all four law officers. (Indeed, none of the law officers had participated in the debate, despite the nature of the issue).[40] Government dissension was awfully palpable.

What had gone wrong? The government presumably expected to win the vote. A year later, referring to the Commons' vote, the Lord Chancellor said, "I frankly confess that I expected an answer in a different sense . . ." And the *Daily Telegraph* stated that Morrison had believed there was a majority for the death penalty and

---

37 Ibid., col. 1017 (Hogg), 1066 (Elwyn Jones). And see col. 1015 (John Paton, Labour MP, and former secretary of the NCADP), col. 1093 (Reginald Paget, Labour MP). See also Lord Elwyn-Jones, *In My Time: An Autobiography* (1983), chap. 10.

38 *New Statesman*, 24 Apr. 1948, p. 326.

39 The other two Cabinet ministers (Arthur Creech Jones and Philip Noel-Baker) were abroad. The nine ministers who voted for retention were Attlee, Morrison, Bevin, Ede, Arthur Woodburn (Scottish Secretary), A. V. Alexander (Minister of Defence), George Isaacs (Minister of Labour), George Tomlinson (Minister of Education), and Tom Williams (Minister of Agriculture). Six of them were from working-class backgrounds. Two other Cabinet ministers, Lords Jowitt and Addison, were in favour of retention, but they could not vote in the Commons.

40 Mass-Observation Archive, TC 72, Box 1, File E; *The Times*, 16 Apr. 1948; Christoph, *Capital Punishment*, p. 51; Morgan, *Labour in Power*, p. 62.

thus the free vote would go in the government's favour.[41] It seems, then, that the government miscalculated abolitionist strength on their own benches and wrongly expected there would be enough Opposition members to see them through. One can only wonder why the government did not do more to divine the mood and intention of their own supporters.

We are on firmer ground in saying that the government had failed to think through the full consequences of a defeat. For they now had to defend a policy they disliked in the House of Lords where they had few supporters and where the Conservative majority would doubtless delete the clause. If the clause came before the Commons again, the Home Secretary would have to ask the House to insist on a clause that the government opposed. Those who had abstained on the first occasion would be free to vote in support of abolition, while the ministers who were against the clause on the first occasion would be compelled to vote for the abolition that they previously opposed. If the Lords held firm, moreover, the government would be faced with a clash between the two chambers. Then the Lords would be able to maintain that they were defending the opinion of the Labour government, not to mention the will of the people, against the Commons' free vote, and there would be a long delay in the passage of the Criminal Justice Bill.

In the aftermath of the abolitionist triumph, ministers agreed that the government must accept the Commons' decision and must ask the House of Lords to accept the new clause. The Cabinet also agreed with Ede's proposal that no death sentence for murder should be carried into effect while Parliament was still considering the Criminal Justice Bill. The House was duly told of this change in the exercise of the prerogative of mercy in capital cases, and the judges were asked to forego the black cap, the presence of the chaplain, and the "Lord have mercy on your soul," when a sentence of death was given.[42]

Second, it became clearer still that parliamentary opinion and public opinion were at odds on the issue of capital punishment. Three opinion polls appeared in quick succession, indicating that the abolition or suspension of the death penalty was rejected by between two-thirds and three-quarters of respondents (see Table 7.1).[43] Neither sex, age, social class, geographic location, nor religious persuasion made much

41 *Hansard*, Lords, vol. 155, 28 Apr. 1948, col. 546; *Daily Telegraph*, 7 Jun. 1948.
42 See CM (48) 28th conclusion, Cabinet meeting, 15 Apr. 1948, TNA, CAB 128/12. See the Home Secretary's statement on the prerogative of mercy in capital cases in the Commons, 16 Apr. 1948, and Ede's letter to the Lord Chief Justice, 19 Apr., in HO45/21958/884452/202A. Ede's announcement that he intended to advise His Majesty to commute every death sentence by conditional pardon to a sentence of penal servitude for life was eventually deemed to be unconstitutional, and Ede had to make another statement to the House on 10 Jun. 1948. See CM (48) 37th conclusions, Cabinet meeting, 8 Jun. 1948, CAB 128/12.
43 See Mass-Observation Archive, File No. 2996, Capital Punishment Survey, Supplement No. 1, p. 14: "Results of the Three Surveys on the Experimental Abolition of the Death Penalty." This table was reproduced in L. R. England, "Capital Punishment and Open-Ended Questions," *Public Opinion Quarterly*, vol. 12 (1948), p. 413 (Table 1). These figures are in marked contrast to the Gallup poll of November 1938, when 45 per cent chose abolition.

difference to the result. Mass-Observation found that there was a steady rise in approval with increasing education (though even among those with higher secondary education, only 21 per cent approved of the suspension measure) and that political affiliation influenced opinion (yet only 19 per cent even of Labour supporters approved of the measure).[44] Perhaps the most significant finding was the discovery by Mass-Observation that "the principle of a 'life for a life' is very much alive in many people's minds still . . . "[45] Two-fifths of Mass-Observation's respondents spontaneously gave a reason for their attitude. Among those who disapproved of abolition, 40 per cent felt it would result in an increase of crime. This was the most frequently-expressed reason. Yet 26 per cent cited the principle of retribution, prompting Mass-Observation to advise the *Daily Telegraph*, which published their poll: "It is well for both parties to know how deeply entrenched still in the minds of hundreds of thousands of citizens is the principle of retribution, quite irrespective of the merely *practical* merits or demerits of abolition."[46]

If the government hoped to persuade the House of Lords to accept the new clause, they could have chosen no worse advocate than the Lord Chancellor. Arguing in the most backhanded manner that he, the head of the judiciary, was opposed to the experiment, but that the Lords should nonetheless make it, was hardly calculated to win over such determined opponents as Lords Simon and Samuel. In the second day's debate, Jowitt was more forthright still:

> I was a party to a bargain. I agreed that this matter should be left to a free vote, and I agreed to stand by the result of that free vote . . . I do not suggest for a moment, however, that your Lordships are bound . . . your Lordships have constitutionally . . . the perfect right to send the clause back to another place for further consideration if you are so minded.[47]

44 See *Daily Express*, 29 Apr. 1948, p. 1; Gallup, *Public Opinion Polls*, p. 174; *Daily Telegraph*, 28 May 1948, p. 1; Mass-Observation Archive, File No. 2996, Capital Punishment Survey, and File No. 3001, Three Surveys on Capital Punishment; Christoph, *Capital Punishment*, pp. 43–4, 53–7. For most surveys, Gallup Poll findings were based on samples of 1,000 interviews conducted in some 100 sampling points. Its poll findings were at this date published in the *News Chronicle*. The Mass-Observation survey interviewed over 6,000 people aged 16 and over throughout England, Wales, and Scotland and used an "open-end" question ("How do you feel about the death penalty for murder being given up for 5 years?"), which allowed scope for spontaneous expressions of opinions. For more on M-O, see Angus Calder, "Mass-Observation 1937–1949," in Martin Bulmer (ed.), *Essays on the History of British Sociological Research* (Cambridge, 1985), pp.121–36.

45 Mass-Observation Archive, File No. 2996, Capital Punishment Survey, p.9.

46 Mass-Observation Archive, TC 72, Capital Punishment Survey, Box 1, File B, May 1948 ("Mass Observation and Opinion Polls"), emphasis in the original. M-O's finding gained confirmation in August 1948 when Gallup asked the question: "What do you think is the main reason for sentencing a murderer to death—because he deserves it, or because it will stop other people committing murders?" The result was: Desert, 45 per cent; Stop others, 43 per cent; Don't know, 12 per cent. See Gallup, *Public Opinion Polls*, p. 180.

47 *Hansard*, Lords, vol. 155, 28 Apr. 1948, cols. 545–6. See also *Hansard*, Lords, 27 Apr. 1948, cols. 396–9.

And, of course, many of the Lords were so minded.

Again, I will not attempt to give a comprehensive review of the four days of debate in the Lords. Suffice it to emphasize three important points. The first is that what has been called the "law-and-order group" among the law lords, which emerged with the post-war rise in recorded crime, were in full cry. Lord Oaksey, a Lord of Appeal (who, as Lord Justice Lawrence, had acted as president of the Nuremberg Tribunal in 1945), was an assertive retentionist with regard to both corporal and capital punishment, for both retributive and deterrent reasons. "Is this the time in which to introduce this change in the law?" he asked the House (shades of Lords Eldon and Ellenborough). "It seems to me somewhat difficult to justify putting to death your enemies" (in Germany), he argued, "and at practically the same time abolish the penalty of death in your own country." Additionally, the time was not ripe "because there is a lack of discipline in the country which gives rise to this wave of crime."[48] He was ably seconded by the Lord Chief Justice, Lord Goddard, or "Lord God-damn," as Churchill styled him. In what was his maiden speech, Goddard delivered a furious assault on those who believed "that punishment should never be punitive, only reformative." Large numbers of criminals were not sentenced for reformative purposes, said Goddard, but to show that such conduct would result in punitive consequences. He continued,

> If the criminal law of this country is to be respected, it must be in accordance with public opinion . . . I cannot believe that the public opinion (or I would rather call it the public conscience) of this country will tolerate that persons who deliberately condemn others to painful and, it may be, lingering deaths should be allowed to live.

The conclusion was foregone: "I believe that there are many, many cases where the murderer should be destroyed."[49]

Second, the bishops of the Church of England provided choral backing for the legal leads. Only the Bishop of Chichester voted for abolition. A more representative figure was Mervyn Haigh, the Lord Bishop of Winchester. The Criminal Justice Bill, he remarked, was "infected at some points by an excessive fear of punishment. I certainly view with some alarm the extent to which the door is opened to the opinions and influence of more medical men and more

48 *Hansard*, Lords, vol. 155, 27 Apr. 1948, cols. 430–1. In the later debate, Oaksey concluded his speech by declaring, "It is all wrong to say that punishment has nothing to do with retribution. There are certain cases which shock the conscience of every ordinary man." *Hansard*, Lords, vol. 157, 20 Jul. 1948, cols. 1047–8. See also Stevens, *Law and Politics*, pp. 360–1.

49 Ibid., cols. 490–4. Goddard also said that the 20 King's Bench judges were all in favour of retaining the death penalty. In late June, however, he had to admit that he had been in error; two judges had since told him that they supported the proposal to suspend the death penalty for five years. See *The Times*, 1 Jul. 1948; Fenton Bresler, *Lord Goddard: A Biography of Rayner Goddard, Lord Chief Justice of England* (1977), p. 184 and note.

TABLE 7.1 Public opinion on experimental abolition of the death penalty

Attitude	Daily Express	British Institute of Public Opinion (Gallup)	Mass-Observation*
Approve	14	26	13
Disapprove	77	66	69
Degrees of murder			7
Mixed feelings			4
Miscellaneous			2
Don't know	9	8	5

Source: Mass-Observation Archive, TC 72, Capital Punishment Survey, Box 1, File B, May 1948, reproduced with permission of Mass-Observation.

*Figures based only on those who had heard of the experiment. A blank indicates that this category was not included in the published results.

psychiatrists." Haigh took the opportunity to remind the Lords of "the primitive framework whereby punishment is awarded by the State in a quite objective way":

> . . . I believe that the deepest point is not just whether the death penalty deters a certain number of people from committing murder . . . but what the effect of abolishing the death penalty on the education of the conscience of the community as a whole will be; how far it will affect the general sense of the wickedness of wickedness, the general sense of the criminality of crime, and the general sense that some crimes are infinitely more heinous than others.[50]

The death penalty, he concluded, still aroused among large numbers of people "what I can only describe as a quasi-religious sense of awe."[51]

Thirdly, a number of speakers recommended the alternative course of limiting the infliction of the death penalty to certain categories of the gravest cases. Lord Samuel, for example, suggested that all murderers should be reprieved except in four categories: political assassins, murderers of police officers, murderers of prison officers, and murders of a "planned and callous character."[52] Soon schemes of grading murders would be all the rage. On 2 June, the Silverman clause was defeated by 181 votes to 28.[53] The rest of the bill was approved by the Lords, even the abolition of corporal punishment.

50 *Hansard*, Lords, vol. 155, 27 Apr. 1948, col. 426.
51 Ibid., col. 427.
52 Ibid., cols. 415–8.
53 Ibid., vol. 156, 2 Jun. 1948, cols. 102 and ff. The total number voting was large by upper chamber standards, pointing to the role of "backwoodsmen," or Conservative peers who came out only on emotive occasions. See P. A. Bromhead, *The House of Lords and Contemporary Politics, 1911–1957* (1958), pp. 47 and 218, n. 2.

IV

Confronted by a Lords' revolt, what could the Labour government do? The press response to the Lords' vote gestured towards a compromise clause, establishing degrees of murder. The *News Chronicle*, for example, advised the government "that there were comparatively few in the House of Lords who desire the permanent retention of the death penalty in its present form." Leading the charge for a compromise clause was Lord Chancellor Jowitt. He had been struck by the Archbishop of Canterbury's opinion during the Second Reading debate that the country could not now go back to the status quo. In addition, he wished to avoid a clash with the House of Lords at a moment when the press was waxing lyrical about how the Lords' delaying power had been used in the public interest. Jowitt feared that if the abolition clause was restored in the Commons, the Lords would again reject it, since they would know that, at a time when the Labour government aimed to reduce the Lords' veto power from two years to one, they had no better case for demonstrating their value as a revising chamber.[54]

The day following the Lords' vote, the Cabinet, on the advice of the Home Secretary, decided to recommend to the PLP that they accept a compromise clause retaining the death penalty for certain specified classes of murder. The Lord Chancellor had drafted a clause to this end. The Cabinet hoped that a majority of the PLP might be persuaded to vote in favour of such a compromise, especially since they could be told that the clause had been unanimously approved by the Cabinet. The Attorney-General, Shawcross, was obviously not at this Cabinet meeting, since, to judge from his memoirs, he felt strongly that the clause suspending the death penalty should be restored by the Commons. Browbeaten by Attlee and Morrison not to split "on an issue on which public opinion was so clear," Shawcross agreed to vote with the government, but then resign (an act he never took).[55]

On June 9, Ede, Cripps, and Morrison persuaded the PLP to accept the compromise clause.[56] The next task, which was never likely to be easy, was to draft an acceptable clause. The new clause was eventually drafted on the basis that the penalty for murder should ordinarily be life imprisonment, but that the death penalty should be retained for those types of murder that were the main cause of public anxiety, and for which the deterrent effect of the death penalty was likely to be more powerful than it was in other cases. The clause did not attempt to define degrees of murder or to distinguish between types of murder according to the moral gravity of the crime. Nor was it drawn so as to include premeditated murders and exclude unpremeditated ones.

Instead, the clause reserved the death penalty for (i) murder incidental to the commission of offenses of robbery, burglary, and housebreaking, violence by gangs,

---

54 *News Chronicle*, 4 Jun. 1948. See also *The Times*, 3 Jun. 1948, p. 5; minute of S. Hoare, Assistant Undersecretary of State, 2 Jun. 1948, HO45/21962/884452.
55 Shawcross, *Life Sentence*, p. 168.
56 See *News Chronicle*, 10 Jun. 1948, p. 1.

offences involving the use of explosives, and sexual offences; (ii) murder committed in the course of resisting or avoiding arrest, of escaping from lawful custody, or obstructing the police or persons assisting the police; (iii) murder by the "systematic administration" of poison; (iv) murder of a prison officer; and (v) for a second murder. In effect, the clause divided murder into two broad categories: capital and non-capital. The Home Office calculated that if this clause became law, the number of actual executions would be reduced by more than half, and the number of cases in which the sentence of death was pronounced by even more.[57]

The compromise clause was introduced in the Commons by Shawcross in a more vigorous manner than might have been expected of a confirmed abolitionist. Winston Churchill, Opposition leader, and other Conservative members then had a field day pointing out the anomalies and illogicalities in the clause. "All the most frequent types of murder," said Churchill,

> that is to say, wounding, stabbing, strangling, drowning, etc., committed for all the most wicked motives, jealousy, greed, revenge, etc., will not carry the death penalty, because that penalty will only apply in such cases if the offence is committed by three or more persons.

Both parties had issued three-line whips, so, unsurprisingly, the Commons agreed to substitute the government's new clause by 307 votes to 209.[58]

As Shawcross handed the baton to the Lord Chancellor, he warned that the clause was difficult to defend on its intrinsic merits. He had tried in his speech to justify the various categories for which the government had retained the death penalty, on the ground that it would operate as a deterrent in these cases:

> This argument rather breaks down in regard to the poisoning case, the truth being that we included this, and, indeed, one or two of the other categories [e.g., two murders], not because the death penalty was a deterrent, but because public opinion demands its imposition by way of retribution in these types of case. As, however, we are sticking to the view . . . that the death penalty cannot possibly be justified on the ground of retribution, we can hardly admit that any of the categories in which we are retaining the death penalty are included on that ground.

Jowitt replied the day after the Lords' debate on the compromise clause to say he had had "a very uncomfortable time" with the hanging clause and that "Simon was almost unbearable, making a speech full of 'malice aforethought.'"[59] Lord Simon certainly pulled no punches. "[T]his clause is simply shot to pieces," he said, "this

---

57 Maxwell minute, 29 Jun. 1948, TNA, HO45/21962/884452.
58 *Hansard*, Commons, vol. 453, 15 Jul. 1948, col. 1442.
59 Shawcross to Jowitt, 19 Jul. 1948; Jowitt to Shawcross, 21 Jul. 1948, in TNA, LCO 2/3341.

clause is rightly denounced as being a quite impossible and utterly absurd provision." Alas, Templewood, the leader of the abolitionists in the Lords, also declared the clause to be unworkable. And even Jowitt, in a study of half-heartedness, conceded that possibly he had gone "a little too far in assenting to this scheme. I daresay it is not very well drafted."[60] Not surprisingly, the clause was decisively rejected by 99 votes to 19.

The opposition to the compromise clause points again to the strength of the morality of blame and desert. The clause was a deliberate attempt to avoid questions of retribution and degrees of culpability. Capital murders were not defined by reference to moral guilt, for they were neither the most abhorrent murders, nor those that had been most clearly premeditated. This entire approach stuck in the craw of all retributivists. They were not willing to accept a system in which the wicked might be more severely punished than the very wicked. To be acceptable to them, a compromise clause would have had to be based firmly and squarely upon degrees of heinousness.[61]

The nettle was back in the government's hand. Ede advised the Commons on 22 July to drop the compromise clause. Morrison seconded this advice, reminding the House that the main issue was whether they were going to save a measure "for making a big landmark in the progressive administration of criminal justice and the criminal law." The government won the vote by 215 to 34. Only 129 of the 215 were Labour members, and thus two-thirds of the party voting strength failed to take part (including 14 senior ministers).[62] On 30 July 1948, the Criminal Justice Act received the Royal Assent.

V

The outcome of the tug-of-war between 1945 and 1948 was to leave the law of capital punishment exactly as it was. For an abolitionist movement that had anticipated the final triumph of a century-long campaign to abolish the death penalty in Britain, this was a deeply disappointing result. Abolitionists had looked forward to providing the capstone to the Criminal Justice Act, the symbolic emblem of a new penal future that "liberal progressives" had so patiently constructed throughout the interwar years. Instead, they had traveled for nine months on a Parliamentary switchback, which came to a halt at its starting point. Parliament passed the kind of law that the government had asked for in November 1947, one shorn of a clause to abolish or suspend the death penalty. It had been a

---

60 *Hansard*, Lords, vol. 157, 20 Jul. 1948, cols. 1055, 1070.
61 Cf. the discussion of the 1957 Homicide Act in Christie, "Power of Life and Death," pp. 365–7.
62 Norman Brook minute, 21 Jul. 1948, TNA, PREM 8/739; CM (48) 53d conclusions, Cabinet meeting, 22 Jul. 1948, CAB 128/13; *Hansard*, Commons, vol. 454, 22 Jul. 1948, cols. 707–11, 750; Mass-Observation Archive, TC 72, Box 1, File E. In the event, Attorney-General Shawcross did vote with the government, for which Attlee thanked him. See Shawcross, *Life Sentence*, p. 169.

tortuous journey, one marked by ironies, dilemmas, embarrassments, and recriminations. It was not the ride the abolitionists had paid for, and it could, they felt, have been avoided.

The government had a huge majority in the Commons, a large segment of which was avowedly abolitionist. The press, moreover, was far from retentionist in sentiment. In the abolitionist corner were *The Times, News Chronicle, Manchester Guardian, Daily Mirror, Daily Herald,* and *Reynolds News,* plus such weeklies as the *Observer, Spectator, Economist,* and *New Statesman.*[63] There can have been few issues raised by the post-war Labour government that attracted such widespread press backing. This was due, in part, to the merely suspensory nature of the amendment. As *The Times* argued, a five-year experiment would lead to evidence whereby a lasting decision could be taken.[64] How, then, could the government temporize in this matter, defer to the Conservative peers, and fail to offer clear leadership?

All this overlooked the peculiar character of capital punishment. It may in principle be the apex of the country's penal system, but in practice governments have treated it as a special case. The death penalty called up the strongest emotions; it touched the deepest fears and values. Few people were without opinions on the state's right to exact death; few governments were willing to go ahead of opinion on so volatile and unpredictable an issue. Fearing an emotionally-charged controversy, parties and governments kept their heads down. Parties made no mention of capital punishment in their manifestos, lest a commitment either way became a hostage to fortune. When in power and when made to confront the issue, governments trusted to the free vote, to Parliament as a body of private consciences, to the fiction that capital punishment was an issue of public morality that cut across party lines.

By refusing to treat capital punishment as an integral part of their legislative program, the Attlee administration opened a Pandora's box of troubles. Only when the government faced up to their responsibilities was the box closed, but between the opening and the closing, confusion reigned. Having decided that the death penalty should be retained, the Labour Cabinet lacked the courage to make it government policy. Consequently, what the majority of Cabinet ministers believed was necessary—to retain capital punishment—was left to a free vote of the Commons, which unexpectedly went in favour of abolition. A measure without strong government backing was doomed in the House of Lords where Conservative and retentionist feeling predominated. The Lord Chancellor's lacklustre performance was an effective nod and a wink to the peers to resist abolition. Jowitt had the

---

63 See *The Press and Its Readers: A Report Prepared by Mass-Observation for the Advertising Service Guild* (1949), pp. 81–4. Editorially opposed to the suspension of the death penalty were the *Daily Telegraph, Daily Mail, Daily Express,* and *Daily Graphic.* As the report also made clear, however, the press "has had little opinion-forming influence on this issue." With the single exception of the *Daily Worker,* the Communist Party newspaper, "the majority of readers of *every* paper are against suspension" (p. 82, emphasis in original).

64 *The Times,* 14 Apr. 1948, p. 5.

sanguinary support, moreover, of His Majesty's judges, especially Lord Chief Justice Goddard, whose reign of retributive bombast was underway. The upper chamber's *lex talionis* was reinforced, finally, by the weight of public opinion. The Lords could legitimately claim that on the issue of capital punishment they were closer to the *vox populi* than the Commons. It was hard to deny the finding that close to three in every four people were unfavourable to abolition, other than by pleading that public opinion was uninformed, a doubtful argument for a People's Party. When the peers resisted, the government declined to face them down, adopting instead the face-saving formula of degrees of murder, so shot through with philosophic contradictions and practical illogicalities that it took the issue to new risible depths. What had gone so wrong? "Funk Rule!" the *Daily Mirror* concluded, by which it meant the lack of clear leadership on a vital moral and legal issue.[65]

One other factor was decisive in the failure to abolish capital punishment. The post-war years proved much less propitious for reform of the criminal code than abolitionists were expecting. In the thirties, parliamentary, public, and even judicial opinion seemed to be moving towards abolition, in tandem with a strong desire to recalibrate the principles of punishment for all criminal offenders. The prison commissioners themselves were in the van of a broad-based campaign to demote retribution in favour of rehabilitation. The 1938 Criminal Justice Bill would have given legislative warrant to the reformative treatment of prisoners. Between 1939 and 1947, however, the rate of reported crime rose markedly, and the very act of homicide appeared to take on a more malevolent character. In this setting, the renewed attempt to abolish the death penalty sounded the alarm. It aroused those who believed that the anti-social tendencies proceeding from the war had far from spent their force, to proclaim that this was not the time to be weakening the penal armoury. Corporal punishment could not be saved; all the more reason, then, to cleave to the death penalty. Retaining the gallows was not only about deterring murder, as important as that mandate remained; it was also about satisfying, expressing, and educating the public instinct to condemn crimes that menaced the community. The Lord Bishop of Winchester had said as much in closing his speech on the Criminal Justice Bill in 1948,

> I urge that the question to be considered is not simply whether there will be a few more murders or a few less, but the whole attitude of the British people to what I have described as the criminality of crime, and to the majesty of the whole system of law from top to bottom.[66]

---

65   *Daily Mirror*, 11 Jun. 1948, p. 2. The fact that a reprise of the 1948 events was enacted in 1956, when a Conservative administration confronted the same issue, suggests that it was the character of capital punishment, not the particular party handling the issue, that influenced these events. See chap. 9 *infra*. See also Nigel Nicolson, *People and Parliament* (1958; reprint, Westport, 1974), p.86.

66   *Hansard*, Lords, vol. 155, 27 Apr. 1948, col. 428.

It is this final factor that prompts the conclusion that the turbulent post-war conflict over the death penalty marks a critical moment in criminal justice history. In the wake of the First World War, the jurisprudential axioms of personal responsibility, deterrence, and a due proportion between crime and punishment retained much of their authority. In the criminal courts, rehabilitation was honoured more in the breach than the observance. Yet the tide was turning between the wars. Recorded crime rose slowly, prison populations declined, and innovations such as open prisons were introduced. A progressive reformism, which had points in common with a positivist criminology, guided penal practice. And it shaped the legislative climax of the era, the Criminal Justice Bill. By rights, the post-war Labour government should have launched an era of unashamed rehabilitation, in which the gallows were dismantled once and for all. That it did not is surely testimony to the enduring political, judicial, and public resistance to the reforming ethos. It meant that for a while longer yet, penal debate would be consumed by the agitation to get rid of the last remaining human sacrifice.

VI

In late September 1948, Frank Newsam, the new Permanent Secretary, recommended to Home Secretary Chuter Ede a royal commission on the following lines: "To consider whether the time has come when capital punishment should be abolished and, if not, to what extent it is necessary to retain it for purposes of deterrence and the protection of society." Allowing the Royal Commission to review the whole question, including abolition, went beyond what the Cabinet had decided in July, yet, said Newsam,

> it hardly seems possible to appoint a Royal Commission and tell them at the outset that the Government have decided that capital punishment should be retained, and that all that the Commission is asked to do is to say what sort of crimes should carry the death sentence.[67]

In fact, this was exactly the limited role the royal commission was ultimately given.

Not all Cabinet members were eager to re-open the debate. Arthur Woodburn, Secretary of State for Scotland, preferred to rely upon "the more liberal exercise of the Prerogative as a means of translating into practice what seemed to be the view of those who, while opposed to complete abolition, feel that some modification of the existing system is justified." Lord Chancellor Jowitt told Ede, "I confess that I am sorry to hear that the matter is to be brought up again so soon." The Cabinet Secretary, Norman Brook, advised Prime Minister Attlee that the summer's debate in both Houses on capital punishment surely justified the existing law, under which "death is prescribed as the penalty for all murders, but it is left to the Home Secretary's administrative discretion to decide in each case whether the penalty shall be exacted." In the development of Home Office practice, said Brook, account should be taken of the "general

---

67   TNA, HO45/25084/837371/95, Newsam, 28 Sep. 1948.

disposition to feel that capital punishment should be reserved for a small minority of cases." "In these circumstances," Brook queried, "may not the appointment of a Royal Commission be a waste of time and effort?"[68] Even so, in early November, the Home Secretary recommended to his Cabinet colleagues the appointment of a Royal Commission on Capital Punishment, with terms of reference that included the question of abolition. The Cabinet endorsed the proposal, but restricted the enquiry to the issue of whether liability to suffer the death penalty should be limited or modified.[69] On 18 November, Ede told the Commons that the government had decided to appoint a royal commission, the terms of reference for which would be announced later, though it was implicit in his statement that the commission would be asked to consider only the question of whether liability to the death penalty should be limited or modified.[70]

We need first to record how frequently the death penalty was being invoked, since it was these figures which informed and guided the work of the royal commission.[71] Above all, we need to examine how many persons were committed for trial for murder, how many persons were actually executed, and why there was such a difference between these two figures. In practice, as the commission would discover, the law was mitigated, such that capital punishment "falls very far short of a threat of instant and certain death to every murderer."[72] Between the moment of committal for trial at the assize courts for murder and actual execution, there were a large number of "escape valves." Between 1900 and 1949, of the 3,130 persons committed for trial at the assizes for murder (2,176 men, 954 women), 658 were acquitted or not tried. Additionally, 428 were found insane on arraignment and 798 were found guilty but insane; thus, of all those committed for trial for murder, almost 40 per cent (1,226 of 3,130) were deemed mentally abnormal, either before trial or by a jury, and were not executed.[73] This led abolitionists to argue that

---

68 Ibid., Jowitt to Home Secretary, 4 Nov. 1948; PREM 5/235, Norman Brook to Prime Minister, 6 Nov. 1948.

69 TNA, CAB 128/6, CM (48) 69, 8 Nov. 1948.

70 *Hansard*, vol. 458, 18 Nov. 1948, col. 564; *Hansard*, vol. 460, 20 Jan. 1949, cols. 329–31; *The Times*, 21 Jan. 1949, p. 4.

71 The figures also guided academic commentators, for example H. L. A. Hart, "Murder and the Principles of Punishment: England and the United States," *Northwestern University Law Review*, vol. 52 (1957), pp. 442–3.

72 The true starting figure, of course, was the incidence of murders known to the police. Between 1900 and 1949, 7,454 murders were known to the police. The 50 years average (1900–49) for England and Wales was 149.1 murders known to the police, or 3.89 per million of population. (Serial killers accounted for only a small proportion of all murders; Philip Jenkins has suggested an average of 2.3 murders per annum: "Serial Murder in England 1940–1985," *Journal of Criminal Justice*, vol. 16 [1988], p. 5). This figure soon began to fall. In 1,674 cases, the suspect committed suicide. 4,173 were arrested on suspicion of murder, but only 3,130 were ultimately sent for trial at the assizes. See Report of the Royal Commission on Capital Punishment 1949–1953 (Cmd. 8932), 1953, Appendix 3, Table 3 (hereafter cited as RCCP).

73 At a murder trial, the accused's mental condition was relevant in one of two ways: the accused could be found insane and unfit to plead, or he could be found guilty but insane, which was in effect an acquittal. Both pleas were subject to the stringent test of the M'Naghten Rules. The rules had been written by the House of Lords in 1843 and

murder was primarily a crime of those so disordered in mind that the deterrent effect of punishment was of no effect.[74] Only 1,210 people were convicted and sentenced to death (1,080 men, 130 women). Of the 1,080 men sentenced to death, 528 or almost half were for murder of wife, parent, sweetheart, or lover. Of the 1,210, 23 had their conviction quashed on appeal, 34 were detained during His Majesty's Pleasure, 506 were reprieved and had their sentence commuted to penal servitude for life (390 men, 116 women),[75] and 47 were certified insane and respited to Broadmoor (45 men, two women).[76] Thus, 632 were actually executed over this fifty-year period, or 52.2 per cent of those sentenced to death (621 men and 11 women), making an execution rate of 13 a year between 1900 and 1949.[77] There was, in all, only one execution for every five people committed for trial for murder; only one execution for every two sentenced to death.[78]

Two factors in particular made for mitigation of the law. One was the tendency of juries to add to their conviction a recommendation to mercy. Of the 1,210 persons convicted and sentenced to death, the jury recommended 468 to mercy (360 men, 108 women), of whom 348 (245 men, 103 women) were reprieved. Significantly, in 211 of the 348 reprieved cases, the judge had concurred with the jury's recommendation. In all, a recommendation to mercy was made in 39 per cent of all murder convictions (33 per cent of the men and 83 per cent of the

stated that ". . . to establish a defence on the ground of insanity, it must be clearly proved that, at the time of the committing of the act, the party accused was labouring under such a defect of reason, from disease of the mind, as not to know the nature and quality of the act he was doing; or if he did know it, that he did not know he was doing what was wrong."

74 RCCP, Appendix 3, Table 1, pp. 298–301, and Table 8, p. 311. See Sir Edward Troup, *The Home Office* (2nd ed. revised, 1926), p. 70.

75 This sentence did not typically mean life, of course. Of the 253 commuted death sentence cases where release was authorized between 1920 and 1948, 58 (or 23 per cent) were released after less than five years' detention, 141 (or 56 per cent) after less than ten years' detention, and 236 (or 93 per cent) after less than 16 years' detention. See Home Office, *Capital Punishment* (Cmd. 7419), 1948, p. 1.

76 Between 1 Jan. 1930 and 31 Dec. 1955, male murderers formed 43.19 per cent of male admissions to Broadmoor, female murderers 75.95 per cent of the female admissions. See TNA, HO291/96.

77 The death penalty was, in practice, confined to murder, except for wartime executions for treason. In addition, eighteen US soldiers (over half of whom were African Americans) were executed for murder or rape (or a combination of the two) in England during the Second World War, under the Visiting Forces Act 1942. See J. Robert Lilly and J. Michael Thomson, "Executing US Soldiers in England, World War II," *British Journal of Criminology*, vol. 37 (1997), pp. 262–88.

78 RCCP, Table 4, pp. 304–5. In Scotland, only eight death sentences were imposed in the fifteen years between 1929 and 1944. None was carried out. This was largely the result of the acceptance by Scottish courts of a doctrine of diminished or impaired responsibility, which, if established, reduced the crime from murder to culpable homicide. Thus, by the attitude of the courts, and the exercise of the prerogative, the death penalty had been virtually abolished in Scotland. During this time crimes of violence did not increase. See CP (47) 310, 17 Nov. 1947, "Criminal Justice Bill: Capital Punishment," memo by Secretary of State for Scotland, CAB 129/22.

women), and reprieves were granted to 74 per cent of those recommended to mercy (68 per cent of men and 95 per cent of women).[79] The second and related mitigating factor was the exercise of the Royal Prerogative of Mercy. The jury's recommendation to mercy was made to the Home Secretary, who reviewed every capital case before the law was allowed to take its course. In the first half of the twentieth century, 45 per cent of the persons sentenced to death for murder had been reprieved. The figure for women alone was much higher. The majority of murders committed by women were killings of children by mothers, where a reprieve almost invariably followed. Of the 130 women sentenced to death, 102 had killed a child. As a result, in 116 of 127 cases (leaving aside two women who were certified insane and one who had her conviction quashed by the Court of Criminal Appeal), or in 91 per cent of cases, the sentence was commuted. In the case of women, the argument for the deterrent effect of execution was nugatory. The proportion of cases in which the sentence of death was commuted or respited remained fairly constant over the entire fifty years, 1900–49. Extenuating circumstances sufficient to justify a reprieve were typically found in cases of unpremeditated murders committed in a state of excessive emotion, murders where there was considerable provocation, and murders committed without intent to kill, as during a quarrel, or in a state of drunkenness. A prisoner's youth, sex, or mental condition might also prompt a reprieve.

VII

The first act on behalf of any royal commission is to find a chairman. It was Edward Bridges, Permanent Secretary to the Treasury, who recommended Sir Ernest Gowers "who has had very wide experience and is a person of distinguished mind."[80] Newsam, Ede, and Attlee all agreed. Gowers had been in the public service since 1920, when he became Permanent Undersecretary for Mines, and had chaired *inter alia* the 1946 Committee on Closing Hours of Shops (with great skill according to Barbara Wootton).[81] One of the members of the Royal Commission on Capital Punishment more recently wrote of Gowers' "gift for assimilating swiftly the central parts of an issue."[82] On 20 January, Attlee announced the setting

---

79 Ibid., Table 10, pp. 312–3. In absolute numbers, of the 135 women condemned to death in England and Scotland from 1900 to 1949, only 13 or one in ten were executed. On the reluctance to send women to the gallows, see Michael Ignatieff's comment: "The quality of a Home Secretary's mercy has always been strained by a degree of patriarchal mysticism about the distinctive mental irresponsibility of the female sex:" "Hanging Women," *Observer*, 10 Jul. 1983, p. 25. The public seem to have shared this sentiment when a reprieve was denied to Ruth Ellis, for whom (see *infra*) public support for hanging sharply if momentarily declined.

80 TNA, HO45/25084/837371/95, Edward Bridges to Newsam, 25 Nov. 1948.

81 R. W. Burchfield, "Gowers, Sir Ernest Arthur (1880–1966)," rev., *Oxford Dictionary of National Biography* (Oxford, 2004); Barbara Wootton, *In A World I Never Made* (1967), p. 253.

82 Leon Radzinowicz, *Adventures in Criminology* (1999), p. 255.

up of the royal commission, under the chairmanship of Gowers, with the following terms of reference:

> To consider and report whether liability under the criminal law in Great Britain to suffer capital punishment for murder should be limited or modified, and, if so, to what extent and by what means, for how long and under what conditions persons who would otherwise have been liable to suffer capital punishment should be detained, and what changes in the existing law and the prison system would be required . . .

Abolitionists were furious. Why, having decided to submit the question of capital punishment to the attention of a royal commission, did the government hamstring the commission by excluding from the terms of reference the question of abolition?[83]

The government took some time to appoint the members of the royal commission. Indeed, the names were not announced until April 1949, half a year after Ede's first mention of the government's intention to appoint a royal commission.[84] The initial list of persons to be considered for membership that had gone before the Prime Minister elicited the riposte: "I am not much impressed by this list nor, I think, will be public opinion."[85] Chuter Ede defended his choices, including Sir Alexander Maxwell, former chairman of the Prison Commission and former Permanent Undersecretary of State to the Home Office, and Leon Radzinowicz of the Department of Criminal Science at Cambridge, whose first volume on the *History of English Criminal Law and its Administration* (1948) was largely devoted to the history of capital punishment, and of whom the judges thought highly "as an academic lawyer."[86] What one might call the "expert" side of the commission also included Dr. Eliot Slater, physician in psychological medicine at the National Hospital for Nervous Diseases, and George Montgomery, professor of Scots Law at Edinburgh. To these, Ede tried to add "some common sense people to balance them," and representatives of a wider public opinion.[87] However, Ede wanted no bishops: "in view of the attitude which the bishops have taken to this question, I

83 *The Times*, 28 Jan. 1949, p. 5, letter signed by Lord Templewood, George Benson, Cicely Craven, and Theodora Calvert; *Economist*, 29 Jan. 1949, p. 185. The NCADP no longer existed, so the Howard League had to take over the abolitionist struggle: Jones, *Margery Fry*, p. 225.
84 *Hansard*, vol. 464, 28 Apr. 1949, col. 355.
85 TNA, HO45/25084/837371/95, Attlee, 23 Jan. 1949.
86 Ibid., Ede to Attlee, 14 Mar. 1949. See Anthony Bottoms, "Sir Leon Radzinowicz," *Independent*, 1 Jan. 2000, p. 7; Terence Morris, *Guardian*, 1 Jan. 2000, p. 16; R. Hood, "Radzinowicz, Sir Leon (1906–1999)," *Oxford Dictionary of National Biography* (Oxford, 2004). Morris noted that the RCCP was the first "on a criminological topic to include a criminologist among its members": see "British Criminology: 1935–48," *British Journal of Criminology*, vol. 28 (1988), p. 32. See also See Duncan Fairn, "Maxwell, Alexander (1880–1963)," *Oxford DNB* (2004).
87 Ibid.

do not think it would be wise to have a bishop on the Commission."[88] Nor was the legal profession heavily represented. The only practicing lawyer on the commission was Norman Fox-Andrews, KC, Recorder of Bournemouth, who, according to Radzinowicz, "was a classical embodiment of the traditional English lawyer of the period . . . instinctively proud of things as they were."[89] James Christoph made three useful observations about the twelve commission members: one, "they were representative of fields of activity rather than of distinct points of view or 'interests' in the usual sense of the word"; two, the group was divided equally between experts and lay figures; and three, "none of them had voiced his [or her] views publicly during the late controversy, and none was conspicuously identified with either side."[90] Last but not least, the secretary to the commission was Francis Graham-Harrison, the consummate civil servant, previously assistant private secretary to Prime Minister Attlee. He it was, claimed Radzinowicz, who "quietly proved to be the pillar of the commission," and who would ultimately write up almost the entire report of the royal commission.[91]

The commission held its first meeting on 27 May 1949, when they decided immediately to take written and oral evidence from the Home Office and the Scottish Home Department, and agreed to solicit evidence from people and organizations with some claim to expertise. In all, 118 witnesses gave evidence before the commission, and 29 others supplied memoranda or letters. The minutes of evidence were published as they were collected, so later witnesses could read what had already been said, and the press could keep the issue of capital punishment in the news if not the headlines. Starting in August 1949, the commission met in public to hear evidence on two days each month, and did so for the next year and a half. In addition, questionnaires were sent to officials and governments in Commonwealth countries and in eight American states; and commissioners visited institutions and took evidence from criminologists and prison officials in Europe and the United States.[92] As Hermann Mannheim later noted, the commission employed the conventional techniques associated with royal commissions: oral and written evidence and foreign inquiries. No attempt was made to sample public opinion on any of the commission's principal recommendations.[93] Little attention was paid to the crime of murder or to the types of murderer, apart from a thumbnail sketch of fifty case-histories of murder in England and Scotland between 1931 and 1951 (two-thirds of whom were reprieved, one-third executed), which the commission used in the first pages of their report to illustrate "the multifarious

---

88 Ibid., Shawcross to Ede, 18 Mar. 1949; Ede to Shawcross, 22 Mar. 1949.
89 *Adventures*, op cit., p. 258.
90 See *Capital Punishment and British Politics* (1962), p. 79.
91 *Adventures*, pp. 255–6. For Graham-Harrison, see *The Times*, 28 Jan. 2002; *Independent*, 26 Jan. 2002 (obit. by Michael Moriarty).
92 See Max Grunhut, "Murder and the Death Penalty in England," in Thorsten Sellin (ed.), "Murder and the Penalty of Death," *Annals of the American Academy of Political and Social Science*, No. 284, Nov. 1952, p. 165. See also Christoph, op cit., pp. 79–81.
93 Mannheim, *British Journal of Delinquency*, vol. 4 (1954), pp. 169–70.

variety of the crimes for which death is the uniform sentence."[94] The report did at least state that murder was not, in general, "a crime of the so-called criminal classes."

The first set of witnesses up to January 1950—the Home Office, the police and prison services, the Director of Public Prosecutions, and the judiciary—defended the status quo, leading Gowers in November 1949 to write to Barbara Wootton:

> So far the deepest impression made on me is the astonishing force of *vis inertiae* of the existing state of affairs merely because it is the existing state of affairs. So far all our evidence has been that everything connected with the death penalty is perfect and nothing needs changing in any respect.[95]

Yet Gowers knew that confirmed abolitionists, who might have been more critical of the status quo, were being kept at arm's length by the commission. Lord Guthrie submitted a memorandum advocating the abolition of capital punishment, a view counter to that of the majority of Scottish judges. His memo was circulated, but he was not invited to give oral evidence "since this might prove an inconvenient precedent if other persons sought to give evidence before the Commission in favour of abolition."[96] By January 1950, the *New Statesman* and the *Howard Journal* were complaining that the only witnesses had been a stream of retentionists, all advancing the "departmental view" that there was nothing wrong with capital punishment, execution by hanging, or the system of reprieves. "Of course," said the *Howard Journal*, "this façade of unanimity is false."[97] Inevitably, in view of their role in the administration of the death penalty, the judges stole the show in these early months. This was particularly true of Lord Justice Denning and Lord Chief Justice Goddard.[98]

The two senior judges advised that the exercise of the royal prerogative to reprieve murderers was used on too many occasions, and that the sentence of death should be passed only in cases where the crime was of a heinous and brutal character, and where the penalty was likely to be exacted. For Denning, the ultimate justification of any punishment was not that it was a deterrent, but that it was "the emphatic denunciation by the community of a crime." There were murders that demanded the ultimate denunciation, namely the death penalty. But he proposed a

---

94 RCCP, Appendix 4, pp. 320–5.
95 Quoted in Ann Scott, *Ernest Gowers: Plain Words and Forgotten Deeds* (Basingstoke, 2009), p. 161.
96 TNA, HO301/2, CP 2nd meeting, 4–5 Aug. 1949.
97 See Christoph, op cit., pp. 82–3; Peter Richards, *Parliament and Conscience* (1970), p. 42; Harry Potter, *Hanging in Judgment: Religion and the Death Penalty* (New York, 1993), p. 155.
98 See R. Goff, "Denning, Alfred Thompson, Baron Denning," *Oxford DNB* (2014); K. J. M. Smith, "Goddard, Rayner, Baron Goddard," *Oxford DNB* (2010). Goddard was Lord Chief Justice for 12 years from 1946 to 1958. As *The Times* obituary, 31 May 1971, p. 8 stated: "he led the reaction . . . against the view that all crime is a symptom of disease, and that the idea of punishment is an irrelevant or immoral anachronism."

three-fold reclassification of culpable homicide: murder, manslaughter, and unlawful killing, the object of which was to confine murder to those cases that could be described as "murder most foul," where death was the appropriate penalty, thereby ensuring that the prerogative to reprieve was sparingly exercised. Radzinowicz asked him if a 40-per-cent reprieve rate was too high, to which Denning replied, "I should have thought that for the law to be in conformity with public feeling it should be in the region of 10 per cent."[99] Lord Chief Justice Goddard also focused on the discrepancy between the number of people sentenced to death and the number executed, stating that too many were reprieved. Unlike Denning, who thought the M'Naghten Rules should be brought more into line with the medical definition of insanity, Goddard held firm to the rules. This caused him to object to the reprieve of Thomas John Ley for the "chalk pit murder," who was clearly insane at his trial in March 1947, Goddard recognized, but who refused to allow his counsel to raise the defence of insanity. Goddard insisted that Ley knew he was committing murder. He was sentenced to death. A few days before his execution, however, Ley was reprieved by and respited to Broadmoor, where he died of a stroke ten weeks later. Dr. Slater presumed Goddard would not have wished Ley to hang, receiving the startling reply, "I should have thought it was very proper that he should have been hanged." Slater tried again, suggesting that the medical point of view would be that the disease had made such wickedness possible, to which Goddard replied,

> If that is the medical point of view, I am afraid, frankly, that it does not appeal to me at all. If that was the case, I think it is one of the reasons why he should be put out of the way.

Finally, these two judges saw no reason to reprieve solely on account of age or sex, or to dispense with the symbolic custom of putting on a black cap—the nine-inch square of black silk the judge placed on top of his short bench wig as he delivered the sentence of death. They thought it undesirable, also, to leave it to the discretion of the trial judge whether or not to pass the capital sentence for murder.[100]

The views of the judiciary were largely seconded by the Archbishop of Canterbury, Geoffrey Fisher, who in his written submission advised curtailing capital punishment to murders in which the sentence would be carried out, in order to sustain the quasi-religious function of the penalty:

99 RCCP, *Mins. of Evidence*, 1 Dec. 1949, p. 207–8; q. 2559, p. 209; q. 2570, p. 210; q. 2627, p. 213. See *The Times*, 2 Dec. 1949, p. 2. See also Stevens, *Law and Politics: The House of Lords as a Judicial Body, 1800–1976* (Chapel Hill, 1978), pp. 499–501.

100 RCCP, *Mins. of Evidence*, 5 Jan. 1950, q. 3111, p. 248; q. 3219, p. 255; qq. 3251–3, p. 258; q 3212, p. 255. See also *The Times*, 6 Jan. 1950, p. 4. For a later response to Goddard's "astonishing ignorance of mental abnormality," see Bernard Levin, "Brother Savage," *Spectator*, 16 May 1958, p. 629.

> . . . it is a very grave thing that the solemn formula of the death sentence should almost as often as not be followed by a reprieve which cancels it. It is not only the formula that is solemn. The whole action of which the formula is the expression is profoundly solemn. In it the community acts through the agency of the jury and of the Judge. It is an action taken with a deep sense of responsibility before God and before man, by which a fellow citizen, a fellow human being, is to be deprived of his life on earth and be sent to the Higher Court of God's judgment.[101]

A mere empty formula, said Fisher, "is a degradation of the majesty of the law and dangerous to society." He was ready, however, to give juries the power to decide if there were extenuating circumstances sufficient to permit the substitution of life imprisonment for hanging, which might in turn be the most effective way of bringing capital punishment to an end:

> . . . juries themselves will become in some sense over a period the reflection of public opinion in this matter. If the public feeling that they must retain this penalty decreased, it would reveal itself in the frequency with which juries came to add that rider, and, indeed, you might almost get to the stage when capital punishment would be abolished, not by law but by usage. That, it seems to me, is perhaps the best possible way to reach its abolition.[102]

For his pains, Fisher suffered the indignity of being interrupted by flamboyant abolitionist Mrs. Van der Elst, who rose from her seat and shouted: "Are you a Christian? Do you think Christ would have said what you have said today? He was executed . . . It is not the job for an archbishop to come here and say the things you have said."[103] Gowers might well have agreed with the sentiment. Six years later, in a note to William Beveridge who had warmly received Gowers' new book, *A Life for a Life?*, the chairman of the royal commission declared that he had been prompted to write the book by "a strong desire to show up the sorry stuff talked by the three Prelates—Fisher, Haigh, and Hawkin—and to contrast it with the simple Christian approach of Temple and Bell."[104]

The proposals of the "sacred hierarchies" of Law and Church sought to limit the number of death sentences and executions, as a means of reinforcing the denunciatory efficacy of capital punishment. By reserving death for the more heinous murder cases in which no extenuating circumstances sufficient to justify clemency

---

101 RCCP, *Mins. of Evidence*, 3 Feb. 1950, p. 333.
102 Ibid., q. 4127, p. 338. See also Potter, *Hanging in Judgment*, op cit., pp. 156–8.
103 See Charles Neilson Gattey, *The Incredible Mrs. Van der Elst* (1972), pp. 206–7; *The Times*, 4 Feb. 1950, p. 2.
104 Beveridge Papers, VI/53, Gowers to Beveridge, 27 Mar. 1956. Mervyn Haigh was bishop of Winchester: see *The Times*, 21 May 1962, p. 12. William Temple was Archbishop of Canterbury, 1942–4: see Adrian Hastings, "Temple, William," *Oxford DNB*, 2004. George Bell was Bishop of Chichester.

could be found, they hoped to make capital punishment morally more acceptable, and less prone to the ignominy of reprieve.

VIII

As the evidence accumulated, the royal commission met in private to begin piecing their way to a final report. The minutes of these thirty-one meetings stretching over three years provide our only window on to the workings of the commission, and of the views and contribution of at least a few of the individual members. Inevitably, in view of the evidence received, the two questions which the commission discussed time and again were whether the number of executions should approximate as closely as possible to the number of sentences of death; and whether the exercise of the royal prerogative was the appropriate weapon to restrict the scope of the death penalty, or whether the law should be changed to conform more closely to what the commission thought was its proper scope.[105] On the first question, the commission accepted that one of the main objects of their inquiry was to find some method of reducing the disparity between the number of persons sentenced to death and the number eventually executed.[106] On the second question, chairman Gowers did not believe there were any specific classes of cases in which the royal prerogative ought to be more freely exercised, especially since the commission was recommending a change in the law for some categories of case, namely suicide pacts and persons under 21. However, he thought the Home Secretary should be "increasingly bold in advising the exercise of the Royal Prerogative, and should gradually extend its scope in the direction of greater leniency."[107] In fact, Gowers put forward the following long-term strategy:

> Public opinion would almost certainly move steadily towards support of abolition, but in other countries abolition had come only after capital punishment had been in abeyance for a considerable period. He suggested, therefore, that the right course would be for the Secretaries of State to move gradually towards complete abeyance, keeping in step with, or perhaps a little ahead of, public opinion. The advantage of this policy was that it could be halted or even reversed at any time if it was found to result in an increase of murders or if the state of public opinion made it expedient to do so.[108]

The commission endorsed the chairman's idea of a wider use of the prerogative, only Mr. Fox-Andrews dissenting. Sir Alexander Maxwell added, however, that the fundamental flaw in the law of murder was the single automatic sentence, and that it was wrong in principle to rely on the royal prerogative to achieve justice. It

105 TNA, HO301/2, CP (12th) meeting, 1–2 Jun. 1950: Interim Conclusions.
106 TNA, HO301/7, CP (conclusions) 6, 25 Jun. 1951: Principal questions to be considered by the Commission, No. 4.
107 Ibid., No. 20.
108 TNA, HO301/2, CP (15th) meeting, 7–8 Sep. 1950.

would never be possible to dispense with the royal prerogative, he argued, but the frequency of its exercise should be diminished: "If the proportion of reprieves could be reduced from the present 45% to 10%, that would be a valuable reform." So great a reduction, the secretary interjected, could only be achieved by either establishing degrees of murder (which commissioners had rejected) or giving the judge or jury power to find extenuating circumstances.[109]

The commission considered it was impracticable to give such discretion to the judge, in view of the reluctance of the judiciary to assume this responsibility and the danger of a conflict of views, real or apparent, between judge and Home Secretary. This left only the grant of discretion to the jury, which was discussed at length in the commission's July 1951 meeting. Maxwell was strongly in favour of substituting a sentence of life imprisonment for a sentence of death if the jury found extenuating circumstances; his former colleague, Sir Frank Newsam, attending the meeting by invitation, was decidedly against, on the grounds that "the State was not justified in requiring jurors to bear such a heavy personal responsibility . . . of sending a fellow creature to the scaffold." The chairman brought the discussion to a close by pointing out that the effect of giving discretion to the jury would be not simply to reduce the disparity between the number of death sentences and the number of executions, but also to reduce the number of persons executed, "since juries would find extenuating circumstances in cases where at present the Home Secretary found no grounds for interfering with the sentence of death."[110] One is left with the impression that the commission was willing, by way of the royal prerogative and jury discretion, to drive the death penalty into complete abeyance.

This was particularly true of Sir Alexander Maxwell, that "sincere, and even passionate liberal," in Robert Pittam's assessment.[111] On one issue after the next, Maxwell led the charge to restrict the scope of the death penalty, typically in opposition to the stance taken by Dr. Radzinowicz, whose views were not without merit. Radzinowicz opposed raising the age limit to 21 "both because the sentence ought not in principle to be determined automatically by the age of the offender and because most atrocious crimes were sometimes committed by offenders between 18 and 21."[112] Each case, he argued, ought to be considered on its merits, whether by jury or Home Secretary. Maxwell recognized the difficulty of drawing a rigid line at a particular age, but "he did not feel that the raising of the age would so seriously impair the deterrent effect of capital punishment as to outweigh the

---

109 Ibid., CP (19th meeting), 1 Mar. 1951.
110 Ibid., CP (21st meeting), 5–6 Jul. 1951.
111 Pittam, *Home Office, 1782–1982* (1981), p. 8.
112 Between 1936 and 1956, 53 persons (48 male, five female) between the ages of 18 and 21 at the time of the crime were sentenced to death for murder, or about 10 per cent of all murder convictions. Of the 53, 37 were reprieved, three were removed to Broadmoor, and 13 were executed. Thirty-five had been recommended to mercy by the jury, of whom 27 were reprieved, one was sent to Broadmoor, and seven were executed. See TNA, HO291/104.

advantages of relieving young offenders from the liability to be sentenced to death." Here was one way of limiting the scope of the death penalty, without impairing the deterrent value of capital punishment.[113] Ultimately, the commission split on raising the age limit, six in favour, five against.

In answer to the question whether the M'Naghten rules in practice exempted from responsibility all those who ought to be so exempted, Radzinowicz declared that the rules did not result in injustice. At the most there should be an extension of the rules, not their complete abrogation, which anyway the judges would strongly oppose. Maxwell begged to differ:

> . . . the position seemed to be that Judges applied the M'Naghten Rules only when they themselves considered that the prisoner was sane but were afraid that the jury would find him insane. There could be no justification for applying the Rules in this way; the sole result was to confuse the jury and prevent them from hearing the truth about the prisoner's state of mind from the medical witnesses.[114]

A set of rules defining what degree of insanity rendered a person irresponsible would be convenient, for sure, but it was impracticable to frame one. The jury should decide the issue of irresponsibility on the facts of each case, said Maxwell, "unfettered and unguided by any legal yard stick." The M'Naghten Rules should be abrogated, replaced by the simple formula: "that the accused was by reason of insanity or mental deficiency not responsible for his actions at the time of the act or omission with which he is charged."[115]

According to Radzinowicz in his 1999 memoir, "at no time during these four years did any member give the slightest hint whether, in the light of our proceedings and inquiries, he or she was moving in the direction of endorsing the abolitionist or the retentionist cause."[116] This is highly improbable. It was well known that Dr. Slater favoured abolition. Alexander Maxwell was thought to be "at heart" abolitionist as early as 1948, and we have seen with what force he pressed the royal commission to restrict the scope of the death penalty. On the other side, no one could have been in any doubt that Mr. Fox-Andrews believed in the deterrent efficacy of capital punishment and was content with the status quo. Nor does Sir Leon's declaration square with Gowers' comment to Terence Morris and Louis Blom-Cooper that "throughout the entire period of the Commission's

113 TNA, HO301/2, CP (26th meeting), 6–7 Mar. 1952; CP (27th meeting), 3–4 Apr. 1952; TNA, HO301/7, CP (Conclusions) 11: Persons under 21 years of age, memo by Mr. Radzinowicz.

114 Ibid., CP (17th meeting), 4–5 Jan. 1951, Criminal responsibility and the M'Naghten Rules; CP (28th meeting), 1–2 May 1952, Insanity and Mental Abnormality.

115 Ibid. The commission endorsed their previous decision (CP 21st meeting) to recommend that the M'Naghten Rules be abrogated and that a simple formula in terms similar to those suggested by Maxwell should be substituted.

116 *Adventures*, op cit., p. 259.

work Radzinowicz had been alone amongst its members in never giving the least hint of where he stood on the issue of abolition."[117] This suggests Radzinowicz was the only member to keep his powder dry. As for Gowers himself, he told Bishop Bell in January 1953 that having started the inquiry without a strong opinion either way, he ended it "as a whole-hearted abolitionist—not emotionally but intellectually." He did not go public with his conversion, however, until 1956 in *A Life for a Life?* [118]

The commissioners' deliberations finally reveal how they negotiated the terms of reference and conceived of the central problem confronting them, which in turn dictated the shape and content of the report they presented in September 1953, four years and four months after the appointment of the commission. This can be encapsulated as follows: the commission's terms of reference had specifically precluded them from considering the fundamental question whether capital punishment should be abolished. This had placed them in a delicate and artificial position. They were asked to find a halfway house between the existing position and the abolition of capital punishment. Yet the application of the death penalty had already been so greatly restricted that there was little scope for further limitation. Murder was an anomaly in English law, in that it was the only offence for which the courts had no power to fit the punishment to the individual crime. Such an anomaly could be justified only if all murders were homogeneous, but all murders were not homogeneous, and the public did not require the imposition of the most severe punishment in all cases. In practice, the anomaly was corrected by administrative action, but such action had serious defects, most notably the discrepancy between the number of persons sentenced to death and the number executed, and the use of the royal prerogative, not as an exceptional remedy but virtually as an additional court of appeal. How, then, to remedy the defects?

IX

The commission recommended certain minor alterations in the existing system—namely that the sentence of death should not be passed on anyone under 21 years of age; that the M'Naghten Rules should either be abrogated (leaving the jury to determine whether a person was sufficiently mad or mentally defective to be held irresponsible for the act) or enlarged to cover cases "where the accused, as a result of insanity or mental deficiency, did not know the nature and quality of the act, or did not know that it was wrong, or was unable to prevent himself from committing it," the formula proposed by the British Medical Association; and also that the Home Secretary should give greater weight to the consideration of epilepsy and psychopathy in exercising the royal prerogative.[119]

---

117 T. Morris, "British Criminology: 1935–48," *British Journal of Criminology*, vol. 28 (1988), p. 32, note 30.
118 Gowers, *A Life for a Life? The Problem of Capital Punishment* (1956), p. 8.
119 RCCP, chap. 10, Final Conclusions, p. 213.

Four more radical solutions were also examined, three of them being rejected, namely classifying murders in order to confine the death penalty to the most heinous ("the object of our quest is chimerical and . . . it must be abandoned," said the report); enacting a narrower statutory definition of murder; and giving judges a discretion to choose death or a lesser sentence. Only the fourth solution—to give discretion to the jury to decide in each case whether there were such extenuating circumstances as to justify a lesser sentence than death—was thought to stand the slightest chance of eliminating the existing defects of the law.[120] A jury finding of extenuating circumstances would preclude the judge from passing sentence of death. The result of the recommendation would be to reduce the number of cases in which a person convicted of murder was sentenced to death and subsequently reprieved. It would also "enable the wide differences in moral guilt to be determined by the Court as a matter of right instead of by the executive as a matter of grace," in Gerald Gardiner's words.[121] The commission "embraced this idea with about as much enthusiasm as a man embracing a hedgehog," in J. E. Hall Williams' words.[122] If the merits of this proposal were thought to be outweighed by its disadvantages, the report stated, in a sentence first crafted by Radzinowicz,

> the conclusion to our mind would be inescapable that in this country a stage has been reached where little more can be done effectively to limit the liability to suffer the death penalty, and that the real issue is now whether capital punishment should be retained or abolished.[123]

This was an issue for Parliament and the nation. And this was, Christoph correctly concluded, "the closest the Royal Commission came to allowing the uninvited guest [the abolitionist] to take his place at the head of the council table."[124]

How was the 500-page report (including 200 pages of statistical tables and appendices) and the 89 recommendations and conclusions greeted publicly, and what impact did the royal commission have upon the capital punishment debate? The criminal lawyers and criminologists of the day were not uncritical of the report,[125] but Edward Glover concluded, ". . . never in the history of penological

---

120 Ibid., p. 214; TNA, HO301/2, CP (30th meeting), 3–4 Jul. 1952.
121 Gardiner, "A Symposium on the Report of the Royal Commission on Capital Punishment: Legal Aspects," *British Journal of Delinquency*, vol. 4 (1954), p. 161.
122 Williams, "Report of the Royal Commission on Capital Punishment, 1949–1953," *Modern Law Review*, vol. 17 (1954), p. 63.
123 RCCP, chap. 10, Final Conclusions, p. 214; Radzinowicz, *Adventures*, op cit., p. 265. For Radzinowicz's influence on the arrangement of the report, see TNA, HO301/2, CP (23rd meeting), 1–2 Nov. 1951; Ibid., CP (31st meeting), 7–8 Aug. 1952. See also RCCP, chap. 14, Summary of Conclusions and Recommendations, pp. 274–83.
124 Christoph, op cit., p. 88.
125 Hermann Mannheim remarked, "[The report] has made hardly any contribution to our knowledge of the crime of murder." See "A Symposium on the Report of the Royal Commission on Capital Punishment: Concluding Remarks," *British Journal of Delinquency*, vol. 4 (1954), p. 171. Cf. Radzinowicz's acceptance of this criticism: *Adventures*, op cit., p. 263.

literature has such a devastating indictment of capital punishment been set before the public that is ultimately responsible for its maintenance." Terence Morris waxed more lyrical still: the Gowers' report "ranks as one of the great social documents of our age . . . which in both language and scholarship is easily the equal of any of the great Victorian 'blue books.'"[126] These statements have the ring of special pleading. They were excessive praise for a report that was renowned more for what it did not recommend—the abolition of the death penalty—than for what it did, and for proposals that ranged from the technical to the recondite, the bulk of which were destined to have only a marginal impact on the administration of the death penalty. A more sober response, but none the worse for that, came from H. L. A. Hart, professor of jurisprudence at Oxford:

> What then is the upshot of the mass of information assembled in this Report? It seems to me to be this. The Report shows that the death penalty is a clumsy instrument; and that we use it very largely in the dark. It is clumsy because its use by the law courts is only made tolerable by an anomaly, the intervention in nearly half the cases by the executive. And we use it in the dark because there is no evidence that it has the desired effect on our social life.[127]

Moreover, the royal commission effectively silenced the national debate on capital punishment for close to five years, during which time 84 people were hanged in England and Wales, all the time giving the stage to witnesses who reaffirmed the denunciatory and deterrent necessity of capital punishment, who attacked the use of executive clemency and the frequency of reprieves, and who claimed, as *The Times* opined, "we have little to reproach ourselves with about the way in which the community uses [the gallows]."[128] What we now know to be the last gasps of judicial resistance to abolition were on full display. The Lord Chief Justice was against raising the age of execution of youths from 18 to 21; saw no reason not to hang women; and was in favour of retaining the black cap: "I think you want to make it a very solemn occasion, and I think those things which emphasise the solemnity of the occasion are all to the good." For the Archbishop of Canterbury, the death penalty served a quasi-religious function of denouncing wrongdoing. There is merit in the view that the commission at least passed the buck back to Parliament with the rider that the present law was incapable of amendment except through abolition. But this was to lead to Churchill's Conservative government delaying even discussing the content of the report, let alone acting upon the

---

126 Glover, "A Symposium on the Report of the Royal Commission on Capital Punishment: Psychiatric Aspects," *British Journal of Delinquency*, vol. 4 (1954), p. 168; T. Morris and L. Blom-Cooper, *A Calendar of Murder: Criminal Homicide in England since 1957* (1964), dedication; Morris, *Crime and Criminal Justice since 1945* (Oxford, 1989), p. 87, note 25; Morris quoted in Ann Scott, *Ernest Gowers*, op cit., p. 154.
127 Hart, "Capital Punishment: A review of the argument," Third Programme, broadcast 6 Jan. 1956, enclosed in TNA, HO291/98.
128 *The Times*, 24 Sep. 1953, p. 7.

commission's recommendations, so frightened was it of allowing the genie of abolition out of the parliamentary bottle. The government's refusal to act on the report led Cabinet Secretary, Norman Brook, to say to Prime Minister Churchill, "The work of this Royal Commission occupied 4½ years and cost £23,000 . . . [and] seems to have been a lamentable waste of public time and money."[129] Christoph was surely right to conclude: " . . . the activities of the Royal Commission on Capital Punishment would not have been sufficient to excite public or Parliamentary attention in such a way as to bring about changes in basic attitudes."[130]

X

During these years of political stalemate over the royal commission's report, it was three individual murder cases—those of Timothy Evans, Derek Bentley, and Ruth Ellis—that brought the death penalty to public, press, and parliamentary attention, to the point that public support for the death penalty momentarily ebbed. Indeed, it is arguable that these three cases, plus the work of the newly-formed National Campaign for the Abolition of Capital Punishment, did more to revive abolitionist sentiment than the royal commission ever did. Above all, the royal prerogative of mercy was manifestly found wanting between 1953 and 1955.

On 10 March 1950, *The Times* contained the following news in brief:

> Timothy John Evans, 25, lorry driver, of Rillington Place, Notting Hill, W., was executed yesterday at Pentonville, for the murder of Geraldine, his 14-months-old daughter, on December 2. Evans was sentenced to death at the Central Criminal Court on January 13.[131]

Evans was convicted of the murder of his daughter; a charge of murdering his wife was not proceeded with, though evidence for both murders was considered in his trial. The state's chief witness had been John Reginald Christie, who lived in the same house.[132] In one of his statements, Evans had accused Christie of killing Mrs. Evans. As Philip Allen, Assistant Secretary, informed the secretary of the Royal Commission on Capital Punishment, an informal medical inquiry was held:

> there is no suggestion that Evans is certifiably insane, but the circumstances of the crime are such that the Secretary of State wishes to know more about his mental condition before deciding whether there are grounds for recommending a reprieve.[133]

129 PREM 11/1241, Brook to Prime Minister, 30 Jul. 1954.
130 Christoph, op cit., p. 92.
131 *The Times*, 10 Mar. 1950, p. 3.
132 Ludovic Kennedy, revised by Robert Brown, "Christie, John Reginald Halliday (1899–1953)," *Oxford DNB* (2012).
133 TNA, HO301/2, CP (15th meeting), 7–8 Sep. 1950; TNA, HO45/25645, Allen, 1 Mar. 1950.

Home Secretary Ede refused to grant a reprieve. Three years later, and shortly before the publication of the report of the royal commission, the bodies of six women were discovered in John Christie's ground-floor flat and backyard. One of the bodies was Christie's wife. Christie was arrested and confessed to the six murders. He also admitted that he had strangled Mrs. Evans, but denied murdering the Evans' baby. On 25 June 1953, Christie was sentenced to death.[134] As newspaper editor, Harold Evans, no relation, wrote many years later:

> If Timothy Evans and John Christie were both killers, we were being asked to accept that there were two stranglers of women in the same two-up, two-down house, operating independently and in ignorance of one another. Both men used the same method of strangulation . . . Both confessed to "using a piece of rope," and not just any piece of rope but one "off a chair." Both disposed of the strangling ligature; both concealed their victims' bodies; both temporarily used the same place of concealment; both wrapped their victims' bodies in blankets; both left them without shoes; both left them without underclothing.[135]

Parliamentary concern at the possibility of a miscarriage of justice led the Home Secretary, Sir David Maxwell Fyfe, to appoint John Scott Henderson, QC, to inquire into both cases. The inquiry was held in private, and took only one week, since Christie was awaiting execution. It concluded that there had been no miscarriage of justice. Evans was responsible for the murder of *both* his child and his wife. Christie's statement that he had murdered Mrs. Evans was said to be untrue.[136] A day later Christie was hanged. Many considered Scott Henderson's report to be a whitewash, and several books appeared asserting Evans's innocence.[137] In the Commons' debate on the Henderson report, Geoffrey Bing quite reasonably asserted that if it had been known at Evans' trial that Christie, the principal witness, had already murdered two women, hidden their bodies temporarily in the very washhouse where Evans was accused of hiding the bodies (subsequently burying them in the garden), "Evans would have been bound to be acquitted."[138] In the Commons debate on capital punishment in February 1955, former Labour Home Secretary, Chuter Ede, entered the stunning admission that he would "have given a different decision on the exercise of the prerogative of mercy," had he known of the other bodies hidden in 10 Rillington Place. He added, "I hope no future Home Secretary

---

134 See Jerry White, *London in the Twentieth Century* (2001), p. 271; Frank Mort, *Capital Affairs: London and the Making of the Permissive Society* (New Haven, 2010), chap. 3, esp. pp. 104–38.

135 Harold Evans, *My Paper Chase* (New York, 2009), pp. 293–4. Cf. Christoph, op cit., pp. 101–2.

136 TNA, HO291/104.

137 R. T. Paget and S. Silverman, *Hanged—and Innocent?* (1953); Michael Eddowes, *The Man on Your Conscience* (1955). See also Peter Richards, *Parliament and Conscience* (1970), p. 44; Christoph, op cit., pp. 102–3.

138 *Hansard*, vol. 518, 29 Jul. 1953, col. 1437.

will ever have to feel that, although he did his best, in fact, he sent a man who was not guilty as charged, to the gallows."[139] Ede's words, the *Daily Express* reported, "fell with shattering emphasis on MPs' ears." Michael Foot wrote in the *Daily Herald* a week later, Ede's assertion "should have made even the most barefaced defender of the death penalty squirm."[140] The Evans case shook the popular belief in the infallibility of English justice. This was important, since the execution of the innocent was the factor most likely to deprive the death penalty of its moral force and legal justification.

On 3 November 1952, Christopher Craig, aged 16, and Derek Bentley, aged 19, broke into a warehouse in Croydon. A gun battle with the London police ensued, during which Craig killed P. C. Miles, the shot that killed him being fired fifteen minutes *after* Bentley had been taken into custody. Both youths were found guilty of murder, Bentley on the grounds of constructive malice, the legal expedient whereby a party to a common purpose must assume common responsibility for anything that occurs in the course of pursuing that purpose. The jury recommended mercy for Bentley. Craig, under 18, the legal age for hanging, was sentenced to life imprisonment; for Bentley, Goddard put on his black cap and sent him to the gallows.[141] Goddard's clerk, Arthur Smith, later insisted that Goddard was "profoundly distressed" when Bentley was not reprieved.[142] This hardly squares with Goddard's behaviour. On the day after the trial, Goddard wrote to the Home Secretary:

> . . . I regret to say I could find no mitigating circumstances in Bentley's case. He was armed with a knuckle-duster of the most formidable type that I have ever seen and also with a sharp pointed knife and he called out to Craig when he was arrested to start shooting.[143]

It is true that the general expectation was that Bentley would be granted a reprieve. There were many reasons in the case for the use of the royal prerogative: his youth (barely over the legal age for hanging); his mental condition (he was rejected by the army as a Grade 4 Mentally Deficient, and had a history of epilepsy); he was under arrest when the fatal shot was fired; and, finally, accomplices were never executed unless the principal (in this case Craig) was executed too.[144] However, the murder had occurred during a moral panic over youthful criminal violence. It was commonly alleged in the press that the authorities were indifferent to the present crime wave.[145] Also the victim was a policeman. The question throughout the country now became, "Should Bentley hang?"[146]

139 *Hansard*, vol. 536, 10 Feb. 1955, col. 2084. See K. Jefferys, "Ede, James Chuter Chuter-, Baron Chuter-Ede (1882–1965)," *Oxford DNB* (2008).
140 *Daily Herald*, 18 Feb. 1955, enclosed in TNA, HO291/94.
141 See Anthony Mockler, *Lions Under the Throne* (1983), pp. 284–5.
142 Smith, *Lord Goddard: My Years with the Lord Chief Justice* (1959), p. 166.
143 TNA, HO291/225, Goddard to Home Secretary, 12 Dec. 1952.
144 See Christoph, op cit., pp. 98–9.
145 See TNA, PREM 11/350.
146 Harry Hopkins, *The New Look: A Social History of the Forties and Fifties in Britain* (1963), p. 215.

At the time, it was unknown why the Home Secretary, David Maxwell Fyfe, had refused a reprieve, a decision announced on 26 January 1953, which, he later wrote, "brought down on my head a storm of vituperation without parallel in my career."[147] Thousands of letters poured into the Home Office and the House of Commons, the majority against the Home Secretary's decision. About 80,000 people wrote to the Bentley family deploring the verdict.[148] The most we learn from Maxwell Fyfe's memoirs is: "In the Bentley case I had the additional question of the possible effects of my decision upon the police force, by whom the murder of a police officer is justly regarded as the most heinous of crimes."[149] It was a familiar argument that England's unarmed police force needed the deterrent threat of the gallows. In 2003, criminologist Nigel Walker said that the Scottish Office was shocked at the refusal to commute Bentley's death sentence, and they had blamed Newsam, the permanent head of the Home Office "who was more reluctant than Cunningham [permanent head in the Scottish Office] to interfere with death sentences." Later, wrote Walker, Kenneth Clarke told the Commons "that Maxwell Fyfe had been advised by his civil servants not to let Bentley be hanged, but had overridden them."[150] To judge from the official papers this is evidently the case. On 16 January, Newsam minuted,

> This is a very difficult case . . . The precedents indicate that mercy would not be out of place in this case. But it is of course possible to take a different view having regard to the present prevalence of crimes of violence. My own view is towards leniency but S of S will no doubt wish to discuss before coming to a decision.

On the same day, Philip Allen reviewed the case, emphasizing Bentley's youth, and the fact that he did not attack the police or try to escape from them and rejoin Craig. Allen concluded,

> Shocking though this murder was, it is suggested that it would on the whole be right to give effect to the jury's recommendation to mercy, principally on the ground . . . that it would not seem right to exact the extreme penalty from the accomplice when the principal offender is escaping with his life.

He finally queried, "Respite and commute to imprisonment for life?"[151] On 22 January, Maxwell Fyfe wrote,

---

147 *Political Adventure: The Memoirs of the Earl of Kilmuir* (1964), p. 207. See also D. J. Dutton, "Fyfe, David Patrick Maxwell, earl of Kilmuir (1900–67)," *Oxford DNB* (2004).

148 TNA, PCom9/2312.

149 *Political Adventure*, p. 206. See also Fenton Bresler, *Lord Goddard* (1977), p. 257.

150 Nigel Walker, *A Man Without Loyalties: A Penologist's Afterthoughts* (Chichester, 2003), p. 81.

151 TNA, HO291/225, Newsam, 16 Jan.; Allen, 16 Jan. 1953. See Brian Cubbon, "Allen, Philip (1912–2007)," *Oxford DNB* (2011).

After anxiously weighing all these considerations, and after consulting the trial judge, I have come to the conclusion that there are not sufficient grounds to justify me in recommending any interference with the due course of the law. I have therefore decided that the law must take its course.[152]

The Opposition in the Commons sought a motion urging the Home Secretary to reconsider his position of declining to reprieve Bentley, but the Speaker ruled that "while a capital sentence is pending, the matter should not be discussed in the House." Silverman had already interjected, "Is the House to wait until Bentley is dead before it is entitled to say that he should not die?" R. T. Paget was even more indignant,

A three-quarter-witted boy of 19 is to be hanged for a murder he did not commit, and which was committed 15 minutes after he was arrested. Can we be made to keep silent when a thing as horrible and as shocking as this is to happen?[153]

Bentley was executed in Wandsworth Prison on 28 January 1953.[154] Forty-five years after the execution, in 1998, three Court of Appeal judges quashed the conviction, Lord Bingham, the Lord Chief Justice, ruling that Goddard's summing up had been "a highly rhetorical and strongly-worded denunciation of both defendants and of their defences." And, "the summing up in this case was such as to deny the appellant that fair trial which is the birthright of every British citizen."[155] The case also gave the lie to Sir John Anderson's statement in the 1948 debate on capital punishment that a reprieve was granted whenever there was "a scintilla of doubt."[156]

In the case of Ruth Ellis, the question at issue was not her guilt, but the appropriateness of the punishment. On Easter Sunday, April 28, 1955, Ellis, 28 years of age, a divorcee with two small children, waited outside a Hampstead pub in London for her lover, David Blakely, by whom she had been made pregnant, and whom she believed had been unfaithful to her. When he appeared, she shot him four times. At her trial the defence contended that the crime was committed without malice and under provocation. Thirteen days before the shooting, Ellis was hit in the stomach by Blakely, causing a miscarriage. A psychiatrist testifying for the defence described the murder as a crime of

---

152 Ibid., Maxwell Fyfe, 22 Jan. 1953. See also Stevens, *Law and Politics*, op cit., p. 424.
153 CAB 128/26, CC (53) 5th conclusions, 27 Jan. 1953; *Hansard*, vol. 510, 27 Jan. 1953, cols. 848, 851.
154 In late 1965, Roy Jenkins agreed to the re-burial of Bentley's body, which had been asked for when he was first executed: TNA, PCom9/2312.
155 *Regina v Derek William Bentley* (Deceased), Court of Appeal, Criminal Division, 30 Jul. 1998, transcript of Smith Bernal Reporting Ltd; *The Times*, 31 Jul. 1998, p. 41. See also K. B. Bucknall, "Derek William Bentley (1933–1953)," *Oxford DNB* (2004).
156 John Wheeler-Bennett, *John Anderson: Viscount Waverley* (New York, 1962), p. 388.

passion. Ellis, however, refused to plead insanity. On the other side, the prosecution (and the press initially) put rather more emphasis upon her job as a nightclub hostess in the seedier part of Mayfair, her platinum blonde looks, and her drinking habits. As for the judge, Sir Cecil Havers, he instructed the jury that insufficient evidence existed to reduce the crime from murder to manslaughter, and refused to allow counsel to argue provocation as a defence.[157] She was convicted of murder and sent to the gallows. The Home Secretary, Gwilym Lloyd George, was pressed to use the prerogative. Hundreds of letters poured into the Home Office appealing for a reprieve; some were petitions containing multiple signatures. One appeal was from Dr. Mary Kidd who presented findings on the pre-menstrual syndrome.[158] Hanging a woman was rare. Only 13 had been hanged since 1900; over 90 per cent were reprieved. At the last minute, new evidence appeared indicating that she had been drinking with another admirer, Desmond Cussen, who had handed her the loaded gun, and driven her to the scene of the murder. A stay of execution would have been in order while the new evidence was examined, but such was not granted.[159] Ruth Ellis was executed on 13 July 1955, the last woman to be executed, as it turned out. Outside Holloway Prison, large crowds gathered behind a large police cordon, one section of the crowd chanting "Evans-Bentley-Ellis."[160] The public and the press, especially the *Spectator* under Ian Gilmour's editorship, had by now decided that the case for a reprieve was overwhelming.[161]

The Home Office had been unmoved. On 4 July, nine days before the execution, Assistant Undersecretary of State, Philip Allen, had minuted,

> A serious view has always been taken of the deliberate use of firearms in this country to commit crime; and it is difficult to see what extenuating features there are in this case to warrant a merciful view being taken of this premeditated shooting.

On the next day, Sir Frank Newsam, Permanent Undersecretary of State, declared,

> I have considered this case very carefully and I regret to say that I can find no sufficiently extenuating circumstances to justify leniency. It would be a bad day for this country if we adopted the doctrine of crime passionel.

---

157 See Jane Dunn, "Ruth Ellis (1926–1955)," *Oxford DNB* (2004); David Kynaston, *Family Britain 1951–57*, op cit., p. 489; J. Minkes and M. Vanstone, "Gender, Race and the Death Penalty: Lessons from Three 1950s Murder Trials," *Howard Journal* , vol. 45 (2006), pp. 416–18.
158 TNA, HO291/236. Also HO291/237 and 238.
159 See *Guardian*, 19 Jan. 1999, p. 3.
160 *The Times*, 13 Jul. 1955, p. 8.
161 See Simon Courtauld, *To Convey Intelligence: The Spectator, 1928–1998* (1999), pp. 35–7; *Spectator*, 15 Jul. 1955, pp. 81–2; ibid., 22 Jul. 1955, p. 110.

On 11 July, the Home Secretary, Gwilym Lloyd-George, presented his conclusions:

> There may be circumstances in a capital case where special considerations apply to a woman which would not be applicable in the case of a man. [No reference was made at this point to Ellis' miscarriage] . . . I can find no such special circumstances, however, in the present case. The crime was a pre-meditated one and was carried out with deliberation. The prisoner has expressed no remorse . . . [He had consulted the trial judge.] He told me that he was unable to suggest any mitigating circumstances . . . If a reprieve were granted in this case, I think that we should have seriously to consider whether capital punishment should be retained as a penalty.
>
> After much anxious thought I have come to the conclusion that this is a case in which the law should be allowed to take its course.[162]

"The outcry against the execution of Ruth Ellis," wrote executioner, Albert Pierre-point, 20 years later, "was the last great sentimental protest against capital punishment in Great Britain."[163] So great was the public trauma over the case that it moved the needle, albeit temporarily, in favour of abolition. The Gallup Polls indicate that in October 1953, a few months after the Christie execution, 73 per cent wished to retain the death penalty, only 15 per cent wanted abolition. By July 1955, following Ellis's execution, the percentage wishing to retain the penalty fell to 50 per cent, with 37 per cent favouring abolition.[164] *Picture Post* decided to launch a new campaign, "the largest and longest they have conducted on any subject and will last at least a year if hanging does not end before."[165] Abroad, the execution produced a feeling of deep revulsion towards England. R. M. A. Hankey wrote from the British Embassy in Stockholm to Foreign Secretary, Harold Macmillan, to report,

> that the repugnance with which Swedish public opinion regards capital pun-ishment . . . has again been manifested on the occasion of the hanging of Mrs. Ruth Ellis . . . The campaign in the press has been quite exceptionally vio-lent—indeed I can think of no issue since I arrived in March 1954, which has given rise to comparable criticism of our policy or institutions . . . Capital punishment is looked upon as a blot upon a noble escutcheon.[166]

162 TNA, HO291/235: Allen, 4 Jul.; Newsam, 5 Jul.; Lloyd-George, 11 Jul. 1955.
163 Pierrepoint, *Executioner: Pierrepoint* (1974), p. 207. See also L. Seal, "Ruth Ellis and Public Contestation of the Death Penalty," *Howard Journal of Criminal Justice*, vol. 50 (2011), p. 493.
164 *Gallup International* (1976), vol. 1, p. 308; TNA, HO291/98, letter from Public Rela-tions Office; *News Chronicle*, 22 Jul. 1955, enclosed in HO291/94.
165 TNA, HO291/92, David Linton to Lloyd-George, 15 Jan. 1956.
166 TNA, HO291/94, Hankey to Macmillan, 19 Jul. 1955. Many years later, Bernard Levin thundered, "the decision not to commute her sentence was probably the grossest single injustice done by the Home Office in modern times . . ." in *The Times*, 31 Mar. 1987. In 2003, Ellis's sister asked the Court of Appeal to quash the murder conviction and

Within a month of Ruth Ellis' execution, a new National Campaign for the Abolition of Capital Punishment (NCACP) was formed. In July 1955, Arthur Koestler suggested to Victor Gollancz that they collaborate in founding a national campaign, and launch a full-scale assault upon the death penalty.[167] Koestler, born into a Hungarian Jewish family, was a novelist, journalist, and critic, best known for his anti-totalitarian novel, *Darkness at Noon*. He had personal experience of waiting in prison for execution in 1937 during the Spanish Civil War (see *Dialogue with Death*). Victor Gollancz was a renowned progressive publisher, organizer of the Left Book Club, described in an *Observer* profile as "a passionate moralist, an ardent and non-denominational Christian and a socialist of ethical rather than utilitarian enthusiasm."[168] At the first meeting of the executive committee on 11 August, Koestler and Gollancz were joined by Canon John Collins of Christian Action, the latter describing himself as "a kind of gadfly within the Churches,"[169] Gerald Gardiner QC, a future Labour Lord Chancellor, and Reginald Paget, MP. This new crusade was clearly the child of left-wing or pacifist figures.[170] Hugh Klare, secretary of the Howard League, was present in an advisory capacity only, since the League did not wish to damage its other penal reform work by directly associating itself with a no-holds-barred propaganda campaign.[171] Sydney Silverman was kept off the committee since he and Gollancz were at daggers drawn.[172] On 25 August, Gollancz as chairman wrote to the press announcing the national campaign, which would be largely educational: books and pamphlets "covered in fierce yellow" would be published and distributed, large public meetings organized, letters sent to the press and MPs, and appearances on radio and television—and partly one of creating opportunities for abolitionists to express their conscience, such as abstaining from any entertainment on the eve of an execution.[173] These latter projects were never employed since no executions were held from the campaign's inception until the passage of the 1957 Homicide Act. The NCACP was more of a pressure group than a mass movement, despite the title it took. By the end of 1955, 17,000 had declared their support; by February 1956, the number had reached over 26,000. Its first large-scale public activity was a meeting at the Central Hall, Westminster, on 10 November 1955, with Gerald Gardiner as the main speaker. By January 1956, Gollancz was telling *Picture Post* readers that capital punishment would be abolished during 1956 "provided that abolitionists pull their full weight."[174]

substitute a verdict of manslaughter on the grounds of provocation and/or diminished responsibility. The appeal was rejected.

167 John Grigg, "The Do-Gooder from Seville Gaol," in Harold Harris, *Astride the Two Cultures: Arthur Koestler at 70* (New York, 1976), p. 125.

168 "Profile," *Observer*, 11 Mar. 1956, p. 4. See also Sheila Hodges, "Gollancz, Sir Victor (1893–1967)," *Oxford DNB* (2004).

169 Canon John Collins, *Faith Under Fire* (1966), p. 119.

170 Nigel Nicolson, *People and Parliament* (Westport, 1958; reprint 1974), p. 87.

171 Iain Hamilton, *Koestler: A Biography* (1982), p. 260.

172 David Cesarani, *Arthur Koestler: The Homeless Mind* (1999), p. 434.

173 *Manchester Guardian*, 25 Aug. 1955, letter from Gollancz, enclosed in HO291/94. See also Enid Jones, *Margery Fry: The Essential Amateur* (1966), p. 235; Christoph, op cit., pp. 113–15.

174 *Picture Post*, 7 Jan. 1956, p. 5, enclosed in TNA, HO291/92; Peggy Duff, *Left, Left, Left: A Personal Account of Six Protest Campaigns 1945–65* (1971), p. 107.

In addition, Gollancz rushed into print with a small tract, *Capital Punishment: The Heart of the Matter* (1955), which ignored empirical arguments about the statistics of deterrence in favour of a religious or moral appeal, what he called the "absolute" case against capital punishment.[175] Gerald Gardiner wrote *Capital Punishment as a Deterrent and the Alternative* (1956), a reasoned, logical, and convincing analysis of the weaknesses of the case in support of the death penalty.[176] The trinity was completed by Koestler's *Reflections on Hanging* (1957), a passionate and polemical indictment of the death penalty and its judicial defenders, notably his *bete noir*, Lord Goddard.[177] Koestler's biographer, Iain Hamilton, observed that disrespectful things had been said about the judiciary before, "but never quite so stingingly, so woundingly, with such a disgraceful lack of respect for a sacred 'tradition.'"[178]*Reflections* reached a wide audience via serialization in the *Observer* in early 1956, before publication in April. Ian Gilmour gave it a friendly review in the *Spectator*, noting that Koestler "dewigs the judges with entertaining ruthlessness," concluding with: "Two months ago Mr. Gerald Gardiner slaughtered the case for capital punishment; Mr. Koestler now dances on its grave."[179] The book was followed by a compilation, by Koestler and Cynthia Jefferies, of the case-histories of those executed between 1949 and 1953, published in the *Observer* on 14 April under Koestler's pseudonym of Vigil, later as a pamphlet, *Patterns of Murder*. It was a familiar catalogue, wrote John Grigg, of "people caught in tragic personal circumstances, acting under the stress of sudden violent emotion."[180]

XI

The Royal Commission on Capital Punishment pulled together a mass of information about the death penalty: the frequency of executions, the superiority of hanging over alternative methods of execution, the range of murders a single penalty had to satisfy, and the workings of the royal prerogative. In the teeth of much of the evidence from judicial and clerical witnesses, the commission's report paid little attention to the "moralist" issues of retribution and denunciation. And it advised against basing "a penal policy in relation to murder on exaggerated estimates of the uniquely deterrent force of the death penalty."[181] In its recommendations, the commission put forward ways in which the law of

175 Ruth Dudley Edwards, *Victor Gollancz: A Biography* (1987), p. 639; Potter, *Hanging in Judgment*, op cit., p. 170.

176 Asa Briggs, "Time and the Rope," *Observer*, 26 Feb. 1956, p. 10.

177 *The Times*, 8 Jul. 1983, in Rolph papers, 1/4/3; Potter, op cit., p. 171.

178 Hamilton, *Koestler*, op cit., p. 270.

179 *Spectator*, 13 Apr. 1956, pp. 502–4.

180 Hamilton, op cit. p. 262; Arthur and Cynthia Koestler, *Stranger on the Square* (1984), p. 221; Grigg, "The Do-Gooder," op cit., p. 127.

181 RCCP, paras. 55–68 of the report, and Appendix 6 (pp. 328–80); para quoted in Christoph, *Capital Punishment and British Politics*, op cit., p. 86. See also TNA, HO291/ 1020, Capital Punishment as a Deterrent. Wrote Gowers, American criminologist, Thorsten Sellin, "was easily the most sensible and knowledgeable witness we had" on the justification of capital punishment. See Beveridge Papers, VI/53, Gowers to Beveridge, 27 Mar. 1956. Sellin could find no answer one way or the other in the data on

murder could be improved and the death penalty modified. It gathered evidence from a wide range of mandarins, judges, bishops, and penal reformers, evidence that left no doubt of the enduring conviction, notably within the judicial fraternity, that the gallows could not be dispensed with. Of course, the royal commission could not pass judgment on the only issue of political import, abolition. As H. L. A. Hart told his radio audience,

> It will be remembered that the Commission's terms of reference actually postulated the retention of the death penalty. They had to consider not the general question, whether it should be abolished but whether the use of it should be limited.[182]

How influential was its report likely to be, if it could offer no judgment on the retention or abolition of the penalty itself? Yet the report recommended abandoning the grading of murders, what it called the "chimerical" quest to confine the death penalty to the most heinous murders. And between the lines of the report ran the conclusion, evident to all, that the outer limits of restricting to what and to whom the death penalty should apply had been reached, and the only question for Parliament and the country to decide was that of abolition. For five years, however, the royal commission deflected parliamentary and public attention from the question of abolition, and its report was too nuanced to change public opinion or spur parliamentary activity. The mobilization of public opinion against hanging was motivated much more by engagement with personal cases. Emotions aroused by the individual execution was far more compelling, and the refrain of "Evans-Bentley-Ellis" a more effective rallying cry for the abolitionist cause.

the deterrent effect of the death penalty. His conclusions were hailed as a victory by abolitionists.
182 See Hart, "Capital Punishment: A Review of the Argument," Third Programme talk, broadcast on 6 Jan. 1956, enclosed in TNA, HO291/98.

8

PENAL PRACTICE IN A CHANGING SOCIETY

A fundamental re-examination of penal methods, based on studies of the causes of crime, or rather of the factors which foster or inhibit crime, and supported by a reliable assessment of the results achieved by existing methods, could be a landmark in penal history and illumine the course ahead for a generation. Such a re-examination . . . need not—and indeed should not—be purely pragmatic. If it were not merely to assess past progress, but also to point the way forward, it must concern itself with the philosophy as well as the practice of punishment.

Penal Practice in a Changing Society, February 1959

I

The implementation of the provisions of the Criminal Justice Act 1948 was quickly overtaken by the pressure of events. It has been well said that crime and prison overcrowding were the two claws of the pincer holding post-war penal policy and practice in its grip. The growth of crime, the propensity of the higher courts to increase sentence lengths, the increase in the prison population, and the related intensification of prison overcrowding, gave the executive no breathing space in which to develop the remand centres, detention centres, and corrective training and preventive detention prisons that the Act made available to the courts. This did not prevent the courts from acting as if such facilities already existed. For the next decade, the prison commissioners had their backs to the wall. Yet these difficult times never dented their faith in the treatment and training of prisoners. They held fast to the set of ideas which reached its apogee in the concept of "the rehabilitative ideal." Not only was this progressive stance not deflected, it was further endorsed in the end-of-decade White Paper, *Penal Practice in a Changing Society*, which set the course for penal administration in the following decade. It is the purpose of this chapter to evaluate the numerical landscape in which the prison commissioners were forced to operate, the ways in which they responded to the dire conditions in the local prisons, where the bulk of the prison population still fetched up, and the impact of R. A. Butler, the Home Secretary, who, in Frank Pakenham's opinion, "took more palpable interest in penal reform than any predecessor since Winston Churchill fifty years earlier."[1] Butler was determined to make an impact on penal policy, as he had done on educational policy during the war years. His 1959 White Paper looked forward to an ambitious prison-building program, to renewed faith in prison treatment and training, and to more research into the effectiveness of the different training regimes. Was it, however, the landmark document for which it has so often been lauded?

In *Causes of Crime*, Lord Pakenham's Nuffield Foundation investigation, the year 1951 was identified as the worst year yet for crime. "It was this year's figures more than any other," said Pakenham, "that gave substance to the general concern over the post-war crime wave."[2] On the first day of December 1952 under the heading "Growth of Serious Crime," *The Times* analyzed this increase of crime. Compared with before the war, the number of indictable offences (the more serious crimes and most larcenies) known to the police had nearly doubled. Of the 524,506 indictable offences in 1951, 355,407 were larceny (an increase of 78 per cent on 1938); 95,946 were housebreaking (an increase of 95 per cent); 9,716 were receiving (an increase of 183 per cent); 14,633 were sexual offences (an increase of 192 per cent); and 6,516 were violence against the person (an increase of 139 per cent). While the figures for property crimes had fluctuated over the years since the war's end, "violence and sex . . . show an almost uninterrupted upward climb." The most violent group was that aged 21–30, in which convictions had increased by 209 per cent on 1938. Another worrying statistic was that boys and girls aged 8 to 14 formed a fifth of the total of all persons found guilty of indictable offences in 1951. Indeed, as a proportion of the population of their age, the peak year for offenders found guilty of indictable offences was 14, followed by 13 and 15. Already, commentators were musing on the paradox, as Pakenham phrased it,

> of a declining moral standard against a background of material improvement.
> Here . . . lay the next great task for the social reformers of our generation; to
> find out what had gone wrong or was still missing in the Welfare State.

Already, the Welfare State was being blamed, as Terence Morris put it, "for having sapped the moral fibre of the nation."[3]

---

1 Frank Pakenham, *Five Lives* (1964), pp. 149–50. See Ian Gilmour, "Butler, Richard Austen (1902–1982)," *DNB 1981–85* (Oxford, 1990), p. 66.
2 Pakenham, *Causes of Crime* (1959), p. 19. Pakenham also dated his connection with criminology from this *Times* article (Ibid., p. 17).
3 *The Times*, 1 Dec. 1952, p. 7. Pakenham, op cit., p. 17; T. Morris, "Contemporary Trends in Crime and Its Treatment," in P. Bean and D. Whynes (eds.), *Barbara Wootton: Social Science and Public Policy* (1986), p. 179.

Yet this turned out to be but the start of the upward curve of recorded crime. Recorded crime per head of population (allowing for demographic change) increased by only 5 per cent between 1947 and 1957. There was even an encouraging fall in crime between 1952 and 1956. It was after 1957 that the increase of recorded crime scaled the heights, increasing constantly at 10 per cent per annum. Between 1957 and 1967, recorded crime increased by 121 per cent. A disturbing feature of the figures for the later 1950s was the increasing involvement of the 17–21 age group in offences of violence against the person and breaking-and-entering offences. Only part of this entire experience can be attributed to a greater propensity of the public to report offences, to recent increases in police strength, and to improvements in the police mode of recording crime.[4]

II

How did the judiciary respond to these alarming trends in crime? It did not take long for Lord Chancellor Jowitt to accept the approach of the Lord Chief Justice, Rayner Goddard, and other high court judges that, in the absence of corporal punishment, longer sentences of imprisonment would have to be passed. "We have to try to see what happens," Jowitt declared in the House of Lords in March 1950, "as the result now of not awarding the short sentence with a sentence of whipping, and of awarding the longer sentences which cannot now be cut down by the use of corporal punishment." Goddard required no extra encouragement. As Lord Pakenham observed in his 1958 study, ". . . the Lord Chief Justice has lent his immense personal and official prestige to a stern sentencing policy in pursuit of law and order . . ."[5] In the same year, Gerald Gardiner, a bencher of the Inner Temple,

4   See R. Hood and A. Roddam, "Crime, Sentencing and Punishment," in A. H. Halsey and J. Webb (eds.), *Twentieth Century British Social Trends* (2000), pp. 680–3; T. Morris, *Crime and Criminal Justice since 1945* (Oxford, 1989), pp. 90–1, 96–7; N. Howard Avison, "Changing Patterns in Criminal Behaviour," in Hugh Klare and David Haxby (eds.), *Frontiers of Criminology* (Oxford, 1967), p. 69; Criminal Statistics 1984 (Cmd. 9621), 1985, p. 33 (Table 2.2). See also Hugh Klare, "Criminal Statistics, England and Wales, 1949," *Howard Journal*, vol. 8 (1951), p. 116; L. Radzinowicz, "Changing Attitudes Towards Crime and Punishment," *Law Quarterly Review*, vol. 75 (1959), pp. 398–9; H. Mannheim, "Developments in Criminal Law and Criminology in Post-War Britain," *Journal of Criminal Law, Criminology and Police Science*, vol. 51 (1961), p. 600.
5   *Hansard* (Lords), vol. 166, 21 Mar. 1950, col. 321; "Lord Goddard on Approved Schools," *The Times*, 9 Dec. 1952, p. 3; Pakenham, *Causes of Crime*, op cit., p. 79. Other senior judges sang from the same hymnal for the rest of the decade. Three young men were sentenced to imprisonment for firing a shotgun at another youth. Mr. Justice Hilbery told one of them, "It is not accurate to say that the sentence should fit the criminal and not the crime . . . it would be a strange thing if we were to pass sentence having merely the interest of the individual criminal and disregard the interest of the many millions who form the law abiding society in which the criminal moves and lives." *The Times*, 12 Nov. 1959, p. 3. See also Lord Justice Denning, "'English Law and the Moral Law,'" *The Listener*, 25 Feb. 1954, p. 333: "But there is little doubt that to all ordinary people retribution is the very essence of punishment . . . the ultimate justification of any punishment is not that it

remarked on "[t]his excessive proneness on the part of our higher courts to impose very long sentences," which could not alone be explained, he felt, by a rise in more serious crime. He called in aid a 1956 study by T. S. Lodge, statistical adviser to the Home Office, who had shown that the average sentence for breaking and entering in English courts in 1952 was three and a half times as long as in the Scottish courts. However, Lodge's enquiry did not reveal whether the difference between the two countries could be explained by the type of court which dealt with these offenders (summary or higher court), by the nature of the offences committed, or by the character of the offenders.[6] The *Criminal Statistics* for 1956 confirmed the increased length of sentence at the English higher courts for breaking and entering, compared with 1938, and revealed a slightly lower increase in length of sentence for violence against the person, and a higher increase for sexual offences. If the average length of sentence in 1938 is taken as 100, the figures for 1956 were 155 for breaking and entering, 130 for violence against the person, and 177 for sexual offences. Also, Hermann Mannheim found that in all four main categories of offences (against the person, nonsexual; against the person, sexual; against property with violence; and against property without violence), "there has been a general, usually very striking, decline in sentences under six months, a slight decline of sentences over seven years, and an increase in sentences between these two extremes." More specifically, Mannheim highlighted the fact that while in 1938 only 373 men received sentences of 18 months to ten years, the figure for 1954 was 1,672, more than four times as many.[7]

Interpreting these figures is not entirely straightforward. An increase in average sentence length could reflect the greater seriousness of crimes committed; judicial compensation for an increase in remission to one-third of the sentence (even though judges were not expected to take remission into account when fixing sentence); or judicial acceptance of the confident assertions of penal reformers and administrators about the reformative potential of prolonged imprisonment and the deleterious effect of short prison sentences. Since proportionately more non-custodial sentences were being passed, replacing short prison sentences, the average length of the remaining sentences of imprisonment was bound to be longer. At least, in part, however, the

is a deterrent; but that it is the emphatic denunciation by the community of a crime." Kenneth Younger wrote a letter of reply to Mr. Justice Devlin's Maccabaean lecture on the enforcement of morals, in which he regretted "a climate of judicial opinion in which moral indignation and the feelings of 'the man on the Clapham omnibus' were coming to be elevated above rational analysis and study as the best guide to the treatment of offenders." *The Times*, 7 Nov. 1959, p. 7.

6   Gardiner, "The Purposes of Criminal Punishment," *Modern Law Review*, vol. 21 (1958), p. 227; T. S. Lodge, "A Comparison of Criminal Statistics of England and Wales with those of Scotland," *British Journal of Delinquency*, vol. 7 (1956), pp. 58–60; TNA, HO291/504: Fox's memo, 13 Feb. 1957.

7   J. P. Martin, "Criminal Statistics 1956," *Howard Journal*, vol. 10 (1958), p. 48; Mannheim, "Comparative Sentencing Practice," *Law and Contemporary Problems*, vol. 23 (1958), p. 567–8. See also Brian MacKenna, "A Plea for Shorter Prison Sentences," in P. R. Glazebrook (ed.), *Reshaping the Criminal Law* (1978), pp. 422–4 (Tables 1 and 2).

increase in sentence length reflects the judicial response to the rise in crime with more deterrent and preventive sentences. The Court of Criminal Appeal guided the courts of assize and quarter sessions in expanding the tariff, or normal range of sentence, at least at the upper end for more serious offences.[8] In addition, the criminal courts used the new sentences of corrective training and preventive detention with some frequency, often handing down eight or ten years' preventive detention for small thefts.

Yet, the increase in length of prison sentences should not be allowed to mask the wholesale change in sentencing policy in the post-war years, of which it was only one part.[9] For a start, prison use declined in these years, even for sexual and violent offences. As Mannheim documented, for all five main groups of offences, sentences of penal servitude (until 1948) and imprisonment, as a percentage of all sentences imposed by the higher courts, fell in each of the three time periods 1934–8, 1946–50, and 1951–54. What he called "an unbroken downward trend" was especially marked for sexual offences and offences against property with violence. The percentage of penal servitude and imprisonment imposed for sexual offences fell from 61.5 in 1946–50 to 47.2 in 1951–4. The same trend was evident for *all* custodial sentences. In the higher courts, the percentage of custodial sentences (including imprisonment, preventive detention, corrective training, borstal training, and detention centres) imposed upon persons aged 17 and above, fell from 67.1 per cent in 1947 to 54.3 per cent in 1957 (returning to 60.1 per cent in 1967). Magistrates courts followed suit. The percentage of custodial sentences imposed upon persons aged 17 and above, fell from 20.2 in 1947 to 14.9 in 1957. For 17 to 20-year-olds convicted of indictable offences the trend was less clear cut. The Criminal Justice Act 1948 brought about an immediate drop in the number of young offenders sentenced to imprisonment, from 2,756 in 1948 to 1,339 in 1949, yet in the 1950s the higher courts resorted more often to the use of imprisonment and less often to the use of borstal training, and they were encouraged by the Court of Criminal Appeal to use sentences of between nine months' and two years' imprisonment for young offenders convicted of serious offences. Receptions under sentence of imprisonment of young offenders aged 17–20 rose to 2,911 in 1962.[10]

Another important feature of the marked change in sentencing policy was the fact that the main replacement for prison was no longer probation but the fine. Mannheim showed that between 1938 and 1955 the percentage of males fined for indictable offences rose from 15 to 36 in the 17–21 age group and from 27 to 45 in the 21 and over age group. By contrast, the percentage of males placed on probation for such offences fell from 42 to 26 in the 17–21 group and from 18 to 12 in the 21 and over age group.[11]

8   See D. A. Thomas, "Appellate Review of Sentences and the Development of Sentencing Policy: The English Experience," *Alabama Law Review*, vol. 20 (1968), pp. 204–10.
9   See H. Mannheim, "Some Aspects of Judicial Sentencing Policy," *Yale Law Journal*, vol. 67 (1958), p. 977.
10   Mannheim, "Comparative Sentencing Practice," op cit., pp. 564, 568–9 (Tables II and VII); R. Hood, *Borstal Re-assessed* (1965), p. 73; C. Nuttall and K. Pease, "Changes in the Use of Imprisonment in England and Wales 1950–1991," *Criminal Law Review*, May 1994, pp. 317–20.
11   Ibid., pp. 563–6 (Tables I, III, IV).

These trends were true mainly of the magistrates' courts, but the higher courts were not unaffected. The 1948 Act extended the higher courts' power to impose fines for all offences except murder, and the courts took advantage of the new power across all the main groups of offences, and particularly for sexual offences. The proportion of fines imposed for sexual crimes rose from 2.5 per cent in 1946–50 to 15.1 per cent in 1951–4. Table 8.1 encapsulates this entire change in sentencing policy in both higher and lower courts:

TABLE 8.1 Trends in sentencing in England and Wales for male and female offenders combined aged 17 and over, 1938–60

Sentences as percentage of those found guilty

	Custodial measure	Probation	Fine	Discharge
Higher courts (Assize and Quarter Sessions)				
1938	63	19	1	16
1950	63	17	7	13
1960	54	23	14	9
Magistrates' courts (persons found guilty of *indictable* offences only)				
1938	22	22	29	25
1950	18	12	49	17
1960	13	13	56	14

Source: Nigel Walker, "Crime and Penal Measures," in A. H. Halsey (ed.), *Trends in British Society since 1900* (Macmillan, 1972), Table 15.1, reproduced with permission of SNCSC.[12]

These figures combine male and female offenders, masking the fact that probation was used twice as frequently, and prison one-third less frequently, for women than for men. Of all offenders convicted of indictable offences at all courts in 1951, nearly a third of the females were placed on probation (the figure for males was one-fifth). In addition, the figures do not reveal the considerable variation between individual courts. Some quarter sessional courts imposed prison sentences in less than a third of their cases, others in over two-thirds; some had a probation rate of over 50 per cent, others of only 5 per cent. So, too, for magistrates' courts: during 1951 to 1954, the percentage of prison sentences imposed on male offenders over 21 for indictable offences ranged from a minimum of 7.8 per cent to a maximum of 47.3 per cent.[13] It

12 These figures also appear in A. Bottoms, "Limiting Prison Use: Experience in England and Wales," *Howard Journal*, vol. 26 (1987), p. 178 (Table 3), 180. Cf. Hood and Roddam, op cit., pp. 690–1 (Table 20.5).

13 See H. Mannheim, "Some Aspects of Judicial Sentencing Policy," op. cit., 978; idem., "Penalties to Fit the Crime," *The Times*, 27 Nov. 1957, p. 11; Leslie Wilkins, "A Small Comparative Study of the Results of Probation," *British Journal of Delinquency*, vol. 8 (1958), p. 201.

is possible, though improbable, that such differences were solely a function of the kind of offences and offenders appearing before the different courts.

Again, interpretation of the figures is far from evident. Was the decline in the proportionate use of probation a sign of the greater discrimination on the part of magistrates' courts in the selection of probationers? Was it a recognition by courts that probation officers were overworked? Or was it a hardening in the attitudes of judges and magistrates, making them less willing to try the kind of positive reform that probation offered, and so less willing to replace prison by probation. When it came to the decline of prison use, were courts increasingly inclined to reserve imprisonment for what they regarded as dangerous, persistent, or notably culpable offenders? And why did the fine become the basic penalty in the post-war period, for indictable as well as non-indictable offences? Did the growth in the proportion fined indicate a high incidence of crimes which the court did not regard as serious? Was the fine seen as an appropriate substitute in an age of affluence for the short prison sentence? What we can say for sure is, first, that the fine was no longer connected with imprisonment, as it had been in the early part of the century, by virtue of the default of payment mechanism. In the post-war era, the proportion of fines enforced by imprisonment was less than 1 per cent. Secondly, the use of the fine went against the grain of the rehabilitative ideal. As Tony Bottoms noted, the period between 1945 and 1965 was characterized by the paradox of rehabilitation as the dominant "positivist" ideal, coinciding with the growth of an essentially "classical" punishment in the form of the fine. The paradox is to be explained, said Bottoms, by the credenda of the different penal stakeholders:

> The concept of scientific rehabilitation gained its dominant hold mainly upon probation officers, senior prison personnel, government officials and academics. The judges and magistrates in the courts, however, were relatively isolated from this development; and they apparently saw the fine as an increasingly appropriate penalty during the same period (perhaps connected with the growth to a full employment economy at the time).[14]

And, thirdly, the judiciary's use of the fine won endorsement in the sixties from the Home Office's new manual for sentencers, *The Sentence of the Court*, which revealed that "[f]ines were followed by the fewest reconvictions compared with the expected numbers for both first offenders and recidivists of almost all age groups."[15]

---

14 Anthony Bottoms, "Neglected Features of Contemporary Penal Systems," in D. Garland and P. Young (eds.), *The Power to Punish: Contemporary Penality and Social Analysis* (1983), p. 193.
15 *The Sentence of the Court* (1969), pp. 71–3.

III

After surveying the trends in crime and sentencing, it can come as no surprise to discover that the number of people in custody increased in the post-war period. The number of prisoners received under sentence (including prisons, borstals, and detention centres) were as follows: 1938, 31,993; 1948, 36,802; 1960, 42,810; 1968, 49,258. The average daily population of men and women in custody was as follows: 1938, 11,086; 1948, 19,765; 1958, 25,379; 1968, 32,461.[16] These numbers were largely a function of male prisoners; the daily average population of females remaining small (between 800 and 1,000) and stable. There is little doubt that the trends in both crime and sentencing had an impact on these figures, but in what proportions? In the *Criminal Statistics* for 1956, it was calculated that of the increase of 9,000 persons in prison between 1938 and 1954, 6,000 (or two-thirds) were ascribable to the increased number of convictions for indictable offences, and the remaining one-third to the longer sentences imposed by the higher courts.[17]

The prison commissioners were caught off guard. During the first half of 1952, the prison population rose at a rate exceeding anything previously experienced, by nearly 1,000 in three months alone. By June 1952, the prison population reached a peak of 24,100.[18] This remarkable increase in population occurred just when the prison commissioners were faced with changes in the prison system required by the 1948 Act, notably the passing of longer sentences on persistent offenders sent to corrective training and preventive detention. Judges tended to sentence irrespective of the facilities for executing the sentences. By 1957, the preventive-detention population had settled at between 1,200 and 1,500, and four prisons were occupied by these men. The result was severe prison overcrowding, with the consequent resort to multiple occupancy of cells; 5,680 prisoners were sleeping three to a cell by 1952. Overcrowding was at its worst in the decrepit local prisons, which held 15,000 of the 1952 total of 20,500 prisoners, and where it was aggravated by an increase in the number of remand prisoners, and the increased average time these

16 N. Walker, "Crime and Penal Measures," op cit., p. 531 (Table 15.4); A. Bottoms, "Limiting Prison Use: Experience in England and Wales," *Howard Journal*, vol. 26 (1987), p. 178 (Table 1), 181; *Prisons and the Prisoner: The Work of the Prison Service in England and Wales* (1977), p. 156 (Table 3).

17 J. P. Martin, "Criminal Statistics, 1956," *Howard Journal*, vol. 10 (1958), p. 44; A. W. Peterson, "The Expanding Prison System 1954–1963," *Criminal Law Review* (1964), p. 573. However, Home Secretary David Maxwell-Fyfe informed Prime Minister Churchill in August 1952 that the disturbing increase in the prison population "seems to be due almost entirely to the general increase in crime and the increased numbers sent to prison, and not to any significant extent to the passing of longer sentences . . . The average length of sentence imposed by the courts, excluding sentences of three months or less, was 10.52 months in 1947, 10.86 months in 1948, 11.66 months in 1949, 11.34 months in 1950 and 11.35 months in 1951." See TNA, PREM 11/29.

18 Twenty-four thousand was the highest prison population recorded since shortly after the establishment of the Prison Commission in 1877. Expressed as a percentage of the total population of the country, however, it was lower than the period 1880–1910. See J. C. Spencer, "Some Recent Developments in the English Prison System," *British Journal of Delinquency*, vol. 4 (1953–4), p. 40.

prisoners were held on remand. About 40 per cent. of the 18,000 untried prisoners remanded in custody each year were not subsequently received back into custody after conviction; they were dealt with by some method not involving detention. Yet recent pronouncements by the Lord Chief Justice were calculated to make magistrates cautious in granting bail.[19] A large proportion of prisoners were still being sentenced to short terms. Sentences of five weeks or less constituted no less than 26.7 per cent of all receptions (male and female) in 1951. Out of approximately 32,000 people sent to prison in that year, over 23,000 (or 72 per cent) had sentences of six months or less (the figure for women prisoners was even higher). At best, then, only one-third of all the prisoners received were committed for the length of time (over six months) considered necessary for effective training. However, in terms of daily average population or cell-space occupied, prisoners serving sentences of six months or less accounted for only 22 per cent; prisoners sentenced to 18 months' and over made up 60 per cent of the prison population, their number having increased five times since 1938.[20]

Having established the statistical landscape that the Home Office and prison commissioners had to negotiate in the post-war years, we now need to examine, first, how the Prison Commission sought to develop its prison training programme, despite the pressure of numbers, and, second, how the Home Office turned to the Advisory Council on the Treatment of Offenders to find ways to alleviate prison overcrowding. In 1952, the chairman of the Prison Commission, Lionel Fox, published *The English Prison and Borstal Systems* in the International Library of Sociology and Social Reconstruction, describing the development of prison administration during the past fifty years, and discussing the methods to be pursued in the light of the Criminal Justice Act 1948. The Act provided that rules should be made for "the training of prisoners," in the forefront of which was the statement: "The purposes of training and treatment of convicted prisoners shall be to establish in them the will to lead a good and useful life on discharge, and to fit them to do so." Fox's book was favourably reviewed in criminological and penal reform circles. Margery Fry heralded its appearance as "an event of great importance in the history of English penology," and lauded the first section, "What Is Prison For?", as a humane statement of the function of imprisonment:

> It is not the lucubration of a Bentham picturing a dream Panopticon, but of one who knows in the utmost detail the difficulties and discouragements of dealing with society's rejects. One admires . . . the courage of such a declaration of principle from a man who exposes himself in making it to the crossfire of those . . . who may accuse him of being too starry-eyed for his position,

---

19 TNA, PCom 9/1760: preparation documents for Lord Pakenham's motion, May 1955; C. H. Rolph, "Prisons and Prisoners," *New Statesman*, 2 Feb. 1957, enclosed in TNA, HO291/504; T. Morris, "Prisons in England and Wales," *British Journal of Delinquency*, vol. 7 (1957), p. 318.

20 Advisory Council on the Penal System, *Sentences of Imprisonment: A Review of Maximum Penalties* (1978), p. 206 (Appendix J); C. H. Rolph, "Prisons and Prisoners," *New Statesman*, 2 Feb. 1957, enclosed in TNA, HO291/504.

and of their opponents who will complain that it is but partially embodied in the organization directed by him.[21]

Fry was prophetic: the statements about the purpose of training and treatment, along with other of the book's claims, were to become hostages to fortune, handy targets for critics of the prisons for the rest of the decade.[22]

In the 1950s, there was a tripartite system of prisons: *regional or training prisons* (Maidstone, Wakefield) for all prisoners, except short-termers, regarded as train-able, including corrective trainees; *central prisons* (Dartmoor, Holloway, Parkhurst) for those serving long sentences of imprisonment or preventive detention; and *local prisons* (Brixton, Liverpool, Manchester, Pentonville, Wandsworth, Wormwood Scrubs, and a slew of county gaols) for men awaiting transfer, or men deemed unsuitable to go elsewhere, "a sort of sump," in Fox's phrase.[23] The locals had a lot of men with very short sentences, largely of the "ordinary class," since the majority of short-sentence "stars" went to "open" local prisons. If the commissioners hoped to reduce the population in local prisons, pressure of accommodation put paid to that. Many long-term and trainable prisoners served a large part or even the whole of their sentences in local prisons. A building programme of some magnitude was needed, but as Philip Allen, deputy chairman of the Prison Commission, 1950–2, said many years later, what hope was there of persuading the Cabinet and the public "that enormous resources should be spent on cosseting criminals rather than on roads, schools, houses and all the rest of the things that more deserving mem-bers of the community were calling for?"[24] Anyway, a commitment to defence expenditure for the Korean War led to a drop in spending on the social services from 18 per cent of gross domestic product in 1952 to 16 per cent in 1955. Only one new secure prison was built, Everthorpe, completed in 1958, the first since Victorian times, apart from Camp Hill in 1912.[25]

21 Fry, "A Great Book," *Howard Journal*, vol. 8 (1953), p. 235. Also Norwood East, "Cri-tical Notices," *British Journal of Delinquency*, vol. 3 (1953), pp. 207–9. See also R. A. Butler, "Fox, Sir Lionel (1895–1961)," *Dictionary of National Biography, 1961–70* (Oxford, 1980), pp. 386–7; *The Times*, 9 Oct. 1961, p. 14.

22 For the most comprehensive account by the Prison Commission of prison population, staffing, classification and training, persistent offenders and preventive detention, young offenders, and after-care in the first post-war decade, see Appendix to Chapter 1, "Review of Development from 1946 to 1955," in *Report of the Prison Commissioners for 1955*, PP, 1956 (Cmnd. 10), pp. 365–86.

23 TNA, PCom9/1822: The Principles Governing the Classification of Prisons, 17 Mar. 1951; Mannheim, "Developments in Criminal Law and Criminology in Post-War Britain," op cit., p. 603; PCom9/1760: Fox to Mancroft, 18 Apr. 1955. Up until 1949, it had been Prison Commission policy to abandon Dartmoor and not to waste money on its improvement. Since then it had been decided that it should be retained, and money went to the maintenance and improvement of the prison. SeePCom9/1320: ACTO, 8 Jul. 1952 minutes.

24 Lord Allen of Abbeydale in conversation with Lord Longford, *Punishment and the Pun-ished* (1991), pp. 32–3.

25 A. W. Peterson, "The Prison Building Programme," *British Journal of Criminology*, vol. 1 (1961), p. 308.

In default of new construction, the prison authorities decided to expand the number of open prisons by taking over disused camps and country houses. One of the first open prisons was established at Leyhill, an open prison for male "stars," serving sentences of three years and above, including reprieved murderers. This was followed by a prison-without-bars for women at Askham Grange, near York. By the mid-fifties, there were five open *local* prisons (including Eastchurch, Kent), four open *regional* prisons (including Sudbury Park, Derbyshire), and one open *central* prison (Leyhill). There was a similar number of open borstals for young male and female offenders. There is little doubt that the creation of the open prison system was one of the most promising developments in the post-war era, fitting testimony to Alec Paterson, famous for the maxim: "You cannot train a man for freedom under conditions of captivity."[26]

Other developments in treatment and training included home leave, already available to borstal trainees, introduced in 1951 for adult prisoners. The first pre-release hostel opened in 1953 in the grounds of Bristol prison, for preventive detainees in the last stages of their long sentence, from which they went out to work in ordinary jobs. Group counselling and group therapy, as a method of helping prisoners to develop a greater degree of self-knowledge, started in the late fifties at Wakefield prison and extended to other prisons. Prison staff were not always favourably inclined towards this experiment, but it was hoped group activity would foster a more humane approach by the staff to the prisoner. Likewise, in 1956, the so-called Norwich system of prison routine was devised as a way of improving the relationship between officer and prisoner. The main features of the system were dining in association, an increase in the hours of work from 26 to 35, and the allocation of groups of prisoners to specific officers who were required to get to know their men personally.[27] Again, the conflict of roles that staff felt—custodian or counsellor—tended to set up barriers to reform. In general, it was a matter of dispute as to what proportion of the staff were prepared to support measures of penal reform, but there was a body of opinion suspicious of reforms, which argued that it only increased the burden on the prison officer. While the prison population practically doubled between 1938 and 1956, personnel increased by only 40 per cent. Prison staff complained about the difficulty of maintaining

---

26 Michael Wolff, *Prison* (1967), p. 54; Joanna Kelley, "Askham Grange—Open Prison for Women," *Howard Journal*, vol. 9 (1955), p. 124; Joan Henry, *Who Lie in Gaol* (1952), *passim*. Henry was transferred to Askham from Holloway during her 1950 prison sentence.

27 R. A. Butler, *Penal Reform and Research* (Liverpool, 1960), pp. 10–13; TNA, PCom9/ 1920; T. Morris, Report of the Commissioners of Prisons for 1958 (1959), *British Journal of Delinquency*, vol. 10 (1960), p. 225; Rev. Peter Timms, former governor of Maidstone prison, in conversation with Longford, op cit., p. 50; Duncan Fairn, "Prisons 1866– 1966," in H. Klare (ed.), *Changing Concepts of Crime and Its Treatment* (Oxford, 1966), pp. 165–7; P. Priestley (ed.), *Jail Journeys: The English Prison Experience since 1918* (1989), pp. 148–9. One habitual prisoner was far from convinced by the "Norwich Experiment": Robert Henry Allerton (with Tony Parker), *The Courage of His Convictions* (1st pub. 1962, 1969 ed.), p. 170.

discipline, and the increasing violence they faced. They also grumbled about the slow promotion and pay, though the Wynn-Parry Committee in 1958 recommended improvements in pay, which the government accepted.[28]

Prison education was improved with the assistance of local education authorities, which offered to organize evening institutes and provide teachers for the purpose. By 1954, 900 classes a week for men and 134 classes a week for women were being held in prison evening institutes.[29] Psychiatric services were also expanded. By 1958, three prisons had a full medico-psychiatric team, composed of psychiatrists and psychologists and psychiatric social workers, though the number of cases dealt with was pitifully small. Still on the agenda was the long-awaited psychiatric prison. The Advisory Council on the Treatment of Offenders had recommended a new institution for mentally abnormal offenders, including the "aggressive psychopath," though they differed from the 1939 East-Hubert report in thinking that courts should have power, after hearing medical evidence, to commit persons direct to the new institution and fix the maximum period of treatment, and that it should not be a penal institution within the prison system, but far removed from the prison atmosphere. ACTO's view was not accepted; the new institution was to be within the prison system. A site was obtained at Grendon Underwood in North Buckinghamshire to accommodate 300 to 350 cases, though it took until 1963 for the new prison to open. The prison authorities thought it could be one of the most important penological advances for many years. For most of the 1950s, however, a psychiatric prison for mentally abnormal inmates remained a pipe dream.[30]

Finally, the Maxwell Committee on Discharged Prisoners' Aid Societies in 1953 recommended the appointment of prison welfare officers, who would be trained social workers; the first was appointed in 1955, employed by the National Association of Discharged Prisoners' Aid Societies. By 1956, they had been appointed at four local prisons. It was the initial step in the provision of social case work rather than material aid for the discharged prisoner. Attempts were made, too, to link the welfare state with the after-care of prisoners, notably the Ministry of Labour, to find work for the released prisoner, and the National Assistance Board for financial aid.[31]

28 J. E. Thomas, *The English Prison Officer since 1850* (1972), p. 189; H. Klare, "Report of the Wynn Parry Committee," *British Journal of Delinquency*, vol. 9 (1959), p. 222; *Report of the Committee of Inquiry into the United Kingdom Prison Services* (Cmnd. 7673), 1979, pp. 17–19.

29 C. T. Cape, "Prison Education—Training for Freedom?", *Howard Journal*, vol. 9 (1954), pp. 56–7.

30 Gardiner, "The Purposes of Criminal Punishment," op cit., p. 128; Advisory Council on the Treatment of Offenders (ACTO), 7 Jul. 1954 minutes in TNA, HO291/19; PCom9/1760.

31 ACTO, 1 Apr. 1954 minutes in TNA, HO291/19; T. P. M. Morris, "Notes and Criticisms," *British Journal of Delinquency*, vol. 7 (1957), p. 319; Gordon Rose, *The Struggle for Penal Reform* (1961), pp. 252–3; G. Mair and L. Burke, *Redemption, Rehabilitation and Risk Management* (2012), pp. 93–4.

This was pretty much the full extent of the Prison Commission's attempts to establish in prisoners "the will to lead a good and useful life on discharge, and to fit them to do so." Most of the new initiatives benefited only a small proportion of prisoners, and apart from open prisons, did little to relieve the overcrowded local prisons. The Achilles heel of prison training remained the poor provision of good quality work for prisoners, aggravated in 1957 by defence cuts and by a trade union movement hostile to the employment of prison labour outside prison walls.[32] The earnings scheme continued to be a source of trouble and indiscipline, the derisory amounts paid doing nothing to diminish the tobacco hunger of prisoners, which brought in its wake the curse of trafficking and tobacco barons. Discipline was still the prison staff's mantra, with solitary cell punishment and bread-and-water diet awarded for the smallest infractions. Occasionally, disturbances (mainly hunger strikes) broke out—at Wandsworth prison in 1954, Dartmoor in 1955, and Birmingham and Cardiff in 1959. And if anything, conditions worsened before they improved. By mid-1961, the local prisons were more overcrowded than they had ever been, with over 7,000 men crammed three in a cell. Overcrowding was not confined to the cells, but also affected workshops. The training prisons and the young prisoners' centres were full, and the wait for a vacancy in one could be long. Escapes reached a disturbing level.[33] It was a sombre picture, and left much for critics of the penal system to sink their teeth into.

IV

Meanwhile, the Home Office turned to the Advisory Council for discussion of ways to combat the prison crisis. No coherent strategy could be expected from a Council asked to deal with precisely defined topics separately, and none emerged, only a few ideas to choke off the supply of prisoners. The Council almost always received guidance from Home Office memoranda, occasionally took evidence from those with the knowledge or experience they lacked, but for the most part they deliberated among themselves.[34] None of the ideas they examined were the subject of any rigorous research before the Council made its recommendations, though George Benson, MP, did his best to introduce what few research results there were.[35]

---

32 TNA, PCom9/1866; HO291/64, CRI 249/4/1. *The Times* on 11 Dec. 1952, p. 7 had declared, "Training, education, recreation, and hard constructive work are now supposed to be the keynotes of prison life, but in few cases can it be said that this is so in fact."

33 George Benson, *Report of a Committee to Review Punishment in Prisons, Borstal Institutions, Approved Schools and Remand Homes, 1951, British Journal of Delinquency*, vol. 2 (1952), pp. 241–2; J. E. Thomas, op cit., p. 190; Robert Adams, *Prison Riots in Britain and the USA* (Basingstoke, 1992), p. 119.

34 For one view of ACTO's role and effectiveness, see Anne Logan, "Women and the Provision of Criminal Justice Advice: Lessons from England and Wales 1944–1964," *British Journal of Criminology*, vol. 50 (2010), pp. 1091–2.

35 Over 40 years later, ACTO member, Leon Radzinowicz, stated, "No doubt some of the reports of the Advisory Council would have certainly gained in substance if more research had gone into them before the final recommendations were reached." See *Adventures in Criminology* (1999), p. 331.

We start with the idea of the suspended sentence, which had been suggested as far back as 1910 by Home Secretary Churchill to cover all minor first offences, and to eliminate short terms of imprisonment, without prejudice to the working of the probation system. The suspension of the *execution* of a sentence of imprisonment was a common feature of foreign penal systems, in France the *sursis a l'execution de la sentence*. England had preferred sanctions (probation and conditional discharge) designed to suspend the *imposition* of a prison sentence. In October 1950, Sir Frank Newsam, Permanent Undersecretary of State, held a department meeting to consider Sir Leo Page's proposal to introduce the suspended sentence as a new method of treatment. Page took the view that probationers did not always understand that they were liable to be punished for the offence for which they were put on probation if they were convicted of a new offence during the probation period. He proposed, therefore, that courts should be empowered to pronounce sentence at the time of the conviction for the original offence, but to postpone its execution. This suspended sentence would be a more effective deterrent, more readily understood by offenders, and would improve the probation system. The suspended sentence, he suggested, could be used either in conjunction with a probation order or alone. If they chose the latter, courts would order a sentence of imprisonment for (say) a year, suspended for (say) three years. This would allow courts to avoid sending an offender to prison while showing their sense of the gravity of the offence. Page offered the idea, then, as both a way of strengthening the force of a probation order, and as an alternative to imprisonment.[36] The department thought the introduction of the suspended sentence might be controversial. In Page's formulation, it would certainly alter the character of the probation order, the essence of which was treatment, not punishment. Newsam wanted the observations of the Lord Chief Justice. The Lord Chief Justice revealed that for some time past, when at the assizes, he had been adopting a plan akin to a suspended sentence:

> If I make a probation order, an order for conditional discharge or a bind over, I tell the prisoner that I am directing the Clerk of Assize to make a note that I consider the proper sentence for the offence which he has committed is so many months and if he commits another offence and so is called up for judgment the Judge before whom he comes will be told of the sentence I thought appropriate.[37]

He did not think that the suspended sentence should come automatically into operation in the event of a further offence, but "probationers and others should understand that a discharge in these circumstances is not an empty formality."

---

36 Sir Leo Page, "The Suspended Sentence," in TNA, LCO2/3357. Minutes of meeting held 25 Oct. 1950 in the Home Office to discuss the suspended sentence, in Ibid. See also Leo Page, *The Young Lag: A Study in Crime* (1950), pp. 302–4.

37 TNA, HO45/25841/887177/36: Lord Chief Justice to Sir Frank Newsam, 15 Nov. 1950.

At this point, the Home Secretary passed the idea to ACTO. The council met in January 1951 to examine the general principles of the proposal. Council members were on the whole sceptical of the proposal, especially in conjunction with probation. The most frequent criticism was that it would involve a court determining what sentence should be served, without knowledge of the future circumstances in which it might operate, and lead to the decision of the second court being coloured by the decision of the first. Dr. Radzinowicz, director of the Department of Criminal Science at Cambridge, added that the scope for the sentence was limited, "since most of those who were put on probation at any rate by courts of summary jurisdiction, were under the age of 17 and could not for that reason be sentenced to imprisonment." Only George Benson gave it a ringing endorsement: ". . . its introduction would relieve the prison and probation services of many persons who would otherwise have been sent to prison or put on probation."[38]

Six months later, the council took evidence from probation officers and the Prison Commission (in the shape of Philip Allen, deputy chairman of the commission). The former claimed that the relationship between probation officer and probationer would be jeopardized by the introduction of the suspended sentence. Allen said the commissioners did not consider a suspended sentence suitable for young offenders; they also felt it was inappropriate in the case of orders involving training (borstal or corrective training), and they were unsure whether the sentence would reduce the number of people going to prison. "On the whole he thought it would not cause any appreciable reduction in the prison population."[39] The council then discussed the use of the suspended sentence apart from probation, Radzinowicz again opposing the idea, arguing that the suspended sentence would not be a greater deterrent than probation or conditional discharge, and that it would create "a confusion of thought between the purposes of probation and imprisonment and would weaken the deterrent effect of imprisonment." Finally, in early 1952, ACTO delivered a report which rehearsed all the objections to the idea of the suspended sentence. They were particularly concerned that if the suspended sentence was used independently of probation, courts would use it in cases in which probation was more appropriate. In disposing of the idea, the council tersely stated, "The suspended sentence is wrong in principle and to a large extent impracticable. It should not be adopted, either in conjunction with probation or otherwise." ACTO recommended that their report not be published since to do so "might stir up controversy in this subject."[40] The council's view had not changed when in 1957 in their report *Alternatives to Short Terms of Imprisonment*, they again rejected the suspended sentence.

38 Ibid: ACTO, 17 Jan. 1951 minutes.
39 Ibid: ACTO, 2 Jul. 1951 minutes.
40 Ibid: ACTO, 1 Apr. 1954 minutes. For ACTO's report on the suspended sentence, see TNA, HO291/19.

In June 1955, Hugh Klare, Howard League Secretary, wrote to the Home Secretary, Gwilym Lloyd-George, to ask him to consider appointing a departmental committee to examine alternatives to some of the short sentences of imprisonment. If the number of prison sentences could be reduced, said Klare,

> the overcrowding, the lack of work and the shortage of staff would all three be favourably affected; and the enforced idleness and the negative regime, which is still the hall-mark of many prisons, could be replaced by that training *for* and *by* work which is one of the declared aims of imprisonment.

The alternatives that the Howard League had in mind were, for civil prisoners, a system of attachment of wages in wife-maintenance and bastardy cases; for first offenders, an attendance centre for adults, and an extension of the provisions of section 17 of the Criminal Justice Act (making it incumbent upon the courts to state in writing their reasons for imposing a prison sentence on persons under 21 years of age) to adult first offenders.[41] Lloyd-George asked ACTO to investigate.

In fact, a year before the Howard League's letter, ACTO had examined a proposal made by George Benson, MP and council member, to apply section 17 to first offenders or persons without previous proved offences. About 8,000 first offenders were sent to prison each year, said Benson. In 1951 such persons formed 26.3 per cent of the total male receptions and 26.5 per cent of the total female receptions. He called in support the result of an investigation published in *Criminal Statistics* 1938, which showed that in terms of reconviction the results of fine, dismissal, and imprisonment were the same, while probation was less successful. This suggested to him that "the operative factor was the shock of appearance in court, not the sentence; and that results would have been little different had the majority of the persons sent to prison been fined or bound over." Benson also pointed out that section 17 had resulted in a 50-per-cent reduction in the number of persons under 21 sent to prison, or "an admission by the courts that prior to this section's coming into force, they had been sending to prison twice as many adolescents as was necessary." There was further evidence of unnecessary imprisonment in the wide variations in the sentencing policy of different courts. In all, the policy of the courts was in need of improvement and guidance from Parliament was desirable. On the first occasion this proposal came before ACTO in April 1954, members thought it merited further examination, though Radzinowicz thought it unlikely that the fall in the number of first offenders sent to prison would be as great as the

---

41 TNA, HO291/19: Klare to Home Secretary, 13 Jun. 1955; *Hansard*, vol. 542, 23 Jun. 1955, col. 1497 (Hyde); ibid., vol. 544, 21 Jul. 1955, col. 535 (Lloyd-George). Hugh Klare believed that penal reform could be achieved most effectively by working closely with the likes of Sir Lionel Fox at the Prison Commission and R. A. Butler at the Home Office. See A. E. Bottoms, "An Introduction to 'The Coming Crisis'" in Bottoms and R. H. Preston (eds.), *The Coming Penal Crisis: A Criminological and Theological Explanation* (Edinburgh, 1980), p. 12. See also D. Barker, "Hugh Klare," *Guardian*, 13 Jul. 2012; Rod Morgan, "Klare, Hugh John (1916–2012)," *Oxford DNB* (2016).

fall in the number of young persons, since "[t]he majority of first offenders sent to prison were so sent for serious offences, for which imprisonment was the only appropriate punishment." At the May meeting, the majority of members were unwilling to commit themselves to support any action, but thought there might be more research into the effects of variations in the sentencing policy of different courts.[42]

In November 1955, ACTO responded to Lloyd-George's request by holding a preliminary discussion of alternatives to short terms of imprisonment. Very quickly, it was decided to set up a sub-committee to examine the whole question of alternatives and report to the council. It was this report that became *Alternatives to Short Terms of Imprisonment* (1957). ACTO focused on those received on conviction with sentences of imprisonment of six months or less, which in 1954 numbered 19,957 or almost 70 per cent of the 28,838 prisoners received on conviction. Magistrates' courts were responsible for the bulk of these short-term receptions (18,647 of the 19,957). The council immediately conceded that the short sentence had valid social and penal functions: "[t]he short sentence has a definite and necessary place in our criminal law. There are many cases in which a sentence of imprisonment is inevitable, but the nature and circumstances of the offence do not require a long sentence." ACTO found it difficult to estimate the numbers of those who might be receiving avoidable prison sentences, but they drew attention to the fact that in 1954 some 4,322 offenders without previous proved offences, and 5,113 offenders with previous proved offences but no previous sentence of imprisonment, were sent to prison for six months or less. ACTO saw no single remedy to the problem of the unessential short term of imprisonment, but made a number of recommendations which were directed primarily at magistrates' courts.[43]

For prisoners in general, the report again ruled against the suspended sentence, relying instead upon heavier fines and the one experimental attendance centre for 17- to 21-year-olds. When it came to special classes of offender, the report had nothing to offer for women imprisoned for child neglect; little to offer for the 3,000 receptions each year of chronic alcoholics (apart from probation with residential treatment for a mental condition); and the introduction of a scheme for attachment of wages for the 5,000 receptions each year of men defaulting on maintenance orders. Finally, the report accepted the Howard League suggestion of extending section 17 of the 1948 Act to adult first offenders, requiring the court to state the reason for its opinion that no other method than imprisonment was appropriate. It also accepted the Magistrates' Association's view that more use could be made of supervision by a probation officer pending payment of a fine (since 2,280 people were imprisoned in default of payment of fines each year, over a third of whom were not allowed time to pay), and that more use could be made by courts of remands for enquiry. And that was it.[44] No mention was made of

42 Ibid: ACTO, 1 Apr. 1954 minutes; ACTO, 27 May 1954 minutes; Prison Sentences on First Offenders, Note by G. Benson, MP.
43 Ibid: ACTO, 22 Nov. 1955 minutes.
44 ACTO, *Alternatives to Short Terms of Imprisonment* (1957).

detention in a detention centre, even though the senior centre at Goudhurst had been open for more than a year when the council began its enquiries. ACTO's report was a cautious and largely inconsequential document. It is very difficult to estimate what impact the combination of recommendations was likely to have on short terms of imprisonment, but one suspects that at most 4,000 of the 19,957 received on conviction with sentences of imprisonment of six months or less, or 20 per cent of the total, would have been spared imprisonment. The final report was sent to the new Home Secretary, R. A. Butler, in May 1957, and forwarded to all justices' clerks shortly afterwards. In June, courts were advised by the Home Office to consider imposing heavier fines, using probation with a requirement for residential treatment in cases of alcoholism, and making greater use of the power to order supervision pending payment of a fine. In December, 1958, an experimental attendance center was opened at Manchester.[45]

Most of ACTO's recommendations were implemented, including applying section 17 (Criminal Justice Act 1948), requiring the court to state the reason for its opinion that no other method than imprisonment was appropriate, to first offenders. This required legislation, to which the government extended only lukewarm support, in view of the reservations about the bill expressed by the lawyers in Cabinet. In May 1957, George Benson told the Home Office that he proposed to introduce a ten-minute rule bill applying section 17 to adults not previously convicted of an offence rendering them liable to imprisonment.[46] In October, R. A. Butler sought the authority of the Home Affairs Committee to give Benson assistance with drafting. The Attorney-General, Sir Reginald Manningham-Buller (whose abrasive style earned him the moniker, Reginald Bullying-Manner), did not want to give government support to Benson's bill. He thought that all lawyers involved in the imposition of sentences

> are anxious to avoid sending a man to prison if that can possibly be avoided; and that they would much regret a Bill such as this which contains a severe reflection on their conduct . . . What it will do is imply that persons have been wrongly sentenced to prison.

Moreover, he continued, "to make it appear now that the chances of a prison sentence are being reduced at a time when there is a great deal of crime is not going to make it easier to maintain law and order."[47] C. C. Cunningham, the new Permanent Undersecretary of State, thought the Attorney-General's belief that the superior courts did not unnecessarily send first offenders to prison, close to true yet irrelevant:

45 TNA, HO291/505.
46 TNA, HO291/64: 9 May 1957.
47 See R. F. V. Heuston, "Buller, Reginald Edward Manningham-, Viscount Dilhorne (1905–1980)," *DNB 1971–80* (Oxford, 1986); *The Times*, 10 Sep. 1980, p. 16. He was a law officer of the Crown for ten years continuously (1951–62) before his appointment as Lord Chancellor.

The unnecessary sentence of imprisonment is primarily a problem of the magistrates' courts, in relation to which the figures collected by the Advisory Council suggest that there may well be room for reduction in the number of first offenders sentenced to imprisonment.[48]

Butler told the Attorney-General that he was very concerned about

the growing congestion in local prisons, where more than 3,000 men are now sleeping three in a cell . . . A good deal of the congestion in local prisons, and even more of the pressure on the staff of local prisons, is caused by the rapid turn-over of short-term prisoners.[49]

The Lord Chief Justice was advised of Benson's bill. Goddard had no objection to applying the principles of section 17 to first offenders in *non-indictable* cases, but wanted the higher courts left out. There were cases, he said,

where in spite of previous good character prison is the only appropriate sentence. In sexual cases . . . the offence and public opinion often demand a degree of severity and this is certainly true in many of the homosexual cases where the element of corruption exists . . . I think it would be most unfortunate to let the idea get abroad that in crime the man is always to be entitled to a first bite before he can be sent to prison.[50]

At the Home Affairs Committee, Lord Hailsham, Lord President of the Council, joined the Attorney-General in opposition to the bill, saying that section 17 applied to the treatment of immature offenders, and the bill could not be regarded as a simple extension of that provision. Courts were often left with no alternative but to sentence an adult first offender to prison. A month later, the same committee asked the Home Secretary to take up with Benson the question of limiting the application of the bill to the magistrates' courts. Butler told Benson "that there is considerable opposition in legal circles to a Bill which extends the provisions of section 17 . . . to first offenders tried before courts of quarter sessions and assizes . . ."[51] Benson agreed

48 See Allen of Abbeydale, "Cunningham, Sir Charles Craik (1906–1998)," *Oxford DNB* (2004); *The Times*, 10 Jul. 1998, p. 25. Cunningham, formerly of the Scottish Office, was Permanent Undersecretary of State from 1957–66, serving four Home Secretaries— Butler, Brooke, Soskice and Jenkins—until he had a falling out with Jenkins over the highly centralized system of administration he had created in the Home Office. See Jenkins, *A Life at the Centre* (1991), p. 182.

49 TNA, CAB 134/1971, Home Affairs Committee, HA (57) 113, memo, 10 Oct. 1957; HO291/64: Attorney-General to Butler, 14 Oct. 1957; Cunningham minute, 21 Oct. 1957; Butler to Attorney-General, 22 Oct. 1957.

50 HO291/64: Butler to Goddard, 22 Oct. 1957; Goddard to Home Secretary, 1 Nov. 1957.

51 CAB 134/1968, HA (57) 23rd meeting, 24 Oct. 1957; CAB 134/2156, LC (57), 26 Nov. 1957; CAB 134/1968, HA (57), 29 Nov. 1957.

to such a limitation. Legal circles had succeeded in ensuring that no aspersions were cast on the infallibility of the higher courts in the matter of sentencing first offenders. The principles governing punishment would not be the same for all courts.

In February 1958, George Benson brought in his bill to restrict the imprisonment of first offenders. He rested the measure on what he called "one of the most remarkable constants in social statistics," the fact that all types of sentence gave exactly the same result in the case of first offenders, a success rate of not less than 80 per cent. In view of this, the House of Commons was entitled to ask courts, before they sent first offenders to prison, to think twice. By so doing they would help to solve the grave problem of prison overcrowding. Before the order for third reading, the Home Office had to decide whether official support would be extended to the bill. R. A. B. decided on "benevolent neutrality."[52] On third reading, Benson agreed to omit imprisonment in default of payment of a fine from the bill, since already courts were required to consider the question of means before imposing imprisonment. He also retreated on the effect the bill would have on overcrowding: "The Bill is not based on a hope that it will make any contribution worth mentioning to the overcrowding of our prisons." The main advantage of the measure was that it would give guidance to magistrates' courts: "If one looks at the sentencing policy of the 1,000 magistrates' courts, the only conclusion that one can draw is that there is no policy, that the whole position is completely chaotic."[53] The bill went through all its remaining stages. A magistrates' court could not pass sentence of imprisonment on an adult first offender unless the court was of opinion, and gave its reasons for that opinion, that no other method of dealing with him was appropriate.[54] In subsequent years, research was undertaken by the Home Office Research Unit and the Prison Commission into the working of the First Offenders' Act 1958, the main finding being that magistrates' courts (as well as higher courts) had given a smaller proportion of prison sentences to first offenders since 1953, and the decrease since 1958 was part of an established trend rather than the result of the First Offenders' Act.[55] In this finding, there was some retrospective justification for the Attorney-General's view that lawyers were already avoiding sending men to prison where possible.

V

None of the Prison Commission's initiatives nor any of ACTO's recommendations served to deflect the growing public and parliamentary critique of the penal system. For the entire decade the prison authorities were on the back foot as one attack after another hit home. The onslaught began in 1951 with an article by Negley

52   *Hansard*, vol. 582, 12 Feb. 1958, col. 399; TNA, HO291/64: RAB, 21 Apr. 1958.
53   *Hansard*, vol. 587, 2 May 1958, cols. 759–60.
54   TNA, HO291/20: ACTO, 26 Jun. 1958 minutes. See also H. M., "Notes and Criticisms," *British Journal of Delinquency*, vol. 9 (1958), p. 134.
55   TNA, 291/65: Notes by Dr. Hammond on the operation of the First Offenders' Act, *circa* May 1964.

Teeters, professor of criminology at Temple University, Philadelphia, on the basis of a six-week tour of some 25 prisons and borstals during the summer of 1949. Teeters recognized the problems confronting the prison authorities, including the shortage of funds to build new prisons, and a shortage of staff, but these did not make him pull his punches. He lambasted the exercise provided for prisoners—the "same senseless walking around in a circle"—the "sheer drudgery" of work that consisted of sewing or repairing mail bags, the poorly lighted cells and the long hours in them, the starchy and monotonous diet, the age of prison buildings, the occasional flogging of prisoners, the shortage of psychiatrists on staff, and the "wide social distance between guards and convicts." He saw no improvement in the treatment programme for women: "It is sterile, drab and monotonous, especially at Holloway. Females, as a rule are a forgotten group." Teeters exempted open prisons and borstals from his condemnatory verdict; and Maidstone prison under the unorthodox leadership of John Vidler emerged unscathed: "His prison is a bee-hive of activity and there is a human relationship between staff and inmates found nowhere else in England." Yet overall Teeters insisted that "there is an almost complete lack of imagination, resourcefulness and dynamics reflected in the traditional aspects of prison life;" "[r]outine and regimentation come first; the prisoner always last."[56]

In response, the editorial board of the *British Journal of Delinquency* and T. C. N. Gibbens of the Institute of Psychiatry, London University, acknowledged Teeter's criticisms on points of detail, yet fell back on the defence that the practical problems faced by the Prison Commission were very serious. As Gibbens stressed, the male prison population had doubled between 1939 and 1949 "without any compensatory building program." At times, however, the defence unwittingly provided evidence for the prosecution. The editorial board of the *Journal* answered Teeter's condemnation of the unconstructive atmosphere in the local prisons by saying,

> but does he know that in 1948, 24 per cent of total receptions on conviction were on sentences not exceeding one month, and another 45 per cent on sentences between one month and six months, which means that more than two-thirds of all convicted prisoners are there on sentences too short for any constructive treatment?[57]

Quite. The Home Secretary was not exempt from pressure on the subject, indeed from the Prime Minister himself in 1952. Churchill had got wind of the reduction in the number of prison staff, an economy directed by the Treasury. He told the Home Secretary, David Maxwell Fyfe, "On no account reduce the number of

56 N. K. Teeters, "The Prison Systems of England," *Journal of Criminal Law and Criminology*, vol. 41 (1951), pp. 578–99. For Vidler, see C. H. Rolph, *Further Particulars* (Oxford, 1987), p. 166.

57 Gibbens, "A Reply to Dr. Teeters' Article on the Prison Systems of England," *Journal of Criminal Law and Criminology*, vol. 41 (1951), p. 590; "Editorial," *British Journal of Delinquency*, vol. 2 (1951), pp. 81–3.

Prison Warders while the prison population is so rapidly increasing. I am also shocked about the '3 in a cell' conditions." Churchill also put his finger on one of the reasons for the increased population, "Owing to the non-infliction of corporal punishment . . . the Judges are imposing far heavier sentences and the prisons are overcrowded to a startling and dangerous degree."[58]

It was in Parliament, however, where the most penetrating critique of the prison system was eventually heard. The Seventh Report from the House of Commons Select Committee on Estimates (session 1951–2) called attention to the state of the 24 local prisons where they found only 8,672 cells for a daily average population of 11,904; to the shortage of prison officers (a further 500 officers would be needed for the three-shift system to be re-introduced); and to an average working week of 22 hours. Underemployment of prisoners had been especially high between 1949 and 1952, owing to a reduction of mat-making, a prison staple, in the face of overseas competition. The Select Committee went deeply into the subject of obtaining orders for manufactured goods from other government departments, and summed up as follows:

> Because orders are insufficient . . . it is impossible to provide enough con-
> tinuous employment . . . the hours worked are short and irregular. Moreover,
> a considerable portion of the work done is routine work of a monotonous
> nature, which is no doubt the only kind of work which a certain small per-
> centage of prisoners are capable of doing, but which is, in fact, being done by
> large numbers of prisoners who are capable of more responsible and intelligent
> work.[59]

In November 1952, Viscount Simon, a former Home Secretary, rose in the House of Lords to call attention to the condition of the prisons. There followed a fatuous debate, full of anecdote and impression, ranging over too many facets of prison life to have any useful effect. In reply, Lord Chancellor Simonds rehearsed the old saws: that 80 per cent of first offenders did not return to prison (for reasons unknown); that cell-sharing was a feature of local prisons and not of the central, regional training, or corrective prisons (though the locals held the bulk of prisoners); that the prison was not a factory, prison officials having no control over the number or quality of their workers; and increased recruitment of prison staff would soon allow the commissioners to extend the three-shift system to all local prisons.[60]

In 1955 and 1956, the House of Lords returned to the fray to greater effect. In May 1955, the Labour peer, Lord Pakenham, introduced a motion on the Report of the Prison Commissioners for 1953. Pakenham had been a prison visitor since the 1930s, he had contributed to Sir William Beveridge's landmark report on social

58 TNA, PREM 11/30; PREM 11/29: Churchill to Home Secretary, 6 Aug. 1952.
59 Quoted in Hugh Klare, "Her Majesty's Prisons," *Howard Journal*, vol. 8 (1953), p. 247, reviewing *Select Committee on Estimates: Prisons, Session 1951–2*; and *Second Report from the Select Committee on Estimates. Prisons, Departmental replies*, Feb. 1953.
60 *Hansard* (Lords), vol. 179, 18 Nov. 1952, cols. 318–72.

insurance (a founding document of the welfare state), and in 1955 he founded the first organization dedicated to the welfare of ex-prisoners, the New Bridge. As one obituarist observed many years later, "he saw politics less as a career and more as part of a moral crusade. Conscience came before party loyalty, heart before the head."[61] In a heartfelt and impassioned speech, the longest of that year in the House of Lords, judged by *Hansard* inches, Pakenham explored two main questions. First, how far was the central purpose of the prison system, which Fox had imagined, being implemented? His answer was emphatic:

> I submit that in respect of the great majority of our convicted prisoners . . . we are completely failing at the present time to live up to our declared purpose. We are doing nothing, or next to nothing, to reform them; indeed, it may well be argued that they are likely to have come out of prison worse than when they went in . . .

Second, what were the reasons for failing to carry out that central purpose, and what could be done "to live up to our professed ideal of the practice?"[62] To illustrate his answer to the first question, Pakenham cited figures to prove that no positive measures of reformation were being taken for 80 per cent of male prisoners, by which he meant the 12,850 in non-training prisons (central and local) out of the 15,400 men serving prison sentences. Only for the 2,500 in regional training prisons, corrective training prisons, and young prisoners' centres were efforts being made to reform the prisoner.[63] At least there they did a full day's work. The "supreme bottleneck" frustrating the efforts to extend the training system was, claimed Pakenham, the shortage of staff. Before the war, the three-shift system for prison staff was in force in all 31 prisons, which made it possible to keep prisoners in the workshops for seven to eight hours a day. Presently, the system was in force in only 12 of the 43 prisons, or just over a quarter. In most prisons, the workshop day was about 4½ hours and prisoners were locked up for the night at 5:30 p.m. So much for Lord Chancellor Simonds's hope in 1952 that the three-shift system would be universally in place in two or three years' time. Pakenham pressed the government to launch a recruitment campaign for prison officers and more assistant governors, with the aim of making the prison service of the future "a true social service."[64]

---

61 P. Stanford, "Lord Longford," *Guardian*, 6 Aug. 2001.
62 *Hansard* (Lords), vol. 192, 4 May 1955, col. 743.
63 Cf. Bottoms' calculation for 1962 in "Towards a Custodial Training Sentence for Adults, I," 1965 *Criminal Law Review* 589–90. Looking at receptions under sentence of imprisonment (including in default of payment of fine) in 1932 and 1962, and accepting that a sentence of 12 months or less was not suitable for effective training, "then 84.4 per cent of those received in 1962 fall into this category, as against 95.3 per cent of those sentenced in 1932." Since the difference between the two years was explicable by the larger proportion of receptions serving imprisonment only in default of fine payment in 1932, "the position seems to be much the same [in 1962] as in 1932." These figures do rather substantiate Pakenham's argument.
64 Ibid., cols. 745–6.

Other speakers added their voices to Pakenham's indictment. Viscount Templewood insisted that the problem of 21,000 men and women was not one of insuperable magnitude:

> Surely it is possible for a State like ours, a Welfare state, with all these immense improvements that we have seen in practically every social service, to face this small problem and to deal with it in a common-sense and urgent manner.[65]

He called for urgent action on "antiquated buildings, over-crowding, under-staffing and under-employment," and he recommended a fundamental review of work in prisons, plus efforts to empty the local prisons of short-term prisoners, including reconsidering suspended sentences. Lord Chorley called upon the government to take research seriously. The Home Office had assisted a number of research projects carried out by university departments (at Oxford, Cambridge, and London to the total tune of £2,500) and the Institute for the Study and Treatment of Delinquency, but "this is still a mere fleabite when one considers the vast extent of this problem." Nor had governments given the Prison Commission the support it deserved: "There are still in existence jails which were condemned long before the First World War and which are not fit to house swine, let alone human beings." And fewer men should be sent to prison:

> It is scandalous that at this late hour there are benches of magistrates, and even judges, who send men to prison for the first time without ever having given the probation officer an opportunity to see what he could do with them.[66]

In reply, the Joint Parliamentary Undersecretary of State for the Home Department, Lord Mancroft, claimed that they were endeavouring to tackle the problem of over-crowding by a programme of prison construction; the problem of staff shortages (1953 and 1954 had seen a slump in recruitment, possibly because of the high pay and convenient hours available in industry in the booming economy) by a new recruiting appeal; and the problem of work by building scores of new workshops and urging purchasing departments to send work the way of the prisons. He insisted that there was little deficiency of work of the better class for prisoners in central, regional, and corrective training prisons. So, too, said Mancroft, "there has been developed what I think is probably the most comprehensive open prison system to be found in any country." He did little to convince the person who had presented the motion. Pakenham closed the debate by saying, "I am putting it as mildly as possible when I say that I am sorry that there has not been any indication of a new approach. But Jericho did not fall at the first sound of the trumpet . . ."[67] The trumpet sounded again in July

65   Ibid., col. 758.
66   Ibid., cols. 783–4.
67   Ibid., cols. 791–9 (Mancroft); 806 (Pakenham). For the numerous briefs prepared for Lord Mancroft, see TNA, PCom9/1760. For press responses to the Lords' debate, see *The Times*, 5 May 1955; *Observer*, 8 May 1955, enclosed in PCom9/1760.

1956, when the Liberal peer, Lord Moynihan, rose to call attention to the prisons and particularly the after-care of prisoners. His opening gambit was to shift the discussion away from crime and moral decline, under the impact of affluence, which Conservative speakers increasingly harped upon, instead placing the onus on the prison system:

> If the present prison system is right, why is it that in times of prosperity, of full employment and of high wages, we have these vast numbers in prison? For we have always been led to believe that the main reasons for crime are unemployment, lack of opportunity and bad wages.[68]

Look at the people in prisons, borstals, and detention centres, he said, "One sees people who have gone wrong once and who, through this initiation, have become recidivists and spend quite a lot of their life committing crimes." Other speakers were similarly indignant about the state of the prisons. Labour peer and medical inspector of schools, Lord Haden-Guest, again described the prisons as in "a condition of swinish filthiness"; while Lord Chorley pressed the Home Office to remove "these sordid prisons from the face of the earth." Once more, Lord Mancroft answered for the government, spending most of his time on the new bridges between prison and freedom, such as pre-release training (including the Bristol pre-release hostel and home leave towards the end of the sentence), and changes in the organization of after-care. He threw in a few more improvements, including the fact that cell lighting had been raised from 20 to 40 watts. Following the debate, a *Times* leading article gave the disquieting verdict that the prison services, in comparison with the other social services, were "Last in the Queue."[69]

In the debate, Lords Moynihan and Chorley had cited the accounts in recent books by ex-prisoners: Peter Wildeblood's *Against the Law* (which Chorley was certain had "shocked everybody who has read it") and Norman Hignett's *Portrait in Grey*. They were not the only prison memoirs written in these years. There was Joan Henry's *Who Lie in Gaol*, published by Victor Gollancz; Anthony Heckstall-Smith's *Eighteen Months*; and Rupert Croft-Cooke's *The Verdict of You All*. These books collectively added to the growing critique of the penal system. They were largely written by "straights," or inmates who were well-educated, middle class, and in no way attached to a criminal lifestyle or identity.[70] Hignett was a solicitor and coroner charged with fraudulent conversion. Heckstall-Smith was a journalist also charged with fraud. In two cases, they were victims of what Croft-Cooke called "the wave of sexual McCarthyism that was sweeping over the authorities . . .

68 *Hansard* (Lords), vol. 199, 31 Jul. 1956, col. 424.
69 Ibid., col 455 (Haden-Guest), 457 (Chorley), 471–86 (Mancroft); Pakenham, *Causes of Crime* (1958), p. 75. See also T. L. Iremonger, *Disturbers of the Peace* (1962), p. 52: "For fifteen years after the war the penal system had such a low priority as to be almost out of the queue altogether."
70 See Steve Morgan, "Prison Lives: Critical Issues in Reading Prisoner Autobiography," *Howard Journal*, vol. 38 (1999), p. 335.

the 'drive' against homosexuals [in 1953–4]."[71] Croft-Cooke was sentenced to nine months' imprisonment on a trumped-up charge of gross indecency. Wildeblood, then diplomatic correspondent for the *Daily Mail*, was sentenced to 18 months' imprisonment for homosexual offences, together with Lord Montagu of Beaulieu and Major Michael Pitt-Rivers, a case that had a direct influence on the appointment of the Wolfenden Committee, whose 1957 report recommended that homosexual acts between consenting adults in private be legalized.[72] Not all these accounts were warmly received. In the *Manchester Guardian*, George Benson, chairman of the Howard League, furiously denounced the accuracy and motives of Joan Henry, and the prison commissioners declined to reappoint her publisher, Victor Gollancz, as a prison visitor. Terence Morris lauded Wildeblood's account, while suggesting that Croft-Cooke's picture of Wormwood Scrubs was "distorted," and that Heckstall-Smith was "less than fair to Maidstone." Yet Heckstall-Smith declared that Maidstone, under John Vidler, "is probably the only prison in the country that is run for the benefit of the prisoners and *not* the officers."[73] What was in these testimonies that was so damaging?

Inevitably, as in the prison memoirs of earlier decades, a good deal of their testimony focused on the degrading living conditions. Slopping-out brought the literary best out of Croft-Cooke ("a curious cortege . . . each man carrying his chamber-pot as though it were an oblation") and Wildeblood ("[t]he general effect, with three landings in view, was rather like some curious Neapolitan slum in which all the domestic chores were being done by men").[74] The coldness was a frequent complaint. The wind whistled through the Old Recreation Hut in Wormwood Scrubs, wrote Wildeblood, "reducing us all to a shivering huddle of creatures who would not have been out of place at Belsen." Joan Henry commented on the short working day at Holloway and the long hours of cell solitude, and Wildeblood thought the main complaint of prisoners was less the discipline or filthy sanitary conditions, but the fact that "no attempt was being made to fit them for life 'outside.' The work which they did in the shops was monotonous and almost useless from the point of view of a future career." In addition to his daily work, Wildeblood was compelled to do a compulsory cell task: "It was a maddening, useless task, sitting there in the dull glow of a 40-watt bulb screwed up high in the ceiling, eternally stitching away at the tough canvas, eight stitches to the inch." The inadequacies of psychiatric treatment were pointed out:

71　R. Croft-Cooke, *The Verdict of You All* (1955), p. 26. See also David Kynaston, *Family Britain 1951–57* (2010), pp. 97–8, 332.
72　For Wildeblood's obituary, see *The Times*, 16 Nov. 1999.
73　For Benson, see Victor Gollancz, *More for Timothy* (1953), pp. 335–6; for Morris, see *British Journal of Delinquency*, vol. 7 (1956), p. 73; A. Heckstall-Smith, *Eighteen Months* (1954), p. 45.
74　R. Croft-Cooke, p. 57; P. Wildeblood, *Against the Law* (1st pub. 1955; 1957), p. 104. And A. Hignett *Portrait in Grey* (1956), p. 137.

Out of 1,000 prisoners at the Scrubs [which Wildeblood noted was "a centre for the psychological treatment of offenders"], only 11 were receiving psychiatric treatment at the time I was there, and only a small proportion of these were homosexuals.[75]

And after-care left much to be desired. Prisoners came out into "an unfriendly world with no job, no home, nothing in your pocket but fifteen shillings from the Discharged Prisoners' Aid Society, and no friends except other criminals."[76] Finally, Heckstall-Smith put flesh on the bare phrase "three to a cell":

> [i]t does not need a vivid imagination to realise the conditions in some of those cells measuring 10 x 7 x 9 feet into which are crammed three prisoners often for eighteen hours out of the twenty-four! They eat, sleep, wash themselves and their socks, and use their chamber-pots in these tiny cells with their two sliding window panes measuring about six inches square.[77]

But these texts were not alone critical of prison conditions; they had a sting in the tail, indicting the prison system *in toto*. Heckstall-Smith hoisted Fox with his own petard, the statement in the Prison Rules concerning the purposes of training and treatment: "I can think of no place less fitted to conform with this cardinal rule than Wormwood Scrubs . . . Everything is without purpose. This strange, grey, drab community exists only to kill time and for no other reason." And later in the book, "In the light of what I have written, is it possible to detect the slenderest shadow of effort to uphold such a rule?"[78] Hignett insisted that rehabilitation was a word that did not reach the prisoner:

> Herein is the central and the essential condemnation of the prison system. The heart of the matter lies not in whether its yoke be heavy or light, or whether its discipline be strict or otherwise. Those matters are relevant only to the deeper question of the merit of imprisonment as a rehabilitative process; and in that merit . . . the present system is conspicuously lacking.[79]

In a word, he concluded, "imprisonment is retribution." Croft-Cooke agreed:

---

75 Shortly afterwards, the *Report on the Organization of the Prison Medical Service* (1964) spoke of the inadequacy of psychiatric training within the service. For the use of electric-shock treatment and oestrogen (a female sex hormone) to "treat" homosexual prisoners, see Kynaston, op cit., p. 554.
76 Wildeblood, pp. 159–61, 168–9, 186; J. Henry, *Who Lie in Gaol* (1952), pp. 41–2.
77 Heckstall-Smith, p. 22.
78 Ibid., pp. 32, 202.
79 Hignett, pp. 201, 217. Even the pinnacle of rehabilitation, Wakefield prison, came out poorly. Hignett wrote, "Wakefield proved to be the most godless and despairingly futile of all the institutions I had visited . . ." (p. 69).

The object of the prison system is, as it has been since the cellular gaols were built in Victorian times, to break a man's will and blast his pride to make him fit for reformers of the old bludgeon-and-Bible school. The object is to deprive him of everything which might enable him to think for himself, raise himself from despondency and fit himself for the future. Claims of any intentions but these are cant.[80]

If something was not done to change the penal system, he concluded, the prison population would reach 100,000 in the next ten years.[81] The last word belongs to Wildeblood. The Scrubs, of which Major Grew was the governor, was known to be the worst prison for first offenders. It was run "as a kind of caricature of the military life." Three of Grew's subordinates even brought to the prison "a typical 'sahib' attitude towards men of colour." Yet "when the stink of Wormwood Scrubs reaches the nostrils of the House of Lords," said Wildeblood, "it seems to be generally assumed that no blame can be attached to Major Grew." In May 1955, two months after his release, Wildeblood was sitting in the Distinguished Strangers' Gallery at the House of Lords. Below him, on the Woolsack, was the Lord Chancellor, Sir David Maxwell-Fyfe, who had sent him to prison. Lord Pakenham, who had visited Wildeblood in prison every three weeks, was speaking. Lord Mancroft later rose to make the government's reply:

> He was a smoothly handsome, youngish man in a beautiful suit, who would not have looked out of place in a motor show-room. His purpose this evening . . . was to sell [their Lordships] an account of the prison administration so grossly ill-informed that I could scarcely prevent myself from unscrewing the nearest brass gargoyle and throwing it at his brilliantined head. "I will gladly deal with the important points which have been raised," purred Lord Mancroft; and then proceeded to ignore every unpleasant detail of prison life which had been exposed, ascribing these to "the sensational crime stories by ex-prisoners which appear in our Sunday newspapers."[82]

In February 1957, there appeared in the *New Statesman and Nation*, an article "Prisons and Prisoners," in the form of an open letter to the new Home Secretary, R. A. Butler, written by C. H. Rolph, a City of London police-officer-turned-journalist, and member of the executive committee of the Howard League.[83] The

---

80 Croft-Cooke, p. 176.
81 Ibid., p. 253.
82 Wildeblood, pp. 155, 158, 178–80. See also Chris Waters, "Disorders of the Mind, Disorders of the Body Social: Peter Wildeblood and the Making of the Modern Homosexual," in B. Conekin et al. (eds.), *Moments of Modernity: Reconstructing Britain 1945–1964* (1999), pp. 135–8.
83 Rolph, "Prisons and Prisoners," *New Statesman and Nation*, 2 Feb. 1957, pp. 135–42. See Anthony Howard, "Hewitt, Cecil Rolph [pseud. C. H. Rolph] (1901–1994)," *Oxford DNB* (2004); *The Times*, 12 Mar. 1994, p. 19.

piece was a fitting end to the campaign of the past few years to get the Government to act. At 12,000 words, Rolph's piece was not for the faint of heart. It sought first to persuade the Home Secretary that the public was ready for his lead, thanks to the recent accounts of prison life by discharged prisoners, and to the stream of blue-books "of growing frankness and pertinacity," which included the report of the Select Committee on Estimates. This was followed by a number of familiar points: the fact that the Home Office knew so little about the effectiveness of the prison system, since so little had been spent on research (despite section 77 of the Criminal Justice Act 1948); and the fact that the penal system "cripples itself with such a dead weight of short sentences." Short sentences for petty thieves, vagrants, civil prisoners, and alcoholics were an exercise in futility, and they needed to be dealt with outside prison. There followed a long and distracting excursus on prison work and the attitude of the trade unions, which sought to exonerate the unions of obstructionism, a charge that had, claimed Rolph, "become little more than a convenient excuse for postponing any real plan for full-scale prison employment schemes at 'the rate for the job.'" The final sections advocated wider use of group therapy in prisons, better training for prison officers, and reorganization of the after-care system. A set of conclusions followed, which did not all arise directly from the evidence in the text. Rolph provided his own critique of the article when he wrote years later, "It is didactic and opinionated, and its peroration is full of things that poor Rab Butler 'must' do without further delay."[84]

Yet Rolph's article prompted an intensive discussion within the Home Office and Prison Commission, initiated by the Home Secretary himself, who read Rolph's piece within days and asked what consideration had been given to these issues in the department or the Prison Commission, and what the official view was of Rolph's suggestions. Lionel Fox, chairman of the Prison Commission, had commented on the article in draft, and esteemed Rolph "as an intelligent, well-informed publicist whose views we may not share but with whom we share a certain community of outlook in our own field." Fox wrote a long response for the Home Secretary, ranging widely, since he saw this as "an occasion when it is not out of place to take a rather radical view of criminal justice as a whole." At the front end, Fox felt strongly that the judicial machinery was not adequate for modern purposes. It was particularly ill-adapted to the penological maxim that courts should choose the sentence most appropriate to the needs of the offender on the basis of a scientific diagnosis of the offender's personality and potential. Too often the prison medical service had only days to complete a report for the court. Nor could the task be completed properly without the remand and observation centres that financial considerations continued to preclude. Fox then took flight:

---

84 Rolph, *Further Particulars* (Oxford, 1987), p. 147. The Friday evening discussion group in Wormwood Scrubs held three days of debate on Rolph's article: Peter Baker, *Time Out of Life* (1961), p. 169. Baker was sentenced to seven years' imprisonment in 1954 for uttering forged documents; he wrote his book in prison, smuggling out notebooks as he wrote.

I am prepared to argue that we never shall get a rational sentencing policy, especially in the superior courts, till our whole mediaeval system of assizes and quarter sessions is swept away, and a system of permanent courts of criminal justice in a few selected centres takes its place. A start has been made with the Old Bailey and the new Crown Court in Lancashire . . . I once persuaded a former Lord Chief Justice, in strict privacy, to share this view. I should not however care to try it on the present Lord Chief Justice.[85]

Fox said he had also discussed with Sir Frank Newsam, Permanent Undersecretary of State, "whether the whole philosophy of our criminal justice, with its concentration on punishment, is not open to question," which was preface to Fox's advocacy of offenders being made to pay compensation or restitution to their victims. When it came to prisons, Fox accepted the emphasis upon human relationships, group therapy, and staffing problems, crediting Hugh Klare, Howard League Secretary, for having moved him in this direction. Such ideas were taking shape in the Norwich experiment, and also "in a gradual indoctrination of the Service through conferences and 'in-service training' courses." As for prison labour, Fox maintained that work on "the mailbag level" was to be found exclusively in the local prisons, occupying only 5,000 out of 12,000 in local prisons, or out of 17,000 in all prisons. A large number of good-class skilled and semi-skilled trades also existed. He was unconvinced, finally, by Rolph's section on the trade unions, stating that "whatever aspect of prison labour is in question, the T[rade] U[nion] reaction is likely to be emotionally prejudiced, suspicious, and often hostile."[86]

Response papers came also from the Criminal Division, from Sir Frank Newsam, and from J. E. S. Simon, Joint Parliamentary Undersecretary of State. Two issues surfaced from these papers: one, the need to develop information about penal methods which could be shared with the courts, in an attempt to shape their sentencing policy; and two, the need to do something about prisons overcrowded with long-sentence prisoners. On the first issue, Newsam wrote, "We shall not, I think, make much advance without more information, particularly information about the effect of different forms of treatment and about the present sentencing policy or absence of policy of the courts." He wanted to make available to the courts the fullest information about the offenders before them, and also "a conspectus of the knowledge available about the effect of various forms of treatment and the trends of their own sentencing policy." Lodge also wrote a paper on how best to organize an expanded research programme. He saw the value of using university departments, but "we have not always been satisfied with what we were able to persuade them to do or with the speed at which they worked." Nor were these departments keen to employ advanced statistical techniques. An expanded Home Office research organization was the answer, thought Lodge, to study the results of treatment of offenders (along the lines of prediction studies), the use of

85 TNA, HO291/504: Fox's memo, 13 Feb. 1957.
86 Ibid.

fines, and the after-care of prisoners.[87] On the second issue, Simon focused on drawing the Lord Chief Justice's attention to the problem caused by long sentences, and on release on licence (possibly via a board of review with judicial, medical, and welfare representation) of all long sentences, over and above earned remission.[88] The Home Secretary directed that plans should be made for an expansion of the research programme both through the universities and by means of a research unit within the Home Office. Treasury authority was obtained for the appointment of two research officers. The Home Secretary also "expressed his urgent wish to see substantial progress with penal reform during his period of office."[89]

VI

In the next two years, the prospects for penal reform improved considerably. On 13 March 1957, after two months in office, R. A. Butler addressed the Commons, the Opposition having asked for a debate on prisons. His speech, said Lord Pakenham, "brought about a new atmosphere of hope overnight." Two years later, Pakenham again stated that the new Home Secretary "raised greater hopes of penal progress than had ever . . . been raised so suddenly in this country."[90] How did Butler achieve this? First, he said that "[t]he biggest initial shock which has come to me in examining this problem" was the paucity of money spent by the department on research. He intended to give "first priority" to expanding the research programme, using the sciences of sociology and statistics. Prison administration, he recognized, was dogged by overcrowding, understaffing, and shortage of prison work. The government was tackling these problems in two ways: by increasing accommodation and by stemming the inflow of prisoners. Building was underway on new prisons, including a psychiatric prison and new borstals. As for the second approach, he intended to study ACTO's report on reducing the number of short sentences of imprisonment, but he stressed the greater need to limit the number of long sentences. The executive could not interfere directly with the sentencing policy of the courts, but it could, said Butler, furnish courts with the fullest information about offenders, and with the results of the different methods of treatment available to the courts. The first tool for this purpose was the remand centre. The understaffing of prisons would be improved, along with staff training, which would emphasize "good case-work technique," and also progress would be made with prison work and earnings. His peroration, while falling short of the literary heights scaled by Churchill, was a positive statement of intent:

---

87 Ibid., "Notes on the Problems Raised by Rolph's Article and Fox's Comments Upon It, Prepared by C Division;" Newsam to Home Secretary, undated; Lodge's memo on research, 6 Mar. 1957.
88 Ibid., memo by J. E. S. Simon, 19 Feb. 1957.
89 Ibid., notes of discussion with Home Secretary, 2 Jul. 1957.
90 Pakenham, *Causes of Crime* (1958), p. 75; *Hansard* (Lords), vol. 215, 8 Apr. 1959, col. 407.

> I believe that we might one day come to think of our prisons not as places of punishment—though that they must be since deprivation of liberty must always be a punishment; not only as places where offenders are trained to be better men and better citizens, which is what they seek, however imperfectly, to be now; but also as places where an offender could work out his own or her own personal redemption by paying his or her debt not only to the society whose order he has disturbed, but to the fellow members of that society whom he has wronged.[91]

The most significant feature of the early deliberations within the Home Office was whether fundamental changes were required in penal sanctions and in the machinery of justice, and if a royal commission should be appointed for the purpose. Butler's was the voice that pressed the department to think expansively. He clearly wanted to do for penal policy what he had earlier done for education policy. Soon after the Commons' debate, Butler asked Lord Chancellor Kilmuir for his views on the appointment in 18 months' time of a royal commission to study the problems of penal reform:

> There has been no major enquiry in this field since the Gladstone Committee of 1895 and after 60 years I think we need to look again in the light of modern knowledge, and in particular, perhaps, of the development of psychology and psychiatric medicine, at our penal sanctions and the machinery by which they are applied.[92]

The three areas that Butler thought would repay study were the sanctions available (and he wondered if more use could be made of compensation and restitution), the methods of treatment (including the desirability of the indeterminate sentence, which had the advantage of combining judiciary and executive in the direction of treatment), and the organization of the courts. With the latter, Butler had in mind a wider use of the semi-permanent court, to ensure that judges had an opportunity to study a report on prisoners before sentencing them. At first, he was thinking of a Royal Commission on Assizes and Quarter Sessions. The Lord Chief Justice was initially doubtful of the need of such an enquiry, believing the courts already received all the help they needed from the prison commissioners and probation officers, and wishing to avoid an impression that the assize system was under scrutiny. He was persuaded otherwise by Sir Lionel Fox, chairman of the Prison Commission. The Attorney-General, Manningham-Buller, was opposed to a large-scale commission, while accepting the case for a more limited enquiry.[93]

91   *Hansard*, vol. 566, 13 Mar. 1957, cols. 1142–55.
92   TNA, LCO2/5113: Butler to Kilmuir, 9 Apr. 1957.
93   Ibid., Attorney-General to Lord Chief Justice, 9 Jan. 1958.

In May, Butler turned to his Advisory Council, addressing them for the first time at their 55th meeting, at which ACTO's sub-committee also presented its report on alternatives to short terms of imprisonment. Butler had no hesitation in declaring that the time had come for consideration of the wider problems of the treatment of offenders. "One thing that strikes me," Butler told council members,

> is that one cannot give much thought to any problem within this field without beginning to ask fundamental questions about what we are doing, why we are doing it, and whether the means we adopt are well-adapted to the ends which we now seek.

It may be, he continued, that the time had come for a comprehensive enquiry into these issues. Council members welcomed this idea, to judge from the minutes of the meeting: "Dr. Radzinowicz pointed out that the last one in this field took place at the end of the nineteenth century and that the time was coming for an authoritative body to take stock and make constructive recommendations." Butler also wanted the publication of ACTO's report on alternatives to short terms of imprisonment, and implementation of the recommendations not requiring legislation. He wanted to make progress with the building programme and with the problems of prison work and earnings, and asked the Council to examine the application of compulsory after-care of offenders sentenced to imprisonment.[94]

By July, the department was considering three lines of action. First, administrative action within the existing law, such as commending ACTO's report on alternatives to short prison sentences to justices, and opening a senior attendance centre for the 17–21 age group. Second, legislation, such as the First Offenders' Bill (this was Benson's bill) and possibly one to compensate the victims of crimes of violence (this was Margery Fry's scheme). Third, study and investigation. As the memorandum produced by Assistant Secretary, Miss Nunn, stated,

> It seems that we have reached a point where reform, if it is not to be confined to tinkering with the present system, must break new ground and involve the examination of assumptions and institutions which have been accepted for generations.[95]

This included fundamental problems of the organization of the courts and the relationship between the courts and the executive. The division also laid out a timetable for a royal commission, which would be announced in autumn 1957 and report in 1961–2, with possibly an earlier interim report on court organization. This timetable would also make it possible to feed research based on prediction

---

94 HO291/20: notes for Home Secretary's speech to ACTO, 3 May 1957; Ibid., minutes of ACTO 55th meeting, 3 May 1957. In June, Mr. Justice Barry replaced Drogheda as chairman of ACTO. Barry was a judge of the Queen's Bench Division.

95 TNA, HO291/504: 15 Jul. 1957.

studies and follow-up of offenders into the Commission's deliberations. A few days later, R. A. B. minuted, "I should like to make a speech in a few weeks' time on the philosophy surrounding all this."[96]

In September 1957, Butler asked Fox for a progress report on prison adminis-tration. Fox presented a mixed report. The Treasury was cooperating on the pro-posals for new prisons and the modernization of existing buildings. Meanwhile the number of prisoners sleeping three in a cell had increased from 2,000 to 2,700, and the commissioners were exploring the possibility of obtaining redundant army depots and barracks. Little advance had been made in relation to prisoner earnings, but on the strength of his recent visits to prisons, Butler insisted that a provision for improved earnings (a few pence per week) be included in next year's estimates. As for prison work, "the situation was alarming," said Fox. The prison population was rising, recruitment of staff meant that a three-shift system at local prisons was in sight, "yet the orders for work were dropping and with the revised defence pro-gramme would doubtless drop more seriously. There was a real danger that pro-gress, both at local prisons and elsewhere, would be prevented by lack of work." The Home Secretary was in discussion with trade union leaders. As the meeting note for the record then stated, "He was convinced, however, that it might become necessary to state publicly in the House of Commons that the attitude of the Trade Unions was hampering penal reform . . ." At the conclusion of the meeting, Butler said he was more and more of the view that if a royal commission were to be appointed, it should be done within the next few months.[97]

For the rest of September, the department struggled with the principal question of whether it was desirable to combine an enquiry on penal reform with one on the organization of the courts. From the point of view of providing a royal com-mission with the fruits of research, there was much to be said for delaying the enquiry on penal reform. Enquiry into court organization was rather more urgent—but was re-organizing the courts before knowing, via a larger enquiry into penal methods, what functions they ought to be performing, to put the cart before the horse? Sir Charles Cunningham, in the Scottish Home Department, soon to replace Sir Frank Newsam as Permanent Undersecretary of state, tried to cut the Gordian knot by asking if consideration of the structure of the courts was inevi-tably linked with consideration of new penal methods:

> If it was so linked it could hardly be undertaken until that investigation had been carried out. Would it not in fact be possible to look at this question of the courts apart from that of penal reform—on the ground that there is exist-ing congestion of business in the Courts of Quarter Sessions and that the

---

96 TNA, HO291/504: RAB minute, 20 Jul. 1957. Home Office discussion on the desir-ability of setting up a royal commission, included the point that "there appeared to be no appreciable body of opinion in Parliament or in the country in favour of penal reform. Experience had cast doubt on the advisability of setting up a Royal Commission in the absence of such pressure." See HO291/64, CRI 249/4/1.

97 TNA, HO291/506: Note for Record of meeting on 4 Sep. 1957.

intermittent visits of the Assize Courts to provincial centres mean that these cases cannot be systematically and quickly disposed of?[98]

Fox wholeheartedly agreed. It would be four years before the research on adult offenders in hand or in contemplation would produce reliable results for the proposed enquiry into penal reform. Yet the existing organization of the courts was already a handicap to the effective carrying out of modern conceptions of penal treatment. Newsam suggested they advise the Home Secretary to appoint a commission on the machinery of justice immediately, and a commission on penal reform later. In late September, Newsam advised Butler that this course had the advantage of an attractive programme of continuing activity. The Home Secretary would be able to say that he was pressing on with practical measures of penal reform (prison work and earnings, etc.); that research was ongoing and once results were available a royal commission would be appointed to examine the fundamental problems of the treatment of offenders; and that a royal commission was being set up to examine the immediate problem of the superior courts. Newsam also saw the main disadvantage of this course: that the royal commission on the machinery of justice

> might be inclined merely to adjust the existing system to cope with the increased volume of crime rather than to consider how the courts can be enabled to perform the increasingly difficult and important, and almost new, task of selecting the appropriate form of sentence.

Or, as he said later, "It involves taking a calculated risk of getting the wrong answers from the first Commission . . ."[99]

Butler responded,

> I am certainly glad that you have put up this major recommendation before the conclusion of your service . . . I reserve my position as to date at which Royal Comm. on Criminal Justice should be appointed & whether the Second Commission will be absolutely necessary (i.e. as a Royal Commission). We might have a different form of follow-up enquiry.[100]

---

98 Ibid: Cunningham to Newsam, 12 Sep. 1957.
99 Ibid: Newsam to Cunningham, 17 Sep. 1957; Newsam to Home Secretary, 25 Sep. 1957.
100 Ibid: RAB note, 28 Sep. 1957. See Allen of Abbeydale, "Newsam, Sir Frank (1893–1964)," *Oxford DNB* (2004); Francis Williams in *Daily Mail*, 13 Feb. 1956, enclosed in TNA, HO291/92. Newsam was Permanent Undersecretary of State from 1948 to 1957. He was a strong personality, with tremendous drive, intolerant of views that differed from his own. He was said to be a good "conferencier" when agreement had to be secured, and a tough decision maker.

This was the start of the burial rites of a Royal Commission on the Penal System, not to see resurrection until the mid-1960s. It was time to return to the Lord Chancellor. Cunningham wrote to Sir George Coldstream to ask for the Lord Chancellor's view on appointing a royal commission on the organization of the higher courts. The Lord Chancellor met with the Lord Chief Justice. The latter was unconvinced of the need to appoint a royal commission. A week later, however, after a further meeting, the LCJ agreed "not to oppose a Royal Commission aimed at considering the organization of the courts in relation to the changing concept of penal methods," and the Lord Chancellor was willing to put the paper to the Cabinet.[101]

In the memorandum for Cabinet, dated 18 October 1957, it was stated that the royal commission would examine the arrangements for the administration of justice in the higher courts, and in particular "consider what alterations are required to ensure that the Courts have before them the material necessary for the proper discharge of the increasingly difficult function of selecting the appropriate sentence." It was added, "We do not propose that this Royal Commission should enquire into the sentencing policy of the courts; this is a subject more germane to the wider inquiry into the treatment of offenders . . ." The proposal was criticized with some vigour by the Cabinet on the ground that it was important "to avoid unnecessary delay between the conviction and sentence" (adjournment to make enquiries about the offender would lead to such delay), and that it was dangerous to adopt "a procedure which would gradually undermine the principle of an itinerant judiciary, which was one of the cardinal features of our legal system." The main opponent was the Attorney-General, Manningham-Buller, who was unconvinced that the courts were seriously hampered in passing sentence by lack of adequate information about offenders. The upshot was that the Home Office had to water down the terms of reference, no longer requiring the royal commission to examine the whole structure and organization of the superior courts, or allowing it to recommend the abolition of, or fundamental changes in, the existing system. And they had to accept an Interdepartmental Committee. The Lord Chancellor was satisfied. The terms of reference left it open to the Committee to recommend the increased use of Crown Courts, like those in Lancashire, "and would avoid any suggestion of a reflection on the work of the judges."[102] When attempting unsuccessfully to recruit Lord Birkett to chair the committee, the Lord Chancellor made it clear: "we do not envisage anything in the nature of a radical review of the Assize system." The Lord Chief Justice recommended Mr. Justice Streatfeild, who accepted the chairmanship. Cunningham considered him "a man of open mind," and suggested "we should be able to rely on the non-judicial members of the Committee to make sure that the penological aspects of the problems under

101 Ibid: Cunningham to Coldstream, 2 Oct. 1957; Cunningham to Home Secretary, 9 Oct. 1957 and 14 Oct. 1957.
102 TNA, CAB 129/89, C (57) 236, 18 Oct. 1957; CAB 128/31, CC (57), 75th conclusions, 22 Oct. 1957; CAB 134/1973, HA (58) 5, 15 Jan. 1958; CAB 134/1972, HA (58), 7 Feb. 1958.

consideration will be given due weight." That role went to Barbara Wootton, Dr. T. C. N. Gibbens, and Professor W. J. H. Sprott.[103]

In late April 1958, the Home Secretary, a full year into his tenure, wrote a note to Cunningham setting out his thinking on the entire issue of penal reform:

> The more I study the penal system the more am I convinced that we must lose no time in laying the foundation for a long term system of reform. I have been long enough employed in tasks of this sort to realise that what matters is launching the scheme. Its execution may have to depend on future circumstances and on other Ministers . . . [N]o one with even a superficial knowledge of the prisons can be content with things as they are.[104]

For a start, a substantial building programme, including the modernization of the old buildings, was required:

> So long as our prisons appear essentially as they were in Victorian times it will be difficult to convince people that there is a change of heart within. It must be still more difficult to overcome the scepticism of the inmates . . . I think we need a forward programme, on a scale quite different from anything we have envisaged before, phased over say five to ten years. I should like to see a comprehensive plan, covering the whole of our prisons and borstals, which we could announce as our objective.

Second, Butler considered it "absurd to try to reform offenders in conditions of semi-idleness and that the key to regeneration lies in useful work, leading to a new self-respect." Surely the time had come, he wrote, "to force this issue with the trade unions. There is a great deal of sympathy for our point of view among the Opposition." Once this was achieved, prisoners' earnings could be improved, and the idea of restitution to the victim of a crime introduced. Finally, he wanted changes in the realm of the young offender, which the Prison Commission were already working on. Butler hoped to prepare the Cabinet in June for decisions on prison reform.

> At the same time we might consider whether we should not draw up a White Paper charting in general terms the course ahead. This would be represented as opening a new chapter in penal reform, and the pressure of public opinion would help to preserve the momentum of the advance.[105]

---

103 TNA, HO291/507: Kilmuir to Lord Birkett, 20 Feb. 1958; Lord Chancellor's Office to Cunningham, 6 Mar. 1958; Cunningham to RAB, 19 Mar. 1958; Graham-Harrison minute, 13 May 1958. For more on the Streatfeild report, see chap. 10 *infra*.
104 TNA, HO291/504, Butler to Cunningham, 28 Apr. 1958.
105 Ibid.

The White Paper would hopefully give inspiration and impetus to the proposed penal reforms.

VII

In late June 1958, Butler sought to recruit Prime Minister Macmillan for his plan of penal reform: "I earnestly hope that you will feel able to support me in what I believe will come to be regarded as a major advance in an important field which successive governments have long neglected." Macmillan responded positively (though Butler described it as one of "indulgent skepticism"):

> It would be a fine thing, both for the Government and for your own satisfaction, if you could leave behind you the same kind of record of your work in the Home Office as you did in the Education Office. I am all for it.[106]

Butler's memorandum for the Cabinet pulled few punches. He informed his colleagues that

> the great majority of men sentenced to imprisonment who are not serving a first sentence have to serve their sentences in the local prisons . . . in grossly overcrowded conditions and without adequate facilities for work or training . . . . Of some 15,000 men now serving sentences of imprisonment only about 4,000 (of whom over 3,000 are serving first sentences) are in central or regional or open prisons.

In the local prisons, nearly 5,000 men were sleeping three in a single cell:

> Any of my colleagues who have visited prisons, especially in the early morning, can obtain a clear Dickensian view of what this means. These local prisons are in themselves quite unsuited to modern conceptions of penal treatment, built as they were 100 years or more ago to serve the purpose of solitary confinement, treadmill hard labour, and brutal repression. They stand as a monumental denial of the principles to which we are committed.[107]

Gross overcrowding and shortage of work "will not make men better citizens; they will grind them down and make them worse." What needed to be done? The number sent to prison had to be reduced. Recent legislation relating to the imprisonment of first offenders would help, and he was considering legislation to

---

106 TNA, PREM 11/4691: Butler to Prime Minister, 27 Jun. 1958; Macmillan to Butler, 28 Jun. 1958. See also *The Art of the Possible: The Memoirs of Lord Butler* (Harmondsworth, 1971), p. 199.
107 TNA, CAB 129/93, C. (58) 136, 30 Jun. 1958: "Prison Reform."

increase the level of fines, as an alternative to imprisonment. Yet this would provide little relief. The total population in prisons, borstals, and detention centres had risen from 20,500 two years ago to over 25,000. *"This is the highest figure in this century."*[108] Three basic needs would have to be satisfied: remand and observation centres for the examination of persons charged with offences and classification of offenders; new accommodation for adult offenders to relieve the pressure on the local prisons; and a specialized system of treatment for young offenders, for which more detention centres were needed. In all, an enlarged building programme. In addition, he was contemplating methods of reducing the number sent to prison, some of which would require legislation, but first he proposed to publish a White Paper setting out the government's proposals. At Cabinet meeting on 3 July, Butler stated that overcrowding, "which was both an effect and a cause of the current increase in crime, had reached a point at which constructive work by prison staffs had become almost impossible." The Cabinet agreed in principle with the Home Secretary's proposals.[109]

The department set about drafting the White Paper. There has been doubt and discussion about who was the main draftsman. The gossip of the day was that C. H. Rolph was its unacknowledged author. It is inconceivable that the Home Office would have outsourced the drafting of a White Paper to a *New Statesman* columnist. C. H. Rolph never claimed he was the author, instead asserting it was written by an Assistant Undersecretary in the Home Office, known to Rolph, but whose name he would not reveal. Departmental papers indicate that a group representing the Prison Commission, the Criminal Department, the Children's Department, and the Research Unit, undertook the preparation of the White Paper, and that it was drafted by Lionel Fox (chairman of the Prison Commission), G. H. McConnell (Assistant Undersecretary of State), T. S. Lodge (head of the Home Office Research Unit), and Francis Graham-Harrison (Assistant Undersecretary of State in charge of the Criminal Department, surely the main contender for Rolph's tease).[110] The Home Secretary stayed closely involved in the process. In early August, he asked Cunningham to introduce "more colour into the Research section," by referring to what research had been done and its meaning: "It is in this part of the Paper that the answer to the Lord Chief Justice can be given, namely that we do not in modern times depend upon the Old Testament only (nor, I believe, does he)."[111] By the end of the month, Butler was worrying about a change in atmosphere: "The public are very anxious about the increase in crime, and in one respect, namely, sexual offences, there is a mild degree of hysteria":

108 Ibid, italics in original.
109 CAB 128/32, CC (58) 52 conclusions, 3 Jul. 1958.
110 C. H. Rolph, *Further Particulars* (Oxford, 1987), p. 148; TNA, HO291/509; PCom9/ 2002, minute to Home Secretary, 29 May 1958.
111 TNA, HO291/509: RAB to Cunningham, 6 Aug. 1958. Butler added, "I think we should explain more fully what an Institute of Criminology does and what it means."

Later this autumn I am to answer 28 bloodthirsty resolutions at the Conservative Conference at Blackpool. It is with the greatest difficulty that we
have chosen one of the 28 which is at least moderate. On this I can make
reasonably calming speech.

However, taking all this atmosphere together, I am sure we should avoid
the mistake of publishing a White Paper . . . which does not take into account
the severely practical attitude adopted by many members of the public towards
what they regard as increased danger to their own life, persons and
property.[112]

He wanted the paper to refer to the success of the police, to the present nature of
penal sanctions, and "the question whether those sanctions can, as the popular
mind imagines, be increased or be made more severe." This new atmosphere may
have made him postpone the idea of an autumn launch for the White Paper.[113]

By October, public and parliamentary interest had clearly been aroused, in part
by the publication of the Criminal Statistics, and in part by the outbreak of racial
violence in Notting Hill in the summer of 1958.[114] Unusually, an entire day of the
debate on the address (or queen's speech) was devoted to the problems of crime
and punishment.[115] The newest version of the White Paper was by now shorter,
which, said Graham-Harrison, allowed the specific proposals for reform and
improvement to stand out more clearly, but

it is also more apparent than before that these proposals do not involve any
very striking or novel developments, and the question whether there is really
sufficient material to justify the issue of a White Paper becomes a very obvious
one.[116]

---

112 Ibid: RAB to Cunningham, 27 Aug. 1958.
113 See Anthony Howard, *RAB: The Life of R. A. Butler* (1987), p. 264.
114 On 16 September, the nine youths who were arrested in the first wave of attacks on
West Indians were each sentenced by Mr. Justice Salmon to four years' imprisonment,
or double the normal sentence. See *Hansard*, vol. 212, 19 Nov. 1958, cols. 632–724;
Butler, *The Art of the Possible*, op cit., p. 208. See also Nigel Walker, *Sentencing in a
Rational Society* (Harmondsworth, 1969; 1972 ed.), pp. 92–3; E. Pilkington, *Beyond the
Mother Country: West Indians and the Notting Hill White Riots* (1988), pp. 127–8; C.
Waters, "'Dark Strangers' in Our Midst: Discourses of Race and Nation in Britain,
1947–1963," *Journal of British Studies*, vol. 36 (1997), pp. 234–5. Graham-Harrison
warned that unless the misconceptions about violent crime were checked, "the Secretary of State's policy of penal reform may well be prejudiced." See TNA, HO291/108.
To add to the Home Office's anxieties (though the case was technically the responsibility of the Minister of Health), Frank Mitchell, "the Mad Axeman," escaped from the
Broadmoor Institution in July.
115 *Hansard*, vol. 594, 31 Oct. 1958, cols. 476–577.
116 HO291/509: RAB to Cunningham, 6 Oct. 1958; Graham-Harrison to Cunningham,
10 Oct. 1958.

All that remained was the title. Butler suggested "Crime and Punishment 1958," which Cunningham thought pretentious and not truly accurate, preferring "Criminal Behaviour: Some Aspects of Prevention and Treatment." RAB changed this to "Penal Practice in a Changing Society: Aspects of Future Development," which had originally been the heading for section III. Burke Trend, Deputy Secretary of the Cabinet, informed the Prime Minister that it was a good White Paper: "well written; forward-looking; and evenly balanced as between the liberal and the severe approaches to this subject, without conceding so much to the former as to be merely sentimental."[117] In December, the draft went before the Cabinet, which approved it in principle, following the standard refrain on the "decline in spiritual values among the younger section of the adult population." Butler was encouraged to mobilize religious and social organizations to strengthen morality in private life. On 2 February 1959, Butler told the Commons that the White Paper was available to all members.[118]

A two-paragraph foreword stated that the White Paper "indicates the problem with which crime confronts us and the agencies which exist to deal with it," and underlined the need for "newly conceived research." "The Paper looks forward to the possibility of a fundamental re-examination of penal philosophy on the basis of the knowledge to be gained in this way . . ." A few pages into the Paper, reference is again made to how a "fundamental re-examination of penal methods . . . could be a landmark in penal history and illumine the course ahead for a generation." This could not be purely pragmatic; "it must concern itself with the philosophy as well as the practice of punishment. It must consider the fundamental concepts underlying our treatment of offenders . . ."[119] We have here an echo of RAB's earlier penchant for a Royal Commission on the Penal System, and a preview of what was appointed in 1964.

The introduction established the growth of crime, the level of prison over-crowding, and the three instruments (an efficient police force, the deterrent effect of the criminal law, and the penal system) on which the country depends "in its war against crime," possibly the first coining of the military metaphor. The main proposals were as follows. The sanctions for the enforcement of the criminal law and the machinery of the courts were being reviewed by the Streatfeild Committee and by the appointment of a Standing Committee on Criminal Law Revision. A research unit had been established in the Home Office, and the government would foster independent research, notably constructive research "into the use of the various forms of treatment and the measurement of their results . . ." The University of Cambridge was prepared, if funds could be found, to establish an Institute of Criminology. (Soon after, Lord Nathan announced a gift of £150,000 by

117 TNA, PREM 11/4691: 15 Dec. 1958.
118 TNA, CAB 129/95, C (58) 251, 12 Dec. 1958; CAB 128/32, CC (58), 85th conclusions, 16 Dec. 1958; *Hansard*, vol. 599, 2 Feb. 1959, col. 31. Butler had written an article in the *Sunday Times*, 16 Mar. 1958, on "Children and Crime: A Question of Responsibility," in which he called for "a proper sense of family responsibility."
119 *Penal Practice in a Changing Society* (Cmnd. 645), presented to Parliament, Feb. 1959.

the Wolfson Foundation, which led to the establishment of the Institute of Criminology at Cambridge under the directorship of Professor Leon Radzinowicz.)
Under development of penal methods, the paper introduced the Prison Commission's proposals for young adult offenders, which ACTO was examining, namely
the single indeterminate sentence of custodial training, integrating borstal and
imprisonment into a single system. The paper did not discuss the treatment of
juvenile offenders (those under 17 years of age) because the government was
awaiting the report of the Ingleby Committee, and anyway the amount of crime
committed by this age group was not increasing excessively. For adult offenders,
the paper focused on the provision of new observation centres, new training prisons, the rebuilding of existing prisons (with better workshops and remunerative
work), improved facilities for psychiatric treatment,[120] and the development of
after-care (a subject ACTO had recently advised upon), all of which would make it
possible for the local prisons to provide "an effective training programme for prisoners with shorter sentences." Finally, an ambitious building programme was proposed, alongside improvements in staffing. The increases in prison officers' pay
proposed by the Wynn-Parry committee had already been accepted.[121]

VIII

How significant was the White Paper? Viscount Templewood was in no doubt: "It
is one of the most remarkable documents issued from the Home Office for many
years. It sets out a comprehensive programme upon which the Home Secretary
intends to start, particularly dealing with the inadequacy of prison accommodation." Yet he added, ". . . there would seem to be nothing in the Home Secretary's White Paper that was not included, or at any rate inherent, in the
programme that I introduced twenty-two years ago, in 1937." Lord Birkett was
impressed by the implied interdependence of criminological research and penal

---

120 By 1962, special centres were in place within the prison service for the psychiatric
treatment of offenders serving prison sentences, whose condition did not warrant their
compulsory detention in a psychiatric hospital. They were at Wormwood Scrubs and
Wakefield prisons, at Holloway for female offenders, and at Feltham Borstal. The largest
was at Grendon Underwood in Buckinghamshire, the institution that had been imagined as far back as 1939, and which was finally opened in 1962, under the direction of
a medical superintendent. See TNA, PCom9/2284; PCom9/2178. See also Elaine
Genders and Elaine Player, *Grendon: A Study of a Therapeutic Prison* (Oxford, 1995). I
have made no close study of the Mental Health Act 1959, the most important landmark
in the treatment of the mentally abnormal in the twentieth century. The greatest
change the Act created was the widening of the categories of mental disorder which
could qualify for consideration by the courts for treatment in hospital instead of a penal
sentence. Hence, the Act diverted a sizeable annual quota of offenders to a more therapeutic milieu than the prisons, to which most of them otherwise would have gone. See
Nigel Walker, "The Mentally Abnormal Offender in the English Penal System," in
Paul Halmos (ed.), The *Sociological Review Monograph*, No. 9 (Keele, 1965).
121 Ibid, *passim.*

reform. The Lords Pakenham, Moynihan, and Silkin were less impressed by the paper, and Lord Stonham (Victor Collins) was positively sceptical:

> . . . before we commit ourselves to the building of more security prisons . . . we should first consider whether enough is being done to keep people out of prison, and, secondly, once they are inside, whether the treatment is designed to ensure that they do not go back.

He continued,

> If by more prisons we mean more of what someone called "crenellated Bastilles", with jangling keys and iron bars and rows of cage-like cells . . . then I say that we want not more but fewer prisons . . . If we were threatened with a 20th century plague we should not put people in a pest-house. Why should we continue to put people who should not be there in the modern pesthouses, the conventional prisons?[122]

Two points in the above are worth underlining. First, if Templewood's reference to his 1937 plans was valid with regard to the proposed building programme, when it comes to the specific penal proposals in the White Paper, it would be more correct to say that they smelled of Lionel Fox's lamp, incorporating ideas that he had developed during his extended chairmanship of the Prison Commission since 1942. Second, taking the White Paper at face value—"It is to the development of the means of dealing with the individual offender who has been sentenced by the courts to some form of *detention* that this Paper is principally directed"—*Penal Practice in a Changing Society* was above all an expansionist prison accommodation programme, and the high watermark of official optimism in prison treatment and training.[123] Butler later claimed that the paper outlined a £20 million building programme, "the largest for one hundred years."[124]

What the White Paper failed to do, as Stonham implied, was consider systematically the ways of keeping people *out* of prison. Yes, there was talk of increasing the number of detention centres and remand centres, along with observation and

---

122 *Hansard*, vol. 215, 8 Apr. 1959, col. 416 (Templewood), 439 (Birkett), 490, and 537 (Stonham). For the positive press response to the White Paper, see Mark Jarvis, *Conservative Governments, Morality and Social Change in Affluent Britain, 1957–64* (Manchester, 2005), p. 21. For Leon Radzinowicz's delayed response, see *Criminology and the Climate of Social Responsibility*, an address to the Howard League, 7 May 1964, p. 14. For the view that the White Paper implicitly accepted that imprisonment "has continued to be repressive and punitive for sixty years," see Dennis Chapman, *Sociology and the Stereotype of the Criminal* (1968), p. 223.

123 See A. Rutherford, *Prisons and the Process of Justice* (1984), p. 24; A. Bottoms and S. Stevenson, "'What Went Wrong?': Criminal Justice Policy in England and Wales, 1945–70," in D. Downes (ed.), *Unravelling Criminal Justice* (Basingstoke, 1992), p. 11; Lord Windlesham, *Responses to Crime*, vol. 2: Penal Policy in the Making (1993), p. 72.

124 Butler, *The Art of the Possible*, op cit., p. 201.

classification centres, and of implementing the intention of section 17 of the 1948 Act, all of which sought to reduce the number of people, especially young ones, spending time in prisons. Yet the other recommendations in ACTO's report, *Alternatives to Short Terms of Imprisonment*—the use of heavier fines, or ordering supervision pending payment of a fine; the use of probation with a requirement for residential treatment in cases of alcoholism; keeping first offenders out of prison— were notable by their absence. Probation was entirely ignored, on the grounds that a committee was to be appointed to survey the workings of the probation service. This is hardly surprising, since the White Paper was essentially a Prison Commission document (plus input from the Advisory Council on the Treatment of Offenders). Unsurprising, too, because the Home Secretary left the specifics in the White Paper to Fox and Co. Butler "had a genuine desire for prison reform without any very clear concept himself of what he wanted to achieve," according to Philip Allen, who served in the Prison Commission and Home Office in the fifties.[125] I might phrase it differently. Butler was more concerned with strategy than with tactics. The White Paper was to serve, as the conclusion stated, "as a chart by which we can plot our course in administering our penal institutions in the difficult years that lie immediately ahead of us." Tactically, it was short on the scale on which, and the rate at which, the government proposed to carry out its programme of action.[126]

In one of those strange historical coincidences, 1959, the year of *Penal Practice in A Changing Society*, also saw the publication of Francis Allen's article, "Criminal Justice, Legal Values and the Rehabilitative Ideal," which described "the dilemmas and conflicts of values that have resulted from efforts to impose the rehabilitative ideal on the system of criminal justice."[127] The writing was not yet on the wall for the rehabilitative ideal, but it was coming under critical academic investigation. George Benson, MP, an early patron of prediction methods in criminology, found no difference in rates of reconviction between borstal training and imprisonment in a young prisoners' centre.[128] Benson recruited Leslie Wilkins to the task of assessing the comparative effects of different kinds of penal treatment on offenders. Wilkins, joint author with Hermann Mannheim of *Prediction Methods in Relation to Borstal Training* (1955), and founding research officer of the Home Office Research Unit, later reflected in an oral interview:

---

125 Lord Allen of Abbeydale in conversation with Lord Longford, *Punishment and the Punished* (1991), p. 35.
126 The White Paper made no reference to capital punishment, since the Homicide Act 1957 (see the next chapter) had momentarily quelled the controversy over the death penalty, and Butler would not have wished to muddy the waters of penal reform by raising the subject.
127 Francis A. Allen, "Criminal Justice, Legal Values and the Rehabilitative Ideal," *Journal of Criminal Law and Criminology*, vol. 50 (1959).
128 Sir George Benson, "Prediction Methods and Young Prisoners," *British Journal of Delinquency*, vol. 9 (1959), pp. 192–4.

The fact that the development of the '55 prediction stuff was one of the first rigorous tests that really demonstrated that extreme differences in treatment modalities made no difference as to recidivism rates was significant. That was probably one of the first nails in the treatment coffin.[129]

129 Interview with Leslie T. Wilkins, 13 Sep. 1978 in John Lamb, *Criminology in the Making: An Oral History* (Boston, 1983), p. 84. See also Wilkins, "Retrospect and Prospect: Fashions in Criminal Justice Theory and Practice," in Don Gottfredson and Ronald V. Clarke (eds.), *Policy and Theory in Criminal Justice* (Aldershot, 1990), p. 187.

9

HOMICIDE ACT 1957

The politics of capital punishment

I

This chapter examines how the Homicide Act 1957 became law. It is a convoluted story of the lengths Conservative governments were willing to go, to retain some semblance of a death penalty for no more than a dozen murderers. Conservative governments were pulled in different directions. They had within their own ranks in the Commons a sizeable minority of fifth column abolitionists, a lock solid majority in the Lords for retention—composed of judicial and clerical advocates and backwoodsmen enthusiasts—and out in the shires party loyalists of a noisy retentionist disposition. Their first instinct was to reject all of the royal commission's recommendations for reforming the law of murder and restricting the use of capital punishment. This was never likely to deter the abolitionist MPs from pressing their case, which the government finally had to confront. Staring defeat in the face following the Commons vote in favour of abolition in February 1956, the Conservative Cabinet decided to take the step which Conservatives in both Houses of Parliament had vehemently opposed in 1948, and which the royal commission had deemed "chimerical": that of grading murders, confining the death penalty to the most heinous—although in the final analysis this became murders that were thought to be the most subject to deterrence. The 1957 Act was the Conservative government's contrivance to save face with its supporters, and to ditch the abolitionists, with little consideration of how the law would be administered in its aftermath. The Act was a product of the worst kind of political chicanery, and, as it turned out, too clever by half. The provision to establish degrees of murder removed the death penalty from nearly all forms of homicide, thereby undermining the retentionist argument that the penalty was a unique deterrent for a unique crime. Henceforth, the argument had to be that only *some* murders were deterred by the death penalty. Former supporters of the death penalty peeled off, including Her Majesty's judges, who could not stomach the glaring anomalies created by the new law. From this point onwards, capital punishment was an empty vessel; a hollow symbol of a bygone age. Yet, as Margery Fry's biographer observed, the 1957 act went far towards abolition, "far enough to set back total abolition for another span of years."[1] The Conservatives, still in power, found themselves unable to administer the last rites to the penalty. They had backed themselves into a corner, with only two ways out: either restore the death penalty for *all* convicted murders, or concede abolition. It became evident that only the election of a Labour government could untie the Gordian knot of the Conservatives' making. For more years yet, the death penalty took the oxygen out of the room, and distracted ministers and mandarins from the penal reform that was urgently required.

The most insistent theme is the party politics of capital punishment, which was critical to the 1948 attempt to abolish the death penalty.[2] At one level, the death penalty had little political purchase. Popular support for the death penalty remained high throughout these years, yet it found little systematic political expression. A 1959 Gallup poll ranked capital punishment down at twentieth of 22 issues that might influence the respondents' voting decision at the next general election.[3] Party manifestos rarely if ever referred to capital punishment. Until 1959, indeed, no party made mention in its manifesto of *any* aspect of crime and punishment.[4] For sure, no general election was ever influenced by the issue of capital punishment. Governments tended to steer clear of questions that bared deep-seated moral codes, or of attempts to change longstanding social and moral attitudes. In addition, parliamentary votes on capital punishment were frequently taken outside party politics by allowing a free vote of conscience. Of course, this in turn enhanced the influence of the House of Lords over the criminal law of murder, and notably that of the "sacred hierarchies" of senior judges and clerics. In a matter of conscience, where MPs voted free of party allegiance, it was possible for the Lords to assert their will over their Commons colleagues, without causing constitutional disruption.

Yet this can mislead us. For socialists and all "progressives," said John Sparrow in 1956, the death penalty "stands for a tradition stretching back from Lord Goddard to Lord Eldon; they oppose the death penalty for murder today because a hundred years ago the death penalty was imposed for stealing a card of wool."[5] Labour MP, Roy Jenkins in his 1959 statement of *The Labour Case*, cautioned that "it would be

1   Enid Jones, *Margery Fry: The Essential Amateur* (1966), p. 236.
2   See chap. seven *supra*. See also Douglas Hay, "Hanging and the English Judges: The Judicial Politics of Retention and Abolition," in D. Garland, et al. (eds.), *America's Death Penalty* (New York, 2011), pp. 153–5.
3   T. J. Wright, "Arguing for the Death Penalty: Making the Retentionist Case in Britain, 1945–1979," MA thesis, University of York, 2010, p. 8.
4   This confirms David Faulkner's impression that in the 1950s "criminal justice, apart from capital punishment, had a lower political profile. . ." See *Servant of the Crown: A Civil Servant's Story of Criminal Justice and Public Service Reform* (Hook, 2014).
5   Sparrow, "Heart versus Head on Hanging," *Daily Telegraph*, 27 Feb. 1956, p. 6.

a great mistake to imagine that there is here nothing to choose between the bulk of the two parties"; rather, "the difference between the pattern of votes on the two sides remains enormous."[6] Likewise, in his 1969 assessment of the party politics of capital punishment, journalist Peter Jenkins pointed out that the Conservative Party was predominantly a party of "hangers," and the Labour Party was "abolitionist almost to a man."[7] The proof was in the voting record. On the Second Reading of the 1955 Abolition Bill, 258 Tories voted for retention of the death penalty, only six Labour MPs. On the Second Reading of the Abolition Bill in 1965, 170 Tories voted to retain the gallows, only one Labour MP. Admittedly, Tory abolitionists numbered 47 in 1955, rising to 81 in 1965, a shift of opinion among Conservative parliamentarians that was important to the ultimate passage of suspension of the death penalty in 1965. The strict division of opinion in the Commons was all the more remarkable given that supporters of *both* parties in the country over-whelmingly favoured capital punishment.[8]

How did Peter Jenkins explain why, since the war, the Conservative Party had been the retentionist party and Labour the party of abolition. One possible explanation was that each party conformed to the views of its activists: liberal, middle class, intellectual reformers in Labour constituencies; illiberal, law 'n' order opinion-makers, more sensitive to public opinion or prejudice, in Tory constituencies. There is something to this. Conservative governments bent over backwards to keep the peace within the wider party and at the party's annual conference. Roy Jenkins insisted in 1959 that "the Conservative Party machine in the country is rapidly destroying the institution of 'free votes.'"[9] However, Peter Jenkins preferred a different explanation. He believed the difference between the parties was "of a theological kind." As he explained:

> The Labour Party in general believes that the world can be made a better place by the endeavours of active and enlightened government; the strongest tradition in the Conservative Party is pessimistic about the improvement of society and suspicious that government will only make matters worse. The

6   Roy Jenkins, *The Labour Case* (Harmondsworth, 1959), pp. 137–8.
7   Peter Jenkins, "The Life and Death of the Parties," *Guardian*, 19 Dec. 1969, enclosed in TNA, LCO2/8109.
8   See Neville Twitchell, "Abolition of the Death Penalty," in Peter Dorey (ed.), *The Labour Governments 1964–1970* (2006), pp. 339–40 and Table 18.3, p. 341. Hugh McCleod argued that the part played by the Church of England, especially the bishops, both in defence of the death penalty, and its abolition, has been overstated. He concluded, "The main role in the abolition of the death penalty in Britain was played by the Labour Party which, throughout most of its history, has drawn support disproportionately from religious minorities of all kinds. An analysis of voting by MPs in 1956 showed that Nonconformists, Catholics, Jews, and atheists or agnostics were all much more likely to oppose hanging than were Anglicans. . ." See McCleod, "God and the Gallows: Christianity and Capital Punishment in the Nineteenth and Twentieth Centuries," in K. Cooper and J. Gregory (eds.), *Retribution, Repentance, and Reconciliation* (Woodbridge, 2004), p. 355.
9   Jenkins, *The Labour Case*, p. 139.

two views of government and society correspond closely to the two views of human nature which have vied with each other throughout Christian history . . . One has it that all men are redeemable in this world; the other that some men are beyond redemption and must be treated accordingly. The question of murder and capital punishment brings these deep instincts of the parties to the surface.[10]

As we saw in Chapter 1, some of the earliest supporters of the "positivist" credo, of rehabilitation *contra* retribution, were the socialists and progressives. An integral component of the positivist agenda was the abolition of capital punishment. Within the Labour movement, opposition to the exercise of the death penalty was of such longstanding that Silverman was astonished that abolition did not naturally follow the election victory in 1945. The positivist movement made converts among Conservatives, for sure, such that most penal issues in the post-war decades garnered cross-party support. This was not true of the death penalty.[11] Conservative minister, R. A. Butler, could launch *Penal Practice in a Changing Society*, in many ways the summit of the rehabilitative ideal, yet at the same time resist abolition of the death penalty, even though he knew the death penalty was the greatest contradiction to the task of the penal system – training for responsible citizenship – which he currently administered.

II

We must plot the political path of these years. In mid–October, 1955, prompted by a Howard League memorial signed by hundreds of well-known people (lawyers, scientists, artists, newspaper editors, and religious leaders) urging the government to abolish capital punishment, or failing that to implement the royal commission's recommendations,[12] the Home Secretary, Gwilym Lloyd-George, sought Cabinet

10   Jenkins, "The Life and Death of the Parties," op cit.
11   For this reason, while recognizing the role of Conservative abolitionists, my view is opposed to that of Andrew Hammel, who argued that "the surprisingly non-rancorous nature of the debate on criminal justice policy. . . in the late 1950s and 1960s," the "obscuring of partisan boundaries," was a crucial factor in setting the stage for abolition of the death penalty. Rather, the fortunes of capital punishment were hostage to the balance of power between a Labour Party advocating abolition, and a Conservative Party committed to preserving the penalty. See Hammel, *Ending the Death Penalty: The European Experience in Global Perspective* (Basingstoke, 2010), p. 108.
12   *Manchester Guardian*, 4 Aug.1955, enclosed in TNA, HO291/94. The Cabinet had agreed on 29 Jul. 1954 not to accept the three major recommendations of the royal commission: that the statutory age limit below which the sentence of death may not be imposed should be raised from 18 to 21; that in all other cases the jury should be given discretion to decide whether there are such extenuating circumstances as to justify substituting the sentence of imprisonment for life for sentence of death; and that the test of criminal responsibility laid down by the M'Naghten Rules should be abrogated and that the jury should be left to determine, unfettered by the formula, whether at the time of the act the accused was suffering from a disease of the mind or mentally deficient to

authority to announce that the government had reached the conclusion that they could not accept the main recommendations of the royal commission and did not propose to introduce legislation to deal with the other recommendations. Brook advised the Prime Minister that this announcement "will probably give fresh impetus to the demand that the death penalty should be abolished."[13] The Cabinet agreed to the announcement, which was made on 10 November.[14] A few days later, Sydney Silverman (with the backing of seven Labour, two Conservative, and two Liberal MPs) introduced under the "ten-minute rule" a private member's bill to abolish or suspend the death penalty, which was read for the first time. Newsam at the Home Office had suggested not forcing a division against the bill's introduction. It would not be appropriate to put Whips on against an introduction under the ten-minute rule, he said, "and there would be a risk that without the Whips the Government would be defeated or that an embarrassingly large number of Members would vote in favour of the introduction of the Bill."[15] The government case would have to go by default in order to avoid a division and a head-on clash over the question of abolition. Thereafter, the government declined to give time for a debate on this bill, even though over 200 members put their names to a motion asking for an opportunity to debate the Second Reading.

Yet the Home Secretary informed the Cabinet that the reception accorded to Silverman's bill had revealed "the widespread concern felt in the House of Commons on the subject of the death penalty . . . [and] an unremitting pressure for the further discussion of this matter could now be expected." In the Cabinet discussion, moreover, the view was expressed that opinion in the new Parliament (following the 1955 general election) had moved in favour of abolition, and that it was doubtful whether there would be a majority for retention of the death penalty.[16] This was confirmed by Robert Carr, parliamentary private secretary to Prime Minister Anthony Eden, who informed the PM,

such a degree that he ought not to be held responsible. See PREM 11/1241. The Home Secretary had examined the possibility of announcing before the House rose, the decisions which the government had taken on the recommendations of the royal commission, but, according to Newsam, Permanent Undersecretary of State at the Home Office, "[t]he Ruth Ellis case supervened [she was executed on 13 July 1955] and you thought that, in view of the revival of the campaign for abolition, it was not a suitable moment for an announcement." See TNA, HO291/93, Newsam, 17 Aug. 1955.

13 TNA, PREM 11/ 1241, Brook to Prime Minister, 17 Oct. 1955. See HO291/93. See also "George, Gwilym Lloyd-, first Viscount Tenby (1894–1966)," *DNB 1961–70* (Oxford, 1981), pp. 664–6; *The Times*, 15 Feb. 1967, p. 12. Lloyd-George was an abolitionist in 1948, a retentionist in office.

14 TNA, CAB 128/29, CM (55) 35th conclusions, 18 Oct. 1955; *Hansard*, vol. 545, 10 Nov. 1955, col. 219; *The Times*, 11 Nov. 1955, p. 8.

15 *Hansard*, vol. 546, 15 Nov. 1955, cols. 207–10; TNA, HO291/100, Newsam, 14 Nov. 1955.

16 TNA, CAB 128/29, CM (55) 42nd conclusions, 22 Nov. 1955.

I am becoming rather worried about the Parliamentary position which is developing over the question of Capital Punishment.

I think it is probable that there is now a majority in the House in favour of abolition. A large majority of Opposition Members certainly hold this view and I believe that the minority of Conservative Members who share it, is considerably greater than it has been before and is probably still growing. When we had the Division on Capital Punishment early this year a number of our Members who voted against the trial suspension of hanging, only did so with very real hesitation and I suspect that some of them would vote the other way on any future occasion. On top of this a considerable number of our new Members are in favour of abolition.[17]

As a result, the following sequence of events might occur, Carr warned. If the Silverman Bill dies from the natural causes of parliamentary procedure, the Opposition will try to force a debate. If a debate takes place, a free vote will have to be allowed, in which case the majority in favour of abolition will show itself.

It would then look as if the Government had lost control of the situation and had been pushed against their will by the tide of events. This would be bad for Government prestige and bad also as a way of settling this problem.

The government ought to take the initiative in one of three ways available to them, Carr advised. *Either*: rally support for the status quo among Conservative MPs, otherwise the tide of opinion will continue to run in favour of abolition. "I think the trend in this direction has been accelerated recently by what is thought by many to be the completely negative attitude of the Home Office to all the main recommendations of the Royal Commission's Report." *Or*: the government could take the initiative in proposing reform, for example by suspending the death penalty except for the murder of policemen and prison officers. *Or*: the government could offer a debate and seek the opinion of the House. At least this would be better than having a debate forced upon the government. Above all, Carr concluded, "if we take no positive action we may find ourselves driven into an awkward and dangerous position."[18] On the following day, the Prime Minister announced that the government were ready to have a debate, though not before Christmas. Eden privately recognized that opinion in the new Parliament had moved in favour of abolition, but expected the weight of public opinion, which had not moved in the same direction, to make itself felt when a debate was imminent.[19]

On the day Eden made this announcement, Philip Allen, Assistant Undersecretary of State, and head of the criminal division at the Home Office, considered

---

17 TNA, PREM 11/1241, Carr to Prime Minister, 23 Nov. 1955.
18 Ibid.
19 *Hansard*, vol. 546, 24 Nov. 1955, col. 1653.

one way out of the difficulties facing the government. "One of the difficulties we find in putting forward the arguments in favour of capital punishment," Allen wrote, "is that the most cogent arguments relate not to hanging as such but to the hanging of particular classes of murderer." In other words, the argument pointed towards the creation of degrees of murder, but the attempt failed in 1948, and the royal commission were convinced it could not be done. Allen wondered if the way out of this dilemma lay in the more extensive use of the prerogative: "The Prerogative has the flexibility which legal definition lacks, and it is constantly used for making precise judgments about the wickedness not of a particular class of offence but of a particular murderer." The limits of prerogative were not static:

> they have, for example, moved forward in recent years as a result of the greater weight given to mental and emotional abnormality. It would not require a much greater shift to comprehend a number of cases which are recognizably not in the most heinous class. Probably most of the cases which lie between that class and the present limits of the Prerogative are cases in which a normally fairly decent person has found himself in an intolerable personal situation . . . People in this class kill for reasons inherent in their personal situation which are unlikely to recur: it would not be necessary for the protection of the public to keep them, if they were reprieved, for much beyond the average period . . . Among recent cases which would probably fall on the reprieve side of a new line those of Ruth Ellis, Alec Wilkinson, Richard Gowler and Mrs. Christofi came to mind.[20]

Another straw in the wind came a few days later when the Home Secretary addressed the Conservative Home Affairs Committee, a meeting of 120 Tory back-benchers. Lloyd-George, using a detailed departmental brief, began by stating that in his view capital punishment could be justified only if it had a deterrent effect—if it kept the number of murders lower than they would otherwise be. There was no reliable evidence either way about the effect of capital punishment as a deterrent. According to the royal commission, capital punishment probably was a deterrent, but it did not operate universally or uniformly; the police and prison representatives were convinced of the unique deterrent value of the death penalty on professional criminals (who declined to carry firearms in consequence), but very few of those who committed murder were professional criminals. As for the abolitionist argument that an innocent person may be executed, he felt there was no risk of this, falling back on the old saw: if there is a scintilla of doubt the Home Secretary recommends a reprieve. As for Timothy Evans, "I am satisfied that there is no ground for thinking that an innocent man was hanged in this case. There is

---

20 TNA, HO291/95, Allen to Newsam, 24 Nov. 1955. See Brian Cubbon, "Allen, Philip (1912–2007)," *Oxford DNB* (2011). Allen assisted Newsam, Permanent Undersecretary of State, with death penalty cases.

every reason to think that Evans murdered both his wife and child." Finally, there was no consistent public opinion on this issue.

> Public opinion is swayed very much by a few notorious cases, and does not make itself felt in the great majority of cases . . . Capital punishment seems to me to be an issue on which we shall look in vain to public opinion for a clear lead.

It was an issue for Parliament, though in reaching a decision Parliament must pay heed to public opinion. His concluding words were that "abolition is something that any enlightened society must aim to introduce when it can do so without too great a risk"; the continuing increase in crimes of violence did not suggest that this was the time for abolition.[21] The Home Secretary's address was well received, though Godfrey Nicholson's contribution—that the capital penalty should be exacted only for the most horrible crimes and not for "the ordinary man who murders his wife"—the Prime Minister was informed, "caused general jubilation."[22]

The Home Office began preparing a memorandum for the Cabinet setting out the arguments for and against capital punishment,[23] and drafting a motion for the debate which did not invite a direct decision on the question of abolition, which would leave the law as it was, but modify practice by making more extensive use of the prerogative of mercy. The extreme penalty would be reserved, in effect, for the most heinous cases. The memorandum reiterated the points made by Lloyd-George to the Home Affairs Committee; the draft motion ran into ministerial opposition. James Stuart felt the motion would lead to a general debate about the type of case in which the prerogative would be used in future, which was contrary to the policy of never stating the grounds on which the prerogative had or had not been exercised; and the number of cases in which the death sentence was solemnly pronounced but not carried out would be further increased; which would lead either to pressure to amend the law (to avoid executive interference with the judicial sentence) or pressure to abolish the death penalty (since the penalty was used in relatively few cases). Since they were agreed that the matter could not be dealt with by an amendment of the law, Stuart preferred to face the issue of keeping or abolishing the death penalty, citing the royal commission for support.[24] Lloyd-George held his ground, arguing that "if we are not prepared to accept abolition, and personally I am not, then we must, if possible, avoid a straight vote on the question." A free vote would hazard the risk of defeat: ". . . a defeat in the face of Government advice to retain capital punishment, would put us in a most embarrassing position." He had sought, therefore, "to find a Motion which would

21   TNA, HO291/95.
22   TNA, PREM 11/1241, minute 29 Nov. 1955.
23   This appeared as a Cabinet paper: TNA, PREM 11/1241, CP (55) 202, 16 Dec. 1955.
24   TNA, HO291/95, Stuart to Lloyd-George, 9 Dec. 1955.

command support from all those who are not committed to abolition." He concluded,

> I believe that if the death sentence were not executed in the cases which are now somewhere near the borderline, public opinion would support its retention for the remainder, and while the Royal Commission thought that as a matter of principle the rigidity of the law ought to be mitigated by the law itself and not by the Executive, I doubt if public opinion feels strongly on this point.[25]

Stuart could not see how Lloyd-George's resolution would be any more effective in avoiding the issue of abolition: "Will not the abolitionists put down an amendment to any Government motion which will test the feeling of the House on the question of abolishing or keeping the death penalty?"[26]

At this point it becomes difficult to keep track of the Home Secretary's approach to the issue. To judge from a note to Newsam on 17 December, he had reached the conclusion "that there is no alternative to a decision for or against capital punishment." The abolitionists would not be satisfied to be told that the supreme penalty should only be exacted in the most "heinous cases," since that was the present position. "There seems to me to be no half way house between retention and abolition, and unless we get a decision on this it will go on being raised whenever a 'sensational' case comes to be decided."[27] Yet when Cunningham in the Scottish Office drafted a possible motion which declared that "this House is of the opinion that the death penalty for murder should be retained," and when Newsam responded that the government should not set down "a positive anti-abolitionist motion" (since there could be no free vote on such a motion), Lloyd-George wrote to Stuart:

> . . . we ought to avoid a Motion which raises directly the issue of abolition because it seems to me that if we put down a Motion on the lines suggested by Cunningham inviting the House to support the retention of capital punishment we shall be almost bound to put the whips on. We could not on a Motion of that sort run the risk of a defeat.[28]

He wanted rather to offer a sop to the abolitionists, by suggesting that capital punishment would not be retained forever, offering the motion drafted by Allen to the effect that the House invites the Home Secretary to bear in mind, in his consideration of capital cases, "the abhorrence with which capital punishment is regarded by considerable sections of public opinion." There are times when Lloyd-

---

25 Ibid., Lloyd-George to Stuart, 12 Dec. 1955.
26 Ibid., Stuart to Lloyd-George, 16 Dec. 1955.
27 Ibid.
28 Ibid., Lloyd-George to Stuart, 30 Dec. 1955.

George seems to be brought back into line, and his backbone reinforced, by his senior officials. One constant, however, seems to be the burden he felt in reviewing capital cases and having to decide on reprieve or execution, which is why he advocated greater leniency in the exercise of the prerogative of mercy. Yet ultimately he would bow to Cabinet opinion, abandoning his desire to widen the use of the prerogative.

In early January, the Attorney-General, Manningham-Buller, weighed in. The Law Officers, he said, had doubts about the constitutional propriety of the Home Secretary informing the House that he proposed to make more extensive use of the prerogative, and about the wisdom of giving effect to the royal commission's proposals (on the age of liability to capital punishment, on provocation by words alone, on constructive malice, and on insanity) by way of the prerogative, while leaving the law unchanged. What the Home Secretary was suggesting would only widen the area of executive interference with the judiciary, and increase the number of cases in which the death sentence was pronounced but not carried out.[29] Newsam, however, thought the Law Officers were misinformed, and advised the Home Secretary that he was perfectly entitled to say what were the general principles he followed in considering capital cases.[30] At their 3 January meeting, the Cabinet agreed that capital punishment should be retained, and that it was inadvisable to attempt in the debate to make detailed reference to the manner in which the prerogative would be exercised in future. The terms of the motion for the debate were tabled for the time being. Towards the end of January, however, the Home Secretary submitted a memorandum to the Cabinet on the amendment of the law relating to murder, recommending action on some of the secondary proposals of the royal commission: (a) the abolition of the doctrine of constructive malice; (b) amendment of the law relating to provocation so that words alone could reduce murder to manslaughter; and (c) making it possible for a person who aids, abets, or instigates suicide to be guilty of that offence and not murder.[31]

Lloyd-George had come round to this approach following the publication of a report by a Committee of the Inns of Court Conservative and Unionist Society (chaired by Sir Lionel Heald, a former Attorney-General), entitled *Murder: Some Suggestions for the Reform of the Law Relating to Murder in England*, what the *Economist* labelled a "sociologically amateur pamphlet written by eight Conservative lawyers in their spare time."[32] The report recommended (a) and (b) above, and also the introduction of the Scottish doctrine of diminished responsibility. It sought to restrict the death penalty to those who had a clear intention to kill; it offered a

29 Ibid., Attorney-General to Prime Minister, 3 Jan. 1956.
30 Ibid., Newsam, 3 Jan. 1956.
31 TNA, CAB 128/30, CM (56), 1st conclusion, 3 Jan. 1956; CAB 129/79, CP (56) 27, 28 Jan. 1956; CAB 128/30, CM (56), 8th conclusion, 31 Jan. 1956.
32 For *Murder: Some Suggestions for the Reform of the Law Relating to Murder in England*, see TNA, HO291/104; *Economist*, 18 Feb. 1956, p. 449. See also Peter Rawlinson, "Heald, Sir Lionel Frederick (1897–1981)," *Oxford DNB* (2004).

middle way between the "two extremes" of the existing law and complete abolition. The adoption of these reforms in the law of murder would not have reduced the number of executions, though it would have restricted the number of death sentences passed. But it was not true, as the report claimed, that the effect of these reforms would be that the death penalty would be passed only on those who had committed a heinous crime, confining the debate on retaining the death penalty "to the moral issues upon which we believe it should be decided . . ."[33] Even so, Lloyd-George thought that narrowing the area of disagreement "will impress our supporters and particularly those who are with us on the main issue of retention of the death sentence, but are disturbed about its present scope."[34] At the Cabinet discussion on 31 January, Lloyd-George recommended a debate on a motion "which would provide an opportunity for a clear vote for or against the retention of the death penalty," and advised that the government would have a better chance of persuading the Commons to agree to retention if they offered to introduce legislation on three of the secondary proposals of the royal commission. He had clearly abandoned his advocacy of a more lenient use of the prerogative of mercy. The Cabinet agreed that the Commons' debate would be held on the motion, to be tabled by the back-bencher Sir Lionel Heald, favouring the retention of the death penalty but advocating legislation on the points set out in the Home Secretary's paper. Backbench government supporters were to be allowed a free vote, but members of the government were not free to vote against the motion.[35] In all, the government had decided to stand on proposals they had rejected when responding to the work of the royal commission. The motion was a compromise stitched together to prevent the retentionists from being beaten. The proposals for reform were tactical in nature. To the proponents of abolition, as Christoph so aptly put it, "this was obviously an attempt to launch a lifeboat into which some of the less certain consciences [among Conservative MPs] could gratefully clamber."[36]

Before turning to the February 1956 contest in the House of Commons, the result of which was to compel the government to introduce legislation to restrict the scope of capital punishment, it is helpful to record the *de facto* suspension of the death penalty for two years, while the law was being amended, in spite of the Home Secretary's insistence on scrutinizing each capital case for mitigating factors before exercising the prerogative of mercy. After the February 1956 debate, Lloyd-George stated in the Commons that it would be unconstitutional to abrogate capital punishment by administrative action in anticipation of the amendment of the law, and that each case would be considered on its merits.[37] Yet the belief had been put abroad, both by the press and by Silverman, that the death penalty had been suspended. By April, Lloyd-George wanted to make it clear again to the Commons that the law must be allowed to take its course in cases where there was no ground or room for leniency. This, he told

33 Ibid., p. 18; *The Times*, 19 Jan. 1956, pp. 5, 9.
34 TNA, CAB 129/79, CP (56) 27, 28 Jan. 1956.
35 CAB 128/30, CM (56), 8th conclusion, 31 Jan. 1956.
36 Christoph, op cit., p. 130.
37 TNA, HO291/1026.

Eden, "would greatly relieve my personal position and would ease my conscience."[38] This was not Eden's sense of their prior meeting, which he believed had decided that "there would not be any further executions until the Bill's fate was decided … ."[39] The Lord Chancellor was asked to consider whether it would be proper to announce that no further executions would be carried out while the future of the law was in doubt. Kilmuir advised that it was not open to the Home Secretary to announce in advance that he proposed to recommend a reprieve in every case, but he was entitled in exercising his discretion to take into consideration "the prospect of a change in the law taking place in the future." "He might decide," the Lord Chancellor continued,

> that public sentiment, whatever its view on abolition of the death penalty, would be shocked by a man being hanged when the future law was uncertain. If that were his view it would be a relevant factor for his consideration, but it would not relieve him of the duty of considering each case on its merits.[40]

This did not pacify Lloyd-George. As he told Eden, "I should find it very difficult . . . to recommend a reprieve where the only factor in favour of reprieve was the doubt about the future of the law."[41] It was agreed, however, that if a difficult case occurred, such as a deliberate poisoning for gain or the shooting of a policeman, the Home Secretary would inform his senior colleagues, and it might be that the law would be allowed to take its course. In January 1957, a case that presented no mitigating circumstances, the murder of a shopkeeper, landed on the Home Secretary's desk. The prisoner was an Indian, and the Home Secretary was advised by one of his officials,

> it could hardly be contemplated that the first case after so long an interval in which the law was allowed to take its course should be that of a coloured man . . . The fact that this may be the only ground on which a recommendation can be based illustrates without in any way decreasing the difficulties with which you are faced. If in a case of this kind you recommend a reprieve you may be criticized by the judges, if by no one else, for acting unconstitutionally.[42]

38   Ibid., Lloyd-George to Prime Minister, 13 Apr. 1956.
39   TNA, PREM 11/1241, Eden minute, 15 Apr. 1956.
40   TNA, HO291/1026, Kilmuir, 8 May 1956.
41   Ibid., Lloyd-George to PM, 18 May 1956.
42   Ibid, minute, Jan. 1957.

A reprieve was nonetheless granted. In all, the controversy over capital punishment in Parliament led to the *de facto* suspension of the death penalty for almost two years, from August 1955 to July 1957. The authority of the death penalty continued to ebb away.

Returning to the fray, in early February 1956, sensing the diversionary nature of the government's approach to the debate, the Labour Opposition tabled a motion proposing that capital punishment, as a penalty for murder, should be abandoned for an experimental period. This motion would be taken before a motion tabled by backbench supporters of the government, which meant that if the final speech before the division was to be made from the government side of the House, the debate would have to be held on the basis of a government motion. Hence, the Cabinet agreed to a government motion, inviting the House to declare that, while the death penalty should be retained, the law defining the crime of murder should be amended (though the Cabinet accepted that amendment of the law "would present formidable legal difficulties.")[43] The stage was set for the next set-piece battle between abolitionists and retentionists, which took place on 16 February 1956.

III

Prior to the debate, the press published a number of unscientific surveys of public opinion. The *Sunday Dispatch* (in their 50-Town Test), the *Daily Sketch*, and the *Daily Express* claimed that between 60 and 70 per cent of those surveyed wished to hang the murderers or retain hanging, though between 15 and 25 per cent leaned towards degrees of murder, hanging only the worst cold-blooded killers.[44] It was the *Daily Telegraph*, however, that went to the greatest lengths to sample opinion, commissioning the polling organization, Mass-Observation, to provide a comparison with a similar report on capital punishment in May 1948.[45] In each case, a sample of over 6,000 people was used. In 1956, in reply to the question, "Do you approve or disapprove of capital punishment," opinion divided as follows:

1. 49 per cent said they approved of capital punishment
2. 18 per cent said they disapproved
3. 25 per cent said they had not made up their minds
4. 7 per cent opted for degrees of murder.

People were also asked, "How do you feel about the death penalty for murder being given up for five years?" The pattern of opinion was as follows:

1. 34 per cent approved of the experiment (as compared with 13 per cent in 1948)

43   TNA, CAB 128/30, CM (56) 9th conclusion, 8 Feb. 1956.
44   See *Sunday Dispatch*, 12 Feb. 1956, front page and editorial; *Daily Sketch*, 16 Feb. 1956, front page. See also TNA, HO291/100, Public Opinion Polls; Nigel Nicolson, *People and Parliament* (1958, repr.1974), p. 92.
45   TC Capital Punishment Survey (1956), Box 2, File A, Mass-Observation Archive.

2.   45 per cent disapproved (69 per cent in 1948)
3.   5 per cent had mixed feelings
4.   9 per cent had not made up their minds

Of the 49 per cent who originally said they approved of capital punishment, 17 per cent said they would agree to a trial period without it, suggesting that 49 per cent approving of capital punishment did not necessarily mean 49 per cent in favour of its retention. If unwilling to support abolition in principle, many people were willing to try an experiment in abolition. It did seem to Mass-Observation that "approval of the death penalty may be losing ground."[46] The sex and education of respondents had little influence on the attitude adopted towards a trial suspension, but political and religious affiliation mattered. Labour and Liberal supporters, and Nonconformist, Roman Catholic, and Jewish members were much more in favour of trial suspension. Mass-Observation also revealed that the single, most important influence on opinion had been the hanging of Ruth Ellis. Of those who disapproved of capital punishment, 27 per cent were influenced by the Ruth Ellis case, 11 per cent by the Bentley/Craig case, and 12 per cent by miscarriages of justice. Mass-Observation also collected verbal responses from many people, which illustrated, wrote Mass-Observation to Michael Berry, editor-in-chief of the *Telegraph*, "that a great many people from all class groups consider the matter purely from an emotional point of view."[47] The overall conclusion of the Mass-Observation report was that between 1948 and 1956, a perceptible swing of opinion in favour of abolition had occurred, and in the country as a whole there was a bare majority for retention. The *Telegraph* reported the Mass-Observation survey's findings fairly, yet an associated leader claimed that "public opinion is by no means ready for abolition of the death penalty. This is a fact which should be given due weight when the House of Commons debates the question shortly."[48]

The debate in an excited and crowded House of Commons is easily encapsulated. First, the principal argument was on deterrence, and the strongest argument for hanging was the danger of the professional criminal. The Home Secretary, who turned in a characteristically stolid performance, again called on the evidence given by police and prison officers to the royal commission

> that the existence of the death penalty was the main reason why lethal violence was not more often used in this country and why criminals . . . do not carry firearms . . . The professional criminal is prepared, apparently, to accept imprisonment as an occupational risk, but not hanging . . .[49]

46   Ibid.
47   Ibid., England to Michael Berry, 31 Jan. 1956.
48   *Daily Telegraph*, 6 Feb. 1956, front page and editorial. See also Christoph, op cit., pp. 117, 122–4; Claire Langhamer, "'The Live Dynamic Whole of Feeling and Behaviour': Capital Punishment and the Politics of Emotion, 1945–1957," *Journal of British Studies*, vol. 51 (2012), pp. 432–3.
49   No objective evidence, as far as I'm aware, has ever been offered for this belief, frequently voiced, about professional criminals, firearms, and the death penalty.

After careful study of the commission's report, said Lloyd-George, in a muddy sentence, "I am not able to conclude that capital punishment has no uniquely deterrent effect."[50] He was opposed by Labour heavyweight and former Leader of the House, Herbert Morrison, who was firmly against abolition in 1948, but under the influence of Gowers' conversion, switched to abolition a week before the debate. "[H]aving wrestled with my mind as well as with my conscience and with my emotions about it," said Morrison, "I became increasingly doubtful whether the death penalty is as decisive a deterrent or is more of a deterrent than life imprisonment . . . would be." He also felt that, between 1948 and 1956, "there has been a change in public opinion in favour of abolition or suspension."[51] Secondly, the scale was tipped in favour of the abolitionists by the ineradicable belief that Evans was wrongly convicted, coupled with the belief that public opinion was in favour of abolition. As Arthur Koestler wrote in the aftermath of the debate, "the ghost of Timothy Evans seemed to have taken possession of the collective subconscious of the House."[52] The Home Secretary might profess: "I do not believe that in recent times there is any case in which an innocent man has been hanged . . . I say it after full consideration of the cases of Rowland and Evans."[53] Sir Lionel Heald, Attorney-General at the time of Evans' execution, might insist that both Christie and Evans "were concerned in that murder." The Lord Privy Seal, R. A. Butler, in an unexpectedly robust defence of hanging, might draw the debate to a close by declaring, "no innocent man has been hanged within living memory."[54] Yet all these interventions were trumped by former Home Secretary Chuter Ede, who in moving the abolitionist amendment, made no bones about the Evans case:

> I say that I do not believe that if, between the time the Court of Criminal Appeal gave its decision and the time when the man was hanged, there had been found on those premises those other bodies from which life had been taken by exactly the same *modus operandi* as was used in the case of Mrs. Evans and her daughter—I do not believe that public opinion in this country would have allowed that execution to have taken place.[55]

They were also trumped by Kenneth Younger's statement that the reforms proposed by the government "would have no effect on cases such as the Evans case, the Christie case, the Bentley case, the Ruth Ellis case . . ." The reforms, he said, "cannot affect the likelihood of a mistake, and would leave the consequences of a mistake as shocking as ever."[56] And they were trumped finally by Silverman's

50 *Hansard*, vol. 548, 16 Feb. 1956, cols. 2545, 2547.
51 Ibid., col. 2574–5. See B. Donoughue and G. W. Jones, *Herbert Morrison: Portrait of a Politician* (1973), p. 545.
52 Koestler, *Observer*, 19 Feb. 1956, p. 2.
53 *Hansard*, vol. 548, 16 Feb. 1956, col. 2542.
54 Ibid., col. 2583 (Heald); col. 2643 (Butler).
55 Ibid., col. 2558.
56 Ibid., cols. 2602–3. See Jo Grimond, "Younger, Sir Kenneth (1908–1976)," *Oxford DNB* (2004).

pronouncement that beyond the arguments about deterrence and retribution, there remained in everyone's mind "this fear that from time to time, at 8 o'clock or 9 o'clock in the morning, we take an innocent man out of a cell and break his neck."[57]

It is finally worth noting that both Younger ("I would say that there is a very strong emotional element in the decision which we have to take tonight") and Silverman accepted that the issue was emotional and moral:

> In the end the question which the House of Commons has to decide tonight will not be answered out of the law books and the legal precedents. It will not be answered by statistics. It will not be answered by fine distinctions, nuances of legal or penal theory. In the end, it is a great moral issue which the House of Commons has to decide tonight.[58]

On a free vote, the government's motion went down to defeat, 262–293. Edward Heath's analysis of the voting on the government's motion was as follows. Nine ministers abstained for reasons of conscience—Iain Macleod, Derick Heathcoat Amory, Selwyn Lloyd, Edward Boyle, Robert Carr, Anthony Nutting, J. R. Bevins, Enoch Powell, and Derek Walker-Smith. Forty-eight government supporters had voted against the government motion, including Nigel Nicolson, J. J. Astor, and Bob Boothby.[59] Labour's amendment passed, 292–246. Again, 48 Conservatives voted for abolition (including 18 newly-elected MPs), and nine ministers abstained. As in 1948, a government had misjudged the voting intentions of their own supporters, and the strength of abolitionist feeling in the Commons.

The press response to the outcome was mixed. The *News Chronicle* believed the conscience of the nation had made itself heard; the *Economist* declared "a victory for the cause of public decency"; while the *Daily Mirror* exclaimed, "Pull the Scaffold Down." By contrast, the *Daily Telegraph* and the *Daily Express* chorused "Emotion Wins!"[60] The most thoughtful response belonged to Arthur Koestler, who interrupted his series of extracts in the *Observer* from his forthcoming book, *Reflections on Hanging*, to assess the Commons' debate. If there is a single strand that holds Koestler's article together it is that the "emotionalism" which surrounds the death penalty applies to both camps. "It indicates the depths of moral passion that were stirred up, and the awareness of the symbolic nature of the issue." Koestler dissected the way in which the abolitionists shifted the focus from the wrong

---

57 Ibid., col. 2635.
58 Ibid., col. 2608 (Younger); col. 2634 (Silverman). Silverman was, by common consent, an opinionated, quarrelsome, uncompromisingly honest backbencher, an accomplished debater, with considerable parliamentary skill, from the radical fringe of the Labour Party. He was a gnome-like figure, only five feet tall, with a large head. In his single-minded pursuit of abolition of the death penalty, he puts one in mind of Wilberforce's campaign to end the slave trade. See *The Times*, 10 Feb. 1968, p. 10.
59 PREM 11/1241, Heath, 21 Feb. 1956.
60 TNA, HO291/96, HO Press Summary, 13–18 Feb. 1956.

question—whether the death penalty was a deterrent, which few would deny—to the right question—whether it is "a *unique* and *irreplaceable* deterrent," and established the new base line question: "capital punishment is evil, but is it a *necessary* evil?" On this terrain the abolitionists were assured of victory. They won "by establishing a climate of moral abhorrence against the death cell which put the burden of argument for its retention on their opponents." Yet arguments alone did not add up to the Commons' decision, Koestler wrote, "its ultimate cause was a revolt of moral conscience."[61] Victor Gollancz concluded that capital punishment had virtually been abolished. As he wrote to Lady Eileen Squire the day after the debate, ". . . we had a sensational victory in the Commons last night, and there is no further need for a campaign in the original sense."[62] Koestler did not share his optimism, which lead to an irreparable breach between the two co-founders of the National Campaign to Abolish Capital Punishment.[63] Subsequently, Gollancz was forced to back-peddle, recognizing that a great moral victory had yet to be converted into a final legislative victory—though he continued to tell correspondents that "abolition will almost certainly become law during the next twelve months."[64]

A few days after the debate, the *Daily Telegraph*, no supporter of abolition, in a leader entitled "Emotion Still," announced the publication of "a book which probably contributed more to the vote against hanging than any other single factor."[65] The book was Sir Ernest Gowers' *A Life for a Life?* It was published to ensure maximum readership before the Second Reading of Silverman's bill, but serialization in the *Evening News* brought it to public attention before the 16 February debate. According to Gowers in a 3 February letter, "Every MP has been sent a notice of the book by the publisher. I have sent the Bishop of Chichester a copy and he is lunching here tomorrow to be briefed for his speech in the Lords."[66] In his book, Gowers explained the reasons which had led him personally into the abolitionist camp, including "the right approach for a professedly Christian people," the possibility of hanging an innocent man, and the "objectionable, not to say repulsive, features of capital punishment and the morbid interest they excite." He added the line that caught press attention: "Perhaps the turning-point was when I learned what a large number of applications there were for the post of hangman." Each week, five people, on their own initiative, applied for the post of public hangman. "Any State institution, I thought, that inspires ambitions of that sort in its citizens, and satisfies some of them . . . surely does need to justify itself on utilitarian grounds."[67] The *Daily Telegraph* took this to mean, however,

61   Koestler, *Observer*, 19 Feb. 1956, p. 2.
62   MSS. 157/3/CAP/3/19, 17 Feb. 1956, Modern Records Centre, University of Warwick.
63   Peggy Duff, *Left, Left, Left: A Personal Account of Six Protest Campaigns 1945–65* (1971), pp. 108–9.
64   MSS. CAP/4/9, draft letter, 1 Mar. 1956; CAP/3/33, Gollancz to C. Thorold Pelham, 7 Aug. 1956.
65   *Daily Telegraph*, 20 Feb. 1956, editorial.
66   Quoted in Ann Scott, *Ernest Gowers: Plain Words and Forgotten Deeds* (Basingstoke, 2009), p. 167.
67   Ernest Gowers, *A Life for a Life? The Problem of Capital Punishment* (1956), p. 135.

that even Gowers "was swayed by a natural emotional repulsion," and led it to conclude its leader with:

> In short, a sensible, fair, ethically right and humanely administered system has been sunk by a broadside of emotional sentiments; coupled with the magnetic mine of Sir Ernest Gowers's book. Its explosive content is, in reality, equally emotional, but has been given by the character and attainments of its author the appearance of a judicial opinion.[68]

The trope of the "mawkish sentimentality" of the abolitionists died hard. The *Economist* took a different view. The central theme of the book was that the burden of proof did not lie on the abolitionists but on the retentionists, and that "it is not the abolitionists who are governed by emotion and sentiment but their opponents."[69]

IV

Cabinet ministers seem not to have realized that the vote could go against them.[70] Lloyd-George was dismayed by the outcome. Expecting to win the vote, the Cabinet had authorized Butler to state that the government would accept the view of the House and take action upon it. As the Cabinet Secretary wrote to the Prime Minister, "I foresee great difficulties over this . . . I have much in mind the embarrassments which beset the Labour Government when a similar situation arose in 1948."[71] And as Harold Macmillan wrote in his diary,

> The H of C has voted—on a motion—against the Death Penalty, and by a substantial majority . . . What does HMG do? Introduce a Bill of their own (in which they don't believe) and force it through the H of Lords under the Parlt Act? It's a paradoxical and rather perplexing situation.[72]

Lord Chancellor Kilmuir was informed on the day after the debate that Sir Frank Newsam had advised the Home Secretary to recommend to the Cabinet that the government, instead of they themselves bringing in legislation, ought to afford time for Silverman's bill. Newsam assumed that the House of Lords would throw out Silverman's bill, and it would therefore have to proceed under the Parliament Act. Sir George Coldstream, permanent secretary to the Lord Chancellor, thought this

---

68   *Daily Telegraph*, 20 Feb. 1956, editorial.
69   *Economist*, 10 Mar. 1956, p. 581.
70   See *Economist*, 3 Mar. 1956, p. 543: "Only after the motion was passed do Ministers seem to have considered its implication."
71   TNA, PREM 11/1241, Brook to Prime Minister, 21 Feb. 1956.
72   *The Macmillan Diaries: The Cabinet Years, 1950–1957*, ed. by Peter Catterall (2003), 23 Feb. 1956, pp. 538–9.

plan "would bring the maximum discredit on the Government." The Commons had pronounced for the abolition of the death penalty.

> In a matter of this kind the sooner the will of the people is given effect the better . . . For I believe that the Debate last night (for all its unevenness) reflected the trend of current opinion . . . I fear that if it is decided to wait to see how things go in the Lords . . . on Silverman's Bill, the Government will be accused of disregarding public opinion on a matter on which there has been a decisive Vote of the elected House.[73]

Nonetheless, the Home Secretary wrote to Eden a few days later, suggesting that the government insist upon a House of Commons bill sponsored by those who carried the abolitionist amendment:

> I see nothing undignified or inappropriate in finding time for a measure which has wide and respected support. It seems to me far better for the Government to make way gracefully for those who believe in abolition than to put ourselves into the equivocal position of sponsoring a measure which we have made it perfectly clear we consider to be contrary to the best interests of the country.[74]

This approach would avoid the government having to execute a *volte face*, and avoid putting the 250 MPs who voted with the government and who conscientiously objected to abolition, in the position of having to support government legislation to the contrary effect.

Already, government supporters outside of Parliament were beginning to show their dissatisfaction. Oliver Poole, chairman of the Conservative Party, told Eden that the party was getting the worst of it from both sides. The majority of Conservatives were against abolition and were dissatisfied with the government for allowing the present situation to arise (to which Eden wrote pitifully in the margin, "How could we help it!"). The minority who supported abolition were dissatisfied because the vast majority of Conservatives voted to retain hanging.[75] On 22 February, the Cabinet agreed that the government should find parliamentary time for a Second Reading of the Death Penalty (Abolition) Bill introduced by Silverman, which would be treated as a private member's bill. In discussion, it was opined that this bill would more than likely be rejected by the Lords. "Public opinion on this question was divided and this would, therefore, be a proper occasion for the exercise of the power of the House of Lords to delay the passage of legislation."[76] Eden announced this decision in the Commons.[77] Hugh Gaitskell, Leader of the

---

73 TNA, LCO2/5108, 17 Feb. 1956.

74 Ibid., Lloyd-George to PM, 20 Feb. 1956.

75 TNA, PREM 11/1241, Poole to PM, 22 Feb. 1956.

76 Ibid., CM (56) 16th conclusions, 22 Feb. 1956.

77 *Hansard*, vol. 549, 23 Feb. 1956, col. 574.

Opposition, was upset that Eden was unwilling to introduce a government bill to carry out the intentions of the House. On 12 March, the Death Penalty (Abolition) Bill was read a second time.[78] Members of the government were again free to abstain from voting. As for the further stages of the bill, the Lord President asked his Cabinet colleagues to remember that the bill was likely to be rejected by the Lords, and hence "it was desirable that the Government should take as little responsibility for it as they could during its passage through the Commons."[79] Nevertheless, this compromise solution only aggravated the poor impression which the government was making in the country. As Lord Chancellor Kilmuir stated in his memoirs, "Lloyd George was made to look foolish, as his advice was consistently ignored by the House; and the Government made to look weak and vacillating."[80]

The government were soon faced with the issue of what attitude to take towards amendments designed to retain capital punishment for certain classes of murder. While government spokesmen had previously rejected attempts to define murder or degrees of murder, the Home Secretary thought it would be difficult to oppose amendments designed to preserve capital punishment for the murder of a police constable, the murder of a prison officer by a prisoner, and a second conviction of murder. Such amendments achieved no defensible moral distinction, but it was possible to distinguish between some types of murder on practical utilitarian grounds, that is, to discourage criminals from carrying arms or prison officers from leaving the service, or for offences in respect of which it was particularly likely to be a valuable deterrent. The Home Secretary also felt that if the amendments were approved, the sponsors of the bill "would think that its main purpose had been destroyed."[81] In April, however, Norman Brook advised the Prime Minister that the government would be accused of inconsistency if, having rejected the idea of "degrees of murder," they now supported attempts to introduce that conception. Brook thought the government should refuse either to accept or to reject amendments moved by private members, and, in an extremely forthright statement, wrote,

> At this stage . . . we are not under any obligation to make this a workmanlike measure. Our real aim is to produce in the House of Commons a feeling that it is not, after all, worthwhile to change the existing law. Therefore, up to a

78 *Hansard*, vol. 550, 12 Mar. 1956, cols. 36–146.
79 TNA, PREM 11/1241, CM (56) 20th conclusions, 8 Mar. 1956. See *Economist*, 3 Mar. 1956, p. 543: "There must be a suspicion that Ministers are hoping that the House of Lords will find legal as well as moral arguments for delaying the Bill for the statutory year."
80 *Political Adventure: The Memoirs of the Earl of Kilmuir* (1964), p. 264.
81 TNA, PREM 11/1241, CP (56) 92, 29 Mar. 1956. Also HO291/100, Newsam to Home Secretary, 14 Mar; Newsam to Cunningham (Scottish Home Department), 21 Mar. 1956.

point, it is a good thing that the House should get itself into a tangle over the Bill. At least the Government has no duty to try to prevent this.[82]

Brook also wanted to avoid the potentially embarrassing position of the government giving advice to the House on an amendment, only for the vote to go against them. Eden emphatically agreed.[83]

Between April and June 1956, the Silverman Bill passed successfully through the committee stage, despite the efforts of retentionists to push a series of damaging amendments, thanks largely to the parliamentary skill and tenacity of Silverman himself.[84] The majority for abolition held together, and the Commons gave the bill its Third Reading at the end of June.[85] Now it was the House of Lords' turn. Before then, however, the one-day annual conference of the Conservative Women's National Advisory Committee reminded the government of anti-abolition sentiment in the shires. Women Conservatives overwhelmingly approved a resolution welcoming the amendment to the Death Penalty Bill, which would retain capital punishment in certain circumstances, and urged Tory MPs to persevere in their efforts in order to bring attention to the views of the many women who were strongly opposed to abolition.[86] As Nigel Nicolson observed, "the broad division on party lines in Parliament was reproduced more rigidly among party-workers in the country."[87] The Second Reading of the Death Penalty (Abolition) Bill was taken in the Lords on 9 and 10 July. An unusual number of peers expressed their intention of taking part in the debate. Conservative "backwoodsmen" with inherited titles emerged from obscurity to speak and vote against the Bill. The *New Statesman*, riffing on the parable of the banquet in Luke 14, was hard-hitting:

> From the hills and forests of darkest Britain they came: the halt, the lame, the deaf, the obscure, the senile and the forgotten—the hereditary peers of England united in their determination to use their medieval powers to retain a medieval institution.[88]

According to Lord Silkin, "I believe that the last occasion when this House had a gathering of this kind was during the debates on the Irish Home Rule Bill [in 1912]." According to Lord Kilmuir, "The Chamber, the peeresses' box and the galleries were all packed."[89] No fewer than 333 peers would ultimately vote, or as

82 Ibid., Brook to PM, 9 Apr. 1956.
83 Ibid., Brook to PM, 19 Apr. 1956.
84 See, e.g., *Hansard*, vol. 552, 16 May 1956, col. 2019, an amendment to exclude the armed robber (including the burglar and housebreaker) from the scope of the bill.
85 *Hansard*, vol. 555, 28 Jun. 1956, col. 787.
86 *The Times*, 13 Jun. 1956, p. 6.
87 Nicolson, *People and Parliament*, op cit., p. 87.
88 *New Statesman and Nation*, 14 Jul. 1956, p. 29.
89 *Hansard* (Lords), vol. 198, 10 Jul. 1956, col. 829; Kilmuir, *Political Adventure*, op cit., p. 265.

P. A. Bromhead noted, "250 more than in an average division." Two days after the vote, Harold Nicholson informed Vita Sackville-West,

> Eric [Lord Carnock] came up yesterday to vote in favour of the abolition of hanging Bill. Charlie [Lord Sackville] and Sam [Lord St. Levan] voted against. "Three uncles", Nigel [Nicolson] snorted, "left the back-woods to vote, and only one of them voted the right way!" But he was pleased that all the bishops were on his side.[90]

The Cabinet decided that government spokesmen in the Lords would advise the House to reject the bill, in line with what Salisbury called the evolving "constitutional convention" that the Lords,

> remain free to reject a contentious Bill on Second Reading on the ground that it was not the subject of a mandate from the electorate. No proposal for the abolition of the death penalty had been put to the electorate during the last election and this was a constitutional argument for rejecting the Bill.[91]

This conveniently neglected the fact that in February 1955, only three months before the general election, the Commons had had a full debate on capital punishment, and MPs had openly declared their view on the issue. As for knowing what electors believed, MPs received floods of letters on capital punishment (more even than on the Suez crisis), held meetings with constituents, and read the Gallup polls.[92] Anyway, abolition was never an election issue since it was considered to be a matter of conscience and free votes.

Viscount Templewood opened the batting for the abolitionist side by saying, "It is a short Bill dealing with a long controversy":

> Indeed, I suppose that there never has been a penal question that has been so constantly discussed over the last century and a half and that has led to such an intensity of discussion during the last eight years. Press, public, both Houses of Parliament and the Royal Commission, each in turn has examined the question from every possible angle.[93]

Lord Chancellor Kilmuir, who had agreed with the Marquess of Salisbury, Leader of the House, to say that the government thought it was a "rotten" Bill, presented for the government, drawing upon the statements to be found in the royal commission's report to argue for the retributive and deterrent efficacy of capital

---

90 P. A. Bromhead, *The House of Lords and Contemporary Politics 1911–1957* (1958), pp. 47–8; Harold Nicholson, *Diaries and Letters 1945–1962* (1968), pp. 304–5.

91 TNA, CAB 128/30, CM (56) 47th conclusions, 5 Jul. 1956.

92 Nicolson, *People and Parliament*, op cit., p. 99; TNA, HO291/101, Nicolson to Lord Salisbury, 12 Jul. 1956.

93 *Hansard* (Lords), vol. 198, 9 Jul. 1956, col. 564.

punishment. Again, the armed professional criminal took centre-stage, for whom execution was said to be a real deterrent.[94] In the long debate that followed, Lords Malvern, Milverton, and Tweedsmuir expressed concern that the colonial territories would follow suit and abolish the death penalty, the latter Lord stating, "What might not be too bad in this highly civilized country would be a vastly different thing in countries just emerging from the Stone Age."[95] Viscount Stansgate (William Wedgwood Benn), in a mischievous speech, declared that he was repulsed by the argument that "If you stop hanging whites, it will be more difficult for us to hang blacks."[96]

It soon became clear that by 1956, unlike in 1948, a split had developed between the lawyers and the bishops. While Lord Goddard thundered, in Stansgate's abridgement, about "how horrible murders are, and what a lot of experience he has of their repulsive details," and Lord Tucker lauded the long-term deterrent effect of capital punishment,[97] the Archbishop of York, in his maiden speech, while accepting "the moral necessity of retribution within our penal code," and declaring it fallacious to assume that the New Testament disallowed the taking of life by the state, declared that the death penalty "no longer has the moral dignity of representing, in an absolutely sure and certain way, the will of the community to inflict an unspeakable penalty for an unspeakable crime."[98] The sentiment was seconded by Exeter, Chichester, and Manchester, the latter stating that as long as the death penalty remained, "I do not see how it is possible to go forward with the general plan of prison reform."[99] Only the Archbishop of Canterbury, whom Harold Macmillan described in his diary as "a silly, weak, vain and muddle-headed man," wanted to amend the bill to allow the death penalty to be retained for particular categories of murder, as "a witness to the sacredness of human life and of social order, which no society, perhaps, should ever altogether dispense with . . ."[100] In the end, both archbishops, and eight bishops voted for the bill, and one (Rochester) against it. It should be added that the judges were split, four of the eight Law Lords voting for the bill. Lord Silkin closed the two-day debate by echoing Manchester: "I believe that to-night is one of the climacterics in the history of penal reform."[101] When the division took place, The Times reported, "peers were wedged in an almost solid mass trying to make their way to the lobbies."[102] They rejected the bill by 238 to 95. It was cold comfort for the abolitionists that the number voting for abolition was three times as great as in 1948.

---

94 Ibid., cols. 581–3.
95 Ibid., cols. 593, 644, 673.
96 Ibid., 10 Jul. 1956, col. 785.
97 Ibid., cols. 784, 812. For Goddard's speech, see Ibid., cols. 735–46.
98 Ibid., 9 Jul. 1956, col. 598.
99 Ibid., cols. 629–30. Ibid., 10 Jul. 1956, cols. 694, 715.
100 Ibid, 10 Jul. 1956, cols. 747, 750; The Macmillan Diaries, op cit., p. 577.
101 Ibid., col. 838.
102 The Times, 11 Jul. 1956, p. 10. See also Christoph, op cit., pp. 148–50.

V

At the first Cabinet meeting following the Lords' decision, Salisbury told his colleagues that the speeches of the Archbishop of Canterbury and Lord Samuel, suggesting the government introduce legislation to narrow the scope of the death penalty, had made an impression on the House. This approach would allow the retention of capital punishment to command a wider measure of support throughout the country, and would allow the government to regain the initiative. The bill could be represented as a genuine attempt to reconcile the widely divergent views expressed both in Parliament and in the country.[103] Discussion indicated that there was a substantial body of opinion in the Cabinet in favour of taking this path. If the government gave a positive lead in the matter, they would be justified in using the Whips against a private member's bill to abolish the death penalty, and perhaps it could be defeated without using the Whips. Harold Macmillan, who was against abolition, nonetheless bent the ears of the Prime Minister and the Lord Chancellor with his view that "we must respect the broad decision of the House of Commons against hanging on general principles," and "we must only ask for its retention in special cases on grounds of public order." The exceptions, he thought, should be as few as possible: "the test shd be . . . what exceptions are required in order to preserve the broad structure of a peaceful society." "We don't want to get into philosophizing about degrees of moral guilt."[104] This was preface to an intense ministerial discussion of the content of a government bill. Attorney-General, Manningham-Buller, was first out of the starting gate, advising that a government bill should have two main objectives: to reduce as far as possible the number of cases where persons were tried for murder when it was common knowledge that a conviction would be followed by a reprieve; and to retain the death penalty only in those categories of murder where public opinion could be expected to support retention.[105] Newsam at the Home Office took another stab at the selection of the types of murder for which the death penalty might be retained. Unlike the Attorney-General, Newsam omitted murder by shooting or explosives, and murder by poisoning, since a high proportion of these murderers were reprieved or certified after conviction.[106]

Thereafter, a Committee on the Law of Murder, cut out from the Cabinet, under the Lord Chancellor's chairmanship, met regularly. At its first meeting on 16 July, they discussed the Attorney-General's letter. The discussion suggested that

---

103 TNA, CAB 128/30, CM (56) 48th conclusions, 11 Jul. 1956. On 16 July, Salisbury minuted, "I think that the Govt. will probably be forced to state a view before the Summer Recess, and. . . I think that they certainly ought to do so. Otherwise, they will lose the initiative that they have, by a great stroke of luck, managed to regain. That would be disastrous." See TNA, LCO2/5108.

104 TNA, PREM 11/1747, Macmillan to PM, 23 Jul. 1956; *The Macmillan Diaries*, op cit., p. 577.

105 TNA, LCO2/5110, Attorney-General to Lord Chancellor, 12 Jul. 1956.

106 TNA, CAB 130/119, Memo by Permanent Undersecretary of State, Home Office, 17 Jul. 1956.

while relying on a wider use of the prerogative of mercy was preferable to amending the law,

> the fact had to be faced that reform of the law broadly on the lines suggested was the minimum price which must be paid to attract sufficient support from Government back-benchers for a measure which would preserve the deterrent effect of capital punishment as an instrument in maintaining law and order.

The Chief Whip told the committee that 11 of the 47 government supporters who had voted for the Second Reading of the Silverman bill would be prepared to support a government bill, "provided it offered a liberal measure of reform and went considerably further than the four points [constructive malice, provocation, suicide pacts, and diminished responsibility] with which the Government had previously undertaken to deal."[107] Already, the difficulty of selecting the categories was evident. The Attorney-General wanted murder by poison to remain punishable by death, "as such murders were often premeditated, heartless and cruel, and difficult to prove." He added that he had the support of the Lord Chief Justice.[108] Yet murders by poison included cases of "mercy killing" and murders of children by distraught women, cases that were typically reprieved.

At the back of all these deliberations was the need to forestall or defeat a revived Death Penalty (Abolition) Bill, which might be reintroduced under the Parliament Act (which had reduced from two years to one year the time that the Lords might delay legislation that had continued support in the Commons), and which would in due course abolish capital punishment. The government's position in the country, it was believed, would be weakened if they were to allow an abolition bill to be enacted without taking any positive lead by introducing their own bill. By late September, the Lord Chancellor presented the Cabinet with a bill to retain capital punishment for those forms of murder which most clearly struck at the maintenance of law and order, and were most likely to be deterred by the death penalty. As Kilmuir stated, "It is aimed at the professional criminal, the person who carries a gun, the killer of the agents of law and order, and the rare but dangerous multiple killers of the type of Christie and Heath." It was a middle way between retention and abolition, expressive of middle opinion in the Lords. It would allow the government spokesman at the party conference to accept a resolution advocating legislation. And the Lord Chief Justice did not dissent from the proposal.[109] Against this, Tory abolitionists might support an amendment to convert this bill into an abolition bill; and they might subsequently support the Silverman bill. The Cabinet Secretary advised Eden that

---

107 TNA, CAB 130/119, Committee on the Law of Murder, 16 Jul. 1956.
108 Ibid., 2nd meeting, 18 Jul. 1956.
109 TNA, CAB 129/83, CP (56) 214, 24 Sep. 1956, memo by Lord Chancellor.

the balance of argument is in favour of a Government Bill on the lines proposed . . . It would be a very weak line for the Government to acquiesce now in the Silverman Bill, contrary to all the advice which Ministers have hitherto given to the House.[110]

The Cabinet agreed to the bill, but ministers were told not to disclose the government's intention at the party conference.[111] At the annual conference of the Conservative Party in October, 33 resolutions were submitted on capital punishment, more than on any other single subject, and following a noisy debate conference passed a resolution to oppose the Silverman abolition bill, but to amend the law of murder to limit its application. The Home Secretary was compelled by the uproar on capital punishment to depart from his intention not to speak, presenting a guarded statement that the government were considering the possibility of retaining the gallows but of limiting its use to the worst murderers—the idea he had rejected in February 1955, and the idea the royal commission had rejected.[112]

On 22 October, the Prime Minister was presented with a petition, drawn up by the National Campaign for the Abolition of Capital Punishment, bearing the names of 2,500 leaders in the professions, social services, and trade unions, calling on the government to legislate for abolition of capital punishment. The Church, the press, and the acting profession were well represented. No judge graced the list, but many magistrates, recorders, and prison governors had signed on. As Silverman informed the Prime Minister,

> this is the first occasion since the days of Charles I that a group of distinguished citizens has found it necessary to call upon the Government to govern themselves in accordance with the majority will of the House of Commons.[113]

On the following day, Eden informed the Commons that the government was preparing its own legislative proposals in relation to capital punishment.[114] Abolitionists were deeply disappointed that the government was unwilling to adopt the Death Penalty (Abolition) Bill as a government measure, or at least to provide time for its consideration as a private member's bill in the new session as they had in 1956. This way, certain abolition lay, for the Lords' veto would be nullified— which is exactly why the government demurred from doing any such thing.

---

110 TNA, PREM 11/1747, Brook to PM, 25 Sep. 1956.
111 TNA, CAB 128/30, CM (56) 67th conclusions, 26 Sep. 1956.
112 *The Times*, 13 Oct. 1956, p. 3; TNA, HO291/99; Nicolson, *People and Parliament*, op cit., p. 93.
113 *The Times*, 22 Oct. 1956, p. 3; *Hansard*, vol. 558, 25 Oct. 1956, col. 827. In the petition, the bill passed by the Commons in 1948 is wrongly described as one to abolish capital punishment. It was technically a bill to suspend the death penalty for a period of five years.
114 *Hansard*, vol. 558, 23 Oct. 1956, cols. 486–90.

In a poorly-attended House, the Home Secretary introduced the Second Reading of the Homicide Bill on 15 November, which dealt with two questions: what should constitute murder and how should murder be punished? Some homicides which had hitherto been murder would not be murder in the future, and some homicides which would still be murder would not be punishable by death. The principle of the bill, Lloyd-George said, was

> limiting capital punishment to the minimum essential for the maintenance of law and order. We have selected the capital categories so that they cover the form of murder most inimical to the public peace and most likely to be prevented by the deterrent effect of the death penalty.

Capital punishment was to be confined to murder by professional criminals, murder of agents of law and order, murder by shooting or causing an explosion (the former associated with gang warfare), and murder by the man who makes a practice of murder. The inclusion of murder by shooting, the only category dependent on method rather than context or function, spread the net wide. It meant that most *crimes passionels* would *ipso facto* be capital murders (including the Ruth Ellises), where the deterrent aspect was weakest, but the government had decided it was more important to retain the death penalty in cases of gang warfare or public affrays. In addition, the Home Secretary said that homicides about which the public were uneasy were to be taken out of the category of murder: homicides which were murder only by virtue of the doctrine of constructive malice; homicides by people who, though not insane, were gravely abnormal; homicides under severe provocation by words; and homicides in pursuance of a suicide pact. The number of people sentenced to death but reprieved would fall, because the total number of persons sentenced to death would be lower, and because the capital crimes would be those in which it was not common to find mitigating circumstances.[115] By putting into the same bill reform of the murder law and the provisions establishing degrees of murder, the government had in effect made any independent abolitionist effort extremely difficult, since it was almost impossible, even by significant amendment, to bring the government bill within the provisions of the Parliament Act.

Labour members, who intended to support the Second Reading, nonetheless accused the government of rushing forward to block the Silverman bill in order to prevent the Commons from having its way under the Parliament Act. Anthony Greenwood reminded the Home Secretary that most of the proposals in the bill were included in the compromise clause rejected by the Lords in 1948; a clause which, said George Benson, "was butchered to make a judge's holiday." Degrees of murder had been rejected, said Greenwood, when the government was trying to stem the tide of abolitionist feeling, but now they had to fall back upon it. The new proposals were bound to create more anomalies than were being removed.[116]

115 *Hansard*, vol. 560, 15 Nov. 1956, cols. 1148–51.
116 Ibid., col. 1196 (Benson); cols. 1159, 1166 (Greenwood).

Silverman pointed out the abandonment of deterrence by the Home Secretary, since the latter declared that only some murderers were deterred by the death penalty:

> He [the Home Secretary] must make up his mind whether he accepts the unique deterrent quality of the death penalty or whether he rejects it. If he rejects it, he must reject it for all forms of murder, and if he accepts it, he must accept it for all forms of murder.[117]

Yet the bill removed that deterrent from 80 per cent of those crimes which up to then had been visited with the death penalty.[118] The Commons gave the Homicide Bill an unopposed Second Reading. For the past 12 months, the Commons had spent more time on abolition than on any other subject, including Suez.

In January, in his first speech as Home Secretary, R. A. Butler had to oppose an amendment which sought to retain the death penalty for the poisoner. Butler rested his case on the fact that the bill did not seek to distinguish degrees of murder according to their heinousness or dreadfulness. Moreover, since only five people had been executed for poisoning in the past 30 years, the government did not wish to put persons on a capital charge who, from experience, would not be executed.[119] In early February, in his first major speech, Butler claimed that the bill "accepts abolition, save in relation to certain limited classes of case . . ." As Conservative MP, Peter Kirk, later expressed it, the bill was progressive, not straight-out, abolition.[120] Greenwood returned to the fray, saying that the view was widespread that the bill was

> the Government's method of introducing the abolition of the death penalty by rather back-stage methods. I hope that it means that there will be no more hanging, but I would have preferred us to have abolished hanging, if this is in the Government's mind, by doing it openly . . .

He added, "This is not a penal reform Bill; it is a Tory Party preservation Bill." For purely party ends, the government "have been prepared to make an ass of the law." The inconsistencies, inequities, and illogicalities were glaring, as Greenwood took pleasure in pointing out,

> If he strangles a night watchman in the course of theft he will hang, but if he strangles an eight-year-old girl in the course of rape he will not hang. If he shoots his wife he will hang but if, on the other hand, he kills her by slow and systematic poisoning, he will not.[121]

117 Ibid., cols. 1180–1.
118 See Sydney Silverman, "Murder and the Constitution," *New Statesman and Nation*, 17 Nov. 1956.
119 *Hansard*, vol. 563, 23 Jan. 1957, cols. 266–7.
120 *Hansard*, vol. 564, 6 Feb. 1957, col. 458; col 485 (Kirk).
121 Ibid., cols. 464–7.

The ending of capital punishment would come, he concluded, but not by the present government. Benson agreed with these sentiments: "The Bill really retains little more than a symbolical gallows, and everyone knows that it is only a matter of time before the death penalty is abolished."[122] Silverman suggested that the Tory abolitionists had been reassured by the government that the execution in August 1955 was the last execution that would ever take place:

> In fact, we have seen the end of this obscene futility . . . The condemned cell will be deserted. The morbid, ghoulish death watch for weeks, including three Sundays, is wound up. No more notices outside the prison gates. No more big crowds assembling on execution mornings. No more hammering in the building of the gallows . . . It is a pity that the Government did not allow it decent burial.[123]

J. E. S. Simon, Undersecretary of State at the Home Office, claimed the bill "can properly bring this painful and protracted controversy to an end," and it was read a third time, 217 to 131.[124] Miss Alice Bacon had earlier introduced the original Silverman bill as a private member's bill, but government supporters had talked it out. Had it been read a second time, the Parliament Act would have been activated and the bill passed whether the Lords agreed with it or not.

Would the Lords now butcher the compromise bill? This time the Lords, including the judges, were not inclined to condemn the proposal to retain capital punishment for limited categories of murder. In the Second Reading debate, Viscount Templewood's prediction that the bill could not possibly remain permanent, given the anomalies it created, was followed by a curiously muted speech from Lord Goddard (who had earlier castigated the introduction of degrees of murder as unworkable), in which he merely stated that he and the judges welcomed this bill because it would end the untenable position they found themselves in, of passing sentence of death, only to find that a reprieve was granted in every case, quite unconstitutionally. He trusted that in future the law would take its course in capital murders. "If the law is not to take its course then, in Heaven's name! Let us abolish the whole thing altogether."[125] The most enthusiastic supporter of the bill's middle way was the Archbishop of Canterbury. In the course of his speech, he uttered the startling line that the entire subject "is not one of deep principle but one of expediency." His clerical colleagues disagreed. The Bishop of Chichester believed that moral issues, such as the sacredness of human life, were an integral part of the problem of capital punishment; and both he and the Archbishop of York described the bill as "morally shocking."[126]

---

122 Ibid., col. 486.
123 Ibid., col. 478.
124 Ibid., col. 566.
125 *Hansard* (Lords), vol. 201, 21 Feb. 1957, col. 1196 (Templewood); col. 1202 (Goddard).
126 Ibid., col. 1193 (Canterbury); 1229 (Chichester and York).

Lords Chorley and Pakenham raised an issue that the government agreed to examine again, relating to those people convicted of manslaughter on the ground of diminished responsibility. The bill introduced into English law the doctrine of diminished responsibility, which would supplement the defence of insanity in the M'Naghten Rules. The two Lords recommended that these cases be dealt with by an indeterminate sentence of imprisonment, since many were "serious mental cases, such as that of the [non-certifiable] psychopath."[127] The resulting discussion showed the continued force of judicial opinion. The Home Office would have preferred that a successful plea of diminished responsibility should result in a special verdict of "guilty of murder with diminished responsibility," and an indeterminate sentence. This would have empowered the Secretary of State to order detention either in a prison, in a special institution (like the East-Hubert institution then under construction), or in Broadmoor; to release on licence; and to recall. The Howard League also supported an indeterminate sentence. But the Lord Chief Justice, while disliking the very introduction of diminished responsibility, wanted a verdict of manslaughter and a determinate sentence. His reasons were entirely retributive and anti-psychiatric. He feared that with an indeterminate sentence, prisoners who were really quite sane would escape without due punishment, because prison doctors would report they had recovered from the instability they were suffering at the time of their conviction, and the Home Secretary would have to release them. Goddard wanted to leave the court to pass such sentence as the crime deserved. The Attorney-General sided with the Lord Chief Justice.[128] In view of such judicial opposition, Lord Chorley was told that the government would not amend the bill, but that the judges would have discretion to impose either a fixed sentence or one of life imprisonment.[129] The courts were trusted once again with a very wide discretionary power, at the expense of executive discretion.

The House of Lords passed the Homicide Bill on 19 March. Two days later it received Royal Assent as the Homicide Act 1957. The Act essentially amended the law of murder by resorting to the law of manslaughter. The defences provided in relation to diminished responsibility, provocation, and suicide pacts reduced the offence of murder to that of manslaughter. It now became possible for the accused to plead diminished responsibility, where before it was possible only to plead "guilty but insane." The measure relegated the M'Naghten Rules to the legal lumber room. The flexibility of the penalty for manslaughter allowed judges to pronounce a sentence reflecting his view of the accused's culpability (and occasionally of the accused's chances of reformation). When it came to the grading of

---

127 Ibid., cols. 1210–1 (Chorley); 1224 (Pakenham).
128 TNA, HO291/102: Newsam to Butler, 27 Feb; Butler to Kilmuir, 27 Feb. 1957; Newsam to Butler, 12 Mar; Allen minute, 13 Mar. 1957; *The Times*, 18 Feb. 1957, letter from Hugh Klare, Secretary, Howard League. See also TNA, LCO2/5111, Goddard to Newsam, 12 Mar. 1957.
129 TNA, LCO2/5111, draft letter to Chorley, 13 Mar.; Chorley to Kilmuir, 14 Mar. 1957.

murders, the Act rushed in where the royal commission feared to tread. The Act distinguished between capital murder, which still carried the death penalty, and non-capital murder, the maximum sentence for which was life imprisonment. Capital murders were defined as those committed in the course of theft, murder by shooting, murder to resist arrest, murder of a police or prison officer, and second murders. The government clung to the noose in those cases where killing was most likely to be the work of the professional criminal, and most likely to be deterred by capital punishment. The impetus behind the Act was manifestly political. Many years later, Edward Heath stated,

> Our purpose in preparing that Act was to try—I say it quite openly—to bridge the gap in the Conservative Party between those who believed in capital punishment and the abolitionists. At the same time we hoped that it might succeed in bridging the gap in the House of Commons.[130]

Tory MPs who had previously voted for abolition were probably persuaded to accept this compromise by an understanding that it would get through the House of Lords, and would result in a drastic cut in the number of death sentences.

VI

It was not long before the impact of the Homicide Act 1957 was plain for all to see. First, the Act accelerated the decline in the use of the death penalty. In the first three years of the Act's operation, the rate of executions fell from an annual average of 13 before 1957 to four per year, suggesting that the death penalty might well expire from inanition.[131] Abolitionists, or at least some of them, had long thought that capital punishment would end in this way, not with a bang but a whimper.[132] In particular, the majority of murders within the family, or where a personal relationship linked murderer and victim, were excluded from the death penalty, prompting Glanville Williams to observe that capital punishment had been removed from "nearly all killings of passion and depression."[133] Secondly, the Homicide Act did little to attenuate the reprieve system: just under 40 per cent of the condemned were reprieved, a drop of only 5 per cent from the pre-1957 era;

---

130 *Hansard*, vol. 23, 11 May 1982, col. 618.
131 J. E. Hall Williams, "Developments since the Homicide Act 1957," in Elizabeth O. Tuttle, *The Crusade against Capital Punishment in Great Britain* (1961), Appendix, pp. 164–5. *The Times*, 12 Dec. 1960, p. 8, listed the 29 convictions for capital murder between 16 May 1957 and 31 Oct. 1960. Sixteen men were executed (four of them under 21), ten were reprieved (including the only woman in the list), and, in three cases, verdicts of manslaughter were substituted on appeal.
132 C. H. Rolph, "The Death Penalty," *Current Affairs*, No. 112, 5 Aug. 1950: "I believe that abolition will come within a few years, but that it will steal upon us unawares. It will come, as it has done in so many other countries, not by legislation but by abrogation." See Rolph Papers, British Library of Political and Economic Science.
133 Quoted in Lord Windlesham, *Responses to Crime*, vol. 2 (1993), p. 84.

and the decisions appeared on the surface as arbitrary as ever.[134] Thirdly, the new defence of diminished responsibility was of value to the accused, many of whom would otherwise have been convicted of murder. The proportion of persons found to be suffering from mental abnormality was the same after the Homicide Act as before, but the defence of diminished responsibility began to replace the plea of guilty but insane, since the former defence was found easier to establish than insanity under the M'Naghten Rules. In about two-thirds of the cases in which a plea of diminished responsibility was put forward, it was successful. The great majority of successful pleas were in cases of non-capital murder. A finding of diminished responsibility led to a conviction for manslaughter, the sentence for which was not fixed. Courts made full use of their sentencing discretion in the early 1960s, imposing life imprisonment in 25 per cent of diminished responsibility cases, hospital orders in 50 per cent, and other sentences in 25 per cent of cases.[135]

Fourthly, and most importantly, the Homicide Act was increasingly discredited by the absurdity and injustice of the distinction between capital and non-capital murders, a distinction criticized at the time, both by abolitionists and retentionists, for creating indefensible anomalies. A thief who broke into a dwelling and, in the course of the theft, killed the homeowner or shopkeeper could be convicted of capital murder. A rapist who broke into a home, violated, and killed his victim could be convicted only of non-capital murder. Only murder by shooting was a capital offence, yet there were killings by knife and other weapons that were anywhere near as premeditated. And the most premeditated of all murders, death caused by poisoning, was exempt from capital punishment. The most problematic category of capital murder was murder in the course or furtherance of theft. By this provision, the authors of the 1957 Act had hoped to deter "professional criminals" who made a living from burglary, housebreaking, and robbery—men of rational calculation and thus subject to being deterred. Yet many of those hanged for theft-murder in no way resembled the professional thief. As the interim report of the Homicide Research Project at Bedford College discovered, "The armed robber figured infrequently among the theft-murder cases which contained mainly the petty, amateur thief who in a panic hit out rather too violently at the owner who came upon the intruder in his house or shop."[136]

---

134 As Lizzie Seal wrote, "demonstrating that the Act had not been successful in restricting the death sentence to the 'death worthy'": *Capital Punishment in Twentieth-Century Britain* (2014), p. 25, note 137.

135 TNA, HO291/1019; Barbara Wootton, *Crime and Penal Policy* (1978), p. 140. A number of those convicted of manslaughter after a plea of diminished responsibility were subsequently transferred from prison to psychiatric hospitals, the number increasing after November 1960 when the Mental Health Act 1959 came into force.

136 MSS. 16B/5/2/9, "Criminal Homicide in England and Wales, 1957–1968, An Interim Report of the Homicide Research Project, Legal Research Unit, Sociology Department, Bedford College, University of London, Oct. 1969, p. 2, Modern Records Centre, University of Warwick. Baroness Wootton of Abinger pressed the Lord Chancellor on whether those who had been convicted of capital murder under Section 5(1)

The first fruits of the new law confirmed this judgment, starting with the very first execution under the 1957 Act. John Vickers, aged 22, a man of exemplary character (having previously stolen only a bike lamp), removed from his mother at age 2, and reared by his grandparents, broke into a small shop in Carlisle to steal money from the till. Surprised by the 72-year-old woman shopkeeper, and aware that she recognized him, Vickers knocked her down and kicked her in the face several times. He admitted striking her but denied intending to kill. At the Cumberland assizes, Vickers admitted he had gone to the shop to rob the woman after hours, and was thus open to the verdict of capital murder in the course or furtherance of theft. Three Court of Criminal Appeal judges differed as to whether this was a case of capital murder; a special court of five judges reheard the appeal and dismissed it; the Home Secretary refused a reprieve. Vickers was executed in Durham prison on 23 July 1957.[137]

The death penalty was also applied in cases where *nothing* was stolen. In June 1960, four young men, full of Dutch courage, decided to rob someone on a secluded towpath in Hounslow. Alan Jee came along; he was struck by one of the men, falling to the ground. Francis Forsyth kicked Jee repeatedly around the head to keep him quiet, while Norman Harris rifled Jee's pockets. Harris stopped when he saw blood on his hands, and the gang ran off. Jee died from his injuries two days later. One of the men who acted as lookout was convicted of non-capital murder and given life imprisonment. Another gang member, under 18 years of age, was ordered to be detained at Her Majesty's Pleasure. Forsyth, aged 18, and Harris, aged 23, were convicted of capital murder in the course or furtherance of theft and sentenced to death. Abolitionist MP, Sydney Silverman, wrote to Home Secretary Butler appealing for mercy. The crime was "utterly inexcusable," said Silverman, yet both were young, both were redeemable. Even the prosecution had conceded that they had not meant to kill, and Harris had struck no blow; and though robbery was in their minds, nothing was stolen. Silverman added, "If the crime was murder it was only just murder. Parliament, when it passed the Homicide Act, did not expect the death penalty to be inflicted when nothing was stolen and there was no intent to kill."[138] Leading abolitionists and a number of cultural figures penned a letter to *The Times* begging that Forsyth at least not be executed: "There could be no greater affront to either the Christian or the humanist

---

"can properly be described as professional criminals." See *Hansard* (Lords), vol. 227, 24 Jan. 1961, col. 1103. See also Christopher Hollis, *The Homicide Act* (1964), chap. 5.

137 *The Times*, 24 Jul. 1957, p. 4; Gerald Gardiner Papers, British Library, vol. 9 A, Add. MS 56463, folio 103. Likewise, in April 1958, Frank Stokes, aged 44, struck a 75-year-old widow with a hammer in her home in Northumberland when she refused the hourly rate he wanted for gardening work. He denied stealing from her home, though he was found with the victim's purse. Theft was not the motive for the crime yet it was the theft that sealed his fate. The brutal killing alone would not have attracted execution. He was hanged in Durham prison on 3 Sept. 1958. Peter Richards concluded that Stokes "was executed for theft, not for murder." See *Parliament and Conscience* (1970), p. 50.

138 TNA, HO291/367, Silverman to Home Secretary, 5 Nov. 1960.

conscience than to kill, in cold blood, a youth of 18, whatever his crime."[139] Forsyth and Harris were executed at Wandsworth and Pentonville prison, respectively, on 10 November 1960. In both these cases, it was not the murder which decided the hanging, but the theft. Yet a month after these executions, John Rogers, aged 20, was convicted of the capital murder of a Bristol taxi driver, whom he shot through the back of the head. Rogers admitted setting out with the intention of robbing a taxi driver to get money to attend the Beaulieu jazz festival. Following an appeal to the Court of Criminal Appeal, which substituted a manslaughter verdict, and an appeal by the government to the House of Lords, which restored the verdict of capital murder, Rogers was finally reprieved by the Home Secretary.[140]

The National Campaign for the Abolition of Capital Punishment was surely right to claim that the 1957 Act had neither a moral nor a rational basis. It was essentially unworkable because of three major difficulties. First, the Act sought to limit capital punishment to the worst murders, but what did "worst murders" mean? Most people, one suspects, meant murders that were committed with the greatest degree of brutality, yet these were typically committed by the insane or the aggressive psychopath. Or were premeditated murders the worst? Secondly, if premeditated murders were to be selected, people's lives would depend on the jury's idea of what "premeditated" meant? Time was the crucial factor, but how long premeditated—60 seconds or 60 minutes? Thirdly, between deliberate poisoning and the mercy killing was a spectrum of cases of varying circumstance. It was impossible to put one's finger down at any point on the spectrum and say—all to the left, to die; all to the right, to live, since the immediate next case would be almost exactly the same. As the National Campaign's pamphlet, *The Fallacy in the Homicide Act*, concluded,

> The Homicide Act was apparently intended to confine the punishment of death in the main to murders by professional criminals. But this . . . it has proved inherently incapable of doing; and, as those are not necessarily the worst murders, public opinion is increasingly critical of a criminal statute which has no moral basis.
>
> The imposition of capital punishment for some, but not all, murders is based on the assumption that there are two classes into which murders can fairly and justly be divided. But this is not true. The fact is, as the Home Office said to the Royal Commission: "There are not in fact two classes of murder, but an infinite variety of offences which shade off by degrees from the most atrocious to the most excusable."

In short, the Homicide Act was a bad Act. "It was an attempt, in defiance of the unanimous report of the Royal Commission, to do that which is inherently

139 *The Times*, 1 Nov. 1960, p. 13.
140 *The Times*, 21 Oct. 1960, p. 4.

impossible."[141] The Act stands as a prime example of a negative reform, serving to undermine the death penalty and hasten its abolition.[142] Yet for a few more years, the death penalty survived, a powerful symbol of an enduring retributive consciousness, propelling public opinion in punitive directions, and undermining any attempt to create a new structure of punishment.

141 See Gerald Gardiner Papers, British Library, vol. 8 A, Add. MS 56462; Rolph Papers, BLPES, 1/4/1, *The Fallacy in the Homicide Act*. True to form, the government's contention that hanging would be a deterrent to one kind of murderer and not to another, was based, as Hollis wrote, "on a merely arbitrary say-so. There was no beginning of an attempt at any statistical or scientific evidence to justify the drawing of the line at the precise point where it is drawn." See *The Homicide Act* (1964), p. 56.

142 Christie Davies has argued compellingly that the Homicide Act, with its emphasis upon deterrence, or what Davies calls the replacement of "moralist" criteria by "causalist" criteria in deciding who should be executed, signalled that the death penalty was no longer a retributory punishment. This made it much harder for what Davies calls the "sacred hierarchies" of militarists, judges, and clerics in the House of Lords to defend the death penalty. "Since [the judges] had previously supported capital punishment as being a just retribution, they were disturbed by a system in which the wicked were often more severely punished than the very wicked." They came to prefer "total abolition to selective execution by category on the basis of presumed deterrence." This all marks for Davies the strange death of moral Britain, of conservative Britain, and of the Conservative party, "whose ideology was tied to the idealization and maintenance of a particular traditional, hierarchical order." See Davies, *The Strange Death of Moral Britain* (2004), pp. 72–7, 107; idem., "The British state and the power of life and death," in S. J. D. Green and R. C. Whiting (eds.), *The Boundaries of the State in Modern Britain* (Cambridge, 1996), p. 367. This argument is restricted to the moral reasoning of the small elite of active parliamentarians, which was surely at odds with much of the moral reasoning of the man/woman in the street, not to mention the moral stridency of the popular press. Even so, it is an argument that is relevant to the final stages of abolition in the 1960s.

10

THE HIGH-WATER MARK OF REHABILITATION

> My agreement to the general principles in the [1961 Criminal Justice] Bill must not be taken as implying that I have abandoned my desire to have some re-introduction of corporal punishment. Whatever the Advisory Council report, I have still strong views on the matter.
>
> *Lord Chief Justice Parker to C. C. Cunningham, 14 Nov. 1960: HO291/369.*

I

If the 1959 White Paper was the high watermark of the treatment ethic, if the first prison rule became in 1964 that the "purpose of the training and treatment of convicted prisoners shall be to encourage and assist them to lead a good and useful life," if the sixties are the decade in which the rehabilitative ideal is thought to have reached its zenith, the "flogging lobby" did not go gently into the night, and the judiciary did not claim, as Foucault imagined, "the honour of curing or rehabilitating."[1] Years later in a radio conversation with psephologist, Robert McKenzie, R. A. Butler lamented the fact that "birching and flogging . . . haunted me almost every week of my time at the Home Office" And not only in his capacity as Home Secretary: ". . .blood-curdling demands were annually made for [birching's] restoration and quite clouded my time as Chairman of the party," he recorded in his memoirs.

Indeed I did not gain ascendancy over the critics until 1961 at the party conference at Brighton where, following on a decisive and unanimous report

---

1   See Introduction *supra.*

from my Advisory Council, I spoke for forty minutes and carried the whole audience after a prolonged debate.[2]

The endurance of the issue of corporal punishment ought not to have surprised Butler, however, since controversy had never subsided. Her Majesty's Judges were especially adept at keeping the pot boiling, particularly the heavy-handed prompts of Lord Chief Justice Goddard and his successor, Lord Parker, to reintroduce what they insisted was a deterrent penalty. This chapter first recreates the controversy over corporal punishment, which was not finally resolved until 1961–2. It also examines the Criminal Justice Act 1961, which implemented the recommendations of the Advisory Council's report, *The Treatment of Young Offenders*. The Act was in line with the rehabilitative ethos, in that it created a quasi-indeterminate sentence of custodial training for young adults between 17 and 21, with the prison commissioners, not the court, deciding how long an offender remained in custody. At first, the judiciary accepted this restriction on their sentencing discretion, but later the worm turned and they began to chafe under the restriction. Likewise, the judiciary, via the Court of Criminal Appeal, laid down its own rules for the use of corrective training and preventive detention, the two measures in the 1948 Criminal Justice Act to deal with persistent offending, rules that led to fewer such sentences, and to the Advisory Council's recommendation to abandon both measures. The rehabilitative ideal was still unable to carry all before it.

As early as March 1950, in the House of Lords, Earl Howe drew the Labour government's attention to remarks made by the Lord Chief Justice and Mr. Justice Streatfeild at recent trials, regretting that crimes of brutal violence could no longer be punished by flogging, and asked if there had been an increase in violent crime since the abolition of corporal punishment in September 1948, and whether the government would consider the re-imposition of corporal punishment in cases of violent crime. On this occasion, Lord Chancellor Jowitt provided figures which suggested that the abolition of flogging had not had an adverse effect on cases of robbery with violence and armed robbery.[3] A week later, the Lords held a two-day debate on "Crimes of Violence." The proposal being canvassed was to restore the power of the superior courts to have adult criminals flogged. Corporal punishment could be inflicted on adults before 1948 for the following offences of robbery under the 1916 Larceny Act: armed robbery, robbery in company with one other person or more, and robbery with personal violence. Opening the debate, Lord Lloyd insisted that judges could be trusted to use such a power wisely. "It is, I think, significant," said Lloyd,

---

2   "A Lifetime in the Jungle—Lord Butler in conversation with Robert McKenzie," *Listener*, vol. 86, 22 Jul. 1971, p. 110; *The Art of the Possible: The Memoirs of Lord Butler* (1st pub. 1971; Harmondsworth, 1973), p. 202.

3   *Hansard* (Lords), vol. 166, 14 Mar. 1950, cols. 189–92.

that so many judges should have publicly stated their opinion that not merely is corporal punishment a deterrent . . . but that in many instances a sentence of corporal punishment coupled with a short term of imprisonment is a much more appropriate sentence than the long term of imprisonment which at the present moment is the only alternative.[4]

Lord Oaksey prayed in aid his 12 years as a King's Bench Judge to claim that flogging was a deterrent; Viscount Templewood (president of the Howard League), Lord Samuel (former Home Secretary), and the Lord Archbishop of York all disagreed.[5] Evidence from the Cadogan Committee was batted back and forth once again. This set the stage for Lord Goddard's intervention. While deploring the abolition of all forms of corporal punishment, he did not demand its re-imposition, at least not yet, since he wished to avoid the continual alteration of penalties. But be warned, he said, the alternative would be heavy sentences of imprisonment, even for young offenders, and allowance would have to be made for the one-third remission that applied to prison sentences. Already the prisons were overcrowded and the prisons were understaffed. He himself preferred to hand down a good whipping and a short prison sentence.[6] In a leading article on the day after the Lords' debate, *The Times* opined that the restoration of corporal punishment found "only a hesitant support," and the Cadogan report held up well to critical examination. The *Times'* leader also pointed out that the post-war wave of violent crime occurred in the years when it was still punishable with flogging, suggesting that the penalty failed to deter. If the crime wave was not brought under control, however, "the popular demand for its resumption may become irresistible."[7]

A larger controversy erupted in 1952 with the Lord Chief Justice front and centre. At the annual Lord Mayor's annual banquet at the Mansion House on 2 July, replying to the Lord Mayor's toast to Her Majesty's Judges, the Lord Chief Justice took the opportunity to speak about the increase in crimes of violence, and to suggest that the remedy for "gangsterism" (the "cosh-boy" was the talk of the press) was to restore corporal punishment: "and to extend it, not limit it." When it came time for the Lord Chancellor, Lord Simonds, to propose the health of the Lord Mayor, he took the unusual step of responding to Goddard, stating that "it is not established that the removal of flogging has resulted in an increase in the number of crimes for which the penalty would formerly have been imposed."[8] This put the cat among the pigeons. In a letter to *The Times* next day, George

---

4 *Hansard* (Lords), vol. 166, 21 Mar. 1950, col. 318.
5 Ibid., col. 345 (Oaksey), col. 333 (Templewood), col. 350 (Samuel), col. 338 (York).
6 Ibid., cols. 459–67.
7 *The Times*, 24 Mar. 1950, p. 7. See also *The Times*, 20 Mar. 1950, p. 5.
8 Fenton Bresler, *Lord Goddard: A Biography of Rayner Goddard, Lord Chief Justice of England* (1977), pp. 225–6; E. Grimshaw and G. Jones, *Lord Goddard* (1958), pp. 115–17. See also Brian Abel-Smith and Robert Stevens, *Lawyers and the Courts: A Sociological Study of the English Legal System 1750–1965* (Cambridge, Mass., 1967), p. 302.

Benson, chairman of the Howard League, reminded Goddard that from 1939 to 1948 corporal punishment was used more frequently, yet robbery with violence quadrupled; since the abolition of corporal punishment, this crime had fallen in number. He added the sting: "That the Lord Chief Justice should advocate the re-introduction of corporal punishment on grounds so glaringly contradicted by facts cannot but shake confidence in judicial wisdom and in judicial ability to interpret evidence."[9] The attention of the Cabinet was also drawn to the LCJ's public speech, the Lord Chancellor and the Home Secretary remarking that the statistical evidence did not bear out Goddard's contention.[10] Yet already, Earl Howe had declared his intention of tabling a motion in the House of Lords to call attention to crimes of violence and ask whether existing penalties were adequate.[11] The debate took place on 22 October.

The Lord Chief Justice spoke second in the debate. His opening was character-istically dramatic. From the evidence of his postbag, he said, in rural districts and in London, "many old people are terrified to answer a knock on the door." What followed was a rambling mess of figures and anecdotal evidence, much too heavy on the figures, in the course of which Goddard recommended that "the superior courts should be given power, in their discretion, to inflict corporal punishment for all forms of felonious violence . . . for felonious wounding, wounding of police with intent to evade arrest and for attempted murder." This provoked the Lord Chancellor to say,

> . . . it is suggested today in your Lordships' House that not only should we reverse the legislation of 1948, but that we should extend the penalty of cor-poral punishment in a degree which surpasses anything that has been permis-sible over the last 130 years. Is not that in the nature of panic legislation?

Her Majesty's Judges (Oaksey, Schuster, and Tucker) lined up to pronounce that corporal punishment was a deterrent.[12] These debates were beginning to take their toll, as was the goading of the press. In Cabinet, on the following day, Prime Minister Churchill

> thought it would be unwise for the Government to close their minds to the possibility of restoring this penalty if the case for doing so were fully

9   *The Times*, 5 Jul. 1952, p. 7.
10 TNA, CAB 128/25, CC (52), 65th conclusions, Cabinet, 3 Jul. 1952. The extent of government and House of Lords' attention to crimes of violence is evident from the following citations: TNA, PREM 11/27, Prime Minister Churchill to Home Secretary David Maxwell-Fyfe, 2 Apr. 1952, Home Secretary to Churchill, 3 Apr. 1952; "Papers Relating to the Large Number of Crimes Accompanied by Violence Occurring in Large Cities," ordered by the House of Lords, 23 Mar. 1950; PREM 11/2921, Churchill to Home Secretary, 3 Jul. 1952, Home Secretary to Churchill, 8 Jul. 1952.
11 *Hansard* (Lords), vol. 177, 10 Jun. 1952, cols. 7–8.
12 *Hansard* (Lords), vol. 178, 22 Oct. 1952, cols. 849–60; col. 907 (Lord Chancellor Simonds); col. 879 (Oaksey), col. 883 (Schuster); col. 890 (Tucker).

established and public opinion hardened in favour of it. There had been a great increase in crime and the prisons were overcrowded: the problem of prison administration would be eased if, through having discretion to impose corporal punishment, the courts sentenced fewer offenders to long terms of imprisonment.[13]

The Lord Chancellor held the line, reiterating the point he had made the day before: the demand voiced in the Lords "that it should be available as a penalty for all crimes of violence involved reverting not merely to 1948 but substantially to 1827, when felonies were punishable by death and misdemeanours by whipping."[14] The 1948 Act should be given a longer trial, said Simonds, but the Prime Minister wanted a fuller discussion on the question.

This took place on 20 November 1952. Cabinet members had been briefed in advance by the Home Secretary, David Maxwell Fyfe, who gave short shrift to the argument that the return of flogging would bring relief to the overcrowded prisons:

> If corporal punishment had been available as a judicial penalty for all crimes of violence to the person, and if all the men sentenced since the beginning of 1947 to more than two years' imprisonment for such offences had been flogged and had not been sent to prison, the present prison population (which is just over 20,500) would be reduced by less than 1,000.[15]

Nevertheless, he felt the agitation for the re-introduction of flogging could not be ignored, given the level of crimes of violence, and so recommended a new inquiry into corporal punishment to be undertaken by either a royal commission or another departmental committee. The prime minister also had the benefit of the views of his Cabinet Secretary, Norman Brook, who felt that before deciding in favour of an enquiry, the Cabinet ought to assess "the *political* difficulties of passing legislation restoring corporal punishment."[16] It was an emotional issue, said Brook, and the division of opinion would not follow party lines. It would be difficult to avoid allowing a free vote, which might lead to embarrassment for the government. Brook recommended seeing how Wing Commander Eric Bullus' private member's bill to restore flogging for crimes of violence fared in February. If the bill were rejected on Second Reading, the government would not need to take the matter further; if the bill were approved, the government could appoint a committee of enquiry. In Cabinet, however, Churchill opposed the appointment of a new enquiry. He wanted the government to be free to introduce legislation. If corporal punishment were re-introduced, possibly on a five-year experimental

13   TNA, CAB 128/25, CC (52) 89th conclusions, Cabinet 23 Oct. 1952.
14   Ibid.
15   TNA, CAB 129/56, C (52) 386, 4 Nov. 1952, Corporal Punishment as a Penalty for Crimes of Violence, Memo by the Home Secretary.
16   TNA, PREM 11/2921, Brook to Prime Minister, 19 Nov. 1952.

basis, Churchill thought it should be available for all crimes of violence or brutality. He also stated, ". . . if a plebiscite could be held on this question, the majority of the people of this country might be found to be in favour of reintroducing this penalty."[17] In response, the Home Secretary reiterated that the increase in crimes of violence was to be found not in robbery with violence, but in offences "for which corporal punishment had not been available for nearly 100 years." Any legislation ought to be preceded by a new enquiry, and anyway legislation had little chance of success in the Commons. The Cabinet decided to hold off on an enquiry, and encourage a free expression of the views of the House of Commons on the Second Reading of the private member's bill.

In early December 1952, Goddard again attracted public attention by his remarks in a case of armed robbery by two brothers aged 14 and 17, both of whom had previously been placed on probation. The younger was sent to approved school, the elder to borstal training. At his most irascible, impetuous, and crudely emotional, the Lord Chief Justice declared the boys needed "a good larruping" (*larrup*: Suffolk dialect word, to beat, thrash [someone]): "What they want is to have somebody who would give them a thundering good beating, and then perhaps they would not do it again."[18] Goddard failed to mention that the papers before him revealed that the two boys, from a broken home, were already beaten nightly, which became public knowledge. The response was predictable. In a *Daily Herald* piece entitled, "O Wordy Judge!" Michael Foot queried which Goddard was in the court: the judge or the "propagandist," the judge or the "would-be lawmaker?" Lord Chorley accused the Lord Chief Justice of "leading a crusade to bring back this form of punishment."[19]

In the run-up to the introduction of Wing Commander Bullus' Bill there were a number of developments. First, the Advisory Council on the Treatment of Offenders addressed the issue at their January 1953 meeting. Dr. Radzinowicz observed that an analysis of persons convicted of robbery with violence in 1950, completed by the Cambridge Department of Criminal Science, showed that two-thirds were "hardened criminals with a long record of crime," and unlikely to be deterred by corporal punishment. Margery Fry thought that enquiry should be made into the mental characteristics of those convicted of violent crime, and that offenders should be made to compensate the victims of violent crime. ACTO submitted a unanimous recommendation against the restoration of corporal punishment as a judicial penalty.[20] Second, a Gallup poll published in the *News Chronicle* showed that of those questioned, some two-thirds favoured corporal punishment for persons committing crimes of violence. On the very day of the Second Reading debate, the Magistrates' Association announced the result of a ballot of their members: of the 6,298 votes cast, 4,412 were in favour of re-

---

17 TNA, CAB 128/25, CC (52) 99th conclusions, 20 Nov. 1952.
18 Bresler, op cit., pp. 229–30; *The Times*, 4 Dec. 1952, p. 3, Central Criminal Court.
19 Ibid., p. 231.
20 TNA, HO291/19, ACTO 13 Jan. 1953 minutes.

introducing corporal punishment, 1,886 against.[21] And third, the figures for offences of robbery with violence known to the police during 1952 showed some increase over the figures of 1951 (rising from 800 to 1,003). The Cabinet was familiar with these developments as they took the decision to declare in the Second Reading debate that Bullus' bill had serious defects, and that there had been insufficient time to judge the effect as a whole of the Criminal Justice Act 1948. Hence, it would be premature to restore corporal punishment.[22] In the Commons' debate, the bill's proponents made much of the need to trust the judges and not allow psychiatrists to usurp judicial authority, but following a very effective speech by Home Secretary, David Maxwell Fyfe, the Commons rejected the bill to restore the penalty by 159 votes to 63.[23]

II

There the issue rested until the arrival of R. A. Butler as Home Secretary. Butler may have hoped that the retirement of Lord Chief Justice Goddard in 1958 would help matters. Alas, Goddard's successor, Lord Parker, while a humane judge for the most part, believed that the courts were not stern enough in their response to violent crime. In early September 1959, in a most injudicious speech in Canada, which Butler personally resented, Parker put his judicial authority behind the return of corporal punishment. As if this were not bad enough, he said the same to the annual meeting of the Magistrates' Association on 22 October:

> I am a believer in corporal punishment . . . Nobody suggests going back to the "cat"; . . . What harm can there be in the cane or the birch? It has got just that amount of indignity about it which is really a deterrent.[24]

Little wonder that Butler faced criticism from Conservative backbenchers. In early November, Gerald Nabarro asked the Home Secretary if he knew that with regard to crimes of violence,

---

21 TNA, PREM 11/2921, *News Chronicle*, 20 Dec. 1952, Gallup Poll. See also Ian Gibson, *The English Vice: Beating, Sex and Shame in Victorian England and After* (1978), p. 185.

22 TNA, CAB 129/59, C. (53) 51, 6 Feb. 1953, Corporal Punishment; PREM 11/2921, Brook to Churchill, 9 Feb. 1953; CAB 128/26, CC (53) 9th conclusions, Cabinet 11 Feb. 1953.

23 *Hansard*, vol. 511, 13 Feb. 1953, cols. 782–92. On 26 November 1957, a petition bearing 87,000 signatures appealing for severer measures against crimes of violence was submitted to the Home Office by the sometime Lord Mayor of Birmingham and the "flogging vicar," Rev. John Jackson of Sparkhill, Birmingham: *The Times*, 27 Nov. 1957, p. 7.

24 TNA, HO291/367: Lord Chief Justice's observations; Anthony Howard, *RAB: The Life of R. A. Butler* (1987), pp. 271–2. For Lord Parker of Waddington (1900–1972), see *The Times*, 16 Sept. 1972, p. 14. Parker was Lord Chief Justice from 1958 to 1971.

there is evidently complete unanimity of view between the present Lord Chief Justice, his predecessor, Lord Goddard, and myself, together with many of my distinguished hon. Friends on these benches, that a proper policy ought to be "whack the thugs"?[25]

The rest of the debate was in this vein. As the *Guardian* correspondent concluded, in the new Parliament "the flogging lobby would not be content to play it mild." Butler knew that the question of giving courts a power to impose sentences of corporal punishment was certain to be raised during the debates on the Criminal Justice Bill dealing with the young offender. He chose to shield himself from further attack on this politically sensitive issue by asking the Advisory Council to consider whether there were grounds for reintroducing corporal punishment, in the light of the great increase in offences of violence against the person since the war, committed especially by young people aged between 14 and 21. Cunningham, the Permanent Undersecretary of State, was a member of ACTO, but Butler agreed that he should absent himself on such a controversial subject.[26]

ACTO recognized that corporal punishment was a matter on which strong and conflicting opinions were sincerely held, and thus felt obliged to sample a wide range of opinion. In a new approach to the solicitation of evidence, Mr. Justice Barry, ACTO chairman, invited private individuals and organizations to submit their views. Over the next six months, 3,500 letters came in, largely from the big industrial cities. Over three-quarters were in favour of re-introduction of corporal punishment, with only 17 per cent against.[27] ACTO also invited a large number of individuals and organizations to give their views in writing or orally, or both. Judicial opinion was particularly probed. The Lord Chief Justice agreed to submit his views in writing as preface to giving oral evidence. In a closely-argued memorandum, Lord Parker said that the press had portrayed him as an emotional advocate of meeting violence with violence. Not so, he said. "My emotional

---

25 *Hansard*, vol. 612, 5 Nov. 1959, col. 1180.
26 Howard, op cit., p. 272; TNA, HO291/792, Butler to Mr. Justice Barry, 21 Jan. 1960; Ibid., AC/212, Corporal Punishment, Memo by the Home Office, 1 Mar. 1960; HO291/20, ACTO meeting, 9 Mar. 1960. Butler's note, 7 Mar., in reply to Cunningham: "I think I would prefer you to find some excuse for not attending for this subject. No excuse need be given. It is v. highly political indeed." See also Medical Correspondent [Dr. Peter Scott], "Is Flogging a Remedy?" *The Times*, 27 Jan. 1960, p. 11.
27 See Anne Logan, "Women and the Provision of Criminal Justice Advice: Lessons from England and Wales 1944–1964," *British Journal of Criminology*, vol. 50 (2010), p. 1088. See also Jonathan Silvey, "The Criminal Law and Public Opinion," [1961] *Criminal Law Review*, pp. 353–4. ACTO also took notice of the results of a Gallup poll on corporal punishment, which appeared in the *News Chronicle*, 21 Mar. 1960. The poll showed that 74 per cent of the population over 16 considered that corporal punishment should be the penalty for some offences. The Home Office Research Unit advised that there was little agreement on which offences should be subject to this punishment. See TNA, HO291/802, AC/216, memo by the ACTO Secretary, E. R. Cowlyn, 26 May 1960; Appendix A by Silvey of the HORU, 4 May 1960.

approach is all against corporal punishment. I dislike the idea of it and I say this having been on more than once occasion at the receiving and the giving end of the cane." His only concern was whether there was sufficient reason why the courts should not have this weapon to combat the vast increase in crime since the Cadogan report of 1938. He pointed out that the overwhelming majority of people in the country were in favour of some form of corporal punishment, and this was consistent as to sex, age, and class. His main argument was that corporal punishment was a general and individual deterrent, so the courts should have it in their armoury. Re-introduction would encourage parents and schoolteachers to use it again; and the crime wave required that the courts have all possible deterrents available. He finally suggested that it should be imposed only after a warning, viz: "if you do this again you will be thrashed." This would mean that first offenders would not be thrashed.[28]

Lord Parker also took soundings of the other judges of the Queen's Bench Division. Of the 26 judges whose opinion Parker received, only four were against the re-introduction of the penalty. The other 22 judges were entirely or generally in agreement with Parker's memorandum, though most would not make warning a condition precedent. Mr. Justice Streatfeild wanted to make corporal punishment available in regard to all ages for any crime involving violence, and also for rape, attempted rape or indecent assault, sexual intercourse with girls under 13 and buggery and indecent assault on boys under 13. Mr. Justice Finnemore thought the reformatory value of prisons was slight, and corporal punishment was more merciful:

> I do not criticize the Notting Hill sentences [of the white youths who assaul-ted West Indian men during racially-motivated riots in August–September 1958], as there was no real alternative, but four years for a youth of 18, I confess, makes my blood run cold. To such an age it is like eternity and what will he be like when he comes out? A thrashing (a severe one) would, I believe, have created just as much public impression and therefore done as much good with less ultimate suffering by the youths. And I am sure they would never have come back for more.[29]

ACTO could have been left in no doubt that the Judges of the Queen's Bench Division wanted the re-introduction of corporal punishment for some offenders and some offences. Mr. Justice Barry also sought the views of the judges of the Probate, Divorce and Admiralty Division (where there was a sharp division of opinion concerning reintroduction for offenders under the age of 21); the Court of Appeal (only Lord Justice Sellers responded, saying he had doubts about corporal punishment, preferring a greater use of the fine); and the Lords of Appeal in Ordinary (Lords Tucker, Reid, and Oaksey favoured reintroduction; Lords

28   TNA, HO291/836, Memo on Corporal Punishment, AC/217.
29   Ibid., Appendix A, Appendix B (Mr. Justice Finnemore).

Somervell of Harrow, Denning, Simonds, Morris of Borth-y-Gest, and Keith of Avonholm were against). Lord Denning was troubled by the delay between offence and punishment; after this delay "the infliction of corporal punishment is more vengeful than deterrent or reformative." Lord Keith was the only one to suggest that "in these days of sex equality it is somewhat illogical to introduce inequality in forms of punishment." Goddard, the former Lord Chief Justice, declined to submit evidence, telling Barry,

> to some . . . who are interested in the subject I am considered an unredeemed old sadist who wants to flog or hang everyone I can! It does not happen to be . . . true, but possibly the mere fact that I express some opinion might convince some people that they should take the opposite view.[30]

In all, enquiry of the judges of other divisions of the High Court and of the Court of Appeal, and of the judicial members of the House of Lords, revealed a good deal of divergence.

At its 60th meeting in June 1960, ACTO began by taking oral evidence, starting with the Lord Chief Justice. The latter added to his memorandum. Reintroduction would be unnecessary, he said, if homes and schools provided better discipline, if there was certainty of detection of offenders, and if the courts had adequate weapons to combat the increase of crime—but these conditions were not fulfilled. If corporal punishment were brought back, said Parker, he hoped it would seldom be inflicted, but it should be available for a greater range of offences. For older offenders, for any serious offence of actual or threatened violence; for juveniles, for serious offences of any kind. He then made the claim that corporal punishment was largely retributive for older offenders, "but with young offenders it has only a small element of retribution." Presumably he thought for juveniles it was entirely deterrent, though in his earlier memo he had stated that "any self-discipline is indirectly reformatory." In short, as Parker had told the annual conference of the National Association of Probation Officers in April, he hoped that ACTO would report that "the balance of advantage" lay in favour of re-introducing the penalty:

> If it took the form of birching or caning, after warning, and limited to say the under 21, it would go a long way to meet my point of view. I would not then confine its imposition to any particular offences but have it available for all offences.[31]

---

30 TNA, HO291/838, AC/214, including Appendices A–D, Apr–May 1960; HO291/837: Denning to Barry, 30 Apr. 1960; Keith of Avonholm to Barry, 1 May 1960; Goddard to Barry, 30 Apr. 1960.
31 TNA, HO291/836, the Lord Chief Justice oral evidence, 1 Jun.; ibid., Frank Dawtry, General Secretary of the National Association of Probation Officers to E. R. Cowlyn, Secretary of ACTO, 26 Apr. 1960; *The Times*, 25 Apr. 1960, p. 8.

Oral evidence was also taken from prison governors (who were evenly divided on the value of corporal punishment as a deterrent); borstal governors and wardens of detention centres (who believed corporal punishment would be an impediment to constructive training methods); the National Association of Probation Officers (which reported that only 10 per cent of the membership was in favour of restoration); the Institute for the Study and Treatment of Delinquency (long opposed to flogging); the Magistrates' Association (the Council of which was opposed to restoration for any type of offence or offender); the Royal Medico-Psychological Association (unanimously opposed to re-introduction); and six MPs, led by Sir Thomas More, representing a group of 43 members who wanted to see birching and caning for crimes of violence against the person introduced for a five-year trial period. The Association of Chief Police Officers declined to give evidence, but Colonel Young, an ACTO member, believed that the majority of police officers of all ranks were against re-introduction, on the grounds that it would only lead to greater violence. ACTO also issued a press notice inviting individuals and groups to send in their views, which many did, including the Society of Labour Lawyers (whose officers included Gerald Gardiner, future Lord Chancellor, and Sir Frank Soskice, future Home Secretary, and which sought to disabuse the public of the belief that judges had any training in penology, psychology, or the treatment of prisoners); the chairmen of the Metropolitan Juvenile Courts (who did not want restored to the juvenile court the power to order boys to be whipped); and a handful of prisoners, the latter evenly split between pro and anti. ACTO's report would conclude that the consensus of opinion among correspondents and witnesses was that if the penalty were to be brought back, "it should be available for a wider range of offences (particularly offences of violence) than before its abolition in 1948; and that it should be available for juveniles convicted of any offence . . ."[32]

At ACTO's 63rd meeting in July, each member of the council stated in turn his or her conclusion. Mr. Justice Barry went first, stating that those who wanted corporal punishment re-introduced had failed to prove their case. Further, the new methods of treatment provided by the 1948 Act had not been fully developed. There was, for example, a shortage of detention centres. ACTO's own recommendations on the treatment of young offenders would hopefully soon be passed into law.

> . . . it would therefore be retrogressive to introduce corporal punishment without waiting to see whether those methods proved effective. For those reasons, he had come definitely to the conclusion that the Council should not recommend the reintroduction of corporal punishment.

32 TNA, HO291/20, AC/222, ACTO 60th meeting, 1–2 Jun. 1960. See also HO291/ 817, /825, /833, /845, and /861.

The other council members stated their views, which were substantially in agreement with those expressed by the chairman. A letter from Judge Sir Basil Nield indicated that he wanted the re-introduction of judicial corporal punishment for males under 21 for offences of violence, in order to plug the gap between borstal and probation, which the detention centre was not yet fulfilling. He was alone in his view.[33] The full report was ready by November 1960, coinciding with the Second Reading of the Criminal Justice Bill.

ACTO's report, *Corporal Punishment*, began with the statistical evidence for the deterrent efficacy of the penalty. While finding the evidence inconclusive—despite statistical appendices that were almost as long as the report itself—the council firmly agreed with the Cadogan committee "that judicial corporal punishment has no special or unique influence as a deterrent, and we think that for that reason it is unlikely to affect the incidence of crime." The council also argued that it was necessary to allow the provisions of the 1948 Act to be implemented in full. In all, ACTO came out strongly against the reintroduction of corporal punishment as a judicial penalty for any offender and any criminal offence, though the conclusion seemed to encourage courts to use severe and exemplary punishment in cases of offenders convicted of crimes of violence, for which purpose the existing powers of the court were said to be adequate. Even so, positive training won out over purely punitive methods. Corporal punishment represented the very antithesis of the treatment ideal, and its re-introduction was deemed to be a retrograde step. Not even the judicial heavyweights could overturn this penal philosophy. Expert advice triumphed over expressions of judicial and popular opinion.[34]

On 17 November 1960, Butler warned the Cabinet that in the debate on the Second Reading of the Criminal Justice Bill, to be held later that day, pressure would come from a section of the government's supporters for the reintroduction of corporal punishment, and amendments to the bill might subsequently be moved. He intended to resist these.[35] When introducing the debate, Butler made it clear that the government accepted the findings of ACTO's report. Speakers for the Opposition (Mr. Gordon Walker, Miss Alice Bacon) were pleased by the exclusion of flogging from the range of punishments for young offenders. Only one voice was raised in favour of corporal punishment. Butler wrote to Cunningham on the following day, "We had on the whole a good debate and a good day. The floggers were nowhere but will rear their heads again in Lords, and on Report."[36] Amendments were indeed floated in both Houses. Yet clauses permitting corporal

33 TNA, HO291/21, ACTO 63rd meeting, 28 Jul. 1960; HO291/797, Judge Sir Basil Nield to Colwyn, 7 Mar. 1960 and 26 Jul. 1960.
34 Home Office, *Corporal Punishment*, Report of the Advisory Council on the Treatment of Offenders, (Cmnd. 1213), 1961; HO291/22, ACTO 65th meeting, 2 Nov. 1960. See also HO291/834 for statistics provided by the HORU, AC/219, AC/220, AC/223.
35 TNA, CAB128/34, CC (60), 58th conclusions, Cabinet 17 Nov. 1960.
36 *Hansard*, vol. 630, 17 Nov. 1960, cols. 565–7 (Butler), col. 578 (Walker), col. 667 (Bacon); TNA, HO291/375, RAB to Cunningham, 18 Nov. 1960. See also *Daily Mirror*, 14 Nov. and 18 Nov. 1960.

punishment in attendance centres and detention centres were ultimately withdrawn; and the vote on the Report Stage in favour of corporal punishment for young offenders on a second or subsequent conviction of a violent crime mustered only 67 votes against 259. In the House of Lords, Lord Parker used the occasion of the Second Reading to advocate for corporal punishment, and criticize the arguments in the Advisory Council's report. If reintroduction meant putting the clock back, so be it: ". . . why should we shrink from it, especially when it is the hooligans themselves who have retarded the clock?" However, Lord Denning declared against corporal punishment, and Lord James of Rusholme, headmaster of Manchester Grammar School, effectively brought the entire debate on corporal punishment to a resounding close:

> If I may state my own view . . . it is that judicial corporal punishment is practically ineffective, morally dubious and, very often, psychologically harmful—and when I say "psychologically harmful," I do not mean to the criminal; I mean to the community that inflicts it. I think that most of those of us who are actively concerned with young people will be delighted that Her Majesty's Government have resisted the clamour of opinion and sentiment on this matter.[37]

All that remained was for Butler to see off the revolt at the Conservative Party conference in the fall of 1961, which he did with aplomb.[38]

III

The revolt over corporal punishment during the passage of the Criminal Justice Bill never truly materialized. From this point on the campaign to reinstate judicial corporal punishment only intermittently made itself heard. The Home Office focused on the clauses of the Criminal Justice Bill 1961.[39] The background to the

37 TNA, BN 29/297; *Hansard*, vol. 638, 11 Apr. 1961, cols. 57–146; 12 Apr. 1960, cols. 290–8; *Hansard* (Lords), vol. 230, 1 May 1961, col. 1106 (Parker), cols. 1121–2 (Denning), cols. 1130–1(James). See also J. E. Hall Williams, "'The Hide of the Thug,'" *British Journal of Criminology*, vol. 2 (1961), p. 81.

38 Howard, *RAB*, op cit., p. 286.

39 See TNA, CAB 134/1976, HA (59) 14th meeting, 24 Jul. 1959; CAB 134/1980, HA (60), 18th meeting, 29 Jul. 1960; CAB 134/1980, HA (60) 20th meeting, 17 Oct. 1960; HO291/356: Legislation Committee, LC (60) 56, 21 Oct. 1960; LC (60) 24th meeting, 26 Oct. 1960; "An Instalment of Penal Reform," *Economist*, 17 Sep. 1960, pp. 1064–5. In August 1959, Butler had been concerned about the depressing comments made in the press about the Annual Report of the Prison Commissioners. According to Cunningham's letter to Sir Lionel Fox, 25 August, Butler was concerned about the reception given to the Criminal Justice Bill "if it has to be introduced against a background of continually increasing crime and of the unreduced overcrowding in prisons which is hampering constructive work among prisoners. Will the Bill be regarded as too trivial or too academic in face of a practical problem of the greatest urgency?": TNA, HO291/351.

bill was, first, the alarming upsurge in the amount of crime committed by young people, which had led to considerable pressure on the accommodation in borstals and young prisoners' prisons. The number of offenders under 21 serving sentences of borstal training or imprisonment had increased by almost 40 per cent from 3,400 in late 1956 to 4,700 in June 1958. Second, young offenders, including many with no previous convictions, continued to be sentenced to imprisonment by magistrates' courts, almost three-quarters of whom received sentences of less than six months. And, third, ACTO's report, *The Treatment of the Young Offender*, had been submitted to the Home Secretary in July 1959, and published in October.[40]

The main recommendations in the report, in line with the prison commissioners' plans, were to integrate Borstal and imprisonment into a single system of "custodial training" with a minimum of six months and a maximum of two years (thereby lowering the existing borstal range of nine months to three years), the actual length to be determined by the commissioners. The aim was to carry a stage further the exclusion of young adults between 17 and 21 years of age from prisons, and extend to all young offenders sentenced to custodial treatment "the benefits of individual study and treatment," with the beneficial side effect of reducing the total demands on accommodation. The principle of the indeterminate sentence, with the prison commissioners and not the court deciding how long an offender remained in custody, was to be extended to more young offenders. However, courts would still have the power to imprison young offenders in default of payment of a fine (for a period proportionate to the amount outstanding), and the power to give a determinate sentence of imprisonment in one of three forms: for three years and above; of not less than 18 months and not more than three years (if the youth had served one indeterminate sentence and was again convicted: in short, for the failures of the indeterminate sentence); or of six months or less (though such sentences were to be abolished when enough places in detention centres were available). There were to be two fixed sentences of detention in a detention centre of three months' and six months' duration. In the report written by the sub-committee, George Benson asked for a sentence of detention of below three months to be available for comparatively trivial offences, but his reservation did not appear in the final report.[41]

Similar changes in the penal treatment of young women were also recommended. Compulsory after-care would follow a detention centre sentence (of one year from the date of release) and an indeterminate sentence (of two years from date of release), with the sanction of recall. ACTO recognized the need for careful selection and classification of offenders sentenced to custody, for which more remand centres were needed, but they still prioritized the provision of detention centres above that of remand centres. Finally, in a strangely dismissive reference to

40 Home Office, *The Treatment of Young Offenders*, Report of the Advisory Council on the Treatment of Offenders (1959).
41 TNA, HO291/20: AC/208, Report of the Sub-Committee on the Treatment of Young Offenders, Reservation by Sir George Benson.

research, the report admitted that no evaluation of the effectiveness of existing methods had informed the report, yet it felt this was no reason for delay in making the proposed changes. Evidently, as J. P. Martin was to observe, it was not yet accepted "that policymaking should be guided by a scientific evaluation of the results achieved by different methods of treatment."[42]

In the lead up to the Second Reading, the Home Office wobbled momentarily, in large part because of a minute by Dennis Vosper, Joint Parliamentary Under-secretary of State, who was worried about the bill:

> I think the public are very expectant about this Bill in the sense that they expect its passage to produce a great change, whereas it will do no such thing. The more I look at the Bill the more I realize that it will have little or no visible effect at all but will merely set the seal upon administrative actions which are already in progress. We talk a great deal about the new measures of treatment now becoming available and this spells detention centres to many of those who will support us against the re-introduction of corporal punishment. I think they are awfully good, but their failure rate is still some thirty per cent or more, and it would seem to be quite wrong to expect them to deal with more than a limited category of young offenders.[43]

Vosper wanted the department to mobilize the full panoply of developments, including the interim report of the Royal Commission on the Police, "to show that we are really determined to deal with what may be the biggest menace on the social front." He was convinced that the detention centre, the attendance centre, and adequate fines provided better deterrents than corporal punishment, "but I think it is a mistake to blur the edges of this type of punishment by confusing it with rehabilitation. It seems to me to be essentially a deterrent." Vosper's apprehensions were catching. The Home Secretary wrote to Cunningham,

> We shall be introducing a very light measure which will arouse the criticism that our policies are not severe enough. I do not see any way round this except by reference to penalties . . . I think we shall do this alright but we want to be quite sure that we show we are being strict as well as progressive . .
>
> .
>
> The upshot is that during the summer holidays we search for severity and stand in front of our looking glasses making grim faces.[44]

---

42 Martin, "A Note on Paragraph 17," *British Journal of Delinquency*, vol. 10 (1960), p. 217. In the same review of *The Treatment of Young Offenders*, Mannheim wrote, "The Committee has done no specific research, but . . . it is at least a concession to the idea of research that it is not altogether laughed out of court but gently put into cold storage." (p. 219).

43 TNA, HO291/367, Vosper to Home Secretary, 25 Jul. 1960.

44 Ibid., Butler to Cunningham, 30 Jul. 1960.

Cunningham sought to steady the ship by suggesting, against the grain of previous executive advice, that the courts "can no doubt be made aware of the widespread view that certain types of offender should be treated more severely." Also, he advised placing the new measure in the context of a plan of campaign pursued on several fronts by administrative action, investigation, and the building of new institutions.[45]

It was doubtless for these reasons that the first part of Butler's speech on Second Reading, rather than laying out the measures to be found in the Criminal Justice Bill (which the Lord Chancellor did so effectively in the House of Lords), dealt with "eight different methods of fighting crime."[46] Among the weapons with which to fight crime, he referred to the police, probation officers, and the prison service, then to the Streatfeild Committee on the machinery of the superior courts, Lord Ingleby's Committee on the treatment of juveniles, and the Advisory Council's report on corporal punishment, and finally to the other penalties available to the courts, which he claimed were more than adequate for the punishment of serious crime, and the government's building program, which included the provision of 12 detention centres by early 1962, centres "which have been most strongly pressed for by the courts." Only then did he explain the provisions that established a new pattern for the treatment of young offenders, and the extended scope of compulsory after care for both young and adult offenders discharged from custody.[47] The bill also included a clause allowing the transfer of all of the functions of the prison commissioners to the Home Secretary, on the ground that all forms of provision for the treatment of offenders should be dealt with comprehensively. As Butler told the Cabinet, "What I have in view . . . is that what is now the Prison Commission should eventually become part of a wider organization covering all Home Office responsibilities for criminal justice and the treatment of offenders." Vosper was less convinced by the transfer; it would be fine as long as the Home Secretary is energetic and progressive, but "it deprives the Prison Commission of the initiative which they might otherwise have, even though the Secretary of State of the day might be lethargic."[48]

---

45 Ibid., Cunningham to Butler, 16 Aug. 1960.
46 In the draft notes for the Lord Chancellor's speech on the Second Reading of the Criminal Justice Bill, Cunningham expressly omitted a revealing paragraph on the dismal state of the prisons. The paragraph stated that the local prisons were more overcrowded than they had ever been, with over 7,000 men crammed three in a cell, an overcrowding that also affected the workshops. The training prisons and the young prisoners' centres were full, and the wait for a vacancy in one could be long. Escapes had reached a disturbing level, and recently there had been concerted indiscipline in a number of prisons. See TNA, HO291/373.
47 *Hansard*, vol. 630, 17 Nov. 1960, cols. 562–77; *Hansard* (Lords), vol. 230, 1 May 1961, Lord Chancellor, Viscount Kilmuir, cols. 1054–67.
48 TNA, HO291/360, Memo by Home Secretary for Home Affairs Committee, HA (60) 116, 21 Jul. 1960; HO291/367, Vosper minute, 11 Nov. 1960. Tony Brennan considered it a fiction, however, that the commission was independent before 1963: personal interview, 20 Jan. 2000 in the Athenaeum.

In August 1963, the sections of the Criminal Justice Act 1961, which restricted the power of the courts to sentence young offenders to imprisonment came into force. How should we judge the Act? Above all, the scope of the indeterminate sentence was extended; greater powers were accorded the prison commissioners at the expense of the courts. The argument on behalf of the indeterminate sentence was that it was essential if institutions were to treat or reform their inmates. One difficulty with the argument was that it assumed that treatment would work. Yet the research that existed was already trending in an unfortunate direction for the treatment model. As George Benson told the Commons on the Second Reading debate of the Criminal Justice Bill,

> I think that . . . we have struck what is possibly a fundamental fact in our penal law, and that law can be stated quite simply. "On a given type of individual all forms of penal treatment give identical results."[49]

In addition, integrating prisons and borstals into one system altered the image and role of borstal training. The latter, wrote criminologist D. A. Thomas, "has ceased to be regarded primarily as a special rehabilitative measure and must now be considered as a general purpose sentence fulfilling deterrent as well as reformative purposes . . ." Or, as Lord Parker, LCJ stated in *Angell*, "Borstal training is in fact a series of institutions, forming a spectrum from pure schooling at one end to near-imprisonment at the other . . ."[50] Even so, the Act placed a mandatory restriction on the judges' sentencing powers. In addition to the indeterminate sentence, the Act raised the minimum age for imprisonment by quarter sessions or assizes from 15 to 17. Imprisonment was to remain, but to be restricted to those cases that were so serious that committal to prison was unavoidable. Judges could no longer operate a tariff system, or distinguish between the culpability of X and Y by a few months' difference in sentence, at least for all sentences of 7–35 months (with the exception of the repeat offender). The Act's significance, for D. A. Thomas, was "that it was the first serious attempt to control by legislation the exercise of the discretion in sentencing which judges had become accustomed to think of as their own prerogative."[51] Lord Parker welcomed the restriction on the power of the courts, even claiming that all Her Majesty's Judges would welcome it—and then went one step further:

49 *Hansard*, vol. 630, 17 Nov. 1960, col. 599. Benson meant that the different forms of penal treatment had no decided effect on the *rate of reconviction* of an offender.
50 R. Hood, *Borstal Re-Assessed* (1965), p. 75; J. E. Hall Williams and D. A. Thomas, "The Use of Imprisonment and Borstal Training for Young Offenders under the Criminal Justice Act, 1961—II," [1965] *Criminal Law Review*, p. 187 for *Angell* (1964); Ibid., III, p. 280.
51 Thomas, "Sentencing Reform: England and Wales," in C. Clarkson and R. Morgan (eds.), *The Politics of Sentencing Reform* (Oxford, 1995), p. 126.

> Indeed, at some later date I myself should welcome what I may call a senior indeterminate sentence to apply to those in the next age group, when it becomes a question of: "Shall they go to prison or shall they go to corrective training?"[52]

Yet it was not long before it was being reported that judges strongly resented the restriction on their power to sentence young offenders to imprisonment.

Finally, the 1961 Act expressed the intention to place greater reliance on detention centres. This was fraught with difficulty. The Act installed large variations in the length of punitive detention, three months, six months, and with cumulative sentences, nine months. There was no consensus on the overriding purpose of the centres: was it a positive training alternative to prison (which the graft of compulsory after care was meant to enhance), or was it a "short, sharp shock," a harsh deterrent, the price for the abolition of corporal punishment? It all depended on the political persuasion of the audience. And would the increased number of men passing through the centres each year (which rose from 2,000 in the late fifties to 6,000 in the mid-sixties) damage their effectiveness?[53] The research papers by Max Grunhut had concluded that the success of short punitive detention was dependent upon good selection procedures.[54] Selecting those offenders suitable for the disciplinary regime would be more difficult, however, if many more offenders were sent there, when remand centres were still so thin on the ground. If the detention centre was used too widely, and especially for more criminally sophisticated offenders, it could degenerate, Grunhut feared, into "a mere name for short prison sentences."[55]

IV

The Criminal Justice Act 1961 was the most substantial legislative consequence of *Penal Practice in a Changing Society*. The White Paper also foreshadowed a reorganization of the higher courts and the preparation of pre-sentence reports for the information of the courts. To this end, an interdepartmental committee on the business of the criminal courts had been set up under Mr. Justice Streatfeild, which reported in February 1961. The former chairman of the Prison Commission, Sir Lionel Fox, had set great store by this committee. He long believed that a rational

---

52 *Hansard* (Lords), vol. 230, 1 May 1961, col. 1103.
53 During the debates on the Criminal Justice Bill, it was announced that a detention centre for girls would be established. Moor Court, Stoke-on-Trent, Staffordshire was opened in September 1962.
54 Grunhut, "After-Effects of Punitive Detention," *British Journal of Delinquency*, vol. 10 (1960), pp. 180–4, 192.
55 Ibid., p. 193. At this date, only preliminary work had started on the construction of the first all-age, combined remand and observation centre sited at Risley, near Warrington. See also Anne Dunlop and Sarah McCabe, *Young Men in Detention Centres* (1965), pp. 5–10; John Muncie, "Failure Never Matters: Detention Centres and the Politics of Deterrence," *Critical Social Policy*, vol. 28 (1990), p. 58.

sentencing policy required a new system of permanent courts, similar to the Crown Courts at Liverpool and Manchester (as opposed to the peripatetic assizes and intermittent sitting of quarter sessions),[56] which would allow courts to receive information before sentencing from "observation and classification centres," sited adjacent to the remand centres for young offenders. These centres would provide full medico-psychological and social information to the courts. Diagnosis would work hand in glove with sentencing. At present, by contrast, there was a wide diversity in the scale and quality of the information. Take, for example, the statutory reports from the prison commissioners when offenders were eligible for certain forms of sentence (borstal training, corrective training, and preventive detention). The time available for making the reports varied greatly as between one case and another, because the courts deciding on the sentence sat at fixed intervals. It was a matter of chance whether an adequate report, an inadequate report, or no report worth the name was produced to guide the disposing court in its treatment of the offender. Little wonder there were such variations in the courts' sentencing practice.[57] Alas, the Streatfeild Committee, persuaded by the legal profession, who argued that full-time criminal judges grew stale or even prosecution-minded, decided that it was not "desirable at the present time to extend the Crown Court system to other areas." Instead, the committee reinforced the existing arrangement of courts, suggesting supplementary assizes, legally continuous quarter sessions, and transfer of cases to those courts that might hear the case soonest. Streatfeild was rather more constructive in the arrangements for providing courts with information.[58]

The report prefaced its recommendation with the important recognition that the "tariff system," or fixing a sentence proportionate to the offender's culpability, was no longer the only factor in deciding on sentence. Other objectives had come to the fore: the protection of society from the habitual offender, the need to deter potential offenders, and the need to deter or reform the individual offender. "The development has been most obvious," said the report, carried away by its own optimism, "in the increased weight which the courts give to the needs of the offender as a person . . . sentences are increasingly passed with the deterrence or

---

56   There was a total of 60 assize towns, which were visited three (in some cases fewer) times a year by a judge or judges of the Queen's Bench Division of the High Court. Each town was on one of seven circuits. "Gaol delivery" had always been regarded as the main function of the itinerant judiciary. In the London area the Central Criminal Court (the Old Bailey) acted as the court of assize. There were also 166 courts of quarter sessions, 71 county and 95 borough sessions. The borough sessions were presided over by a recorder. About 75 per cent of the cases tried on indictment were tried at quarter sessions.

57   TNA, HO291/507: Memo by Home Office and prison commissioners, SC 3, 11 Jul. 1958; SC 81, Further memo, 10 Apr. 1959; Hugh Klare, "The Problem of Remand in Custody for Diagnostic Purposes," in Modern Records Centre, Warwick University, MSS 16B/5/2.

58   Home Office and Lord Chancellor's Office, *Report of the Interdepartmental Committee on the Business of the Criminal Courts* (Cmnd. 1289), 1961, pp. 120–2.

reform of the offender as the principal objective . . ."[59] These newer objectives called for information not only about past events (the seriousness of the offence and the offender's record) but also about future events (the likely effect on an offender of a particular sentence). How could practical effect be given to the principle that a penal sentence should be fitted to the needs of the individual offender? The essential features of the Streatfeild Committee's proposals were as follows. Judges should be given full background knowledge of types of penal treatment, their purpose, and their effect. The report gave particular support to the development of prediction studies. To this end, a handbook ought to be prepared containing information about penal methods and the results of research into their effects. Judges also should have full information about the individual offender and his background. Since it was desirable that sentence follow immediately on conviction, reports on accused persons should be prepared before trial; if this were not possible, the case should be adjourned to enable a report to be made prior to sentence. Finally, arrangements should be systematized to secure pre-sentence reports in cases where they were most likely to be useful (all offenders up to the age of 30, and all first offenders above that age), and to improve the content of the reports.[60]

Home Office Circulars to implement the new reporting facilities went out in June 1963, its implementation synchronized with that of the Criminal Justice Act. The new scheme was not mandatory; it was at the discretion of the courts to decide how far they would adopt it. The police would provide information about the offender's criminal record; prison governors would assess his suitability for particular forms of custodial sentence; and probation officers would provide information about his personal history and characteristics.[61] Streatfeild proved influential in the growth in volume of social enquiry reports by probation officers in the 1960s and beyond. Some criminologists have doubted the impact they have had on courts' decisions, but they most likely encouraged sentencers to think outside "the tariff."[62] Yet Streatfeild was concerned with sentencing as a technical problem of allocation, and never stopped to question the appropriateness of the available penalties to which an offender might be allocated. The greatest disappointment was felt for the rejection of permanent crown courts, as a result of which Lionel Fox's plans for observation and remand centres for adults had to be largely abandoned. Only one such place was opened, the Risley remand centre, close to the Lancashire crown courts, with space for 400 men, 150 young adults, and 60 females. Adult remand prisoners continued to fetch up in the remand wings of local prisons. The legal profession had successfully closed ranks to stymie the reorganization of the

59 Ibid., p. 76.
60 Ibid., pp. 122–6. See J. E. Hall Williams, "Report of the Interdepartmental Committee on the Business of the Criminal Courts," *British Journal of Criminology*, vol. 2 (1961), pp. 67–78; idem., *Modern Law Review*, vol. 24 (1961), pp. 360–5.
61 TNA, HO291/525.
62 A. E. Bottoms and W. McWilliams, "Social Enquiry Reports Twenty-Five Years After the Streatfeild Report," in P. Bean and D, Whynes (eds.), *Barbara Wootton: Social Science and Public Policy* (1986), pp. 246–7.

courts, which in turn dashed all hopes for a new approach to remand in custody for diagnostic purposes, and *a fortiori* any serious improvement in sentencing practice.

An interesting side-note remains. Streatfeild's proposal to create a research base for sentencing initially fluttered the dovecotes at the Home Office. The Lord Chief Justice expressed support for a "sentencer's handbook," but the department was unsure what could be produced given the present ignorance about the probable effects of sentences. Miss Nunn wrote to Lodge to say,

> You will probably share our first reaction that there is as yet little or anything on these lines that could be given to the courts on which it would be reasonable and practicable for them to base a sentencing policy.

Yet three months later, Nunn was more optimistic,

> We have had in mind for some time that we ought to interest the courts in the results of research into the results of particular types of sentence, & we hope ultimately to develop prediction to the point where it will enable a court to compare the probability of success of a particular offender under two or more different methods of treatment. This is some way ahead . . .[63]

A slim handbook was prepared in the Home Office entitled *The Sentence of the Court*, with the sub-title *A Handbook for Courts on the Treatment of Offenders*. It was published in 1964, with a revised edition in 1969.[64] The handbook was long on description of available sentencing measures, short on discussion of research results, which anyway were open to different interpretations. To what extent the publication of these tables in 1964 influenced courts' sentencing practices going forward is unknown, but it is unlikely that publication influenced many sentencing decisions, unless it was a wider use of the fine.

V

Penal Practice in a Changing Society promised a review of preventive detention. The White Paper stated that it was too early to know if this method of dealing with recidivism was achieving what the 1948 statute anticipated, and research was underway into the courts' use of the method and into its effectiveness. The past decade had revealed a number of issues:

> It has been suggested, for example, that more people who are still relatively young have been sentenced to preventive detention than was originally

63 TNA, HO291/535; HO291/510: Nunn to Lodge, 22 Apr. 1959; Nunn minute, 15 Jul. 1959.

64 Home Office, *The Sentence of the Court: A Handbook for the Courts on the Treatment of Offenders* (1st pub. 1964; 2nd ed. 1969). See also R. M. Jackson, *Enforcing the Law* (Harmondsworth, revised ed. 1972), p. 201.

contemplated; and that others, though they have long criminal records, have not been guilty of offences of the more serious kind.[65]

Butler used his Advisory Council to an inordinate degree, so it was quite in character that he should ask it to evaluate preventive detention and recommend what should be done with it. For whatever reason, he did not ask ACTO to evaluate the other measure for the persistent offender, corrective training. It is the latter, however, with which we begin this estimate of the 1948 provisions for persistent offenders.

Under section 21 of the Criminal Justice Act 1948, in the case of an offender of 21 years of age or over, whose criminal record showed that he was becoming a professional criminal, a court of assize or quarter sessions could sentence him to not less than two or more than four years' corrective training, sentences long enough to enable methods of training to be applied. It was to be imposed on a criminal "with a view to his reformation and the prevention of crime."[66] After two-thirds of the sentence had been served the offender was eligible for release on conditional licence. No novelty was claimed for the method of corrective training. "Corrective training," wrote the chairman of the prison commission,

> is a new name in our penal terminology, but it does not describe any new method of treatment or training: it is the statutory application of an existing method to a category of prisoners selected not by the administrative classification system but by the Courts.[67]

The method was the system of training applied in the regional training prisons. During 1950, the 40 per cent of places allotted to "trainable ordinaries" at Wakefield and Maidstone were gradually filled by corrective trainees, allocated by the centre at Reading prison (transferred to Wandsworth in early 1951). In addition, the training prisons of Sudbury (an open prison) and the Verne at Portland (a semi-open prison) received corrective trainees, as did Askham Grange for women. The main features of the regime were hard industrial work, with some trade training; an evening programme of education and recreation; free association at meals and in the evenings; the exercise of personal attention by the prison staff; the development of responsibility among the prisoners; and supervision on discharge. However, not all corrective trainees were found suitable for training in the regional prisons, so

---

65 *Penal Practice in a Changing Society* (Cmnd. 645), Feb. 1959, p. 19.

66 D. A. Thomas described corrective training, along with detention in a detention centre, as two further forms of rehabilitative sentence provided by the Criminal Justice Act 1948. He added, "It is primarily in the use of these special sentences that the rehabilitative theory finds expression in the sentencing policy of the Court [of Criminal Appeal]." See "Theories of Punishment in the Court of Criminal Appeal," *Modern Law Review*, vol. 27 (1964), p. 563.

67 L. W. Fox, *The English Prison and Borstal Systems* (1952), p. 307. See also J. D. McClean, "Corrective Training—Decline and Fall," [1964] *Criminal Law Review*, pp. 748–9.

other prisons or parts of prisons were set aside with a regime of strict discipline and security: Chelmsford, Nottingham, Liverpool, Wormwood Scrubs, and Durham for men, with Holloway for women. It was estimated in 1948 that there were then in custody some 5,743 prisoners who on their next conviction would be eligible for a sentence of corrective training. For the ten months ending February 1950, 1,291 men and 63 women were sentenced to corrective training. By January 1951, 2,129 men (1,247 in corrective training prisons, only 367 in regional training prisons), and 91 women (mostly in Holloway) were under corrective training. Clearly, most of those selected for the new treatment were not thought suitable for regional training. The bulk of prisoners, for whom "there is little hope of spontaneous co-operation," to use the words of the official publication, *Prisons and Borstals* (1950), was being sent to corrective training prisons. Parts of two local prisons (Manchester and Pentonville), moreover, received men removed as unsuitable for training, usually because of bad behaviour in ordinary corrective training prisons.[68]

There was considerable incertitude among the judges in the early years concerning the purpose or objective of corrective training. They went from enthusiasm—as shown in the use made of the sentence (in the first three years over 3,000 men were sentenced to corrective training)—to confusion. At first, the Court of Criminal Appeal described corrective training, in Lord Goddard's words, as "extended Borstal treatment to try to train a man instead of merely imprisoning him;" or in Justice Birkett's words, as "an extension of the principles underlying Borstal training," even as the prison commissioners continued to insist that the purpose of the Act was not to provide a new form of training.[69] By early 1950, it was dawning on the Court that there was little difference between corrective training and imprisonment. Judicial bewilderment led to a meeting between the prison commissioners and the judges as a result of which the latter accepted that, to quote Lord Goddard's opening remarks in *Ledger*, "the discipline and effects of a sentence of corrective training are different from the discipline and effects of a sentence of simple imprisonment."[70] Even then not all was plain sailing. In *McCarthy*, in substituting a sentence of 18 months' imprisonment for three years' corrective training, Devlin argued that since corrective training was "in substance a form of imprisonment," it was necessary when passing a sentence of three years' training "to bear in mind that it is a sentence of three years' imprisonment and to consider whether that is the right length."[71] Just proportions would not be denied. The courts' interpretation of eligibility and sentence length only added to this initial confusion. While the Act did not lay down any upper age limit for a corrective training sentence, the Court in *Boucher* decided that such a sentence ought not to be given to a person over 30 years of age, and certainly not to a person of

68 Ibid., pp. 310–11; R. Hinde, *The British Penal System 1773–1950* (1951), pp. 187–8; *Prisons and Borstals* (1950), pp. 40–2.
69 *Barrett* (1949) 34 Cr. App. R. 3; McClean, op cit., p. 749.
70 *Ledger* (1950), 1 All E. R. 1104, per Lord Goddard at p. 1105.
71 *McCarthy* (1955) 1 W. L. R. 856. See also J. Ll. J. Edwards, "A New Doctrine in Criminal Punishment," *Law Quarterly Review*, vol. 72 (1956), pp. 117–19.

over 35.[72] Cases had been known of men between 40 and 50 being sentenced to training in the early 1950s; in 1954, only 61 out of 513 sentenced to corrective training were over 30 years, and only one (a woman) was over 40. As for length of sentence, the Act fixed the minimum period of corrective training at two years. However, in *Grant*, the Court decided that three years should be the minimum for a training sentence.[73] In 1950, out of a total of 1,216 such sentences, 30 per cent were for two years, 54 per cent for three years. In 1954, out of a total of 513 sentences, only six per cent were for two years, 80 per cent for three years. A *Practice Direction* in 1961, however, encouraged courts to pass two-year sentences if they felt this would provide an adequate period of training. In 1962, over half (186 out of 314) of the total number were two-year sentences.[74]

As the years went by the popularity of the sentence declined. By the mid-fifties, about 400 persons per annum were sentenced to corrective training, or less than half the number in 1950, and by 1962 the figure was down to 263. The contraction was a combination of Court of Appeal rulings, the experience gained by prison governors and courts of the type of prisoner for whom corrective training was suitable, and the disappointing reconviction rates of discharged trainees. Of those trainees discharged in 1952, two-thirds had been reconvicted by the end of 1954, three-quarters by the end of 1959.[75] This is not to suggest that the reconviction rate for corrective trainees was any worse than that for recidivists of the same age-group sentenced to shorter terms of imprisonment, a conclusion about which would require an analysis of matched samples. It is to suggest that the impression of corrective training's failure, based on reconviction rates, affected the use of the sentence. To be sure, the prison authorities were dealing with unpromising material, to judge from the reports of prison governors. The trainees were accused of being irresponsible, apathetic, and near unemployable. Typically, also, they had "form" beyond the statutory requirements for the sentence, many having over six previous convictions of indictable offences, almost exclusively breaking and entering and larceny (only a tiny number were convicted of sex or violent crimes), and many with prior experience of borstal and prison.[76]

Yet, at least in part, the uncooperativeness of the trainee was a function of his sense of injustice at the nature of the sentence. The supposed advantages of training were largely illusory, and the licence and recall conditions were a burden not shared by those undergoing simple imprisonment.[77] Frank Norman, sentenced to

---

72 *Boucher* (1952) 36 Cr. App. R. 152; *The Times*, 14 Oct. 1952, p. 11.

73 *Grant* (1951) 34 Cr. App. R. 230.

74 45 Cr. App. R. 100; Edwards, op cit., note 8, p. 120. See also H. B. Wilson, "Developments in the Penal System 1954–63," [1964] *Criminal Law Review*, p.641; D. A. Thomas, "Theories of Punishment in the Court of Criminal Appeal," *Modern Law Review*, vol. 27 (1964), pp. 552–3.

75 *The Times*, 2 Dec. 1952, p. 5; McClean, op cit., p. 757.

76 McClean, op cit., p. 753.

77 *The Times*, 7 May 1962, p. 13. See also A. E. Bottoms, "Towards a Custodial Sentence for Adults," II, (1965) *Criminal Law Review*, p. 654.

three years' corrective training for false pretences, confirmed the sense of injustice on both counts. As he wrote on the first,

> This is supposed to be corrective training at least that is what the judge said when he sentenced me. This being the case when I came here I expected something I don't know what but something. The two years that I have done here I might just as well [have] done in an ordinary nick. I have been cheated . . . the difference between Corrective Training and ordinary bird is none egsistant [sic].[78]

This sort of resentment was only heightened by corrective trainees increasingly serving their sentences alongside men sentenced to imprisonment, particularly from 1960 onwards. Anthony Heckstall-Smith, sentenced to 18 months for fraud, insisted, "The CT prisoners in Maidstone lived almost exactly the same life as I did myself." And on the second count, Norman wrote,

> When you get CT you do not get any remition [sic] of sentence at least not in the true sence [sic] of the word, what happens is you get say three years like I did out of that you do two years of it in the nick that is if you don't loos [sic] any time. When you have finished doing this they let you go, but you are still not free the rest of the time you have to go on licence . . . If you break any of the tearms [sic] of the licence you can be recalled without having to go to court . . .[79]

Can anything be said in favour of corrective training? Only that a few hundred prisoners, notably those sent to regional training prisons, experienced a more constructive regime than if they had been sent to local prisons on shorter sentences, which would have been their lot in the absence of corrective training; and that corrective training prisons set a standard in terms of work, education, and a late-stage hostel system to which the regime of other medium-length sentences might aspire. The prison commissioners were of the view as early as 1955 that corrective training was making a real contribution to the problem of reducing recidivism which was not reflected in the reconviction rate, arguing that a large number of men had been saved from a life of crime, and that had these prisoners continued "doing time" in local prisons they would have fetched up in preventive detention.[80] How they knew this is not vouchsafed us. Years later, Lord Allen of

---

78 Norman, *Bang to Rights: An Account of Prison Life* (1958), p. 140. Joan Henry also remarked of female trainees: ". . . they are supposed to go to places set aside solely for corrective trainees; but as these places are not yet ready, they are treated exactly the same as any other prisoner . . . Many of them would much prefer to have been given an ordinary prison sentence . . . they consider themselves to be the cream of prison society." See *Who Lie in Gaol* (1952), p. 69.

79 Heckstall-Smith, *Eighteen Months* (1954), p. 62; Norman, op cit., p. 158.

80 TNA, PCom9/1760: Fox to Mancroft, 28 Apr. 1955.

Abbeydale exonerated the Home Office for the measure's lack of success: ". . . the fact that corrective training failed was not our fault—unfortunately, the judges failed to understand it."[81] This is to pass the buck. Judges may have restricted the sentence to a youthful group of recidivists, yet the prison authorities never objected to the exclusive selection of prisoners young enough to be reformable; and judges were at least willing to dispense with just proportions and send young men to training for three-year terms. Indeed, the courts' eager use of the new measure took the Prison Commission by surprise; the necessary accommodation was not ready, and was in such a rudimentary state that it was difficult for courts to espy any difference between corrective training and imprisonment. Moreover, if the poor quality of corrective trainees is at issue, it surely had something to do with the quality of the reports prepared by prison governors. These erred on the side of the need for training, rather than the will and capacity of prisoners to benefit from it. If judges did not always follow the lead of these reports—in 1954, out of 1,005 offenders declared to be suitable for corrective training, only 450 were sentenced to it—they gave corrective training to only 17 who were reported as *unsuitable* by the prison authorities. Wherever the buck should stop, few mourned the passing of corrective training when it came time to change the procedures for handling persistent offenders.

By early 1964, Arthur Peterson, chairman of the Prison Commission, believed that it would simplify prison administration if they no longer had to treat corrective trainees as a separate class. The abolition of corrective training "could be justified solely on the grounds that it is now the aim that all sentences of imprisonment for two years or more should be regarded as training sentences."[82] Since this had been true of prison administration since at least 1948, the query surely arises: why then was the sentence ever invented?

VI

The eligibility for the new system of preventive detention was based on three factors: age, previous convictions, and present offence. The age of 30 was the lower limit; three previous convictions on indictment since the age of 17 punishable by a term of at least two years' imprisonment were required (and on at least two of those occasions the offender had been sentenced to imprisonment, borstal, or corrective training); as was a present conviction for an indictable offence punishable in the same way. If satisfied that detention was required for public protection, courts could sentence the offender to a term of not less than five or more than 14 years' preventive detention. In a memorandum to all courts, the Home Secretary immediately declared that while the Prevention of Crime Act 1908 had been confined to "cases of professional criminals with a long record of crime, who

---

81 Lord Allen in conversation with Lord Longford, *Punishment and the Punished* (1991), pp. 34–5.
82 TNA, HO291/927, Peterson to Brennan, 14 Feb. 1964.

are a danger to society," the qualification for preventive detention under the 1948 Act was "much wider than the definition of 'habitual criminal' in the Act of 1908 . . ." Hence, "It may be expected that much larger numbers will be sentenced to preventive detention, including a high proportion of the most difficult and dangerous prisoners in the country."[83] Detainees were to progress "through a series of establishments of different types, each of which will serve a particular purpose, their total effect being to break up the monotony of a long sentence." The first stage, one of observation and awaiting a vacancy in a central prison, would take place in a local prison, for anything up to two years. The second stage would be spent in one of the two central prisons, Dartmoor or Parkhurst (women detainees in Holloway). The third stage would prepare the detainee for release on a conditional licence. Those entering the third stage, on the recommendation of an advisory board, would be eligible for licence when they had served two-thirds of their sentence; the prisoners who did not graduate to the third stage would be released after five-sixths of the sentence had been served.[84]

The Home Secretary's memorandum to courts was predictive in one regard: the numbers sentenced to preventive detention shot up, the new system commending itself to judges as a way of dealing with the habitual criminal. By late 1954, 1,375 men were serving preventive detention sentences; Parkhurst prison was full of them (670 detainees), and they had overflowed to Nottingham, Northallerton, and Chelmsford prisons.[85] It was not long before the new system was in difficulty, however. At Parkhurst in the early years, there was an arson attempt and a number of razor-slashing incidents among the prisoners, followed by a concerted hunger strike involving 400 prisoners.[86] The cause of this indiscipline was thought to be the intense dislike on the part of the prisoners for the new system governing release on licence. In 1955, the chairman of the Prison Commission, conceded that the two disappointing features were the unwillingness of detainees to accept "the element of limited indeterminacy in the system," and "the inability of the Advisory Board to find more than a trifling proportion of men suitable for the Third Stage."[87] In 1952, the advisory board selected only 38 out of 223; in 1953, only 14 out of 136. Over the entire decade, four-fifths of all preventive detainees received only one-sixth remission of their sentence, since they were considered to be unlikely to do well on release. In a note by the prison commissioners for the information of ACTO, it was stated,

83 *Prisons and Borstals*, op cit., p. 42.
84 Ibid., p. 43.
85 C. H. Rolph, "Prisons and Prisoners," *New Statesman and Nation*, 2 Feb. 1957, p. 136.
86 TNA, PCom9/1760. See also John C. Spencer, "Some Recent Developments in the English Prison System," *British Journal of Delinquency*, vol. 4 (1953–4), p. 47. Part of the problem was the location at Parkhurst of three different categories of men in the same institution: long-term "ordinary" prisoners, the 40 or so men still serving preventive detention under the 1908 Act, and 400 or so serving preventive detention under the 1948 Act.
87 Ibid., Fox to Mancroft, 28 Apr. 1955.

> The governor and staff [of Parkhurst] are strongly of opinion that the system is not and never will be either understood or accepted and is a primary cause of unrest and indeed bitterness among the prisoners . . . They are all conditioned to the idea that so long as they behave they will get out on a fixed date that they can foresee from the beginning. They regard the operations of the Advisory Board with complete cynicism.[88]

At their meetings in November 1954 and February 1955, ACTO member Benson, relying on his knowledge of the Borstal prediction studies, thought the method of selection was "unscientific and unjustified," and pressed for the principle of one-third remission. Other members referred to the difficulty of making any forecast of whether a man would go straight on release. Even so, ACTO concluded that the existing system should continue but that further research should be carried out.[89]

As with corrective training, so with preventive detention, the sentencing policy of the courts imposed constraints on the new system. While the number of such sentences went up, judges were still sparing in their use of the measure. The prison commissioners estimated that about 10 per cent of those eligible for preventive detention received the sentence. Research by the Home Office Research Unit later recorded that in 1956 only 13 per cent (or 178) of the 1,384 men eligible for preventive detention at sentencing stage were sentenced to it. (It might be added that 14 per cent of those who were not sentenced to preventive detention, though liable for it, were given probation, and 75 per cent were given terms of imprisonment of below five years).[90] In addition, the courts, uneasy still about the preventive theory of sentencing, began to lay down their own rules concerning the use of preventive detention. The statute was fairly precise, but the Court of Criminal Appeal added its own refinements, particularly in the area of sentence length and eligibility. The legal minimum for PD sentences was five years, but the Court declared in *Sedgwick* that seven years was the "irreducible minimum," and it should generally be eight years or longer.[91] The result was a striking decline in the number of sentences below seven years, and a predominance of those between seven and ten years. This might be taken as a sign of the court's desire to protect the public against the habitual offender, but it also seemed to owe a lot to its desire to factor into length of sentence what it claimed was the one-third remission.[92] In fact, as we have seen, most detainees received only one-sixth remission. Fixing such a high minimum only served to create an even wider chasm between ordinary imprisonment and preventive detention. The minimum age for a PD sentence was

---

88 TNA, HO291/19: Note by prison commissioners, AC/174, 27 Oct. 1954.
89 Ibid., ACTO minutes, 3 Nov. 1954; 10 Feb. 1955. See also HO291/881: PD/2, ACTO, Sub-Committee on Preventive Detention.
90 TNA, HO291/507, further memo by Home Office and prison commissioners, 10 Apr. 1959.
91 Edwards, "A New Doctrine," op cit., p. 122.
92 H. Mannheim, "Some Aspects of Judicial Sentencing Policy," *Yale Law Journal*, vol. 67 (1958), pp. 961–81.

fixed by statute at 30. The court varied any sentence where the offender was younger than 35, and by its 1962 *Practice Direction*, which declared that too many PD sentences were being passed, held that preventive detention "should in general . . . only be given as a last resort and to those nearing 40 years of age or over."[93] Retributive proportionality also limited the use of the sentence. The court took a number of long preventive detention sentences down to 18 or 12 months' ordinary imprisonment, on the ground that the sentence was out of proportion to the offence. In *Grimwood* (1958), eight years' preventive detention was reduced to two years' imprisonment for a theft of 14 shillings from a domestic gas meter, the court stating that a sentence "ought really to have relation to the gravity of the crime itself."[94] And in the late fifties, the court even pioneered a liberal approach to the "inadequate recidivist," whereby a sentence of PD was varied to probation plus voluntary residence in a private hostel, in an attempt to avoid the offender's complete institutionalization.[95]

The problem with courts seeking to restrict PD sentences to those of an older age, to those with institutional experience, to those who had made no attempt to go straight but had speedily committed another offence, and to those who had committed the same kind of offence on each occasion, was that it plotted a straight line to the incompetent petty persistent offender not the "dangerous" criminal. In 1950, of the 213 sentences of PD, five were for violence against the person, five for sexual offences, and one for robbery. The figures were almost identical in 1959.[96] This group represented less than 10 per cent of those sentenced to preventive detention. The professional robber, the sexual molester, or the man of violence typically received a sentence of imprisonment, though most were for

---

93   *The Times*, 27 Feb. 1962, p. 3. The direction, which was issued after consultation with the prison commissioners, stated *inter alia*: "Recent experience in this Court has shown that too much use is being made of the power to impose preventive detention. Indeed in over 30 per cent of appeals sentences of preventive detention have been varied by the substitution of periods of imprisonment." See also "A Serious Gulf: Aims of Prison Sentences," letter from T. Morris and L. Blom-Cooper, *The Times*, 7 Mar. 1962; Glanville Williams, "The Courts and Persistent Offenders," [1963] *Criminal Law Review*, p. 732. This policy was also applied to female persistent offenders: see Ann Smith, "Penal Policy and the Woman Offender," in P. Halmos (ed.), *The Sociological Review Monograph*, No. 9 (1965), p. 119–20.

94   See Regina v. Jenner, *The Times*, 15 May 1956, p. 5. A man with sixteen convictions for petty larceny since 1942 received seven years' preventive detention for stealing a pair of shoes which he sold for 7s. 6d. The court substituted a sentence of 18 months' imprisonment, the PD sentence being out of proportion to the offence. See R. v. Grimwood [1958] *Criminal Law Review*, p. 403. See also *Sentences of Imprisonment: A Review of Maximum Penalties*, Report of the Advisory Council on the Penal System (1978), pp. 49–50.

95   D. A. Thomas, "Appellate Review of Sentences and the Development of Sentencing Policy: The English Experience," *Alabama Law Review*, vol. 20 (1968), pp. 205–7; idem., *Principles of Sentencing* (1970), pp. 22–5.

96   TNA, HO291/920, ACTO sub-committee on preventive detention, PD/34: memo by Home Office and Prison Commission, "The Use of Imprisonment as an Alternative to Preventive Detention," Appendix A.

three years or less. Sixty per cent of PD sentences were imposed upon those convicted of more serious offences against property, notably breaking and entering. Those who committed these offences but who did not receive preventive detention were rarely sentenced to more than three years' imprisonment. It is the final 30 per cent of those sentenced to PD, those convicted of less serious offences against property, notably larceny and false pretences, that brought the measure into disrepute. Those who committed these offences but who did not receive preventive detention were rarely sentenced to more than two years' imprisonment. These were the petty swindlers and pilferers, whose main distinction was inadequacy or incompetency not innate wickedness, and whose hauls were small change. It meant that the refrain that had been heard ever since 1908 was voiced again: preventive detainees were nuisances not dangers. As Nigel Walker rightly concluded, "courts were being influenced not so much by the type of offence as by the pattern of the criminal career—the number of previous convictions, or of offences "taken into consideration" at the stage of sentence, and the length of time for which the offender had kept out of "trouble since his last discharge from prison."[97] An offence committed immediately after release from prison, as Charles Patrick Smith, released after a stint of seven years' preventive detention, learned to his cost, could get you sent back (in the cold legalese of R. E. Seaton, chairman of London Sessions) "to the place whence you came . . . and this time it will be for ten years."[98] As early as 1959, Lord Stonham called out this iniquitous system:

> I say that sentences of from seven to ten years on these human derelicts who have never done more (even if they have done it often) than steal something worth £1 cannot be approved by public opinion . . . I say that to immure a man for one-fifth of his adult life for such offences is worse than transportation . . . For this type of offender, and indeed in my view for any offender, the present system of preventive detention is hopelessly wrong, a gross waste of public money, and it helps strain the prison system to breaking point.[99]

VII

In April 1961, Home Secretary Butler asked ACTO to mount a full-scale review of the sentencing practice of the courts, the nature of the preventive detention regime, and the element of indeterminacy in the sentence. The first meeting of the sub-committee charged with the review was held on 7 July 1961. The number then serving PD sentences was over 1,300, of whom 28 were women. Detainees

---

97   Walker, "The Habitual Criminal: An Administrative Problem," *Public Administration*, vol. 41 (1963), p. 270. See also T. E. James, "Preventive Detention in 1961 in the Court of Criminal Appeal," [1962] *Criminal Law Review*, pp. 352–9; Leslie Wilkins, "Persistent Offenders and Preventive Detention," *Journal of Criminal Law, Criminology, and Police Science*, vol. 57 (1966), p. 316.
98   Tony Parker, *The Unknown Citizen* (Harmondsworth, 1st pub. 1963; 1966), p. 42.
99   *Hansard* (Lords), vol. 215, 8 Apr. 1959, cols. 539–40.

comprised less than five per cent of the prison population. The sentence was given about 200 times a year, as against 12,000 sentences of simple imprisonment. As they did when examining judicial corporal punishment, the sub-committee first requested evidence from the Lord Chief Justice on the sentencing practice of the Queen's Bench Judges. Lord Parker replied that for every five sentences of PD given on assize, 100 or more were given by quarter sessions, so the best he could do was to offer the experience of the Court of Criminal Appeal in reviewing sentences given by quarter sessions.[100] As E. R. Cowlyn in the Home Office told the sub-committee chairman, the Lord Bishop of Exeter, "There is, in fact, no recognised machinery for obtaining the collective views of judges . . ."[101] The LCJ and Mr. Justice Ashworth, the constant presidents of the Court of Criminal Appeal, turned in a memorandum that succinctly laid out the circumstances under which the court found a preventive detention sentence to be appropriate. The statutory provisions in regard to age and previous convictions were the bare minimum without which detention could not be imposed. The prisoner should also have served at least one term of imprisonment of more than three years, showing he was "a person who cannot be deterred from a criminal career by a substantial term of imprisonment," and that a longer term of detention was needed to protect the public. An exception, however, was "the inveterate cycle thief or false pretender, none of whose offences were sufficiently serious to warrant a substantial period of imprisonment." The statement revealingly continued,

> Though it can be said that such a man is merely a nuisance, causing annoyance and inconvenience, a time, we recognise, comes when the section of the public, often poor people upon whom he preys, need protection, even more than from a persistent bank robber or wage snatcher.[102]

It should be clear in these cases, they wrote, that all attempts at reform had failed, and the sentence be imposed "only as a last resort when such offences have reached large figures." It was also essential to consider good conduct since last release from prison (holding down a job for at least 12 months since last release told against preventive detention) and the nature of the current offence (if a relatively trivial offence, or of a different nature from previous offences, detention should not be imposed). At the other end of the scale, the court laid increasing emphasis on the desirability of imposing a long sentence of imprisonment rather than preventive detention when it was justified by the gravity of the offence. In all, the court had clearly superimposed on the minimum qualifications a more stringent set of qualifications; indeed, it had created a reasonably clear set of rules by its frequent interventions. Yet uncertainty not to say conflict of views concerning the sentence

---

100 TNA, HO291/887: Lord Parker to Mr. Justice Barry, 6 Oct. 1961.
101 Ibid: Cowlyn to Exeter, 24 Oct. 1961.
102 TNA, HO291/887, ACTO sub-committee on preventive detention, PD/12: memo by LCJ and Mr. Justice Ashworth, Dec. 1961.

still prevailed, to judge from the fact that in 1961, the percentage of successful appeals against a sentence of PD was 34 (or 18 out of 53), very much higher than the 7 per cent success rate in appeals against a sentence other than preventive detention.[103]

ACTO was also privy to the findings of the Home Office Research Unit's study, published in 1963 as *Persistent Criminals: A Study of All Offenders Liable to Preventive Detention in 1956* by W. H. Hammond and Edna Chayen; and of the psychiatric survey of preventive detainees by the Cambridge Institute of Criminology carried out by D. J. West, published in 1963 as *The Habitual Prisoner*. Along with "observations on some of the characteristics of men sentenced to preventive detention," by R. S. Taylor, senior psychologist at Wandsworth prison, which appeared in the *British Journal of Criminology* in 1960, the research base of ACTO's report was stronger than any previous report. Dr. West's study of 100 recidivist prisoners (half of them preventive detainees, the other half "intermittent recidivists"), using interviews and case-history data, was essentially a study of the psychology of recidivism. It confirmed that no more than ten per cent of the detainees were a danger to the public; the remainder were subject to what Gordon Trasler, in his review of the study, described as "a crippling degree of social incompetence—in their work, their financial affairs, their personal relations and family ties."[104] Only in the regimented conditions of a prison could they survive without anxiety. The Hammond and Chayen study revealed what had long been suspected. Preventive detention was given to only a small proportion of persistent offenders. An offender liable to the sentence had about the same chance of being given a non-custodial sentence as a sentence of preventive detention. In addition, the majority of detainees had already been given three or more sentences (mostly short-term imprisonments) since first becoming liable to preventive detention, but only about one-fifth had ever received corrective training. Courts sentenced those with the *worst criminal histories* to preventive detention, and sentenced offenders convicted of the *most serious offences* to long sentences of imprisonment. And two types of detainee could be distinguished, persistent offenders with more serious offences (notably breaking and entering) and older men with long criminal records whose offences were not serious, which raised the question whether there ought to be a system of differential methods of treatment and degrees of security within the preventive detention system. In terms of subsequent reconvictions, the study revealed no evidence that PD was more effective than other sentences. According to the 1959 report of the Central After-Care Association, between 47 and 53 per cent of preventive detainees discharged between 1952 and 1957 were reconvicted. Nor was there much difference between the rate of conviction of those detainees who served five-sixths

---

103 Ibid. Also PD/26, "Decisions of the Court of Criminal Appeal," 26 Mar. 1962.
104 Trasler, "Preventive Detention: A Symposium," *British Journal of Criminology*, vol. 4 (1963), p. 184. See also West, *The Habitual Prisoner* (1963); Taylor, "The Habitual Criminal: Observations on Some of the Characteristics of Men Sentenced to Preventive Detention," *British Journal of Criminology*, vol. 1 (1960), pp. 21–36.

of their sentence and those who served two-thirds, though men released after serving two-thirds tended to be reconvicted after a rather longer interval.[105]

The sub-committee of ACTO visited all the prisons where detainees were held; took oral evidence from prison staff, prisoners, judges, and after-care representatives; and written evidence from a number of Recorders and the Howard League. In addition, three of their number paid what can only be seen as a token international visit to a penal colony in Luxembourg. In December 1962, ACTO signed off on the proposals in the report of the sub-committee on preventive detention. At this final meeting, the Bishop of Exeter stated that the sub-committee had taken objection to three main features of preventive detention: one, the prisoner was being punished for his record; two, there was a wide gap between the minimum sentence of detention and the maximum sentence of imprisonment which was likely to be given for the same offence; and three, the element of indeterminacy. On the last point, the sub-committee hoped no delay would be brooked in accepting their interim recommendation that all detainees should become eligible for release on licence after serving two-thirds of the sentence, thus abolishing the element of indeterminacy. "But it had also seemed to them," said Exeter, "that the system as a whole was full of injustice, little used and not a particularly effective deterrent." Yet the sub-committee saw no reason why the length of sentences of ordinary imprisonment should not be determined by the offender's record. Moreover, said Exeter,

> . . . society was clearly justified in detaining the inadequate but persistent offender for a long period, on the ground of his inability to keep himself from preying on society. Thus it was recommended that the statute abolishing preventive detention should specifically give the courts power to pass long sentences of imprisonment which would have regard to the offender's antecedents and to the need to protect the public. The sub-committee had in mind that the persistent offender should receive sentences of imprisonment gradually increasing in length.[106]

The sub-committee recognized that persistent offenders must be dealt with, but it did not wish to create a separate, special category of offender, and it did wish to bridge the gap between the minimum sentence of PD, in practice seven years, and the term of imprisonment awarded in precisely the same circumstances.

ACTO sent the report to the Home Secretary for publication.[107] It recommended that preventive detention should be abolished and that, pending its abolition, all preventive detainees should be eligible for release after serving two-thirds

---

105 W. H. Hammond and Edna Chayen, *Persistent Criminals: A Study of All Offenders Liable to Preventive Detention in 1956* (1963), A HORU Report., *passim*. See also TNA, HO291/877, PD/33, note by T. S. Lodge, May 1962, main results of HORU study of PD.
106 TNA, HO291/22, ACTO minutes, 12 Dec. 1962. Also HO291/862.
107 *Preventive Detention*, Report of ACTO (1963).

of their sentence. In fact, the Home Secretary moved with alacrity to implement the council's interim recommendation, and on a cold day in March 1963, according to Nigel Walker, "a small company of slightly startled preventive detainees were thrust out of their centrally heated prisons to face an unwelcoming world."[108] The public were to be protected in the future from the persistent criminal by encouraging courts to deal with these offenders by longer sentences of imprisonment. The proposal would allow courts to make use of the whole range of sentences of imprisonment for persistent offenders. Thus the minor persistent offender who had on the previous occasion received, say two years' imprisonment, might on the next occasion, having committed a similar offence, be sentenced to three, four, or five years' imprisonment, rather than "jump," as he was liable to under the existing system, from two years' imprisonment to seven years' preventive detention. For most offences, the existing maxima were high enough for the purpose the report had in mind; for some offences, however, the power of the court needed strengthening. Thus, courts would be empowered to pass sentences of up to ten years' imprisonment on persistent offenders convicted of crimes presently punishable for a term of five years or more. So, for example, it would be possible to award longer sentences to those convicted of housebreaking with intent to commit a felony (present maximum seven years' imprisonment), and to those convicted of obtaining goods by false pretences (present maximum five years' imprisonment). The provision was not to affect the court's power to impose a longer sentence than ten years' imprisonment where this was already permitted by law (for instance, for burglary or housebreaking with larceny). The report finally suggested that a new type of institution with a less secure regime should be available for offenders of inadequate personality, and homes or hostels should be established where persistent offenders could be accommodated on discharge.

VIII

How should we evaluate the report? Let us first underline the fact that the main object of the ACTO recommendations was that there should be a gradual and not a sudden increase in the length of sentence passed on persistent offenders. The general philosophy or principle underlying the report was that a persistent offender might properly receive sentences of imprisonment of increasing length without the need for any special procedure to designate such sentences as being of a preventive character. This was the present practice of the courts; a man's record was customarily taken into account in imposing an ordinary sentence; ACTO's proposal represented no very radical change in sentencing policy. As the report stated,

> Many statutes provide for increased penalties for second and subsequent offences, thereby recognising that persistence in the same offence should attract heavier punishment . . . We think that it follows from this principle that

108 Walker, "The Habitual Criminal," op cit., p. 271.

the weight of a persistent offender's past misdeeds may come to be of more account in determining the sentence than the seriousness of his latest offence.[109]

In this way, it would be possible to get rid of the excessive contrast between the length of a normal sentence for many offences and the length of a sentence of preventive detention. It would also avoid the necessity to treat preventive detainees as a special class for purposes of prison treatment. ACTO wanted the appropriate method of training to be selected by the prison authorities within the maximum period fixed by the court. The ACTO report envisaged, moreover, that for most offences this policy could be pursued without any change in the existing maximum sentences. The *sole* object, we repeat the *sole* object, of the recommendation in paragraph 63 was to provide for a few types of offence (such as frauds and false pretences) for which the existing maximum was so low that it allowed no room for a gradual increase in sentences.[110] I would contend, therefore, that the critical attention that was lavished upon this subordinate feature of the proposal, the "extended" sentence of imprisonment, served to mask the essential proposal of the report, which was for a gradual accumulation of sentence for persistent offenders.

In August 1963, the new Conservative Home Secretary, Henry Brooke, alerted the Lord Chief Justice to his plan to put before the Home Affairs Committee of the Cabinet proposals for legislation to implement ACTO's recommendations.[111] This spurred Lord Parker to voice disagreement to two of ACTO's proposals: the 10-year maximum, which "would mean a grave curtailment of the Courts powers," and the limitation of the new preventive sentence to offences carrying five years or more. On the first point, Parker argued for a sentence of 12 years, to ensure that courts would actually pass sentences of nine or ten years, which even with remission would result in an effective sentence length of seven or eight years, or something equivalent to what was currently awarded to preventive detainees. On the second point, he urged strongly that sexual offences carrying a maximum of two years (namely indecent assault on a female, the procuration offences, and many attempt cases, such as to have intercourse with a girl under 13) should be brought within the scope of any new powers to deal with persistent offenders. The entire tone of the Lord Chief Justice's letter suggested to Cunningham, the Permanent Undersecretary of State, that "(in contrast with his apparent readiness last January to welcome the ultimate abolition of preventive detention) he now wants to see it kept under another guise." Conceding these two points, Cunningham believed, "would represent a radical departure from the whole tenor of the Council's recommendations."[112] Brooke decided to ask for the views of the Lord Chancellor and the Attorney-General on Parker's two points, telling his colleagues

109 *Preventive Detention*, Report of ACTO (1963), para 60, p. 24.
110 Ibid., p. 25.
111 TNA, HO291/927, Draft memo for Home Affairs Committee, Jun. 1963.
112 Ibid: Lord Parker to Cunningham, 10 Jul. 1963; Cunningham minute, 23 Aug. 1963.

that he could not adopt the proposal to make the maximum sentence 12 years, but that he would meet the Lord Chief Justice by providing that the new preventive sentence should apply to persons convicted of offences carrying a maximum sentence of *two* years or more, instead of *five* years or more. This was a remarkable concession to judicial opinion, creating an excessive contrast between the normal maximum sentence of two years and a maximum of ten or even 12 years for persistence. Yet the other senior law officers fully endorsed it and more. Lord Dilhorne, the Lord Chancellor, thought there was great force in the Lord Chief Justice's points: "I agree that the courts should have power to put away persistent sexual offenders for long periods," and "I think the maximum should be fourteen years." In the blink of an eye, Dilhorne added another two years to the extended sentence, taking the maximum to that of preventive detention. He added that the qualifications for the new sentence, in terms of age and previous convictions, should be defined rather more precisely than ACTO was proposing. Sir John Hobson, the Attorney-General, who had been a member of the ACTO subcommittee for a time, endorsed the 12-year maximum, and also called for a definition of the "persistent offender." Hobson finally remarked that the main problem of persistent offending was "the passive inadequate deviant," one of the categories described by Drs. Hammond and West, for whom he thought a cross between an open prison, a mental institution, and an old people's home in some remote place was required: "The idea would be to provide a kind of poor man's St. Helena rather than a Devil's island."[113]

Arthur Peterson, chairman of the Prison Commission, the only official who seemed to truly understand ACTO's proposals, was horrified to learn of these judicial amendments. The gradual increase in the length of sentence, which is what ACTO proposed, was important from the point of view of treatment, said Peterson. It did not create "the same resentment as a sudden increase," and allowed the prison staff to focus their efforts on persistent offenders "at a stage in their career when the sentence is long enough to provide some constructive training but not so long as to lead to institutionalization." If legislation were introduced on the lines advocated by the Lord Chancellor and Attorney-General, the effect would be to replace preventive detention by a special type of imprisonment sentence, with possibly the same maximum and the same qualifications (the only difference being that there would be no minimum sentence), thereby requiring the prison authorities to provide special treatment for those offenders designated by the courts as persistent offenders, with all the disadvantages that the system of preventive detention was heir to. If a special sentence were retained, moreover, a varied system of treatment for distinct groups of prisoners would be needed, if those of inadequate personality were to be helped. Peterson also feared that if corrective training as well as preventive detention was abolished and the courts were given power to impose longer sentences on persistent offenders of any age over 21, the

113 Ibid: Brooke to Dilhorne, 3 Sep. 1963; Dilhorne to Brooke, 10 Sep. 1963; Hobson to Brooke, 18 Sep. 1963.

courts were likely to impose longer sentences in considerable numbers of cases with the result that the prison population in general, and the number of persistent petty offenders serving long sentences in particular, would increase.[114]

In March 1964, the Home Secretary wrote to inform the Lord Chief Justice of the lines on which his mind was running. In terms of length of sentence, Brooke proposed that in the case of an offender convicted of an offence for which the normal maximum was two years or more, the court could impose a sentence of *double the maximum* length or of 14 years, whichever was the lesser. He claimed that this approach would avoid a sudden jump in the maximum from two or five to 14 years, and would statutorily relate the new maximum sentence to the gravity of the offence which was the occasion of its imposition. Brooke also proposed that an extended sentence should not be imposed on conviction for an offence which had been committed after more than three years from the date of the offender's last release from prison, which echoed existing practice in the case of preventive detention.[115] Lord Parker supported this approach, though he objected to allowing an extended sentence to all persistent offenders of 21 and over, floating instead the suggestion, which he first made in 1959, of "an indeterminate sentence—a kind of senior Borstal—for those in their twenties . . . for any sentence that merited more than two years and less than four years." It may be the Lord Chief Justice feared that an extended sentence starting at 21 years of age would involve so wide a discretion and so extensive an age range that there were bound to be considerable varieties in sentence, which the Court of Criminal Appeal would have to sort out. He himself expressed his concern in the following way:

> I cannot help feeling that, since for serious offences a prisoner can be dealt with suitably within the maximum, an extended sentence is only required for the petty offender and then only as a last resort when he is at least 35 or even 40.[116]

Peterson agreed with Lord Parker that prisoners between 21 and 30 should be sentenced with the object of reform not to protect the public, but Brooke simply replied to the effect that the idea of an indeterminate sentence was one for the Royal Commission on the penal system, which the Home Office had under consideration. Shortly afterwards, however, Brooke wrote to Parker to recommend the counting of qualifying convictions and sentences from the age of 21, thus making the operative lower age limit for the new sentence closer to 24, and imposable only where prior substantial experience of prison had failed to reform the offender. In addition, he suggested a proviso, echoing the provision restricting the imprisonment of first offenders, that in the case of an offender aged 35 or younger, the court should be required

114 Ibid: Peterson to H. B. Wilson, 24 Oct. 1963. See Brian Cubbon, "Peterson, Sir Arthur William (1916–1986)," *Oxford DNB* (2004).
115 Ibid: Brooke to Parker, 19 Mar. 1964.
116 Ibid: Parker to Brooke, 24 Mar. 1964.

to consider all other methods of dealing with him before imposing an extended sentence of imprisonment.[117]

At last, on 10 July 1964, the proposals went before the Home Affairs Committee, which raised no objection. Precise statutory qualifications for the new sentence were included on the grounds that if the matter were left to the courts, they would have to lay down their own criteria and it was preferable that these should be prescribed by Parliament.[118] The government's intentions were made known on 23 July in reply to questions in both Houses. A bill to introduce the new law could not be brought in until after the general election, however, because no parliamentary time remained for fresh legislation.[119] The new Labour government's 1965 White Paper, *The Adult Offender*, proposed to abolish corrective training and preventive detention, and replace it with a similar though scaled-down extended sentence. The Labour Home Secretary, Frank Soskice, considered that the previous government's proposals "would amount to little more than the continuance of preventive detention under another name."[120] Hence, the new administration intended to empower the courts to sentence a persistent offender to up to ten years' imprisonment where the ordinary maximum term for the offence was five years or more and not more than ten years; and to up to five years' imprisonment where the ordinary maximum term was two years or more and not more than five years. The statutory definition would be so framed, moreover, to catch the "real menace to society," not the nuisance. Hope springs eternal. The persistent offender would qualify for one-third parole on licence, but whatever the date of release, he would be on licence until the whole of the sentence had expired. These proposals found their way into the 1967 Criminal Justice Act.

The courts used the new sentence cautiously. Twenty-seven extended sentences were awarded in 1968, rising to a peak of 129 in 1970; it was downhill from that point. The offences for which the sentence was given were mainly burglary; the number of violent and sexual offences could be counted on the fingers of one hand. Confusion was added to caution when in *DPP v. Ottewell* (1968) the House of Lords held that a sentence could be extended even if it did not go beyond the maximum penalty, but simply beyond the ordinary sentence that the judge might otherwise have imposed; and that the sentence could be used as a way of ensuring release on licence.[121] This decision did not, however, lead to any greater use of the sentence.

The prison commissioners thought it an illogical criticism to say that three in every four preventive detainees were later reconvicted. The measure, they insisted,

---

117 TNA, HO291/928: Brooke to Parker, 8 May 1964.
118 TNA, CAB 134/2056, Home Affairs Committee, HP (64) 114, 1 Jul. 1964; CAB 134/2054, HP (64), 23rd meeting, 10 Jul. 1964; HO291/928.
119 *Daily Telegraph*, 24 Jul. 1964, enclosed in TNA, HO291/928.
120 TNA, CAB 134/2001, H (65) 87, 2 Aug. 1965, "Persistent Offenders and Parole." See *The Adult Offender* (Cmnd. 2852) 1965.
121 [1968] 3 Weekly L. R. 621; [1968] 3 All E. R. 153; [1968] 52 Cr. App. R. 679. See also J. E. Hall Williams, *The English Penal System in Transition* (1970), pp. 209–13; *Sentences of Imprisonment: A Review of Maximum Penalties*, op cit., pp. 53–4; Thomas, *Principles*, op cit., pp. 283–6.

was always intended for offenders whose careers had shown them to be beyond cure. As Lionel Fox advised Lord Mancroft, "Thus nearly 1,200 persistent offenders are at present 'out of circulation' for periods of from 7–14 years. This achieves the primary purpose of the Act."[122] Yet it was impossible for the commissioners to deny that for sixty years, one measure after another to deal with the habitual criminal had become dismal failures. The legislative and executive branches of government had never managed to convince the judiciary to use the "positivist" escape clause from tariff restraints that the law allowed. The newest reincarnation was no more successful. The extended sentence was never needed. The courts had developed their own response to dealing with the serious and persistent offender. They used the tariff or life sentence for really serious crime. For the inadequate persistent offender, and increasingly for the intermediate recidivist, judges used probation. They didn't require the power to go beyond the existing maxima to punish persistence. Did the courts do what ACTO had actually proposed, gradually increasing sentence length for persistence? It is hard to be categoric. Only to the degree, one suspects, that the tariff entertained. One can only conclude that the search for a measure to deal with the persistent offender was the most fruitless search in all of English penal history.

IX

The Criminal Justice Bill, which introduced the most far-reaching reform of the system of criminal justice since 1948, had been under consideration since Labour returned to power in 1964. Soskice secured a place for a Criminal Justice Bill in the legislative programme for 1965–6, but the bill was edged out by other legislation, despite the strong support in October 1965 of Lord Chancellor Gardiner and Attorney-General, Sir Elwyn Jones. The next Home Secretary, Roy Jenkins, took up the cause. In April 1966, he asked for urgent consideration, with a view to inclusion in the Criminal Justice Bill, of provisions that would make a substantial reduction in the number of prisoners sentenced to terms of less than six months. In July, Jenkins took these proposals before the Home Affairs Committee of the Cabinet.[123] A sentence of six months, claimed Jenkins, blunts rather than sharpens the deterrent effect of imprisonment, and overcrowded the gaols with prisoners for whom no effective remedial treatment could be provided. He proposed tackling the problem in four ways: by introducing suspended sentences; by amending the law of drunkenness; by changing the procedure for the enforcement of fines; and by restricting remands in custody. Courts would have discretion to suspend a prison sentence of between six months and two years for any offence. For sentences of six months or less, there would be a statutory fetter on the courts' discretion, requiring them to suspend such sentences where the offender had not been in prison or borstal before. Jenkins recognized that the Lord Chief Justice, the Recorder of London, and a number of metropolitan magistrates

122 TNA, PCom9/1760, Fox to Mancroft, 28 Apr. 1955.
123 TNA, CAB 134/2853, H (66) 73, Home Affairs Committee, 27 Jul. 1966, "Criminal Justice Bill: Short Terms of Imprisonment," memo by Home Secretary.

opposed the suspended sentence, "mainly on the ground that for some offences the deterrent impact of the penalty is all-important and that there are cases where an immediate short sentence is the appropriate treatment even for a first offender," but he thought these objections could be met by removing offences of personal violence or sexual assault from the provision for compulsory suspension.[124] It is hard to accept Lord Windlesham's claim, therefore, that the suspended sentence "had been pressed on the Home Secretary by an enthusiastic judiciary."[125] Compulsory suspension represented the most substantial restriction ever imposed by Parliament on the normal discretion of the courts to sentence within the legal maxima.[126] Magistrates were denied the power to impose sentences of immediate imprisonment on offenders who had not previously been sentenced to imprisonment or borstal training, a denial the Magistrates Association opposed until the provision was repealed in 1972.

The bill would also allow the Home Secretary to make an order providing that the offence of being drunk and disorderly was no longer punishable with imprisonment, when satisfied that sufficient accommodation was available for the treatment of those convicted of that offence. Changes in the procedure for the enforcement of fines had the object of reducing the number of persons sent to prison in default of payment; and obliging courts to offer bail in certain types of minor offences sought to restrict remands in custody. Jenkins had been informed by R. S. King in the Prison Department that these proposals, plus parole, would immediately reduce the prison population by approximately 2,000 men and 100 women. The decline in the number of receptions into prison would be larger, and would bring some administrative relief. Ominously, King also wrote, "The long term effect seems likely almost exactly to balance the increase in [prison] population expected by 1975 if current sentencing policy is maintained . . ."[127] And this calculation was doubtless based on the assumption that the proposals would work as expected.

In August the bill went before the Cabinet. As Burke Trend explained to the Prime Minister,

> The proposals are designed to let long-sentence prisoners out of prison on licence under supervision [the parole system], if this seems likely to promote their rehabilitation without risk to the public; and to prevent people being sent to prison at all for short sentences up to six months, which are useless for training purposes and divert prison staff from the more important business of training long-term prisoners.[128]

124 Ibid.
125 Lord Windlesham, *Responses to Crime*, vol. 2: *Penal Policy in the Making* (Oxford, 1993), p. 121.
126 TNA, HO291/1246: Graham-Harrison to Home Secretary, 31 Jan. 1967.
127 TNA, HO291/468; HO291/481: W. H. Hammond, The general relevance of research findings to proposals in the Criminal Justice Bill, 6 Dec. 1966.
128 TNA, PREM 13/999, Trend, 3 Aug. 1966.

The parole system would allow a prisoner to be released after serving one-third of his sentence or 12 months, whichever was the longer, to enable selected prisoners to be released on licence when they had reached a "peak" in their prison training. This proposal introduced a modicum of indeterminacy into fixed-term sentencing (in addition to the borstal sentence and life imprisonment). A six-year sentence of imprisonment meant that a prisoner would serve between two years (the one-third parole eligibility point) and four years (the two-thirds remission point) in prison, according to the chances of the offender re-establishing himself in the community on release. Trend added that there were also proposals to deal with persistent offenders by abolishing preventive detention and corrective training, and replacing them with an extended sentence (to which the parole system would apply), proposals to increase the maximum fines for many offences, and proposals "to reduce the bias of our present criminal procedure in favour of the accused [such as majority verdicts by juries]." Corporal punishment in prisons was ended (against the wish of the Prison Officers' Association), and the Home Secretary was empowered to require courts to consider social inquiry reports on offenders before passing custodial sentences. And, finally, the bill gave formal effect to the enlargement of the probation service into a probation and after-care service, combining the existing voluntary and statutory responsibilities for after-care, in the way that ACTO had recommended in their 1963 report, *The Organisation of After-Care*. The bill was published in late November, the Home Secretary telling the lobby correspondents,

> If we can eliminate from our prisons many of the types of people who are at present cluttering them up and clogging the machine, we can get down to providing a properly organized regime for those who for the protection of society must be sent to prison. We can then ensure that there is at least a chance that those who go to prison can be trained and, we hope, rehabilitated so that at the end of their sentences they may be able to lead useful lives.[129]

This statement had been the refrain of penal administrators for sixty years or more.

The Second Reading of the Criminal Justice Bill took place on 12 December 1966. Jenkins explained that the penal provisions of the bill revolved around the single theme of keeping people out of prison who did not need to be there. However, by contrast with legislation based on some master plan, the final measure, following numerous amendments imposed by the Commons Standing Committee, was what Sir Philip Allen later called "a pretty fair rag-bag," strapped together by the title of Criminal Justice Act 1967. The Act caused a sharp increase in the average length of prison sentence. The index of average length rose from 93.9 in 1966 to 119.3 in 1968, which was a reflection of the fall in the number of offenders received into prison on short sentences.

It is worth concluding with a brief commentary on the two most innovative measures in the Act: the suspended sentence and parole. The former measure was accepted

---

129 TNA, HO291/477.

without any detailed examination of the use and efficacy of the sentence in countries where it had its origins. Jenkins claimed that the Criminal Justice Act "would give us a penal system more able to do its job in accordance with . . . modern criminological knowledge." Not, it seems, in the case of the suspended sentence, Roger Hood concluding, "[t]here was indeed no basis in criminological knowledge for this change"— though he omits mention of the 1964 Israeli investigation which Nigel Walker profiled in his 1965 article in *The Times*, "Case for More Use of Suspension."[130] The suspended sentence was adopted in 1967 as part of a wider search for ways of reducing the numbers in prison. Jenkins made it clear that he envisaged the sentence as being used only in place of imprisonment, not in lieu of non-custodial measures like probation. In fact, research work soon indicated that the sentence was being used in place of fines and probation as much as of imprisonment. Offenders who, but for the existence of the suspended sentence, would not have been given a custodial sentence were now getting the stigma if not the reality of one. As if this were not bad enough, courts were passing suspended sentences longer in length than the sentences of immediate imprisonment they might otherwise have given, so that when activated in full, the result was a longer stay in custody for the offender.[131] In the case of parole, too, the basis for the measure was anecdotal penology and faith in rehabilitation: the belief on the part of prison governors that prisoners reached a "peak of training" before the one-third remission point, after which deterioration set in. This in turn rested on the prevalent confidence in the rehabilitative ideal. The rationale for parole also included the desire to regulate the size of the prison population. Indeed, for some, parole held out the promise of reducing the prison population immediately, even though Jenkins told the Commons that he would not expect more than 20 per cent of long-term prisoners to be granted parole, and that the daily average prison population would decline by no more than 600.[132]

X

In the sixties, the rehabilitative ideal still had traction. The corporal punishment lobby was defeated, if it did take a hard fight to face down the judiciary. The Criminal Justice Act 1961 integrated borstal and imprisonment into a single system of "custodial training" for young adult offenders between 17 and 21, with a minimum of six

130 R. Hood, "Criminology and Penal Change: A Case Study of the Nature and Impact of Some Recent Advice to Governments," in Hood (ed.), *Crime, Criminology and Penal Policy* (1974), p. 399; Walker, "Case for More Use of Suspension," *The Times*, 13 Apr. 1965, p. 13.

131 A. E. Bottoms, *The Suspended Sentence After Ten Years: A Review and Reassessment* (Leeds, 1980), pp. 4–7; "Limiting Prison Use: Experience in England and Wales," *Howard Journal*, vol. 26 (1987), p. 183; Advisory Council on the Penal System, *Sentences of Imprisonment*, op cit., chap. 13 and Appendix Q; B. Wootton, "The Changing Face of British Criminal Justice," in N. Morris and M. Perlman (eds.), *Law and Crime* (1972), p. 109.

132 Home Office, *Review of Parole in England and Wales* (1981), pp. 1–2; Neil Morgan, "The Shaping of Parole in England and Wales," [1983] *Crim.L.R.* 137–46; Kenneth Younger, "Sentencing," *Howard Journal*, vol. 16 (1977), p. 21.

months and a maximum of two years, the aim being to further exclude young offenders from prisons, and to give them the benefit of individual study and treatment. The provisions of the Criminal Justice Act 1967 included an extended sentence for habitual criminals; the suspended sentence, to diminish the number of short prison sentences; and a system of parole, with prisoners released when they had reached their "peak of training." In 1972, community service orders were added to the penal basket. This really was the high-water mark of the rehabilitative ethic. The suspension of the death penalty in 1965, and its permanent abolition in 1969, was the cherry on the cake.

It is impossible to end this chapter without a prison reality check, however. "Slopping out," or the absence of night sanitation, symbol of the decrepit conditions of the prisons, was still required in 1968, including in the newest prisons of Blundeston (opened 1963), Gartree (1965), and Albany (1967), and would be required in Coldingley, set to receive its first inmates in February 1969. As the Home Office admitted to the Treasury,

> As regards "slopping out," there is no other feature of existing prisons that attracts more criticism . . . It exists in no other prison system in Western Europe, nor in the American Federal system, and successive Home Secretaries have . . . said it must not be allowed to continue in new prisons, although there is no immediate prospect of abolishing it in existing prisons.[133]

The department asked the Treasury to fund an experiment with remote controlled, electric unlocking of cell doors at night in Albany (one wing of 96 cells), which, if successful, would be applied to Coldingley prison. In the meantime, the Home Office took comfort from the fact that the incidence of slopping out at new prisons was, compared with the old "locals," reduced by improved facilities for evening association. Prisoners remained out of their cells until 9:00–9:30 p.m. "and there is thus less recourse to the chamber pot during the night."[134] That this unhygienic and humiliating practice was still almost universal in the penal estate, at the very moment the rehabilitative ideal crested, tells you something about the limits of that ideal.

133 PCom9/2002.
134 Ibid., 7 May 1969. "Slopping out" continued in many prisons until the mid-1990s, for which see the Epilogue, *infra*. In 1969, Hugh Klare told the annual general meeting of the Howard League for Penal Reform: "In spite of growing points such as Grendon, the psychiatric prison hospital, or Coldingley, the new industrial prison, the prisoner seems to me to be no better off than he was 20 years ago." Quoted in Younger, "Sentencing," p. 18.

11

ROYAL COMMISSION ON THE PENAL SYSTEM, 1964–1966

Whether it was the inordinate breadth of its terms of reference, the chemistry of the relationships between some of the strong-minded commissioners and the chairman's inability to control them, or the fact that the incoming Wilson Government had its own ideas about penal policy which it wanted to implement immediately without waiting for the Commission are matters for historians to argue about.

Sir Henry Brooke, son of the Home Secretary who appointed the Royal Commission on the Penal System, in the Foreword to L. Blom-Cooper and S. McConville, The Case for a Royal Commission on the Penal System (2014).

I

In April 1957, in one of his first acts as Home Secretary, R. A. Butler wrote to Lord Chancellor Kilmuir asking for his views on the appointment, in 18 months' time, of a royal commission to study the problems of penal reform with which they would be confronted in the next decade:

There has been no major enquiry in this field since the Gladstone Committee of 1895 and after 60 years I think we need to look again in the light of modern knowledge, and in particular, perhaps, of the development of psychology and psychiatric medicine, at our penal sanctions and the machinery by which they are applied.[1]

Kilmuir conveyed interest in the project, adding: "Here again I agree in principle with your views . . ."[2] At the 3 May meeting of the Advisory Council on the

1 TNA, LCO2/5113: Butler to Kilmuir, 9 Apr. 1957.
2 Ibid, Kilmuir to Butler, 12 Apr. 1957.

Treatment of Offenders, Butler raised the idea of a comprehensive inquiry into the penal system. ACTO members welcomed an enquiry, Dr. Radzinowicz pointing out "that the last one in this field took place at the end of the nineteenth century and that the time was coming for an authoritative body to take stock and make constructive recommendations."[3] On 30 May, ACTO presented its report, *Alternatives to Short Terms of Imprisonment*, the conclusion to which recognized that there were issues—such as offenders making restitution for their crimes or remands for enquiry—that went beyond the "narrow sector of penology" that the report dealt with. The report's final sentence then declared,

> We have been struck by the fact that there has been no authoritative inquiry for a long time into such fundamental problems as the objects of punishment, the suitability of the existing methods of dealing with offenders, the desirability of introducing new ones, and the procedure for determining what is the appropriate method in a particular case—problems which lie at the root not only of our work as defined by this inquiry but of that of the Council itself.[4]

The signatories included Margery Fry, George Benson, and Leon Radzinowicz.

Two years later, the 1959 White Paper, *Penal Practice in a Changing Society*, set out the case for a fundamental re-assessment of penal methods which "could be a landmark in penal history and illuminate the course ahead for a generation." To point the way forward, however, the examination must not alone pragmatically assess past progress,

> it must concern itself with the philosophy as well as the practice of punishment. It must consider the fundamental concepts underlying our treatment of offenders, and examine not only the obligations of society and the offender to one another, but also the obligations of both to the victim.[5]

In the House of Lords' debate on the White Paper, Lord Silkin welcomed the possibility of "a fundamental re-examination of penal philosophy on the basis of knowledge to be gained as a result of the establishment of this institute [of Criminology at Cambridge]."[6] Silkin went on to suggest that a royal commission might be appointed to examine the causes of the increase in crime, and the most effective ways of handling and preventing crime. With such cross-party support, it seemed only a matter of time before a fundamental review of penal policy and practice would be launched. In fact, it took until 1964 before the Royal Commission on the Penal System was appointed in what turned out to be the tail end of 13 years of Conservative rule. Two years later, the Labour government agreed to dissolve

3   TNA, HO291/20, ACTO minutes, 3 May 1957.
4   Home Office, *Alternatives to Short Terms of Imprisonment*, Report of ACTO, 1957, pp. 19–20.
5   *Penal Practice in a Changing Society* (Cmnd. 645), Feb. 1959, p. 7.
6   *Hansard* (Lords), vol. 215, 8 Apr. 1959, col. 469.

the royal commission, which by then had split evenly between those commissioners who wanted to continue working, and those who wished to stop. Never before had a royal commission been dissolved without reporting. It is the aim of this chapter to examine the extraordinary rise and fall of the Royal Commission on the Penal System.[7]

Criminologists never linger long over this failed royal commission, if they refer to it at all; they prefer to put their time into reports that resulted in administrative or legislative change. I would contend, however, that there are occasions when failure can tell you anywhere near as much as success can. In this case, the failure of the Royal Commission on the Penal System speaks volumes for the pragmatic and pedestrian character of criminological research, for the English aversion to exploring the issues of penal values and penal philosophy, and for the inability of penal reformers to create the rehabilitative programme they had promised for so long and which they were finally asked to provide. The royal commission had a golden opportunity to provide a blueprint for the future. A new set of guiding penal principles could have been declared, a new penal structure envisaged, the abatement of imprisonment pushed further, and the treatment and training ethos protected against the cold retributive winds that began to blow after 1970. Failure to report was a severe blow to the rehabilitative ideal.

II

R. A. Butler made way in July 1962 for Henry Brooke, a well-meaning Home Secretary, though not the man to do more than add a little to modern penology. Brooke was particularly interested in delinquency, appointing an Advisory Committee on Juvenile Delinquency in February 1964 to examine the origins and causes of delinquency.[8] He too was confronted by the unyielding problem of prison overcrowding, a problem more firmly in the lap of the department following the dissolution of the independent life of the Prison Commission.[9] On 1 April 1963, on the first day in eighty-six years that there were no prison commissioners, Lord Stonham, a blunt and determined Labourite, with personal knowledge of the prison and after-care system, rose in the House of Lords to call attention to the disparity between the government's penal policy and the practice in the prisons, as

---

7   Ann Oakley, *A Critical Woman: Barbara Wootton, Social Science and Public Policy in the Twentieth Century* (2011), p. 257, observed: "The extraordinary story of this Commission has never yet been told in full. . ." For whatever reason, the article by A. E. Bottoms and S. Stevenson, "'What Went Wrong?': Criminal Justice Policy in England and Wales, 1945–70," in D. Downes (ed.), *Unravelling Criminal Justice* (Basingstoke, 1992), made no mention of the Royal Commission on the Penal System.

8   *The Times*, 13 Feb. 1964, p. 6; [1964] CrimLR 251. See R. Blake, "Brooke, Henry (1903–84)," *Dictionary of National Biography: Missing Persons* (Oxford, 1993), pp. 91–2.

9   *Hansard* (Lords), vol. 246, 21 Feb. 1963, col. 1441, Prison Commissioners Dissolution Order; *The Times*, 1 Apr. 1963, p. 11. *The Times*, 6 Feb. 1963, p. 11, considered it "A Step Backwards;" Duncan Fairn thought it of great advantage: "Prisons 1866–1966," in H. Klare (ed.), *Changing Concepts of Crime and Its Treatment* (Oxford, 1966), p. 168.

revealed in *Inside Story*, a report submitted to the Home Office in August 1962 by a group of ex-prisoners, and published by the Prison Reform Council.[10] The authors were nuclear disarmers, notably members of the committee of 100, imprisoned for direct action demonstrations. The same movement also spawned *Gate Fever* by Jane Buxton and Margaret Turner, imprisoned for six months in Holloway.[11] They were, as Christopher Driver said, "the 20th century's latest middle-class invasion of the British penal system."[12] The 30 young men and women had experiences in 12 different prisons in 1961–2, notably Brixton, Holloway, and Wormwood Scrubs. Their sentences ranged from one week to eight months. Stonham encapsulated their prison experiences by stating, "A man is ill-fed, appallingly clothed, surrounded by every difficulty and incredible meanness, not only financially but spiritually, in his efforts to keep clean, and has his self-respect as a man torn to shreds."[13] Earl Jellicoe, Minister of State at the Home Office, claimed in response that many of the criticisms were misleading "in that they suggest that the conditions which are said to exist in certain establishments may be typical of the system as a whole."[14] Yet even he could not defend the conditions and overcrowding, typical of the large closed local prisons like Pentonville. A month earlier, the department had received Terence and Pauline Morris's report on Pentonville, a critical study of the prison and its highly disciplined staff, sponsored by the Home Office through Dr. Mannheim. The book was one of the earliest products of the sociological turn in criminology, though the authors concluded, "It is at the psychological level that imprisonment is a painful, depriving and destructive experience."[15] The Home Office thought the work presented "a reasonably fair picture of conditions in

10 *Hansard* (Lords), vol. 248, 1 Apr. 1963, col. 356; Direct Action Committee, "Suggestions for Immediate Reform of Penal Institutions" (1962); *Inside Story* (1963). See also S. J. Carroll, "'Fill the Jails': Identity, Structure and Method in the Committee of 100, 1960–1968," D. Phil thesis, University of Sussex, 2010, chap. 5.

11 Few female offenders were imprisoned by this date. Of every 100 women convicted and sentenced by the courts in England and Wales during 1963, 70 per cent were fined, 14 per cent discharged, 10 per cent awarded probation, and only 4 per cent confined in institutions (either prisons or borstals). See Ann D. Smith, "Penal Policy and the Woman Offender," in Paul Halmos (ed.), *The Sociological Review Monograph*, No. 9 (Keele, 1965), p. 116.

12 Buxton and Turner, *Gate Fever* (1962); Driver, *The Disarmers: A Study in Protest* (1964), pp. 170–81.

13 *Hansard* (Lords), vol. 248, 1 Apr. 1963, col. 359.

14 Ibid., col. 417.

15 T. and P. Morris, "The Experience of Imprisonment," *British Journal of Criminology*, vol. 2 (1962), p. 358. Dennis Chapman believed the publication of Pentonville "has dispelled for all who have read it ignorance about the physical, social, and psychological nature of prison": *Sociology and the Stereotype of the Criminal* (1968), p. 222. See also Alison Liebling, "Pentonville Revisited: An Essay in Honour of the Morris' Sociological Study of an English Prison, 1958–1963," *Prison Service Journal*, issue 209 (2013), pp. 29–34; Ibid., T. Morris, "A Lifetime with Pentonville," pp. 36–40. Pentonville was then a maximum-security prison for recidivist prisoners. The population was 1,250, with 650 allocated three prisoners to a cell, the rest in single cells.

Pentonville *at the time of research*."[16] The emphasis was meant to imply that the report depicted the prison four years ago, since when two new governors and the appointment of more young prison officers had led to improvements. However, it was arranged for the Home Secretary to visit Pentonville prior to the report's publication, and for Home Office Ministers to visit other prisons.

In the meantime, the last chairman of the Prison Commission, Arthur Peterson, undertook to find ways of reducing the population in closed local prisons. He returned with three expedients: first, reducing the number of receptions of civil and untried prisoners and of those on conviction for drunkenness; second, reducing the period of detention by increasing the rate of remission (especially on longer sentences, by allowing prisoners to earn *additional* remission), by making more use of the hostel parole scheme, and by introducing an indeterminate sentence; and third, what Peterson considered to be the only effective expedient, transferring prisoners to open prisons, taking the figure from the present 3,200 men up to at least 5,000.[17] Three factors limited the rate of expansion of the open prison system, however. First was the rate of absconding. The second was finding enough "ordinary," as distinct from "star," prisoners capable of attaining the higher standard of behaviour and discipline. And the third was the willingness of prisoners to accept the conditions of life in an open prison: sleeping in dormitories, the difficulty of receiving visits from family, and the expectation of a greater sense of personal responsibility.[18] Duncan Fairn, Assistant Undersecretary of State in the prison department, agreed that the only effective way to relieve pressure on the closed locals was to have more open prisons. By contrast, it would be difficult to enable prisoners to earn extra remission: "To promise prisoners extra remission for industry & then not to be able to let them work would create mutiny."[19]

Out of this internal discussion emerged the idea of a new White Paper. It originated with Lord Jellicoe. In the wake of the Lords' debate on 1 April, Jellicoe offered his personal suggestions about the prisons. He dealt with the building

16 TNA, PCom 9/2230. The Home Office review of the manuscript added, "Then many of the staff were old and not well inclined to 'reform' and the Marwood execution had seriously affected morale in the prison." See, however, David Faulkner, *Servant of the Crown: A Civil Servant's Story of Criminal Justice and Public Service Reform* (2014), p. 35: ". . . I remember the concern and disbelief which [the Morris'] report caused among my senior colleagues and I saw its impact on the sometimes wishful thinking that was prevalent at the time." Faulkner was seconded to the Prison Commission in 1963.

17 Ibid., Peterson, 11 Apr. 1963.

18 TNA, HO291/22: minutes of ACTO 68th meeting, 12 Dec. 1962; AC/240, "Use of Open Prisons," Memo by Home Office and Prison Commission. There was also the NIMBY factor. Plans for an open prison for 600 men on a redundant Royal Naval Air station at Ford, Sussex in April 1959, aroused public opposition from the owners of a nearby private girls' school and from hoteliers in Worthing. A public enquiry was held. Home Secretary Butler went forward with the prison, telling the PM, "If we are ever to get on with the programme in the White Paper, we cannot hold up development. Things are really shocking in some prisons." See PREM 11/2621, Butler to PM, 20 Apr. 1959.

19 Ibid., R. D. Fairn to Peterson, 24 Apr. 1963.

programme (the need to end three prisoners in a cell, and to stop building prisons that perpetuated the "beastly practice" of slopping out and that were designed, like Grendon, in antediluvian ways), work for prisoners (including a full day's pay for a full day's work), aftercare, and lastly, a stock-taking in the shape of a White Paper.[20] A month later, Brooke asked the department to prepare a White Paper to take stock of the five years since *Penal Practice*, which would incorporate the recent ACTO reports on preventive detention and aftercare, compensation for victims of crimes of violence, and the review of the prison medical service. He wished to provide evidence of constructive Home Office activity.[21] In September 1963, F. H. Gwynn, Deputy Undersecretary of State, sent Cunningham, the Permanent Undersecretary of State, a first draft of a White Paper entitled "Developments in Penal Practice," which he had some doubts about: "There is precious little in the draft that is new or exciting; and it is far from being as finished a document as 'Penal Practice in a Changing Society.' But perhaps it will pass muster as a progress report."[22] The White Paper was published in April 1964 as *The War Against Crime in England and Wales 1959–1964*, of which more in a moment.

Alongside the idea of a White Paper ran discussion of the re-examination of the entire penal system. The department believed both that there was a case for "a fundamental re-examination of penal matters and what prison population should be provided for, as it was doubtful if society should aim to provide for a population of 30,000," and also that the time was not yet ripe for a full review, given the state of the research programme. Cunningham reiterated the second point in late July: "There were strong grounds for thinking that this should be deferred at least for a year or two, when sufficient results of research should be available to enable the enquiry to be scientifically based from the outset." Cunningham believed that scientific research into the nature of criminal behaviour was in its infancy. "If an inquiry were set up too soon," he advised Brooke, "it might mean that the opportunity to make a major advance in penal policy would be missed . . ." Nor did he think a royal commission was the most suitable instrument for a critical examination of the main purposes (retribution, deterrence, reform) of the penal system. He worried, too, that finding members for a royal commission would be difficult in view of the paucity of people with expert knowledge of the penal system.[23] Arthur Peterson thought the reconstitution of ACTO was preferable to the appointment of a royal commission, recognizing that ACTO would have to be invited "to undertake an inquiry which would be sufficiently far-reaching to appear likely to lead to a major advance in penal treatment." He then suggested that ACTO should first examine the hostel scheme for young and adult offenders undergoing institutional treatment. Cunningham appreciated Peterson's position,

20 Ibid., Jellicoe's Note, 5 Apr. 1963.
21 Ibid., Meeting on Prisons, 2 May 1963; HO291/516, Note on Home Secretary's conference on prisons, 22 May 1963.
22 TNA, BN29/455, Gwynn to Cunningham, 13 Sep. 1963.
23 TNA, PCom9/2230, Meeting on Prisons, 2 May 1963; HO291/516; HO291/518, Cunningham's minute to Home Secretary, 13 Aug. 1963.

and agreed that "we should not run the risk, by launching an over-ambitious inquiry into the penal system as a whole, of arresting more limited but valuable advances upon which quicker agreement could be reached."[24] He advised Brooke, therefore, to reconstitute ACTO and ask it to review in a comprehensive manner the means available to the courts for the treatment of offenders.[25]

By September 1963, it was agreed for the Home Secretary to discuss with the chairman of ACTO whether a reconstituted Advisory Council would be a suitable body to undertake a radical examination of penal methods. He reported back to Cunningham:

> It was with a very open mind about the relative suitability of ACTO or a Royal Commission for the fundamental inquiry we have under consideration, that I entered upon my discussion with Mr. Justice Barry this morning . . . Though I am not yet ready to reach a definite decision either way, the outcome of an hour's talk with him was to incline me rather more towards choosing a Royal Commission.[26]

ACTO was perhaps too large a body, Brooke went on, with members who regarded the work as an occupation for such hours as they could spare: "I think an altogether different degree of application would be needed of the people charged with the inquiry we are concerned to set on foot." He envisaged a new and smaller team of eight to ten members under a new chairman. A department note put the other side: ". . . to appoint a Royal Commission might build up too great an expectation of radical innovations, and would give rise to criticism that reform would be unduly delayed while the Commission was at work."[27] ACTO might be better, therefore, for an enquiry proceeding in stages, dealing first with young offenders before extending to a wider field. The autumn 1963 draft of the White Paper concluded with an announcement of a review of the penal system to be carried out by ACTO. It is mildly astonishing that using ACTO for such a re-evaluation of the entire penal system was seriously considered. The council had only ever examined discrete topics *seriatim*, rarely if ever offering solutions that went beyond existing penal arrangements. The role of an advisory council was not to keep the whole subject with which they were concerned under critical scrutiny. In fact, their reports were largely peripheral to the main issues faced by the penal system. They rejected the suspended sentence, gave political cover to the Home Secretary on corporal punishment, suggested a few limited alternatives to short terms of imprisonment, put the final nail in the coffin of preventive detention, and took a slightly more radical approach to after-care.[28] In fact, Brooke decided to

24 TNA, HO291/518, Peterson to Cunningham, 15 Aug. 1963.
25 Ibid., Cunningham to Home Secretary, 22 Aug. 1963.
26 TNA, HO291/516, Brooke to Cunningham, 2 Oct. 1963.
27 Ibid., Note of meeting held 25 Nov. 1963.
28 Home Office, *The Organisation of After-Care*, Report of ACTO (1963). The Home Secretary accepted ACTO's recommendation that the existing voluntary and statutory

appoint a royal commission.[29] It was thought that sufficient research material was available, at least for young offenders, where the commission would begin its work; and by the time it turned to adult offenders, two or three years later, more research results would be available.

A draft for the Home Affairs Committee of the Cabinet was prepared. Tony Brennan, assistant secretary in the Criminal Department, who would eventually be appointed secretary to the Royal Commission, offered his take on the draft paper, revealing that he had a different approach to how the commission should work. The division of the enquiry into young and adult offenders, wrote Brennan,

> carries the risk that the Royal Commission will not get sufficiently down to fundamentals. It seems to be common ground among all who have considered this that we need to look at our penal philosophy from first principles: to consider afresh the relationship between the offender and society and the purposes which penal sanctions should serve.[30]

Such a study, he continued, needed to precede any attempt to make recommendations about specific methods and institutions, though, in turn, he thought the philosophy on which the commission would base its recommendations had to emerge from study of the material on the nature of criminality and the effectiveness of existing methods. In short, Brennan had in mind a three-stage enquiry: study of crime and its treatment; study and critique of penal theory; and formulation of recommendations. This was an ambitious agenda, going well beyond mere pragmatic review. The legal hierarchy then weighed in.[31] Lord Chancellor Dilhorne, assuming without cause that any proposals would be in the direction of "softer" treatment of offenders, expressed "very considerable misgivings about the wisdom of setting up a Royal Commission on this at this time." It would not allay the anxiety about the extent of crime; it would not solve the problem of courts passing lenient sentences; it would do nothing to strengthen the means of preventing

responsibilities for after-care of those discharged from penal establishments should be combined, and entrusted to an enlarged though still decentralised probation and after-care service, *pace* a dissenting memorandum that argued for an independent after-care system, a new central service controlled nationally. See TNA, HO291/22, minutes of 69th meeting of ACTO, 16 Jul. 1963; *Hansard*, vol. 253, 5 Dec. 1963, cols 1018–1100; *Problems of the Ex-Prisoner*, Report of the Pakenham/Thompson Committee (1961).

29 TNA, HO291/518, Brooke minute, 8 Jan. 1964. A month later, the Home Office recognized that the term of appointment of members of ACTO had expired, and its reconstitution had to be considered. It was thought that ACTO might study subjects without overlapping the work of a royal commission, but "there was an obvious difficulty in having two bodies concurrently engaged in a study of penal matters, and it might be difficult to find sufficient qualified persons to man both." Reconstitution of ACTO was postponed. See TNA, BN29/455, note of meeting held 5 Feb. 1964.

30 Ibid: Brennan minute, 22 Jan. 1964.

31 Cunningham reminded the Home Secretary, "Lord Kilmuir and Lord Goddard were consulted about a similar proposal (which they resisted) in 1957." See BN29/455, 24 Jan. 1964.

crime and catching criminals; and an announcement now "will look rather like an election gimmick . . ."[32] Parker, LCJ, rushing off to the Stafford assizes, kept his reply brief yet positive:

> I agree with you that there is a real need for a fundamental re-examination of our penal system and I welcome the idea that it should have the widest possible terms of reference.
>
> As to timing, I think that the present time is opportune. It is clearly a long term project and I see no advantage in waiting until further research has been undertaken or the results of the present research have come into being.[33]

He also did not wish the enquiry to delay progress with the building of new institutions. The Attorney-General, Sir John Hobson, welcomed a comprehensive enquiry, and felt certain "it must be a Royal Commission if it is to carry sufficient weight with the Judges and the public." He entered the caveats, however, that the causes of crime should be part of the remit, without which "the efforts of the penologists are like buildings set on the sea shore without any consideration or understanding of the tides"; and that sentencing practice and powers should be investigated, since "[t]his is the sieve through which the customers of the penologists must be provided. This is the place where the balance between curing the criminal and deterring others from becoming criminals must be precariously held."[34] Cunningham spoke against both caveats: no one in the present state of knowledge could hope to define the causes of crime; and it would be sufficient for the commission to consider the methods of selecting offenders for particular types of treatment, since this would enable them to consider whether the courts were the right people to make the selection and whether they had the right means of making it.[35]

Before the Home Affairs Committee in February 1964, the Home Secretary argued that the development of ways of dealing with offenders "has been unco-ordinated and fragmentary: we have not, at least for very many years, paused to examine our penal philosophy, and to consider whether it is best served by the methods and organisations we employ." An enquiry into penal philosophy and practice could be deferred no longer in view of the crime increase and of the public feeling that existing methods of training offenders were insufficiently effective. He wanted a royal commission to cover the ground in two stages: a review of the treatment of offenders up to the age of 21, followed by an enquiry into the

---

32 Ibid: Dilhorne to Brooke, 10 Feb. 1964. He also wrote, "It will not, I think, look sensible to appoint a Royal Commission unless the results of research are now available to them." And concluded, "I think that perhaps the greatest contribution that could now be made to crime prevention would be the cessation of the practice of two and sometimes three prisoners sharing a cell."

33 Ibid: LCJ to Brooke, 7 Feb. 1964.

34 Ibid: Hobson to Brooke, 10 Feb. 1964.

35 Ibid: Cunningham to Brooke, 12 Feb. 1964.

treatment of adult offenders, "including a fundamental examination of penal theory." Meanwhile, the enquiry would not prevent improvements in existing methods as were called for. Brooke added, "It was desirable that the Government should be seen to be taking an initiative, not least in view of the forthcoming publication by the Labour Party of a full statement on penal policy."[36] There was general support for a royal commission, though the Home Affairs Committee thought it desirable to publish, simultaneously with the announcement of the appointment of a royal commission, a White Paper explaining the need for a comprehensive review of penal policy and practice, and asked for the terms of reference to include consideration of the factors which fostered or inhibited crime. Again, Cunningham advised against the latter:

> To direct a Royal Commission to investigate the causes of crime would be to give it a task so vague and wide-ranging that hardly anything would be excluded from its scope. We do not really know what the causes of crime are—to a limited extent they may be the pressures of social and economic environment; to a much greater extent they are probably causes very deep in human nature. A Royal Commission which had to explore both the psychological and social reasons for delinquent behaviour would, I fear, never really reach the stage of considering how delinquents—whatever the cause of their delinquency—should be treated.[37]

The next stage was to receive Cabinet support. In advance of the Cabinet meeting, Burke Trend advised the Prime Minister that the White Paper was not the strongest document. The list of what had been done since 1959 in "the war against crime" was far from impressive (including as it did the Street Offences Act, the Betting Act, and the Committee on Sunday Observance), and the paragraphs explaining the need for a review were devoted to juvenile offenders. Trend went on to raise a number of telling questions:

> The explanation looks a bit thin and possibly invites the question why, if the various inquiries mentioned in the earlier part of the draft [the Streatfeild Committee Report; the Royal Commission on the Police; the Departmental Committee on the Probation Service] have done their work properly, it is now necessary to have a comprehensive enquiry. Alternatively, if the

36 TNA, CAB 134/2055, HP (64) 23, Royal Commission on Treatment of Offenders, Memo by Home Secretary, 12 Feb. 1964; CAB 134/2054, 5th meeting, 14 Feb. 1964.

37 TNA, HO291/518: Cunningham to Brooke, 21 Feb. 1964; HO219/519. A week earlier, Tony Brennan had taken a different tack on the causes of crime: "The Royal Commission clearly cannot be asked to undertake a comprehensive investigation of causes which. . . would open up a vast sociological field. But some appreciation of causes will be inseparable from a study of the treatment of offenders if it is accepted that one of the objectives of treatment is, where possible, to remove the cause of criminal behaviour so as to prevent its repetition." See HO291/518, Brennan minute, 13 Feb. 1964.

comprehensive enquiry was necessary, why was it not undertaken before the inquiries into the particular aspects of the field?[38]

At the Cabinet meeting on 12 March, it was agreed that a royal commission should be appointed, but there was concern about the White Paper. Some felt the title "The War Against Crime in England and Wales" was over-dramatic; some felt that greater prominence was needed for the reasons which led the government to believe it was time for a comprehensive review. Brooke was asked to revise the draft again "with a view to its publication before Easter, in order to forestall the expected publication of the report of a committee set up by the Labour Party under Lord Longford to consider penal policy."[39] In mid-March, Cunningham also returned to the White Paper, telling Brooke that he doubted the wisdom of going ahead with it. Much of the material for it, he advised, had gone into the reports of the children's department and the prison department; a separate White Paper on compensation for victims of crimes of violence was ready for publication; and the debates on the police bill had already publicized developments in the police service. Cunningham concluded,

> As a result there is nothing new at all in the White Paper. It will inevitably be compared with "Penal Practice in a Changing Society," which was a major statement of penal policy, with the forthcoming Scottish report—which proposes major changes in relation to young offenders—and with the forthcoming report of the Longford Committee, which is unlikely to be inhibited by considerations of what is immediately practicable.[40]

Despite the considerable unease about the White Paper among Cabinet members and within the department, Brooke would not be denied.[41]

III

The War Against Crime in England and Wales 1959–1964 was published in April 1964. Like its predecessor, *Penal Practice in a Changing Society*, the White Paper claimed that the crime rate was rising inexorably, and public concern was widespread, though the evidence for both claims was rather thin. Following a few paragraphs on the increase in crime, the paper turned to the war against crime, emphasizing the role of the police and the community; to improvements in the administration of justice, the criminal law, and criminological research; and to changes in the treatment of offenders and after-care, before concluding with the

38 TNA, PREM 11/4691, Trend to Prime Minister (Sir Alec Douglas-Home), 11 Mar. 1964.
39 TNA, CAB 129/117, CP (64) 67, Memo by Home Secretary, 10 Mar. 1964; CAB 128/38, CM (64) 18th conclusions, 12 Mar. 1964.
40 TNA, HO291/518, Cunningham to Home Secretary, 16 Mar. 1964.
41 TNA, CAB 128/38, CM (64) 20th conclusions, 24 Mar. 1964.

declaration that the time was ripe for a fundamental review of the whole penal system. Taken together, the White Paper stated over-confidently, "it represents a comprehensive and formidable armoury for intensifying the war against crime."[42] The White Paper was in fact a pretty rum document, a bricks-without-straw mission on behalf of a Home Secretary whose initiatives on crime were partly motivated by a wish to create a reputation as something other than an accident-prone politician who had gravitated upwards during a long period of Tory rule. The document paled into insignificance at the side of *Penal Practice in a Changing Society*. Like *Penal Practice*, the White Paper included an appendix on the research published by the Home Office Research Unit (notably *Delinquent Generations* and *Persistent Criminals*) and the universities, the latter dominated by the first policy-oriented fruits of the Institute of Criminology (namely *Attendance Centres* and *Habitual Prisoner*), and the ongoing research from the same sources, most of which was in an early stage of development. This did not bode well for the comprehensive enquiry of the penal system.[43]

The two most recent government White Papers had now expressed faith in the contribution that criminology could make to the reform of the criminal justice system. How well placed was criminology to deliver what was expected of it? The discipline was at this date characterized by three main features. The first was the collective influence of the three émigré criminologists, Hermann Mannheim at the London School of Economics, Max Grunhut at Oxford, and Leon Radzinowicz at Cambridge, who were shaped by an "intellectual framework" so well described by Lucia Zedner:

> . . . they shared a common vision of the discipline as scientific, practical, empirical, and purposive. Its purpose, was, above all, to secure by scientific investigation a body of knowledge about crime and criminals that would provide the foundations of informed policy development.[44]

They also shared a belief in what Leon Radzinowicz called "the socio-liberal compromise," with its faith in the capacity of the state to engineer an improved system of criminal justice as an integral cog of the welfare state.[45] The second feature of the criminological discipline was the establishment of the Home Office

---

42 *The War Against Crime in England and Wales 1959–1964* (Cmnd. 2296), Apr. 1964, p. 14.
43 Ibid., Appendix A and B.
44 Zedner, "Useful Knowledge? Debating the Role of Criminology in Post-war Britain," in L. Zedner and A. Ashworth (eds.), *The Criminological Foundations of Penal Policy* (Oxford, 2003), p. 206. See Roger Hood, "Hermann Mannheim (1889–1974) and Max Grunhut (1893–1964)," in J. Beaton and R. Zimmermann (eds.), *Jurists Uprooted: German-speaking Émigré Lawyers in Twentieth-Century Britain* (Oxford, 2004), pp. 728–34. See also L. Radzinowicz, "Mannhein, Hermann," *Dictionary of National Biography 1971–80* (Oxford, 1986), pp. 543–4; John Croft, "Hermann Mannheim—a Biographical Note," in T. Grygier et al (eds.), *Criminology in Transition* (1965), pp. xiii–xix; 295–301.
45 Ibid., p. 210.

Research Unit in 1957 and the Cambridge Institute of Criminology in 1959, and particularly the close links between these two bodies. As David Garland observed, ". . . the research agenda pursued by the Cambridge Institute . . . was heavily influenced by immediate policy needs. Indeed, for the most part, it was scarcely distinguishable from the in-house research of the Home Office . . ."[46] This was never more evident than in September 1959, when the Home Office Research Committee agreed to support the Cambridge Institute's research programme for the first four or five years with a £5,000 grant.

The grant was provided for six research projects that were approved by the Home Office, projects with clear-cut practical value: *Crimes of Violence in London* (F. H. McClintock), *Social Consequences of Conviction* (J. P. Martin), *Costs of Crime* (Martin), *Psychiatrists' Reports to Magistrates Courts* (D. J. West), *The State of Crime* (Radzinowicz), and *The System of Recording Crimes* (McClintock). By 1961, the Institute was reporting six enquiries as completed or nearing completion, along with four long-term projects. In addition to four of the previously mentioned projects (no mention was made again of *Psychiatrists' Reports* or *The System of Recording Crimes*), there was *Attendance Center Orders* (McClintock), *Robbery in the Metropolis* (McClintock and E. H. Gibson of the Home Office Research Unit), *Offenders as Employees* (Martin), *Interludes of Honesty in the Careers of Persistent Thieves* (West), *Psychopathic Traits in Preventive Detainees* (West), and the *Family Development Study* (West). While the White Paper spoke of the need to give pride of place to elucidating the causes of crime, the Institute, with Home Office sanction, chose to centre their research programme "upon certain specific, well defined, criminological and penological problems; plucked out, as it were, of the vast real field of crime and its control."[47]

The third feature of the criminological enterprise at this date was the imperious role of Leon Radzinowicz himself. In his manifesto for the Institute, *In Search of Criminology*, he again indicated his priorities: "descriptive analytical accounts of the state of crime, of the various classes of offender, of the enforcement of criminal law [and] of the effectiveness of various measures of penal treatment."[48] Radzinowicz

46 Garland, "Of Crimes and Criminals: The Development of Criminology in Britain," in M. Maguire et al. (eds.), *Oxford Handbook of Criminology* (Oxford, 1994), p. 56. See also Richard F. Sparks, "Britain," in *The International Handbook of Contemporary Developments in Criminology*, vol. 2 (1982), p. 87; J. P. Martin, "The Development of Criminology in Britain 1948–60," *British Journal of Criminology*, vol. 28 (1988), pp. 42–4; D. Garland, "Obituary: F. H. McClintock," *British Journal of Criminology*, vol. 35 (1995), pp. 134–5; Garland, "Ideology and Crime: A Further Chapter," in A. Bottoms and M. Tonry (eds.), *Ideology, Crime and Criminal Justice* (Cullompton, Devon, 2002), pp. 5–6.

47 TNA, HO291/575: Home Office Research Committee, minutes of 10th meeting, 20 Sep. 1959; Research Programme of the Institute of Criminology, note of meeting held at Home Office, 12 Nov. 1959; Radzinowicz, *The Study of Criminology in Cambridge* (Cambridge, 1961), pp. 7–10. See also Home Office, *The Cambridge Institute of Criminology: Its Background and Scope*, A Report by Sir Leon Radzinowicz (1988), pp. 92–6.

48 Radzinowicz, *In Search of Criminology* (Cambridge, Mass., 1962), p. 175. See also Anthony Bottoms, "Sir Leon Radzinowicz," *Independent*, 1 Jan. 2000, p. 7; R. Hood, "Radzinowicz, Sir Leon (1906–1999)," *Oxford Dictionary of National Biography* (Oxford,

had a profound influence on the development of the fledgling discipline of criminology, and showed laudable moderation in the face of the more out-landish aims and claims of the positivist credo, yet he also encapsulated his own approach to criminology in the phrase, "towards a pragmatic position." *In* was empirical, piecemeal, functional, policy-oriented research; *Out* was philosophical and theoretical research, the examination of first principles, the master plan or grand strategy, the comprehensive solution. Criminological research had no higher ambition than to serve as a weapon in the "war against crime." Yet this pragmatic, policy-oriented brand of criminology had not by 1964 produced more than an eclectic set of research findings: the concept of the "delinquent generation," Wilkins' investigation of the effects on subsequent delinquency of being born and raised under wartime condi-tions, a hypothesis later discredited by the data; a statistical analysis of time spent awaiting trial (commissioned by the Streatfeild Committee); and studies evaluating the supposed effects and achievements of particular penal measures (on the pattern of the paradigmatic 1955 study by Mannheim and Wilkins, *Prediction Methods in Relation to Borstal Training*, the first volume in the Home Office Research Series). Already, said Wilkins in 1965, "[i]t came to appear that it did not matter what was done, offenders recidivated or not quite independently of the type of treatment."[49] If any further corroboration were needed of the short commons supplied by criminology, it was evident in what *The Times* described as "the woefully inadequate part in the recent Home Office booklet for the courts [*The Sentence of the Court*, 1964] on the results of treatment."[50] Even R. A. Butler, architect of the Home Office Research Unit and the Institute of Criminology, was forced to declare by 1974, "it is now increasingly recognized that it is a painfully slow business to produce con-clusive findings of direct practical importance."[51]

2004); Idem., "Professor Sir Leon Radzinowicz," *British Journal of Criminology*, vol. 37 (1997), p. ii. *In Search of Criminology* also contained the sentence: ". . . in the present state of knowledge, the very attempt to elucidate the causes of crime would be better put aside."

49 Wilkins, "Evaluation of Penal Treatments," in P. Halmos (ed.), *The Sociological Review Monograph*, No. 9 (Keele, 1965), p. 244. See Home Office, *Delinquent Generations* by Leslie Wilkins (1960); A. A. Walters, "Delinquent Generations?" *British Journal of Criminology*, vol. 3 (1963), p. 391.

50 *The Times*, 30 May 1964, p. 9. This editorial appeared on the same day as the article by L. Radzinowicz, "Sentencing Policy in Criminal Cases," ibid., p. 9.

51 Lord Butler, "The Foundation of the Institute of Criminology in Cambridge," in R. Hood (ed.), *Crime, Criminology and Public Policy* (1974), p. 9. It could be argued that a fourth feature of the criminological enterprise at this date was the influence of psycho-analysis, especially in the study and treatment of juvenile delinquency. The Institute for the Scientific Treatment of Delinquency (ISTD), one of the main advocates of psy-choanalysis, published the first issue of the *British Journal of Delinquency*. See M. Shapira, *The War Inside: Psychoanalysis, Total War, and the Making of the Democratic Self in Postwar Britain* (Cambridge, 2015), chap. 6.

IV

The War Against Crime was published at the same time as the announcement in both Houses of Parliament on 16 April of the setting up of a royal commission with the following terms of reference:

> In the light of modern knowledge of crime and its causes and of modern penal practice here and abroad, to re-examine the concepts and purposes which should underlie the punishment and treatment of offenders in England and Wales: to report how far they are realized by the penalties and methods of treatment available to the courts, and whether any changes in these, or in the arrangements and responsibility for selecting the sentences to be imposed on particular offenders, are desirable: to review the work of the services and institutions dealing with offenders, and the responsibility for their administration: and to make recommendations.[52]

Almost immediately, the Prime Minister, Sir Alec Douglas-Home, confused the issue. In reply to a question, he intimated that "the terms of reference include an inquiry into the causes of crime," which they didn't. In the House of Lords, Longford, unaware of the government's determination to pre-empt his own report, was mystified by the timing:

> The Government have had many years during which to propose a Commission of this sort, and that it should come in the last months of a dying Government is, frankly, amazing to those of us who sit on this side of the House, and no doubt to others. I think I need only say now that the matters with which the Royal Commission are concerned are highly urgent, and the House will realise that a future Labour Government could not possibly be retarded in the steps it might take by the fact that this Royal Commission had been set up.[53]

Viscount Blakenham was ready with his riposte:

> I do not think this is a matter on which there is any political controversy and I would point out that the Labour Government, I believe, appointed a Royal Commission within less than a year of the General election in 1950—the Royal Commission on Capital Punishment.[54]

The response of *The Times* was bang on target. The royal commission had been given two tasks: first, metaphysical; second, organizational. The terms of reference expected the commission "to get their theory right first and then to examine its

52 *Hansard*, vol. 693, 16 Apr. 1964, col. 601.
53 *Hansard* (Lords), vol. 257, 16 April 1964, cols. 605–6.
54 Ibid., col. 606.

practical applications. This is sensible . . . It is better to make the attempt to fashion a new cogent, and informed philosophy." If this could be done, "and it would be unworldly to underestimate the difficulties," the Commission could proceed to examine the range of tools to do the job, including a parole system, the indeterminate sentence, and the suspended sentence. The editorial was less convinced by an interim report on young offenders: "The study should be treated as a whole, and to rush it would rob it of most of its value."[55]

Who was to chair the royal commission? The department thought it would not be appropriate to appoint the Lord Chief Justice as chairman.[56] Cunningham initially put forward Lord James of Rusholme, Lord Devlin, and Lord Shawcross. Brooke was at first sight attracted by Shawcross. The Treasury suggested Lord Amory, Chancellor of the Exchequer, 1958–60. Tony Brennan, secretary of the royal commission, wondered about Lord Devlin

> in view of the criticism which his views on the relation between law and morality have attracted. It is true that the Royal Commission will not be directly concerned with questions of jurisprudence, but they can hardly avoid touching on them.

Lord Kilmuir was sounded about the chairmanship, but he was not prepared to undertake it.[57] The Lord Chancellor, Dilhorne (formerly Manningham-Buller), then forced his way into the discussion, insisting that the chairman should be a judge. Brooke told the Prime Minister that he did not share this view. He did not want a chair who was "personally associated either with the sentencing function of the judiciary or with the administration of the penal system." Dilhorne countered,

> The Lord Chief Justice and the Queen's Bench judges are primarily responsible for the administration of the criminal law. They have wide discretion as to the sentences they impose, and they are concerned with both the deterrent effect of their sentences and the prospect of securing the reform of the offender.

---

55 *The Times*, 17 Apr. 1964, p. 15.
56 TNA, BN29/455, ". . . it was the Home Office view that it would not be appropriate to appoint the Lord Chief Justice as Chairman of a Royal Commission. Indeed, it was better that the Chairman should not be a member of the judiciary." HO291/518, Brooke minute, 19 Mar. 1964: "I can see. . . that [the Lord Chancellor] is going to argue strongly that the Commission's eventual report will not carry conviction in the legal world, unless I agree to have a Judge as chairman," to which Cunningham replied: "The danger is that if it carries conviction in the legal world it will not do so elsewhere." Cunningham told the Home Secretary on 27 Apr. 1964 that "in the course of conversation at the Police College last weekend, more than one of the senior police officers present expressed the hope that a judge would not be appointed as Chairman of the Royal Commission on the Penal System." See HO291/520.
57 TNA, HO291/520.

Anything which appears to diminish their status has an adverse effect on the administration of justice and the appointment of someone other than a judge to preside over the Royal Commission would in my view be taken to imply that there was no judge fit to preside.[58]

He suggested Lord Justice Salmon or Lord Upjohn. The Prime Minister thought Lord Amory "would be admirable but asked whether he knew enough about the law to move with any familiarity among the sort of issues that would be involved." Three weeks later, Brooke minuted that the Prime Minister had said to him informally that on further consideration Amory was not the ideal man to chair the Commission. Yet two days later the PM decided to ask Amory to serve as chairman! Amory was troubled on two counts. One, his qualifications, which the PM reassured him about. Two, the fear that the Opposition would see him as a political appointee. The Leader of the Opposition, Harold Wilson, was approached on the subject, and he expressed no objection to Amory. Amory accepted the chalice. He wrote to Brooke, "I have grave doubts about my capacity but only hope things will work out all right."[59] Viscount Amory was a genial man of diligence and duty, with a reticent disposition, more the empiricist than the idealist, and with no close acquaintance with penal matters, though active in the campaign to end capital punishment in the late 1940s. His appointment was announced on 29 May 1964. The *Guardian* considered the appointment "an unexpected one, but Lord Amory has always shown a special interest in the problems and welfare of young people . . ."[60]

As for members of the commission, Brennan, who wanted no more than 14 or 15 appointees (Brooke wanted to keep the number to 12), suggested H. L. A. Hart or Glanville Williams as the academic lawyer; Leon Radzinowicz "the obvious claimant" as criminologist; Exeter, "whose philosophical training should be useful for a broad inquiry of this sort" as Churchman; Dr. Pearce as psychiatrist; and Professor Lafitte or Titmuss as sociologist. Brooke wanted to omit Lady Wootton, said Brennan, "and although her claims are strong I think the position she has already adopted on certain matters within the purview of the Royal Commission must probably, in any event, disqualify her." Brooke also wanted some members aged between 35 and 50. Peterson could not suggest anyone: "The younger group of research workers (Dr. and Mrs. Morris; Dr. Charlotte Banks) would not, I imagine, be acceptable."[61] Cunningham advised, "There are few people in this age

58   Ibid., Dilhorne to Prime Minister, 6 Apr. 1964.
59   Ibid., Amory to Brooke, 15 May 1964.
60   *Guardian*, 30 May 1964 in Ibid; *The Times*, 30 May 1964 in PREM 11/4691. See also John Ramsden, "Amory, Derick Heathcoat, first Viscount Amory (1899–1981)," *Oxford DNB* (2004); *The Times*, 21 Jan. 1981, p. 16. David Donnison later underlined the cardinal role of the chairman, stating: "A really good chairman can create an effective committee against heavy odds, but even a good committee is unlikely to be effective if it has a poor chairman." See "Committees and Committeemen," in M. Bulmer (ed.), *Social Research and Royal Commissions* (1980), p. 14.
61   TNA, BN29/1034, Peterson, 3 Apr. 1964.

group who are sufficiently prominent in their fields to have a strong claim for inclusion." There was R. G. Andry, a psychologist and assistant editor of the *British Journal of Criminology*, who was said to have "a robust common sense." Leslie Wilkins suggested Alan Little, sociologist at the London School of Economics, but Lafitte and Radzinowicz had prior claims as sociologist and criminologist *du jour*. In June, Brooke sent the Prime Minister preliminary descriptions of the list of members they were considering. The PM thought the members were very experienced, but asked if "enough of them will have a fresh approach. We want the Royal Commission to take a new look at these problems." Cunningham advised Brooke to inform the PM that it was their intention that the Royal Commission "should work through committees, and that younger men should be appointed to them. The Commission will, therefore, be in the nature of a senior body . . ."[62] In all, five women and ten men were initially appointed. What were their credentials?

The women: *Lady Hester Adrian*, a magistrate, member of the Ingleby Committee on Children and Young Persons and the Royal Commission on Mental Health, and wife of the Master of Trinity College, Cambridge[63]; *Sylvia Fletcher-Moulton*, a magistrate, member of the Departmental Committee on Sunday Observance, chair of the south-eastern area of the National Union of Conservative Associations, whose claim had been personally pressed by the Home Secretary; *Bee (Beatrice) Serota*, chair of the London County Council Children's Committee, a magistrate and member of ACTO, and Labour Chief Whip for the Greater London Council[64]; *Barbara Warburton*, chair of the London Juvenile Courts; and *Lady Wootton of Abinger*, a peer who accepted the Labour Whip, juvenile magistrate, former member of the Streatfeild Committee on the Business of the Criminal Courts, and author of *Social Science and Social Pathology* (1959), an excoriating critique of the popular explanations of criminal behaviour, in the course of which she demolished the psychoanalytic approach to criminology, and gave the kiss of death to "grand theory."[65]

The men: *David Basnett*, a moderate trade unionist (National Union of General and Municipal Workers) and a member of the Home Secretary's Advisory Committee on Juvenile Delinquency[66]; *Sir Herbert Edmund-Davies*, High Court Judge (fresh from sentencing the Great Train Robbers to 20 and 30 years in prison), and a member of the Criminal Law Revision Committee;[67] *Dr. T. C. N. Gibbens*,

62   TNA, HO291/520, Brooke to Prime Minister, 8 Jun. 1964; PM to Brooke, 10 Jun. 1964; Cunningham to Brooke, 17 Jun. 1964.
63   D. Thom, "Adrian, Hester Agnes, Lady Adrian (1899–1966)," *Oxford DNB* (2004).
64   John Davis, "Serota, Beatrice, Baroness Serota (1919–2002)," *Oxford DNB* (2009); *Guardian*, 22 Oct. 2002, p. 22.
65   See Ann Oakley, *A Critical Woman*, op cit., p. 257; A. H. Halsey, "Wootton, Barbara Frances, Baroness Wootton of Abinger (1897–1988)," *DNB 1986–1990* (Oxford, 1996)," pp. 491–3. See also T. Morris, "In Memoriam: Barbara Wootton 1897–1988," *British Journal of Sociology*, vol. 40 (1989), pp. 310–8; N. Walker, *A Man Without Loyalties: A Penologist's Afterthoughts* (Chichester, 2003), p. 98.
66   *The Times*, 26 Jan. 1989, p. 16.
67   *Independent*, 1 Jan. 2014.

lecturer in Forensic Psychiatry at the London Institute of Psychiatry, and former member of the Streatfeild Committee; *Thomas Iremonger*, Conservative MP for Ilford North, a magistrate, and member of the General Council of the Institute for the Study and Treatment of Delinquency[68]; *J. E. MacColl*, Labour MP for Widnes, and chair of the London Juvenile Court, who resigned when he took office in the Labour government, to be replaced in May 1965 by *Sam Silkin*, barrister and Labour MP for Camberwell, Dulwich[69]; *R. E. Millard*, Clerk of the Peace, Clerk of the Buckinghamshire County Council, and member of the Departmental Committee on Criminal Statistics. *J. N. Morris*, physician and epidemiologist, professor of social medicine, London University, director of the Social Medicine Research Unit of the Medical Research Council, and member of the Advisory Committee on Juvenile Delinquency[70]; the *Rt. Rev. R. C. Mortimer*, Bishop of Exeter, theologian, and member of ACTO[71]; *Leon Radzinowicz*, Wolfson Professor of Criminology and Director of the Institute of Criminology, and member of ACTO[72]; and *Lord Wheatley*, Senator of the College of Justice in Scotland, and former Labour MP.[73]

In addition to the chairman, the royal commission was 15-strong, larger than Brooke wanted. It was probably too large, and part cause of the difficulty the chairman experienced in restraining its "centrifugal tendencies," and in developing a consensus on the essential issues. It was a heterogeneous collection: the statutory trade unionist, seven magistrates (two of whom were MPs), two judges, a psychiatrist, a bishop, a professor of social medicine, a clerk of the peace, and two criminologists. Some were merely FOB, Friends of Brooke, including those known to him via service on the Advisory Committee on Juvenile Delinquency. Indeed, the delinquency sector of the penal system was heavily represented on the commission. Three commissioners, Exeter, Radzinowicz, and Serota were members of ACTO. Three commissioners, Serota, Gibbens, and MacColl were serving on the Labour Party's Study Group, which was about to publish its report, *Crime: A Challenge to Us All*. Apart from Amory, no one had any business experience, and no one had served in the police or prison service.[74]

---

68 *The Times*, 20 May 1998, p. 23. See Iremonger, *Disturbers of the Peace* (1962).
69 Archer of Sandwell, "Silkin, Samuel Charles, Baron Silkin of Dulwich (1918–1988)," *Oxford DNB* (2004); *The Times*, 19 Aug. 1988, p. 14.
70 Tom Arie, "Morris, Jeremiah Noah (1910–2009)," *Oxford DNB* (2013).
71 J. R. Porter, "Mortimer, Robert Cecil (1902–1976)," *DNB 1971–1980* (Oxford, 1986), pp. 595–6; *The Times*, 13 Sept. 1976, p. 16.
72 See fn. 48 *supra*.
73 D. M. Ross, "Wheatley, John Thomas, Baron Wheatley (1908–1988)," *Oxford DNB* (2004).
74 See *Daily Express*, 5 Aug. 1964. See also "Royal Commission Reporting," in M. Bulmer (ed.), op cit., p. 186. Tony Brennan, Assistant Secretary in the Home Office, was appointed Secretary of the Royal Commission.

V

The royal commission had barely been announced in mid-April before the alarms were sounded. The first tocsin was the address delivered three weeks later by Professor Leon Radzinowicz to the Howard League for Penal Reform, on 7 May 1964, which was published as *Criminology and the Climate of Social Responsibility*. Radzinowicz did not yet know he was a member of the royal commission (even the chairman's name was not released until 29 May), but he must have known his seat was being warmed, and his lecture was surely in the nature of a pre-emptive strike. "Reforming zeal, reforming utterances, reforming schemes," said Radzinowicz, were suddenly all the rage. Coming to what he defined as "the crux of the matter," he declared, "I can recollect no similar period when matters of penal reform and criminology have figured so prominently in the political contest." He had in mind the Conservative's White Paper, *The War Against Crime*, and the Labour Party's Study Group report on the causes of crime and penal reform, which was close to being published, and whose recommendations, Alice Bacon had told the Commons on 27 April, would be acted upon by the incoming Labour government.[75] The final section of Radzinowicz's address turned to the royal commission. He set out in these few pages the core beliefs that would shape his performance as commission member and as leader of what would become known as "the dissident minority." First, he compared the restricted terms of reference of the Gladstone Committee of 1895 with the far-from-narrow ones of the new commission, including what he called the "troubled and treacherous waters" of the causes of crime. Secondly, he questioned the value of arguing over the principles of punishment. What appealed to the public imagination, he claimed, was not "arguments about first principles," but "the successful salvage operation—the well-directed attempt to retrieve and to mend." After all, the establishment of approved schools, the borstal system, open prisons, and hostels for prisoners had all started as "practical experiments to meet what were recognized as practical needs." In an earlier publication, he had shown scepticism about the role that criminological research played in penal reform:

> Treatment by probation, the borstal system, the juvenile courts . . . were not devised on the strength of fresh and precise criminological knowledge. They can be shewn (sic) to have evolved . . . under the influence of growing social consciousness, of religious movements and philanthropic stimulus, from some temporary measure, or just from straightforward commonsense, supported by experience.[76]

"It is this empirical approach," he concluded, "rather than jurisprudential disquisition on the calculus of utility in punishment that has produced progress."

75   *Hansard*, vol. 694, 27 Apr. 1964, col. 85.
76   Radzinowicz, *In Search of Criminology* (Cambridge, Mass., 1962), pp. 178–9.

Accordingly, further progress would be achieved by the commission "only if it selects . . . a series of specific and related themes and tackles them in their appropriate order."[77]

The themes he had in mind were hardly miniscule. They included the role of the juvenile court, youth courts for young adult offenders, replacements for preventive detention and corrective training, the concept of the indeterminate sentence, parole on American lines, a hostel network, the organization of after-care, sentencing tribunals, and the organization of research. This list does not suggest that Radzinowicz was deeply troubled by the scope of the inquiry, despite his comment 35 years later about "our suicidal terms of reference."[78] What troubled him more, as Roger Hood correctly identified, was the method of work characteristic of royal commissions: the garnering of oral and written evidence from the usual list of organizations and individuals, "the great bulk of which," said Barbara Wootton, a year after the collapse of the Royal Commission on the Penal System, "consists, in my experience, of expressions of opinion unsupported by any factual foundation."[79] Radzinowicz put forward measures to ensure a royal commission "adapted to modern conditions," to ensure a more efficient and scientific approach. These included a sizeable secretariat, the collaboration of government and university research units, and research commissioned from "specialized working parties . . . drawing as widely as possible on the younger generations of criminologists." It remained to be seen if any of these measures would be adopted.

The second alarm came with the publication in June 1964 of *Crime—A Challenge to Us All*, the report of the Labour Party's Study Group under Lord Longford's chairmanship, which had been appointed in December 1963 "to present the next Labour Government with a firm basis for action designed to tackle the problem of crime at its roots . . ."[80] The 15 signatories to the report included no fewer than eight members of the next Labour government—Longford (Leader of the House of Lords), Gardiner (Lord Chancellor), F. Elwyn Jones (Attorney-General), Anthony Greenwood (Colonial Secretary), Margaret Herbison (Minister of Social Security), Alice Bacon (Minister of State at the Home Office), James MacColl (Parliamentary Secretary to the Minister for Housing and Local Government), and Reg Prentice (Minister of State at Education and Science). Also signing the report were Dr. Gibbens and Bee Serota, who would serve on the royal commission (along with James MacColl); and Terence Morris, one of the younger generation of criminologists, co-author of the sociological study, *Pentonville*, and Xenia Field,

---

77 Radzinowicz, *Criminology and the Climate of Social Responsibility*, an address to the Howard League for Penal Reform, 7 May 1964 (Cambridge, 1964), esp. pp. 20–2, 24–6.

78 Radzinowicz, *Adventures in Criminology* (1999), p. 346.

79 R. Hood, "Criminology and Penal Change: A Case Study of the Nature and Impact of Some Recent Advice to Governments," in Hood (ed.), *Crime, Criminology and Penal Policy* (1974), p. 386; Wootton, *In a World I Never Made* (1967), p. 256.

80 *Crime—A Challenge to Us All*, Report of the Labour Party's Study Group, Jun. 1964, p. 1.

prison reformer and author of *Under Lock and Key: A Study of Women in Prison*. In a Lords' debate in the following month, Longford had good cause to describe his group as "quite as strong a team of experts as a Royal Commission is likely to collect." Individuals giving oral or written evidence to the study group in a personal capacity, moreover, included long-time penal reformer Lord Stonham (soon to be Parliamentary Undersecretary at the Home Office), and Lady Wootton (who would serve on the Royal Commission).

To forestall delinquency, the Longford report, taking a page from the Kilbrandon Report (on Children and Young Persons, Scotland) and going further, recommended the setting up of a Family Service, under the central direction of a new Family Department of the Home Office, and Family Service Departments at local authority level. The majority of children with difficulties (including delinquents) would be dealt with by agreement between parents and the Family Service. Where agreement could not be reached, there would be family courts, instead of juvenile courts, the proceedings in which would be civil not criminal for children below school-leaving age. Children would no longer suffer the stigma of court appearance. For adult offenders, the report recommended the abolition of capital punishment; statutory compensation for victims of violent crimes; changes in sentencing policy and practice; strengthening of the probation service and the introduction of the suspended sentence; measures to overcome the gross overcrowding of prisons; the transformation of prisons into places for rehabilitation through social training; special institutions for alcoholics, drug addicts, and mentally ill offenders; extension of the hostel scheme; the introduction of a parole system; and after-care for all offenders as part of a combined probation and after-care service. The report finally attached a notice of intent, stating that a number of the matters which the royal commission had been asked to examine had already been the subject of review and on which action was overdue. "We consider that action to deal with many of these urgent problems should not be held up by the Royal Commission's proceedings."[81] The document was a product of Fabian or social democratic thinking. In the very first section, the standard assault on the Welfare State for weakening the country's moral fibre was countered by an attack upon "the get-rich-quick ethos of the affluent society—Tawney's acquisitive society." It was a report on an ambitious scale, though the general level of argument was not particularly profound, and the recommendations were not particularly novel. As the editorial in *New Society* opined, Longford was "stimulating rather than definitive." "By and large on penal practice they do no more than sensibly reflect current progressive thought, much of it already adopted by the Home Office; but on prevention they come up with some radical suggestions which deserve careful thought."[82] As Terence Morris was to remark many years later, what was unique about the Longford group was that "a political leader who was about to assume

81   Ibid., p. 3. For a review by John Mack, see *British Journal of Criminology*, vol. 5 (1965), pp. 103–6.
82   *New Society*, 18 Jun. 1964, p. 3.

power had actually invited the [penal] reformers in to advise in advance of legislation."[83] M. J. Moriarty had already said something similar: "In general . . . it is unusual for an incoming government to bring with it anything approaching a detailed blueprint of penal policy."[84] In other words, the Labour government had its own agenda. This fact is what most undermined the workings, and what led directly to the collapse, of the Royal Commission on the Penal System. This all emerges clearly from a close perusal of the Home Office papers on the subject.

VI

The first meeting of the royal commission took place on 7 October, one week before the 1964 general election, which was won by the Labour Party with an overall majority of four seats. Almost immediately, therefore, the question arose of the relationship between the Home Office and the royal commission. The new Home Secretary, Frank Soskice, spoke with Lord Amory on 4 November at Buckingham Palace. They discussed "how the Royal Commission . . . might carry on its work whilst the Department would no doubt also be considering changes in penal administration from time to time." Amory welcomed the idea of the department asking the commission to comment upon any change the department would like to implement, and said: "It would be a great pity if the Department and the Royal Commission proceeded independently of each other working upon the same subject in their thinking without each knowing how the thoughts of the other were progressing." Amory later told Soskice that he had shared their understanding with the royal commission, which had welcomed the idea, "so as to minimize the chance that any early legislation you may be thinking of might clash with our thinking at the time."[85] Already, however, the royal commission was getting defensive, undoubtedly aggravated by the new Joint Parliamentary Undersecretary of State's speech in the House of Lords on 10 November. Lord Stonham stated that the government looked forward to considering the views of the royal commission, "but vitally necessary improvements cannot be held up pending the Commission's Report."[86] He went on to indicate the directions in which the Home Secretary wished to move. It was a conventional though extensive agenda: the possible application to England of the Kilbrandon Committee's proposals for juvenile offenders; keeping young people out of prison; replacing preventive detention; an allocation centre for long-term prisoners to identify those for whom "an early and intensive training for rehabilitation" was appropriate; improvement in the conditions of work, working hours, pay, and standards of food and clothing in the prisons; the introduction of a parole system, and the launch of the probation

---

83 Morris, *Crime and Criminal Justice since 1945* (Oxford, 1989), p. 114.

84 Moriarty, "The Policy-Making Process: How It Is Seen from the Home Office," in N. Walker (ed.), *Penal Policy-Making in England* (Cambridge, 1977), p. 132.

85 TNA, HO291/539: Soskice to Cunningham, 5 Nov. 1964; Amory to Soskice, 13 Nov. 1964. See R. Pearce, "Soskice, Frank (1902–1979)," *Oxford DNB* (2004).

86 *Hansard* (Lords), vol. 261, 10 Nov. 1964, col. 314.

and after-care service—all very much in line with the recommendations of the Longford Committee.[87]

At the end of November, H. B. Wilson, Assistant Undersecretary of State in the Criminal Department, described what he understood from Brennan was the general feeling of the royal commission about consultation with the Home Office,

> namely that, to put it crudely, they wd hope not to be regarded as a sort of super-ACTO to whom the S of S wd make a practice of referring specific questions. They want . . . to concentrate on getting on with their task of reviewing the penal system as a whole.[88]

Cunningham tried to advise Soskice on the issue of how far he, as Home Secretary, should exercise freedom of action in the field of penal reform, pending the outcome of the Commission's lengthy deliberations. Amory had already indicated that he did not want to compartmentalize the thinking of the Commission by focusing on a particular aspect in isolation. "It may be, therefore," said Cunningham, "that the Commission would not . . . welcome being asked, in effect, to make a series of interim reports or recommendations on specific points referred to them *ad hoc.*" On the other hand, it seemed only courteous to inform the commission of any major proposals for change in areas within their terms of reference, and give them the chance to comment. "Otherwise the Commission may well feel that their usefulness is in doubt and some members may not wish to continue."[89]

Amory met with Home Office ministers at the end of November, when he told them that the commission were inclined to focus on juvenile delinquency to begin with, as they had been asked to do by the previous government. This would keep them busy until the end of 1965 (a very optimistic forecast, according to Brennan); they would require two years after that to study the wider field of adult offenders. Soskice replied to the effect that the government could not feel themselves precluded from introducing measures of penal reform while the commission was studying the matter, and that ministers recognized that the commission would not be able in every case to abandon their work programme in order to examine points referred to them by the department. Yet, "If, without prejudicing their broad survey of the whole field, the Royal Commission felt able to deal with particular aspects of it in separate reports, as they were contemplating with juvenile delinquency, the Government might well find this helpful."[90] A few days later, Cunningham was already referring to "the difficult situation which I think may develop in relation to the Royal Commission on the Penal System."

---

87   Ibid., col. 316.
88   TNA, HO291/539: Wilson minute, 26 Nov. 1964.
89   Ibid., Cunningham to Soskice, 27 Nov. 1964.
90   Ibid., G J. Otton, 1 Dec. 1964, note of Amory's talk with HO ministers on 30 Nov.

The risk, I think, is that if the Government go ahead with legislation about preventive detention, possibly approved schools and possibly about a parole system, before the Royal Commission have expressed any view, the Commission, or at least some of its members, may feel that there is no point in going on with the work. I am told that this view is already being expressed by some members of the Commission privately.[91]

And he included a "we told him so" in his minute to Gwynn, Deputy Undersecretary of State:

Our difficulties . . . would have been very much less if, as we recommended, we had had a reconstituted advisory council to which, although it was under contract to review the penal system as a whole, we could have referred from time to time specific proposals for changes in the law or major administrative developments.

In fact, he wondered if a similar, albeit unorthodox, course should be followed even with the royal commission. If the Home Secretary wanted to introduce a bill to deal with preventive detention, approved schools and parole, could the RCPS be asked to review these three matters by way of sub-committees, and asked to report by, say, the end of July 1965? Of course, he recognized the obvious difficulty that approved schools could hardly be considered in isolation from other methods of dealing with young offenders, or parole in isolation from the arrangements for dealing with adult offenders.[92]

Things went from bad to worse. Brennan told G. J. Otton, Soskice's private secretary, that the royal commission was worried on a number of counts, which he expressed in a set of questions. Was the commission working to the priorities which would best assist the new government? What did the government expect from the commission on topics that the government was eager to push forward? Was the commission doing, or planning to do, work which government action would make nugatory? Since the commission had decided at their third meeting on 10–11 November to give priority to young offenders, they ought to know, said Brennan, whether or not the government intends to await the royal commission's views on the profound changes in existing treatment raised by the Kilbrandon and Longford reports. Brennan finally fought for the original purpose of appointing a royal commission:

. . . I believe that if the Commission tried to produce a series of reports, as if it had taken over the role of ACTO, it would be at great risk of prejudicing the fundamental review expected of it and of losing impact when it makes its final recommendations. I am sure that whatever the Commission has to

91 Ibid., Cunningham to Gwynn, 3 Dec. 1964.
92 Ibid.

recommend, particularly if it is of a radical kind, will be more likely to get public acceptance if it is presented as part of a coherent philosophy and system.[93]

Amory now pressed the Home Secretary to set out the government's priorities for consideration at the commission's fourth meeting on 15–16 December. The Home Secretary responded by saying that he hoped the commission would produce an interim report on young offenders by the end of 1965. Also, the government contemplated the introduction, when preventive detention and corrective training were abolished, of some form of parole system, and he asked the commission to report their views on parole by summer 1965. The day before the commission met, Alice Bacon, Minister of State, wrote to the Home Secretary, insisting that action be taken on behalf of children and young people:

> In this whole field there has got to be a great deal of trial and error and I believe that there is much that can be done even though it is, as so much of our work in this field, experimentation.[94]

At the December meeting, royal commission members differed in their view about the commission's relationship with the government. Iremonger had no doubt: it was not the commission's function

> to act as the Government's adviser on ad hoc questions of policy. The Commission's work would only realise its full value if major reforms were kept in suspense until it had reported; if it was left free to explore thoroughly and at its own pace; and if its eventual views could be presented as a whole.

Likewise, Miss Fletcher-Moulton thought the penal system had for years suffered the ill-effects of piecemeal legislation: "The Commission now had the opportunity of making a fundamental re-appraisal of the system and of producing a report covering the entire field." And Lord Wheatley thought the commission "would have to decide to plan its work independently of the Government's programme." On the other side, Professor Morris thought the commission "should beware of adopting an inflexible attitude to the Government's request for advice." Dr. Gibbens suggested arriving at a "negotiated settlement" with the government: "an attempt might be made to draw up a list of topics on which the Commission could report speedily and a similar list of topics upon which the Government would require early advice." Neither he nor Millard nor Warburton, however, believed it practicable to produce an interim report on parole by mid-1965, or in isolation from the associated topics of the indeterminate sentence, the suspended sentence,

93 Ibid., Brennan to Otton, 4 Dec. 1964.
94 Ibid., Bacon minute to Soskice, 14 Dec. 1964. See C. M. P. Taylor, "Bacon, Alice Martha, Baroness Bacon (1909–1993)," *Oxford DNB* (2004).

and hostel provision and after-care. Dr. Radzinowicz and Lady Wootton focused on the commission's terms of reference as preface to calling for a further exchange of views between the commission and the Home Secretary. Radzinowicz said that

> he had from the outset been troubled by the breadth of the Commission's terms of reference and the length of time which . . . would be needed for the Commission to complete a study of the great number of topics which the terms of reference covered.

A full examination of the issues raised by young offenders alone would take four to five years:

> It was therefore essential for the Commission to single out from the possible field of study a few central topics for concentrated examination and report. The Government's desire to take action should be accepted by the Commission, and its need for advice on particular topics would help . . . such a selective approach provided that the Government accepted that its programme could be carried out only in constructive collaboration with the Commission . . .[95]

Lady Wootton thought the royal commission should consider asking for a revision of its terms of reference: "These required a broad and fundamental re-appraisal of the concepts and purposes of the penal system whereas the Home Secretary now appeared to be looking for detailed advice on selected and specific matters."[96] The discussion was adjourned to January, when the meeting between the Home Secretary and the commission would, said Brennan, "explore frankly and informally possible solutions to the dilemma with which the Government and the Commission are confronted."[97]

At the 12 January meeting, to judge from Soskice's subsequent letter to Amory, presenting his understanding of the "agreement" reached, the royal commission said it expected to take four years or more to complete its task, and they did not expect to be able to produce interim reports on parole or on the treatment of juveniles before the end of the year. Many members saw considerable difficulty in advising the government on individual aspects of the penal system in advance of reaching conclusions over the entire field. In these circumstances, wrote the Home Secretary,

95 TNA, HO307/14, RCPS, minutes of 4th meeting, 15–16 Dec. 1964.
96 Ibid.
97 TNA, HO307/7: Brennan's note for meeting with the Home Secretary on 12 Jan. 1965. Cunningham had told Gwynn on 22 Dec. 1964, "According to Professor Radzinowicz, the Commission are now disposed to offer to do their best to produce a report on the parole system by next Autumn, and to endeavour also to submit some sort of interim report on the means of selecting the appropriate method of treatment for adolescent offenders."

it seems to me that the Commission should settle and carry out its programme of study as it would have done had no question of amending legislation arisen. On this basis, a report dealing with the whole of its terms of reference may perhaps be expected four or five years from now. In the meantime, the Government will proceed with such legislative proposals as it thinks desirable, recognizing that the Commission may wish in its report to recommend that they should be abandoned or modified. I for my part will see that the Commission are informed at the earliest possible stage of our legislative proposals [principally in the treatment of young offenders and of parole for adults with long terms of imprisonment].[98]

The royal commission were, it seems, reluctant to commit themselves to offering comments on particular government proposals, and were unwilling to accept that there was an "agreement." Indeed, on the day after the meeting, an unsigned minute, most probably by Brennan, indicated that the writing was on the wall:

A substantial minority, including some of the weightier members, of the Commission is not disposed to accept that the Commission could act as the Home Secretary's letter proposes. They think that it would be artificial for the Commission to be considering matters which were the subject of legislation; and that even if the Commission could bring itself to make recommendations on these matters they would be likely to be treated as academic on the grounds that it was too soon to judge whether the Government's legislation had been on the right lines.

   This minority of the Commission is accordingly disinclined to continue the effort to discharge the Commission's all-embracing terms of reference: and it is disposed to think that the terms of reference, minus the topics on which the Government propose to legislate, would be so emasculated as not to justify the continuance of the Royal Commission. The minority accept that there remain important matters for consideration. But they see that as more appropriate to a body on the lines of ACTO which can consider specific matters on request.[99]

A narrow majority of the commission, said the minute, was anxious to carry on, without amendment of the terms of reference, on the lines suggested in the Home Secretary's letter. But two resignations were said to be probable, and there could be five or six. The minute added a telling paragraph:

The minority are influenced by an impression . . . that the Home Secretary, while prepared to make "polite noises," in fact finds the Commission's existence an embarrassment. They might be prepared to think again if persuaded

98   Ibid., Soskice to Amory, 12 Jan. 1965. See also TNA, HO291/546, Otton, 13 Jan. 1965.
99   TNA, HO291/546, confidential unsigned minute, 13 Jan. 1965.

that he really saw a job for them, and that they were not merely being invited to carry on as the least embarrassing solution politically. The minority consider, in this atmosphere, that the Commission's eventual report would be liable to be a "flop."

Consideration of this by the Commission is bedeviled by the imprecision of the Government's intentions.[100]

It was unclear, for example, whether the proposed legislation on young offenders would be confined to the under 16's or whether the legislation would affect the 16–21 age group. It was unclear whether the proposed parole legislation implied that the Home Secretary's mind was made up on major aspects of prison treatment. Cunningham tried to persuade Soskice to give Amory a firm assurance before the 27 January meeting that he wished the commission to go on with its long-term study, and to be a bit more precise about what he had in mind for young and adult offenders. Amory, it was added, was anxious "to use his influence to ensure that the Commission does not disintegrate."[101] Home Office Ministers were having none of this. They felt the Home Secretary had made his position clear at the 12 January meeting,

and that he should not, by spelling out in detail the action he wished the Government to take in the next Session or two, inhibit the Government's freedom of action in a way which might be most unacceptable to Government supporters who favoured early advance on the lines of the Longford Report.[102]

A draft was circulated on 19 January for discussion at the meeting on the 27th signed by six members: Lady Adrian, Dr. Gibbens, the Bishop of Exeter, Leon Radzinowicz, Lady Wootton, and Bee Serota. The message was unequivocal:

The fact that major legislation appears to be pending in the near future greatly alters the situation in which the Royal Commission finds itself. The immediate investigations now required are not the proper work of a Royal Commission.

---

100 Ibid.
101 Ibid., Cunningham to Soskice, 18 Jan. 1965. Cunningham wrote, "[Lord Amory] made it clear. . . that there is no unanimity on the Commission in favour of continuing with its work. There is a strong and influential minority who feel that, in the light of what you said at your meeting with the Commission, it would be premature for them to attempt to discharge their terms of reference. This minority may well resign from the Commission—using the argument that until the fundamental changes which they believe you have in contemplation have been carried out it is premature to attempt any comprehensive assessment of the present methods of penal treatment. . . I think there is also an impression in the minds of some members of the Commission that you would really like it to pass out of existence."
102 Ibid., Otton minute, 21 Jan. 1965.

Further, having taken a quick look at the whole field contained in our terms of reference, we are of the opinion that a Royal Commission, as now constituted, is not a good instrument for the purpose of long-term research. We advise that such long-term research would be better done by a permanent Research Council established within, but independent of, the Home Office, capable of working in small working parties, employing expert researchers and having at its service all the resources of money and talent available.

Lastly, we believe that a period of active major legislation is not an opportune one for conducting the kind of assessment and philosophical appreciation envisaged in our terms of reference. We believe, however, that a Royal Commission set up some years hence could be of great service.[103]

The middle paragraph has clear echoes of Radzinowicz's address to the Howard League. For whatever reason, Radzinowicz said nothing about this *January 1965* revolt in his account of "The Death of a Royal Commission" in *Adventures in Criminology*.

It is worth pausing to point the significance of this evidence. The threatened resignation of six members of the royal commission, what Cunningham called "the dissident minority," came only *three* months after the commission's first meeting, and in the wake of only its *fifth* meeting. All the commission had managed to discuss by this point was how justice should be dispensed to young offenders, having considered the Ingleby, Kilbrandon, and Longford committees' reports at its December meeting. Yet at this meeting, the commission were still considering their programme of work: whether they should even continue with their consideration of the young offender, whether they should shift focus to those aged 16–21 or to adult offenders. By this date, too, barely any evidence had been submitted by government departments, legal and penal organizations, or individuals; there hadn't been time to put the submissions together. The bulk of evidence arrived between May and November 1965. There had been no time even for Lord Amory's indecisive leadership to become a major source of discontent, though the actions of the minority hardly reflected great respect for the chairman. There was a feeling among close to half the membership that the terms of reference were unprecedentedly wide, that the task set them was too large—though this did not yet rest upon the experience of getting down to work. The essential problem that led to the decision by six commissioners to throw in the towel was the relationship between the royal commission and the government. The royal commission found itself working in an atmosphere of great uncertainty; standing on ground that was shifting under its feet. Major changes and innovations in the penal system, which the new Labour government were eager to introduce, were hard to reconcile with the royal commission's task of producing a balanced, cohesive, long-term plan for

103 TNA, HO307/7: RCPS/N/26, circulated on 19 Jan. for discussion at meeting on 27 Jan. 1965, at the request of the six members who signed it: Lady Adrian, Dr. Gibbens, Bishop of Exeter, Leon Radzinowicz, Barbara Wootton, and Bea Serota.

the entire penal system. Thus, the proposal to introduce a parole system raised in an acute form the questions of what the concepts and purposes of the penal system as a whole should be. Any piecemeal reporting by the commission, as they were being pressed to deliver, could only undermine the impact of the final report. This was underlined by the events of the following days.

On 20 January, the day following circulation of the minority's draft, Soskice wrote to Amory to emphasize his wish that the royal commission should proceed with its comprehensive review of the penal system. "I fully recognise that it will take a considerable time;" said Soskice, "but its results should provide us with a basis of future policy over the whole field of penal treatment for the first time since the Gladstone report of 1895." There was no incompatibility, he insisted, between a wide-ranging review and the development of some parts of it. To bolster this request, Brennan set out for the commission the issues that were unaffected by the projected legislation, notably the place of imprisonment in the penal system, and specifically the objectives of imprisonment (in terms of the balance between "punishment," "containment," and "therapy"), a blueprint for a system to meet those objectives, and the means by which the prison population could be reduced. There was also work to do in the selection of sentences, such as the extent to which the determination of sentence should be a judicial function. In short, there was much for the commission to do. On 27 January, the commission met to consider the future, having before it the suggestion from six members that a short report should be produced "indicating that it feels unable to continue its work in the changed circumstances." In fact, the commission decided that it would continue its work. Brennan explained to Cunningham how the decision was reached:

> The majority spoke forcibly against the arguments for winding-up, and the minority, who were undoubtedly influenced by the Home Secretary's letter of 20 January, may best be described as being prepared to acquiesce in the majority view without being at all satisfied that their own misgivings were unfounded. It was pretty evident from the discussion that these misgivings were due, as much as to the Government's legislative plans, to doubts that they have harboured all along about whether the Commission is capable of doing the enormous job that has been set it. I am afraid this means that we shall be working . . . with some members whose enthusiasm is less than whole-hearted, but we shall have to make the best of it.[104]

Just how much less than wholehearted became evident a week later when the Bishop of Exeter, spokesman for the minority, told Soskice that six of the commission were "very disturbed in mind":

> We are very anxious to do nothing which would embarrass the Government, and we are very anxious to do everything we can to help with Penal Reform,

104 TNA, HO291/546, Brennan to Cunningham, 27 Jan. 1965.

but we are very far from certain that serving on the Royal Commission is the best way of helping . . . Could you possibly spare the time to see us, quite off the record and alone, except for the two Ministers of State?[105]

Brennan and Lord Amory were quite unaware of this request. As Soskice's private secretary, Otton, said to Cunningham, "Surely S of S cannot agree to this without asking them first to clear their lines with Lord Amory?" Soskice declined to meet the dissidents. Exeter replied to Soskice, expressing disappointment:

If we are unable to discuss our difficulties informally with you, we may find ourselves in a very difficult position. In the circumstances, because we are deeply concerned with Penal Reform and the direction which it should take, we have decided that we will continue to serve on the Commission . . . Nevertheless, our doubts about the value of this Royal Commission . . . as an instrument for promoting the right reforms in the penal system remain. We hope that as the work of the Commission progresses our doubts will be removed. But we think we should tell you that we still have these doubts and, if they are not removed by the end of the year, we shall have to re-consider our position.[106]

Professor Morris wrote to Amory on 1 February, declaring that "we must now get down to hard work and would rather we attempted too much than too little . . . In short: full steam ahead."[107]

At this point, the royal commission ceased to give priority to young offenders, and took as their central topic of study, imprisonment and its place in the penal system. At the same time, the commission began to resort to sub-committees to accomplish their task. Ultimately, there would be four sub-committees: research, concepts and purposes, sentencing, and treatment. Brennan accepted the need for sub-committees, without which the commission's work would never be done, but he recognized the objections to them: they would lead to fragmentation of the commission's work, and sub-committees might go off in directions contrary to the commission's general thinking.[108]

The papers emanating from these sub-committees are painful reading. The research sub-committee were first out of the gate. Almost immediately, however, they found themselves discussing the government's legislative intentions. Significantly, four of the five present at the second meeting on 2 December were of the dissident minority. The sub-committee concluded that the choice of priorities in research was impossible until the commission had arrived at a firm programme

105 Ibid., Exeter to Soskice, 28 Jan. 1965.
106 Ibid., Otton to Cunningham, 1 Feb. 1965; Exeter to Soskice, 15 Feb. 1965.
107 TNA, HO307/17, Morris to Amory, 1 Feb. 1965.
108 HO307/7, note by Brennan, 7 Jul. 1965.

of work. Lady Adrian was adamant that the full commission should consider its policy with regard to impending legislative changes before the sub-committee attempted a review of the research data available and required. The remaining meetings of the research sub-committee were taken up with considering possible subjects of research and the collection of data, especially concerning the prison population.[109] The treatment and sentencing sub-committees did not meet until July 1965. The former began by listing a host of questions that needed answering under the three main heads of custodial, non-custodial, and semi-custodial treatment. By November 1965, the treatment sub-committee were considering budding small panels to study individual topics, possibly inviting criminologists to assist in the work of each panel. And by January 1966, they were looking at information on foreign practice collected by the secretariat, all largely unsifted, since the commission had not been able to indicate specific questions or areas on which foreign information was required.[110] The sentencing sub-committee began by assessing the data they would need to collect, by consideration of the use of fines, and by discussion of alternatives to imprisonment (weekend arrest, semi-detention, and work release). Yet by November 1965, the sub-committee were still trying to decide what they should focus upon: "who should sentence" or the range of sentences and questions of sentencing practice? They decided to focus on the latter issue, while recognizing that their work would be subject to the commission's conclusion on "concepts and purposes."[111] As late as February 1966, moreover, Amory and Wheatley were meeting to define more exactly the respective responsibilities of the sentencing and treatment committees.[112] The concepts and purposes committee held its first meeting in October 1965. The royal commission had tried examining concepts and purposes of the penal system in their early meetings, but had been forced to conclude that there was an insufficient meeting of minds to make it useful to continue. A year later, the sub-committee first decided that members should acquaint themselves with the literature surrounding the Hart-Devlin debate (on the legal enforcement of morality, sparked by the publication of the Wolfenden Report on Homosexual Offences and Prostitution), and that a seminar would be arranged with selected outside experts on penal philosophy. The latter soon took the form of "a confrontation between philosophers and social scientists." By December 1965, it was agreed that the committee would have to relate their penal philosophy to modern hypotheses about the nature and causes of criminality, and they recruited

109 HO307/5, RCPS: Research Sub-Committee, minutes of 2nd meeting, 2 Dec. 1964. See also HO307/14, RCPS, minutes of 4th meeting, 15–16 Dec. 1964. At the 8th meeting on 16 Dec. 1965, the research sub-committee examined a proposal for a survey of the prison population by Dr. Banks, which quickly descended into a discussion of overcrowding.
110 TNA, HO307/3, minutes of Treatment sub-committee.
111 HO307/4, minutes of Sentencing sub-committee.
112 HO307/6, 2nd Joint meeting of Sentencing and Treatment Committees, 1 Feb. 1966.

Nigel Walker to assist them, and Professor Sprott to help them with "criminal sub-cultures." The sub-committee had become a glorified seminar.[113]

The collection of evidence and the interviewing of witnesses was no more constructive. Written evidence poured in from all the obvious sources: government departments; penal, legal, and medical bodies; professional associations of police, probation and prison officers; and individual judges, magistrates, and prisoners. The proposals within this evidence were quite predictable, the bulk of which concerned the purpose and effects of imprisonment. The various bodies argued that there was a too ready resort to imprisonment as a penal measure, that reformation was incapable of being achieved in prison conditions, that prisoners should be paid "full wages" or "the rate for the job," and that there should be more resort to semi-detention or semi-liberty in order to avoid disruption to the offender's working and family life. Almost without exception the proposals were made in broad terms. Witnesses advanced general principles without exploring in detail whether they were capable of practical application. Few or none of the pronouncements were based on any hard data. However, most of the innovations made by the Criminal Justice Act 1967 were recommended by witnesses: suspended sentence; parole; larger fining powers for magistrates' courts; and restriction on magistrates' courts' power to impose imprisonment for default in payment of fines.[114] The oral evidence was equally flawed. Nigel Walker's "bizarre" experience as a witness may not have been universal, but is emblematic of the limitations of oral evidence-gathering: "As soon as I began to give my views on the proper aims of sentencing . . . they began to argue with each other, unchecked by the Chairman and uninterrupted by me."[115]

VII

At this point, it is necessary to return to the chronology we have been tracking, to illustrate, if further illustration were needed, that the royal commission and Home Office were unable to develop a stable partnership. There was a major flap in March 1965 when Minister of State, Alice Bacon, told a couple of press representatives that she had been seeing which proposals of Longford and Kilbrandon could be embodied in future legislation. This prompted the *Daily Express* and the *Guardian* to announce that the laws for children were to be changed without waiting for the royal commission to complete their work. A White Paper would be published in the summer, with legislation in the next parliamentary session. *The*

---

113 HO307/2, RCPS, minutes of meetings of Concepts and Purposes Committee; Appendix B to minutes of 5th meeting, 18 Jan. 1966, discussion with Nigel Walker. See also HO291/542, HO memo on concepts and purposes of punishment and treatment, 5 Nov. 1964.

114 RCPS, *Minutes of Evidence Taken Before the Commission, vol. 1: Government Departments; vol. 2: Miscellaneous (e.g., Magistrates' Association, Society of Labour Lawyers); vol. 3: Miscellaneous Bodies (e.g., Prison Officers' Association, National Association of Probation Officers); vol. 4: Individual Witnesses,* HMSO (1967). See also TNA, HO291/1401, Advisory Council on the Penal System, Research sub-committee, Review of Evidence submitted to the Royal Commission on the Penal System, May–Jun. 1968.

115 Walker, *A Penologist's Afterthoughts,* op cit., p. 112.

Times went so far as to say that the future of the commission "may be in doubt."[116] To smooth the commission's ruffled feathers, Soskice was forced to state in the Commons that the government still wanted the comprehensive review.[117] In June, the idea of appointing a vice or deputy chairman of the royal commission, to take the chair in Amory's absence, became a bone of contention. When Amory raised the idea, Radzinowicz and Lady Adrian resisted such an appointment, "apparently seeing this as amounting to something more than a designation of a deputy to take the chair," according to Brennan. "This fuss over the Vice-Chairmanship is," said Brennan, ". . . symptomatic of the factionalism of the Commission, and the suspicion by some members of others."[118] This was followed in August by publication of the government's White Paper, *The Child, The Family and The Young Offender*, containing the government's proposals to abolish the juvenile courts and to introduce "Family Councils."[119] The White Paper attracted a storm of criticism from the legal lobby and probation officers.[120] Lady Adrian told Amory that she did not feel that "the circulation, a bare two weeks before publication . . . of a summary of the Government's proposals in the White Paper . . . really amounts to keeping the Commission informed of their thinking about legislative reforms."[121] The White Paper came as a surprise to the commission in that it had gone wider than they were expecting by proposing changes to the treatment of young adults as well as juveniles. Soskice tried harder with the proposals for parole and a new sentence for persistent offenders, alerting Amory to them at the beginning of October, and saying he hoped to issue a White Paper in due course.[122] In mid-October 1965, at the invitation of the Home Secretary, Amory gave a brief outline of the lines upon which the royal commission's thinking was forming. His report spoke volumes:

> In its first year, the Royal Commission had directed its thoughts towards a broad review of the penal system in an effort to establish common ground amongst the members and adumbrate the lines upon which the Commission

116 *Daily Express*, 2 Mar., *Guardian*, 2 Mar. 1965 enclosed in HO291/546; "Inquiry on Crime May Be Dropped," *The Times*, 5 Mar. 1965, p. 8; HO291/546, Brennan to Cunningham, 4 Mar. 1965.

117 *Hansard*, vol. 710, 8 Apr. 1965, col. 95.

118 TNA, HO307/39, Radzinowicz, 16 Jun.; Brennan, 25 Jun. 1965.

119 Home Office, *The Child, the Family and the Young Offender* (Cmnd. 2742), Aug. 1965.

120 Less extreme changes were ultimately announced in a 1968 White Paper, which served as preface to the Children and Young Persons Act of 1969. Most criminologists see the 1969 Act as the highpoint of the rehabilitative ideal. As Tony Bottoms and Simon Stevenson wrote, the Act "contained the most developed application of welfare principles to criminal justice ever seen in an English statute, and as such was the culmination of a range of measures which can be traced back to the first decade of the twentieth century." See "'What Went Wrong?': Criminal Justice Policy in England and Wales, 1945–70," in D. Downes (ed.), *Unravelling Criminal Justice* (Basingstoke, 1992), p. 36. See also Bottoms, "On the Decriminalization of English Juvenile Courts," in R. Hood (ed.), *Crime, Criminology and Public Policy* (1974), p. 320.

121 HO307/7, Adrian to Amory, 25 Aug. 1965.

122 HO291/546, Soskice to Amory, 1 Oct. 1965; 7 Dec. 1965.

would wish to approach the very large problems with which it was confronted. So far it had not formulated agreed proposals and though its thinking on some subjects such as parole, indeterminate sentences, and an up to date penal philosophy were crystallizing they remained, as yet, largely in an inchoate state. Even though this was the case, the Royal Commission was perturbed lest the work upon which it was engaged should be in any way prejudiced or pre-empted by action taken by the Home Office.[123]

It was unlikely anything would be achieved by a commission constantly craning its neck to see what the government was doing.

Soskice had failed to secure a place in the autumn session for a Criminal Justice Bill to incorporate the proposals for the adult offender, which would appear instead in the White Paper, *The Adult Offender*.[124] As the Home Secretary explained in a memo for the Cabinet in late November,

> The central feature of my proposals is to select by a careful process all those prisoners who are capable of being reclaimed for society and bringing them back into society under a considerably extended parole system which would apply, not merely to ordinary and star prisoners, but also to the recidivist prisoners as well.[125]

At the Cabinet meeting, Soskice introduced his White Paper by saying, "the Government might be liable to incur criticism from liberal opinion if they did not soon make a distinctive contribution to the reform of the penal system."[126] The White Paper was never destined to make much of a splash, since apart from the new proposals on parole and persistent offenders, the measures were more a continuation of existing plans to improve the condition of prisoners and their re-integration in the community than new departures. In large parts, the paper read more like an annual report of the prison department.

The White Paper was Soskice's swan song, since he was replaced as Home Secretary in late December by Roy Jenkins. Jenkins told Amory at the end of January 1966 that he hoped the royal commission would give their general thoughts on the two White Papers by September. Such a report would have an impact on the department's proposals for legislation. In fact, the end was nigh. Exeter submitted a paper on 23 February for a commission meeting on 1 March, in which he recommended that the royal commission be discharged and an advisory council on the penal system constituted in its place.[127] This represented the views of the dissident minority. It soon became clear that the majority were not willing

123 HO291/547, meeting held 14 Oct. 1965.
124 Home Office, *The Adult Offender* (Cmnd. 2852), Dec. 1965.
125 TNA, CAB 129/123, C. (65) 164, 30 Nov. 1965: "The Adult Offender: Draft White Paper," memo by Home Secretary; PREM 13/999, Burke Trend, 1 Dec. 1965.
126 TNA, CAB 128/39, CC (65) 67th conclusions, Cabinet, 2 Dec. 1965.
127 HO307/7.

to liquidate the commission, but Jenkins told Amory that if it proved impossible for the commission to agree on a short report, "he would not be disposed to appoint additional members to fill the vacancies caused by the resignation of the minority."[128] On 5 April, Amory (along with Mr. Justice Davies, Wheatley, Morris, Millard, and Iremonger) called to see Cunningham. The six members who had decided to resign had written to the Prime Minister asking that either the royal commission should be formally dissolved or they should be allowed to tender their resignation. The remaining eight wished to complete a report by the end of the year, and asked for new members to be appointed to the commission. If additional appointments were not made, Warburton and Fletcher-Moulton intended to resign. Amory asked for an interview with the Home Secretary "so that I could offer a personal explanation of the position . . . I need not say how distressed I am at the present deplorable situation."[129]

The letter to the Prime Minister, which the signatories wanted published, pleaded that a royal commission was not the right kind of body to undertake a comprehensive review of the penal system. "The comprehensive solution—if indeed there is one at all—will only be reached as a result of long, painstaking and expertly-guided research and experiment."

> We are convinced that in these days of rapid and urgently needed change in the penal system the necessarily somewhat leisurely approach of a Royal Commission, composed of persons heavily engaged in other occupations and unable to devote more than a small portion of their time to the work of the Commission, is unsuitable. What is needed is not a slow deliberate survey of the field by a body which reports its conclusions at an arbitrarily chosen moment. For by then both the penal system itself and the society in which it operates will have changed. What is needed is a continuous survey of the penal system by a body in continuous existence.[130]

The letter recommended the formation of a permanent advisory council "to hold the penal system under continuous review, to order enquiries or research into particular parts of the field and to co-ordinate the various enquiries and researches which are going on at any one time." Amory and Jenkins agreed that the Home Secretary would meet the royal commission, inform them that the government had decided that the commission should be wound up, that a standing advisory council would be appointed, and all this would be made public. As Cunningham wrote, "There is some hope that if the matter is dealt with in this way the dissentient members may refrain from publishing their letter of resignation."[131] The Prime Minister informed the Commons of the dissolution of the royal commission on 27

128 HO291/546.
129 HO291/554, minute to Home Secretary, 5 Apr. 1966; Amory to Cunningham, 6 Apr. 1966.
130 HO291/546, Minority of RCPS to Prime Minister, 5 Apr. 1966.
131 Ibid., Cunningham to Gwynn, 18 Apr. 1966.

April 1966, in the course of which he insisted that this outcome had *not* been caused by the publication of the two White Papers.

> While it is true that, when the Royal Commission was set up, we on this side said that we would reserve the right . . . to get on with urgent legislation without waiting for the Royal Commission to report, in fact this has not been one of the issues . . . This could have been a difficulty . . . but it was not.[132]

We beg to differ.

Inevitably, there were personal dimensions to the failure of the royal commission. During the 18 months the commission was at work, members had an unfortunate tendency to form into cabals, perhaps best described as pessimists and optimists. The dissenting six would meet for lunch or a drink at Brown's Hotel. The most constructive members, those who wanted to succeed with the task they had been given, were Mr. Justice Edmund-Davies, Sam Silkin, and Professor Morris. In fact, Morris regarded the royal commission as the greatest failure of his life.[133] Clearly there were tensions between individual members. In his psychoanalytically-infused autobiography, Leo Abse described how

> the essential pragmatism of Radzinowicz clashed with the restless perfectionism of my friend . . . Sam Silkin. These formidable protagonists became locked in a fatal struggle: over the corpse of the Commission they were to continue to view each other unforgivingly.[134]

Tony Brennan, secretary to the Commission, was as disappointed as Silkin at the outcome, indicting Radzinowicz, it has to be said, as spoiler-in-chief.[135] Radzinowicz had sounded the tocsin even before appointment to the commission, and in his autobiography posed the question, "how could I bring myself to serve on the Commission?" He states that he considered it was his duty as the first professor of criminology in the country

> to accept this responsibility and to do all I could to help to salvage as much as possible. Thus, when I accepted the invitation I was pretty certain that this would be a stony path to follow, and one very likely to be met by bitterness and sadness at the end of it.[136]

Clearly a pessimist from day one. He was also unsympathetic to abstract talk about "concepts and purposes" or the principles of penal policy. Penal change, he believed, did not require unanimity of view on principles. And, lastly, Lord Amory

132 *Hansard*, vol. 727, 27 Apr. 1966, col. 707.
133 Ann Oakley, *A Critical Woman*, op cit., p. 259.
134 Abse, *Private Member* (1973), p. 126.
135 Interview with Tony Brennan, 20 Jan. 2000 in the Athenaeum.
136 Radzinowicz, *Adventures*, op cit., pp. 336–7.

undoubtedly found it difficult to hold a fissiparous membership together, and the Home Secretary, Frank Soskice, was in wretched health, politically inept, indecisive to a fault, and, claimed Tony Benn, "entirely in the hands of his civil servants."[137]

Yet the Commission's failure cannot be laid at the feet of personal animosities or personal incompetence, as distracting as these were. What of the reasons for failure offered by the resigning commissioners? They argued, in effect, that the open-ended terms of reference ensured the Commission was always on "mission impossible." Lord Windlesham concurred. After citing the terms of reference, he wrote, "It was a vast task. The Commission was being asked to frame a philosophy for criminal justice and to measure the performance of penal proceedings against it."[138] Correct, but this was exactly what was required—and was the task really beyond the wit of an effective Royal Commission? If this was not its task, why bother setting it up in the first place? Relatedly, the resigning commissioners were dismissive of judgments on moral and political issues, deeming them inappropriate for the work of the royal commission. Yet its preferred alternative was to rely on the *in seriatim* accumulation of proposals, eschewing all sense of an integrated penal system, in which one piece inevitably interacted on the others. Again, the point of the royal commission was surely to make political and ethical judgments, and to have an eye to the system of criminal justice *in toto*. In addition, the resigning commissioners, including most of the academic criminologists on the commission, argued that the science of criminology was far from ready to respond to the requirements the commission wished to place on it. Only a handful of published books and papers existed on the effectiveness of different methods of treatment. Again, correct, but did the commissioners do anything to improve the position; did they hire staff, plan, pilot, and launch fresh research? The answer is, not really. A survey of a 15 per cent sample of the total prison population was eventually commissioned, one outcome being Richard Sparks' excellent *Local Prisons*, but this all paled in comparison with the research work initiated by the US President's Commission on Law Enforcement and Administration of Justice between 1965 and 1967. None of the reasons for resignation offered by the "dissident minority" holds any substantial body of water.

The royal commission's failure was a function of politics, more strictly the change in government. Thirteen years out of power, Labour was eager to implement the ideas they had developed about young offenders, parole, and other matters. The new government was not going to wait for Henry Brooke's commission to complete their work. In the context of a more intense political activism, the representative, investigative and deliberative style of policy building was too slow

---

137 Cecil King, *The Cecil King Diary 1965–1970* (1972), p. 19; Benn, *Out of the Wilderness: Diaries 1963–67* (1987), p. 284. See also "Lord Stow Hill," *The Times*, 16 Nov. 1979.
138 Windlesham, *Responses to Crime*, vol. 2: *Penal Policy in the Making* (Oxford, 1993), p. 100.

and unresponsive. Government White Papers, presaging early legislation, gave the kiss of death to the royal commission.[139]

VIII

In the knowledge that the royal commission would not be reporting, the Home Office began to look afresh at a number of subjects, using a paper entitled "Sentencing Policy" by Parliamentary Undersecretary of State, Victor Stonham, as their starting point, which built on his remarks in the Commons' debate on prison after-care in December 1963.[140] This document was more thoughtful than anything the royal commission produced. Lord Stonham's paper questioned the policy of passing short prison sentences. Statistics indicated that of the 42,239 men received into prison in 1963, 23,764 (50.4 per cent) were serving sentences of three months or less, 33,745 (73 per cent) were serving sentences of six months or less, and 38,927 (85.5 per cent) were serving sentences of 12 months or less. This meant that, allowing for remission, three out of four men sent to prison were only there for a few days up to a maximum of four months, or as Stonham put it, "3 out of 4 men are sent to prison solely as a punishment" (by which he meant for too short a time for any training to occur). The figures for women prisoners were even more tilted towards the short sentence: seven out of eight women were sent to prison for a few days to four months. These numbers were enlarged further by the committal to prison of 30,000 persons remanded in custody. For Stonham, this proved that "the concept of retribution still dominates the judicial process, and the belief still persists that the suffering must be adjusted to the sin." Yet society was punishing itself, said Stonham, "in maintaining a vast and expensive prison system when only one man in seven and one woman in twenty has committed a crime deemed to merit confinement in prison for more than eight months." He suggested, therefore, that "we consider ways of ensuring that we do not send to prison, offenders who are at present receiving sentences of 6 months or less." This would reduce the prison population by 25 per cent. For this, there would have to be action on remands in custody, fine defaulters, and debtor prisoners; alternative ways of handling alcoholics; prohibition of prison sentences on summary conviction of first offenders; the suspended sentence; and semi- or weekend detention. Stonham also proposed delegating the function of sentencing to a professional treatment tribunal. In conclusion he declared,

> I am convinced that if we are to evolve a dynamic penal policy there must be, for the majority of offenders, a lessening of the aggressiveness inherent in sentencing, together with an increasing acceptance of the offender as a person

139 I recognize that my conclusion is in harmony with that of Lord Windlesham, *Responses to Crime*, vol. 2: *Penal Policy in the Making* (Oxford, 1993), p. 103.
140 TNA, HO291/547: "Sentencing Policy," 7 May 1965. For Stonham (1903–1971), see *The Times*, 23 Dec. 1971, p. 12. He had long felt that prison treatment was ill adapted to rehabilitation, and that the after-care system for prisoners was pitifully inadequate.

who must, whenever possible, be kept within the community; and when the protection of society requires imprisonment of the criminal, we must use every endeavour to ensure that he is drawn back into the community, not exiled.[141]

Before changes could be made in these directions, however, the department found itself sidetracked by issues of prison security. English prisons were holding a growing number of long-term prisoners, sentenced to fixed sentences of over 14 years' imprisonment or life imprisonment. In 1958, the number of male offenders received with fixed sentences of 14 years and over was two. In 1961, there were 15 (including one of 42 years), in 1964, 16 (including seven of 30 years), and in 1966, 15. At the end of 1958, there were 139 prisoners serving life sentences (including detention "during Her Majesty's Pleasure"); five years later the figure was 329, and by December 1968, it was 598.[142] This was related to a number of factors: changes in the pattern of crime (particularly the growth in violence); the appearance of the complete professional criminal (for whom violence was a tool of the trade); and the impact of the 1965 Act abolishing the death penalty. Long, fixed sentences of 30 years or more were still reserved for such egregious crimes as spying or the Great Train Robbery, but the standard they set led to inflation down the line in the length of prison sentences.[143] Likewise, the Act to abolish the death penalty empowered judges to recommend a *minimum* period which should elapse before a prisoner serving life for murder was released: an unwritten judicial *quid pro quo* for the ending of capital punishment.[144]

In August 1964, Charles Wilson, a mail train robber serving 30 years, was sprung from Birmingham Prison. A year later, another mail train robber, Ronald Biggs escaped from Wandsworth.[145] Each escape attracted exceptional press coverage. In November 1965, the Home Secretary, fearing an armed attempt to rescue certain of the train robbers held in Durham Prison, accepted a military guard of eight armed soldiers for two weeks from the Secretary of State for Defence.[146] The climax to this litany of escapes came in October 1966, when the spy George Blake, serving a sentence of 42 years' imprisonment, the longest fixed-term sentence imposed in England in modern times, escaped from Wormwood Scrubs.[147] When two days later three more prisoners escaped from Wandsworth, Home Secretary Roy Jenkins had no option but to appoint an enquiry into prison escapes and

141 Ibid.
142 Home Office, *People in Prison* (Cmnd. 4214), Nov. 1969, pp. 18–19.
143 *The Times*, 17 Apr. 1964, p. 14; 3 *Weekly L. R.* [1964], 593–609, 28 Aug. 1964; TNA, HO291/929, "Great Train Robbery: Disparity of Sentences": LCJ Parker to Sir Philip Allen, 10 Apr. 1968; Rupert Cross, "Sentencing the Serious Offender," *Listener*, 18 Mar. 1965, p. 401.
144 L. Radzinowicz talking to Hugo Young, "Date of Release—1999," *Sunday Times*, 9 Mar. 1969, p. 13.
145 J. E. Thomas, *The English Prison Officer since 1850: A Study in Conflict* (1972), p. 213; A. Rutherford, *Prisons and the Process of Justice* (1984), pp. 76–8.
146 TNA, PREM 13/366, Home Secretary phone call to Prime Minister, 19 Nov. 1965.
147 TNA, PREM 13/952, note to PM, 22 Oct. 1966.

security, asking Lord Mountbatten to head it.[148] These events have already received considerable attention; suffice it to say here that Mountbatten recommended a four-fold security classification of inmates. Category A prisoners were to be the highest risk for whom escape had to be made impossible. The 250–300 prisoners so categorized would be concentrated in a newly-constructed prison on the Isle of Wight, since, as Mountbatten told a meeting of prison governors, he had been "appalled at the conditions under which men are kept in the maximum-security blocks at Parkhurst, Durham and Leicester."[149] Frank Soskice had first considered the idea of a special prison security wing to house convicted murderers and dangerous criminals at Albany Prison on the Isle of Wight in April 1965.[150] The Home Office was not convinced by the idea of a British Alcatraz, however, so they asked the Advisory Council on the Penal System to consider the type of regime appropriate for category-A prisoners.[151] The task was devolved to a sub-committee of the advisory council, under the chairmanship of Leon Radzinowicz. By widening its terms of reference, the sub-committee was able to reject a policy of concentration, and recommend instead the dispersal of category-A prisoners to four existing prisons.[152] Critics of the policy of dispersing maximum-security prisoners have long argued that it led to the imposition of higher standards of security on more prisoners than Mountbatten's grand design for concentration would have done. This, in turn, is said to have increased prison costs, provoked inmate unrest, reversed the trend towards enabling prison officers to play a more positive part in the rehabilitation of prisoners (which the Prison Officers' Association had called for as recently as November 1963), and snuffed out many constructive educational and employment programmes.[153] The critics have a point, though was this state of affairs so different to that which existed before Mountbatten? In the large local prisons, for example, people sentenced to several years of imprisonment for violence or robbery had been treated in the same way as the tramp who came in for

148 Ibid., note to PM, 24 Oct. 1966; *The Times*, 25 Oct. 1966, pp. 1, 8, and 13. See also Philip Allen, "A Young Home Secretary," in A. Adonis and K. Thomas (eds.), *Roy Jenkins: A Retrospective* (Oxford, 2004), p. 69. Allen was Permanent Undersecretary of State at the Home Office, 1966–72.

149 Home Office, *Report of the Inquiry into Prison Escapes and Security by The Earl Mountbatten of Burma* (Cmnd. 3175), Dec. 1966, reprint 1971; TNA, HO278/17; HO278/18, notes for Mountbatten's meeting with governors, 12 Dec. 1966. See also Thomas, op cit., pp. 214–7; Rutherford, op cit., pp. 78–9.

150 *The Times*, 12 Apr. 1965, p. 5.

151 *The Times*, 22 Feb. 1967, p. 19.

152 Home Office, *The Regime for Long-Term Prisoners in Conditions of Maximum Security*, Report of the Advisory Council on the Penal System (1968). For a colourful account of service on the Radzinowicz sub-committee, see Leo Abse, *Private Member* (1973), pp. 125–34.

153 TNA, HO278/6, memo from Prison Officers' Association to the Commission of Inquiry into Prison Security, Appendix I, "The Role of the Modern Prison Officer." See Alison Liebling, "A 'Liberal Regime within a Secure Perimeter'? Dispersal Prisons and Penal Practice in the Late Twentieth Century," in A. Bottoms and M. Tonry (eds.), *Ideology, Crime and Criminal Justice* (2012), chap. 5.

seven days for being drunk. They were in cells on the same landing, used the same exercise yard, worked side by side in the same workshop, all under conditions of maximum security.

However, there is no question that security became of paramount importance for the prison system from the late 1960s. Home Secretary Jenkins wrote years later, "in general I overreacted to this ephemeral public (or press) hysteria about escapes, and tilted the emphasis of prison regimes too much towards security and away from training and work."[154] Category-A men were transferred to Parkhurst, Wormwood Scrubs, and Wakefield. New maximum-security dispersal prisons were opened at Gartree, Albany, and Long Lartin. In 1969, the White Paper, *People in Prison*, declared that one of the two aims of the prison service was "humane containment," the other being training or rehabilitation. Yet the same document reported that 9,000 prisoners were sleeping two or three in a cell, and predicted a rise in the prison population to 40,000 by 1972 (a number exceeded by July 1970).[155] The White Paper, as Richard Sparks wrote at the time, "sets out the present strategy of the English prison system, and sketches a strategy for that system in the future":

> But *People in Prison* may also mark the end, in England, of the whole peno-logical era which began with the publication of the Gladstone report in 1895. A major objective of English penal policy during that time—indeed, the objective which more than anything else has characterized the penology of the past 75 years—has been to keep as many offenders as possible out of prison. But it is possible, even likely, that this objective is no longer realistic.[156]

His words were prophetic. The prison went from being "the last-resort terminus on a continuum of reformatory treatment," in David Garland's words, to "a mechanism of exclusion and control."[157] In the last fifty years, we have witnessed a remarkable growth in the prison population and a decline in prison conditions. In May 2016, there were 85,335 people in prison.

IX

Returning, finally, to the Royal Commission on the Penal System, the lesson drawn by Leon Radzinowicz from its failure, in which he played a central role, was that a clearly articulated penal strategy is a fool's errand. Only pragmatic, single-issue evaluation makes any sense. In the context of a change of government and of greater political activism in the realm of penal policy, one can see how this

154 Jenkins, *A Life at the Centre* (1991), p. 205; *The Times*, 9 Dec. 1969, letter from Frank Norman. See also Louis Blom-Cooper, *The Penalty of Imprisonment* (1988), The Tanner Lectures, Cambridge, p. 30.
155 Home Office, *People in Prison* (Cmnd. 4214), Nov. 1969, p. 7.
156 Sparks, *Local Prisons: The Crisis in the English Penal System* (1971), p. 89.
157 Garland, "Ideology and Crime," op cit., p. 11.

conclusion might have been reached. The Labour government wanted to burnish its reputation for enlightened thinking about penal matters, and to move forward expeditiously with penal reform. There was no political advantage to waiting four or five years for a royal commission, appointed by the previous administration, to deliver its master-plan. A re-appointed advisory council would have served the new government better, since it could have advised upon proposals in the two White Papers without delay. Indeed, this was the kind of counsel the new Advisory Council on the Penal System was ultimately charged to deliver in the wake of the commission's dissolution.

Yet it is equally possible to argue that the royal commission missed a once-in-a-generation opportunity to plot the direction of penal policy, to frame a philosophy and coherent strategy for the inter-connecting sectors of the criminal justice system.[158] At the Second Reading of the Criminal Justice Bill on 12 December 1966, MPs from both sides of the House were heard bemoaning the dissolution of the Royal Commission on the Penal System. From the left, Sam Silkin stated,

> I deeply regret that it has not been possible to deal with the whole penal system in a far more radical and fundamental way than the Bill is able to do and to survey the whole concepts and purposes, in particular, of the custodial part of our system and to deal radically with them. I must criticize it on the basis of its . . . lacking a comprehensive philosophical base. I believe that that base could have been provided . . . by the Royal Commission, which unfortunately died . . . [I]t seems to me to be a tragedy that we now have to grope forward lacking a clear definition of the concepts and purposes of the penal system that we are operating . . .[159]

From the Right, Quintin Hogg wanted "a new appraisal of the fundamental assumptions of our penal system, a new rational and coherent approach to English criminal law." The Home Secretary had abandoned such an approach, said Hogg,

> when he condoned what I can only describe as the sabotage of the Royal Commission on the Penal System by a minority of its members . . . We shall pay for many years for that ill-considered and rash termination of what was already an overdue inquiry.[160]

158 There have been attempts to revive the idea of a royal commission on crime and punishment "to propound a sound and authoritative penal philosophy for the 21st century." See *The Times*, 10 Apr. 1995, p. 17; ibid., 3 Jun. 1996. See also Sean McConville, "Committees of Inquiry and Penal Policy in England," *Swedish Journal of Political Science*, vol. 1 (1981), pp. 23–7; Sir Louis Blom-Cooper and Sean McConville, *The Case for a Royal Commission on the Penal System* (Hook, Hampshire, 2014).

159 *Hansard*, vol. 738, 12 Dec. 1966, col. 171. Silkin's sentiment was endorsed by royal commission member, T. Iremonger MP, "Britain's Penal System Lacks Clarity of Purpose," *The Times*, 26 Apr. 1967, p. 11.

160 *Hansard*, vol. 738, 12 Dec. 1966, col. 77.

The failure to provide a blue-print for the future meant that when disillusion-ment with the "rehabilitative ideal" set in, as studies of the effectiveness of penal measures led to the belief that "nothing works," and as a new criminology shif-ted the focus from crime to the judicial system's responses to it—there was nothing to fall back on.[161] As Sparks wrote shortly afterwards, "there is little by way of well-articulated philosophy or principle that can guide the reorganization of the criminal justice system in the wake of the abandonment of the 'rehabili-tative ideal.'"[162] The system was defenceless—and here is the cruel irony—against a criminology that took seriously questions of penal philosophy. The texts that made the running in the field of criminal justice in the following decade were not the reports of the Advisory Council on the Penal System, but *Struggle for Justice*, prepared for the American Friends Service Committee, and *Doing Jus-tice* by Andrew Von Hirsch. Issues of theory and questions of social and penal values were at the heart of these studies. For that reason, they were able to shape the contours of penal policy, though unfortunately and unwittingly in the direction of an authoritarian penal policy. "Nothing works" was rebranded as "prison works." The rehabilitative ideal, which had struggled for over 70 years to become rehabilitative practice, was rather easily swept away by the recrudescence of a retributive judicial philosophy of "just deserts."[163]

161 R. L. Martinson, "What Works—Questions and Answers about Prison Reform," *The Public Interest*, vol. 35 (1974), p. 22.
162 Sparks, "Britain," op cit., pp. 90–1.
163 See Epilogue to this book, *infra*.

12

ABOLITION OF THE DEATH PENALTY

> The death penalty . . . has been an obstacle in the way of progress, since it symbolizes the negation of a curative approach to crime prevention. But its removal won't make much of an advance possible, if the price abolitionists are eventually willing to pay is agreement to some supposedly deterrent alternative, such as a gargantuan fixed term of punitive imprisonment to be imposed at judicial discretion on the basis of "deserts".
>
> *Giles Playfair, Spectator, 1 January 1965*

I

The final chapter brings the long history of capital punishment to a close. The anomalies of the Homicide Act 1957 were so indefensible that even the Lord Chief Justice and his judicial colleagues withdrew their support, and were heard favouring abolition over the status quo. The number of executions each year dropped into single figures; while public opinion remained staunchly retentionist. When in 1964, Labour returned to office, after 13 years in Opposition, it seemed only a matter of time before abolition was successful. Even then, the government had to accept *suspending* the death penalty for five years rather than outright *abolition*. The penalty for murder would now be the indeterminate sentence of life imprisonment, which gave the Home Secretary full discretion to determine the prisoner's date of release. This did not sit well with the judges, who tried in the House of Lords, first to allow the trial judge to give a fixed sentence for murder, and secondly, to give courts a power to recommend a minimum period during which the prisoner should not be released. They were successful with the second amendment, and the Commons did not demur. It is clear that judges were uneasy with the executive having the premier role in the sentencing and release of murderers, which the indeterminate life sentence required. Judges still wished to have some say in marking the tariff for murder, some chance to air their denunciatory view of punishment. In 1969, Parliament finally agreed permanently to abolish the death penalty. No longer would the gallows cast its long shadow over the entire penal system. Unfortunately for penal reformers, the final removal of the gallows coincided with a marked turn against the rehabilitative ideal.

At the close of 1960, capital punishment again inserted itself into domestic politics. At this date, there had been 29 convictions for capital murder in England and Wales since 16 May 1957. Twenty-one were convicted of murder in the course of theft, five of murder by shooting, and three of murder of a policeman in the course of his duty. In addition, one offender was sentenced to death under section 6 of the Homicide Act, having been convicted of two murders committed on different occasions. First, the National Campaign for the Abolition of Capital Punishment, which had been in suspended animation since the passing of the Homicide Act, launched a new campaign, the aim of which was to end hanging by 1962. A final attempt was to be made to convince doubters that the death penalty was neither necessary as a deterrent nor morally justified as an act of State, even though the NCACP's executive committee was privy to a disappointing estimate, in the wake of the 1959 general election, which put abolitionist MPs at 299, retentionist MPs at 305, with 26 "doubtful."[1] Secondly, Miss Alice Bacon tabled an official Opposition amendment to the Criminal Justice Bill, then in standing committee, seeking to prevent the sentence of death being passed on convicted murderers under the age of 21.[2] The political correspondent of *The Times* predicted that in relation to Bacon's amendment, Butler "will not be ready to see the Homicide Act eroded piece by piece in this way just as the abolitionist campaign is being renewed and intensified."[3] And, thirdly, Silverman had a motion on the Commons Order Paper, calling the Home Secretary to account for refusing to recommend a reprieve in the cases of Forsyth and Harris, the "towpath" murderers.[4]

Butler's problem, according to the *Times'* correspondent, was two-fold: first, his recommendations for a reprieve, if too plentiful, would strengthen the argument for further liberalization of the law; and second, the fact that he could not reveal the factors in the decisions to reprieve was "liable to create confusion in the public mind on issues that already have a considerable emotional admixture." *The Times* recognized the strain that such decisions imposed upon Butler. Indeed, his own memoirs refer to this "hideous responsibility," each decision requiring him to shut himself away for two days or more, "with only the Office, the Judiciary, and

---

1   *Observer*, 11 Dec. 1960, enclosed in Rolph Papers, 1/4/1, British Library of Political and Economic Science; NCACP, Minutes of EC meeting, 19 Jul. 1960; 15 Nov. 1960, Rolph 1/4/1.
2   TNA, HO291/367, Criminal Justice Bill: The Law of Murder; BN 29/297, Criminal Justice Bill, Notes on Amendments; CAB 128/34, CC (60) 62nd conclusions, 8 Dec. 1960.
3   *The Times*, 12 Dec. 1960, enclosed in Rolph Papers, 1/4/1.
4   Ibid.

occasionally my old friend David Kilmuir, the Lord Chancellor, to counsel me."[5] If, as some believed, Butler was a closet abolitionist, and if he later confessed that by the time he left his post, "I began to see that the system could not go on," he nonetheless sent more murderers to the scaffold than any other post-war Home Secretary—28 executions in all, starting in July 1957 with John Vickers (murder in the course of theft) and ending in April 1962 with James Hanratty (murder by shooting).[6]

In early February 1961, Butler wrote to the Cabinet, "I am under considerable pressure to do something about capital punishment." A number of government supporters wanted him to restore the death penalty for all murders, a proposal that attracted a considerable section of public opinion. Butler then described the views of the two main protagonists, starting with retentionist opinion, as preface to a proposal to leave the law unchanged:

> It is argued that the murder rate has risen, that many of the murders which arouse the strongest feelings (in particular, sex murders) are not capital, and that the present distinction between capital and non-capital murder can no longer be defended. The abolitionists, on the other hand, while agreeing that the present law is anomalous and indefensible, argue, as they have always done, that there is no evidence that the death penalty has a uniquely deterrent effect, and that the only thing to do is to abolish it altogether.
>
> If a change in the present law were to be made, these seem to be the alternatives—to restore the death penalty for all persons convicted of murder, or to abolish it altogether. I do not think that it would be practicable or desirable to try to modify the present categories of murder for which the death penalty is available.[7]

The settlement of 1957, Butler argued, had been designed to retain the death penalty for "those crimes which were thought to be most prejudicial to law and order," and the intention had always been to reassess the Act after five years (which meant March 1962). There were two issues in these circumstances: the more the government implied an intention to review the law, "the more we are bound to give the impression that we shall then change it one way or the other"; and the longer the issue was shelved, "the nearer we get to an election; and we do not want this to become an election issue." Even so, said Butler, *"I am disposed to think the right course is to play the matter long."* At present, he argued, an abolition bill

5   *The Art of the Possible: The Memoirs of Lord Butler* (Harmondsworth, 1973), p. 203. Cf. Churchill's comment to Wilfred Scawen Blunt, as reported by Violet Bonham Carter, "'it had become a nightmare to him to have to exercise his power of life and death in the case of condemned criminals, on an average of one case a fortnight.'" See Bonham Carter, *Winston Churchill: An Intimate Portrait* (New York, 1965), p. 174.
6   Anthony Howard, *RAB: The Life of R. A. Butler* (1987), p. 253.
7   TNA, CAB 129/104, C. (61) 20, 8 Feb. 1961, Capital Punishment: Memo by Home Secretary.

would not commend itself to the majority of government supporters, or to public opinion; and a bill for restoring the death penalty for murders not then capital would be opposed by the Opposition and "by a strong minority of our own people."[8]

Butler also took the opportunity to respond to Ludovic Kennedy's new book, *Ten Rillington Place*, which had exposed the many discrepancies in the case against Timothy Evans, and refreshed the belief that Evans was wrongly convicted of the murder of his child. Kennedy suggested that the real murderer was the serial killer John Christie, himself hanged in 1953. Butler's view was that, in the absence of any new facts, "whether Evans was guilty or not, *it cannot now be established that he was innocent of the murder of the child.*"[9] Accordingly, there could be no question of giving him a free pardon, and no point in having a further enquiry. As *Tribune*, the socialist magazine, succinctly concluded, "acquittal would mean having to admit that an innocent man was hanged, and that would mean admitting that the same thing could happen again."[10] Prior to the Cabinet meeting, in counselling the Prime Minister, Norman Brook made no bones about his view of the Homicide Act:

> There is growing recognition that the Homicide Act 1957 was a mistake. It was inherently unsound to distinguish between capital and non-capital murder—and experience is emphasizing the anomalies to which this gives rise.
>
> On the other hand, if the law is to be changed, there are only two alternatives—to restore the death penalty for all murders or to abolish it altogether. And on this public opinion is pretty evenly divided.[11]

Brook endorsed Butler's decision to play it long, and advised that in any future reference to an experimental period, it would be wiser to speak of "at least five years." A few days later, the Cabinet endorsed Butler's approach to these matters. The only issue to arouse dissent was the Evans case. The Colonial Secretary, Iain Macleod, taking a leaf out of the abolitionists' playbook, observed,

> . . . that it was arguable that Evans would not have been convicted of the murder of his child if the court had had before them evidence now available which suggested that his wife had been murdered by Christie. More generally, it seemed possible that Evans would not have been convicted if the court had been aware of the other murders committed by Christie at 10, Rillington Place.[12]

Butler replied, "even if this were so, there could be no possibility at this date of establishing that Evans was innocent of the murder of the child," and hence, he

8   Ibid., emphasis in the original.
9   Ibid., emphasis in the original. See Kennedy, *Ten Rillington Place* (1961).
10 *Tribune*, 24 Mar. 1961, in Rolph 1/4/1.
11 TNA, PREM 11/3686, Brook to PM, 10 Feb. 1961.
12 TNA, CAB 128/35, CC (61) 6th conclusions, 13 Feb. 1961.

reiterated, there could be no question of giving him a free pardon and no point in holding a fresh enquiry. There was general support in Cabinet for the Home Secretary's view, though it was suggested that in any public statement, "it would be inexpedient to refer to a need to establish Evans' innocence. It would be preferable to refer to the representations on his behalf as directed to proving that he had been wrongfully convicted."[13]

At the meeting of the Commons Standing Committee on the Criminal Justice Bill on 23 February, the clause raising the age limit for capital punishment from 18 to 21 was defeated by a single vote. Conservative MP, William Deedes, said he might have supported the clause had he felt that sentences of 20–25 years might be imposed, but there was no hope of that.[14] In April, at Report Stage, the Opposition again tried to raise the age limit to 21, resulting in a three-hour debate on the new clause. Michael Foot claimed the Home Secretary already drew a distinction between those over and those under 21 in his exercise of the Royal Prerogative, so why not make it the law. Silverman reminded the House that the entire thrust of the Criminal Justice Bill was the further restriction of the penalty of imprisonment for young adult offenders: "How can we reconcile the choice of a limit of 21 as the age below which imprisonment ought not to be imposed . . . with the retention of the gallows and the hangman at the age of 18?" The clause was voted down by 229 to 144, illustrating once more the illogic in penal reform that the death penalty aroused.[15]

Butler also had to fight his corner against his own supporters. There was considerable public disquiet that life imprisonment neither provided public protection nor marked the public opprobrium for the crime. In June 1961, a motion on the Order Paper, signed by more than fifty Conservative MPs, asked the government to introduce legislation "to ensure that a sentence of life imprisonment for this crime [non-capital murder] shall be for a period of not less than twenty-five years . . ." In correspondence with Edward Gardner, MP, which was later made public, Butler was at pains to convince his colleague that many of those convicted of non-capital murder, especially where there were no mitigating features, would likely serve longer than nine years—the period served, in an average case, by a man whose sentence was commuted to life imprisonment before the Homicide Act.[16] The opposition came to a head in mid-October at the 1961 Conservative Party conference. A motion was forced by delegates calling for the return of capital punishment to cover all murders where insanity was not proven (and corporal punishment to cover all crimes of violence). Butler defended the Cabinet's view of capital punishment, claiming

13 For the Commons' debate on the Evans case, see *The Times*, 16 Jun. 1961, p. 21.
14 *Guardian*, 24 Feb. 1961, in Rolph 1/4/1.
15 *Hansard*, vol. 638, 11 Apr. 1961, col. 187 (Foot); Ibid., 12 Apr. 1961, col. 266 (Silverman).
16 TNA, HO 291/1021: Gardner to Butler, 12 Jun. 1961; Butler to Gardner, 4 Jul. 1961; Rolph 1/4/3.

in passing that the annual average of murders had "hardly risen." In a stage-managed operation, a more liberal amendment was moved, which won the day, scotching the reintroduction of capital (and corporal) punishment.[17]

II

Butler's passing reference to the annual average of murders was based upon an analysis of murder that he had directed the Home Office Research Unit to complete in early 1961, when there was considerable disquiet about the incidence of murder. Seventeen murders in the first 23 days of January were the figures given to the public, including murders of children in circumstances of revolting brutality. A draft of HORU's report was available to the Home Office in early August, and Cunningham, the Permanent Undersecretary of State, informed Butler that the report confirmed the department's view that the Homicide Act had not led to an appreciable increase in the number of non-capital murders committed (or in the number of specific kinds of murder, for example of young girls for sexual motives). Nor did the HORU report suggest that the increase in non-capital murders had been greater than that in those types of murder for which the death penalty was retained.[18] In its appropriate red cover, *Murder* was published two weeks after the party conference. The report expressed no opinions; it was content to let the facts in 41 tables of figures speak for themselves. The most telling finding was that there was no change in the proportion of murder of the type that remained capital; the figure was about 14 per cent at either side of the 1957 Act, suggesting that the death penalty made no difference.[19] The press had the first opportunity to pass judgment on the report. In a sober leading article, *The Times* remarked that the report "confirms the picture of murder as a crime which has been remarkably stable in its incidence over the last thirty years when the increase in population is taken into account." Moreover, the distinction made in the Homicide Act was operating roughly as intended, "capital murderers are mainly thieves who kill in pursuit of criminal activities, while non-capital murder is more likely to be committed in the heat of emotion by persons of violent temperament." There was some evidence, however, of a trend towards "an increasing number of murders by persons already criminal." The proportion of convicted murderers with criminal records had increased from 26 per cent in the two years before the Homicide Act, to 36 per cent in the next three years. Previous convictions were primarily for property offences in both time periods.[20]

---

17   Mark Jarvis, *Conservative Governments, Morality and Social Change in Affluent Britain, 1957–64* (Manchester, 2005), pp. 56–7.

18   TNA, HO291/109, Cunningham to Home Secretary, 3 Aug. 1961.

19   *Murder: A Home Office Research Unit Report* (1961).

20   *The Times*, 26 Oct. 1961, enclosed in HO291/109. See also T. Morris and L. Blom-Cooper, *A Calendar of Murder: Criminal Homicide in England since 1957* (1964), p. 281.

A more detailed presentation of the report's findings led *The Times* to conclude, "Quarrels, violent rage, insanity, and suicidal despair accounted for most murders."[21] The *Economist* underlined the fact that "murder is largely a family affair":

> Of the 51 child victims in 1960 (out of a total of 166 murders), nearly three-quarters were murdered by a parent or other relative; of the 71 women, over half were murdered, or suspected of being murdered, by their husbands.

It was because family murders bulked so large that almost one-third of all murderers committed suicide immediately after their crime. If life was to be saved, then, a deterrent penalty was less important "than investigating the kind of mental breakdown that leads to family murders," to quote the report. The *Economist* recognized, however, that retentionists would point out that the total number of murders (including those classified as manslaughter under section 2 of the Homicide Act), had increased since the Act came into force; the annual average in the last three years was 160, compared with 143 before the Act. And that the proportion of men with previous convictions had increased from a quarter to over a third.[22]

In November, the House of Lords discussed the Home Office report on murder. It was very much a Labour Lords affair, and so inclined towards abolition. Indeed, the Earl of Longford regretted the fact that "[w]e do not get the untrammeled thoughts of the opponents of abolition." Lord Stonham, who rose to call attention to the report, sought first to establish the four main facts the report catalogued beyond a reasonable doubt. First, "there is no appreciable increase in murder over the years," to which he added, "It is clear that the Homicide Act has not produced a murder wave. The tragic increase in the general crime rate is not reflected in the murder rate. Murder is a crime apart." Second, the figures of deaths recorded as murders by the police were misleading. No more than 30 per cent of the total were convicted and sentenced for murder, and thus held to be responsible for their actions, and this figure was the same either side of the 1957 Act. (One-third of the suspected murderers committed suicide, another 35 per cent were insane or succeeded with a plea of diminished responsibility). Moreover, less than half of the 30 per cent, or about one in seven of the total, were murders now defined as capital murders, and again this proportion was unchanged either side of the Act. As such, "suicidal despair, insanity and violent rage account for the overwhelming majority of murders." Few of the people composing this majority had previous convictions, and for whom, therefore, "hanging is no deterrent." Third, the contraction in the use of the death penalty had not led to an increase in murder. The proportion of non-capital murders had declined, thereby "reducing the number of what I may call 'unnecessary' murder verdicts." Fourth, "the hopes that the retention of the death penalty for capital murder would prove a deterrent have not been fulfilled." Despite the death penalty, the number of murders in pursuance of theft had sharply increased, especially murder with robbery. The report proved that "it does not matter whether you hang or not, the number of

---

21 *The Times*, 25 Oct. 1961, enclosed in HO291/109.
22 *Economist*, 28 Oct. 1961, enclosed in HO291/109.

capital murders will be the same."[23] Abolitionists liked the argument that the death penalty was not an especially effective deterrent, but it is the weakest of Stonham's four points. The report did not prove anything either one way or the other; no one could say what the murder rate would have been in the case of capital murders had the death penalty not been kept. Yet the point informed Stonham's peroration, "This Report proves that observance of the hanging ritual serves no purpose at all . . . I plead for its abolition . . ."

In the same debate, Lord Kennet hoped the booklet would be a turning point on capital punishment, and Lord Taylor thought the report marked the beginning of the end for the death penalty. Mortimer, the Lord Bishop of Exeter, reminded the House that the Lower House of the Convocation of Canterbury (representing the clergy of the South of England) had recently passed unanimously a resolution advocating the abolition of capital punishment. Mortimer, an erstwhile retentionist, endorsed the proposed reform to abolish capital punishment "for it would be more consistent with the humane instincts of our nation and more congruent with the principles of Christian mercy."[24] Viscount Kilmuir, the Lord Chancellor, wrapped up the debate by underlining the Cabinet's view that there had been no alarming increase in murder generally, and that there were no grounds for the fears that had been expressed. Inevitably, he put a different spin on some of the figures. While accepting that murder was predominantly a family crime in which "a defenceless relative is the victim of an attack by a person who acts in a state of despair or mental stress, and who often takes his own life," yet one-fifth of all offenders were mentally normal persons who killed strangers. Moreover, 70 per cent of the men convicted of capital murder had previous convictions of other offences, and those convicted of capital murder were mainly persons who killed in pursuit of criminal activities. Finally, Kilmuir advanced three points in support of the compromise reached in the Homicide Act: first, that the distinction created by the Act was operating as intended, since those convicted of capital murder were largely those who killed in pursuit of crime; second, murder was a family crime, and the sentence of death was no longer passed for the majority of such murders; and third, the increase in capital murders committed for gain was much less than the increase in crimes of violence against the person during the same period. In short, the Act contained the minimum number of capital offences compatible with the preservation of law and order. The government's view was that "it is too early to consider any amendment of the Act."[25]

The *Murder* report reinvigorated the efforts of the National Campaign Against Capital Punishment. Gerald Gardiner and Victor Gollancz, joint chairmen of the Campaign, wrote to *The Times* to emphasize that since the 1957 Act, there had been both a small increase in the percentage of capital murders, and a small decrease in the percentage of non-capital murders, "which tends to confirm all the existing evidence that capital punishment is not in practice more deterrent than any alternative punishment."[26] In April,

23   *Hansard* (Lords), vol. 235, 9 Nov. 1961, cols. 435–9; col. 450 (Longford).
24   Ibid., col. 461 (Kennet); col. 486 (Taylor); col. 449 (Exeter).
25   Ibid., cols. 487–99. See also *Guardian*, 10 Nov. 1961, in Rolph 1/4/1.
26   *The Times*, 27 Oct. 1961, enclosed in HO291/109.

1961, the campaign had organized a successful meeting at the Albert Hall at which the crowd was asked to regard themselves as "the shock-troops of abolition." From October 1961 to April 1962, the campaign sent to every MP a weekly sheet dealing with some aspect of the case against capital punishment.[27] In March 1962, Silverman presented to the executive committee of the NCACP a report on a recent parliamentary deputation, in which he said Home Secretary Butler realized that the trend was clearly towards abolition, and that this would undoubtedly come, but that he was not satisfied there was strong enough Conservative support in the Commons to justify government legislation. In July 1962, a deputation from the NCACP (which included the Bishop of Exeter and former Home Secretary, Chuter Ede) went to see the Prime Minister and the Home Secretary. Gerald Gardiner argued that the only way forward was abolition, which "would be in line with the general penal policy of the Government and if we entered the Common Market would prepare us to join a group of countries who, with the exception of France, had abolished Capital Punishment." Again, the Home Secretary said that "the trend was undoubtedly towards abolition but that the time for it had not yet quite come."[28]

Clearly the government had no intention of initiating or permitting further legislation on the subject. The NCACP decided to launch a new agitation when a new Parliament was in session, but the organizers took comfort from a recent speech in favour of abolition by Lord Parker, the Lord Chief Justice, not because of doubts about the moral validity of capital punishment, but because of the anomalies and injustices flowing from the provisions of the Homicide Act;[29] and from a change of episcopal opinion: the unanimous vote in favour of abolition by the Bishops of the Convocation of Canterbury in January 1962, and a similar vote with only one dissentient in the Convocation of York. The resolution at the first convocation was moved by Mervyn Stockwood, Bishop of Southwark, an avowed socialist, who attacked the 1957 Act as appropriate for Alice in Wonderland. Shamefully, with the exception of William Temple, the bishops of the Church of England had taken no part in the movement for abolition before mid-century. However, since 1956, a new generation of bishops had been appointed to both provinces; it was their reappraisal of the moral basis of capital punishment that was behind this change of opinion.[30] The "sacred hierarchy" of judges and clerics was no longer the reliable champion of the death penalty it had been for centuries.[31]

The NCACP's leadership believed that *informed* public opinion was being converted to abolition. Chuter Ede went a step further, suggesting that the movement of

2/ MSS. 157/3/CAP/1/4 and 14, Modern Records Centre.
28 NCACP, Minutes of EC meeting, 13 Mar. 1962 in Rolph 1/4/1; TNA, PREM 11/3686, 5 Jul. 1962, summary of deputation meeting.
29 *The Times*, 4 Sep. 1959, p. 8. Lord Birkett, Lord of Appeal in Ordinary, told Rolph on 26 Jan. 1961: "Personally I shall be glad to see the abolition of the death penalty; but I am not sure of the wisdom of abolishing it altogether at this particular moment."
30 *The Times*, 18 Jan. 1962, p. 11. See also G. I. T. Machin, *Churches and Social Issues in Twentieth-Century Britain* (Oxford, 1998), p. 205; Harry Potter, *Hanging in Judgment: Religion and the Death Penalty in England* (1993), p. 193.
31 See Christie Davies, *The Strange Death of Moral Britain* (2004), chap. 3, "The Death of the Death Penalty and the Decline of the Sacred Hierarchies."

opinion among judges and bishops was "symptomatic of the general change in the balance of the public's attitude."[32] Was he right? On 21 March 1960, the *News Chronicle* published the results of a Gallup poll on capital and corporal punishment. The fieldwork had been conducted in early March; the sample was representative of the British adult population aged 16 and over. Interviews were made at 75 separate sampling points, with interviewers operating quotas set for sex by age, class, and occupation of respondents. As such, the poll was probably a pretty accurate reflection of public opinion. What did it uncover? First is that 74 per cent of the population advocated capital punishment for some offence or other. Measured in this way, support for capital punishment was as high as it had ever been since 1940. The drop in the 1955 figure to 50 per cent reflected the effect of the Ruth Ellis hanging, an effect that had rapidly worn off. Yet not more than 70 per cent agreed on any one form of offence deserving this punishment: killing a policeman in an attempt to escape arrest. For murder following a sexual assault, the figure dropped to 62 per cent, and there was a bare majority of 53 per cent in favour of hanging for murder in connection with burglary. Moreover, among those who supported the death penalty, only 36 per cent thought hanging should be the automatic penalty, while 60 per cent thought the courts should be able to substitute a lesser penalty where there were extenuating circumstances such as age, upbringing, and mental condition.[33]

Another finding was that of the three concepts of punishment—deterrence, retribution, or reclaiming the criminal—a majority (54 per cent) gave deterrence as the major reason for their support of capital punishment; while 44 per cent of those advocating the punishment said their main reason was to punish the criminal for what he had done to his victim. Three-quarters believed that the number of murders would increase if hanging were to be completely abolished. Support for capital punishment cut across boundaries of politics, religion, and class. In all sections of the community there was majority support for some measure of capital punishment, if differences in the level of support for it. The higher the educational level, the greater the opposition to capital punishment. Labour voters were more likely to oppose capital punishment than were Conservative voters, but the Labour vote also included a higher proportion of those who would hang without taking circumstances into consideration. In all, the poll found that four main factions existed on the question of capital punishment: a minority who would never resort to it (22 per cent); a minority who would impose it automatically without regard to extenuating circumstances—for all cases of murder (4 per cent), for certain but not all murders (24 per cent); and the majority (50 per cent) who accepted the death penalty but did not believe that it should be an automatic penalty for murder without regard to extenuating circumstances.[34] A Gallup poll taken two years later found that 70 per cent did not want to abolish the death penalty altogether. And among those who did not want to abolish or didn't know what they wanted, 50

32 PREM 11/3686, 5 Jul. 1962, summary of deputation meeting.
33 See TNA, HO291/802.
34 Ibid.

per cent thought the death penalty was not applied to enough cases of murder, and 52 per cent said they would still support the death penalty if it were proved that an innocent man had been wrongly convicted of a murder and hanged.[35] It was a complex picture, for sure, and there were rays of sunlight for the abolitionist lobby, yet the figures did not suggest that public opinion was moving solidly towards abolition.

In July 1962, Henry Brooke took over from Butler at the Home Office. For the next 18 months, the Homicide Act gave rise to little discussion in Parliament—yet Brooke thought the issue would come to the fore again as the general election drew close.[36] For this reason, he asked the department to update the figures in the HORU report, in order to see if any more definite conclusions could be drawn about the working and effects of the Homicide Act. In fact, the inclusion of figures for 1961 and 1962 did not materially alter the picture provided by *Murder*. Since the Act there had been an increase in the total number of offences (murder and diminished responsibility taken together), but not on a scale to give cause for concern. There was no appreciable change in the proportion of capital to non-capital murders.[37] At the Home Secretary's conference on 24 March 1964, it was agreed that no steps would be taken to promote further discussion of the issue before the end of the present Parliament, though the concluding sentence stated, "All the evidence suggested . . . that the Homicide Act would certainly have to be reconsidered in the next Parliament."[38] Indeed, both Brooke and Prime Minister, Sir Alec Douglas-Home, accepted that the Act was "unworkable in its present form and the next Home Secretary, of whatever party, will have to end the death penalty."[39] There were no compelling grounds for thinking that a new Conservative government would do any such thing, but the Labour Party had nailed its colours to the mast. *Crime—A Challenge to Us All* (June 1964), a report of the Labour Party's Study Group, declared that capital punishment should be abolished.[40]

In August 1964, Gwynne Evans and Peter Allen, Preston-based dairy workers, though unemployed at the time, were executed in Strangeways, Manchester, and Walton, Liverpool, respectively, for the murder of John West of Seaton, Cumberland. They were the last two men to hang, though at the time this could not have been known. This is as appropriate a moment as any to encapsulate statistically the impact of the Homicide Act, the provisions of which were in force between 21 March 1957 and 9 November 1965, when the Murder Act 1965 (abolition of death penalty) came into operation. Fifty-nine males were convicted of capital murder (one woman was convicted but reprieved), of whom 29 were executed, 26 reprieved, and

---

35   *Gallup International*, vol. 1, 1937–64 (1962), pp. 638–9.
36   TNA, HO291/109, Home Secretary to Cunningham, 10 Jan. 1964.
37   Ibid., Cunningham to Home Secretary, 17 Mar. 1964.
38   Ibid.
39   TNA, PREM 11/4690, 22 Sept. 1964. Cited in Liz Homans, "Swinging Sixties: The Abolition of Capital Punishment," *History Today*, vol. 58 (2008).
40   *Crime—A Challenge to Us All*, Jun. 1964, p. 40.

four detained during Her Majesty's Pleasure. The 59 offenders were convicted for murder in the course or furtherance of theft (37), murder by shooting (18), and murder of a policeman (4).[41]

III

On 16 October, after 13 years of continuous Conservative government, the Labour Party was elected with a very slender working majority. When the Murder Bill (abolition of death penalty) received its Second Reading on 21 December, Home Secretary Frank Soskice announced that all capital murderers would be reprieved.[42] The NCACP had informed its Friends in April 1964 that abolition would not be an issue in the election, and that it would not be in the campaign's interest to make it one. Once the new Parliament was elected they would press for abolition. Labour MP for Northampton, Reginald Paget, a strong opponent of the execution of Timothy Evans and Derek Bentley, told Victor Gollancz, "Frankly, we have only got to win the Election in order to abolish Capital Punishment."[43]

Labour MPs and Labour peers had always provided the overwhelming bulk of parliamentary support for abolition. In the 1948 division on abolition, 215 of the 245 abolitionists were Labour (16 were Conservative); in February 1956, 240 of the 292 abolitionists were Labour (48 were Conservative). In another measure of Labour support, the percentage of Labour MPs voting for abolition rose from 54.3 per cent in 1948 to 86.6 per cent in February 1956. The percentage of Labour MPs voting for retention of the death penalty fell from 18.7 per cent in 1948 to 1.9 per cent in February 1956; the percentage of Conservative MPs voting for retention rose from 66.5 to 70.6 per cent between the same years.[44] This is striking evidence of party-line voting, even though the decision was always taken on a free vote. Almost one-third of the Labour members elected to the Commons in 1964 had not served in the previous parliament; they were better educated than their predecessors, many were lawyers or educators, and they more concerned about social and ethical issues. Abolitionist sentiment had increased in the Lords especially among the Labour life peers, following the Life Peerages Act 1958. Almost all the senior figures in the Labour Party had by the 1950s been converted to abolition. The new Lord Chancellor was Gerald Gardiner whose abolitionist credentials were unassailable. In the 1950s, he was joint chairman of the NCACP. According to the new Prime Minister, Harold Wilson, Gardiner "had refused a judicial appointment . . . because he could not accept collective responsibility with his prospective

---

41 Evelyn Gibson, "Murder Statistics for England and Wales," *Anglo-American Law Review*, vol. 1 (1972), p. 506.

42 Soskice was the first Home Secretary during whose term of office no one was hanged: R. Pearce, "Soskice, Frank (1902–1979)," *Oxford DNB* (2004).

43 MSS. CAP/1/62, Apr. 1964, Letter to Friends; CAP/1/63, R. T. Paget to Victor Gollancz, 25 Apr. 1964, Modern Records Centre.

44 See Neville Twitchell, "Abolition of the Death Penalty," in Peter Dorey (ed.), *The Labour Governments 1964–1970* (2006), p. 338, Table 18.2.

brother judges for the enforcement of the death penalty."[45] When Wilson wanted to nominate him for a life peerage, Gardiner asked what a Labour government would do about capital punishment. Wilson said it would be left to a free vote, but it was inconceivable that a House of Commons with a Labour majority would not also be a House in favour of abolition. Gardiner aroused a number of striking portrayals: "an 'El Greco' figure, very tall, with hollow eyes and a pale complexion, and a look of injured innocence," according to Jeremy Hutchinson, QC; "a tight-lipped Quaker liberal . . . a real political innocent, uncertain and unsure of himself," according to Dick Crossman.[46] But the part he played as Lord Chancellor in the final push toward abolition is hard to overestimate.

There were other auguries of impending success. John Grigg, NCACP treasurer, wrote to Victor Gollancz the day after the *Daily Telegraph's* leading article, "Exit the Gallows," appeared, which opined that if the government moves to abolish hanging, "all but the most fanatical retentionists will breathe a sigh of relief." For Grigg, this was bound to have considerable influence "with moderate Conservative opinion . . . To my mind, the 'Daily Telegraph' is the most important citadel that has fallen yet—more important than any number of bishops and professors."[47] The campaign sent the leader to all Conservative MPs and 70 "active" peers. As a result, Mark Carlisle, a new Conservative MP, wrote pledging support. A few days later, Grigg informed Gollancz that the Shadow Home Secretary, Edward Boyle, had declined to join the executive committee, believing

> he can do more to influence waverers if he is not too blatantly committed as a crusader for abolition. In fact, he is, of course, a wholehearted abolitionist, and I gather that the Tory leader in the House of Lords, Lord Carrington, is an abolitionist too.

Grigg agreed with Gollancz that "things really do seem to be working out more hopefully—but it's too early to celebrate."[48]

Only three days after the election, the new Home Secretary, Frank Soskice, invited Lord Gardiner to a meeting "to go through the various things you think we might do." He added, "I am very keen on the Whips being put on when we take steps to abolish the death penalty, as I foresee great difficulty if it is left to a

45 Wilson, *The Labour Government 1964–70* (Harmondsworth, 1974), p. 89. See also Muriel Box, *Rebel Advocate: A Biography of Gerald Gardiner* (1983), *passim*; Robert Stevens, *Law and Politics: The House of Lords as a Judicial Body, 1800–1976* (Chapel Hill, 1978), pp. 431–5.

46 Thomas Grant, *Jeremy Hutchinson's Case Histories* (2016), p. 131; Crossman quoted in Box, *Rebel Advocate*, p. 229. See also N. S. Marsh, "Gardiner, Gerald Austin, Baron Gardiner (1900–1990)," Oxford DNB (2004); Sam Silkin's obituary notice, *Guardian*, 10 Jan. 1990, p. 47: "As Lord Chancellor from 1964 to 1970, Gardiner seemed to have reached his natural pinnacle, yet he sometimes seemed oddly ill at ease. In Cabinet he was never a dominating personality and at times seemed lonely and uncomfortable."

47 MSS. CAP/1/100, Grigg to Gollancz, 27 Oct. 1964, Modern Records Centre.

48 MSS. CAP/1/103, Grigg to Gollancz, 30 Oct. 1964.

free vote."[49] Two days later, Edward Short, Labour's Chief Whip, wrote to Soskice to discuss whether a death penalty bill (abolition) should be a government bill with the whips on, or whether it should even be a government bill. "I must be influenced," said Short,

> by the fact that in a matter of such importance if we were to take it on and be defeated, then the consequences would obviously be serious. Moreover, on a matter of conscience, could we really attempt to Whip in?[50]

He thought the solution was a private member's bill with the Whips off. However, Soskice's Permanent Undersecretary, Cunningham, advised that there was a strong case for government legislation, on the grounds that there was "the major issue whether or not the death penalty, as it now exists, is needed for the preservation of law and order." There was also the concept of diminished responsibility, which the Lord Chief Justice was critical of, an issue on which the government would wish to reach its own conclusions and give effect to in a government bill.[51] Yet, the Cabinet decided on 29 October that the issue would be better raised by means of a private member's bill. On 3 November, the government's intention to provide facilities for a free decision on the issue of capital punishment appeared in the Queen's Speech.[52] The day before, Soskice told the Lord President of the Council, Herbert Bowden, and the Chief Whip that he hoped for a speedy expression of opinion by the Commons in favour of abolition, to justify recommending clemency to those convicted of capital murder, three cases of which were in the pipeline—validating Dick Crossman's withering view that "[we] have to abolish capital punishment so that he [Soskice] won't have to execute a bank robber."[53]

In preparation for a Home Affairs Committee meeting on 6 November, Soskice asked his colleagues to agree that a bill should be drafted for handing to a private member providing for the abolition of capital punishment for murder. The penalty should in all cases be imprisonment for life, subject to release on licence at the Home Secretary's discretion. The memorandum then turned to an issue that would perplex Labour's ministers for the next two weeks: the defence of diminished responsibility. No initiative should be taken, Soskice argued, to alter the law, and so long as the law provided that a successful defence of diminished responsibility reduced the offence to manslaughter, "it seems right that the court should have the same discretion as to sentence as in any other case of manslaughter."[54] This was to

---

49 Gerald Gardiner Papers, vol. 7, Pt. A, Add. MS. 56461A, Soskice to Gardiner, 19 Oct. 1964.
50 TNA, HO291/1018, Short to Soskice, 21 Oct. 1964.
51 Ibid., Cunningham minute, 28 Oct. 1964.
52 TNA, CAB 128/39, CC (64), 4th conclusions, 29 Oct. 1964; *Hansard* (Lords), vol. 261, 3 Nov. 1964, col. 12.
53 TNA, HO291/1018, Lord President of the Council meeting, 2 Nov. 1964; Crossman, *The Diaries of a Cabinet Minister* (1976), p. 61. Roy Jenkins thought Soskice an indecisive Home Secretary: *A Life at the Centre* (1991), p. 175.
54 Ibid., H (64) 3, Home Secretary's memo, 4 Nov. 1964.

reject the Report of the Labour Party's Study Group, which proposed that the sentence following a successful defence of diminished responsibility should, as in the case of murder, be automatically one of life imprisonment, in order to avoid short fixed sentences leading to the release of a man before his mental state made it safe to do so. On the day before the Home Affairs Committee meeting, the Lord Chancellor told Soskice that he felt diminished responsibility should be abolished. If it were not, there would be argument as to whether the result of the verdict should be a life sentence, or lie in the discretion of the judge. Gardiner went on to argue that the sole object of the defence was to prevent the execution of those who, though not insane within the M'Naghten rules, were clearly mentally abnormal. If capital punishment was abolished, "the only logical choice would be between abolishing diminished responsibility or applying it to all crimes."[55] The Scottish Secretary, Willie Ross, could not accept that abolition of diminished responsibility was the logical consequence of abolishing the death penalty, or that the only choice was between abolishing the defence and applying it to all crimes. Ross was concerned less with the merits of the proposal, however, "as for the smooth passage of the Bill."[56] The Attorney-General and Solicitor-General agreed with Ross. They added one further ground, namely "that the abolition of the defence of diminished responsibility might well revive defences based on the M'Naghten Rules and . . . the many controversial problems associated with them. This would, in our view, be a very retrograde step."[57] On 18 November, ministers decided that the bill should not deal with diminished responsibility. At this meeting, the Lord Chancellor told his colleagues that he thought the Lord Chief Justice might argue in the Lords that the bill should include a provision which would give power to a judge to direct, in passing the fixed sentence of life imprisonment, that the prisoner should not be released on licence until he had served a term specified in the direction. The Home Secretary would have nothing to do with this minimum sentence idea, even though he would not be bound by any such recommendation.[58]

The murder bill (abolition of death penalty) received its Second Reading on 21 December 1964. There would be a free vote, but the Cabinet agreed that any Ministers who supported retention should preferably abstain from voting rather than vote against the bill. Ministers were told to inform junior ministers and principal private secretaries accordingly, on the understanding that they would not be pressed to act otherwise than in line with their conscience.[59] Sydney Silverman moved the Second Reading by claiming to be "the only private Member whose Private Member's Bill has been accorded the distinction of a mention in the Queen's Speech, and I take this as a good omen." He insisted that the preservation

---

55 Ibid., Lord Chancellor to Soskice, 5 Nov. 1964.
56 Gerald Gardiner Papers, vol. 7, Pt. A, Add. MS. 56461A, folio 66, Ross to Soskice, 16 Nov. 1964.
57 TNA, HO291/1018, Attorney-General, Sir Elwyn Jones, to Home Secretary, 17 Nov. 1964.
58 Ibid., Cunningham minute, 18 Nov. 1964.
59 TNA, CAB 128/39, CC (64) 15th conclusion, 15 Dec. 1964.

or abolition of the death penalty for murder was not the battle on this occasion. "That battle . . . was won in 1957 in the Homicide Act." The question for the Commons was simply "whether we shall abolish or retain not the abolition of the death penalty for murder, but the exceptions to that abolition which were made in the Homicide Act, 1957." The latter had abolished the death penalty for murder "over about five-sixths of the field."[60] It is not easy to encapsulate a seven-hour debate in the Commons, but some things are evident. The first is that the decision at the end of the evening was based on three main grounds. One, the barbarity of hanging and the morbid effect it had on the public mind. Two, the absence of decisive evidence of its deterrent effect. And three, the anomalies in the present distinction between capital and non-capital murder. This was true, moreover, of both sides of the House. Sir Edward Boyle (Conservative) said,

> I am not ashamed of expressing views held on emotional grounds. I do not think that there is anything wrong with idealism nor with the feeling that capital punishment, that institutionalized and legalized killing, is indeed a somewhat sickening and barbarous ritual and that our society would be better without it.

For Dr. Shirley Summerskill (Labour), "this is essentially a moral issue . . . I believe that unnecessary killing is morally wrong and that death authorised by law is morally wrong." She also said she supported the bill "primarily because it has no compromises, no exceptions, no anomalies." In his maiden speech, Mark Carlisle (Conservative) said he supported the bill

> because of my belief in the sanctity of human life. It is because I believe that it is wrong to take human life that I believe that it is equally wrong whether that life is taken by the individual or by the State.

Carlisle also stated, "Only if it can be shown that the death penalty is a unique deterrent . . . would we be justified in retaining it." Boyle added that the Home Office figures "show very clearly that the majority of capital murderers cannot be deterred."[61]

The second thing that marked the debate was the speech of former Home Secretary, Henry Brooke, which abolitionist R. T. Paget described as

> one of the most distinguished and most important speeches which I have ever heard in the many years I have been in the House—a speech which probably was more effective in moving opinion and affecting votes than any speech we have heard.

---

60 *Hansard*, vol. 704, 21 Dec. 1964, cols. 870–2. See also Emrys Hughes, *Sydney Silverman: Rebel in Parliament* (1969), p. 172.

61 Ibid., col. 985 (Boyle); col. 950 (Summerskill); cols. 919–20 (Carlisle); col. 988 (Boyle).

Ten years ago, said Brooke, he had been a firm opponent of the abolition of capital punishment. He had disliked the Homicide Act, believing that the death penalty should be retained for all murders. In 1962, he became Home Secretary, and immediately asked for a report on the working of the 1957 Act. "I must say with such authority as I can command," he told the House, "that it is useless to study further the possibility of improving the law of murder by retaining the distinction between capital and non-capital murder but drawing a different demarcation line." He added,

> At the end of my time at the Home Office, I had become convinced that the case for retaining the death penalty was no longer strong enough to justify retention and that we were coming to the time when we ought to make trial of abolition.

Brooke did not share the view that

> the taking of life by the State is contrary to moral principle . . . [b]ut I believe that retention of the death penalty can be justified only on the ground that it is a unique deterrent. If it is a unique deterrent, there is justification for it. If it is not, I do not think that the case for it can be upheld.

He then cited figures which he believed undermined the case that the death penalty was a unique deterrent. He ended his speech, however, by declaring support for an amendment, to be pressed in Committee, that would make it incumbent on the government after a period of five years to bring forward an affirmative resolution for a continuance of the operation of the Act.[62]

The third thing that reared its head in the debate, and would dominate proceedings in the House of Lords, was the judge's part in fixing the length of detention in cases of life imprisonment. A week before the debate, Home Secretary Soskice informed the Lord Chief Justice that while he did not favour empowering the court, in passing a life sentence for murder, to specify a minimum period for which the murderer should be detained, he would welcome any memorandum which a trial judge might care to send him after imposing a life sentence for murder, which would be consulted when the release of a murderer on licence was under consideration. Soskice so informed the House during the second reading debate.[63] Yet trouble was clearly brewing. Parker, LCJ, appreciated Soskice's willingness to consult the judiciary, but this did not meet the LCJ's view that

> the Judge ought to be able to say something publicly when sentencing the prisoner which in a bad case would have a deterrent effect and incidentally

62 Ibid., cols. 993 (Paget); 905–15 (Brooke).
63 Ibid., cols. 929–30 (Soskice); TNA, HO291/1023, Soskice to Lord Chief Justice Parker, 14 Dec. 1964.

would also help to allay the public anxiety which arises from the oft quoted average period before release.[64]

(He was referring to the common though mistaken idea that Home Secretaries regarded nine years as the right term of imprisonment for a murderer to serve). Hence, Lord Parker reserved the right to seek an amendment to meet this point.

The Second Reading in the Commons, on a free vote, was carried by a resounding 355 votes to 170. Only one Labour MP voted against the bill, while 81 Conservative MPs or just over a quarter (26.6 per cent) voted for it.[65] A Gallup poll for the *Daily Telegraph* in January 1965 illustrated that the Commons and the public were wide apart on the issue. Among the British public, abolitionists were outnumbered by more than three to one. To the question, "Should the death penalty be abolished altogether, or not?", 70 per cent chose "Do not abolish it," 23 per cent chose abolition. As many as 33 per cent of retentionists advanced retribution ("the punishment most fitting the crime") as the main reason for advocating hanging. Seventy per cent of respondents believed that the number of murders would increase if hanging were to be abolished.[66]

Both in standing committee, and on the floor of the House of Commons, almost all amendments to the bill were defeated, including one making the penalty for murder a minimum of 25 years' imprisonment unless the court directed otherwise (Edward Gardner). One amendment succeeded, proposed by Henry Brooke, limiting the period of operation of the bill by providing that it would expire on 30 July 1970 "unless Parliament by affirmative resolution of both Houses otherwise determines." In effect, the death penalty would not be abolished but would be suspended for five years. If the Act expired, in default of resolutions, the provisions of the Homicide Act, with all its anomalies, would automatically come back into operation. That Brooke of all people would want to return to an Act he had only recently lambasted in the Commons beggars belief. Towards the end of June 1965, Silverman wrote to all MPs to say that the new clause, which had carried in committee, "involves such a constitutional absurdity that no democratic Parliament should accept it and I propose on Report to move to delete the Clause from the Bill." In an abrupt about-turn, however, on 1 July, the Cabinet decided that there was no time for a contentious Report Stage. Time could be provided for the bill in the present session only if Silverman made no attempt to disturb Brooke's new clause limiting the duration of the bill to five years. Silverman was so informed.[67]

---

64 HO291/1023, Parker to Soskice, 18 Dec. 1964.
65 See Brian Block and John Hostettler, *Hanging in the Balance* (Winchester, 1997), p. 239; N. Twitchell, op cit., p. 332.
66 *Daily Telegraph*, 22 Jan. 1965, enclosed in TNA, HO307/113.
67 TNA, HO291/1025, Silverman letter, 22 Jun. 1965; CAB 128/39, CC (65) 35th conclusions, 1 Jul. 1965; HO291/1025, minute, 12 Jul. 1965.

IV

Attention switched to the House of Lords. In early February 1965, Victor Gollancz wrote to the Earl of Harewood to tell him that Silverman "has reason to believe that the second reading in the Lords may be moved by the Archbishop of Canterbury." Gerald Gardiner, moreover, would step down from the Woolsack to close for the abolitionist side. "All this being so, there really does seem a good chance that the backwoodsmen will be overawed, and we shall get the Bill through."[68] Michael Ramsey (Canterbury) had reservations about taking charge of the bill, but agreed to pilot it through.[69] It seems Lord Dilhorne (Sir Reginald Manningham-Buller) was horrified by this news. According to historian, Harry Potter, "He thought it monstrous if the impression were given that the enemies of the Bill were less moral than its advocates." Dilhorne wrote to Ramsay begging him not to introduce the bill on Second Reading. In June, Canterbury stepped aside, and the task fell to Baroness Wootton of Abinger. She wrote to the Lord Chancellor: ". . . it is imperative that we should win this time, and would be disastrous if one were to put a foot wrong."[70] For two days in July the Lords debated the bill.

Again, it is difficult to encapsulate a debate of fifty-six speeches. The person who came closest to doing so was the left-winger, Gerald Kaufman, in a piece for the *New Statesman* entitled "The Lords and Hanging." The debate, wrote Kaufman, "was a tedious shambles." Only five of the participants, he declared, gave speeches of "any notable quality": Wootton, Shawcross, Alport, Reay, and the Lord Chancellor. Shawcross began by lamenting the frightening increase in crime, before swerving into "a relentless exegesis of the abolitionist argument." Lord Alport contributed "a devastatingly dour little indictment of the Homicide Act"; and Lord Reay, in a maiden speech on his 28th birthday, "employed an array of statistics to batter a bemused House into punch-drunk admiration."[71] Louis Blom-Cooper thought Reay's speech "remarkable both for its lambent humanity and its fierce insistence on riveting attention to the known facts."[72] Most of the other speeches, said Kaufman, fell into two categories. The abolitionist side inclined to the personal reminiscence, some, such as that of the Earl of Harewood, who had never spoken in the Lords before ("and the prospect of doing so fills me with horror"), "were, through their simplicity, mildly touching." Lord Chorley wished "to testify rather than to argue," depicting the abolitionist campaign as a crusade:

---

68 MSS. CAP/3/118, Gollancz to Earl of Harewood, 5 Feb. 1965, Modern Records Centre.

69 Michael Ramsey had succeeded Geoffrey Fisher as Archbishop of Canterbury in 1961.

70 Potter, *Hanging in Judgment*, op cit., p. 200; Gerald Gardiner Papers, vol. 7, Pt. A, Add. MSS. 56461A, folio 110, Wootton to Gardiner, 23 Jun. 1965.

71 Kaufman, *New Statesman*, 23 Jul. 1965, enclosed in MSS. 157/10/CAP/29, Modern Records Centre.

72 Blom-Cooper, "Murder (Abolition of Death Penalty) Act 1965," *Modern Law Review*, vol. 29 (1966), p. 185.

I think that we crusaders are now getting close to Jordan. We see Jerusalem across the Jordan of your Lordships' House. I hope that tomorrow evening we shall decide to cross the river.

Among the retentionists, the tendency was "to insist that available statistical evidence [concerning the ineffectiveness of hanging as a deterrent to murder] was not to be relied upon," and to rest their case upon "conventional wisdom" or "informed opinion," leading to Lord Francis-Williams's rebuke: "The noble Viscount, Lord Dilhorne, does not accept this evidence. He thinks that hanging is a deterrent. My Lords, what Lord Dilhorne thinks is not evidence."[73] According to Kaufman, the Earl of Kilmuir's speech, which accused "the Bench of Bishops and every other part of this House" of "sneering" at the public, and abolitionists of never "expressing sympathy for the person murdered or his relatives," aroused "strident anger." And it was sad, he wrote, to see the Marquess of Salisbury, "the exponent of a historically important strain of right-wing Conservatism, decline into a rear-guard spokesman for a tattered cause . . ."[74]

Baroness Wootton moved the Second Reading by recognizing that "there are grave moral issues involved in the principle of this Bill," and that she wished to assume that no civilized person "can contemplate taking the life of another human being in cold blood without deep repugnance." An echo of this sentiment was heard two years later when she wrote *In a World I Never Made* of a secular morality, the first principle of which was a profound sense of the value of human life. On this ground alone, she said, "I am irrevocably opposed to capital punishment in any circumstances, even apart from the cogent arguments as to its ineffectiveness . . ." She also insisted that the public (which, it was always claimed, was not ready for abolition) does not realize that the average number of men hanged each year since the Homicide Act was four "and that the chance of any given murderer being hanged is now under 1½ per cent. That, surely, cannot be an effective deterrent." The step to be taken was thus small: "you are being asked to reduce the chance that a murderer will be hanged from a rate of something of the order of 1½ per cent to zero."[75] The Lord Chief Justice declared he was in favour of abolition, not "on any moral ground," but because of the working of the 1957 Act: "I think I can say that all the Judges are quite disgusted at the results produced by the Homicide Act." He also underlined Wootton's point: deterrence is weakened "if out of 190 murderers some 3 are hanged." The Archbishop of Canterbury, "in trying to set out what I believe to be Christian principles in this matter," insisted upon reclamation: "I mean the possibility of the person being alive, repentant and different." Secondly, he believed that the taking of life as a penalty "does not enhance the sacredness of human life." Finally, in an acclaimed closing speech, the

73 *Hansard* (Lords), vol. 268, 19 Jul. 1965, col. 543.
74 Kaufman, op cit.
75 *Hansard* (Lords), vol. 268, 19 Jul. 1965, cols. 456–7, 463; Wootton, *In a World I Never Made* (1967), p. 173.

Lord Chancellor emphasized that the bishops were on the side of abolition, "and yesterday for the first time in English history a Lord Chief Justice spoke in favour of the Second Reading of a Bill to abolish capital punishment . . ."[76] With that, the bill was read a second time, contents 204, not-contents 104. As Kaufman wrote, the size of the majority suggested that "there may be fewer pitfalls for the bill than was at one time anticipated." Kaufman was not entirely sanguine, however, about the Committee Stage of the bill. Throughout the debate, he wrote, "there throbbed an undercurrent of dissatisfaction with the life sentence for murderers proposed in the bill."[77] The Lord Chief Justice was particularly adamant that something be inserted at Committee Stage to make life imprisonment more of a deterrent, "either by allowing the Judges to impose as an alternative to life imprisonment a long sentence, or in some other way provide a substituted deterrent."[78]

Her Majesty's Judges had accepted the abolition of the death penalty, but to compensate for the loss of the penalty, now clearly wished to revert to fixed terms of punitive imprisonment to be imposed on the retributive basis of "deserts." The Home Office had known for months that the Lord Chief Justice intended to press an amendment in the House of Lords giving courts a specific power to recommend a minimum period during which the prisoner should not be released. According to Cunningham, the LCJ had said

> a little illogically—that the purpose of this provision was not to ensure that the prisoner remained in custody for that minimum period but to demonstrate to the public the serious view the court took of particular types of murder.

Cunningham was firmly of the view that the judge was in no position to make a worthwhile recommendation when passing sentence: "What the LCJ is saying, in effect, is that the sentence should be not life, but X years plus whatever addition the Home Secretary thinks right. With great respect, this is nonsense."[79] The department held fast to the principle that a life sentence was an indeterminate sentence. It made no sense to empower judges to impose a minimum penalty because a judge necessarily had the murderer before him for but a short period, whereas the Home Secretary, from the periodic reports he received, got to know what sort of person the murderer was and whether he could safely be released.

First, however, the Lord Chief Justice put forward a different kind of amendment: to abolish a fixed penalty for murder, in other words, to prevent life imprisonment from being the only sentence which could be passed. He argued in committee that in a fixed sentence, which he disliked, there was no room for any

76 Ibid., cols. 480–1, 483 (Parker); Ibid., 20 Jul. 1965, cols 633–4 (Canterbury); col. 710 (Lord Chancellor).
77 Kaufman, op cit.
78 *Hansard* (Lords), vol. 268, 19 Jul. 1965, col. 484.
79 TNA, HO291/1023, Cunningham to Otton, 8 Jan. 1965; Cunningham to Gwynn, 17 Feb. 1965.

matters of mitigation. Judges had the quality of mercy and wished to exercise it. "It is a horrifying experience to have to sentence the perpetrator of a mercy killing . . . to life imprisonment, to cast on him the slur of life imprisonment." In addition, he argued that it would enable the judge "to pass a sentence which marks the seriousness of the crime and signifies the public feeling of revulsion." Finally, Parker said the judges should be trusted to give life imprisonment "where there is some mental element involved, some mental aberration where it may well be quite unsafe to let him out if a number of years were given."[80] He was supported in the committee debate by Lords Denning, Reid, and Dilhorne, all arguing in favour of judicial discretion, and against executive encroachment on the functions of the judiciary. The Lord Chancellor reminded Her Majesty's Judges that they were by the amendment seeking "to take for the Judiciary a power which in murder cases they have never had before."[81] In a revealing closing speech, Parker accepted that 80 or 90 per cent of murders involved some aberration of mind, for which cases judges would always use life imprisonment.

> But the idea in this Amendment is that in the odd case—and such cases may be only 5 per cent of the total—the judge at the time can give a sentence which will act as some deterrent . . . such a sentence would be given only in the case of highly professional organized crime . . .[82]

The amendment was carried by 80 votes to 78.

Lord Stonham, junior minister at the Home Office, and Lord Shepherd, Government Chief Whip in the Lords, advised against attempting to reverse the decision in the Lords, but to sweep away the amendment in the Commons. Stonham further advised the Home Secretary,

> if judges were given the opportunity to impose fixed sentences this would have very grave consequences for our penal policy as a whole and would make it impossible for us to maintain our record of success in the rehabilitation and release of murderers.[83]

Soskice sought to persuade the Cabinet to agree to reverse the House of Lords' decision and restore life imprisonment as the only penalty for murder. He argued, first, that the amendment "contravenes the principle that murder is a crime apart and as such must be marked by a special mandatory sentence which, if it is not death, must be imprisonment for life." The life sentence was not the empty formula which had been suggested; no other sentence carried

---

80 *Hansard* (Lords), vol. 268, 27 Jul. 1965, cols. 1213–4, 1217.
81 Ibid., col. 1239.
82 Ibid., col. 1242.
83 TNA, HO291/1204, Stonham to Soskice, 28 Jul. 1965. Stonham added a postscript to his letter: "We lost because our people did not stay to vote. Even retentionists voted with us after hearing the case."

the lifelong disabilities of a life sentence. Allowing the court to sentence a murderer to imprisonment for a fixed term of years would create inconsistencies in the sentences passed:

> A murderer sentenced to a fixed term would have to be released when the sentence expired regardless of whether or not it would be safe to release him; and he would not be subject to licence or to recall. Alternatively, a court might feel impelled to pass an exemplary sentence of inordinate length, and the S of S might then be compelled to detain the murderer long after he could safely and with justice have been released. In other words, the flexibility provided by a life sentence for training and rehabilitation, as well as the control which the Secretary of State can exercise for the protection of the public, would be lost.[84]

The Home Office expected the supporters of the amendment to argue that it enabled the court to pass a manifestly deterrent sentence, yet a life sentence—potentially the severest sentence of all—must surely be seen as a deterrent sentence. And the department hoped that in time it would become apparent that "the worst type of murderer, who would have been hanged before 1957 (or even under the Act of 1957), will serve substantially longer than the majority of those life prisoners who have already been released."[85]

At this point, the Lord Chief Justice, forgoing the sweets of victory, tabled an alternative amendment, to meet the criticisms raised by his first amendment, under which the only sentence would be life imprisonment, but the trial judge would be allowed to recommend the minimum period which should elapse before the offender was released on licence. Parker stated in Committee that this was akin to a restrictive order which a judge could impose in making a hospital order under the Mental Health Act. Above all, it would preserve the right

> for which I have been striving so long, of the trial judge to mark the gravity of the offence, the revulsion of public feeling, in a proper case by giving what appears to be a very long sentence, which it is hoped will deter others and afford some protection to the police, in particular.[86]

The Home Secretary initially resisted this amendment. The recommendation would tend to be regarded, notably by the prisoner himself, as equivalent to a determinate sentence. The murderer would have a natural expectation of release at the end of the minimum period, and if he had to be told that he could not be released at the time expected, it would lead to disappointment and embitterment,

---

84 Ibid., Memo by Home Secretary, undated.
85 Ibid., Notes on Amendments, Lord Parker, Clause 1.
86 *Hansard* (Lords), vol. 269, 5 Aug. 1965, cols. 418–20.

jeopardizing such progress as he had been making.[87] Yet at Committee Stage, Lord Stonham supported the amendment, as long as it was clear that "the recommended minimum period will not necessarily mean the maximum period." So, too, did Baroness Wootton and the Lord Chancellor, the latter satisfied by the fact that the mandatory sentence of life imprisonment, which offered the greatest degree of flexibility, remained intact.[88] In fact, the power to recommend a minimum period was used sparingly by judges, and then only for the "worst" murders. Yet in the 1966 Moors Murders case, Mr. Justice Atkinson made no minimum recommendation, despite describing the accused, Ian Brady and Myra Hindley, as "two sadistic killers of the utmost depravity." From November 1965 to the end of 1972, there were only 45 recommendations, or one in every 12 convictions for murder, most of which ranged in length from 15 to 30 years' detention. The recommendation power was clearly used as an instrument of the denunciatory theory of punishment. As a Bedford College report on homicide later stated,

> The judges have apparently construed the provision as a judicial cudgel against heinous murderers rather than as a shield against the Executive's timidity in declining to release the less morally blameworthy killers at an early date . . . Since no mercy has been tangibly reflected in the judiciary's hard won power to involve itself in penal practice, the Lord Chief Justice's protestations that judges can be merciful and wish to demonstrate it look very hollow.[89]

It remains only to endorse the conclusion of Louis Blom-Cooper and Terence Morris that the view which surfaced in the mid-1990s, that a deal was struck in 1965 between abolitionists and retentionists, by which the "price" of abolition was the retention of the mandatory life sentence for murder, was a canard. On the contrary, there was considerable support in the Lords to get rid of the mandatory sentence, for judges to have power to pass discretionary life sentences. The Home Secretary and the Lord Chancellor held the fort against all such attempts, much preferring the flexibility given by the mandatory life sentence. The discussion at the time had nothing to do with a deal or *quid pro quo*; it was all about whether the judiciary or the executive should have the predominant role in the sentencing of murderers.[90]

---

87 TNA, HO291/1204, Notes on Amendments, Lord Parker, Clause 1.

88 Ibid., col. 421 (Stonham). See also Frank Dawtry, "The Abolition of the Death Penalty in Britain," *British Journal of Criminology*, vol. 6 (1966), pp. 185–6.

89 MSS. 16B/5/2/9, "Criminal Homicide in England and Wales, 1957–1968, An Interim Report of the Homicide Research Project, Legal Research Unit, Sociology Department, Bedford College, University of London, Oct. 1969, p. 68, Modern Records Centre, University of Warwick. See also L. Blom-Cooper, "The Penalty for Murder," *British Journal of Criminology*, vol. 13 (1973), p. 188.

90 Louis Blom-Cooper and Terence Morris, "The Penalty for Murder: A Myth Exploded," *Crim. L. R.* [1996], pp. 707–16; idem., *With Malice Aforethought: A Study of the Crime and Punishment for Homicide* (Oxford, 2004), chaps. 6 and 7.

The bill was given a Third Reading in the House of Lords on 26 October by 169 votes to 75, the Lord Chancellor stating, "I am quite sure that, when the traps have been removed from the prisons, not only shall we be as safe a country but we shall be a much saner and healthier one."[91] He wrote to Victor Gollancz three days later,

> I know you will be as pleased as I was about the Death Penalty Bill. I do not like the five-year clause but capital punishment cannot in fact be restored without discussion.
>
> No one has done more than you have to achieve this result and all abolitionists must be greatly in your debt.[92]

The Commons accepted the Lords' amendments, and on 9 November, the Murder Act 1965 (abolition of death penalty) came into effect, suspending rather than abolishing the death penalty. Barbara Wootton later declared, "surely the most important change in our penal system in the present century."[93] Towards the end of November, C. H. Rolph wrote to Gollancz to suggest a small dinner party for Sydney Silverman:

> It all seems to have gone off rather like a damp squib, probably because of the inordinate delays in the Commons. Surely we ought to celebrate just a bit, and felicitate each other as we toast Sydney?[94]

V

In a macabre juxtaposition, the parliamentary stages of the abolition bill coincided with the final stages of the case of Timothy John Evans, who was hanged for the murder of his infant daughter in 1950. In early February 1965, Ian Gilmour asked Home Secretary Soskice to make an official declaration of Evans' innocence and make arrangements for the transfer of his body to his mother's keeping. The Home Secretary declined to issue a declaration, or appoint a new inquiry (though he had called for one when in Opposition in 1961), but he said he would look sympathetically upon a request to authorize the removal of the remains for private burial, if the abolition bill became law.[95] In mid-May, Lord Byers pressed for a new enquiry. Stonham replied to the effect that the Home Secretary believed "that it would be impossible to reach any definite conclusion on whether or not Evans

---

91   *Hansard* (Lords), vol. 269, 26 Oct. 1965, col. 553.
92   MSS. CAP/1/131, Gardiner to Gollancz, 29 Oct. 1965, Modern Records Centre.
93   Wootton, *Crime and Penal Policy* (1978), p. 138.
94   MSS. CAP/1/154, C. R. Hewitt (C. H. Rolph) to Gollancz, 24 Nov. 1965. Silverman did not live to see the final abolition of the death penalty: *The Times*, 10 Feb. 1968, p. 10, obituary.
95   *Hansard*, vol. 705, 4 Feb. 1965, cols. 125–7.

murdered his child," after a lapse of 16 years.[96] At the end of May, however, the Prime Minister's view was made known to Soskice:

> His view is that the Home Secretary should not rule out a new investigation of the case of Timothy John Evans provided that new evidence can be brought forward or reasonable grounds be shown for doubting the validity of earlier enquiries.

Soskice replied at length to Harold Wilson insisting that any further enquiry could not establish or prove that Evans was innocent. He added,

> What I think should be said is that the jury which tried Evans, had they known the truth about Christie's murders, would probably, whatever other evidence there was against Evans, have acquitted him, upon the ground that they could not banish all reasonable doubts from their minds. It by no means follows that Evans was not guilty in fact.

Wilson's marginal note read, "Not happy, but hold over."[97] In August, following an all-party deputation of MPs, Soskice asked Mr. Justice Brabin to conduct an independent enquiry in public into the case. On 9 November 1965, Evans' body was exhumed and reburied in St. Patrick's cemetery in Leytonstone.[98]

The Brabin report appeared in October 1966.[99] It concluded, in effect, that Evans may have gone to the gallows for the wrong murder. The report said that Evans probably did not murder his baby daughter, the charge on which he was convicted, but that he probably murdered his wife. Those who had long doubted Evans's guilt were disappointed by these speculative conclusions. Yet a few days later, the new Home Secretary, Roy Jenkins, told the Commons that since "it is more probable than not that Evans did not kill his daughter, for whose murder he was tried, convicted and executed," he had recommended to Her Majesty that she grant a free pardon. The free pardon had been signed that morning. Jenkins concluded by saying, "This case has no precedent and will, I hope and believe, have no successor."[100] The long sad story of Timothy Evans was ended by what Frank Dawtry described as "one official line of cold print in the table covering the exercise of the prerogative of mercy" in the *Criminal Statistics* for 1966: "One of the free pardons was in respect of a male person previously executed following conviction of murder."[101]

---

96 *Hansard* (Lords), vol. 266, 18 May 1965, cols. 359–63.
97 TNA, PREM 13/790: D. J. Mitchell to Otton, 31 May 1965; Soskice to PM, 19 Jul. 1965.
98 *The Times*, 20 Aug. 1965; ibid., 27 Aug. 1965, p. 8; Block and Hostettler, *Hanging in the Balance*, op cit., p. 254.
99 *The Case of Timothy John Evans* (Cmnd. 3101), 12 Oct. 1966; *The Times*, 13 Oct. 1966.
100 *Hansard*, 18 Oct. 1966, col. 38.
101 Dawtry, "Criminal Statistics 1966," *Justice of the Peace*, 2 Sept. 1967, enclosed in HO291/1027.

In the immediate aftermath of the abolition of the death penalty, two notorious murder cases led to calls for the reintroduction of the death penalty. The first case also spoke to the gulf that existed between Labour politicians and Labour voters on the issue of hanging. In October 1965, while the abolition bill was passing through Parliament, the Moors murders came to light, for which Ian Brady and Myra Hindley were ultimately convicted. The bodies of two children had been found buried on Saddleworth Moor in Yorkshire. In nearby Nelson, 6,000 signatures were collected demanding the return of the death penalty. Patrick Downey, uncle of one of the murdered children, decided to challenge the premier abolitionist, Sydney Silverman, in his Nelson and Colne seat in the March 1966 general election, standing as an Independent Labour candidate. His platform was to bring back hanging. Silverman was unperturbed, and focused on what he considered to be the key election issue, whether the Labour government should be returned to power. In the end, Silverman increased his majority. Even so, the pro-hanging candidate attracted a remarkable 13 per cent of the vote, or 5,000 of the 37,000 total.[102] In August 1966, three police officers were murdered in a shoot-out with robbers in Shepherd's Bush, London. Sections of the press called for the death penalty to be restored for murder of a policeman, demands that were resisted by the new Home Secretary, Roy Jenkins. Shortly after these murders, Conservative MP Duncan Sandys formed the Society for the Restoration of Capital Punishment, and proposed a national "bring-back-the-rope" campaign. In November, 1966, Sandys sought leave under the ten-minute rule to restore the death penalty for the murder of police or prison officers. Sandys told the House that in the two years since abolition, "as many policemen have been murdered as during the whole of the previous 13 years." Leave was refused by 292 votes to 170.[103]

Clause 4 of the 1965 act provided that the act should remain in force for five years, or until July 1970, and should continue only by affirmative resolution of both Houses. In the lead up to this event, in February 1969, the National Campaign for Abolition of Capital Punishment was reactivated; in March, the London *Evening Standard*'s survey of attitudes to capital punishment again showed that public opinion obstinately refused to accept the lead of the politicians; and in June, Duncan Sandys tried to introduce a bill to ensure that the 1965 Act could be prolonged only by another Act rather than by affirmative resolution.[104] Between September and November 1969, the criminologists weighed in. Professor Leon Radzinowicz of the Cambridge Institute of Criminology, and a member of the

---

102 See E. Hughes, *Sydney Silverman*, op cit., chap. 19; N. Twitchell, op cit., pp. 342–3; Andrew Hammel, *Ending the Death Penalty: The European Experience in Global Perspective* (Basingstoke, 2010), p. 111.

103 See *Hansard*, vol. 736, 23 Nov. 1966, col. 1409; Twitchell, op cit., p. 334; Hammel, op cit., p. 112; Trevor Fisk, "A Student's View," in L. Blom-Cooper (ed.), *The Hanging Question* (1969), p. 77.

104 T. Fisk, op cit; Hugh Klare, "Capital Punishment: Building on Sandys," *New Statesman*, 19 Jun. 1969, p. 958; Ronald Butt, "The Demand for Hanging," *The Times*, 11 Dec. 1969, p. 10; *The Times*, 15 Dec. 1969, p. 1; Gavin Drewry, "Parliament and Hanging: Further Episodes in an Undying Saga," *Parliamentary Affairs*, vol. 27 (1974), pp. 253.

Royal Commission on Capital Punishment, 1949 to 1953, spoke to Lewis Chester of the *Sunday Times* on the theme of "Hanging: Has Abolition Worked?" Radzinowicz did not shy away from the evidence: "Taking the four years each side of [1965] one gets the following total figures for 'capital' murder: prior to abolition— 71; post abolition—161." Murders that would in theory have merited capital punishment had more than doubled. Radzinowicz argued, however, that the increase may be accounted for by factors other than abolition, for example, "a sizeable proportion of the rise in 'capital' murders is simply a reflection of the expanding lawlessness of our society." He also called in aid the royal commission which had concluded that "the deterrence aspect of capital punishment was liable to be grossly exaggerated," and that the figures did not improve when capital punishment was reintroduced after a period of abolition. In conclusion, the country's leading criminologist stated, "It is no use deluding ourselves that hanging a dozen or so offenders a year would have any impact on the murder figures, much less on the pattern of crime."[105]

In early November 1969, the long-awaited Report of the Home Office Statistical Division, *Murder, 1957 to 1968,* was published. The authors, Evelyn Gibson and Stanley Klein, believed that the most striking conclusion to emerge was

> the relative constancy of the murder pattern; it remains mainly a personal or family crime, committed for emotional reasons. Over one-third of murders are done by persons in an abnormal mental state, most of whom commit suicide; and the remainder are largely due to rage, quarrels, jealousy or revenge.[106]

The single most cited statistic in the report, however, was the 130 per cent increase in "capital" murders, of which the main types were murder by shooting and murder in the course of theft. There were 154 in the four years of suspension (1965–8), an average of 38; and 67 in the four preceding years (1961–4), an average of 17. Against this had to be set the difficulty of defining "capital" murder since 1965. As the Home Office researchers said, "The figures since 1965 are inevitably over-estimated since offenders are classified as capital on the basis of circumstances on which doubt might have been thrown in the course of trial if capital murder had been an issue."[107] Also, the increase was a function largely of the rise in murders by shooting followed by suicide. *The Times* concluded that these conclusions were "too tentative to justify the restoration of capital punishment," though it declared the right course was "to extend the period of experimental suspension for a further term."[108]

105 Radzinowicz, "Hanging: Has Abolition Worked?" *Sunday Times,* 21 Sep. 1969, p. 13. See also "Capital Punishment: View of Criminologists," *The Times,* 15 Dec. 1969, p. 9.

106 *Murder 1957 to 1968,* A Home Office statistical division report on murder in England and Wales, by Evelyn Gibson and S. Klein (1969), paras. 11 and 72.

107 Ibid., paras. 19–21. See also Robert Jackson, "Hanging as a Deterrent: the Missing Statistics," *The Times,* 10 Dec. 1969, p. 11.

108 *The Times,* 6 Nov. 1969, p. 11.

As for the timing of the affirmative resolutions, the Prime Minister wanted the business out of the way before the next general election, while Home Secretary, Jim Callaghan wanted to wait for the publication of the Home Office Statistical Division's report. The Lord Chancellor, unhappy about putting off a vote on the affirmative resolutions until after Christmas, wrote to Callaghan,

> I am sure it is a nettle which ought to be grasped and disposed of. I do not want to be too optimistic but I do not really know what we are going to argue about. For the first time in our history there appears to be no national newspaper which is in favour of capital punishment.

Callaghan replied,

> You ask what we are going to argue about, but you do not mention public opinion which we must recognize is very largely against us . . . I have no doubt at all that the right course is to make the Act permanent, but we must not overlook the fact that the most recent polls show that something like 80% of the population are in favour of maintaining the death penalty in some form.

The Cabinet finally decided to proceed with the resolutions in both Houses in December 1969.[109] The Lord Chancellor immediately feared defeat on the resolution in the Lords, and the return of the 1957 Homicide Act.[110] So rattled was he, according to Leo Abse, that he wanted to present "a rationalized compromising Hanging Bill." Abse was horrified, knowing that a third way between an end to hanging and the reactivation of the 1957 Act would be fatal to the abolitionist cause. "Yet here was a Lord Chancellor," wrote Abse, "who for years had eschewed all judicial advancement because of his refusal to sentence any man to death, apparently naively offering signposts to that third way." Fortunately, Abse persuaded the Lord Chancellor to bury the idea of a contingency bill.[111] When the Opposition was told of the government's intention to make the 1965 Act permanent before the five-year period came to an end in July 1970—thus having the effect of truncating the experiment—it tabled a censure motion. On 15 December, Quintin Hogg asked the House to postpone any decision on the 1965 Act until after publication of the murder figures for 1969. In his closing speech, the Home

---

109 TNA, LCO2/8109, Gardiner to Callaghan, 19 Nov; Callaghan to Gardiner, 19 Nov. 1969. According to K. O. Morgan, Callaghan had declared that "he would resign rather than order any further executions." *Callaghan A Life* (1997), p. 297.

110 A letter was drafted to the Prime Minister in which Gardiner said: "We could be fairly confident that on a straight issue the Lords would probably be all right, but recent developments now show that the straight issue is being successfully confused by the Tories with argument over the five year experimental period. . . the Tory leadership, either consciously or unconsciously are playing party politics in seeking to defer the final decision until after the general election." See LCO2/8109.

111 Abse, *Private Member* (1973), pp. 109–13.

Secretary took the wind out of Conservative sails by promising to put before the House the first crude 1969 figures. The motion was defeated, 303 to 241.[112]

The next day the House debated the substantive issue for seven and a half hours. In a packed House, on a free vote, MPs approved the permanent abolition of the death penalty for murder. The voting was 343 for and 185 against, a thumping majority of 158. All three party leaders were in the abolitionist lobby, along with almost all the frontbenches of both main parties. Labour MPs voted by 278 to 2 for the motion.[113] On the following day, attention turned to the House of Lords.[114] According to Harold Wilson, there was "a packed attendance of peers, public and many MPs from the Commons."[115] Two amendments were offered, both to delay a decision: in one case (Lord Brooke) until the middle of the next year (until after publication of the 1969 statistics); in the other case (Viscount Dilhorne) until 31 July 1973. Only Dilhorne's amendment was put to the vote, being defeated by 220 to 174. The abolitionist lobby of 220 included 100 Labour peers, 41 Conservatives, 39 crossbenchers (with no official party loyalty), 22 Liberals, the Archbishop of Canterbury, and 18 of the 19 bishops present. At the end of two days of debate, and following a strong closing speech from the Lord Chancellor, without division the Lords agreed the motion permanently abolishing capital punishment.[116]

VI

It is a remarkable feature of the English penal landscape that not until 1969 did Parliament rid the land of the shadow of the gallows. If by then, the death penalty was a hollow symbol, preserved by hollow men, it had displayed a staying power that is hard to comprehend.[117] What should have been an opening triumph of the rehabilitative movement, removing the penalty most anathema to a policy of training for citizenship, was instead a final act of a rehabilitative movement that was

112 *Hansard*, vol. 793, 15 Dec. 1969, col. 939.

113 *Hansard*, vol. 793, 16 Dec. 1969, cols. 1148–294; *The Times*, 17 Dec. 1969, p. 1.

114 Mrs. Undine Barker, secretary to the Liberal peers, was the unofficial organizer of the abolitionist vote in the Lords. The *Guardian*, 19 Dec. 1969, declared, "Memo to the instant historians already working at the definitive study of hanging and its abolition: keep a chapter for Undine Barker. . ."

115 Wilson, *The Labour Government*, op cit., p. 925.

116 *Hansard* (Lords), vol. 306, 17 Dec. 1969, cols. 1107–21; *The Times*, 19 Dec. 1969, p. 1. Abolition was confirmed in Northern Ireland in 1973, where the last execution was in 1961. Attempts to re-introduce capital punishment—13 times in all—for certain categories of murder, such as terrorism, were all defeated. The Crime and Public Order Act 1998 abolished capital punishment for piracy with violence (last execution, 1860) and treason (last execution, 1946). In 1999, the UK government ratified Protocols 6 and 13 of the European Convention of Human Rights and the Second Optional Protocol to the International Convenant on Civil and Political Rights, which committed the government never to reintroduce the death penalty for any offences.

117 With the exception of France (1981), Spain (1978), and Greece (1975), every other Western European country had abolished the death penalty by 1950, some (Norway, Sweden, Denmark) much earlier in the twentieth century, and some (Portugal, the Netherlands) even in the nineteenth century.

beginning to lose momentum. It is cruelly ironic that at the very moment the icon of retribution was abandoned, penal thought and ultimately penal practice began to run in re-bored retributive grooves. The staying power that is hard to comprehend can only be explained by the fact that Parliament had the final say on the question of abolition. Parliament typically played a subsidiary role in directing the course of penal policy. It was responsible for laying down a legislative framework for administrative and judicial activity, but the development of penal policy and practice was firmly under the direction of the mandarins, and in the discretion of the judiciary. For the most part, also, there was political consensus concerning the main lines of penal policy, and debate tended to be dominated by those who had credentials in legal and penal reform circles. When it came to capital punishment, Parliament was in the driving seat, and consensus was absent. The death penalty entered the political lists. It was an emblem of the ideological differences separating the two main political parties in the twentieth century. It was a question that embodied moral as well as legal considerations, and called forth strong emotions. Those with little or no legal background felt qualified to speak on the issue. The retort that capital punishment was above politics, that governments allowed the individual conscience free reign by way of the free vote, is sophistry. The free vote was employed less as a concession to individual conscience, and more to avoid the defeat that a government motion on a controversial issue might entail. Even then, the ploy could backfire, governments of both political stripes showing themselves incapable of correctly predicting the outcome of free votes. The death penalty was a highly charged political matter. It went to the very heart of the political divide. It was for that reason that it was never likely that a Conservative government would have assumed the responsibility for abolishing the death penalty. This was not something they wanted to their political credit, not something that belonged on their political resume. Abolition succeeded because the Labour government was willing to defy public opinion, and do what it had pledged to do since its inception as a political party, which was to remove what it considered to be the major blot on the penal landscape. Alas, its influence was removed at the very moment that retributivism found a new lease on life.

EPILOGUE

The retributive turn

I

If the 1895 Report of the Gladstone Committee on Prisons marked a watershed in the way prisoners were regarded, historians and criminologists have claimed too much for the report, and for the changes in penal policy which followed. Talk of a transition to a "modern penal complex" is overblown rhetoric. The "positivist" manifesto was by no means the dominant framework of thought in the late Victorian and Edwardian debate on prisons. Penal culture was influenced more by a humanitarian-cum-Christian sensibility and the classic maxims of moral responsibility and just proportion between crime and punishment. As a result, these decades set an early seal on how far the rehabilitative paradigm would be taken by judges, ministers, and mandarins. The years up to 1920, and the two decades that followed, were characterized less by the arrival of individualized, indeterminate measures of treatment, the trademark of the positivist school, than by a remarkable abatement in the use of imprisonment by judges and magistrates.

The sentencing stage was at least as important to what happened to an offender as what went on behind prison walls. Judges and magistrates, moreover, often acted independently of those who inaugurated shifts in penal administration. The judiciary were not known for advocating the amelioration of punishment; they rarely subscribed to the penology that reformers and criminologists urged on them. Yet it was precisely because of their suspicion of these new ideas that the judiciary insisted upon adherence to traditional legal principles of a proportion between crime and punishment. A related feature of this judicial activism was the unwillingness to accept those parts of the rehabilitative programme that required predictive restraint. In principle, the introduction of preventive detention in 1908 allowed judges an escape from notions of retributive justice. Yet the new measure neither erased such notions nor persuaded judges to rush headlong towards preventive sentences.

Executive appeals to the judiciary to use preventive detention for persistent criminals fell on deaf ears. The result was a steady and striking decline in the number
and length of prison sentences between 1880 and 1940.

In the favourable context of a declining prison population between the wars, the
prison commissioners sought to improve the conditions of life for inmates. Yet
when tested against the reactions of prisoners themselves, the ameliorations left
much to be desired. So, too, the commissioners' aspirations to implement new
schemes of classification of prisons and prisoners were defeated by the volume of
offenders still committed for short terms to the local prisons. Likewise, the attempt
to improve prison employment ran into the sand. The continued high proportion
of prisoners working on sewing mailbags gave the lie to claims of betterment in
prison labour. Improvements in the psychological treatment of prisoners were
minimal. Norwood East, the medical prison commissioner, resisted calls to see
most prisoners as in need of psychological remedy, yet even for the small percentage who in his view required treatment, little was available within the prisons.
After-care of prisoners remained the disgrace of the penal system, unable to pivot
from a patchwork system of voluntary agencies to a professional service that could
assist prisoners to find work and housing on discharge.

In the late thirties, Sir Samuel Hoare put the recommendations of the committees
of enquiry into preventive detention, corporal punishment, and allied subjects into an
omnibus measure. The Criminal Justice Bill was a thoroughly departmental project,
strictly pragmatic, devoid of any wider vision. And, anyway, the Second World War
put paid to the bill. In the immediate post-war years, concerns about the crime rate
fostered a more punitive approach to penal matters. This became evident when the
amendment to the 1948 Criminal Justice Act, which came closest to wrecking the
entire measure was the one to abolish the death penalty. For long, the Labour Party
had promised to get rid of the hanging judge. A majority Labour government would
surely deliver on the promise. This was to underestimate the strength of the retributive
counter-attack launched against the attempt to dispense with capital punishment,
particularly from the ranks of the judiciary, the bishops, and Conservative members of
both Houses of Parliament. In the face of this opposition, the Labour government
withdrew the clause to abolish the death penalty, and fell back on the appointment of
the Royal Commission on Capital Punishment.

The royal commission concluded, in effect, that there were no ways of limiting
the liability to capital punishment short of outright abolition. Yet the judges and
bishops made it clear in their evidence that abolition would be firmly resisted.
Abolitionist sentiment was revived in the mid-fifties less by the royal commission's
report and more by three controversial executions. The shift in public opinion
inspired abolitionists in Parliament to try again in 1956 to get rid of the death
penalty. As in 1948, the government underestimated the strength of abolitionist
feeling in the Commons. This impelled the Conservative government to scramble
to regain the political initiative by introducing a bill on degrees of murder, limiting
capital punishment to the most "deterrable" crimes, an approach, which the royal
commission had declared unworkable. The Homicide Act 1957 was a terribly

flawed law, and would in the long run only strengthen the abolitionist cause. In all, the dispute over the death penalty was at its twentieth-century height between 1956 and 1964, in the wake of the royal commission's report. The dispute served to revive retributive sentiment, propel public opinion in punitive directions, and hinder the creation of a uniformly rehabilitative penal policy. The death penalty was a powerful symbol of an enduring retributive penal consciousness.

In the 1950s, penal policy and practice was in the grip of the twin pincers of a growing crime rate and prison overcrowding. The prison population rose, in part because of the increase in the number of convictions for indictable offences, and in part because of longer sentences imposed by the higher courts. This led to severe overcrowding, and to a decade-long critique of the prison system. The Home Secretary turned to his advisory council to combat the prison crisis, and the council came up with a small number of alternatives to short-terms of imprisonment, which had little or no impact on the problem of overcrowding. Even so, Home Secretary, R. A. Butler was determined to make an impact on penal practice, and his 1959 White Paper promised an ambitious prison building program, renewed faith in prison treatment and training, and research into the effectiveness of the different training regimes.

The sixties are considered the decade in which the rehabilitative ideal reached its zenith. For sure, the 1961 Criminal Justice Act created a partially indeterminate sentence of custodial training for young adults aged between 17 and 21, with the prison commissioners not the court deciding how long an offender remained in custody. At first, the judiciary accepted this restriction on their sentencing discretion, though they later chafed under the restriction. At the same time, the Court of Criminal Appeal laid down its own rules for the use of corrective training and preventive detention, the two measures in the 1948 Act to deal with persistent offenders. Their rules led to fewer such sentences, and ultimately to the advisory council's recommendation to abandon both measures. It was the end of an ignominious, 60-year attempt by the prison executive to solve the recidivist problem. In the mid-sixties, the long-awaited Royal Commission on the Penal System was appointed, the first attempt to survey the penal system *in toto* since Gladstone in 1895. It turned into a lamentable failure. There were a number of reasons for the commission's failure, but foremost was the fact that the new Labour government wished to implement penal reform via specific measures more rapidly than the royal commission could accept. It was the final nail in the coffin of the rehabilitative ideal. The royal commission had a rare opportunity to reformulate the guiding principles of sentencing and punishment, to frame a penal structure in which each penalty would contribute to reducing crime, to offer new alternatives to imprisonment, and to recommend restraints on sentencing courts in their use of the short prison sentence. Whether this would have served to repulse the retributive turn after 1970, however, is anyone's guess.

The sixties claimed one long-awaited victory. When in 1964, the Labour Party returned to power, it seemed inevitable that the death penalty would be outlawed.

Even then, the government had to accept *suspending* the death penalty for five years rather than outright *abolition*. The penalty for murder would instead be an indeterminate sentence of life imprisonment, which gave the Home Secretary full discretion to determine the prisoner's date of release. This did not sit well with the judges, who tried in the House of Lords, first to allow the trial judge to give a fixed sentence for murder, and secondly to give courts a power to recommend a minimum period during which the prisoner should not be released. They were successful with the second amendment, and the Commons did not demur. It is clear that judges were uneasy with the executive having the premier role in the sentencing and release of murderers, which the life sentence allowed. Judges still wished to have some say in marking the tariff for murder, some chance to air their denunciatory view of punishment. In 1969, Parliament finally agreed to abolish the death penalty. Unfortunately for penal reformers, the final removal of the gallows, rather than heralding the triumph of the rehabilitative ideal, coincided with a rejuvenated retributivism.

Yet we should be careful about turning this moment into something it was not. The retributive turn is too often presented as a revolution in penal philosophy and practice. Yet was the post-1970 return to retributive ways really so surprising in the wake of the analysis we have presented in this book? It had been evident for some time that rehabilitative strategies were failing to live up to the claim that they would reduce crime and recidivism. Recorded crime in England and Wales doubled between 1955 and 1964, and doubled again by 1975. What little serious criminology there was already pointed to the failure of the individualized treatment model to show any empirical evidence of success in reducing levels of reconviction. It did not need American sociologist Robert Martinson's 1974 article to reveal the supposed shortcomings of rehabilitation programmes.[1] More importantly, "just deserts" had never truly gone away. Sentencing according to tariff calculation was enormously resilient. For all the freight of rehabilitative rhetoric, sentencing and penal practice were largely punitive for most adult offenders. The Victorian prison behemoths were still in use a century or more beyond their original build. For most prisoners, especially the short sentence ones who were in the majority, there never was any treatment or training. With the exception of a few training prisons, the prisons were too overcrowded for any such thing. The bulk of prisoners were still sent to prison for retributive-cum-deterrent reasons; for punishment, not rehabilitation. Prisoners were as poorly educated (in many cases functionally illiterate), poorly trained, unemployable, and frequently as homeless and mentally handicapped as when they were admitted. The surprise is not that retribution gained ascendancy, but that the 1970s are still thought to signify a major rupture in the history of the rehabilitative ideal.

---

1   Martinson, "What Works? Questions and Answers about Prison Reform," *Public Interest*, vol. 35 (1974), pp. 22–54.

II

This is not to deny that the retributive turn strengthened in the 1970s and beyond. To growing domestic doubts about rehabilitation were added a spate of publications from across the Atlantic. The most influential report was that of a study group of the American Friends Service Committee, *Struggle for Justice* (1971), which condemned the treatment model as "theoretically faulty" (incorrectly believing that crime resulted from the pathologies of individual offenders); "systematically discriminatory in application" (discriminating against the poor and the young), and "inconsistent with some of our most basic concepts of justice" (liberty from prison being based on the impressionistic evidence of caseworkers to which offenders were rarely privy).[2] This was followed by Andrew von Hirsch's edition, *Doing Justice* (1976), in which a group of American liberals issued the Luther-like proclamation: "Certain things are simply wrong and ought to be punished. And this we do believe." Criminologist Nigel Walker responded, "The retributive justification of punishment, regarded for so many recent decades as the sick man of penology, is clearly up and about again."[3]

This liberal retributivism adopted the name of "just deserts" or "back-to-justice," since it sought to pare punishment down to its bare essentials: denunciation of moral iniquity and just retribution for it. The main assumptions or principles were laid down. Offenders were responsible for their own behaviour. Punishment was a blaming institution. Punishment was justified not on the grounds that it would reduce the future likelihood of crime, but that it honoured the moral agency of the offender. Penalties should be distributed according to the degree of blameworthiness of the criminal conduct. The aim was to allow the crime and prior criminal record to dictate the penalty, without reference to the social characteristics or pathologies of the offender. There should be fixed and determinate sentencing with an established tariff for each offence. And prisoners should have the benefit of due process. Criminological theory came into line. Social and psychological explanations of crime, the sovereign currency of penal welfarism, made way for the view of offenders as rational actors who had chosen to do wrong and hence merited punishment (though the notion of the pathological predator driven by individual defects lived on). This is not the place to provide a detailed explanation of why the rehabilitative ideal was so easily undermined and replaced by retributive thinking.[4] Suffice it to suggest that, in keeping with the evidence presented in this book, the rehabilitative ideal never truly established its legitimacy, not least among prisoners themselves, and retributivist ideas in the realm of criminal justice were never vanquished.[5] As Francis Allen stated in the 1970s,

2   American Friends Service Committee, *Struggle for Justice* (New York, 1971). See also A. E. Bottoms, "An Introduction to 'The Coming Crisis,'" in Bottoms and R. H. Preston (eds.), *The Coming Penal Crisis* (Edinburgh, 1980), p. 3.

3   Andreas von Hirsch (ed.), *Doing Justice* (New York, 1976); Nigel Walker, *British Journal of Criminology*, vol. 18 (1978), p. 79.

4   David Garland offered his explanation in *The Culture of Control* (Oxford, 2001), chap. 3, "The Crisis of Penal Modernism."

5   This leads some people to claim that reform in prison has not failed; it has never been tried. Francis Allen referred to "the persistent tendency toward the debasement of the

the notion of just deserts has survived . . . because it expresses a basic moral intuition: persons ought not to be subjected to the rigorous and stigmatic sanctions of the criminal law unless their conduct has merited it. There seems every reason to believe that this intuition will exert a continuing influence on the penal policy now emerging as it has . . . on policies of the past.[6]

In the 1970s and 1980s it was still unclear where penal policy and practice would ultimately settle. The law of unintended consequences quickly reared its head. If the original thrust of the "just deserts" movement was to minimize penal coercion, fixed sentencing turned out to be inflationary. The prison population reached a peak of 51,000 in 1988. The 1980s also saw an increase in prison staff of over 50 per cent, reflecting the government's massive investment in the prison system, the largest prison building programme for a hundred years. In 1990, and the following year, however, a more philosophically coherent sentencing and penal policy seemed to be emerging. In February 1990, the government put out the White Paper, *Crime, Justice and Protecting the Public*. It clarified the objectives which sentencing should seek to meet:

> The first objective for all sentences is denunciation of and retribution for the crime. Depending on the offence and the offender, the sentence may also aim to achieve public protection, reparation and reform of the offender, preferably in the community. This approach points to sentencing policies which are more firmly based on the seriousness of the offence, and just desserts [sic] for the offender.[7]

Deterrence, by contrast, was rarely seen as a proper aim of sentencing. The paper was uncompromising in the role it mapped out for imprisonment. "Nobody now regards imprisonment, in itself, as an effective means of reform for most prisoners . . . imprisonment has to be justified in terms of public protection, denunciation and retribution."[8] On April Fool's Day 1990, prisoners in one of England's Gormenghast prisons, Strangeways in Manchester mutinied. For 25 days, prisoners engaged in the most destructive riot in English penal history, and unrest spread to 20 other prisons across the country. The riots, wrote Derek Lewis, director-general of prisons between 1992 and 1995, "represented the nadir in the fortunes of the Prison Service."[9] An independent public enquiry was appointed under the direction of Lord Justice

rehabilitative ideal in practical application" (in part due to lack of funding), evidence, he wrote, that could justify the assertion "that rehabilitative theories of penal treatment have never been accorded a fair trial." See "The Rehabilitative Ideal and Its Modern Critics," in idem., *The Decline of the Rehabilitative Ideal: Penal Policy and Social Purpose* (New Haven, 1981), p. 56.

6 Allen, "What Future for the Rehabilitative Ideal?" in idem., *The Decline of the Rehabilitative Ideal*, op cit., p. 69.

7 Home Office, *Crime, Justice and Protecting the Public*, Cm 965 (1990), p. 6, para 2.9.

8 Ibid., p. 6, para 2.7.

9 Lewis, *Hidden Agendas* (1997), p. 2.

Woolf. The Woolf Report, co-signed by Judge Stephen Tumin, was published nine months later, 600 pages in length, widely hailed as the most significant examination of the prison system since the Gladstone Report of 1895.[10] The report recommended a better balance in prisons between the needs of security, control, and justice. It proposed that the decrepit and degrading conditions in many prisons should be improved, that prisoners should be treated with dignity, that regimes should be constructive, and that staff should be better trained. One proposal was the abolition by 1996 of the unhygienic procedure of "slopping out," symbol of the squalor of English prisons.[11] The government's subsequent White Paper, *Custody, Care and Justice*, published in September 1991, endorsed the vast majority of Woolf's 204 proposals and 12 core recommendations, and displayed a commitment to a broadly rehabilitative purpose for prisons. Before much progress was made on Woolf's proposals, the government translated the 1990 White Paper into legislation, the Criminal Justice Act 1991, which installed desert as the primary rationale of sentencing, except for the few cases where an incapacitated sentence for public protection was thought to be required. Rehabilitative considerations were to be important when choosing between community orders of a similar severity, and as justification for probation orders and supervision after early release from prison. Automatic release of prisoners at the halfway point in their sentences was also enacted. These changes drove the prison population down to 40,600 in 1992.

Enter Michael Howard, who as Home Secretary in October 1993, told the Conservative Party conference, "Let us be clear. Prison works. It ensures that we are protected from murderers, muggers and rapists—and it makes many who are tempted to commit crime think twice." "Nothing works" was replaced by "prison works." This heralded the government's retreat from the 1991 Act. In the White Paper *Protecting the Public* (1996) and the Crime (Sentences) Act, 1997, deterrence and incapacitation became prominent, with tougher sentences for repeat offenders, despite Lord Chief Justice Taylor's description of the proposed mandatory minimum sentences as ill-conceived, "a denial of justice," and subverting the function of the court.[12] The effect on judges and magistrates of Howard's clarion call and the subsequent legislation was to increase the use of jail and lengthen sentences, sending the penal system into crisis. The prison population rose by 50 per cent between 1993 and 1998; it almost doubled between 1992 and 2008, including a sharp rise in the number of both black and female prisoners. The cause of the growth in the prison population was a tougher sentencing process. Sentencers were passing more custodial sentences, under pressure in part from press and Parliament. Fewer than half those convicted at Crown Courts were sentenced to immediate custody in 1993; by 2000, it was 63 per cent. And average

---

10   *Prison Disturbances April 1990: Report of an Inquiry by the Rt. Hon. Lord Justice Woolf (Parts I and II) and His Honour Judge Stephen Tumin (Part II)*, (1991).

11   The Minister of Prisons, Ann Widdecombe, announced that "slopping out" was history in 1996. David Ramsbotham (Chief Inspector of Prisons), was impelled to disagree: ". . . having just visited Dartmoor, I had to say publicly that 'slopping out' had not yet ended there or in a number of other prisons." See *Prisongate: The Shocking State of Britain's Prisons and the Need for Visionary Change* (2005), p. 79.

12   *Hansard* (Lords), vol. 572, 23 May 1996, col. 1026.

Crown Court sentence lengths rose dramatically. Only 6 per cent convicted by magistrates went to prison in 1993; but 15 per cent in 2001. The parole board was more cautious about releasing prisoners on licence; and offenders were more likely to be recalled to prison following a breach of licence conditions, and more likely to be sent to prison for breach of a community order. By 2011, the prison population peaked at 88,000; in May 2016, there were 85,335 people in prison in England and Wales, up from 45,000 in 1992, despite a decreasing crime rate. At 149 per 100,000 population, the incarceration rate is still well below America's figure of 707 per 100,000, but it is far greater than other European countries like Germany or Holland. The prison system is overstretched, underfunded, and in disarray.

In November 2016, the central focus of the Queen's Speech was prison reform, and a renewed focus on rehabilitation. The reform package included the creation of six "reform prisons," which were to be given greater freedoms in relation to budgets, staffing and testing new approaches. The Second Reading of the Prisons and Courts Bill, a measure that sought to enshrine into law that a key purpose of prison is to reform and rehabilitate offenders, as well as punish them for the crimes they have committed, took place in March 2017. The bill was not passed before Parliament was dissolved on 3 May 2017. This is a promising development if only because the history of prisons shows that maintaining standards for the treatment of those held in custody relies upon those with rehabilitative motives. As Francis Allen stated 40 years ago: "It is a historical fact that the great reforms in the physical and moral conditions of institutional life have been accomplished largely by persons whose humanitarian impulses were joined with rehabilitative aspirations."[13]

If faith in the rehabilitative enterprise has gradually revived since the 1980s, it is unlikely that rehabilitation will again be the primary objective of the penal system, at least not in the sense of rehabilitating the individual prisoner as an end in itself. No research supports the notion that imprisonment *per se* can be rehabilitative. The high reconviction rates of ex-prisoners alone indicate the reverse. Instead, it is more likely that "just deserts" will continue to make the running as the primary aim, with rehabilitation or penal welfarism restricted essentially to community-based penalties, and to supervision following custody, and with better provision on a voluntary basis of treatment programmes in prisons, whether medical, educational, or vocational. If this approach is to work, however, the courts must once again, as they did between 1880 and 1940, recalibrate the tariff of punishment, abate the use of imprisonment, and shorten the length of prison sentences. Whether judges have the disposition to do this, and whether politicians and the press will allow them to do this, remains to be seen.

---

13   Allen, "What Future for the Rehabilitative Ideal?" in idem., *The Decline of the Rehabilitative Ideal*, op cit., pp. 80–1.

BIBLIOGRAPHY

Order of Bibliography

A. Archives

Robin Page Arnot Papers: University of Hull Library
William Henry Beveridge Papers: London School of Economics Library
Gerald Gardiner Papers: British Library
Viscount Gladstone Papers: British Library
Victor Gollancz Papers: Modern Records Centre, University of Warwick
Howard League Minute Books: Modern Records Centre, University of Warwick
Arthur Creech Jones Papers: Bodleian Library, Oxford University
Mass Observation Archive: University of Sussex

National Campaign Against the Death Penalty Papers: Modern Records Centre, University
    of Warwick
Cecil H. Rolph Papers (Cecil Rolph Hewitt): London School of Economics Library
John A. Simon, 1st Viscount Simon Papers: Bodleian Library, Oxford University
Viscount Templewood Papers: Cambridge University Library
The National Archives, London

Cabinet Records:

CAB 23 Minutes and Conclusions, 1916–1939
CAB 24 Memoranda, 1915–1939
CAB 71 Lord President's Committee
CAB 128 Cabinet Conclusions
CAB 129 Cabinet Memoranda
CAB 130 Ad Hoc Committees
CAB 134 Home Affairs Committee

Home Office Papers:

HO 45 Registered Papers
HO 144 Registered Papers, Supplementary
HO 291 Criminal Files
HO 301 Royal Commission on Capital Punishment: Evidence and Papers
HO 307 Royal Commission on the Penal System: Evidence and Papers
Home Office Children's Department: BN29
Lord Chancellor's Office Papers: LCO2

Prime Minister's Office Records:

PREM 5 Patronage Papers
PREM 8 1945–51 (Clement Attlee)
PREM 11 1951–64 (Winston Churchill, Anthony Eden, Harold Macmillan, Alec Douglas-
    Home)
PREM 13 1964–70 (Harold Wilson)

Prison Commission Papers:

PCOM 7 Registered Papers
PCOM 9 Registered Papers, Series 2
Treasury papers: T161

B. Other Unpublished Material

Carroll, S. J., "'Fill the Jails': Identity, Structure and Method in the Committee of 100,
    1960–1968," D. Phil thesis, University of Sussex, 2010
McGowen, R. E., "Rethinking Crime: Changing Attitudes towards Law-Breakers in
    Eighteenth and Nineteenth-Century England," Ph.D. dissertation, University of Illinois
    at Urbana-Champaign, 1979
Wright, T. J., "Arguing for the Death Penalty: Making the Retentionist Case in Britain,
    1945–1979," MA thesis, University of York, 2010

C. Parliamentary Papers and Official Publications

i. Annual Reports

Annual Reports of the Commissioners of Prisons
Judicial Statistics
Criminal Statistics

ii. Reports of Royal Commissions, Select Committees and Departmental Committees

Report of the Commissioners Appointed to Inquire into the Working of the Penal Servitude Acts (Kimberley Commission), Minutes of Evidence, Parliamentary Papers, PP, 1878–1879 (C.-2368.-1) XXXVII

Report from the Departmental Committee on Prisons, PP, 1895 (C. 7702) LVI

Minutes of Evidence to the Departmental Committee on Prisons, PP, 1895 (C. 7702-I) LVI

Report from the Departmental Committee on Habitual Offenders, Vagrants, Beggars, Inebriates, and Juvenile Delinquents (Scotland, 1895)

Report of the Indian Jails Committee, 1919–20, PP, 1921 (Cmd. 1303) X

Report of the Committee Appointed to Inquire into the Pay and Conditions of Service at the Prisons and Borstal Institutions in England and Scotland and at Broadmoor Criminal Lunatic Asylum, 1923 (Cmd. 1959)

Report of the Departmental Committee on Sexual Offences against Young Persons, PP, 1924–1925 (Cmd. 2561) XV

Report of the Select Committee on Capital Punishment, PP, 1930–31 (15) VI

Report by Mr. Herbert du Parcq, K.C., On the Circumstances Connected with the Recent Disorder at Dartmoor Convict Prison, PP, 1931–1932 (Cd. 4010) VII

Report of the Departmental Committee on Persistent Offenders, PP, 1931–1932 (Cmd. 4090)

Report of the Departmental Committee on Imprisonment by Courts of Summary Jurisdiction in Default of Payment of Fines and Other Sums of Money, PP, 1933–1934 (Cmd. 4649) XI

Report of the Departmental Committee on the Employment of Prisoners, Pt. II: Employment on Discharge, PP, 1934–1935 (Cmd. 4897) XI

Report of the Royal Commission on Capital Punishment, 1949–1953 (Cmd. 8932), 1953

Report of the Interdepartmental Committee on the Business of the Criminal Courts (Cmnd. 1289), 1961

Royal Commission on the Penal System, Minutes of Evidence Taken Before the Commission, vol. 1: Government Departments; vol. 2: Miscellaneous; vol. 3: Miscellaneous Bodies; vol. 4: Individual Witnesses, HMSO (1967).

Report of the Committee of Inquiry into the United Kingdom Prison Services, PP, 1979 (Cmd. 7673)

iii. Returns

Copy of Circular, dated 21 June 1911, issued by the Secretary of State to Police Authorities, PP, 1911 (Cmd. 5629), LXV

iv. Official Publications

Hansard (Parliamentary Debates): House of Commons; House of Lords
Abatement of Imprisonment, British Library State Papers, B.P. 2/4 (15), 1910
Prisons and Borstals, 1945; 1950
Capital Punishment, 1948
Alternatives to Short Terms of Imprisonment, Advisory Council on the Treatment of Offenders, 1957

Penal Practice in a Changing Society, 1959

The Treatment of Young Offenders, Advisory Council on the Treatment of Offenders, 1959

Corporal Punishment, Advisory Council on the Treatment of Offenders, 1961

Delinquent Generations, by L. Wilkins, 1st. pub., 1960; 1961

Murder: A Home Office Research Unit Report, 1961

Preventive Detention, Advisory Council on the Treatment of Offenders, 1963

The Organisation of After-Care, Advisory Council on the Treatment of Offenders, 1963.

The Sentence of the Court: A Handbook for the Courts on the Treatment of Offenders, 1st pub. 1964; 1969

The War Against Crime in England and Wales 1959–1964, 1964

The Adult Offender, 1965

The Child, the Family and the Young Offender, 1965

Report of the Inquiry into Prison Escapes and Security by the Earl Mountbatten of Burma, 1966, reprint 1971

The Case of Timothy John Evans, 1966

The Regime for Long-Term Prisoners in Conditions of Maximum Security, Advisory Council on the Penal System, 1968

People in Prison, 1969

Habitual Drunken Offenders, Report of the Working Party, 1971

Prisons and the Prisoner: The Work of the Prison Service in England and Wales, 1977

Sentences of Imprisonment: A Review of Maximum Penalties, Advisory Council on the Penal System, 1978

Her Majesty's Commissioners 1878–1978, by K. Neale, Home Office, 1978

Home Office 1782–1982, 1981

Review of Parole in England and Wales, 1981

The Cambridge Institute of Criminology: Its Background and Scope, Report by L. Radzinowicz, 1988

Crime, Justice and Protecting the Public, 1990

Prison Disturbances April 1990: Report of an Inquiry by the Rt. Hon. Lord Justice Woolf (Parts I and II) and His Honour Judge Stephen Tumin (Part II), 1991.

The Principles and Limits of the Penal System, Commission on English Prisons Today, 2009

v. Party Political Publications

Report of the Annual Conference of the Independent Labour Party, 1916

Youth Astray, Report on the Treatment of Young Offenders Published by the Conservative Party Committee on Policy and Political Education, Conservative Central Office, 1946

Murder: Some Suggestions for the Reform of the Law Relating to Murder in England, Committee of the Inns of Court Conservative and Unionist Society, 1956

Crime: A Challenge to Us All, Report of the Labour Party's Study Group, June 1964

vi. Other Publications

Problems of the Ex-Prisoner, Report of the Pakenham/Thompson Committee, 1961

Inside Story, Prison Reform Council, 1962

vii. Law Cases

Criminal Appeal Reports

King's Bench Division Reports

Queen's Bench Division Reports

D. Books, Essays, and Journal Articles

Unless otherwise stated the place of publication is London.

Abel-Smith, B., and Stevens, R., *Lawyers and the Courts: A Sociological Study of the English Legal System 1750–1965*, Cambridge, Mass., 1967

Abse, L., *Private Member*, 1973

Acton, H. B., *The Philosophy of Punishment*, 1969

Adams, R., *Prison Riots in Britain and the USA*, Basingstoke, 1992

Addison, P., *Churchill on the Home Front 1900–1955*, 1992

Addison, P., "Churchill and Social Reform," in Blake, R. and Louis, W. R. (eds.), *Churchill*, New York, 1993

Alderman, R. K., "Discipline in the Parliamentary Labour Party 1945–1951," *Parliamentary Affairs*, 18, 1965

Allen, F., "The Wakefield Scheme," *The Humanist*, 2, 1925

Allen, F. A., "Criminal Justice, Legal Values and the Rehabilitative Ideal," *Journal of Criminal Law and Criminology*, 50, 1959

Allen, F. A., "The Juvenile Court and the Limits of Juvenile Justice," in Allen, F. A., *The Borderland of Criminal Justice: Essays in Law and Criminology*, Chicago, 1964

Allen, F. A., "The Decline of the Rehabilitative Ideal in American Criminal Justice," *Cleveland State Law Review*, 27, 1978

Allen, F. A., "The Law as a Path to the World," *Michigan Law Review*, 77, 1978

Allen, F. A., *The Decline of the Rehabilitative Ideal: Penal Policy and Social Purpose*, New Haven, 1981

Allen, P., "A Young Home Secretary," in Adonis, A. and Thomas, K. (eds.), *Roy Jenkins: A Retrospective*, Oxford, 2004

Allerton, R. H. (with Parker, T.), *The Courage of His Convictions*, 1st pub. 1962; 1969

American Friends Service Committee, *Struggle for Justice*, New York, 1971

Andrews, A., "Results of Preventive Detention," *Howard Journal*, 1, 1921

Attlee, C., *The Social Worker*, 1920

Ashworth, A., *Reducing the Prison Population in the 1980s: The Need for Sentencing Reform*, NACRO, 1983

Avison, N. H., "Changing Patterns in Criminal Behaviour," in Klare, H., and Haxby, D. (eds.), *Frontiers of Criminology*, Oxford, 1967

B.2.15, *Among the Broad-Arrow Men: A Plain Account of English Prison Life*, 1924

Badinter, R., *La Prison Republicaine (1871–1914)*, Paris, 1992

Bailey, V. (ed.), *Policing and Punishment in Nineteenth Century Britain*, 1981

Bailey, V., "Churchill as Home Secretary: Prison Reform," *History Today*, 35, 1985

Bailey, V., *Delinquency and Citizenship: Reclaiming the Young Offender, 1914–1948*, Oxford, 1987

Bailey, V., "The Fabrication of Deviance: 'Dangerous Classes' and 'Criminal Classes' in Victorian England," in Rule, R., and Malcolmson, R. (eds.), *Protest and Survival: Essays for E. P. Thompson*, 1993

Bailey, V., "The Shadow of the Gallows: The Death Penalty and the British Labour Government, 1945–51," *Law and History Review*, 18, 2000

Baker, F. E., "Star Convicts," *Howard Journal*, 4, 1936.

Baker, P., *Time Out of Life*, 1961

Barton, A., and Brown, A., "Dartmoor: Penal and Cultural Icon," *Howard Journal*, 50, 2011

Baxendale, A., *Before the Wars: Churchill as Reformer (1910–1911)*, Oxford, 2011

Behlmer, G., *Child Abuse and Moral Reform in England, 1870–1908*, 1982

Beirne, P., *Inventing Criminology: Essays on the Rise of Homo Criminalis*, New York, 1993

Bell, J. (ed.), *We Did Not Fight*, 1935

Benn, T., *Out of the Wilderness: Diaries 1963–67*, 1987

Benney, M., *Gaol Delivery*, 1948

Benney, M., *Low Company: Describing the Evolution of a Burglar*, 1936

Benson, G., "Report of a Committee to Review Punishment in Prisons, Borstal Institutions, Approved Schools and Remand Homes (1951)," *British Journal of Delinquency*, 2, 1952

Benson, G., "Prediction Methods and Young Prisoners," *British Journal of Delinquency*, 9, 1959

Bligh, M., *Doctor Eurich of Bradford*, 1961

Block, B., and Hostettler, J., *Hanging in the Balance*, Winchester, 1997

Blom-Cooper, L., "Murder (Abolition of Death Penalty) Act 1965," *Modern Law Review*, 29, 1966

Blom-Cooper, L., "The Penalty for Murder," *British Journal of Criminology*, 13, 1973

Blom-Cooper, L., *The Penalty of Imprisonment*, 1988

Blom-Cooper, L., and Morris, T., "The Penalty for Murder: A Myth Exploded," *Criminal Law Review*, 1996

Blom-Cooper, L., and Morris, T., *With Malice Aforethought: A Study of the Crime and Punishment for Homicide*, Oxford, 2004

Blom-Cooper, L., and McConville, S., *The Case for a Royal Commission on the Penal System*, Hook, Hampshire, 2014

Blunt, W. S., *My Diaries*, New York, 1922

Bosanquet, B., *The Philosophical Theory of the State*, 1910

Bosanquet, B., *Some Suggestions in Ethics*, 1918

Bottoms, A., "Towards a Custodial Training Sentence for Adults," *Criminal Law Review*, 1 and 2, 1965

Bottoms, A., "On the Decriminalization of English Juvenile Courts," in Hood, R. (ed.), *Crime, Criminology and Public Policy*, 1974

Bottoms, A., *The Suspended Sentence after Ten Years: A Review and Reassessment*, Leeds, 1980

Bottoms, A., "An Introduction to 'The Coming Crisis'," in Bottoms and R. H. Preston (eds.), *The Coming Penal Crisis: A Criminological and Theological Explanation*, Edinburgh, 1980

Bottoms, A., "Neglected Features of Contemporary Penal Systems," in Garland, D. and Young, P. (eds.), *The Power to Punish: Contemporary Penality and Social Analysis*, 1983

Bottoms, A., and McWilliams, W., "Social Enquiry Reports Twenty-Five Years After the Streatfeild Report," in Bean, P., and Whynes, D. (eds.), *Barbara Wootton: Social Science and Public Policy*, 1986

Bottoms, A., "Limiting Prison Use: Experience in England and Wales," *Howard Journal*, 26, 1987

Bottoms, A., and Stevenson, S., "'What Went Wrong?': Criminal Justice Policy in England and Wales, 1945–70," in Downes, D. (ed.), *Unravelling Criminal Justice*, 1992

Bottoms, A., "The Philosophy and Politics of Punishment and Sentencing," in Clarkson, C., and Morgan, R. (eds.), *The Politics of Sentencing Reform*, Oxford, 1995

Boulton, D., *Objection Overruled*, 1967

Bowden, P., "Pioneers in Forensic Psychiatry. Maurice Hamblin Smith: The Psychoanalytic Panacea," *Journal of Forensic Psychiatry*, 1, 1990

Bowden, P., "Pioneers in Forensic Psychiatry: William Henry de Bargue Hubert (1905–1947): Reformer and Expert Witness," *Journal of Forensic Psychiatry*, 7, 1996

Box, M., *Rebel Advocate: A Biography of Gerald Gardiner*, 1983

Bresler, F., *Reprieve: A Study of a System*, 1965

Bresler, F., *Lord Goddard: A Biography of Rayner Goddard, Lord Chief Justice of England*, 1977

Branson, N., *Poplarism 1919–1925: George Lansbury and the Councillors' Revolt*, 1979

Brittain, V., "The Forgotten Prisoner," in *Prisoners' Circle: Essays by Ex-Prisoners*, Prison Medical Reform Council, 1943

Brockway, A. F., *Prisons as Crime Factories*, 1919

Brockway, A. F., *A New Way with Crime*, 1928

Brockway, A. F., *Inside the Left*, 1942

Brockway, A. F., *Towards Tomorrow: The Autobiography of Fenner Brockway*, 1977

Bromhead, P. A., *The House of Lords and Contemporary Politics, 1911–1957*, 1958

Brookshire, J. H., *Clement Attlee*, Manchester, 1995

Brown, A., and Clare, E., "A History of Experience: Exploring Prisoners' Accounts of Incarceration," in Emsley, C. (ed.), *The Persistent Prison: Problems, Images and Alternatives*, 2005

Brown, A., "The Amazing Mutiny at the Dartmoor Convict Prison," *British Journal of Criminology*, 47, 2007

Brown, A., "Challenging Discipline and Control: A Comparative Analysis of Prison Riots at Chatham (1861) and Dartmoor (1932)", in Johnston, H. (ed.), *Punishment and Control in Historical Perspective*, 2008

Brown, A., *Inter-War Penal Policy and Crime in England: The Dartmoor Convict Prison Riot, 1932*, Basingstoke, 2013

Brown, I., "A Commissioner Calls: Alexander Paterson and Colonial Burma's Prisons," *Journal of Southeast Asian Studies*, 38, 2007

Brown, W. J., *Prison Problems*, Prison Reform Council, 1946

Bryder, L., "The First World War: Healthy or Hungry?", *History Workshop*, 24, 1987

Butler, R. A., *Penal Reform and Research*, Liverpool, 1960

Butler, R. A., *The Art of the Possible: The Memoirs of Lord Butler*, Harmondsworth, 1971

Butler, R. A., "The Foundation of the Institute of Criminology in Cambridge," in Hood, R. (ed.), *Crime, Criminology and Public Policy*, 1974

Buxton, J., and Turner, M., *Gate Fever*, 1962

Cahalan, M., "Trends in Incarceration in the United States since 1880," *Crime and Delinquency*, 25, 1979

Calder, A., "Mass-Observation 1937–1949," in Bulmer, M. (ed.), *Essays on the History of British Sociological Research*, Cambridge, 1985

Calvert, E. R., *Capital Punishment in the Twentieth Century*, 1927; 5th ed. 1936

Calvocoressi, P., *Nuremberg: The Facts, the Law and the Consequences*, New York, 1948

Camp, J., *Holloway Prison: The Place and the People*, 1974

Cape, C. T., "Prison Education: Training for Freedom?" *Howard Journal*, 9, 1954

Carlen, P., "Psychiatry in Prisons: Promises, Premises, Practices and Politics," in Miller, P., and Rose, N. (eds.), *The Power of Psychiatry*, Oxford, 1986

Carpenter, E., *England's Ideal and Other Papers on Social Subjects*, 1895

Carpenter, E., *Prisons Police and Punishment*, 1905

Carter, H., *The Control of the Drink Trade: A Contribution to National Efficiency 1915–1917*, 1918

Carter, V. B., *Winston Churchill: An Intimate Portrait*, New York, 1965

Catchpool, T. C., *On Two Fronts*, 1918

Catterall, P. (ed.), *The Macmillan Diaries: The Cabinet Years, 1950–1957*, 2003

Ceadel, M., *Pacifism in Britain 1914–1945*, Oxford, 1980

Cesarani, D., *Arthur Koestler: The Homeless Mind*, 1999

Chapman, C., "War and Criminality," *Sociological Review*, 9, 1916–1917

Chapman, C., *The Poor Man's Court of Justice: Twenty-Five Years as a Metropolitan Magistrate*, 1925

Chapman, D., *Sociology and the Stereotype of the Criminal*, 1968

Cheney, D., "Dr. Mary Louisa Gordon (1861–1941): A Feminist Approach to Prison," *Feminist Legal Studies*, 18, 2010

Choppen, V., "The Origins of the Philosophy of Detention Centres," *British Journal of Criminology*, 10, 1970

Christoph, J. B., *Capital Punishment and British Politics*, 1962

Churchill, D., *Crime Control and Everyday Life in the Victorian City*, Oxford, 2017

Churchill, R., *Winston S. Churchill: Companion Volume*, 2, Boston, 1969

Clayton, G. F., *The Wall Is Strong*, 1958

Cohen, H., "The Court of Criminal Appeal," *Quarterly Review*, 230, 1918

Cohen, S., *Folk Devils and Moral Panics: The Creation of the Mods and Rockers*, 1972

Collins, J., Canon, *Faith under Fire*, 1966

CornishW. R., and Hart, J., *Crime and Law in Nineteenth Century Britain*, Dublin, 1978

Courtauld, S., *To Convey Intelligence: The Spectator, 1928–1998*, 1999

Cox, P., "Girls, Deficiency and Delinquency," in Wright, D., and Digby, A. (eds.), *From Idiocy to Mental Deficiency*, 1996

Craven, C., "The Report of the Departmental Committee on Persistent Offenders," *Howard Journal*, 3, 1932

Craven, C., "The Progress of English Criminology," *Journal of Criminal Law, Criminology and Police Science*, 24, 1933

Craven, C., "English Prisons: Two Points of View," *Howard Journal*, 4, 1936

Croft, J., "Hermann Mannheim—a Biographical Note," in Grygier, T., Jones, H., and Spencer, J. (eds.), *Criminology in Transition*, 1965

Croft-Cooke, R., *The Verdict of You All*, 1955

Cronin, H., *The Screw Turns*, 1967

Cross, J. A., *Sir Samuel Hoare: A Political Biography*, 1977

Crossman, R., *The Diaries of a Cabinet Minister*, 1976

Crowley, R., "The Role of Sterilisation in the Prevention of Mental Defect and Disorder," *Howard Journal*, 4, 1934

Davidson, M., *The World, the Flesh and Myself*, 1962

Davie, N., "Criminal Man Revisited? Continuity and Change in British Criminology, c. 1865–1918," *Journal of Victorian Culture*, 8, 2003

Davies, C., *Bad Girls: A History of Rebels and Renegades*, 2018

Davies, C., "The British State and the Power of Life and Death," in Green, S. J. D., and Whiting, R. C. (eds.), *The Boundaries of the State in Modern Britain*, Cambridge, 1996

Davies, C., *The Strange Death of Moral Britain*, 2004

Davies, D.S., "The Court of Criminal Appeal: The First Forty Years," *Journal of Society of Public Teachers of Law*, 1, 1951

Davies, M. et al., *Criminal Justice*, 2nd ed., 1998

Davitt, M., *The Prison Life of Michael Davitt, Related by Himself*, Dublin, 1882

Davitt, M., "Criminal and Prison Reform," *Nineteenth Century*, 36, December 1894

Dawtry, F., "The Abolition of the Death Penalty in Britain," *British Journal of Criminology*, 6, 1966

DeLacy, M., *Prison Reform in Lancashire, 1700–1850*, Stanford, 1986

Dennis, N., and Halsey, A. H., *English Ethical Socialism*, Oxford, 1988

Dernley, S., *The Hangman's Tale: Memoirs of a Public Executioner*, 1989

Devon, J., *The Criminal and the Community*, 1912

Dingle, A. E., "Drink and Working-Class Living Standards in Britain, 1870–1914," *Economic History Review*, 25, 1972

Donnison, D., "Committees and Committeemen," in Bulmer, M. (ed.), *Social Research and Royal Commissions*, 1980

Donoughue, B., and Jones, G. W., *Herbert Morrison: Portrait of a Politician*, 1973

Downing, K., and Forsythe, B., "The Reform of Offenders in England, 1830–1995: A Circular Debate," *Criminal Justice History*, 18, 2003

Drewry, G., "Parliament and Hanging: Further Episodes in an Undying Saga," *Parliamentary Affairs*, 27, 1974

Driver, C., *The Disarmers: A Study in Protest*, 1964

Du Cane, E. F., "The Duration of Penal Sentences," *Fortnightly Review*, 33, 1883.

Du Cane, E. F., "The Prison Committee Report," *Nineteenth Century*, 38, 1895

Du Cane, E. F., "The Prisons Bill and Progress in Criminal Treatment," *Nineteenth Century*, 43, 1898

Duff, P., *Left, Left, Left: A Personal Account of Six Protest Campaigns 1945–65*, 1971

Dunlop, A. and McCabe, S., *Young Men in Detention Centres*, 1965

East, W. N., "Critical Notices," *British Journal of Delinquency*, 3, 1953

East, W. N., "In Memoriam: Maurice Hamblin Smith," *Howard Journal*, 4, 1936

East, W. N., "The Modern Psychiatric Approach to Crime," *Journal of Mental Science*, 85, 1939

East, W. N., and Hubert, W. H., *Report on the Psychological Treatment of Crime*, 1939

East, W. N., *The Adolescent Criminal*, 1942

East, W. N., *Society and the Criminal*, 1949

East, W. N., "Medical Aspects of the Criminal Justice Act 1948," *Journal of Criminal Science*, 2, 1950

Eddowes, M., *The Man on Your Conscience*, 1955

"Editorial," *Howard Journal*, 1, 1922

Edwards, J. Ll. J., *The Law Officers of the Crown*, 1964

Edwards, J. Ll. J., "A New Doctrine in Criminal Punishment," *Law Quarterly Review*, 72, 1956

Edwards, R. D., *Victor Gollancz: A Biography*, 1987

Elkin, W. A., "Progress of Criminal Justice Bill," *The Penal Reformer*, 6, 1939

Elkin, W. A., "English Prisons in Six Years of War," *Howard Journal*, 7, 1946–1947

Ellis, H., *The Criminal*, 1890

Ellmann, R., *Oscar Wilde*, New York, 1988

Elwyn-Jones, F., Lord, *In My Time: An Autobiography*, 1983

Emsley, C., "The History of Crime and Crime Control Institutions, c. 1770-c. 1945," in Maguire, M., Morgan, R., and Reiner, R. (eds.), *The Oxford Handbook of Criminology*, Oxford, 1994

England, L. R., "Capital Punishment and Open-Ended Questions," *Public Opinion Quarterly*, 12, 1948

Evans, H., *My Paper Chase*, New York, 2009

Fairn, D., "Prisons 1866–1966," in Klare, H. (ed.), *Changing Concepts of Crime and Its Treatment*, Oxford, 1966

Faulkner, D., *Servant of the Crown: A Civil Servant's Story of Criminal Justice and Public Service Reform*, Hook, 2014

Feeley, M., "The Decline of Women in the Criminal Process: A Comparative History," in Knafla, L. (ed.), *Criminal Justice History*, 15, 1994

Field, S., *Trends in Crime and Their Interpretation: A Study of Recorded Crime in Post War England and Wales*, 1990

Fielding, S., Thompson, P., and Tiratsoo, N., *"England Arise!": The Labour Party and Popular Politics in 1940s Britain*, Manchester, 1995

Fisk, T., "A Student's View," in Blom-Cooper, L. (ed.), *The Hanging Question*, 1969

Forsythe, W. J., "National Socialists and the English Prison Commission: The Berlin Penitentiary Congress of 1935," *International Journal of the Sociology of Law*, 17, 1989

Forsythe, W. J., *Penal Discipline, Reformatory Projects and the English Prison Commission, 1895–1939*, Exeter, 1990

Forsythe, W. J., "Mental and Social Diagnosis and the English Prison Commission 1914–1939," *Social Policy and Administration*, 24, 1990

Forsythe, W. J., "Reformatory Projects in British Prisons, 1780–1939: Recent Writings and Lessons from the Past," in Robert, P. and Emsley, C. (eds.), *History and Sociology of Crime*, Pfaffenweiler, 1991

Forsythe, W. J., "Women Prisoners and Women Penal Officials 1840–1921," *British Journal of Criminology*, 33, 1993

Forsythe, W. J., "Loneliness and Cellular Confinement in English Prisons 1878–1921," *British Journal of Criminology*, 44, 2004

Foucault, M., *Discipline and Punish: The Birth of the Prison*, 1975; reprint 1977

Fox, L. W., *The Modern English Prison*, 1934

Fox, L. W., "A Survey of the Prison Administration for England and Wales since 1945," *Howard Journal*, 8, 1951

Fox, L. W., *The English Prison and Borstal Systems*, 1952

Freeden, M., "Eugenics and Progressive Thought: A Study in Ideological Affinity," *Historical Journal*, 22, 1979

Fry, S. M., "A Great Book," *Howard Journal*, 8, 1953

Fry, S.M., "The State in Its Relation to Law-Breakers," *Friends Fellowship Papers*, May 1920

Fry, S.M., "Prison Labour," *Howard Journal*, 4, 1934

Fry, S.M., "The 'Penal Reform' Bill," *Fortnightly*, 151, 1939

Fry, S.M., "The Future Treatment of the Adult Offender," *Agenda*, 1943

Fry, S.M., "The Criminal Justice Bill," *Political Quarterly*, 19, 1948

Fyfe, D. P., *Political Adventure: The Memoirs of the Earl of Kilmuir*, 1964

Gallup, G. H. (ed.), *The Gallup International Public Opinion Polls: Great Britain 1937–75*, 1, New York, 1976

Galsworthy, J., *Justice*, New York, 1910

Galton, F., "Terms of Imprisonment," *Nature*, 20, June 1895

Gard, R. L., *The End of the Rod: A History of the Abolition of Corporal Punishment in the Courts of England and Wales*, Boca Raton, 2009

Gard, R. L., *Rehabilitation and Probation in England and Wales 1876–1962*, 2014

Gardiner, A., "In Memoriam: Dr. M. Hamblin Smith," *Penal Reformer*, 3, 1936

Gardiner, G., "A Symposium on the Report of the Royal Commission on Capital Punishment: Legal Aspects," *British Journal of Delinquency*, 4, 1954

Gardiner, G., "The Purposes of Criminal Punishment," *Modern Law Review*, 21, 1958

Gardiner, G., and Curtis-Raleigh, N., "The Judicial Attitude to Penal Reform," *Law Quarterly Review*, 65, 1949

Garfinkel, H., "Conditions of Successful Degradation Ceremonies," *American Journal of Sociology*, 61, 1956

Garland, D., "The Criminal and His Science: A Critical Account of the Formation of Criminology at the End of the Nineteenth Century," *British Journal of Criminology*, 25, 1985

Garland, D., *Punishment and Welfare: A History of Penal Strategies*, Aldershot, 1985

Garland, D., "British Criminology before 1935," *British Journal of Criminology*, 28, 1988

Garland, D., *Punishment and Modern Society: A Study in Social Theory*, Chicago, 1990

Garland, D., "Criminological Knowledge and Its Relation to Power: Foucault's Genealogy and Criminology Today," *British Journal of Criminology*, 32, 1992

Garland, D., "Of Crimes and Criminals: The Development of Criminology in Britain," in Maguire, M., Morgan, R., and Reiner, R. (eds.), *The Oxford Handbook of Criminology*, Oxford, 1994

Garland, D., "Obituary: F. H. McClintock," *British Journal of Criminology*, 35, 1995

Garland, D., *The Culture of Control: Crime and Social Order in Contemporary Society*, Oxford, 2001

Garland, D., "Ideology and Crime: A Further Chapter," in Bottoms, A., and Tonry, M. (eds.), *Ideology, Crime and Criminal Justice*, Cullompton, Devon, 2002

Garland, D., "Beyond the Culture of Control," *Critical Review of International Social and Political Philosophy*, 7, 2004

Garland, D., "Modes of Capital Punishment: The Death Penalty in Historical Perspective," in Garland, D. et al. (eds.), *America's Death Penalty*, New York, 2011

Garnett, E. (ed.), *Letters from John Galsworthy 1900–1932*, 1934

Gatrell, V. A., "The Decline of Theft and Violence in Victorian and Edwardian England," in Gatrell, V. A., Lenman, B., and Parker, G. (eds.), *Crime and the Law*, 1980

Gatrell, V. A., *The Hanging Tree: Execution and the English People, 1770–1868*, Oxford, 1994

Gattey, C. N., *The Incredible Mrs. Van der Elst*, 1972

Genders, E., and Player, E., *Grendon: A Study of a Therapeutic Prison*, Oxford, 1995

Gibbens, T. C., "A Reply to Dr. Teeters' Article on the Prison Systems of England," *Journal of Criminal Law and Criminology*, 41, 1951

Gibson, E., and Klein, S., *Murder 1957 to 1968: A Home Office Statistical Division Report on Murder in England and Wales*, 1969

Gibson, E., "Murder Statistics for England and Wales," *Anglo-American Law Review*, 1, 1972

Gibson, I., *The English Vice: Beating, Sex and Shame in Victorian England and After*, 1978

Gibson Mackenzie, T. B., "The British Prison," *Fortnightly Review*, 137, 1932

Gilbert, M., *Plough My Own Furrow: The Story of Lord Allen of Hurtwood as Told through His Writings and Correspondence*, 1965

Gilbert, M., *Winston S. Churchill*, 8, Boston, 1988

Glover, E., "The Diagnosis and Treatment of Delinquency," in Radzinowicz, L., and Turner, J. W. (eds.), *Mental Abnormality and Crime*, 1944

Glover, E., "A Symposium on the Report of the Royal Commission on Capital Punishment: Psychiatric Aspects," *British Journal of Delinquency*, 4, 1954

Glover, E., *The Roots of Crime*, 1960

Godfrey, B. S., "Sentencing, Theatre, Audience and Communication: The Victorian and Edwardian Magistrates' Courts and Their Message," in *Les Temoins Devant La Justice: Une Histoire des Status et des Comportements*, Rennes, 2003

Godfrey, B. S., et al., "Explaining Gendered Sentencing Patterns for Violent Men and Women in the Late-Victorian and Edwardian Period," *British Journal of Criminology*, 45, 2005

Godfrey, B. S., et al., *Serious Offenders: A Historical Study of Habitual Criminals*, Oxford, 2010

Godfrey, B. S., et al., *Crime, Regulation and Control During the Blitz*, 2016

Gollancz, V., *More for Timothy*, 1953

Gordon, M., *Penal Discipline*, 1922

Goring, C., *The English Convict: A Statistical Study*, abridged ed., 1919

Gorringe, T., *God's Just Vengeance: Crime, Violence and the Rhetoric of Salvation*, Cambridge, 1996

Gottschalk, M., *The Prison and the Gallows: The Politics of Mass Incarceration in America*, Cambridge, 2006

Gowers, E., *A Life for a Life? The Problem of Capital Punishment*, 1956

Graham, J. W., *Conscription and Conscience: A History, 1916–1919*, 1922

Grant, T., *Jeremy Hutchinson's Case Histories*, 2016

Green, T. H., "Principles of Political Obligation," in Nettleship, R. L. (ed.), *Works of Thomas Hill Green*, 2, 1886; 5th impression, 1906

Greenleaf, W. H., *The British Political Tradition*, New York, 2, 1983

Grey, D., "Women's Policy Networks and the Infanticide Act 1922," *Twentieth Century British History*, 21, 2010

Griffith, J., *Judicial Politics since 1920*, Oxford, 1993

Grigg, J., "The Do-Gooder from Seville Gaol," in Harris, H. (ed.), *Astride the Two Cultures: Arthur Koestler at 70*, New York, 1976

Grimshaw, E., and Jones, G., *Lord Goddard*, 1958

Grosskurth, P., *Havelock Ellis*, New York, 1980

Grunhut, M., *Penal Reform*, 1948

Grunhut, M., "The Treatment of Persistent Offenders," *Journal of Criminal Science*, 2, 1950

Grunhut, M., "Murder and the Death Penalty in England," in Sellin, T. (ed.), *Murder and the Penalty of Death*, Annals of the American Academy of Political and Social Science, 284, 1952

Grunhut, M., "After-Effects of Punitive Detention," *British Journal of Delinquency*, 10, 1960

Guest, E. R., "'Criminal Science' and Punishment," *Journal of Comparative Legislation and International Law*, 30, 1948

Gwyn, W. B ., "The Labour Party and the Threat of Bureaucracy,"*Political Studies*, 19, 1971

Haldane, R. B., *An Autobiography*, 1929

Hall, P., Land, H., Parker, R., and Webb, A., *Change, Choice and Conflict in Social Policy*, 1975

Hamilton, I., *Koestler: A Biography*, 1982

Hammel, A., *Ending the Death Penalty: The European Experience in Global Perspective*, Basingstoke, 2010

Hammond, W. H., and Chayen, E., *Persistent Criminals: A Study of All Offenders Liable to Preventive Detention in 1956*, 1963

Hammond, W. H., "A Study of the Deterrent Effect of Prison Conditions," *Howard Journal*, 15, 1977

Hammond, W. H., "Doing Time," *New Society*, June 1977

Harding, C., "'The Inevitable End of a Discredited System'? The Origins of the Gladstone Committee Report on Prisons, 1895," *Historical Journal*, 31, 1988

Harding, C., and Wilkin, L., "'The Dream of a Benevolent Mind': The Late Victorian Response to the Problem of Inebriety," *Criminal Justice History*, 9, 1988

Harris, J., "The Webbs, the Charity Organisation Society and the Ratan Tata Foundation: Social Policy from the Perspective of 1912," in Bulmer, M., Lewis, J., and Piachaud, D. (eds.), *The Goals of Social Policy*, 1989

Harris, J., "Political Thought and the Welfare State, 1870–1940: An Intellectual Framework for British Social Policy," *Past and Present*, 135, 1992

Harris, J., *Private Lives, Public Spirit: A Social History of Britain 1870–1914*, Oxford, 1993

Harris, P., "Moral Progress and Politics: The Theory of T. H. Green," *Polity*, 21, 1989

Harrison, B., *Peaceable Kingdom: Stability and Change in Modern Britain*, Oxford, 1982

Hart, H. L., "Murder and the Principles of Punishment: England and the United States," *Northwestern University Law Review*, 52, 1957

Harvey, T.E., "The Home Secretary's Opportunity," *Contemporary Review*, 152, 1937

Harvey, T.E., "The Criminal Justice Bill," *Contemporary Review*, 155, 1939

Haskell, T. L., "Capitalism and the Origins of the Humanitarian Sensibility," parts 1 and 2, *American Historical Review*, 90, April and June 1985

Havighurst, A. F., *Radical Journalist: H. W. Massingham (1860–1924)*, Cambridge, 1974

Hawkins, G., "Prison Labor and Prison Industries," *Crime and Justice*, 5, 1983

Hay, D., "Time, Inequality, and Law's Violence," in Sarat, A., and Kearns, T. R. (eds.), *Law's Violence*, Ann Arbor, 1992

Hay, D., "Hanging and the English Judges: The Judicial Politics of Retention and Abolition," in Garland, D., McGowen, R., and Meranze, M. (eds.), *America's Death Penalty*, New York, 2011

Heckstall-Smith, A., *Eighteen Months*, 1954

Hendrick, G., *Henry Salt: Humanitarian Reformer and Man of Letters*, Urbana, 1977

Hennessy, P., *Cabinet*, Oxford, 1986

Hennessy, P., *Never Again: Britain, 1945–51*, New York, 1994

Henriques, U., "The Rise and Decline of the Separate System of Prison Discipline," *Past and Present*, 54, 1972

Henry, J., *Who Lie in Gaol*, 1952

Heuston, R. F., *Lives of the Lord Chancellors, 1940–1970*, Oxford, 1987

Hewart, G., "Alternatives to Imprisonment," in Hewart, G., *Essays and Observations*, 1930

Hignett, A., *Portrait in Grey*, 1956

Himmelfarb, G., *Poverty and Compassion: The Moral Imagination of the Late Victorians*, New York, 1991

Hinde, R., *The British Penal System 1773–1950*, 1951

Hirst, F. W., *The Consequences of the War to Great Britain*, 1934

Hobhouse, H., *I Appeal unto Caesar*, 1917

Hobhouse, S., "The Silence System in British Prisons," *Friends' Quarterly Examiner*, July 1918

Hobhouse, S., *An English Prison from Within*, 1919

Hobhouse, S., and Brockway, A. F., *English Prisons To-Day: Being the Report of the Prison System Enquiry Committee*, 1922

Hobhouse, S., *Forty Years and an Epilogue: An Autobiography*, 1951

Hollis, C., *The Homicide Act*, 1964

Holt, W., *I Haven't Unpacked: An Autobiography*, 1939

Holt, W., *I Was a Prisoner*, 1935

Homans, L., "Swinging Sixties: The Abolition of Capital Punishment," *History Today*, 58, 2008

Home, W. D., *Now Barabbas*, 1947

Home, W. D., "The Worst of Prison," *Picture Post*, 15 March 1947

Home, W. D., *Half-Term Report*, 1954

Hood, R., *Borstal Re-Assessed*, 1965

Hood, R., "Criminology and Penal Change: A Case Study of the Nature and Impact of Some Recent Advice to Governments," in Hood, R. (ed.), *Crime, Criminology and Penal Policy*, 1974

Hood, R., and Roddam, A., "Crime, Sentencing and Punishment," in Halsey, A. H. and Webb, J. (eds.), *Twentieth Century British Social Trends*, 2000

Hood, R., "Hermann Mannheim (1889–1974) and Max Grunhut (1893–1964)," in Beatson, J., and Zimmermann, R. (eds.), *Jurists Uprooted: German-speaking Émigré Lawyers in Twentieth-Century Britain*, Oxford, 2004

Hopkins, H., *The New Look: A Social History of the Forties and Fifties in Britain*, 1963

Howard, A., *RAB: The Life of R. A. Butler*, 1987

Howard, P., "The English Court of Criminal Appeal," *American Bar Association Journal*, 17, 1931

Hughes, E., *Sydney Silverman: Rebel in Parliament*, 1969

Hunt, G., Mellor, J., and Turner, J., "Wretched, Hatless and Miserably Clad: Women and the Inebriate Reformatories from 1900–1913," *British Journal of Sociology*, 40, 1989

Ignatieff, M., *A Just Measure of Pain: The Penitentiary in the Industrial Revolution, 1750–1850*, New York, 1978

Ignatieff, M., "State, Civil Society, and Total Institutions: A Critique of Recent Social Histories of Punishment," in Tonry, M., and Morris, N. (eds.) *Crime and Justice: An Annual Review of Research*, 3, Chicago, 1981

Iremonger, T. L., *Disturbers of the Peace*, 1962

Jackson, R. M., *Enforcing the Law*, 1967; 1972

Jackson, R. M., *The Machinery of Justice in England*, Cambridge, 1972

Jacobson, S., "Inside Holloway Prison," *Picture Post*, 13 September 1947

Jacot, B. L., "Women in Prison," *Quarterly Review*, 271, 1938

James, T. E., "Preventive Detention in 1961 in the Court of Criminal Appeal," *Criminal Law Review*, 1962

Jarvis, M., *Conservative Governments, Morality and Social Change in Affluent Britain, 1957–64*, Manchester, 2005

Jefferys, K. (ed.), *Labour and the Wartime Coalition: From the Diary of James Chuter Ede, 1941–1945*, 1987

Jenkins, P., "Serial Murder in England 1940–1985," *Journal of Criminal Justice*, 16, 1988

Jenkins, R., *The Labour Case*, Harmondsworth, 1959

Jenkins, R., "On Being a Minister," in Herman, V., and Alt, J. E. (eds.), *Cabinet Studies: A Reader*, 1975

Jenkins, R., *A Life at the Centre*, 1991

Jewkes, Y., and Johnston, H., "The English Prison During the First and Second World Wars," *Prison Service Journal*, 198, 2011

Johnston, H., "Gendered Prison Work: Female Prison Officers in the Local Prison System," *Howard Journal*, 53, 2014

Johnston, H., "Prison Histories, 1770–1950s," in Jewkes, Y., Bennett, J., and Crewe, B. (eds.), *Handbook on Prisons*, 2016

Jones, E. H., *Margery Fry: The Essential Amateur*, 1966

Jones, D. C. (ed.), *The Social Survey of Merseyside*, 3, 1934

Jones, H., *The Working Faith of the Social Reformer*, 1910

Jones, H., and Cornes, P., *Open Prisons*, 1977

Jowitt, W ., 1st Earl Jowitt, "Message from Britain: The Lord Chancellor's Address in Cleveland,"*American Bar Association Journal*, 33, 1947

Kelley, J., "Askham Grange—Open Prison for Women," *Howard Journal*, 9, 1955

Kennedy, L., *Murder Story*, 1954

Kennedy, L., *Ten Rillington Place*, 1961

Kennedy, L., *On My Way to the Club: The Autobiography of Ludovic Kennedy*, 1989

Kennedy, T. C., "Public Opinion and the Conscientious Objector, 1915–1919," *Journal of British Studies*, 12, 1973

Kennedy, T. C., *The Hound of Conscience: A History of the No-Conscription Fellowship, 1914–1919*, Fayetteville, Ark., 1981

Kenney, A., *Memories of a Militant*, London, 1924

King, C., *The Cecil King Diary 1965–1970*, 1972

Kisch, E. R., *Consistent Principles in Criminal Punishment*, 1939

Klare, H., *Anatomy of Prison*, 1960

Klare, H., "Criminal Statistics, England and Wales, 1949," *Howard Journal*, 8, 1951

Klare, H., "Her Majesty's Prisons," *Howard Journal*, 8, 1953

Klare, H., *People in Prison*, 1973

Klare, H., "Report of the Wynn Parry Committee," *British Journal of Delinquency*, 9, 1959

Knowles, C. M., "The Problem of the Old Offender," *Police Journal*, 4, 1931

Koestler, A., *Reflections on Hanging*, New York, 1957

Koestler, A., and Koestler, C., *Stranger on the Square*, 1984

Kramnick, I., and Sheerman, B., *Harold Laski: A Life on the Left*, 1993

Kynaston, D., *Family Britain 1951–57*, 2010

Lacey, N., "In Search of the Responsible Subject: History, Philosophy and Social Sciences in Criminal Law Theory," *Modern Law Review*, 64, 2001

Lamb, J., *Criminology in the Making: An Oral History*, Boston, 1983

Langhamer, C., "'The Live Dynamic Whole of Feeling and Behaviour': Capital Punishment and the Politics of Emotion, 1945–1957," *Journal of British Studies*, 5, 2012

Laqueur, T. W., "Bodies, Details, and the Humanitarian Narrative," in Hunt, L. (ed.), *The New Cultural History*, Berkeley, 1989

Lawton, L. J., "The Law and Public Opinion," in *The Riddell Lecture*, 1975

Leslie, S. (compiler), *Sir Evelyn Ruggles-Brise: A Memoir of the Founder of Borstal*, 1938

Lewis, D., *Hidden Agendas: Politics, Law and Disorder*, 1997

Lewis, E. O., "Mental Deficiency and Criminal Behaviour," in Radzinowicz, L. and Turner, J. W. (eds.), *Mental Abnormality and Crime*, 1944

Liebling, A., "A 'Liberal Regime within a Secure Perimeter'? Dispersal Prisons and Penal Practice in the Late Twentieth Century," in Bottoms, A., and Tonry, M. (eds.), *Ideology, Crime and Criminal Justice*, 2012

Liebling, A., "Pentonville Revisited: An Essay in Honour of the Morris' Sociological Study of an English Prison, 1958–1963," *Prison Service Journal*, 209, 2013

Lilly, J. R., and Thomson, J.M., "Executing US Soldiers in England, World War II," *British Journal of Criminology*, 37, 1997

Llewellyn Smith, H., *The New Survey of London Life and Labour*, 9, 1935

Loader, I., "Fall of the 'Platonic Guardians': Liberalism, Criminology and Political Responses to Crime in England and Wales," *British Journal of Criminology*, 46, 2006

Lodge, T. S., "A Comparison of Criminal Statistics of England and Wales with those of Scotland," *British Journal of Delinquency*, 7, 1956

Logan, A., "Women and the Provision of Criminal Justice Advice: Lessons from England and Wales 1944–1964," *British Journal of Criminology*, 50, 2010

Logan, A., *The Politics of Penal Reform: Margery Fry and the Howard League*, 2018

Lombroso, C., *L'Uomo delinquent*, Milan, 1876

Lombroso, C., and Ferrero, W., *The Female Offender*, New York, 1916

Lytton, C., *Prisons and Prisoners*, New York, 1914

Macartney, W., *Walls Have Mouths: A Record of Ten Years' Penal Servitude*, 1936

Machin, G. I., *Churches and Social Issues in Twentieth-Century Britain*, Oxford, 1998

MacKenna, B., "A Plea for Shorter Prison Sentences," in Glazebrook, P. R. (ed.), *Reshaping the Criminal Law*, 1978

MacKenzie, N., and MacKenzie, J., *The First Fabians*, 1977

Mair, G., and Burke, L., *Redemption, Rehabilitation and Risk Management: A History of Probation*, 2012

Mallet, B., Sir, "The Social Problem Group," *Eugenic Review*, 23, 1931

Mannheim, H., "Comparative Sentencing Practice," *Law and Contemporary Problems*, 23, 1958

Mannheim, H., "The Report of the Departmental Committee on Corporal Punishment," *Modern Law Review*, 2, 1938

Mannheim, H., *The Dilemma of Penal Reform*, 1939

Mannheim, H., *Social Aspects of Crime in England Between the Wars*, 1940

Mannheim, H., "Crime in Wartime England," *The Annals of the American Academy of Political and Social Science*, 217, 1941

Mannheim, H., *War and Crime*, 1941

Mannheim, H., "A Symposium on the Report of the Royal Commission on Capital Punishment: Concluding Remarks," *British Journal of Delinquency*, 4, 1954

Mannheim, H., *Group Problems in Crime and Punishment*, 1955

Mannheim, H., "Some Aspects of Judicial Sentencing Policy," *Yale Law Journal*, 67, 1958

Mannheim, H., "Comparative Sentencing Practice," *Law and Contemporary Problems*, 23, 1958

Mannheim, H., "Developments in Criminal Law and Criminology in Post-War Britain," *Journal of Criminal Law, Criminology and Police Science*, 51, 1961

Marrot, H. V., *The Life and Letters of John Galsworthy*, 1935

Martin, J. P., "Criminal Statistics 1956," *Howard Journal*, 10, 1958

Martin, J. P., "A Note on Paragraph 17," *British Journal of Delinquency*, 10, 1960

Martin, J. P., "The Development of Criminology in Britain 1948–60," *British Journal of Criminology*, 28, 1988

Martinson, R. L., "What Works? Questions and Answers about Prison Reform," *The Public Interest*, 35, 1974

Maser, W., *Nuremberg: A Nation on Trial*, New York, 1979

Mason, E. W., *Made Free in Prison*, 1918

Mass-Observation, *The Press and Its Readers: A Report Prepared by Mass-Observation for the Advertising Service Guild*, 1949

Mathiesen, T., *Prison on Trial: A Critical Assessment*, 1990

Matza, D., *Deliquency and Drift*, 1964

Maxwell, A. "Penal Reform, 1898–1948," *Magistrate*, 8, 1948

Maxwell, A., "Treatment of Crime," Sidney Ball Lecture, 16 November 1937, *Barnett House Papers*, 21, 1938

McCall, C., *'They Always Come Back'*, 1938

McClean, J. D., "Corrective Training—Decline and Fall," *Criminal Law Review*, 1964

McCleod, H., "God and the Gallows: Christianity and Capital Punishment in the Nineteenth and Twentieth Centuries," in Cooper, K., and Gregory, J. (eds.), *Retribution, Repentance, and Reconciliation*, Woodbridge, 2004

McClintock, F. H., and Avison, N. H., *Crime in England and Wales*, 1968

McConville, S., *A History of English Prison Administration, 1750–1877*, 1981

McConville, S., "Committees of Inquiry and Penal Policy in England," *Swedish Journal of Political Science*, 1, 1981

McConville, S., *English Local Prisons, 1860–1900: Next Only to Death*, 1995

McConville, S., "Hearing, Not Listening: Penal Policy and the Political Prisoners of 1906–1921," in Zedner, L. and Ashworth, A. (eds.), *The Criminological Foundations of Penal Policy*, Oxford, 2003

McGowen, R., "Civilizing Punishment: The End of the Public Execution in England," *Journal of British Studies*, 33, 1994

McHugh, J., "The Labour Party and the Parliamentary Campaign to Abolish the Military Death Penalty, 1919–1930," *Historical Journal*, 42, 1999

McKibbin, R., *Classes and Cultures: England 1918–1951*, Oxford, 1998

McWilliams, W., "The Mission to the English Police Courts 1876–1936," *Howard Journal*, 22, 1983

McWilliams, W., "The Mission Transformed: Professionalisation of Probation Between the Wars," *Howard Journal*, 24, 1985

Meacham, S., *Toynbee Hall and Social Reform, 1880–1914*, New Haven, 1987

Mead, G. H., "The Psychology of Punitive Justice," *American Journal of Sociology*, 23, 1918

Melossi, D., "Changing Representations of the Criminal," *British Journal of Criminology*, 40, 2000

Minkes, J., and Vanstone, M., "Gender, Race and the Death Penalty: Lessons from Three 1950s Murder Trials," *Howard Journal*, 45, 2006

Mockler, A., *Lions under the Throne*, 1983

Morgan, K. O., *Labour in Power, 1945–51*, Oxford, 1985

Morgan, K. O., *Labour People*, Oxford, 1987

Morgan, K. O., *The People's Peace: British History, 1945–1990*, Oxford, 1992

Morgan, K. O., *Callaghan: A Life*, Oxford, 1997

Morgan, N., "The Shaping of Parole in England and Wales," *Criminal Law Review*, 1983

Morgan, S., "Prison Lives: Critical Issues in Reading Prisoner Autobiography," *Howard Journal*, 38, 1999

Morgan, T., *Churchill: Young Man in a Hurry 1874–1915*, New York, 1982

Moriarty, M. J., "The Policy-Making Process: How It Is Seen from the Home Office," in Walker, N. (ed.), *Penal Policy-Making in England*, Cambridge, 1977

Morris, N., "The Criminal Justice Bill 1947—A Cook's Tour," *Res Judicatae*, 4, 1948

Morris, N., *The Habitual Criminal*, Cambridge, Mass., 1951

Morris, N., and Hawkins, G., "Rehabilitation: Rhetoric and Reality," *Federal Probation*, 34, 1970

Morris, R. M., "'Lies, Damned Lies and Criminal Statistics': Reinterpreting the Criminal Statistics in England and Wales," *Crime, History and Societies*, 5, 2001

Morris, T., "Notes and Criticisms," *British Journal of Delinquency*, 7, 1957

Morris, T., "Prisons in England and Wales," *British Journal of Delinquency*, 7, 1957

Morris, T., "Report of the Commissioners of Prisons for 1958 (1959)," *British Journal of Delinquency*, 10, 1960

Morris, T., and Morris, P., "The Experience of Imprisonment," *British Journal of Criminology*, 2, 1962

Morris, T., and Morris, P., *Pentonville*, 1963

Morris, T., "Contemporary Trends in Crime and Its Treatment," in Bean, P., and Whynes, D. (eds.), *Barbara Wootton: Social Science and Public Policy*, 1986

Morris, T., "British Criminology: 1935–1948," *British Journal of Criminology*, 28, 1988

Morris, T., *Crime and Criminal Justice since 1945*, Oxford, 1989

Morris, T., "In Memoriam: Barbara Wootton 1897–1988," *British Journal of Sociology*, 40, 1989

Morris, T., and Blom-Cooper, L., *A Calendar of Murder: Criminal Homicide in England since 1957*, 1964

Morris, T., "A Lifetime with Pentonville," *Prison Service Journal*, 209, 2013

Morrison, W. D., "The Study of Crime," *Mind*, 4, October 1892

Morrison, W. D., "Are Our Prisons a Failure?" *Fortnightly Review*, 55, April 1894

Morrison, W. D., "Prison Reform, I: Prisons and Prisoners," *Fortnightly Review*, 63, May 1898

Morrow, J., "Ancestors, Legacies and Traditions: British Idealism in the History of Political Thought," *History of Political Thought*, 6, 1985

Mort, F., *Capital Affairs. London and the Making of the Permissive Society*, New Haven, 2010

Morton, J.H., "Alcoholics in Prison," *Howard Journal*, 2, 1929

Moseley, S., *The Convict of To-Day*, 1927

Muncie, J., "Failure Never Matters: Detention Centres and the Politics of Deterrence," *Critical Social Policy*, 28, 1990

Nellis, M., "British Prison Movies: The Case of 'Now Barabbas'," *Howard Journal*, 27, 1988

Nuttall, C., and Pease, K., "Changes in the Use of Imprisonment in England and Wales 1950–1991," *Criminal Law Review*, May 1994

Nicholson, H., *Diaries and Letters 1945–1962*, 1968

Nicolson, N., *People and Parliament*, 1958; reprint, Westport, 1974

Norman, F., *Bang to Rights: An Account of Prison Life*, 1958

Oakley, A., *A Critical Woman: Barbara Wootton, Social Science and Public Policy in the Twentieth Century*, 2011

Olivier, M. (ed.), *Sydney Olivier: Letters and Selected Writings*, 1948

Orwell, G., "Decline of the English Murder," in Orwell, G., *Decline of the English Murder and Other Essays*, Harmondsworth, 1965

Page, L., *Crime and the Community*, 1937

Page, L., "Outcasts or Human Beings?" *The Listener*, 1937

Page, L., "The Discharged Prisoner," *Howard Journal*, 5, 1938

Page, L., "Soft Justice," *Quarterly Review*, 571, 1947

Page, L., *The Sentence of the Court*, 1948

Page, L., *The Young Lag: A Study in Crime*, 1950

Paget R. T., and Silverman, S., *Hanged—and Innocent?* 1953

Pailthorpe, G. W., *What We Put in Prison*, 1932

Pailthorpe, G. W., *Studies in the Psychology of Delinquency*, Medical Research Council, 1932

Pakenham, F., *Causes of Crime*, 1959

Pakenham, F., *Earl of Longford, Five Lives*, 1964

Pakenham, F., Lord Longford, *Punishment and the Punished*, 1991

Parker, T., *The Unknown Citizen*, Harmondsworth, 1st pub. 1963; 1966

Paterson, A., *German Prisons*, 1922

Paterson, A., "Should the Criminologist Be Encouraged?" *Transactions of the Medico-Legal Society*, 26, 1933

Paterson, A., "The Present Policy of the Prison Commission," *The Magistrate*, 5, 1938

Pattenden, R., *English Criminal Appeals 1844–1994*, Oxford, 1996

Pearson, G., *Hooligan: A History of Respectable Fears*, 1983

Peet, H. W., "Some Fruits of Silence," *Friends Quarterly Examiner*, April 1920

Pellew, J., *The Home Office 1848–1914*, 1982

Pellew, J., "Law and Order: Expertise and the Victorian Home Office," in MacLeod, R. (ed.), *Government and Expertise: Specialists, Administrators and Professionals, 1860–1919*, Cambridge, 1988

Penal Reform League, *The Spirit of Punishment*, 1910

Peterson, A. W., "The Prison Building Programme," *British Journal of Criminology*, 1, 1961

Peterson, A. W., "The Expanding Prison System 1954–1963," *Criminal Law Review*, 1964

Pethick-Lawrence, Lord, *Fate Has Been Kind*, 1942

Phelan, J., *Jail Journey*, 1940

Pierrepoint, A., *Executioner: Pierrepoint*, 1974

Pilkington, E., *Beyond the Mother Country: West Indians and the Notting Hill White Riots*, 1988

Pollitt, H., *Serving My Time*, 1940

Potter, H., *Hanging in Judgment: Religion and the Death Penalty in England*, New York, 1993

Potts, W. A., "The Birmingham Scheme," *British Medical Journal*, 3 April 1920

Powell, A., and Blight, E. C., "Poor Law Relief" in Llewellyn Smith, H., Sir (ed.), *The New Survey of London Life and Labour*, 1, 1st pub. 1930; 1934

Pratt, J., "Towards the 'Decivilizing' of Punishment?" *Social and Legal Studies: An International Journal*, 7, 1998

Pratt, J., *Punishment and Civilization: Penal Tolerance and Intolerance in Modern Society*, 2002

Pratt, J., "The Acceptable Prison: Official Discourse, Truth and Legitimacy in the Nineteenth Century," in Gilligan, G., and Pratt, J. (eds.), *Crime, Truth and Justice*, 2004

Priestley, P. (ed.), *Jail Journeys: The English Prison Experience since 1918*, 1989

Purvis, J., "The Prison Experience of the Suffragettes in Edwardian Britain," *Women's History Review*, 4, 1995

Rackstraw, J. W., "Vagrancy and Petty Crime," *Howard Journal*, 2, 1929

Radzinowicz, L., "The Present Trend of English Penal Policy," *Law Quarterly Review*, 55, 1939

Radzinowicz, L. and Turner, J. W., (eds.), *Mental Abnormality and Crime*, 1944

Radzinowicz, L., "The Assessment of Punishments by English Courts," in Radzinowicz, L., and Turner, J. W. (eds.), *The Modern Approach to Criminal Law*, 1945

Radzinowicz, L., "The Persistent Offender," in Radzinowicz, L., and Turner, J. W. (eds.), *The Modern Approach to Criminal Law*, 1945

Radzinowicz, L., *Sir James Fitzjames Stephen*, 1957

Radzinowicz, L., "Changing Attitudes towards Crime and Punishment," *Law Quarterly Review*, 75, 1959

Radzinowicz, L., *The Study of Criminology in Cambridge*, Cambridge, 1961

Radzinowicz, L., *In Search of Criminology*, Cambridge, Mass., 1962

Radzinowicz, L., "Criminology and the Climate of Social Responsibility," address to the Howard League, 7 May 1964

Radzinowicz, L., *Ideology and Crime*, New York, 1966

Radzinowicz, L., and Hood, R., "Judicial Discretion and Sentencing Standards: Victorian Attempts to Solve a Perennial Problem," *University of Pennsylvania Law Review*, 127, 1979

Radzinowicz, L., and Hood, R., "Incapacitating the Habitual Criminal: The English Experience," *Michigan Law Review*, 78, 1980

Radzinowicz, L., and Hood, R., *The Emergence of Penal Policy, A History of English Criminal Law and Its Administration from 1750*, 5, 1986

Radzinowicz, L., *Adventures in Criminology*, 1999

Rae, J., *Conscience and Politics: The British Government and the Conscientious Objector to Military Service, 1916–1919*, 1970

Ramsay, M., "British Penal Policy: The Shackles of the Past," *Contemporary Review*, 1980

Ramsay, M., "Two Centuries of Imprisonment," *Research Bulletin (Home Office Research and Planning Unit)*, 14, 1982

Ramsbotham, D., *Prisongate: The Shocking State of Britain's Prisons and the Need for Visionary Change*, 2005

Rich, C. E., *Recollections of a Prison Governor*, 1932

Richards, B., "Psychology, Prisons and Ideology: The Prison Psychological Service," *Ideology and Consciousness*, 2, 1977

Richards, P. G., *Parliament and Conscience*, 1970

Richter, M., "T. H. Green and His Audience: Liberalism as a Surrogate Faith," *Review of Politics*, 18, 1956

Richter, M., *The Politics of Conscience: T. H. Green and His Age*, 1964

Roberts, H. E., "Years of Struggle: The Life and Work of Robin Page Arnot," *Labour History Review*, 59, Autumn 1994

Roberts, R., *The Classic Slum*, Manchester, 1971

Robin, G., "The Executioner: His Place in English Society," *British Journal of Sociology*, 15, 1964

Rolph, C. H., "The Death Penalty," *Current Affairs*, 112, 5 August 1950

Rolph, C. H., *Further Particulars*, Oxford, 1987

Roodhouse, M., *Black Market Britain, 1939–1955*, New York, 2013

Roper, W. F., "A Comparative Survey of the Wakefield Prison Population in 1948," *British Journal of Delinquency*, 1, 1950

Rose, A. G., "Some Influences on English Penal Reform, 1895–1921," *Sociological Review*, 3, 1955

Rose, G., *The Struggle for Penal Reform*, 1961

Rose, G. N., "The Artificial Delinquent Generation," *Journal of Criminal Law, Criminology and Police Science*, 59, 1968

Rose, M. E., "The Success of Social Reform? The Central Control Board (Liquor Traffic) 1915–21," in Foot, M. R. D. (ed.), *War and Society*, 1973

Rose, N., *The Psychological Complex: Psychology, Politics and Society in England, 1869–1939*, 1985

Rubin, G. R., "Law, Poverty and Imprisonment for Debt, 1869–1914," in Rubin, G. R., and Sugarman, D. (eds.), *Law, Economy and Society: Essays in the History of English Law 1750–1914*, Abingdon, 1984

Ruck, S. K., "Developments in Crime and Punishment," in Radzinowicz, L., and Turner, J. W. (eds.), *Penal Reform in England*, 1st. ed. 1940; 2nd ed., 1946

Ruck, S. K., (ed.), *Paterson on Prisons*, 1951

Ruggles-Brise, E., *The English Prison System*, 1921

Ruggles-Brise, E., *Prison Reform: At Home and Abroad*, 1924

Rusche, G., and Kirchheimer, O., *Punishment and Social Structure*, 1939; New York, 1968

Rutherford, A., *Prisons and the Process of Justice: The Reductionist Challenge*, 1984

Rutherford, A., *Prisons and the Process of Justice*, 1984

Rutherford, A., "Lessons from a Reductionist Era," in Robert, P., and Emsley, C. (eds.), *History and Sociology of Crime*, Pfaffenweiler, 1991

Ryan, M., *The Acceptable Pressure Group: Inequality in the Penal Lobby, a case study of the Howard League and RAP*, Farnborough, 1978

Ryan, M., *Penal Policy and Political Culture in England and Wales*, Winchester, 2003

Schooling, J. H., "Crime," part 2, *Pall Mall Magazine*, 15, 1898

Salt, H. S., *Seventy Years among Savages*, 1921

Scott, A., *Ernest Gowers: Plain Words and Forgotten Deeds*, Basingstoke, 2009

Scott, D., and Spear, F., "Counterblast: 100 Years On: Constance Lytton/Jane Warton Prisons and Prisoners," *Howard Journal*, 53, 2014

Scott, H., *Your Obedient Servant*, 1959

Scull, A., *The Most Solitary of Afflictions: Madness and Society in Britain, 1700–1900*, New Haven, 1993

Seal, L., "Ruth Ellis and Public Contestation of the Death Penalty," *Howard Journal*, 50, 2011

Seal, L., *Capital Punishment in Twentieth-Century Britain*, 2014

Seal, L., "Perceptions of safety, fear and social change in the public's pro-death penalty discourse in mid twentieth-century Britain," *Crime, History and Societies*, 21, 2017

Searle, G. R., *Eugenics and Politics in Britain, 1900–1914*, Leyden, 1976

Shadwell, A., *Drink in 1914–1922: A Lesson in Control*, 1923

Shapira, M., *The War Inside: Psychoanalysis, Total War, and the Making of the Democratic Self in Postwar Britain*, Cambridge, 2015

Sharpe, J. A., *Judicial Punishment in England*, 1990

Shawcross, H., *Life Sentence: The Memoirs of Lord Shawcross*, 1995

Shetreet, S., *Judges on Trial*, Amsterdam, 1976

Silvey, J., "The Criminal Law and Public Opinion," *Criminal Law Review*, 1961

Simmons, H. G., "Explaining Social Policy: The English Mental Deficiency Act of 1913," *Journal of Social History*, 11, 1977–1978

Simpson, H. B., "Crime and Punishment," *Edinburgh Review*, 482, 1922

Size, M., *Prisons I Have Known*, 1957

Smith, A., *Women in Prison*, 1962

Smith, A., "Penal Policy and the Woman Offender," in Halmos, P. (ed.), *The Sociological Review Monograph*, 9, 1965

Smith, A., *Lord Goddard: My Years with the Lord Chief Justice*, 1959

Smith, D., "Juvenile Delinquency in Britain in the First World War," *Criminal Justice History*, 11, 1990

Smith, H. L. (ed.), *Britain in the Second World War*, Manchester, 1996

Smith, M. H., "Habitual Women Drunkards," *The Magistrate*, 3, 1934

Smith, M. H., "Medical Examination of Delinquents," *Journal of Mental Science*, 68, 1922

Smith, M. H., *Prisons and a Changing Civilization*, 1934

Snowden, P. V., *An Autobiography*, 1934

Sparks, R. F., *Local Prisons: The Crisis in the English Penal System*, 1971

Sparks, R. F., "Britain," in *The International Handbook of Contemporary Developments in Criminology*, 2, 1982

Spencer, J. C., "Some Recent Developments in the English Prison System," *British Journal of Delinquency*, 4, 1953–1954

Stallybrass, W. T., "A Comparison of the General Principles of Criminal Law in England with the Progetto Definitivo Di Un Nuovo Codice Penale of Alfredo Rocco," *Journal of Comparative Legislation and International Law*, 15, 1933

Stephen, J. F., "The Punishment of Convicts," *Cornhill Magazine*, 7, 1863

Stephen, J. F., *A History of the Criminal Law of England*, 2, 1883

Stevens, R., *Law and Politics: The House of Lords as a Judicial Body, 1800–1976*, Chapel Hill, 1978

Stevens, R., *The Independence of the Judiciary*, Oxford, 1993

Stockdale, E., "A Short History of Prison Inspection in England," *British Journal of Criminology*, 23, 1983

Stokes, J., *In the Nineties*, Chicago, 1989

St. John, A., *Prison Regime*, 1913

Sutherland, E. H., "The Decreasing Prison Population of England," *Journal of Criminal Law and Criminology*, 24, 1933

Taylor, H., "Rationing Crime: The Political Economy of Criminal Statistics since the 1850s," *Economic History Review*, 51, 1998

Taylor, H., "Forging the Job: A Crisis of 'Modernization' or Redundancy for the Police in England and Wales, 1900–1939," *British Journal of Criminology*, 39, 1999

Taylor, H. A., *Jix. Viscount Brentford*, 1933

Taylor, I., Walton, P., and Young, J., *The New Criminology*, 1973; 4th impression, 1977

Taylor, R. S., "The Habitual Criminal: Observations on Some of the Characteristics of Men Sentenced to Preventive Detention," *British Journal of Criminology*, 1, 1960

Teeters, N. K., "The Prison Systems of England," *Journal of Criminal Law and Criminology*, 41, 1951

Templewood, V., *Crime and Punishment*, Cambridge, 1947

Templewood, V., *Nine Troubled Years*, 1954

Thomas, D. A., "Theories of Punishment in the Court of Criminal Appeal," *Modern Law Review*, 27, 1964

Thomas, D. A., "Appellate Review of Sentences and the Development of Sentencing Policy: The English Experience," *Alabama Law Review*, 20, 1968

Thomas, D. A., *Principles of Sentencing*, 1970

Thomas, D. A., *Constraints on Judgment: The Search for Structured Discretion in Sentencing, 1860–1910*, Cambridge, 1979

Thomas, D. A., "Sentencing Reform: England and Wales," in Clarkson, C., and Morgan, R. (eds.), *The Politics of Sentencing Reform*, Oxford, 1995

Thomas, J. E., *The English Prison Officer since 1850: A Study in Conflict*, 1972

Thomas, J. E., "The Influence of the Prison Service," in Walker, N. (ed.), *Penal Policy-Making in England*, Cambridge, 1977

Tolstoy, L., *What I Believe*, Geneva, 1888

Trasler, G., "Preventive Detention: A Symposium," *British Journal of Criminology*, 4, 1963

Trenaman, J., "English Prisons in 1947," *Howard Journal*, 7, 1948–1949

Troup, E., *The Home Office*, 2nd ed. rev., 1926

Tsuzuki, C., *Edward Carpenter, 1844–1929*, Cambridge, 1980

Tumin, J. S., "Inspector of Prisons," in *Asking Around: Background to the David Hare Trilogy*, New York, 2001

Turner, G. D., "Five Years of Progress in Penal Administration," *Contemporary Review*, 138, 1930

Tuttle, E., *The Crusade against Capital Punishment in Great Britain*, 1961

Twitchell, N., "Abolition of the Death Penalty," in Dorey, P., (ed.), *The Labour Governments 1964–1970*, 2006

Ulam, A. B., *Philosophical Foundations of English Socialism*, Cambridge, Mass., 1951

Valier, C., "Psychoanalysis and Crime in Britain during the Inter-War Years," *British Society of Criminology, Selected Proceedings*, 1, 1998

Valier, C., *Crime and Punishment in Contemporary Culture*, 2004

Vellacott, J., *Bertrand Russell and the Pacifists in the First World War*, Brighton, 1980

Vincent, A., and Plant, R., *Philosophy, Politics and Citizenship: The Life and Thought of the British Idealists*, Oxford, 1984

von Hirsch, A. (ed.), *Doing Justice*, New York, 1976

Walker, N., "The Habitual Criminal: An Administrative Problem," *Public Administration*, 41, 1963

Walker, N., "The Mentally Abnormal Offender in the English Penal System," in Halmos, P. (ed.), *The Sociological Review Monograph*, 9, Keele, 1965

Walker, N., *Sentencing in a Rational Society*, Harmondsworth, 1st pub. 1969; 1972

Walker, N., "Crime and Penal Measures," in Halsey, A. H. (ed.), *Trends in British Society since 1900*, 1972

Walker, N., and McCabe, S., *Crime and Insanity in England*, 2, Edinburgh, 1973

Walker, N., *A Man Without Loyalties: A Penologist's Afterthoughts*, Chichester, 2003

Wallhead, R. C., "In Jail," *Socialist Review*, 15, 1918

Walters, A. A., "Delinquent Generations?" *British Journal of Criminology*, 3, 1963

Waters, C., "'Dark Strangers' in Our Midst: Discourses of Race and Nation in Britain, 1947–1963," *Journal of British Studies*, 36, 1997

Waters, C., "Disorders of the Mind, Disorders of the Body Social: Peter Wildeblood and the Making of the Modern Homosexual," in Conekin, B., Mort, F., and Waters, C. (eds.), *Moments of Modernity: Reconstructing Britain 1945–1964*, 1999

Watson, J., *Meet the Prisoner*, 1939

Watson, J., "The Prison System," in Radzinowicz, L., and Turner, J. W. (eds.), *Penal Reform in England*, 2nd ed., 1946

Watson, S., "Malingerers, the 'Weakminded' Criminal and the 'Moral Imbecile': How the English Prison Medical Officer Became an Expert in Mental Deficiency, 1880–1930," in Clark, M., and Crawford, C. (eds.), *Legal Medicine in History*, Cambridge, 1994

Webb, B., and Webb, S., *English Prisons under Local Government*, 1922; reprint, 1963

Weinbren, D., "Against All Cruelty: The Humanitarian League, 1891–1919," *History Workshop Journal*, 38, 1994

West, D. J., *The Habitual Prisoner*, 1963

Wheeler-Bennett, J., *John Anderson: Viscount Waverley*, New York, 1962

White, J., *London in the Twentieth Century*, 2001

Wiener, M. J. (ed.), "Special Issue: Humanitarianism or Control? A Symposium on Aspects of Nineteenth Century Social Reform in Britain and America," *Rice University Studies*, 67, Winter 1981

Wiener, M. J., "Some Images of Man and their Relation to the Administration of the Criminal Law in Britain, 1830–1914," in Watkin, T. G. (ed.), *Legal Record and Historical Reality*, 1989

Wiener, M. J., *Reconstructing the Criminal: Culture, Law, and Policy in England, 1830–1914*, Cambridge, 1990

Wiener, M. J., *Men of Blood: Violence, Manliness and Criminal Justice in Victorian England*, Cambridge, 2004

Wiener, M. J., "Murderers and 'Reasonable Men': The 'Criminology' of the Victorian Judiciary," in Becker, P., and Wetzell, R. (eds.), *Criminals and Their Scientists: The History of Criminology in International Perspective*, Cambridge, 2006

Wilde, O., *The Soul of Man and Prison Writings*, Oxford, 1990

Wildeblood, P., *Against the Law*, 1st pub. 1955; 1957

Wilkins, L. T., "A Small Comparative Study of the Results of Probation," *British Journal of Delinquency*, 8, 1958

Wilkins, L T.., "Evaluation of Penal Treatments," in Halmos, P. (ed.), *The Sociological Review Monograph*, 9, Keele, 1965

Wilkins, L. T., "Persistent Offenders and Preventive Detention," *Journal of Criminal Law, Criminology, and Police Science*, 57, 1966

Wilkins, L. T., "Retrospect and Prospect: Fashions in Criminal Justice Theory and Practice," in Gottfredson, D., and Clarke, R. V., (eds.), *Policy and Theory in Criminal Justice*, Aldershot, 1990

Williams, F., *Nothing So Strange*, 1970

Williams, G., "The Courts and Persistent Offenders," *Criminal Law Review*, 1963

Williams, J. E., "Report of the Royal Commission on Capital Punishment 1949–1953," *Modern Law Review*, 17, 1954

Williams, J. E., "Sex Offences: The British Experience," *Law and Contemporary Problems*, 25, 1960

Williams, J. E., "Developments since the Homicide Act, 1957," in Tuttle, E. O. (ed.), *The Crusade against Capital Punishment in Great Britain*, 1961

Williams, J. E., "'The Hide of the Thug,'" *British Journal of Criminology*, 2, 1961

Williams, J. E., "Report of the Interdepartmental Committee on the Business of the Criminal Courts," *British Journal of Criminology*, 2, 1961

Williams, J. E., *The English Penal System in Transition*, 1970

Williams, J. E., and Thomas, D. A., "The Use of Imprisonment and Borstal Training for Young Offenders under the Criminal Justice Act, 1961," part 2, *Criminal Law Review*, 1965

Wilson, H. B., "Developments in the Penal System 1954–1963," *Criminal Law Review*, 1964

Wilson, H., *The Labour Government 1964–70*, Harmondsworth, 1974

Windlesham, D., *Responses to Crime, Penal Policy in the Making*, 2, Oxford, 1993

Winter, J. M., *Socialism and the Challenge of War*, 1974

Winter, J. M., *The Great War and the British People*, 1986

Wintle, F. E., "Preventive Detention at Work," *Howard Journal*, 1, 1921

Wolff, M., *Prison*, 1967

Wood, S., *Shades of the Prison House*, 1932

Woods, H. J., "Religion in the City of Cells," *The Congregational Quarterly*, 4, 1926

Wootton, B., *Social Science and Social Pathology*, 1st pub. 1959; 1967

Wootton, B., *In A World I Never Made*, 1967

Wootton, B., "The Changing Face of British Criminal Justice," in Morris, N., and Perlman, M. (eds.), *Law and Crime*, 1972

Wootton, B., "Official Advisory Bodies," in Walker, N. (ed.), *Penal Policy-Making in England*, 1977

Wootton, B., *Crime and Penal Policy*, 1978

Younger, K., "Sentencing," *Howard Journal*, 16, 1977

Zedner, L., *Criminal Justice*, Oxford, 1st pub. 2004; 2010

Zedner, L., *Women, Crime and Custody in Victorian England*, Oxford, 1991

Zedner, L., "Women, Crime, and Penal Responses: A Historical Account," in Tonry, M. (ed.), *Crime and Justice: A Review of Research*, 14, Chicago, 1991

Zedner, L., "Dangers of Dystopias in Penal Theory," *Oxford Journal of Legal Studies*, 22, 2002

Zedner, L., "Useful Knowledge? Debating the Role of Criminology in Post-War Britain," in Zedner, L., and Ashworth, A. (eds.), *The Criminological Foundations of Penal Policy*, Oxford, 2003

E. Journals, Newspapers, and Works of Reference

American Bar Association Journal
British Medical Journal
Daily Chronicle
Daily Express
Daily Herald
Daily Mail
Daily News
Daily Sketch
Daily Telegraph and Morning Post
Economist
Eugenic Review
Evening Standard
Guide to the Records of the Lord Chancellor's Department, by P. Polden, 1988
Independent
John Bull
Journal of Mental Science
Journal of Social Forces
Justice of the Peace
Lancet
Law Times
Listener
Magistrate
Manchester Guardian
Nation
Nation and Athenaeum
News Chronicle
New Statesman and Nation
Observer
Picture Post
Police Journal
Prison Officers' Magazine
Prison Service Journal
Spectator
Sunday Dispatch
Sunday Times
The Times
Times Literary Supplement
Transactions of the Medico-Legal Society

F. Biographical Entries

Adrian, Hester Agnes, Lady Adrian (1899–1966), by D. Thom, *Oxford Dictionary of National Biography* (hereafter *Oxford DNB*), 2004
Allen, Philip (1912–2007), by B. Cubbon, *Oxford DNB*, 2011

Amory, Derick Heathcoat, first Viscount Amory (1899–1981), by J. Ramsden, *Oxford DNB*, 2004

Anderson, John, first Viscount Waverley (1882–1958), by G. C. Peden, *Oxford DNB*, 2016

Bacon, Alice Martha, Baroness Bacon (1909–93), by C. M. P. Taylor, *Oxford DNB*, 2004

Bentley, Derek William (1933–53), by K. B. Bucknall, *Oxford DNB*, 2004

Birkett, (William) Norman (1883–1963), by C. Rogers, *Oxford DNB*, 2004

Bowen, Elizabeth Dorothea Cole (1899–1973), by D. Toomey, *Oxford DNB*, 2004

Brook, Norman Craven, Baron Normanbrook (1902–67), by K. Theakston, *Oxford DNB*, 2011

Brooke, Henry (1903–84), by R. Blake, *Dictionary of National Biography: Missing Persons*, Oxford, 1993

Buller, Reginald Edward Manningham-, Viscount Dilhorne (1905–80), by R. F. V. Heuston, *Dictionary of National Biography, 1971–80*, Oxford, 1986

Butler, Richard Austen (1902–82), by I. Gilmour, *Dictionary of National Biography, 1981–85*, Oxford, 1990

Christie, John Reginald Halliday (1899–1953), by R. Brown, *Oxford DNB*, 2012

Cunningham, Sir Charles Craik (1906–98), by Allen of Abbeydale, *Oxford DNB*, 2004

Denning, Alfred Thompson, Baron Denning (1899–1999), by R. Goff, *Oxford DNB*, 2014

Du Cane, Sir Edmund Frederick (1830–1903), by B. Forsythe, *Oxford DNB*, 2004

Du Parcq, Herbert (1880–1949), by G. R. Rubin, *Oxford DNB*, 2004

Ede, James Chuter Chuter-, Baron Chuter-Ede (1882–1965), by K. Jefferys, *Oxford DNB*, 2008

Ellis, Ruth (1926–55), by J. Dunn, *Oxford DNB*, 2004

Fox, Sir Lionel (1895–1961), by R. A. Butler, *Dictionary of National Biography, 1961–70*, Oxford, 1980

Fry, (Sara) Margery (1874–1958), by T. L. Hodgkin, *Oxford DNB*, 2007

Fyfe, David Patrick Maxwell, earl of Kilmuir (1900–67), by D. J. Dutton, *Oxford DNB*, 2004

Gardiner, Gerald Austin, Baron Gardiner (1900–90), by N. S. Marsh, *Oxford DNB*, 2004

George, Gwilym Lloyd-, first Viscount Tenby (1894–1966), *Dictionary of National Biography, 1961–70*, Oxford, 1981

Gladstone, Herbert John, Viscount Gladstone (1854–1930), by H. C. G. Matthew, *Oxford DNB*, 2010.

Goddard, Rayner, Baron Goddard (1877–1971), by K. J. M. Smith, *Oxford DNB*, 2010

Gollancz, Sir Victor (1893–1967), by S. Hodges, *Oxford DNB*, 2004

Gowers, Sir Ernest Arthur (1880–1966), by R. W. Burchfield, *Oxford DNB*, Oxford, 2004

Hancock, Dame Florence May (1893–1974), by J. Hannam, *Oxford DNB*, 2004

Heald, Sir Lionel Frederick (1897–1981), by P. Rawlinson, *Oxford DNB*, 2004

Hewart, Gordon, first Viscount Hewart (1870–1943), by R. Stevens, *Oxford DNB*, 2008

Hewitt, Cecil Rolph [pseud. C. H. Rolph] (1901–94), by A. Howard, *Oxford DNB*, 2004

Hoare, Samuel (1880–1959), by R. J. Q. Adams, *Oxford DNB*, 2004

Isaacs, Rufus Daniel, first marquess of Reading (1860–1935), by A. Lentin, *Oxford DNB*, 2011

Klare, Hugh John (1916–2012), by R. Morgan, *Oxford DNB*, 2016

Lushington, Sir Godfrey (1832–1907), by J. Pellew, *Oxford DNB*, 2009

Mannhein, Hermann (1889–1974), by L. Radzinowicz, *Dictionary of National Biography 1971–80*, Oxford, 1986

Maxwell, Alexander (1880–1963), by D. Fairn, *Oxford DNB*, 2004

Morris, Jeremiah Noah (1910–2009), by T. Arie, *Oxford DNB*, 2013

Mortimer, Robert Cecil (1902–76), by J. R. Porter, *Dictionary of National Biography, 1971–1980*, Oxford, 1986

Newsam, Sir Frank (1893–1964), by Allen of Abbeydale, *Oxford DNB*, 2004

Paterson, Sir Alexander Henry (1884–1947), by C. Smith, *Oxford DNB*, 2004

Peterson, Sir Arthur William (1916–86), by B. Cubbon, *Oxford DNB*, 2004

Radzinowicz, Sir Leon (1906–99), by R. Hood, *Oxford DNB*, 2004

Ruggles-Brise, Sir Evelyn John (1857–1935), by P. Priestley, *Oxford DNB*, 2004

Scott, Sir Harold Richard (1887–1969), by Anon., *Oxford DNB*, 2011

Serota, Beatrice, Baroness Serota (1919–2002), by J. Davis, *Oxford DNB*, 2009

Silkin, Samuel Charles, Baron Silkin of Dulwich (1918–88), by Archer of Sandwell, *Oxford DNB*, 2004

Silverman, (Samuel) Sydney (1895–1968), by S. McCabe, *Dictionary of National Biography, 1961–70*, Oxford, 1980

Soskice, Frank (1902–79), by R. Pearce, *Oxford DNB*, 2004

Temple, William (1881–1944), by A. Hastings, *Oxford DNB*, 2004

Troup, Sir Charles Edward (1857–1941), by P. Bartrip, *Oxford DNB*, 2004

Younger, Sir Kenneth (1908–76), by J. Grimond, *Oxford DNB*, 2004

Webster, Richard Everard, Viscount Alverstone (1842–1915), by F. D. Mackinnon, *Oxford DNB*, 2004

Wheatley, John Thomas, Baron Wheatley (1908–88), by D. M. Ross, *Oxford DNB*, 2004

Wootton, Barbara Frances, Baroness Wootton of Abinger (1897–1988), by A. H. Halsey, *Dictionary of National Biography, 1986–1990*, Oxford, 1996

INDEX